NOTABLE PLAYWRIGHTS

NOTABLE PLAYWRIGHTS

Volume 1

Kōbō Abe – Susan Glaspell

1 – 372

Edited by

CARL ROLLYSON

Baruch College, City University of New York

SALEM PRESS, INC.

Pasadena, California   Hackensack, New Jersey

All the essays in this set originally appeared in *Critical Survey of Drama, Second Revised Edition,* 2003, edited by Carl Rollyson. Some new material has been added.

∞ The paper used in these volumes conforms to the American National Standard for Permanence of Paper for Printed Library Materials, Z39.48-1992 (R1997)

Library of Congress Cataloging-in-Publication Data

Notable playwrights / editor, Carl Rollyson.
    p. cm. – (Magill's choice)
Includes bibliographical references and indexes.
    ISBN 1-58765-195-5 (set : alk. paper) – ISBN 1-58765-196-3 (vol. 1 : alk. paper) – ISBN 1-58765-197-1 (vol. 2 : alk. paper) – ISBN 1-58765-198-X (vol. 3 : alk. paper)
    1. Drama–Bio-bibliography–Dictionaries. 2. Drama–Biography–Dictionaries. 3. Drama–History and criticism–Dictionaries. I. Rollyson, Carl E. (Carl Edmund) II. Series.
    PN1625.N68 2005
    809.2'003–dc22

2004011762

First Printing

PRINTED IN THE UNITED STATES OF AMERICA

Contents – Volume 1

Publisher's Note vii
List of Contributors ix
Complete List of Contents xiii

Abe, Kōbō 1
Aeschylus 6
Albee, Edward 15
Anouilh, Jean 30
Aristophanes 42
Ayckbourn, Sir Alan 51

Baraka, Amiri 61
Beaumarchais, Pierre-Augustin Caron de 74
Beckett, Samuel 83
Behan, Brendan 91
Bogosian, Eric 99
Brecht, Bertolt 104
Byron, George Gordon, Lord 116

Calderón de la Barca, Pedro 131
Čapek, Karel 142
Chekhov, Anton 153
Chikamatsu Monzaemon 166
Chin, Frank 173
Churchill, Caryl 181
Cocteau, Jean 187
Congreve, William 195
Corneille, Pierre 210
Coward, Noël 222

Dryden, John 230
Durang, Christopher 241
Dürrenmatt, Friedrich 248

Eliot, T. S. 257
Euripides 270

Farquhar, Gseorge 283
Foote, Horton 289
Friel, Brian 295
Frisch, Max. 306
Fugard, Athol. 315

García Lorca, Federico 329
Genet, Jean. 342
Gilbert, W. S.. 356
Glaspell, Susan 367

Publisher's Note

Notable Playwrights contains biographical sketches and critical studies of 106 of the most important and best-known dramatists from antiquity to the present day. Publication of this set completes Salem Press's adaptation of all its Critical Survey sets in the Magill's Choice line of books, which now includes *Short Story Writers* (1997), *Notable Poets* (1998), *Notable American Novelists* (1999), and *Notable British Novelists* (2001),

The essays in *Notable Playwrights* originally appeared in Salem's *Critical Survey of Drama, Revised Edition* (2003), which combined and updated earlier editions and added entirely new essays. The 106 essays in *Notable Playwrights* constitute one-sixth of the profiles in *Critical Survey of Drama*; however, the editors of *Notable Playwrights* have taken special care to include the dramatists whose plays are most often studied in high school and undergraduate literature and drama courses. The set should thus cover the writers of greatest interest to students.

Coverage. Of the 106 playwrights covered in *Notable Playwrights*, 72 are English-language writers and 34 are foreign-language writers whose works are widely studied in translation. Thirty-three are American playwrights, and 30 are British. Among the 42 playwrights from other countries are 12 from France; 4 each from Germany and Greece; 3 each from Italy, Japan, and Spain; and 2 from Canada. The Geographical Index of playwrights in volume 3 lists all the playwrights covered by the countries and regions from which they come and with which they are associated.

The collection of playwrights in *Notable Playwrights* reflects the development of drama from ancient Greek and Roman playwrights up to European, American, Asian, and African writers of the present century. Among the many movements and dramatic genres represented by playwrights in this set are postmodernism (27 playwrights), comedy (15), absurdism (14), modernism (12), and expressionism (8). The Categorized Index of playwrights in volume 3 lists all the writers by the genres and movements with which they are most closely associated.

Organization and Structure of the Set. Essays in *Notable Playwrights* are arranged alphabetically by playwrights' names: From Kōbō Abe through Paul Zindel. Each volume's table of contents is followed by a complete list of the playwrights covered in the set's three volumes. In addition to the indexes already mentioned, volume 3 contains a glossary of Dramatic Terms and Movements, a Time Line listing the playwrights by their birthdates, and a general Subject Index.

Every essay is organized under the same basic subject headings. The essays open with their playwrights' full names and details of their births and deaths, followed by these sections:

Principal drama: Lists the writer's major plays through 2003, providing full titles and dates of production (pr.) and publication (pb.).

Other literary forms: Describes the writer's work in genres other than drama to help students differentiate authors known primarily as dramatists from those who are equally well known for their work in other genres.

Achievements: Discusses the writer's honors, awards, and other tangible recognitions and sums up the writer's influence and contributions to drama and literature.

Biography: Offers a condensed biographical sketch with vital information from birth up to the writer's latest activities.

Analysis: Provides an overview of the writer's development as a writer, with attention to recurrent themes and genres that lead into subsections on major plays and aspects of the writer's work as a dramatist. This section examines the plays that are most representative of the playwright's best and most significant work and offers examples of the techniques and themes found in these plays.

Other major works: Lists the playwright's principal works in nondramatic genres, such as screenplays, fiction, poetry, and nonfiction.

Bibliography: Lists published secondary sources that are appropriate for students. All these bibliographies have been updated through 2003.

Contributor byline: Identifies the essay's original contributor, as well as the scholar or scholars who have updated it.

The editors of Salem Press wish, once again, to thank the 121 scholars who wrote and updated the essays used in *Notable Playwrights*. Their names are listed at the beginning of volume 1. We are especially grateful to Carl Rollyson, of the City University of New York's Baruch College, for serving as the project's Editor.

List of Contributors

Patrick Adcock
Henderson State University

Jacob H. Adler
Purdue University

Thomas P. Adler
Purdue University

Andrew J. Angyal
Elon College

Stanley Archer
Texas A&M University

Gerald S. Argetsinger
Rochester Institute of Technology

Philip Bader
Independent Scholar

Lowell A. Bangerter
Original Contributor

Thomas Banks
Ohio Northern University

Theodore Baroody
American Psychological Foundation

David Barratt
Independent Scholar

Ronald H. Bayes
Original Contributor

Kirk H. Beetz
Original Contributor

Rebecca Bell-Metereau
Original Contributor

Milton Berman
University of Rochester

Cynthia A. Bily
Adrian College

Franz G. Blaha
University of Nebraska, Lincoln

Robert G. Blake
Elon University

Harold Branam
Savannah State University

Gerhard Brand
California State University, Los Angeles

Timothy Brennan
University of Minnesota

J. R. Broadus
Original Contributor

Mitzi Brunsdale
Mayville State College

Lorne M. Buchman
California College of Arts & Crafts

Ralph S. Carlson
Azusa Pacific University

Thomas Gregory Carpenter
Lipscomb University

C. L. Chua
California State University, Fresno

Richard N. Coe
Original Contributor

Robert T. Corum, Jr.
Independent Scholar

J. D. Daubs
Independent Scholar

Frank Day
Clemson University

Elliott A. Denniston
Missouri Southern State College

Margaret A. Dodson
Independent Scholar

Lillian Doherty
University of Maryland

Henry J. Donaghy
Idaho State University

Susan Duffy
Original Contributor

Ayne C. Durham
Original Contributor

Stefan Dziemianowicz
Independent Scholar

Rodney Farnsworth
Original Contributor

Anne Fletcher
Southern Illinois University, Carbondale

Howard L. Ford
University of North Texas

Steven H. Gale
Kentucky State University

Peter W. Graham
Virginia Polytechnic Institute and State University

Ira Grushow
Franklin and Marshall College

Angela Hague
Middle Tennessee State University

Elsie Galbreath Haley
Metropolitan State College of Denver

Shelley P. Haley
Original Contributor

Robert W. Haynes
Texas A&M International University

William J. Heim
University of South Florida

Holly Hill
John Jay College

Peter C. Holloran
New England Historical Association

John R. Holmes
Franciscan University of Steubenville

Joan Hope
Independent Scholar

Glenn Hopp
Howard Payne University

Eril Barnett Hughes
East Central University

William Hutchings
University of Alabama, Birmingham

Rhona Justice-Malloy
Central Michigan University

B. A. Kachur
University of Missouri, St. Louis

Albert E. Kalson
Purdue University

Irma M. Kashuba
Original Contributor

Nancy Kearns
Mercer University, Atlanta

Howard A. Kerner
Polk Community College

Leigh Husband Kimmel
Independent Scholar

Anne Mills King
Prince George's Community College

Matthew J. Kopans
University of Pittsburgh

Mildred C. Kuner
Hunter College, City University of New York

Gregory W. Lanier
University of West Florida

Norman Lavers
Arkansas State University

Katherine Lederer
Southwest Missouri State University

Stanley Longman
University of Georgia

Robert McClenaghan
Independent Scholar

Richard D. McGhee
Arkansas State University

Barry Mann
Independent Scholar

Patricia Marks
Valdosta State College

Joseph Marohl
Original Contributor

Richard A. Mazzara
Original Contributor

Jennifer Michaels
Grinnell College

Anne Newgarden
Independent Scholar

Evelyn S. Newlyn
Virginia Polytechnic Institute and State University

Sally Osborne Norton
University of Redlands

George O'Brien
Georgetown University

Robert H. O'Connor
North Dakota State University

Robert M. Otten
Marymount University

Cóilín D. Owens
George Mason University

Sidney F. Parham
St. Cloud State University

David B. Parsell
Furman University

Peter Petro
University of British Columbia

Victoria Price
Lamar University

Maureen Puffer-Rothenberg
Valdosta State University

J. Thomas Rimer
University of Pittsburgh

James W. Robinson, Jr.
Independent Scholar

Carl Rollyson
Baruch College, City University of New York

Joseph Rosenblum
University of North Carolina, Greensboro

Matthew C. Roudané
Independent Scholar

Irene Struthers Rush
Independent Scholar

Susan Rusinko
Bloomsburg University

Murray Sachs
Brandeis University

Arthur M. Saltzman
Missouri Southern State College

June Schlueter
Lafayette College

Fredericka A. Schmadel
Indiana State University

Hugh Short
Original Contributor

R. Baird Shuman
*University of Illinois at Urbana-
    Champaign*

K. M. Sibbald
Original Contributor

Thomas J. Sienkewicz
Monmouth College

Genevieve Slomski
Independent Scholar

August W. Staub
University of Georgia

Judith Steininger
Milwaukee School of Engineering

Eric Sterling
Auburn University

Roy Arthur Swanson
University of Wisconsin, Milwaukee

Daniel Taylor
Bethel College

Judith K. Taylor
Northern Kentucky University

Thomas J. Taylor
University of Akron

Currie K. Thompson
Gettysburg College

Jonathan L. Thorndike
Belmont University

Gordon Walters
Independent Scholar

Craig Werner
University of Wisconsin

Barbara Wiedeman
Auburn University, Montgomery

Thomas N. Winter
University of Nebraska

Robert F. Willson, Jr.
University of Missouri

Michael Zeitlin
University of Toronto

Complete List of Contents

Contents–Volume 1

Abe, Kōbō, 1
Aeschylus, 6
Albee, Edward, 15
Anouilh, Jean, 30
Aristophanes, 42
Ayckbourn, Sir Alan, 51
Baraka, Amiri, 61
Beaumarchais, Pierre-Augustin
  Caron de, 74
Beckett, Samuel, 83
Behan, Brendan, 91
Bogosian, Eric, 99
Brecht, Bertolt, 104
Byron, George Gordon, Lord, 116
Calderón de la Barca, Pedro, 131
Čapek, Karel, 142
Chekhov, Anton, 153
Chikamatsu Monzaemon, 166
Chin, Frank, 173

Churchill, Caryl, 181
Cocteau, Jean, 187
Congreve, William, 195
Corneille, Pierre, 210
Coward, Noël, 222
Dryden, John, 230
Durang, Christopher, 241
Dürrenmatt, Friedrich, 248
Eliot, T. S., 257
Euripides, 270
Farquhar, George, 283
Foote, Horton, 289
Friel, Brian, 295
Frisch, Max, 306
Fugard, Athol, 315
García Lorca, Federico, 329
Genet, Jean, 342
Gilbert, W. S., 356
Glaspell, Susan, 367

Contents–Volume 2

Goethe, Johann Wolfgang von, 373
Goldsmith, Oliver, 385
Gray, Simon, 395
Gregory, Lady Augusta, 404
Hakim, Tawfiq al-, 412
Handke, Peter, 422
Hansberry, Lorraine, 431
Havel, Václav, 440
Hellman, Lillian, 447
Henley, Beth, 457
Howe, Tina, 464
Hwang, David Henry, 471
Ibsen, Henrik, 480

Inge, William, 493
Ionesco, Eugène, 501
Jonson, Ben, 516
Kushner, Tony, 526
Lagerkvist, Pär, 531
McCullers, Carson, 542
Mamet, David, 551
Marlowe, Christopher, 563
Middleton, Thomas, 578
Miller, Arthur, 587
Mishima, Yukio, 602
Molière, 610
O'Casey, Sean, 621

Odets, Clifford, 630
O'Neill, Eugene, 640
Orton, Joe, 651
Osborne, John, 659
Parks, Suzan-Lori, 668
Pinero, Arthur Wing, 674
Pinter, Harold, 685

Pirandello, Luigi, 697
Plautus, 705
Priestley, J. B., 711
Racine, Jean, 723
Rattigan, Terence, 734
Rostand, Edmond, 743

Contents–Volume 3

Ryga, George, 751
Sartre, Jean-Paul, 760
Schiller, Friedrich, 773
Shaffer, Peter, 783
Shakespeare, William, 795
Shange, Ntozake, 827
Shaw, George Bernard, 835
Shepard, Sam, 850
Sheridan, Richard Brinsley, 861
Simon, Neil, 873
Sondheim, Stephen, 885
Sophocles, 890
Soyinka, Wole, 901
Stoppard, Tom, 914
Strindberg, August, 925
Synge, John Millington, 935
Terence, 944
Tremblay, Michel, 950
Valdez, Luis Miguel, 961

Vega Carpio, Lope de, 969
Voltaire, 979
Wasserstein, Wendy, 988
Wilde, Oscar, 994
Wilder, Thornton, 1004
Williams, Tennessee, 1016
Wilson, August, 1032
Wilson, Lanford, 1039
Wycherley, William, 1048
Yeats, William Butler, 1057
Zindel, Paul, 1064

Dramatic Terms and Movements, 1074
Time Line, 1098
Geographical Index, 1103
Categorized Index, 1107
Subject Index, 1113

NOTABLE PLAYWRIGHTS

Kōbō Abe

Born: Tokyo, Japan; March 7, 1924
Died: Tokyo, Japan; January 22, 1993

Principal drama • *Seifuku*, pr., pb. 1955; *Yūrei wa koko ni iru*, pr. 1958, pb. 1959 (*The Ghost Is Here*, 1993); *Omae ni mo tsumi ga aru*, pr., pb. 1965 (*You, Too, Are Guilty*, 1978); *Tomodachi*, pr., pb. 1967 (*Friends*, 1969); *Bō ni natta otoko*, pr., pb. 1969 (*The Man Who Turned into a Stick*, 1975); *Gikyoku zenshū*, pb. 1970; *Imeiji no tenrankai*, pr. 1971 (pr. in U.S. as *The Little Elephant Is Dead*, 1979); *Mihitsu no koi*, pr., pb. 1971 (*Involuntary Homicide*, 1993); *Gaido bukku*, pr. 1971; *Midoriiro no sutokkingu*, pr., pb. 1974 (*The Green Stockings*, 1993); *Ue: Shin doreigari*, pr., pb. 1975; *Three Plays*, pb. 1993

Other literary forms • A man of myriad talents, Kōbō Abe first established himself in the literary world as a novelist, but his reputation rests almost equally on his dramatic works. His first published work, in 1947, was a collection of poetry entitled *Mumei shishū* (collection of nameless poems). His best-known novel is *Suna no onna* (1962; *The Woman in the Dunes*, 1964), and his *Daiyon kanpyōki* (1958-1959, serial; 1959, book; *Inter Ice Age 4*, 1970) is science fiction. Abe also wrote short stories, some of which are collected in *Four Stories by Kōbō Abe* (1973), political essays, screenplays, film scripts, and film criticism.

Achievements • Kōbō Abe received the Second Postwar Literary Prize (1951) for his short story "Akai mayu" (1950; "The Red Cocoon," 1966). Later in the same year, he was given the twenty-fifth Akutagawa Prize for the title story in his collection *Kabe* (1951; walls), a surrealistic work. His 1967 play *Friends* was awarded the Tanizaki Jun'ichirō Prize. For most of the forty years preceding his death in 1993, Abe was a central figure among avant-garde artists in Japan. In 1975, Columbia University conferred on him the honorary degree Doctor of Humane Letters. He was frequently mentioned as a likely Nobel Prize candidate, but his death in 1993 prevented realization of that honor.

Biography • Although Kōbō (Kimifusa) Abe's parents lived in Manchuria, China, where his father worked as a doctor, he was born in Tokyo in 1924 because his father had brought the family back to Japan in order to conduct some research. His mother, like his father, was from the northern Japanese island of Hokkaido, and she had written novels as a young woman. The young Abe and his mother moved to Hokkaido temporarily in 1931 to avoid the Japanese invasion of the Chinese mainland.

Both Manchuria and Hokkaido are important in that they represent the only frontier lands that many Japanese would ever have the opportunity to experience, and they were also the only places where the significance of "being Japanese" was not a given. Those living in these marginal places were not completely excluded nor were they wholly accepted by mainstream Japanese society. This fact is reflected in Abe's writings, in which he portrays Manchuria as a bleak, flat, hostile place and Hokkaido as a land of promise, a Japanese "Wild West." Though Abe grew up in a colonial setting, his school books were those issued by the Ministry of Education in Japan, so he had read textbook descriptions about the landscape of Japan with its mountains, rivers, and

(Library of Congress)

cherry blossoms, but in Manchuria, he knew only plains and no cherry trees. On occasions when he was scolded by teachers, he was told that "a child back home would never do such a thing," reinforcing in Abe's mind the fact that he was not a typical Japanese. Abe has commented on how he grew to doubt the significance of belonging to any nation or to any society.

In 1943, Abe entered medical school in Tokyo at the strong urging of his father, and although Abe took no pleasure in his studies, the training may have contributed to his ability to make precise descriptions and to look on situations and on people with emotional detachment. He remarked jokingly that he was allowed to graduate only on the condition that he never practice medicine. Abe began writing fiction upon his graduation from medical school. His first long work, *Owarishi michi shirube ni* (the road sign at the end of the road) was published in 1948. When Abe was in his early twenties, he met and married Machiko Yamada, who would be his lifelong companion and artistic collaborator. A brilliant artist in her own right, she designed the covers for most of Abe's books as well as sets for the Abe Studio productions. They had one child, a daughter, Neri, who became a physician and writer in Tokyo.

In Manchuria the concept of the "harmony of the five races" had instilled in Abe a sense of the equality of all peoples, but when he watched the behavior of the Japanese, which contrasted so greatly with what he had been taught, he felt frustration and anger. This experience may have contributed to his attraction to the Japanese Communist Party, which he joined. Even before his writing began to receive literary awards, Abe was involved with party operations. Trips to Eastern Europe in the late 1950's provided direct exposure to a communistic society, and he became disillusioned. It was, however, in this part of the world that his work first received international attention. Abe's play *Friends*, the story of a man whose home is invaded by unwanted visitors, slipped past the censors and provided its audiences with an allegorical comment on their own situation.

Abe's criticism of the Japanese Communist Party led to his expulsion from the party. Following a period of poverty and hardship in which he and his young wife lived in Tokyo and sold charcoal and pickles on the street, the 1950's proved to be very productive and increasingly prosperous for Abe. He published more than a dozen short stories, four major novels, a collection of political essays, and a collection of film criticism. He also staged seven plays, released a film that he had written, and broadcast a dozen radio plays or teleplays.

The 1960's were also successful, and Abe's work included the works for which he is best known: the stage play *Friends* and the novel *The Woman in the Dunes*. Other major works of the period include the novels *Inter Ice Age 4*, *Tanin no kao* (1964; *The Face of Another*, 1966), and *Moetsukita chizu* (1967; *The Ruined Map*, 1969); the stage play *You, Too, Are Guilty*; and the film versions of *The Woman in the Dunes* and *The Face of Another*. In 1971, Abe formed his own theater troupe, the Abe Studio. For the next seven years, the studio held one or two productions a year, most of them written by Abe. He worked not only on scripts but also on sets, lighting, direction, and musical scores. Abe continued his work in various genres throughout the 1980's, but in the early 1990's, his health began to fail. The last novel he would see in print, *Kangarū nōto* (*The Kangaroo Notebook*, 1996), was published in 1991. In 1992, he was hospitalized and died of heart failure on January 22, 1993.

Analysis • Kōbō Abe's background may have been a prime influence in his coming to occupy a central position among Japanese avant-garde writers. Though he was born in Japan, being brought up in Manchuria isolated him from mainstream Japanese life. The sense of alienation and utter isolation he experienced provided one of the most powerful themes that would emerge in almost all his work. Many of Abe's sources were not Japanese; therefore, his work appealed to an international audience, and a substantial number of his plays were translated into English and other languages. Although Abe's earlier works were relatively structured and linear, they were characterized by social satire, allegory, and black humor. The later experimental plays moved away from allegorical social criticism toward allegories involving dream imagery, and some of the later plays were freely created in rehearsals.

Seifuku • Two themes that would be evident in much of Abe's later work, the censure of others' suffering and the rejection of what Abe felt to be Japan's self victimization, are particularly clear in this 1955 play, *Seifuku* (uniform). In this allegorical play, a broken old soldier who wears the ragged uniform of a colonial police officer and is stranded at a port in North Korea in 1945 represents Japan's colonial experience, which left the nation impoverished and unable to shed its disgrace. In the old soldier, the play depicts the Japanese colonial spirit, which has been broken and is stranded on a foreign shore, unable to return home. All the characters fulfill an allegorical role: the innocent youth of Korea, the conscience of Japan, and the spirit of Japanese womanhood, symbol of hearth and home.

Friends • In *Friends*, his most successful play, Abe critiques Japanese communal values, which he views as stifling of individual creativity. One evening, a family of strangers bursts into the apartment of a man who enjoys his solitude in order, they say, to save him from his loneliness. Although he resists their forced companionship, he is unable to remove them from his home. Finally, he dies, a victim of their aggressive communality. The play portrays the consequences of social pressures and the kind of mandatory communal spirit a communist totalitarianism would inflict on the citizenry. Abe had broken with the Communist Party just a few years before the play appeared.

The Man Who Turned into a Stick • Abe dealt with the theme of the exploitation of one group of people by another in a number of his plays, but perhaps the consequences of this behavior are most clearly investigated in *The Man Who Turned into a Stick*. Abe explained the play as depicting the alienation occurring in modern society, in which a sticklike man who has no reason for existence except being used by others is punished from within himself precisely for being a stick. The man turns into an actual stick, falling from the roof of a department store as his son watches. Two characters have to find the stick and take it with them to Hell, where they are employed specifically to gather up all the sticks into which many people have turned. The message is clear: In a world in which people are merely tools—the source of another's livelihood—there is no room for mercy or sentimentality.

The Green Stockings • By depicting characters who could not possibly exist, Abe intended to administer a shock to the theatrical form. *The Green Stockings* moves away from Abe's socially critical works toward interior-oriented plays with dreamlike allegorical qualities with no obvious reference to the exterior, real world. Pajama-clad Man stands center stage against the backdrop of a dreamscape of an immense wild field. Man, initially a narrator, turns into a nameless main character, a go-between for the performers and the audience. Man is obsessed with lingerie and, in an effort to transcend everyday existence, raids clotheslines for items, including green stockings, on Mondays and Fridays. Not satisfied, Man attempts suicide, and although a doctor offers him a new life as a grass-eating man, his emptiness prevails. The play poses the difficult question of whether reality, fiction, and dream are distinguishable even in one's mind.

Ue: Shin doreigari • Built around a hoax in which two characters pretend to be an exotic species of animal, *Ue: Shin doreigari* (the new slave hunters) may be the quintessential Abe Studio production. A professor receives a box containing a pair of *ue* along with instructions and a note reading "Limited only by your imagination! You may put these remarkable creatures to any use you wish." Actually, the *ue* are the sister of the professor's daughter-in-law and her husband, participating in a game to extort money from the professor by his son. At first dubious, the professor succumbs to a yearning to believe that animals that look just like human beings could exist. The fake *ue* become human, and the rest of the household also assume animal identities that correspond to their latent qualities.

The Little Elephant Is Dead • The full Japanese title for this play when it was performed in the United States is *Kozō wa shinda: Nikutai + ongaku + kotoba + imeiji no shi* (*The Little Elephant Is Dead: Bodies + music + words = image poem*). This title demonstrates what happens when words are supplanted by integrated but diffuse information. As Abe's last play, it provides a good means of measuring the departures from his earliest works as well as the continuities. The play is especially difficult to comprehend, for the underlying "logic" is not logic, but the illogic of a world of dreams. *The Little Elephant Is Dead* comes as close to a purely gestural theater as is possible.

Other major works

LONG FICTION: *Owarishi michi shirube ni*, 1948; *Baberu no tō no tanuki*, 1951; *Mahō no chōku*, 1951; *Kiga dōmei*, 1954; *Kemonotachi wa kokyō o mezasu*, 1957; *Daiyon kanpyōki*, 1958-1959 (serial), 1959 (book; *Inter Ice Age 4*, 1970); *Ishi no me*, 1960; *Suna no onna*, 1962 (*The Woman in the Dunes*, 1964); *Tanin no kao*, 1964 (*The Face of Another*, 1966); *Moetsukita chizu*, 1967 (*The Ruined Map*, 1969); *Hako otoko*, 1973 (*The Box Man*, 1974); *Mikkai*, 1977 (*Secret Rendezvous*, 1979); *Hakobune sakuramaru*, 1984 (*The Ark Sakura*, 1988); *Kangarū nōto*, 1991 (*The Kangaroo Notebook*, 1996); *Tobu otoko*, 1994.

SHORT FICTION: *Kabe*, 1951; *Suichū toshi*, 1964; *Yume no tōbō*, 1968; *Four Stories by Kōbō Abe*, 1973; *Beyond the Curve*, 1991.
POETRY: *Mumei shishū*, 1947.
NONFICTION: *Uchinaru henkyō*, 1971.
MISCELLANEOUS: *Abe Kobo zenshū*, 1972-1997 (30 volumes).

Bibliography

Goodman, David. *Japanese Drama and Culture in the 1960's: The Return of the Gods.* Armonk: M. E. Sharpe, 1988. This translation of five plays representative of the period provides commentary by a leading Japanese critic. The central thesis is that the decade of the 1960's was characterized by disillusionment with the radical politics of the pre-World War II era and a quest for viable alternatives.

Olsen, Lance. *Ellipse of Uncertainty: An Introduction to Post-modern Fantasy.* New York: Greenwood Press, 1987. The first study to examine the intersection of fantasy and postmodernism in literature. Olsen develops working definitions of these terms and then analyses various postmodernist fantasy works. Accessible to intellectually mature undergraduates.

Shields, Nancy K. *Fake Fish: The Theater of Kōbō Abe.* New York: Weatherhill, 1996. Provides plot summaries of the plays that were produced in the Abe Studio, the theater group that Abe began in 1971. Also discusses techniques used and themes developed in the plays and provides descriptions of Abe's rehearsal sessions.

Yamanoguchi, Hisaaki. "In Search of Identity: Abe Kōbō and Ōe Kenzaburō." In *The Search for Authenticity in Modern Japanese Literature.* Cambridge, England: Cambridge University Press, 1978. Compares and contrasts works of Abe Kōbō and Ōe Kenzaburō, both of whom are concerned with the solitude of men and women alienated from contemporary society and suffering from a loss of identity. Notes that Abe shares a greater kinship with contemporary European writers such as Franz Kafka than other Japanese writers do.

Victoria Price

Aeschylus

Born: Eleusis, Greece; 525-524 B.C.E.
Died: Gela, Sicily; 456-455 B.C.E.

Principal drama • Of the more than 80 known plays of Aeschylus, only 7 tragedies survive in more or less complete form: *Persai*, 472 B.C.E. (*The Persians*, 1777); *Hepta epi Thēbas*, 467 B.C.E. (*Seven Against Thebes*, 1777); *Hiketides*, 463 B.C.E.? (*The Suppliants*, 1777); *Oresteia*, 458 B.C.E. (English translation, 1777; includes *Agamemnōn* [*Agamemnon*], *Choēphoroi* [*Libation Bearers*], and *Eumenides*); *Prometheus desmōtēs*, date unknown (*Prometheus Bound*, 1777)

Other literary forms • A few surviving epigrams and elegiac fragments show that Aeschylus did not limit himself to drama but also experimented with other forms of poetic expression. The ancient *Life of Aeschylus* mentions that the playwright lost a competition with the poet Simonides to compose an elegy for the heroes of Marathon. Although Aeschylus's entry was judged to lack the "sympathetic delicacy" of that of Simonides, the elegy, fragments of which were discovered in the Athenian agora in 1933, projects the dignity and the majesty that mark Aeschylus's dramatic style. It is doubtful that Aeschylus's surviving tombstone inscription is autobiographical, despite such ancient authorities as Athenaeus and Pausanias, because the epigram mentions the place of Aeschylus's death.

Achievements • The earliest of the three ancient Greek tragedians whose work is extant, Aeschylus made major contributions to the development of fifth century B.C.E. Athenian tragedy. According to Aristotle's *De poetica* (c. 334-323 B.C.E.; *Poetics*, 1705), it was Aeschylus who "first introduced a second actor to tragedy and lessened the role of the chorus and made dialogue take the lead." This innovation marks a principal stage in the evolution of Greek tragedy, for although one actor could interact with the chorus, the addition by Aeschylus of a second actor made possible the great dramatic agons, or debates between actors, for which Greek tragedy is noted. Aeschylus also is the probable inventor of the connected trilogy/tetralogy. Before Aeschylus, the three tragedies and one satyr play that traditionally constituted a tragic production at the festival of the Greater Dionysia in Athens were unconnected in theme and plot, and Aeschylus's earliest extant play, *The Persians*, was not linked with the other plays in its group.

All the other surviving plays of Aeschylus were almost certainly part of connected groups, although the *Oresteia*, composed of the extant *Agamemnon*, *Libation Bearers*, and *Eumenides*, is the only connected tragic trilogy that survived intact. However, the loss of the *Oresteia*'s satyr play, *Proteus*, makes observations on Aeschylus's use of connected tetralogies (three tragedies and one satyr play) nearly impossible. In fact, there is no certain evidence that Aeschylus always used the connected group in his later productions, and imitations of this dramatic form by other fifth century B.C.E. playwrights are not firmly documented. The triadic form of the *Oresteia*, however, has certainly had a great influence on the development of modern dramatic trilogies. Aeschylus's brilliant use of the chorus as protagonist in *The Suppliants* may have been another significant innovation.

6

Until the discovery in 1952 of a papyrus text, *The Suppliants* was universally considered the earliest surviving Greek tragedy, and the central place of the chorus of Danaids was thought to reflect the choral role of early tragedy. As a result of the play's revised dating to 463 B.C.E., *The Suppliants'* chorus is now viewed as demonstrating a deliberate attempt to make the chorus a part of the action of the tragedy. Certainly, the chorus of *The Suppliants* is the earliest known example of a Greek tragic chorus, traditionally nondramatic and reflective, transformed into a significant dramatic participant. Although later dramatists rarely borrowed this choral technique, *The Suppliants'* chorus underscores Aeschylus's originality and experimentation in the development of Greek tragedy.

Aeschylus's historical play *Persai* (472 B.C.E.; *The Persians*, 1777) must also be mentioned as the only extant Greek tragedy based directly on historical events rather than on mythology. At least two other historical tragedies are known to have been produced in the early fifth century B.C.E., both by Phrynichus: *Capture of Miletus* (492 B.C.E.), based on the fall of that Greek city to the Persians in 494, and *Phoenissae* (c. 476 B.C.E.), based on the naval battle of Salamis in 480. Themistocles, the Athenian victor at Salamis, was Phrynichus's *choregus*, or producer. Aeschylus's *The Persians*, then, is clearly an imitation in the main of Phrynichus's *Phoenissae*, but it is impossible to judge whether Aeschylus derived from the play the idea to depict the Greek victory from the perspective of the defeated Persians. This ability to divest his historical tragedy of jingoism and propaganda makes Aeschylus's *The Persians* a universal statement on the tragic cause and meaning of defeat.

Aeschylus was known in antiquity for his spectacular stagecraft and especially for his use of stage trappings, special effects, and costuming. Examples of Aeschylus's skilled attention to such visual elements of drama include his dramatic employment in *Agamemnon* and *Libation Bearers* of stage machinery such as the *eccyclema*, a wheeled vehicle used to display the interior; his striking use of altars and tombs in *The Suppliants* and in *Libation Bearers*; his fondness for spectral appearances, such as the ghosts of Darius in *The Persians* and of Clytemnestra in *Eumenides*; and the terrifying costuming of the chorus of Furies in *Eumenides*, said to have been so effective that it caused miscarriages among pregnant spectators. Aeschylus's plays were held in such great esteem in the late fifth and fourth centuries B.C.E. that posthumous revivals of his works were granted special license to compete at the Greater Dionysia and often won first prize.

The famous debate between the ghosts of Aeschylus and Euripides in Aristophanes' comedy *Batrachoi* (405 B.C.E.; *The Frogs*, 1780) is perhaps the best ancient statement of Aeschylus's dramatic and literary

(Library of Congress)

significance. Aeschylus's plays were widely adapted by Roman tragedians, who in the second and first centuries B.C.E. still had access to the entire Aeschylean corpus, but Seneca's *Agamemnon* (c. 40-55 C.E.; English translation, 1581) is the only surviving example of such Roman imitation. The first complete ancient edition of the Aeschylean corpus was not made until the late fourth century B.C.E. by the orator Lycurgus. This edition became the basis of the definitive Alexandrian edition by Aristophanes of Byzantium in the second century B.C.E. The seven surviving plays are probably the result of a school selection made by the fifth century C.E.

The work of Aeschylus was unknown in Western Europe from early medieval times until the fifteenth century, when the impending fall of Constantinople to the Turks brought many Byzantine scholars to the West. The first printed edition of the extant plays was the Aldine edition of Venice, in 1518. Perhaps because of the difficulty of Aeschylus's poetic language, which is generally indirect and metaphoric, Aeschylus's extant corpus has not been as directly influential as the works of Sophocles and Euripides have been on the history of tragedy since the Renaissance. Nevertheless, Aeschylus is recognized today as a brilliant dramatist whose contributions to the fifth century B.C.E. Athenian theater have made him a "father of Western tragedy."

Biography • The life of Aeschylus can be pieced together from ancient sources, especially from several biographies that survive in the manuscript tradition that are probably derived from an Alexandrian volume of biographies, perhaps by Chamaeloon. Aeschylus was born in about 525-524 B.C.E. in the Attic town of Eleusis. His father, Euphorion, was a Eupatrid (an aristocrat) and probably very wealthy.

As a youth, Aeschylus witnessed the fall of Pisistratid tyranny in Athens and the beginnings of Athenian democracy, and he later lived through the Persian invasions of mainland Greece in 490 and 480 B.C.E. He is said to have fought at Marathon in 490, where he lost a brother, Cynegirus, and at Salamis in 480. Aeschylus's description in *The Persians* of the great sea battle of Salamis suggests that he was an eyewitness. Ancient reports that Aeschylus also fought in other battles of the Persian Wars, including Artemisium in 480 and Plataea in 479, are more doubtful. Aeschylus's well-known patriotism may have led to the tradition of his being involved in all these battles. Aesychlus lived in an age not only of the citizen-soldier but also of nationalistic and political poetry, and allusions to contemporary issues can be found in Aeschylus's plays.

In addition to the historical play *The Persians*, other political references in the extant Aeschylean corpus include those in *Eumenides* to the reform of the Athenian Areopagus by Ephialtes in 462 and to the Athenian alliance with Argos in 458. Evidence for Aeschylus's connections with the Eleusinian Mysteries is contradictory. In *The Frogs*, Aristophanes implies that Aeschylus was initiated into this famous mystery cult of his native city; however, in *Ethica Nicomachea* (335-323 B.C.E.; *Nicomachean Ethics*, 1797), Aristotle states that Aeschylus was accused of revealing the secrets of the mysteries in a play, and Clement of Alexandria asserts that Aeschylus was acquitted of this charge by proving that he had not been initiated. Scholars have searched the surviving plays and fragments for such a revelation, but none has been found. Certainly, the religious piety that pervades the extant plays makes conscious revelation most unlikely.

Aeschylus's dramatic career probably began very early in the fifth century B.C.E. with his first dramatic production at the Greater Dionysia between 499 and 496. His first tragic victory, for unknown plays, was won in 484, and he earned at least twelve more victories in his lifetime and several more posthumously. *The Persians*, presented in 472 together with the lost *Phineus* and *Glaucus Potnieus*, is Aeschylus's earliest extant play and won first prize. That the *choragus* of this group was Pericles, the great Athenian general and statesman, may suggest Aeschylean sympathy for Periclean political reforms. A second production of *The Persians* was probably made within a few years at the court of Hieron, tyrant of Gela in Sicily, where Aeschylus also wrote a play called *Aetnae*, now lost, in honor of Hieron's founding of the city of Aetna in 476 B.C.E. Aeschylus's Sicilian connections can be readily explained by noting that Hieron, like other Greek tyrants, such as Polycrates of Samos and the Pisistratids of Athens, was a great patron of the arts and attracted to his court many poets and philosophers, including Pindar, Bacchylides, Simonides, and Xenophanes.

Aeschylus had certainly returned to Athens by 468 B.C.E., for he lost in the Greater Dionysia of that year to Sophocles, who won his first tragic victory. In the next year, however, Aeschylus was victorious with *Laius, Oedipus,* and the extant *Seven Against Thebes*, a tragic group often called Aeschylus's Theban trilogy. Evidence suggests that Aeschylus produced his Danaid trilogy, including the extant *The Suppliants* and the lost *Egyptians* and *Danaids*, in 463, when he was victorious over Sophocles. This trilogy was formerly dated on stylistic grounds as early as 490, but subsequently discovered evidence has caused scholars to revise their conclusions about Aeschylus's dramatic development and about the evolution of Greek tragedy in general. Aeschylus's surviving trilogy, the *Oresteia*, was produced in Athens in 458 B.C.E. and was followed shortly by the poet's second trip to Gela, where he died and was buried in 456-455. The Gelans erected the following tombstone inscription in the poet's honor:

> This memorial hides Aeschylus, the Athenian, son of
>   Euphorion
> Who died in wheat-bearing Gela.
> The sacred battlefield of Marathon may tell of his great
>   valor.
> So, too, can the long-haired Mede, who knows it well.

Conspicuously absent from this epitaph is any reference to the literary accomplishments of Aeschylus, who is remembered only as a patriotic Athenian. The author of *The Persians* and *Eumenides* would have wanted no other eulogy. Aeschylus had at least two sons, Euaeon and Euphorion, both of whom wrote tragedies. In 431 B.C.E., Euphorion defeated Sophocles as well as Euripides, who produced his *Mēdeia* (*Medea*, 1781) in that year. Aeschylus's nephew Philocles was also a tragedian; according to an ancient hypothesis (an introductory note providing information about the play) to Sophocles' *Oidipous Tyrannos* (c. 429 B.C.E.; *Oedipus Tyrannus*, 1715), one of Philocles' productions was even considered better than Sophocles' play.

Analysis • Despite the fifth century B.C.E. Athenian political and religious issues that are diffused more often in Aeschylus's tragedies than in those of Sophocles and Euripides and that demand some historical explanation for the modern reader, the plays of Aeschylus still possess that timeless quality of thought and form that is the hallmark of classical Greek literature and that has made the themes of Aeschylean drama forever contemporary. Although Aeschylus's intense Athenian patriotism and probable support for Periclean democratic reforms is fairly well documented in his biographical sources and is reinforced by the dramatic evidence, it is his attention to theological and ethical issues and especially to the connection between Zeus and justice and to the rules governing relationships among humans and between humanity and divinity that provide a central focus for his tragedies.

It cannot be a coincidence that all seven extant tragedies, while less than one-twelfth of his total corpus, reflect a constant Aeschylean concern with the theme of human suffering and its causes. Again and again, the plays of Aeschylus suggest that human suffering is divine punishment caused by human transgressions and that people bring on themselves their own sorrows by overstepping their human bounds through *hybris*, hubris or excessive pride. At the same time, the role of the gods, and especially of Zeus, in this sequence of human action and human suffering is of particular interest to Aeschylus, whose plays seek in Zeus a source of justice and of fair retribution despite the vagaries of an apparently unjust world.

The Persians • *The Persians*, Aeschylus's earliest surviving tragedy, analyzes this system of divine retribution in the context of the unsuccessful invasion of Greece by the Persian king Xerxes in 480-479 B.C.E. Instead of the jubilant Greek victory ode that this drama could have become in the hands of a less perceptive artist, *The Persians*, presenting events from the viewpoint of the defeated Persians rather than that of the victorious Greeks, transforms the specific, historical events into a general, universal dramatization of defeat and its causes, of hubristic actions and their punishment.

The tragedy, set in the palace of Xerxes at Sousa, far from the events with which it is concerned, sacrifices the immediacy of the battlefield for a broadened perspective. The Persian defeat at Salamis is dramatically foreshadowed in the parodos, or choral entrance song, in which description of the magnificent departure of the Persian forces contrasts with the chorus's fear of impending disaster. A central cause of this apprehension is the yoking of the Hellespont, which the Persian king had ordered to facilitate departure, and, with overweening pride, to punish the sea for inhibiting Darius's earlier expedition against Greece. The chorus of elders does not speak here specifically of hubris, but of *ate*, an untranslatable Greek word implying "blindness," "delusion," "reckless sin," and "ruin." At the climax of the parodos, the ropes that bind the Hellespont become a metaphor for the nets of *ate* from which no mortal "who enters is able to escape."

Foreshadowing is continued in the first episode, in which the queen mother Atossa describes to the chorus a vision of Xerxes' defeat, which has troubled her at night. The chorus's response to this dream is the suggestion that the queen sacrifice to the chthonic powers and especially to the dead Darius, but before Atossa can act on this advice, a messenger arrives with news of the disaster at Salamis. This scene is an example of the structural and dramatic variety open to the Greek dramatist with Aeschylus's introduction of the second actor. The messenger's opening lines are in the traditional anapestic meter reserved for entrances and are followed by an epirrhematic passage in which the messenger speaks in iambic trimeter while the chorus responds in sung lyrics. No details of the battle are provided by the messenger until the queen requests them, and there follow several messenger reports, one listing Persian losses, another describing the sea battle at Salamis, a third the nearby land battle, and, finally, one announcing the losses in the fleet on the return journey. These reports are interrupted by brief interchanges between the messenger and the queen, in which both speakers respond in two or more lines of trimeter.

Rarely in this early play can be found the rapid stichomythia, or conversation in alternate lines of trimeter, that is later used so effectively by two or more speakers in Greek tragedy. The messenger scene substantiates the earlier fears of the queen and the chorus with the reality of defeat, and the dramatic effect of the series of speeches is like a sequence of disastrous waves on the Persian nation. The choral ode that follows the messenger scene is a lyric lament over the disaster and contrasts vividly in its pathos with the majesty of the parodos, in which the expedition's departure was described.

The messenger scene dramatizes the actuality of the Persian defeat, but the causes of this defeat are not explained until the second episode, in which Atossa and the chorus call forth the ghost of Darius as they had planned to do before the arrival of the messenger. It is Darius who, as a ghost, has the atemporal perspective to link cause and effect and to explain the defeat of his son Xerxes. When the disaster of Salamis is announced to him, Darius's initial response is that "some great divine force has made Xerxes unable to think clearly," and he then elaborates by linking both Zeus and Xerxes himself as agents in the disaster. Darius says that Xerxes' senses were diseased when he yoked the Hellespont: "Although a mortal, he thought to have power over all the gods, but not with good counsel."

Zeus did not stop Xerxes in his folly because "god joins in when a man hastens [his own destruction]," a doom that Xerxes "in his youthful boldness unwittingly accomplished." Thus, it is Xerxes' senseless pride, his haughty attempt to become more than human, which is his downfall, and the gods, especially Zeus, not only acquiesce but also assist in this downfall. Darius makes this most explicit in his prophecy of the Persian defeat at Plataea (479 B.C.E.), in which he speaks specifically of "*hybris* blossoming forth and having the fruit of *ate*" and of Zeus who is "a harsh accountant and punisher of excessively arrogant thoughts." This dramatically central episode ends with Darius advising the absent Xerxes to be more moderate. The arrival of the defeated Xerxes in the exodos, or last scene, is, in a sense, an undramatic but necessary anticlimax to the psychopomp of Darius in the second episode. The scene with Xerxes is a purely lyric lament in which no further dramatic or thematic development is achieved. There is, in fact, no reference in the exodos to the appearance of Darius or to his explanation of events.

The drama ends with Xerxes, still unconscious of his own fatal role in the disaster, giving himself over to uninhibited lamentation. This ignorance is a significant feature of Greek tragedy, and of Aeschylean tragedy in particular, a fact that has been obfuscated by Aristotelian criticism. In his *Poetics*, Aristotle placed great emphasis on a tragic fall (peripeteia) linked with recognition (anagnorisis) and tragic flaw (hamartia). Most Greek tragedies cannot be successfully interpreted through Aristotelian terminology; certainly not *The Persians*, in which there is no recognition (anagnorisis) of his tragic flaw (hamartia) by Xerxes. The disastrous effects of Xerxes' pride are well developed in *The Persians*, but they are developed for Atossa, the chorus, and the audience, not for Xerxes.

Agamemnon • The theological and ethical system suggested in *The Persians* can also be seen in *Agamemnon*, a play in which the theme of pride and its punishment is complicated by the issues of blood guilt and family curse. The plot is not historical in the modern sense of the word, but rather mythical, which, for the Greeks, was also historical, and it is concerned with the homecoming of Agamemnon, the leader of the Greek forces in the Trojan War, and with his subsequent brutal murder by his wife, Clytemnestra, and his cousin Aegisthus.

The story is at least as old as Homer, who uses it in the *Odyssey* (c. 725 B.C.E.; English translation, 1614), but it is impossible to determine whether the stark thematic contrasts between the Aeschylean and Homeric versions are a result of an intermediary source or Aeschylean innovation. In Homer, the tale is used as an exemplum of filial duty and feminine deception: Telemachus should show as much fidelity to his missing father as Orestes did to his late father, Agamemnon, and on his visit to Hades, Odysseus is warned by the ghost of Agamemnon to beware of the guile of women. In Aeschylus's *Agamemnon*, the death of the king is not simply a result of the deception of Clytemnestra; rather, the play is a dramatized quest for the deeper causes of events, causes that are seen as a combination of past and present deeds, individual and collective guilt, and human and divine motivation.

The parodos of *Agamemnon* deals with the past. In this unusually long entrance song, the chorus of elders reflects forebodingly on the crucial event surrounding Agamemnon's departure for Troy—the sacrifice by Agamemnon of his own daughter Iphigenia. This sacrifice presented a dilemma for Agamemnon. On the one hand, it was clear that Zeus was sending him against Troy because Troy broke the Greek custom of *xenia*, or guest-friendship, in the theft of Helen, wife of Agamemnon's brother Menelaus, by the Trojan prince Paris. On the other hand, the departing Greeks had offended the goddess Artemis, who would not permit departure until Iphigenia was sacrificed. Agamemnon was thus placed in the impossible situation of either offending Zeus or killing his own daughter. He reluctantly chose the latter course.

Significantly, the chorus's narration of these events is broken by the famous "Hymn to Zeus." In this prayer, occurring at the narrative point at which Agamemnon must make his decision, the chorus turns to Zeus as a source of wisdom, as a god who "has led men to think, who has set down the rule that wisdom comes through suffering." These lines, often considered the heart of *Agamemnon*, if not of the entire *Oresteia*, underscore Zeus's central role in dramatic events. Agamemnon dies not only because he killed Iphigenia, but also because of Zeus's didactic system of learning through suffering (*pathei mathos*).

The lessons of Zeus's instruction are explained in the first choral ode, a song of victory for the fall of Troy in which the chorus argues that the city fell by the lightning stroke of Zeus because of Paris's insolence in stealing Helen. It is in reference to Paris that the chorus says that "someone has denied that the gods deign to care about mortals who trample upon the beauty of holy things." Yet, by the end of the ode, Zeus's anger is not only directed toward Paris but also toward someone else who has caused so many war dead, who has become "prosperous beyond justice." Although his name is not mentioned, it is clear that this man is Agamemnon.

The hubris of Agamemnon, implied in the first ode, becomes more explicit in the second episode, when a messenger arrives to confirm the fall of Troy and to report that even the temples of the gods at Troy have been destroyed. The burden for this unwarranted and insolent offense against the gods must fall squarely on the shoulders of Agamemnon, as commander, and is an act of hubris similar to Xerxes' yoking of the Hellespont. Agamemnon's hubris is dramatically confirmed in the famous third episode, often called the "Carpet Scene" because of the purple carpet that Clytemnestra craftily laid in the path of her returning husband, supposedly as a gesture of respect but actually for Agamemnon's spiritual destruction. Agamemnon himself refers to this carpet as an honor befitting the gods alone and asks that he should be respected as a mortal, not a god. Nevertheless, Clytemnestra is able to coax her husband across the fatal tapestry by the mention of Priam, Agamemnon's defeated Trojan rival, who, in his Eastern opulence, would certainly have accepted the honor. So, the Greek king walks on the carpet into his palace and his death, not without an apotropaic prayer that "no god strike him from afar" as he does so.

Although hubris is not mentioned in this scene, there is no need to do so. Agamemnon's act is in itself visual proof of the king's overweening pride, of his excessive self-esteem. Agamemnon dies, then, for his own sins. There are, however, further considerations: There is Cassandra, a Trojan princess whom Agamemnon has brought home as his slave and mistress. Cassandra is another proof of Agamemnon's pride; he has what a god could not have. Cassandra, a prophetess of Apollo, had dedicated her virginity to the god. When she refused the god's sexual advances, Apollo punished her by making her prophecies never believed but always true.

Aeschylus uses this prophetic skill of Cassandra to great effect in the climactic fourth episode, in which the prophetess repeatedly predicts the king's and her own imminent deaths, but no one believes her. At the same time, Cassandra adds another perspective to the death of Agamemnon by mentioning "small children crying for their own death." This is a reference to the crime of Agamemnon's father, Atreus, who had killed his nephews, Aegisthus's brothers, and served them for dinner to their father, Thyestes. Cassandra's prophetic abilities thus serve to clarify the causes of Agamemnon's death, just as the ghost of Darius did Xerxes' downfall. In this way, Aeschylus manipulates Greek belief in prophecy and in ghosts to great dramatic effect.

By the time that Agamemnon's death cries ring from the palace, the king's death has been shown to be not only the result of his own sins of pride but also the result of blood guilt, of the sins of his father. The net in which Clytemnestra and Aegisthus capture Agamemnon is no simple affair, but an entangled web of his own and his father's making, of human and divine cause and effect. This web engulfs Agamemnon in the first play of the *Oresteia* and engulfs his son in the remaining two plays. Xerxes in *The Persians* had been caught in a similar net of pride, and such links of theme and imagery between these two plays, which together represent Aeschylus's earliest and latest extant plays, suggest a continuity of thought in the Aeschylean corpus centered around hubris and its consequences. Variations on this theme can be found in the other surviving plays, such as *The Suppliants*, in which a just but mysterious Zeus is seen as the protector of the good and the punisher of evil, and *Seven Against Thebes*, in which human and divine will together with blood guilt again coalesce into disaster.

Despite its diversity, the Aeschylean corpus presents a peculiar cohesion of thought. Although the lessons derived from dramatic events may be lost on Aeschylus's main characters, such as Xerxes and Agamemnon, for whom there is no "learning through suffering," the lesson of Aeschylus's plays is directed especially to the audience, not only a fifth century B.C.E. Athenian audience but also a more universal one for whom the Aeschylean play is a timeless attempt to explain the causes of human suffering through a complicated chain of cause and effect, of human action and divine punishment. Through a masterful combination of great poetry and ingenious stagecraft, Aeschylus presents in his plays the outstanding moral issues of his day and of all time.

Prometheus Bound • *Prometheus Bound*, the seventh play in Aeschylus's manuscript tradition, cannot be firmly dated and contains so many problems and idiosyncrasies of meter, languages, staging, and structure that a large number of modern scholars have come to question Aeschylean authorship. The arguments on both sides of the authorship debate have been thoroughly discussed by C. J. Herington in *The Author of the "Prometheus Bound"* (1970) and by M. Griffith in *The Authenticity of "Prometheus Bound"* (1977), and the debate has remained a stalemate. If this play was written by Aeschylus, it must have been written toward the end of Aeschylus's lifetime, probably after 460, and may have been part of a connected trilogy including the lost *Prometheus Lyomenos* (unbound) and *Prometheus Pyrphoros* (fire-bearer).

Bibliography

Bloom, Harold, ed. *Aeschylus.* Philadelphia: Chelsea House, 2001. Part of a series on dramatists meant for secondary school students, this book contains essays examining the work and life of Aeschylus. Includes bibliography and index.

Connacher, D. J. *Aeschylus: The Earlier Plays and Related Studies.* Buffalo, N.Y.: University of Toronto Press, 1996. A study of the Greek dramatist's earlier works, with particular emphasis on his technique. Includes bibliography.

Goward, Barbara. *Telling Tragedy: Narrative Technique in Aeschylus, Sophocles, and Euripides.* London: Duckworth, 1999. The author examines the function of narrative in the works of Aeschylus, Sophocles, and Euripides. Includes bibliography and index.

Griffith, M. *The Authenticity of "Prometheus Bound."* New York: Cambridge University Press, 1977. Discusses the question of whether Aeschylus wrote *Prometheus Bound.*

Harrison, Thomas E. H. *The Emptiness of Asia: Aeschylus' "Persians" and the History of the Fifth Century.* London: Duckworth, 2000. An examination of Aeschylus's *The Persians* from the historical perspective. Includes bibliography and index.

Herington, C. J. *The Author of the "Prometheus Bound."* Austin: University of Texas Press, 1970. An examination of the authorship question regarding *Prometheus Bound.*

Podlecki, Anthony J. *The Political Background of Aeschylean Tragedy.* 2d ed. London: Bristol Classical Press, 1999. In addition to providing literary criticism, the author looks at the politics that pervades much of Aeschylus's work. Includes bibliography and index.

Sullivan, Shirley Darcus. *Aeschylus's Use of Psychological Terminology: Traditional and New.* Montreal: McGill-Queen's University Press, 1997. Sullivan examines the psychological aspects of the language used in Aeschylus's tragedies. Includes bibliography and index.

Taplin, Oliver. *The Stagecraft of Aeschylus: The Dramatic Use of Exits and Entrances in Greek Tragedy.* Reprint. Oxford: Clarendon, 1989. Taplin focuses on Aeschylus's stagecraft, particularly his use of dramatic visual devices.

Thomas J. Sienkewicz

Edward Albee

Born: Virginia; March 12, 1928

Principal drama • *The Zoo Story*, pr. 1959, pb. 1960; *The Death of Bessie Smith*, pr., pb. 1960; *The Sandbox*, pr., pb. 1960; *Fam and Yam*, pr., pb. 1960; *The American Dream*, pr., pb. 1961; *Bartleby*, pr. 1961 (libretto, with James Hinton, Jr.; music by William Flanagan; adaptation of Herman Melville's "Bartleby the Scrivener"); *Who's Afraid of Virginia Woolf?*, pr., pb. 1962; *The Ballad of the Sad Café*, pr., pb. 1963 (adaptation of Carson McCullers's novel); *Tiny Alice*, pr. 1964, pb. 1965; *A Delicate Balance*, pr., pb. 1966; *Malcolm*, pr., pb. 1966 (adaptation of James Purdy's novel *Malcolm*); *Everything in the Garden*, pr. 1967, pb. 1968 (adaptation of Giles Cooper's play *Everything in the Garden*); *Box and Quotations from Chairman Mao Tse-tung*, pr. 1968, pb. 1969 (2 one-acts); *All Over*, pr., pb. 1971; *Seascape*, pr., pb. 1975; *Counting the Ways*, pr. 1976, pb. 1977; *Listening*, pr., pb. 1977; *The Lady from Dubuque*, pr., pb. 1980; *Lolita*, pr. 1981, pb. 1984 (adaptation of Vladimir Nabokov's novel); *The Man Who Had Three Arms*, pr., pb. 1982; *Finding the Sun*, pr. 1983, pb. 1994; *Marriage Play*, pr. 1987, pb. 1995; *Three Tall Women*, pr. 1991, pb. 1994; *The Lorca Play*, pr. 1992; *Fragments: A Sit Around*, pr. 1993, pb. 1995; *The Play About the Baby*, pr. 1998, pb. 2002; *The Goat: Or, Who Is Sylvia?*, pr., pb. 2002; *Occupant*, pr. 2002

Other literary forms • Although Edward Albee has written the libretto for an unsuccessful operatic version of Herman Melville's story "Bartleby the Scrivener," as well as some occasional essays and a few adaptations, he is known primarily for his plays. Albee's unpublished works include a short story and at least one novel written while he was a teenager. *Esquire* published the first chapter of a novel he began writing in 1963 but never completed.

Achievements • Edward Albee is, with David Mamet, Sam Shepard, and August Wilson, one of the few American playwrights to emerge since the 1950's with any claim to being considered a major dramatist ranked among the pantheon of Eugene O'Neill, Thornton Wilder, Arthur Miller, and Tennessee Williams. Since *The Zoo Story* first appeared, Albee has produced a sustained and varied body of work, often of considerably higher quality than his critical and popular reputation would suggest. In the introduction to his most experimental works, the two one-acts published together in *Box and Quotations from Chairman Mao Tse-tung*, Albee sets forth the two "obligations" of a playwright: to illuminate the human condition and to make some statement about the art form itself by altering "the forms within which his precursors have had to work."

Like O'Neill before him, Albee has always been an experimentalist, refusing to go back and repeat the earlier formulas simply because they have proved commercially and critically successful. Although acutely disturbed by the downward spiral and paralysis of will that seem to have overtaken modern civilization and committed to charting these in his work, Albee is not primarily a social playwright, and there is hardly one of his plays that is totally naturalistic or realistic. In form and style, they range, indeed, from surrealism (*The Sandbox*) to allegory (*Tiny Alice*), from the quasi-religious drawing-room play (*A Delicate Balance*) to the fable (*Seascape*), from the picaresque journey (*Malcolm*) to the ritual deathwatch (both *All Over* and *The Lady from Dubuque*), from scenes linked by cinematic techniques (*The Death of Bessie Smith*) to monodrama for a disembodied voice (*Box*), and from traditional memory play (*Three Tall Women*) to postmodern burlesque (*The Play About the Baby*).

Albee has received numerous awards and honors, including two Obie Awards, one in 1959-1960 for *The Zoo Story* and a second in 1993-1994 for sustained achievement, and two Tony Awards for best play, for *Who's Afraid of Virginia Woolf?* in 1963 and for *The Goat: Or, Who Is Sylvia?* in 2002. He was awarded three Pulitzer Prizes in Drama, for *A Delicate Balance* in 1967, *Seascape* in 1975, and *Three Tall Women* in 1994. The New York Drama Critics Circle Award for Best Play was given to three of Albee's dramas: *Who's Afraid of Virginia Woolf?* (1963), *Three Tall Women* (1994), and *The Goat* (2002). Other honors include the Kennedy Center Lifetime Achievement Award (1996) and the National Medal of Arts (1997).

Biography • Born on March 12, 1928, Edward Franklin Albee was adopted at the age of two weeks by the socially prominent and wealthy New Yorkers Reed and Frances Albee. His adoptive father was the scion of the family who owned the Keith-Albee chain of vaudeville houses; his adoptive mother was a former Bergdorf high-fashion model. Albee's deep-seated resentment of the natural parents who abandoned him finds reflection in the child motifs that pervade both his original plays and his adaptations: the orphan in *The Zoo Story* and *The Ballad of the Sad Café*, the mutilated twin in *The American Dream*, the intensely hoped-for child who is never conceived and the conceived child who is unwanted in *Who's Afraid of Virginia Woolf?*, the dead son in *A Delicate Balance*, the child in search of his father in *Malcolm*, the prodigal son detested by a haughty mother in *Three Tall Women*, and the apparently kidnapped child in *The Play About the Baby*. Living with the Albees was Edward's maternal grandmother, Grandma Cotta, whom he revered and would later memorialize in *The Sandbox* and *The American Dream*.

After his primary education at the Rye Country Day School, Albee attended a succession of prep schools (Lawrenceville School for Boys, Valley Forge Military Academy), finally graduating from Choate in 1946 before enrolling at Trinity College in Hartford, Connecticut, where he studied for a year and a half. While in high school, he wrote both poetry and plays. In 1953, Albee was living in Greenwich Village and working at a variety of odd jobs when, with the encouragement of Thornton Wilder, he committed himself to the theater. *The Zoo Story*, written in only two weeks, premiered in Berlin on September 28, 1959; when it opened Off-Broadway at the Provincetown Playhouse on a double bill with Samuel Beckett's *Krapp's Last Tape* (pr., pb. 1958) in January, 1960, it brought Albee immediate acclaim as the most promising of the new playwrights and won for him an Obie Award as Best Play of the Year.

Who's Afraid of Virginia Woolf?, Albee's first full-length work—and still his most famous—opened on Broadway in October, 1962, winning for him both the Drama Critics Circle Award and the Tony Award for the Best American Play of that season; the Drama Jury voted it the Pulitzer Prize, but the Advisory Board of Columbia University overturned the nomination because of the play's strong language and, as a result, John Gassner and John Mason Brown resigned from the jury in protest. Albee went on, however, to win three Pulitzers, for *A Delicate Balance*, *Seascape*, and *Three Tall Women*.

Along with the New York productions of numerous original one-act plays and original full-length works, Albee has done four adaptations for the stage: of Carson McCullers's 1951 novella *The Ballad of the Sad Café*; of James Purdy's 1959 novel *Malcolm*; of Giles Cooper's 1962 play *Everything in the Garden*; and of Vladimir Nabokov's 1955 novel *Lolita*. From the time of his own early successes, Albee has ac-

(AP/Wide World Photos)

tively encouraged the development of other young dramatists and, as part of a production team, has also brought the work of major avant-garde foreign dramatists to New York. Under the auspices of the State Department, he toured behind the Iron Curtain and in South America, and he has become a frequent and popular lecturer on the college circuit, as well as a director of revivals of his own plays.

Albee is an impassioned defender of the National Endowment for the Arts. He has also been actively involved with the international writers association PEN and served as president of the International Theater Institute. After a residency at the University of Houston, Albee directed the world premieres of *Marriage Play* and *Three Tall Women*, both at the English Theatre in Vienna; he also directed *Marriage Play* at the Alley Theatre in 1991 and at the McCarter Theatre in 1992. Between 1993 and 1994, the Signature Theatre Company presented a season of plays by Albee that included the New York premieres of *Finding the Sun, Marriage Play* and *Fragments*. Albee's plays and the actors who perform in them are perennial nominees for Tony and Obie Awards. *The Goat*, Albee's nineteenth play produced on Broadway, won the Tony Award for Best Play in 2002 as well as a New York Drama Critics Circle Award for Best Play. In 1996, he became only the fourth playwright to receive a Kennedy Center Honor. Critic David Richards of *The New York Times* noted that Albee, "increasingly introspective over the years," has countered his disappointment with Broadway (*The Man Who Had Three Arms* saw only sixteen performances in 1983) by becoming "a European playwright."

Analysis • Though he is touted sometimes as the chief American practitioner of the absurd in drama, Edward Albee only rarely combines in a single work both the techniques and the philosophy associated with that movement and is seldom as unremittingly bleak and despairing an author as Beckett. Yet the influence of Eugène Ionesco's humor and of Jean Genet's rituals can be discerned in isolated works, as can the battle of the sexes and the voracious, emasculating female from August Strindberg, the illusion/reality motif from Luigi Pirandello and O'Neill, and the poetic language of T. S. Eliot, Beckett, and Harold Pinter, as well as the recessive action and lack of definite resolution and closure often found in Beckett and Pinter.

As the only avant-garde American dramatist of his generation to attain a wide measure of popular success, Albee sometimes demonstrates, especially in the plays from the first decade of his career, the rather strident and accusatory voice of the angry young man. The outlook in his later works, however, is more that of the compassionate moralist, linking him—perhaps unexpectedly—with Anton Chekhov; one of the characters in

All Over, recognizing the disparity between what human beings could become and what they have settled for, even echoes the Russian master's Madame Ranevsky when she says, "How dull our lives are." Even in his most technically and stylistically avant-garde dramas, however, Albee remains essentially very traditional in the values he espouses, as he underlines the necessity for human contact and communion, for family ties and friendships, which provide individuals with the courage to grow and face the unknown.

Always prodding people to become more, yet, at the same time, sympathetically accepting their fear and anxiety over change, Albee has increasingly become a gentle apologist for human beings, who need one crutch after another, who need one illusion after another, so that—in a paraphrase of O'Neill's words—they can make it through life and comfort their fears of death.

Despite a lengthy career that has, especially in its second half, been marked by more critical downs than ups, Albee has not been satisfied to rest on his successes, such as *Who's Afraid of Virginia Woolf?*, nor has he been content simply to repeat the formulas that have worked for him in the past. Instead, he has continued to experiment with dramatic form, to venture into new structures and styles. In so doing, he has grown into a major voice in dramatic literature, the progress of whose career in itself reflects his overriding theme: No emotional or artistic or spiritual growth is possible without embracing the terror—and perhaps the glory—of tomorrow's unknown, for the unknown is contemporary humanity's only certainty. The major recurrent pattern in Albee's plays finds his characters facing a test or a challenge to become more fully human.

In *The Zoo Story*, Jerry arrives at a bench in Central Park to jar Peter out of his passivity and Madison Avenue complacence; in *The Death of Bessie Smith*, the black blues singer arrives dying at a southern hospital only to be turned away because of racial prejudice; in *Tiny Alice*, Brother Julian arrives at Miss Alice's mansion to undergo his dark night of the soul; in *A Delicate Balance*, Harry and Edna arrive at the home of their dearest friends to test the limits of friendship and measure the quality of Agnes and Tobias's life; in *Seascape*, the lizards Leslie and Sarah come up from the sea to challenge Charlie to renewed activity and to try their own readiness for the human adventure; and in *The Lady from Dubuque*, the Lady and her black traveling companion arrive to ease Jo to her death and help her husband learn to let go. To effect the desired change in Peter, Jerry in *The Zoo Story* must first break down the barriers that hinder communication. Accomplishing this might even require deliberate cruelty, because kindness by itself may no longer be enough: Oftentimes in Albee, one character needs to hurt another before he can help, the hurt then becoming a creative rather than a destructive force.

Along with the focus on lack of communication and on a love and concern that dare to be critical, Albee consistently pursues several additional thematic emphases throughout his works. *The American Dream*, which comments on the decline and fall from grace of Western civilization and on the spiritual aridity of a society that lives solely by a materialistic ethic, also decries the emasculation of Daddy at the hands of Mommy; to a greater or lesser degree. *The Death of Bessie Smith*, *Who's Afraid of Virginia Woolf?*, and *A Delicate Balance* all speak as well to what Albee sees as a disturbing reversal of gender roles (a motif he inherits from Strindberg), though Albee does become increasingly understanding of the female characters in his later works.

Several plays, among them *Who's Afraid of Virginia Woolf?* and *A Delicate Balance*, consider the delimiting effect of time on human choice and the way in which humanity's potential for constructive change decreases as time goes on. Characters in both *A Delicate Balance* and *Tiny Alice* face the existential void, suffering the anxiety that arises over the possibility of there being a meaninglessness at the very core of existence, while characters in several others, including *Box and Quotations from Chairman Mao Tse-tung, All Over,* and *The Lady from Dubuque,* confront mortality as they ponder the distinction between dying (which ends) and death (which goes on) and the suffering of the survivor.

Elsewhere, particularly in *Counting the Ways,* Albee insists on the difficulty of ever arriving at certainty in matters of the heart, which cannot be known or proved quantitatively. Finally, in such works as *Malcolm* and *Seascape,* he explores the notion that innocence must be lost—or at least risked—before there can be any hope of achieving a paradise regained. If the mood of many Albee works is autumnal, even wintry, it is because the dramatist continually prods his audiences into questioning whether the answers that the characters put forward in response to the human dilemma—such panaceas as religion (*Tiny Alice*) or formulaic social rituals (*All Over*)—might not in themselves all be simply illusions in which human beings hide from a confrontation with the ultimate nothingness of existence. In this, he comes closer to the absurdists, though he is more positive in his holding out of salvific acts: the sacrifice to save the other that ends *The Zoo Story,* the gesture of communion that concludes *Who's Afraid of Virginia Woolf?,* the affirmation of shared humanness that ends *Seascape,* and the merciful comforting of the survivor that concludes *The Lady from Dubuque.* If Albee's characters often live a death-in-life existence, it is equally evident that human beings, God's only metaphor-making animals, can sometimes achieve a breakthrough by coming to full consciousness of their condition and by recognizing the symbolic, allegorical, and anagogical planes of existence.

Who's Afraid of Virginia Woolf? • *Who's Afraid of Virginia Woolf?,* which brought Albee immediate fame as the most important American dramatist since Williams and Miller, is probably also the single most important American play of the 1960's, the only one from that decade with any likelihood of becoming a classic work of dramatic literature. In this, his first full-length drama, Albee continues several strands from his one-act plays—including the need to hurt in order to help from *The Zoo Story,* the criticism of Western civilization from *The American Dream,* and the Strindbergian battle of the sexes from that play and *The Death of Bessie Smith*—while weaving in several others that become increasingly prominent in his work: excoriating wit, a concern with illusion/reality, the structuring of action through games and game-playing (here, "Humiliate the Host," "Hump the Hostess," "Get the Guests," and "Bringing Up Baby"), and a mature emphasis on the need to accept change and the potentially creative possibilities it offers. Tightly unified in time, place, and action, *Who's Afraid of Virginia Woolf?* occurs in the early hours of Sunday morning in the home of George, a professor of history, and his wife, Martha, in the mythical eastern town of New Carthage.

After a party given by her father, the college president, Martha invites Nick, a young biology teacher, and his wife, Honey, back home for a nightcap. Through the ensuing confrontations and games that occasionally turn bitter and vicious, both the older and the younger couples experience a radical, regenerative transformation. George, who sees himself as a humanist who lives for the multiplicity and infinite variety that have always characterized history, immediately sets himself up against Nick, the man of science, or, better yet, of scientism, whose narrow, amoral view of inevitability—wherein every creature would be determined down to color of hair and eyes—would sound the death knell for civilization.

Like the attractive, muscular young men from *The American Dream* and *The Sandbox,* Nick is appealing on the outside but spiritually vapid within. If his ethical sense is undeveloped, even nonexistent, and his intellect sterile, he is also physically impotent when he and Martha go off to bed, though his temporary impotence should probably be regarded mainly as symbolic of the general sterility of his entire life. George apparently intends, much as Jerry had in *The Zoo Story*, to jar Nick out of his present condition, which involves being overly solicitous of his mousey, infantile wife. Though experiencing a false pregnancy when Nick married her, Honey, slim-hipped and unable to hold her liquor—her repeated exits to the bathroom are adroitly managed to move characters on and off the stage—is frightened of childbirth. As George detects, she has been preventing conception or aborting without Nick's knowledge, and in this way unmanning her husband, preventing him from transmitting his genes. By the play's end, Nick and Honey have seen the intense emptiness that can infect a marriage without children, and Honey three times cries out that she wants a child. George and Martha were unable to have children—neither will cast blame on the other for this—and so, twenty-one years earlier, they created an imaginary son, an illusion so powerful that it has become, for all intents and purposes, a reality for them.

If not intellectually weak, George, who is in fact Albee's spokesperson in the play, does share with Nick the condition of being under the emotional and physical control of his wife. Ever since the time when Martha's Daddy insisted that his faculty participate in an exhibition sparring match to demonstrate their readiness to fight in the war and Martha knocked George down in the huckleberry bush, she has taunted George with being a blank and a cipher. It is unlikely that he will ever succeed her father as college president—he will not even become head of the history department. Martha claims that George married her to be humiliated and that she has worn the pants in the family not by choice but because someone must be stronger in any relationship. George realizes that if he does not act decisively to change his life by taking control, the time for any possible action will have passed.

In a formulation of the evolutionary metaphor that Albee recurrently employs, George, who, like civilization, is facing a watershed, remarks that a person can descend only so many rungs on the ladder before there can be no turning back; he must stop contemplating the past and decide to "alter the future." Martha, too, seems to want George to take hold and become more forceful; she, indeed, is openly happy when he exerts himself, as when he frightens them all with a rifle that shoots a parasol proclaiming "Bang," in one of the absurd jokes of which Albee is fond. Martha, despite being loud and brash and vulgar, is also sensual and extremely vulnerable. She does indeed love George, who is the only man she has ever loved, and fears that someday she will go so far in belittling him that she will lose him forever. The imaginary son has served not only as a uniting force in their marriage but also as a beanbag they can toss against each other.

When George decides to kill the son whom they mutually created through an act of imagination, Martha desperately insists that he does not have the right to do this on his own, but to no avail. Even if the child, who was to have reached his twenty-first birthday and legal maturity on the day of the play, had been real, the parents would have had to let go and continue alone, facing the future with only each other. As George says, "It was time." He kills the illusion, intoning the mass for the dead. It is Sunday morning, and Martha is still frightened of "Virginia Woolf," of living without illusion, and of facing the unknown. "*Maybe* it will be better," George tells her, for one can never be totally certain of what is to come.

Just as there can be no assurance—though all signs point in that direction—that Nick and Honey's marriage will be firmer with a child, there can be no certainty that

George and Martha's will be better without their imaginary son, though George is now prepared to offer Martha the strength and support needed to see her through her fear. Finally, Albee seems to be saying, human beings must not only accept change but also actively embrace it for the possibilities it presents for growth. The future is always terrifying, an uncharted territory, yet if one does not walk into it, one has no other choice but death.

Tiny Alice • *Tiny Alice* is Albee's richest work from a philosophical point of view; it also represents his most explicit excursion into the realm of the absurd. In it, Albee addresses the problem of how human beings come to know the reality outside themselves, even questioning whether there is, finally, any reality to know. To do this, Albee builds his play around a series of dichotomies: between faith and reason, between present memory and past occurrence, and between symbol and substance.

The play opens with a scene that could almost stand on its own as a little one-act play, demonstrating Albee's wit at its virulent best. A Lawyer and a Cardinal, old school chums and, apparently, homosexual lovers in their adolescence, attack each other verbally, revealing the venery of both civil and religious authority. The Lawyer has come as the emissary of Miss Alice, ready to bequeath to the Church one hundred million dollars a year for the next twenty years; the Cardinal's secretary, the lay Brother Julian, will be sent to her castle to complete the transaction. For Julian, this becomes an allegorical dark night of the soul, a period when his religious faith will be tempted and tested. On the literal level, the play seems preposterous at times and even muddled; the suspicion that all this has been planned by some extortion ring, though it is unclear what they hope to gain by involving Julian, or even, perhaps, that all this is a charade devised by Julian to provide himself with an opportunity for sacrifice, is never quite dispelled.

On the metaphoric and symbolic levels, however, as a religious drama about contemporary humanity's need to make the abstract concrete in order to have some object to worship, *Tiny Alice* is clear and consistent and succeeds admirably. Julian, who earlier suffered a temporary loss of sanity over the disparity between his own conception of God and the false gods that human beings create in their own image, is now undergoing a further crisis. His temptation now is to search out a personification of the Godhead in order to make the Unknowable knowable, by making it concrete through a symbol; he hopes to prove that God exists by making contact with an experiential representation of him. To represent the Deity in this manner is, however, as the Lawyer insists, to distort and diminish it so that it can be understood in human terms. Up to this point, Julian has always fought against precisely such a reduction of the divine.

The symbol that Julian now literally embraces—through a sexual consummation and marriage that is both religious and erotic—is Miss Alice, the surrogate for Tiny Alice. That God in Albee's play is named "*Tiny* Alice" points, in itself, to the strange modern phenomenon of a reduced and delimited rather than an expansive deity. Instead of the real (Miss Alice) being a pale shadowing forth of the ideal form (Tiny Alice), here the symbol (Alice) is *larger* than what it represents, just as the mansion in which the action after scene 1 occurs is larger than its replica, exact down to the last detail, that is onstage in the library. The Lawyer insists that human beings can never worship an abstraction, for to do so always results in worshiping only the symbol and never the substance or the thing symbolized. Furthermore, he causes Julian to question whether that substance has any tangible existence: Is it only the symbol, and not the thing symbolized, that exists? If so, then Julian faces the possibility of nothingness, of there being *nothing there*, of there being only the finite, sense-accessible dimension in which people live and no higher order that provides meaning.

In the face of this dilemma, Brother Julian can either despair of ever knowing his God or make a leap of faith. When the financial arrangements have been completed, the Lawyer, who—like the Butler—has had Miss Alice as his mistress, shoots Julian, who has always dreamed of sacrificing himself for his faith. Martyrdom, the ultimate form of service to one's God, always involves questions of suicidal intent, of doing, as Eliot's hero in *Murder in the Cathedral* (pr., pb. 1935) knows, "the right deed for the wrong reason." Is one dying for self, or as a totally submissive instrument of God? As Julian dies in the posture of one crucified, he demands, in a paroxysm blending sexual hysteria and religious ecstasy, that the transcendent personify itself; indeed, a shadow moves through the mansion, accompanied by an ever-increasing heartbeat and ever-louder breathing, until it totally envelops the room. As Albee himself commented, two possibilities present themselves: Either the transcendent is real, and the God Tiny Alice actually manifests itself to Brother Julian at the moment of his death, or Julian's desire for transcendence is so great that he deceives himself.

The play's ending, while allowing for the person of faith to be confirmed in his or her belief about the spiritual reality behind the physical symbol, is at the same time disquieting in that it insists on the equally possible option that the revelation of transcendence is merely a figment of one's imagination. What Albee may well be suggesting, then, and what brings him to the doorstep of the absurdists in this provocative work, is that there is, finally, nothing there except what human beings, through their illusions, are able to call up as a shield against the void.

A Delicate Balance • *A Delicate Balance*, for which Albee deservedly won the Pulitzer Prize denied him by the Advisory Board four seasons earlier for *Who's Afraid of Virginia Woolf?*, is an autumnal play about death-in-life. A metaphysical drawing-room drama in the manner of Eliot and Graham Greene, it focuses on a well-to-do middle-aged couple, Agnes and Tobias, who are forced one October weekend to assess their lives by the unexpected visit of their closest friends, Harry and Edna (characters in Albee traditionally lack surnames).

The latter couple arrives on Friday night, frightened by a sudden perception of emptiness. Having faced the existential void, they flee, terrified, to the warmth and succor of Agnes and Tobias's home, trusting that they will discover there some shelter from meaninglessness, some proof that at least the personal values of friendship and love remain. As the stage directions imply, an audience should not measure these visitors-in-the-night against the requirements of realistic character portrayal; they function, instead, as mirror images for their hosts, who, by looking at them, are forced to confront the emotional and spiritual malaise of their own lives. Agnes's live-in sister, the self-proclaimed alcoholic Claire—whose name suggests the clear-sightedness of this woman who stands on the sidelines and sees things as they are—understands the threat that Harry and Edna bring with them.

Agnes fears that their guests come bearing the "plague," and Claire understands that this weekend will be spent waiting for the biopsy, for confirmation of whether some dread, terminal disease afflicts this family. Agnes not only has no desire for self-knowledge but also deliberately guards against any diagnosis of the family's ills. As the fulcrum, she is able to maintain the family's status quo only by keeping herself and Tobias in a condition of stasis, insulated from the currents that threaten to upset the "delicate balance" that allows them to go on without ever questioning their assumptions. A somewhat haughty though gracious woman, whose highly artificial and carefully measured language reflects the controlled pattern of her existence and her inability to tolerate or handle the unexpected, Agnes muses frequently on sex roles. A dramatic descendant of Strindberg's male characters rather than of his female characters, she decries all of those things that have made the sexes too similar and have thus threatened the stability of the traditional family unit. From her perspective, it is the wife's function to maintain the family *after* the husband has made the decisions: She only holds the reins; Tobias decides the route. It is Tobias's house that is not in order, and only he, she says, can decide what should be done.

Tobias himself would claim that Agnes rules, but Agnes would counter that this is only his illusion. Clearly, Tobias seems to have relinquished his position of authority after the death of their son, Teddy; at that point, according to their oft-divorced daughter, Julia, now inopportunely home again after a fourth failed marriage, Tobias became a pleasant, ineffectual, gray *non*eminence. Undoubtedly, his insufficiencies as a father have had an adverse effect upon his daughter's relationships with men, and although Tobias rationalizes that he did not want another son because of the potential suffering it might have caused for Agnes, he might equally have feared his own inadequacy as a role model. That Tobias lacks essential self-criticism and decisiveness is suggested by the motto he has cheerfully adopted: "We do what we can." In other words, he takes the path of least resistance, no longer exerting himself to do more than the minimum in his personal relationships.

At one point in the play, Tobias tells a story about his cat and him—a parable similar to Jerry's tale of the dog in *The Zoo Story*—which illustrates Tobias's attitude toward having demands placed on him and being judged. Believing that the cat was accusing him of being neglectful, and resenting this assessment, he turned to hating the cat, which he finally had put to sleep in an act Claire terms the "least ugly" choice. Now, with Harry and Edna's visit, Tobias is again having his motives and the depth of his concern measured. He realizes that if he does not respond positively to their needs, he will be tacitly admitting that his whole life, even his marriage to Agnes, has been empty. In one of the verbal arias for which Albee is justly famous, Tobias begs, even demands, that they remain, though he does not want this burden and disruption. When, despite his desperate entreaties, they insist on leaving, Agnes can calmly remark, "Come now; we can begin the day," satisfied that the dark night of terror is safely passed. Her closing line must, however, be understood as ironic. Although it is Sunday morning, there has been no resurrection or renewal; the opportunity for salvation has been missed, and Tobias must now live on with the knowledge that he has failed, that much of his life has been a sham. As is true of the characters at the end of O'Neill's *Long Day's Journey into Night* (pr., pb. 1956) Tobias's tragedy is that he has come to self-knowledge too late to act upon the new recognition.

Albee's central perception in *A Delicate Balance* appears to be that time diminishes the possibilities for human choice and change. Try as he might, it is now too late for Tobias to break out of the pattern, and so he is condemned to living out his days with an awareness of how little he has become because he lacks the comforting illusions of propriety and magnanimity that Agnes can call on for solace. He has seen his soul and has found it wanting, and things can never be the same again. For Tobias, in what is Albee's most beautiful play, the "delicate balance" that everyone erects as a shelter has tipped, but not in his favor. As Agnes muses, "Time happens," and all that remains is rust, bones, and wind. These are Albee's hollow people for whom the dark never ends.

Seascape • If *Tiny Alice* and *A Delicate Balance* are dark plays, *Seascape* is a play of light, Albee's most luminous work to date. An optimistic tone poem that won for Albee his second Pulitzer, *Seascape* might, indeed, profitably be seen as a reverse image of *A Delicate Balance*, which won for him his first. In the later play, Albee again focuses on a couple in their middle age who ask: Where do we go from here? Are change and growth still possible, or is all that remains a gradual process of physical and spiritual atrophy until death? Nearly the entire first act of *Seascape*—which is primarily a play of scintillating discussion rather than action—is a two-character drama, with the diametrically opposed viewpoints of Nancy and Charlie temporarily poised in a tenuous equilibrium. Nancy's inclination is to follow the urge to ever fuller life, while Charlie is seduced by the prospect of a painless withdrawal from all purposive activity.

The "seascape" of the play's title is the literal setting, but it is also an "escape," for the sea lying beyond the dunes is the archetype of both life and death; if it once symbolized Charlie's will-to-life, it now communicates his willed desire for the inertia of death or, at least, for a kind of premoral existence in which life simply passes. The shadow of Albee's dark plays still falls over *Seascape* in Charlie's initial stance as a man experiencing existential angst, terrified by the premonition of loneliness if Nancy should no longer be with him, fearful that even life itself may be only an illusion. In the face of these terrors—symbolized by the recurrent sound of the jet planes passing overhead—death beckons as a welcome release for Charlie because he has lived well. As his watchword, he chooses "we'll see," just another way of saying that things will be put off until they are blessedly forgotten. Nancy, on the other hand, refuses to vegetate by retreating from life and living out her remaining days in a condition equivalent to "purgatory *before* purgatory," insisting instead that they "*do something*." She understands that if nothing is ever ventured, nothing can be gained.

If Charlie, like Agnes in *A Delicate Balance*, desires stasis, a condition comfortable precisely because it is known and therefore can be controlled, Nancy will make the leap of faith into the unknown, accepting change and flux as a necessary precondition for progress and growth. Nancy accuses Charlie of a lack of "interest in imagery"; if, as Albee has frequently said, it is the metaphor-making ability that renders humanity truly human, then Charlie's deficiency in this regard signals his diminished condition. No sooner has Nancy finished her admonition to Charlie that they "*try* something new" than the opportunity presents itself in the appearance of Leslie and Sarah, two great green talking lizards come up from the sea. Their arrival, a startling yet delightful *coup de théâtre*, raises the work to the level of parable and allegory: Leslie and Sarah, existing at some prehuman stage on the evolutionary scale, serve as recollections of what the older couple's heritage was eons ago—as well as of what Charlie desires to become once again.

Leslie and Sarah, like Harry and Edna in *A Delicate Balance*, are afraid not of the prospect of dying and finding nothingness or the void but of the challenge of becoming more highly developed, which is to say more human and morally responsible creatures. Life in the sea, unterrifying because a known quantity, was also more restricted and limiting. What inspires them to seek something more are the inklings of a sense of wonder, of awe, and of a childlike enthusiasm—qualities Nancy possesses in abundance. Their choice, then, exactly parallels Charlie's: They can make do by settling for less than a full life, or they can expand their lives qualitatively by becoming conscious of themselves as thinking and feeling beings, although that requires a willingness to experience consciously suffering as well as joy. Significantly, it is Charlie, himself afraid, who persuades Leslie and Sarah to remain up on earth rather than descend back into the deep. In the moment of convincing them, he himself undergoes a regenerative epiphany that saves him, too.

At the climactic point in *Seascape*, Charlie, like Jerry in *The Zoo Story* and George in *Who's Afraid of Virginia Woolf?* before him, gives Leslie and Sarah a "survival kit." To accomplish this requires that he hurt them, especially Sarah. Because what separates human beings from the lower animals is precisely their consciousness of being alive, of being vulnerable, and of finally being mortal, Charlie realizes that he can help Leslie and Sarah complete their transformation from beast to human only by making them feel truly human emotions. Playing on Sarah's fear that Leslie might someday leave her and never return, he deliberately, in an action that recalls the necessary violence of Jerry toward Peter, makes Sarah cry; that, in turn, makes Leslie so defensive and angry that he hits and chokes Charlie. Having tasted these human emotions of sorrow and wrath, Sarah and Leslie at first desire more than ever to return to the ooze, to the prehuman security of the sea. What quenches their fears is Nancy and Charlie pleading with them not to retreat, extending their hands to the younger couple in a gesture of compassion and human solidarity.

In aiding Leslie and Sarah on the mythic journey from the womb into the world that, no matter how traumatic, must in time be taken, Charlie simultaneously leaves behind his desire to escape from life and asserts once more his will to live. If Charlie is a representative Everyman, fallen prey to ennui and despair, then Leslie's "Begin," on which the curtain falls, is a declaration of faith, trust, and determination, uttered not only for himself and Sarah but also for all humankind, who must periodically be roused and inspired to continue their journey.

The Man Who Had Three Arms • In *The Man Who Had Three Arms,* Albee abolished the fourth wall of the theater in a manner that reminded many critics of the works of Luigi Pirandello. The play's protagonist, coyly named "Himself," spends much of the drama lecturing to the audience. Himself claims to have been an ordinary man who aspired to little more in life than his marriage, family, and success at work until the morning he discovered a third arm growing out of his back. Seduced by his newfound celebrity, he embarks on a lucrative and highly conspicuous career, exploiting his anomalous "talent" and indulging morally challenging impulses with the seeming approval of an admiring public.

One day, however, the third arm mysterously withers away and disappears, leaving him financially bankrupt, spritiually broken and forsaken by his supporters. Coming on the heels of *The Lady from Dubuque,* which garnered mixed reviews and closed after only twelve performances on Broadway, and the failed adaptation of *Lolita,* which earned Albee some of the worst reviews of his stage career (as well as criticism by the Nabokov estate and the condemnation of several special interest groups), *The Man Who Had Three Arms* struck many critics as a transparently autobiographical play in which a self-pitying Albee lashed out at a public that he felt had celebrated him during his successful years, then abandoned him. Many reviewers, in fact, decried *The Man Who Had Three Arms* as a virtual attack on its audience. Albee concurred, noting that he agreed with Atonin Artaud that at times a dramatist must "literally draw blood." He admitted that the drama was "an act of aggression" and "probably the most violent play I've written," but he also disputed the autobiographical allusions many saw in the play.

The Man Who Had Three Arms closed after sixteen performances, capping a period that marks a low point both personally and professionally for Albee, in which it seemed his relevance and ability to enlighten as well as provoke theater audiences had, like the symbolic third arm of his protagonist, withered away to nothing.

Three Tall Women • With *Three Tall Women,* Albee proved that second acts are possible in a theater career. The play earned him his third Pulitzer Prize and inaugurated a revival of interest in his work that continued through the 1990's and beyond. It is a touchstone for many themes that he has tackled in other dramas, notably the illusions people cling to to distract them from the emptiness of their lives and the disillusionment that comes as aging gradually shuts off the individual's capacity for change and redemption.

The play also reflects a highly original melding of Albee's influences. It is a Chekhovian play in its compassion for its characters, and might almost be seen as Albee's rendition of *Tri sestry* (pr., pb. 1901, revised pb. 1904; *The Three Sisters,* 1920) in its treatment of three heroines who reflect with nostalgia and regret on the choices they have made in their lives. At the same time, its observations on personal decline and its minimalist staging techniques suggest the spare and despairing spirit of the plays of Beckett. The first act establishes the personalities of three distinct characters who are on stage for the entire play.

Woman A is a frail and needy woman in her early nineties. Described in the character notes as "thin, autocratic, proud," she radiates fading glory and dominates the dialogue with memories of her life as a girl from an ordinary family who married into wealth and soon learned the self-deceiving social rituals and hypocrisies of the moneyed class. A has outlived the philandering husband she once loved by more than thirty years. She speaks proudly of her accomplishments but grows childish and petulant when her memory fails or she finds herself physically incapable of activities she could once perform. B, who "looks rather as A would have at fifty-two," serves A as a nurse and caretaker. She is dutiful and understanding and calm to the point of seeming enigmatic. B serves as a buffer between A and C, who "looks rather as B would have at twenty-six" and who shows all the impatience and selfishness one associates with youth.

Though serving A in a vaguely legal capacity, C taunts A with the deficiencies of her age and openly expresses her exasperation with the older woman. There is no action per se in the first act, only verbal exchanges between the three women, who oscillate back and forth between heated, catty arguments with each other and conspiratorial schoolgirl confidences until A suffers an apparent stroke that brings down the curtain on first act. The seemingly naturalistic development of the play collapses in the second half when it becomes apparent that A, B, and C are actually different incarnations of the same character at different ages in her life, a nod (as some critics have suggested) to Beckett's *Krapp's Last Tape* (pr., pb. 1958), in which an aging man labors to reconcile his current self with tape-recorded messages that reflect the person he was on several different birthdays at earlier times in his life. The emotional makeup and personalities of these three tall women are shaped by their expectations and experiences of the moment. A has come to accept that the arc of her life has gradually moved her away from the attractive fantasy of things she hoped for as a young woman—love and happiness—to the cold reality of things she settled for: financial security and social status.

B is embittered by the fresh memory (for her) of the son who despised her for her compromises and acquiescence to disappointment and who ran away from home (and who visits A and curries her favor, much to B's dismay). C is two years younger than the woman she will be when she marries; she clings desperately to the belief that the best times of her life are all ahead of her, when in fact observations from A and B suggest that the best years of her life—the years that A and B might look back on wistfully—are soon to end. Despite the fact that these three women are the same character, each has no sympathy for the others and either resists or repudiates the person that the other is. However, though they act as if irreconcilable toward one another, the three provide one of Albee's most elaborate character mirrorings, yielding a single sympathetic reflection of someone once young, beautiful, and full of hope whose life has devolved into a simple, seemingly pointless struggle to survive.

As in previous plays, Albee provides his characters with an illusion that serves them as a crutch for getting through life: the jewelry the three women are given by their husband. Each interprets the illusion and its significance differently, based on her different self-awareness. C, who is still beholden to the illusions of youth, cherishes her jewelry as "tangible proof . . . that we're valuable." B is of a more cynical frame shaped by her disillusionments and disappointments: She sees no difference between real and fake jewelry "because the fake looks as good as the real, even feels the same, and why should anybody know our business?" Virtually all of A's jewelry is fake: Over the years, she has had to sell her real jewelry to support herself, a type of self-cannibalization that crystallizes the decline into emotional and spiritual entropy at the play's core. In his introduction to the published edition of the play, Albee reveals that *Three Tall Women* grew out of his troubled relationship with his adoptive mother Frankie, whom the characters are meant to represent.

Albee himself appears in the play as the prodigal son, who is present at A's sickbed but does not speak a line. He writes, "As she moved toward ninety, began rapidly failing both physically and mentally, I was touched by the survivor, the figure clinging to the wreckage only partly of her own making, refusing to go under." The play thus makes an interesting bookend to *The Man Who Had Three Arms,* for which Albee appears to have drawn from his personal life to craft a theatrical act of revenge. With *Three Tall Women* he showed it was possible to draw from the same life and fashion a compassionate reflection equally devastating in its honesty.

Marriage Play • *Marriage Play* confines its violence to the stage, where the protagonists, a married couple named Jack and Gillian, alternate between bouts of physical abuse and scenes of tenderness and physical attraction. Jack and Gillian are in some ways reminiscent of the battling couples of *Who's Afraid of Virginia Woolf?,* but the newer play also incorporates the sort of metaphysical speculation that marks much of Albee's later work. *Marriage Play* encapsulates many of the principal themes of Albee's dramatic career.

The Play About the Baby • With *The Play About the Baby,* Albee's career came full circle. The play reprises ideas and themes from earlier plays, albeit in a synthesis that makes it stand apart from the works from which it borrows. Its central conceit, a baby that may just be a figment of the characters' imaginations, seems a self-conscious nod to *Who's Afraid of Virginia Woolf?* and is reinforced by the pairing of a younger and older couple. At the same time, the free-form absurdism of the play calls to mind Albee's debut *The Zoo Story,* with its escalation to an act of dramatic provocation to shock a character out of a complacent frame of mind. Girl and Boy, the younger couple, have apparently had a baby together. Their nemeses are Man and Woman, an older couple—possibly married, possibly not—who first claim to have taken the baby, then proceed to call the baby's very reality in question. While the young couple plead for the return of their child, the older couple taunt them with word games, false memories, and similar challenges that hinder the younger couple's ability to prove who they are and the reality of their child.

The play ends with the couples agreeing—possibly under emotional duress, possibly faced with irrefutable proof—that there is no baby. Although very much a chamber piece, the play shows Albee at his wittiest and builds on distillations of trademark ideas in his dramas, including the notion that individual reality is shaped by needs, and the therapeutic value of an act of cruelty to save people from the illusions that focus their life.

The Goat • Albee's award-winning *The Goat* is, on the surface, a comedy, but it has an underlying tone of tragedy. Like *Who's Afraid of Virginia Woolf?*, it centers on a married couple, successful upper-class New York architect Martin, who has just won the Pritzker Prize, and Stevie, his wife of more than twenty years. This couple, however, has a seventeen-year-old gay son, and the center of their conflict involves Martin's infidelity. His infidelity is revealed during the course of a television interview. Martin explains that although he loves his wife, he fell in love while looking at property in upstate New York. When Martin shows the interviewer, his friend Ross, a photograph of his new love, Ross is shocked to see a photo of a goat—Sylvia. The second act deals, largely humorously, with Stevie's feelings as she comes to terms with Martin's infidelity; she is especially angry and feels unclean when she realizes that Martin had been having sex with both her and the goat for several months. She complains that he has brought her down, and as she exits, she threatens to bring him down as well.

The couple's son, Billy, argues with his father, comparing their sexual preferences, and when they reconcile, a kiss turns sexual. When Ross walks in and sees the kiss, he expresses his disgust, and in return, Martin describes a father being sexually aroused after bouncing his baby on his lap. It is this scene rather than, as might be expected, the references to bestiality that brought shocked responses from the audience. Some critics suggest that this is because Albee's treatment of bestiality is similar to the early treatment of homosexuality in its vagueness. In the last act, Stevie returns, dragging along the body of Sylvia. Martin is grief-stricken, able only to say "I'm sorry." A reviewer for *The New Republic* noted that Albee manages to sympathetically portray Martin, the goat-lover, despite the repugnance that many people feel for those who engage in bestiality.

Bibliography
Amacher, Richard E. *Edward Albee.* Rev. ed. Boston: Twayne, 1982. Taking Albee's career through *The Man Who Had Three Arms*, this study is part biography, part script analysis, and part career assessment. Amacher is best at discussing Albee's "place in the theatre" and his marriage of the well-made play form with the formless Theater of the Absurd. Good second opinion after C. W. E. Bigsby's edition of essays in 1975. Chronology, notes, bibliography.

Bigsby, C. W. E., ed. *Edward Albee: A Collection of Critical Essays.* Englewood Cliffs, N.J.: Prentice-Hall, 1975. Part of the Twentieth Century Views series, this collection includes notable names in theater and scholarship, such as Gerald Weales, Martin Esslin, Richard Schechner, Alan Schneider, Harold Clurman, Philip Roth, and Robert Brustein. They contribute several interpretations of the symbolic aspect of Albee's plays, usually, but not always, in single-play discussions. Chronology and select bibliography.

Bottoms, Stephen J. *Albee: "Who's Afraid of Virginia Woolf?"* New York: Cambridge University Press, 2000. A thorough study of Albee's best-known play.

Bryer, Jackson R. "Edward Albee." In *The Playwright's Art.* New Brunswick, N.J.: Rutgers University Press, 1995. Interview conducted in 1991 that discusses most of Albee's major plays at the time, both successes and failures. Albee reveals himself as clever and articulate as the characters in his plays, and makes pointed statements about the Broadway establishment and its impact on playwriting in America.

"Edward Albee." In *Playwrights at Work.* New York: Modern Library, 2000. Although this interview appeared in the *Paris Review* in 1966, when Albee had taken several critical hits in the wake of his success with *Who's Afraid of Virginia Woolf?*, it captures him in the full flush of his "angry young man" interval and records observations on the art and craft of playwriting that continue to inform his work.

Gussow, Mel. *Edward Albee: A Singular Journey.* New York: Simon & Schuster, 1999. A comprehensive biocritical study of the playwright by a leading cultural critic of *The New York Times*, whose association with Albee extends back to 1962. Written with Albee's cooperation and input, it discusses all his plays in the context of his life and his beliefs as an artist. With photos, bibliography, and index.

Kolin, Philip C., and J. Madison Davis. *Critical Essays on Edward Albee.* Boston: G. K. Hall, 1986. Part of a series of critical essays on American literature, this collection of original reviews (from *The Zoo Story* to *Counting the Ways*), general criticism, and an overview of Albee's importance to world theater is comprehensive and thorough, with some thirty-seven articles, as well as an annotated bibliography of Albee interviews (with its own index).

McCarthy, Gerry. *Edward Albee.* New York: St. Martin's Press, 1987. Stronger than other studies on Albee's theater sense, as opposed to his plays as dramatic literature, this brief but informative overview puts the work in a dynamic, action-and-reaction-oriented structural perspective. Some production stills, index, and brief bibliography.

Roudané, Matthew. *Understanding Edward Albee.* Columbia: University of South Carolina Press, 1987. Organized chronologically, and pairing the plays in each chapter (*Who's Afraid of Virginia Woolf?* gets its own), this study focuses on Albee's plays in a "culture seeking to locate its identity through the ritualized action implicit in the art of theater." Bibliography and index.

_____. *Who's Afraid of Virginia Woolf?: Necessary Fictions, Terrifying Realities.* Boston: Twayne, 1990. A close study of Albee's landmark drama, by one of Albee's most perceptive critics. A followup to the author's *Understanding Edward Albee,* with particular emphasis on the function and purpose of illusion in Albee's dramas.

Wasserman, Julian, ed. *Edward Albee: An Interview and Essays.* Houston, Tex.: University of St. Thomas, 1983. This 1981 interview, on translations, audiences, and similar earthly subjects, has a show-biz tone to it, without much of the transcendental abstractions of later interviews. A good place to start a study of Albee because he articulates his intentions here with some clarity and grace. Wasserman contributes an essay on language; seven other authors offer single-play discussions, not including *Who's Afraid of Virginia Woolf?* but including *The Lady from Dubuque, Seascape,* and *Counting the Ways.*

Thomas P. Adler,
updated by Thomas J. Taylor,
Robert McClenaghan, and Stefan Dziemianowicz

Jean Anouilh

Born: Cérisole, near Bordeaux, France; June 23, 1910
Died: Lausanne, Switzerland; October 3, 1987

Principal drama • *L'Hermine*, pr. 1932, pb. 1934 (*The Ermine*, 1955); *Le Bal des voleurs*, wr. 1932, pr., pb. 1938 (*Thieves' Carnival*, 1952); *Le Voyageur sans bagage*, pr., pb. 1937 (*Traveller Without Luggage*, 1959); *La Sauvage*, pr., pb. 1938 (*Restless Heart*, 1957); *Léocadia*, pr. 1940, pb. 1942 (*Time Remembered*, 1955); *Le Rendez-vous de Senlis*, pr. 1941, pb. 1942 (*Dinner with the Family*, 1958); *Antigone*, pr. 1944, pb. 1946 (English translation, 1946); *Jézabel*, pb. 1946; *Roméo et Jeannette*, pr., pb. 1946 (*Romeo and Jeanette*, 1958); *L'Invitation au château*, pr. 1947, pb. 1953 (*Ring Round the Moon*, 1950); *Ardèle: Ou, La Marguerite*, pr. 1948, pb. 1949 (*Ardèle*, 1951); *La Répétition: Ou, L'Amour puni*, pr., pb. 1950 (*The Rehearsal*, 1958); *Colombe*, pr. 1951, pb. 1953 (*Mademoiselle Colombe*, 1954); *La Valse des toréadors*, pr., pb. 1952 (*The Waltz of the Toreadors*, 1953); *L'Alouette*, pr., pb. 1953 (*The Lark*, 1955); *Ornifle: Ou, Le Courant d'air*, pr. 1955, pb. 1956 (*Ornifle*, 1970); *Pauvre Bitos: Ou, Le Dîner de têtes*, pr., pb. 1956 (*Poor Bitos*, 1964); *Jean Anouilh*, pb. 1958-1967 (3 volumes); *L'Hurluberlu: Ou, Le Réactionnaire amoureux*, pr., pb. 1959 (*The Fighting Cock*, 1960); *Becket: Ou, L'Honneur de Dieu*, pr., pb. 1959 (*Becket: Or, The Honor of God*, 1960); *La Foire d'empoigne*, pb. 1960, pr. 1962 (*Catch as Catch Can*, 1967); *L'Orchestre*, pr. 1962, pb. 1970 (*The Orchestra*, 1967); *The Collected Plays*, pb. 1966-1967 (2 volumes); *Le Boulanger, la boulangère et le petit mitron*, pr. 1968, pb. 1969; *Cher Antoine: Ou, L'Amour raté*, pr., pb. 1969 (*Dear Antoine: Or, The Love that Failed*, 1971); *Les Poissons rouges: Ou, Mon père, ce héros*, pr., pb. 1970; *Le Directeur de l'opéra*, pr., pb. 1972 (*The Director of the Opera*, 1973); *L'Arrestation*, pr., pb. 1975 (*The Arrest*, 1978); *Le Scénario*, pr., pb. 1976; *Le Nombril*, pb. 1981; *Number One*, pr. 1984

Other literary forms • Jean Anouilh is known only for his plays. With the exception of infrequent reviews, he wrote nothing else and was known to refuse requests for occasional pieces with characteristic truculence, professing his inability "to write."

Achievements • Active as a dramatist well past the age of sixty-five, Jean Anouilh wrote nearly fifty plays in roughly as many years, among them five or ten true masterpieces that more than suffice to assure him a position of high distinction in the history of French drama.

Achieving distinction in his mid-twenties with such memorable successes as *Traveller Without Luggage* and *Thieves' Carnival*, Anouilh soon thereafter consolidated his reputation with the thought-provoking *Antigone* to become the preeminent dramatist of wartime and postwar France, reaching both a serious and a popular audience. Among the most instinctively "theatrical" of playwrights, Anouilh proved equally skillful at comedy, melodrama, near-tragedy, and satire, adopting for his efforts a new, if tongue-in-cheek, system of genre classification: In the standard collections of his theater, the pieces are duly classified as "pink" plays, "black" plays, "shining" plays, "grating" plays, and so on.

During the 1950's, Anouilh added, with considerable success, a new category: "costume" plays based, if somewhat less than faithfully, on the characters and incidents of history. Both *The Lark*, which re-creates the life and death of Joan of Arc, and *Becket*, studying the tortured relationship between Thomas à Becket and Henry II, achieved great success worldwide, as did a subsequent film version of the latter, featuring Richard Burton in the title role and Peter O'Toole as the king.

Increasingly involved in the staging and direction of his plays, Anouilh wrote little new for the theater during the 1960's. A subsequent phase of his career, beginning around 1970, brought forth several new plays deemed generally inferior to Anouilh's prior standard, with a tendency toward repetition, yet eminently stage worthy thanks to the author's personal involvement in their production.

For reasons difficult to fathom, Anouilh's plays have fared somewhat less well in English translation than might have been expected, with appreciably better success in Britain than in the United States or Canada. At times ill-served by his translators, even down to the titles of his plays, Anouilh was perhaps too irretrievably Gallic in thought and expression to reach an American audience. Even in America, however, he is destined to be remembered as the most talented, versatile, and representative French dramatist of the mid-twentieth century.

Biography • "I have no biography," wrote Jean-Marie-Lucien-Pierre Anouilh around the age of thirty-five to one of his earliest critics, "and am quite pleased not to have any." Going on to sketch in such bare essentials as a year of law school and two years in advertising, with some desultory work in films, Anouilh observed that he had discovered the theater at an early age and had fortunately (he claimed) never had to resort to journalism. Thus did Anouilh drape about his life a screen of privacy that more or less protected him for the rest of his life. To an even greater degree than in the case of most prolific authors, Anouilh's work was his life, and vice versa.

Anouilh's "life in the theater" began in late 1929 or early 1930, when he succeeded the scenarist and playwright Georges Neveux as secretary to the eminent director Louis Jouvet, who had "discovered" and developed the playwriting talents of Jean Giraudoux, by then France's most eminent dramatist. Almost at once, Anouilh began to try his hand at writing plays, initially without much success; later he withdrew certain of his early efforts from circulation, and they remain to this day in a limbo perhaps well deserved. One of the few anecdotes attaching itself to the playwright's early life holds that on Anouilh's marriage in 1932 to the actress Monelle Valentin, Jouvet "gave" the young couple some opulent stage properties left over from his production of Giraudoux's *Siegfried* (pr., pb. 1928; English translation, 1930) to furnish their otherwise bare apartment.

Not long afterward, with *Siegfried* scheduled for revival, Anouilh and his wife returned home to find their flat stripped clean of furniture. Anouilh, meanwhile, was beginning to attract favorable attention with his attempts at playwriting; a sale of film rights to Hollywood around 1934 proved sufficient to assure his financial independence—despite the fact that the play, *Y avait un prisonnier*, was never filmed and has since been repudiated by its author.

Following the runaway success of *Traveller Without Luggage* in 1937, Anouilh settled into the life of the professional playwright. Divorced from Monelle Valentin, with whom he had one child, Anouilh around 1953 married an actress known professionally as Charlotte Chardon, with whom he had three more children. Soon thereafter, following the success of *The Lark*, Anouilh assumed increasing responsibility in the mounting of his plays, usually in collaboration with the director Roland Piétri.

Only after around 1968, with a cycle of generally superficial plays offered mainly as a pretext for his own involvement in their production, did Anouilh begin to inject an autobiographical element into his work. The character of Antoine de Saint-Flour, featured in several of the plays, is a successful (but harried) writer modeled clearly on the author in the manner of Neil Simon; several of these late plays also portray shabby casino orchestras similar to those in which Anouilh's mother played violin during the author's childhood. In any case, however, Anouilh appears to have been quite justified in attempting to divert public attention away from his life, all the more so as his work provides a most useful and reliable record. It is no exaggeration to say that the life of Jean Anouilh is most readily accessible through the history of the French stage in the mid-twentieth century.

Analysis • The young Jean Anouilh arrived in Paris during one of the richest periods of French dramatic activity since the seventeenth century. Recently rescued from the commercial doldrums by a "Cartel" of four brilliant directors, infused with new life from abroad (German expressionism and the ground-breaking work of Luigi Pirandello), French drama in the late 1920's and the early 1930's enjoyed a genuine renaissance. Jean Giraudoux, previously known as a diplomat and a rather esoteric novelist, was charming even the crowds with his ethereal yet somehow earthy speculations on politics and love, joining such established talents as the Freudian Henri-René Lenormand, the neo-Shakespearean Jean Sarment, and the highly inventive Armand Salacrou, who was just then beginning to hit his stride as a singular interpreter of life as lived in a world of broken (and inevitably breakable) dreams.

Receptive to such influences, Anouilh soon joined his perceptions to his innate sense of theater to forge a dramatic style that was uniquely and unmistakably his own, very much of its time yet destined, at its best, to prove timeless. Today, only the work of Giraudoux has achieved anything even approaching the staying power of Anouilh's finest efforts. Salacrou, at one time Anouilh's closest competitor, fell far behind him during the postwar years and never managed to regain his stride. Sarment and Lenormand, even their best works now hopelessly dated, are all but forgotten except by students of the interwar French theater.

To a large degree, the abiding strength of Anouilh's dramaturgy resides in its basic theatricality, a polyvalent sense of play and playing that recalls and renews the most playful moments in the works of Molière and William Shakespeare. In the words of critic John Harvey, Anouilh discovered the secret early in his career, after *The Ermine*, when he ceased "toiling" at his material and began "toying" with it instead.

The Ermine, although the first of Anouilh's plays to attract widespread recognition, is perhaps the least innovative in its presentation, its originality residing primarily in Anouilh's announcement and treatment of themes that would soon come to characterize his theater. Cast in a naturalistic mold, *The Ermine* contrasts the wealthy Monime with the underprivileged, ambitious Frantz, who will stop at nothing, even murder, in order to win her hand. Monime, however, does not decide that she loves Frantz until *after* he has claimed responsibility for the crime and turned himself in to the authorities. Such hopelessness, usually polarized between rich and poor, would continue to haunt Anouilh's would-be lovers throughout the rest of his career as a playwright.

Although the masterful *Thieves' Carnival* had already been written by the winter of 1936-1937, it was *Traveller Without Luggage*, produced during that season by the illustrious Pitoëffs (Georges and Ludmilla), that truly secured Anouilh's reputation as a dramatist. In total control of his material for the first time, Anouilh moves deftly and playfully between satiric farce and near-tragedy only to conclude, with a self-mocking coup de théâtre at the end, that the concept of tragedy has long since outlived its usefulness. A similar undercutting of tragedy characterizes Anouilh's memorable treatment of time-honored classical themes in *Antigone*, whose heroine consciously gives her life in vain. Both plays, however, were among the first to be classified by their author under the heading of "black" plays, perhaps because they are too bleak and pessimistic to be considered wholly tragic.

Closely related to the "black" plays are the early "pink" plays, ostensible comedies in which, as the author has observed, there are nevertheless woven fine strands of black. Even when cast in the comic mode, Anouilh's personal vision remains profoundly pessimistic, hinting at the corrosive effects of life-as-lived and the frequently intolerable burdens of the past. *Dinner with the Family*, about a married man who rents a house for one evening and hires actors to represent his family in order to impress his would-be second mistress (or wife), is at once the most frankly theatrical and the most successful of the pink plays and remains one of Anouilh's finest achievements.

Owing mainly to the resonant, if ambivalent, success of his *Antigone*, Anouilh in the 1940's acquired a reputation as a "writer-thinker" whose plays merited serious evaluation for their "ideas" alongside the works of such consciously philosophical dramatists as Albert Camus and Jean-Paul Sartre. Anouilh, who had never made any claim to writing anything but playable theater, was miscast in such company, and his "ideas," in consequence, were frequently found wanting. His strongest plays, however, do express a worldview by no means incompatible with Sartre's existentialism or Camus's speculations on the Absurd.

Like Sartre, Anouilh presents characters "in situation" and totally at the mercy of their own actions, with no deity available to rescue them (except in the most blatantly contrived of self-consciously theatrical situations). Long since corrupted by conflicting interests recalling those of Sartre's bourgeois *salauds*, the world inhabited by Anouilh's characters is a disquieting place, with communication among mortals (let alone love) as impossible as in Sartre's *Huis clos* (1944; *No Exit*, 1946), and for most of the same reasons. Dehumanized by poverty, conditioned by their aspirations to expect a world of satisfactions that simply does not exist, the have-nots among Anouilh's characters, spiritual descendants of Frantz in *The Ermine*, experience an awareness of the Absurd not unlike that of the murderous Martha in Camus's *Le Malentendu* (1944; *The Misunderstanding*, 1948).

Anouilh's work, however, differs profoundly from that of Sartre and Camus in that ideas are secondary in importance to the prime value of dramatic art; never presented solely on their own merits, the ideas to be found in Anouilh's theater are of interest to the author only insofar as they help him to present, or the audience to understand, the motivation of his characters. It is therefore more than a bit hyperbolic to see in *Antigone*, as did a number of commentators at the time, a reactionary counterpoise to the existentialist, politically liberal stance of Sartre's *Les Mouches* (1943; *The Flies*, 1946). Given Anouilh's lack of religious belief, it is wholly natural that Antigone be disabused of the faith that supposedly motivates her actions, just as the "sainthood" of Becket in Anouilh's later play will be attributed to wholly aesthetic, nonreligious, and "human" standards of behavior. A number of critics also erred in their assumption that Creon, the pragmatist, emerges somehow as the hero of *Antigone*; there are simply no heroes in Anouilh's theatrical universe, and the playwright's main point throughout the play is to stress the eventual futility of *all* human action.

During the years following World War II, Anouilh expanded his repertory to include such new categories as the "shining" or "brilliant" (*Pièces brillantes*), "grating" (*Pièces grinçantes*), and quasi-historical (*Pièces costumées*) plays. An offshoot of the prewar

Pièces roses, or pink plays, the *Pièces brillantes* offer a particularly sophisticated form of satiric comedy, or comic satire; in the view of critic Lewis Falb, the plays resemble the diamonds recalled in their title in that they are sparkling, many-faceted, yet cold and hard at the center. Perhaps best known of the *Pièces brillantes* is *Ring Round the Moon*. Recalling the ludic wit of Oscar Wilde's *The Importance of Being Earnest: A Trivial Comedy for Serious People* (pr. 1895), *Ring Round the Moon* features twin brothers intended to be played by the same actor, with split-second entries and exits. Also notable among the "brilliant" plays are *The Rehearsal* and *Mademoiselle Colombe*.

Trenchant social satire, never far from the surface in any of Anouilh's plays, rises to a featured position in the "grating" plays, presumably so named because they are designed to set one's teeth on edge. Featuring intentionally disagreeable characters often presented in broad caricature, the "grating" plays recall such early "black" plays as *The Ermine* and *Restless Heart* in their treatment of the necessary compromise between aspirations and reality. *Ardèle* and *The Waltz of the Toreadors*, linked by common featured characters, are perhaps the most notable of the earlier grating plays; others include *Ornifle*, a generally weak reworking of the Don Juan theme, and *Poor Bitos*, a biting political satire juxtaposing World War II and the French Revolution. Anouilh's finest plays during the 1950's, however, were two of his somewhat misnamed "costume" plays, historical at least in setting, which are about as close as he ever came to writing true "plays of ideas." Both *The Lark* and *Becket* remain thought-provoking as well as highly playable, inviting the audience to speculate on what might have been going on in the characters' minds as they performed the actions now duly recorded in the pages of history.

Like Albert Camus in his *Caligula* (wr. 1938-1939, pb. 1944; English translation, 1948), Anouilh made no claim to a faithful re-creation of history, or even to writing "historical" plays. As with Camus, history serves as little more than a pretext—a fecund source of potentially fascinating theatrical characters. Earlier in his career, Anouilh, like Giraudoux and several others just before him, had appropriated the characters and setting of classical mythology to make some very contemporary theatrical statements, of which *Antigone* is the best; during the 1950's, history came to serve him much as mythology had done earlier. Devoid of faith and admittedly uncomfortable with the concept of sainthood, Anouilh in *The Lark* and *Becket* revisits the lives of two saints in order to present them in wholly human terms.

As Anouilh sees them, Joan of Arc and Thomas à Becket are heroic figures, high-principled to be sure, but hardly otherworldly. Joan, offered a reprieve, pragmatically chooses martyrdom in order to provide a shining example for posterity; Thomas, denied the consolation of true belief, has adopted instead an aesthetic standard of behavior that dictates that he do the best possible job at whatever he is supposed to do, even at the cost of his life. Remarkable in their affirmation of basic human dignity, *The Lark* and *Becket* remain among the finest of Anouilh's efforts, equal or superior in vigor to such comparable efforts as Maxwell Anderson's *Joan of Lorraine* (pr., pb. 1946) or T. S. Eliot's *Murder in the Cathedral* (pr., pb. 1935).

Some ten years after the success of *Becket*, Anouilh resumed work on a new cycle of "grating" plays that he had in fact begun even before *Becket* with *The Fighting Cock*, the latter a dark-edged comedy satirizing, among other things, the "postmodern" drama of Samuel Beckett, Eugène Ionesco, and the early Arthur Adamov. By the late 1960's, however, Anouilh had himself assimilated many of the perspectives and techniques of the newer dramatists and had begun incorporating them into his own work. *Les Poissons rouges*, generally considered to be the finest play in the new cycle, dispenses with chronology in order to present various stages in the protagonist's life, all compressed into the space of one particularly trying day. A parallel cycle of "baroque" plays, often featuring some of the same characters, has proved somewhat less successful, but the strongest of them, such as *Dear Antoine*, have been well received in production.

Traveller Without Luggage • Frankly derived from such sources as Giraudoux's *Siegfried,* which deals with an amnesiac veteran of World War I, and Jean Cocteau's *La Machine infernale* (1934; *The Infernal Machine*, 1936), a playful reworking of the Oedipus legend, *Traveller Without Luggage* nevertheless served notice of a new and highly innovative talent. Gleefully exploiting the conventions and resources of the stage, at times assuming the spectator's familiarity with his obvious sources, the young Anouilh both charmed and disconcerted his audiences by proving, at least in theatrical terms, that there is in life no problem too large to run away from.

In skillful parody of the Oedipus legend, Anouilh presented as his protagonist an amnesiac veteran known only as "Gaston," who is presumably in search of his own identity. Unlike Oedipus, however, Gaston will resolutely—and successfully—turn his back on the overwhelming evidence at hand.

Institutionalized for eighteen years since the Armistice, Gaston has been interviewed by nearly three hundred families in search of a missing son or brother, and even as he meets with the prosperous, respectable Georges Renaud, there are supposedly five or six other families just offstage, eagerly awaiting their turn. Considerable tension soon develops between the mounting evidence that Georges Renaud has at last found his brother Jacques and Gaston's increasing revulsion against the character of Jacques as revealed. Jacques, it seems, was for the eighteen known years of his life a most disagreeable fellow who shot birds out of trees, crippled his best friend by pushing him down a flight of stairs, and eventually slept with his brother's wife.

In further parody of the Oedipus material, Gaston keeps asking questions in relentless pursuit of the hideous truth; quite unlike Oedipus, however, he will feel no constraint to live with what he has learned. Over the years, Gaston has apparently envisioned himself as a *tabula rasa* about to acquire the imprint of a joyous childhood, and he will certainly not stop now. Ironically, the cold obstinacy with which Gaston refuses to accept his identity amply proves, to the satisfaction of both the audience and his fellow characters, that he is in fact Jacques Renaud.

Crucial to the developing action is the figure of Georges Renaud's wife, Valentine, whose abiding love for the seemingly unlovable Jacques has survived the eighteen years of his absence. Anticipating by several weeks her husband's planned interview with the "living unknown soldier," Valentine entered the asylum disguised as a laundress, and she maneuvered the unsuspecting Gaston into an amorous encounter. Horrified to learn that he has thus been tricked, Gaston remains unmoved by Valentine's unquestioning love and acceptance—even after the revelation that Valentine had loved Jacques first and had subsequently married his older, established brother only for reasons of financial expediency. Georges, for his part, remains understanding, perhaps even forgiving, but for Gaston that is not enough.

Oddly, the affair with Valentine appears to strike him as the least forgivable of Jacques Renaud's many recorded dastardly deeds, and he remains resolutely "pure," indeed even priggish, in her presence. Valentine, whose love for Jacques has long since been stripped of illusions, urges Gaston to return to the human race, accepting both himself and her. As proof of his identity, she asks him to look for a scar on his back, the remnant of a lover's quarrel shortly before Jacques's departure for the front, when Valentine suspected Jacques of infidelity and jabbed him with a hatpin.

The device of the scar, surely the most obvious of Anouilh's allusions to the Oedipus legend, ironically becomes the agent of Gaston's eventual and unabashedly theatrical deliverance. The scar is there, and Gaston bursts into tears (offstage) when he sees it in the mirror, but it is not long before he craftily turns Valentine's love against her, using the scar as evidence to "prove" that he is in fact someone else. Like the amorous female Sphinx in *The Infernal Machine* who has told Oedipus the answers to the riddle in the hope of winning his affections, Valentine finds herself thrust aside by the machinations of an overweening masculine ego. For Gaston, though, there will be no eventual reckoning or even recognition. In place of tragedy, Anouilh seems to be saying, there is for most people only tedium, made bearable at best by a seemingly limitless capacity for self-delusion.

The controversial ending of *Traveller Without Luggage*, alternately criticized or misconstrued by observers, merely suggests that modern man, his back to the wall, will either seek refuge in daydreams or lie, cheat, and steal. Gaston in effect does both, exchanging his "real" life for one chosen after his fancy. Had Anouilh sent Gaston off to a literal castle in Spain, he could hardly have made his message more explicit; the English country house with "marvelous ponies" will surely do in a pinch. Far from being "rescued" by a *deus ex machina* in the person of the little English boy who needs an adult "nephew" in order to claim his inheritance, Gaston has in fact chosen the thoroughly human hell of anonymity, rejecting Valentine's promise of a life (likened to a full page of writing) "full of spots and crossed-out words, but also full of joys." Gaston's refuge, if such it may be called, is hardly preferable to that of the ostrich.

Nearly forty years after the first performances of *Traveller Without Luggage*, the play's—or Gaston's—basic premise was intriguingly and rather effectively questioned by Eugène Ionesco in a play suggestively titled *L'Homme aux valises* (pr., pb. 1975; *Man with Bags*, 1977). In Ionesco's play, the anonymous protagonist trudges through at least forty years of recent history lugging two heavy suitcases that he doggedly refuses to put down for fear of losing them, and with them his identity. Oddly replicating Valentine's appeals to Gaston, Ionesco makes the point that while identity and heredity may be cumbersome, they are all that one can confidently claim and are at the very least a point of departure for one's actions; without them, one might as well be dead.

The Arrest • Curiously, the theatrical season of *Man with Bags*, 1975, also brought forth a new play by Anouilh titled *The Arrest*, itself a thought-provoking coda to Gaston's concept of identity. Its title no doubt an intentional double entendre embracing cardiac arrest as well, *The Arrest* expands to two hours the final moments in the life of an aging gangster, fatally wounded in a motor accident while fleeing the police. Indebted for its structure to Salacrou's *L'Inconnue d'Arras* (1935), which dramatizes the last thoughts of a suicide, *The Arrest* poses a new, pertinent, and most intriguing question: Is not the deepest (and most futile) human need that of being "understood"?

Breathing his last, the hoodlum Frédéric Walter asks many questions about his life, and is fortunate enough to have them answered by the avuncular Inspector, who, like Victor Hugo's Javert in *Les Misérables* (1862; English translation, 1862), has devoted his life's work to learning the habits and lifestyle of one particular criminal. As Walter prepares to die, the Inspector helps him to "understand" himself far more effectively than any parent, child, wife, mistress, or psychoanalyst ever could. As the Prayer of St. Francis implies, it is far more human to seek to be understood than to understand, and Frédéric Walter is surely no saint. Unlike Gaston, however, he both seeks and finds the truth about himself in highly memorable theatrical terms.

Dinner with the Family • Written soon after *Traveller Without Luggage*, although not staged until some four years later, *Dinner with the Family* is perhaps the strongest and most memorable of Anouilh's "pink" plays, with a highly entertaining restatement of the author's characteristic themes.

Like Gaston of *Traveller Without Luggage*, Georges of *Dinner with the Family* longs for, and seeks to re-create, an idyllic life quite different from the one that he has found himself obliged to lead. A young man of some means, he has rented a charming country house for one evening in order to impress a young woman with whom he has fallen in love; to represent his parents, he has hired an aging actor and actress who at first appear to need a considerable amount of coaching in their roles.

As the action proceeds, the various threads of Georges's dream begin to unravel, if never quite completely. His parents, it seems, are very much alive and very demanding of Georges's time and money, as are his wife, Henriette, and a rather sympathetic mistress named Barbara, who happens to be the wife of Georges's best friend, Robert. It is Barbara who precipitates much of the early action by warning Georges, in a telephone call, that Henriette has threatened to rid the house of freeloaders—his parents included—if Georges does not return at once. As in *Traveller Without Luggage*, considerable tension develops between the protagonist's aspirations and the somewhat more sordid reality of his life. Georges, however, is a more sympathetic character than is Jacques/Gaston; he is portrayed throughout as a fundamentally decent man whose sustained attention to the needs of other people has hampered his own emotional development.

Counterpointed by the presence of the two professional actors, who frequently offer their opinion as to how a particular scene should be played, the various levels of reality and artifice in Georges's life remain in delicate balance throughout the play. His marriage, it seems, was arranged by his parents as a solution to their own financial woes, and they have in fact been sponging off him ever since. His wife, although she professes to love him, may well be incapable of love, and Robert (with his wife) has joined the small army of freeloaders even as he has come to envy and detest his erstwhile boyhood friend. The only sane or sympathetic character in the lot is Barbara, who loves Georges deeply and without illusion. A close spiritual descendant of Valentine Renaud, Barbara alone can see, or will admit, that Georges's life has been nearly devoured by the demands of his family and other hangers-on; in the final analysis, she loves Georges enough to grant him his right to freedom. Isabelle, the charming young woman with whom Georges has fallen in love, may well represent his last chance to "reclaim himself," and Barbara will not stand in his way.

Criticized in its time as false or at the very least incredible, the ending of *Dinner with the Family*, although frankly contrived, now seems prophetic of a later generation in which "fresh starts," if not the rule, are at least no longer the exception. Today it seems almost plausible, if still humorous, that Georges be reunited with Isabelle for their long-delayed evening meal, sometime after which they will go off to the mountains and raise bees. Georges, in fact, may well be the first member of the dropout counterculture to have been portrayed sympathetically on the stage.

Antigone • The best-known and most frequently performed of Anouilh's many plays, rivaled only by *The Lark* and *Becket, Antigone* is certainly one of his strongest efforts, as relevant and resonant today as it was when it first appeared onstage.

Near the last in a long (and sometimes distinguished) line of French plays with a classical setting that began to appear in the late 1920's, including Giraudoux's *Amphitryon 38* (pr., pb. 1929; English translation, 1938) and *Électre* (pr., pb. 1937; *Electra*, 1952), *Antigone* is an even stronger and more original play than it must at first have seemed. Understatedly theatrical in presentation, intended to be played in inconspicuous modern dress, Anouilh's restatement of the Antigone-Creon debate remains one of the theater's most powerful and memorable portrayals of the inevitable conflict between youth and age, between uncompromising idealism and the weathered voice of experience.

Displaying his usual sure sense of theater, Anouilh replaces the traditional Greek chorus with a single dinner-jacketed male figure, recalling the Stage Manager in Thornton Wilder's *Our Town* (pr., pb. 1938). The Chorus, as he is known, steps forward on a stage full of characters to explain, in urbane tones, the role and function of each character in the drama that is to follow. As the action progresses, the Chorus will continue to serve as both the narrator and commentator, with a suitable coda at the end. Given Anouilh's reluctance to make public statements, the words and thoughts of *Antigone*'s Chorus are often quoted, no doubt with some justice, as being those of the author himself.

To a somewhat greater degree than Anouilh's earlier efforts, *Antigone* expresses the author's singular, profound, but often overlooked capacity for "poetry." Eschewing the overblown rhetoric of certain of his predecessors and contemporaries in the theater, Anouilh was nevertheless highly skilled at the creation of poetic imagery, often expressed in a simple, highly memorable conceit or metaphor. In *Antigone*, particularly in the title character's dialogues with her governess and with her fiancé, Hémon, such imagery helps to establish Antigone as a character and fix her in the spectator's mind. As her language shows, Antigone combines the strength of such characters as Valentine and Barbara with the impossible idealism generally associated with the author's male protagonists, making her more than a match for the toughened, world-weary Creon.

By far the most memorable feature of *Antigone* is the stylized yet credible debate between Antigone and her uncle, whose thankless task it has been to clean up the mess created by Oedipus and his family. In one scene, anticipating numerous more modern family quarrels, Creon accuses his niece of resembling her father in her refusal to leave well enough alone; her branch of the family, he observes, tends to ask too many questions and make trouble for everyone. Politically bound to leave one of her dead brothers unburied in order to keep the peace, Creon astonishes the headstrong, idealistic Antigone by informing her that he was unable to tell the two bodies apart and that he honestly does not care which was which; after all, he concludes, both boys were venal scoundrels quite different from the heroes envisioned by their adoring younger sister. Thus disabused of any true motivation for her actions, Antigone nevertheless perseveres in defying Creon's orders, telling him that her "role" is to say no to him and die. Anouilh thus casts in purely heroic terms the refusal hitherto exemplified in the attempts of Gaston and Georges to escape the sordid pettiness of life. Although hers will be a hollow victory, exemplified in death, Antigone at least achieves a grandeur of sorts by refusing to accept her uncle's "adult" world of smoke-filled rooms, trade-offs, and compromise.

First performed during 1944 with World War II still in progress, *Antigone* initially drew both praise and blame from both sides of the political fence. There was little doubt in anyone's mind that Antigone represented the uncompromising, if barely visible, spirit of Free France, or Creon as those who collaborated with the Germans, if need be, in order to keep the country running. Disagreement arose, however, as to which of the characters was more sympathetically presented, and there were those who saw Antigone's martyrdom as sufficiently "meaningless" to render Creon, by default, the true hero of the piece. *Antigone*, however, typical of Anouilh's theater in general, seeks less to make a statement than to reflect the many ambiguities of life itself.

Today *Antigone* still speaks eloquently of youth and age, idealism and compromise, to spectators yet unborn at the time of its first performance.

Ardèle and **The Waltz of the Toreadors** • No doubt somewhat disconcerted by the freight of meaning attached to *Antigone* by numerous spectators, Anouilh during the postwar years appeared to turn his back on "serious" playwriting, preferring instead to occupy himself primarily with comedy and satire. The "shining" plays all date from this period, as do the first of the "grating" plays. Two of the more successful among the latter are *Ardèle* and *The Waltz of the Toreadors*, linked by the common, slightly ridiculous character of General Saint-Pé. An aged version of Georges and other would-be romantic lovers in the earlier "pink" plays, the General has never quite relinquished the dreams of his lost youth, even as he has outwardly accepted all the "necessary" trade-offs, substituting assignations for idylls and bottom-pinching on the stairs for stolen kisses in the garden.

In *Ardèle*, the envious General declares a family crisis when he learns that his hunch-backed sister Ardèle has fallen in love with his son's hunchbacked tutor. A "ridiculous" love such as theirs cannot be allowed to survive, he proclaims. Presumably the love itself survives, but the lovers, alas, do not, choosing double suicide as the only "reasonable" alternative to the corrupt perversions of "love" that they have observed in the behavior of the General himself, his deranged wife Amélie, and other members of the family. Throughout the action, Anouilh steers a tight course between broad farce and melodrama, avoiding bathos through his use of pasteboard caricatures in place of more fully rounded characters. A similar approach obtains in *The Waltz of the Toreadors*, in which the General, even more cynical than before, attempts reunion with a woman who briefly crossed his path nearly twenty years earlier. During the years since, the General has had several more brief encounters with Ghislaine but has thus far resisted the temptation to leave Amélie and elope with her.

Arriving at long last to claim the General as her own, Ghislaine confronts him with purported evidence of his wife's infidelity. After much slapstick and stage business, the charges turn out to be true, but by that time Ghislaine has fallen irretrievably in love with Gaston, the General's painfully shy male secretary. By the final curtain, four of the characters have threatened or attempted suicide, yet all remain alive to contemplate a future fraught with compromise and disillusionment.

As he does in *Ardèle*, in *The Waltz of the Toreadors* Anouilh avoids bathos through the judicious use of caricature; here, however, both the General and his ostensibly insane wife emerge as more fully rounded and therefore credible characters than in the earlier play. The General, very much a weathered version of Anouilh's post-Romantic heroes, elicits the spectator's sympathy as he wonders precisely what has gone wrong in his life, where and when. His wife Amélie, equally credible, has chosen to express her love through jealousy, feigning invalidism for more than a decade in order to keep her basically compassionate husband from deserting her. Grim and unrelenting in its satire of contemporary marriage and morals, *The Waltz of the Toreadors* is nevertheless highly playable and has been successfully filmed.

The Lark • With the notable exception of *Antigone*, Anouilh achieved his greatest worldwide success with two of his "costume" plays—both of them drawn, loosely and somewhat ironically, from the recorded lives of saints. Making no claim whatever to interpret history (a process that he likens to the permanent dismantling of a favorite toy), Anouilh frequently discards or distorts such data as do not happen to suit him, altering chronology if need be in order to render playable the stuff of legend. In both *The Lark* and *Becket*, Anouilh is considerably less concerned with what happened than with what the characters might be able to tell the contemporary audience about itself. His presentation of Thomas à Becket, for example, shaves at least ten years off Becket's real age and deliberately exploits the nineteenth century myth, long since corrected, of Becket's Saxon ancestry. Such distortions, however, serve in the final analysis to create highly entertaining, thought-provoking theater.

Anouilh's mature sense of the theatrical serves him well indeed in *The Lark*, in which several different characters (including Joan herself) take turns narrating (and commenting on) the action in the manner of *Antigone*'s one-man Chorus. As in the earlier play, the action is assumed complete and immutable as the curtain rises; all that remains to be seen is the particular form that the retelling will take. The characters, who at first appear to be actors rehearsing a play-within-a-play, debate among themselves as to how the action will be presented; it is Cauchon who decides that Joan's entire career must be reviewed, rather than only her trial and execution. The action then proceeds in chronological order, interrupted only by the "testimony" of the various participants and witnesses. The scene of Joan's martyrdom, although realistically portrayed, is interrupted in quasi-cinematic style to present an opulent, triumphant final scene depicting the coronation of the erstwhile Dauphin at Rheims.

For critic Lewis Falb, *The Lark* remains a weaker play than *Antigone* precisely because it lacks ambiguity. In *The Lark*, he claims, the boundaries are too well defined to allow for true dramatic tension or suspense; unlike Antigone, Joan is far too obviously right, and she seems to know as much. Nevertheless, *The Lark* remains an impressive effort, frequently revived in production and one of the more memorable plays devoted to the life and death of Joan.

Becket • Anouilh's growing fascination with the adaptation of "cinematic" techniques for the stage, adumbrated in the final scene of *The Lark*, takes over almost completely in *Becket*, by far the longest and most technically complicated of his many plays. Indeed, the text of *Becket* often reads more like a scenario than a play, with abundant flashbacks, rapid scene changes, and highly specific instructions as to how a particular line is to be delivered. It is hardly surprising, therefore, that *Becket* has been equally successful in its well-known film version, which is extremely faithful to the play.

Ranging freely across the conventions of the murder mystery, spy fiction, and broad political satire, Anouilh in *Becket* presents a highly convincing and entertaining portrayal of a close friendship gone sour—with repercussions far beyond personal loss. Containing some of Anouilh's finest, most memorable dialogue, *Becket* shows the audience "not a saint, but a man," a character closely descended from such other demanding protagonists as Antigone and Joan. Inner-directed, secretive, at times seemingly heartless, Anouilh's Thomas is a shrewd political manipulator and pragmatist who carries both in his heart and on his sleeve the defeat of his beloved Saxon people. The defeat, it seems, has made it impossible for Becket to believe in anything except himself and the strict code of personal conduct that has somehow ensured his survival.

When asked by the king if he believes in right and wrong, Becket replies enigmatically that he believes certain actions to be more "beautiful" than others, having long since chosen an aesthetic standard of behavior in the absence of ethical or moral imperatives. When the king, irritated by the clergy, impulsively names Becket chancellor, Becket is at first awed by the responsibility but soon warms to the task, proving himself to be a most adept and manipulative politician with an instinctive sense of power. As he tells the king, his personal code dictates that he do the best—or at least most "beautiful"—job he can at whatever he is called on to do. Such apparent loyalty will eventually rebound on the king, who, seeking to control the clergy by appointing his own man—the somewhat underqualified Becket—as Archbishop of Canterbury, finds that he has unwittingly provided himself with the most formidable and indomitable of adversaries. Becket, committed as usual to performing any appointed task to the best of his ability, dedicates his skills to defending an embattled Church against the Crown. As presented by Anouilh, Becket's apparent change of allegiance is most readily understood by the audience, but not by the king.

Closely balanced between comedy and pathos (or perhaps pathology), Anouilh's Henry II is one of his most masterful if least admirable creations. Weak, petulant, self-indulgent, and henpecked by his wife and mother, Henry emerges as a most incompetent and impulsive ruler, a compulsive womanizer with more than a trace of latent homosexuality. Trembling with rage, he responds to Becket's apparent defection with all the hysteria of an abandoned mistress, seeking mindless vengeance even as he hopes against hope for an eventual reconciliation with his erstwhile friend and boon companion. Anouilh, in whose work the lack or loss of close friendship has always loomed large, achieves remarkable results in his attribution of the king's vengeance to a friend's perceived betrayal. As the king lies almost paralyzed with unrequited love for Becket, unable even to give orders, his henchmen decide to "rescue" him by assassinating Becket, their movements orchestrated by the gradually amplified "beating" of the king's heart.

Unwieldy and expensive to produce, perhaps a shade too long and discursive, *Becket* is nevertheless a superb play. Together with *Antigone*, *The Lark*, and *Traveller Without Luggage*, and perhaps the strongest of the pink and grating plays, it secures Anouilh's international reputation as one of the century's most versatile and significant dramatists.

Bibliography

Carrington, Ildiko de Papp. "Recasting the Orpheus Myth: Alice Munro's *The Children Stay* and Jean Anouilh's *Eurydice*." *Essays on Canadian Writing* 66 (Winter 1998): 191-203. Examines the way in which Munro's characters are recast from Anouilh's *Eurydice* in order to reject his conception of a pure, fated love.

Falb, Lewis W. *Jean Anouilh*. New York: F. Ungar, 1977. Explores Anouilh's life and works. Index and bibliography.

Grossvogel, David I. *The Self-Conscious Stage in Modern French Theatre*. New York: Columbia University, 1958. Explores the history and criticism of twentieth century French theater. Bibliography and index.

Guicharnaud, Jacques. *Modern French Theatre: From Giraudoux to Genet*. 1961. Rev. ed. New Haven, Conn.: Yale University Press, 1972. Examines critical playwrights and prominent themes of modern-day French theater.

Harvey, John. *Anouilh: A Study in Theatrics*. New Haven, Conn.: Yale University Press, 1964. Provides criticism and interpretation of Anouilh's works. Bibliography.

McIntire, H. G. *The Theatre of Jean Anouilh*. London: Harrap, 1981. An introductory survey of Anouilh's plays. Counters the criticism of his work and suggests a new approach to understanding his place in French theater. Bibliography and index.

Pronko, Leonard C. *The World of Jean Anouilh*. 1961. Rev. ed. Berkeley: University of California Press, 1968. Provides criticism and interpretation of Anouilh and examines his place in French theater. Bibliography.

David B. Parsell

Aristophanes

Born: Athens, Greece; c. 450 B.C.E.
Died: Athens, Greece; c. 385 B.C.E.

Principal drama • *Acharnēs*, 425 B.C.E. (*The Acharnians*, 1812); *Hippēs*, 424 B.C.E. (*The Knights*, 1812); *Nephelai*, 423 B.C.E. (*The Clouds*, 1708); *Sphēkes*, 422 B.C.E. (*The Wasps*, 1812); *Eirēnē*, 421 B.C.E. (*Peace*, 1837); *Ornithes*, 414 B.C.E. (*The Birds*, 1824); *Lysistratē*, 411 B.C.E. (*Lysistrata*, 1837); *Thesmophoriazousai*, 411 B.C.E. (*Thesmophoriazusae*, 1837); *Batrachoi*, 405 B.C.E. (*The Frogs*, 1780); *Ekklesiazousai*, 392 B.C.E.? (*Ecclesiazusae*, 1837); *Ploutos*, 388 B.C.E. (*Plutus*, 1651)

Other literary forms • Aristophanes is remembered only for his plays.

Achievements • Because the plays of his contemporaries and rivals have all been lost, it is impossible to credit Aristophanes with specific innovations in the development of Greek comedy. In his eleven surviving plays, however, one can trace an evolution in his own work. Although this evolution corresponds to a broader trend (the movement from Old Comedy to Middle and New Comedy), which in turn was influenced by changes in political and social conditions, Aristophanes' own development as an artist undoubtedly influenced such larger developments as much as it was shaped by them.

Aristophanes was recognized as a great comic poet in his lifetime, winning many first prizes in dramatic competitions and almost never taking less than second prize. His first two plays have been lost, but his third, *The Acharnians*, displays an early mastery of comic technique and a profound unity of theme. Only later did Aristophanes develop unity of action; it was clearly not expected of Old Comedy, which had grown out of two or more heterogeneous elements (including the animal chorus and primitive forms of farce). Indeed, the unity of plot to be discerned in Aristophanes' later comedies (*Lysistrata*, *Ecclesiazusae*, and *Plutus*) is to some extent a compensation for the loss of certain features of the early plays—notably the freedom of the chorus to engage in wild ad hominem attacks and unbridled political satire.

The outstanding features of Aristophanes' art are the audacity of his comic metaphors and the beauty of his choral lyrics. These are best displayed in his early and middle plays, as well as in *The Frogs*, a brilliant post mortem on Greek tragedy and the culture of imperial Athens (the Athenian defeat, marking the end of the Peloponnesian War, was imminent when the play was produced). Though Aristophanes survived his city's defeat and continued to develop as an artist, the postwar plays betray a certain weariness, a flagging of comic invention, corresponding to the political and cultural exhaustion of Athens in the early fourth century B.C.E. Perhaps the greatest single achievement of Aristophanes is the fact that his are the only plays of the Old Comedy to have survived—a tribute, surely, to his superb comic craftsmanship.

Biography • Very little is known of Aristophanes' life; most of what is known has been gleaned from his plays and is therefore vague or uncertain because of the comic content. The only evidence for his birthdate is the fact that he was "very young" when his first play was produced in 427 B.C.E. His first three plays were produced by another man, but it is not known whether this was because of a legal age limit, Aristophanes' inexperience, or simple preference (some of his later plays were also produced by others). He belonged to the *deme* (township) of Kudathenaion, and his father's name was Philippos. Nothing is known, however, of the family's social or economic status. A line in *The Acharnians* has been interpreted to mean that he or his father had land holdings on the island of Aegina, but these may have been acquired during the distribution of Aeginetan land to Athenian citizens after the expulsion of the islanders in 431.

According to the scholiasts, Aristophanes was indicted several times by the demagogue Cleon—whom he attacked in several plays—for usurping citizenship rights and for holding Athens up to ridicule before foreign visitors (the latter charge stemmed from his lost play *The Babylonians*, produced in 426, which portrayed the subject-allies of Athens as Babylonian slaves). Apparently Cleon was unable to make either charge stick, and Aristophanes returned to the attack. *The Knights*, presented in 424 (and which won a first place), portrays Cleon as a venal slave who flatters and cheats his master Demos ("the people" personified). The popularity of the play did not, however, have any effect on Cleon's popularity: A few weeks after it won first prize, Cleon was chosen as one of the city's ten generals for the following year.

From the lists of victors in the dramatic festivals, it can be inferred that Aristophanes was a prolific and popular playwright. The Alexandrian scholars of the third and second centuries B.C.E. knew of forty-four plays attributed to him, forty of which they considered genuine. According to an early fourth century B.C.E. inscription, he also held public office (as *prytanis*, one of the presiding members of the Boulē, the council that set the agenda for the legislative assembly). His last datable play is the *Plutus*, staged in 388; two other plays were staged, perhaps posthumously, by his son Araros. All three of Aristophanes' sons tried their hand at writing comedies, but their works have not survived.

There is one further piece of biographical evidence: the vivid portrait of Aristophanes drawn by Plato in his dialogue the *Symposion* (388-368 B.C.E.; *Symposium*, 1701). As a character in the dialogue, Aristophanes delivers a brilliantly witty speech on the origin of erotic love, which he traces to the "globular" condition of the first mortals. These globular humans had two heads, four arms, and four legs apiece, and were so powerful that the gods felt threatened by them, so Zeus cut each one in half. Sexual love is thus the attraction between "halves" of formerly whole beings. What lovers really seek is indissoluble union with their other halves.

This speech cannot be attributed to the historical Aristophanes. Plato was a great stylist and could easily have invented the whole. Yet the comic myth is akin to those found in Aristophanes' plays, and it sheds an interesting light on the relationship between the comic dramatist and the philosopher Socrates, whom Aristophanes satirized (unfairly, many scholars feel) in his play *The Clouds*. Socrates is also a character in the *Symposium*, and his speech, which follows and rebuts that of Aristophanes, reveals the irreducible opposition between the two men's views of the human condition. As scholar David Grene has put it, what Aristophanes most objected to in Socrates' teaching was the idea that philosophical investigation superseded all other claims on people's attention and energy, including the pleasures of food, sex, and poetry. These pleasures, together with that of competition, which Plato also deplored, are central to Aristophanes' comic vision.

Analysis • Because Aristophanes has had no real literary heirs, or imitators, in subsequent European literature, some discussion of Old Comedy as a genre is in order.

There are good reasons why this genre died out when Athens went into its decline and was never revived. Old Comedy was nurtured and sustained by a constellation of social and political features of imperial Athens, which never came together in quite the same way subsequently.

The fifth century B.C.E. saw the height of Athenian fortunes, and the sense of limitless possibility that the times inspired is reflected in Aristophanes' early plays. Athenian democracy was also at its height. It was a limited democracy, insofar as citizenship was limited, but a direct democracy in which the citizens themselves voted on every proposed law and treaty. There were obvious analogies between the legislative assembly, the popular courts (where juries numbered in the hundreds, sometimes in the thousands), and the theater, where the people assembled in a body on a few festival days each year to see productions subsidized by state taxes. The no-holds-barred approach prevailing in assembly and court debate spilled over into the comedies, which are filled with ad hominem attacks on individuals. Politicians and poets were favorite targets, but a man might be singled out for ridicule because of his appearance, his cowardice in battle, or even his sexual proclivities.

Two unique features of Old Comedy reflect its political and social setting with special vividness. These are the agon and the parabasis. The agon is a contest, partly physical but chiefly verbal, between the protagonist and the chorus. Its rhetoric reflects that of the assembly and law courts (and of Greek tragedy as well, which had a similar relationship to its social and political milieu). The parabasis is an address to the audience in which the comic chorus drops whatever dramatic identity the play imposes on it to speak in the first person, in the poet's own voice. The parabasis may be only tangentially related to the plot and can address any political or social issue, although always in a fantastic vein that must have blunted its political impact.

Scholars disagree considerably on the question of Aristophanes' political purpose and beliefs, though most see him as in some sense conservative—that is, supportive of moderate (as opposed to radical) democracy and of the "traditional" virtues proper to an agrarian, nonimperial economy: peace, political stability, and free trade. It is difficult, though, to elicit any specific political program from the plays, because of their essentially anarchic spirit, which tends to subvert the few sober pronouncements of individual characters. Even if it could be demonstrated from the plays that Aristophanes had such a program, the question of its impact would remain. Here again evidence is slight and ambiguous.

(Library of Congress)

There is no known case in which a comedy demonstrably influenced public policy. Aristophanes produced a whole series of brilliant antiwar plays during the course of the Peloponnesian War (some took first prize), but the war continued. Even the *Peace* of 421, staged the same year the Peace of Nicias between Athens and Sparta was concluded, seems more a reflection of the city's mood than a peace initiative on Aristophanes' part. The attack on Socrates in *The Clouds* is cited by Plato in the *Apologia Sōkratous* (399-390 B.C.E.; *Apology*, 1675; which purports to be Socrates' own defense at his trial) as a source of popular hostility against the philosopher, but *The Clouds* preceded the trial by twenty-five years. What is more, to judge from the *Symposium*, Aristophanes and Socrates belonged to the same circle of friends; surely the poet had no intention of urging any action against the philosopher.

Scholar K. J. Dover has pointed out that Aristophanes survived the advent of oligarchic regimes as well as the democratic backlash that accompanied their overthrow; this would hardly have been possible had he been perceived as a partisan of either. A careful reading of his plays will reveal that they take advantage precisely of the freedom from responsibility that Old Comedy permits to create a world of fantasy and wish-fulfillment. Though Aristophanes addresses real political issues, the solutions he offers are not political but poetic ones.

The Acharnians • *The Acharnians*, Aristophanes' earliest surviving play, deserves close consideration not only because of its intrinsic merit but also because it exemplifies two strands that run throughout his work: a celebration of the joys of peace (with its corollary, an attack on the evils of war) and a fantasy of limitless possibility for the protagonist. These two strands are intimately interwoven, for the "pacifism" of Aristophanes is by no means the selfless and idealistic stance evoked by that word in modern times. His heroes hate war not because it entails the shedding of blood but because it results in a dearth of good things: food, wine, sex, and the freedom to do what one pleases and go where one pleases. Therefore, Dikaiopolis, the hero of *The Acharnians*, after trying in vain to raise the issue of peace negotiations in the assembly, makes his own private treaty with Sparta and proceeds to enjoy the benefits: freedom to celebrate the rural Dionysia, to trade with former enemies for imported delicacies, and to stay at home and feast while General Lamachos goes off to battle with his rations of salt fish and onions.

The agon in this play is a debate between Dikaiopolis and a chorus of Acharnian charcoal-burners (from Acharnai, one of the demes of Attica), who hate the Spartans for ravaging their lands and can think of nothing but revenge. Dikaiopolis wins them over with a comic version of the war's causes (a parody of Herodotus's account of the reasons for enmity between Greece and Asia Minor) and a reminder that poor men have the least to gain from war. Like many of Aristophanes' heroes, Dikaiopolis is a "little man" of middle age or older whose triumph over the powers that be is symbolized by his rejuvenation or restored sexual potency at the end of the play. As Lamachos returns wounded from battle, Dikaiopolis returns drunk from the feast, ready for a night of lovemaking with two courtesans. Yet this play is hardly a straightforward plea for the "little man," for once he has his treaty, Dikaiopolis refuses to extend it to include another farmer whose two oxen have been seized by the enemy.

The consistency of the play lies in its imagery. On the level of dramatic action, each Aristophanic comedy is built on one or more controlling images that assume a life of their own; in the choral odes, these and other images appear in a "crystallized" form. (In Old Comedy, as in Greek tragedy, the choral poetry provides a kind of lyric reflection on the action it interrupts.) In *The Acharnians*, the central comic image is that of wine, which becomes a metaphor for peace thanks to a pun: The Greek for "truce" is *spondai*, literally the "libations" that accompanied ratification of treaties. Dikaiopolis is offered three kinds of *spondai* by the Spartans and picks the best "vintage"—that is, the longest truce. The image is appropriate in other ways as well, for peace was associated with the euphoria of drunkenness and the freedom to celebrate festivals (many of which were curtailed during the war). At the play's end, Dikaiopolis is proclaimed the winner in a drinking contest—a standard feature of the Lenaia, the festival at which the play was produced—and his victory is made to suggest (before the fact) the poet's own victory in the dramatic contest.

It should be obvious that such "pacifism" as the play contains is fully compatible with the most vigorous forms of competition; within the comic universe of his plays, Aristophanes loves a good fight as much as anyone. Nor would his Greek audience have perceived this as a paradox: There was a traditional distinction, going back at least to Hesiod's *Erga kai Emerai* (c. 700 B.C.E.; *Works and Days*, 1618), between useful and destructive *eris*, "strife." Only the latter was considered hateful; rivalry and emulation were encouraged as the means to excellence and prosperity.

Peace • This preoccupation with competition is visible, though somewhat more restrained, in the two other extant antiwar plays of Aristophanes. *Peace* is unusual in that it has no agon; instead, the members of the chorus, farmers from all the city-states, are made to "pull together" (literally and figuratively) as they raise the goddess Peace from the pit to which War has consigned her. Exhumation is only one of a constellation of images presiding over the action of this most earthy play, which opens with two slaves kneading cakes of excrement to feed a giant dung-beetle. The play's hero, Trygaios, mounts the beetle and flies to heaven, where he finds War preparing to pound the Greek cities in a mortar. No pestle is available, however (both the Athenian and the Spartan commanders in chief, Cleon and Brasidas, having recently died), and Trygaios takes advantage of the circumstance to unearth Peace, whose acolyte Opora (Harvest) he then weds. His flight to heaven notwithstanding, Trygaios has less of the entrepreneur about him than does Dikaiopolis. He is willing to share his good fortune with all who desire peace, and he even presents the goddess's other acolyte, Theoria (Ceremony), to the Council as a gift.

Lysistrata • In his generosity, Trygaios anticipates Lysistrata, heroine of the play that bears her name. Though she leads the women of Greece in a successful coup that leaves them in possession of the Acropolis (and the Athenian treasury), her only aim is to induce the men to make peace; she keeps nothing for herself. The motif of competition recurs in the "battle of the sexes" she so cunningly orchestrates. The agon of *Lysistrata* involves two semi-choruses, one of old men and one of old women, who at first shower one another with abuse but are eventually reconciled, forming a single chorus. The attack on the Acropolis that the old men stage, complete with battering rams and torches, is an obvious sexual metaphor. True to their oath to resist their husbands' advances, the women repulse the attack and douse the torches.

Once the men have signed a treaty ending the war, they are admitted for a banquet, and each goes home with his own wife, in a mass version of the "wedding" that so often closes Aristophanes' plays. Frequently in Aristophanes, and notably in Trygaios's address to the Council as he presents them with Theoria, the sexual act itself is described as a struggle, yet another form of contention. That it is an example of "good" strife should be obvious because it is also a form of union, and indeed, Trygaios compares it to various events in the athletic contests, which were among the few truly Panhellenic institutions of the fifth century B.C.E.

Despite these points of comparison, the three antiwar plays differ from one another in important ways, as might be expected from their dates of production. *The Acharnians*, fairly early in the war, allows its hero greater selfishness and irresponsibility than does either of the later plays; the mood of *Peace*, staged in 421 when peace seemed imminent, is more euphoric than that of *Lysistrata* in 411. There is even a note of pathos in Lysistrata's plea for the women left widowed and unmarried by the ongoing war, in which they have no say. The fantasy of unlimited possibility, reflected in Dikaiopolis's private treaty and Trygaios's flight to heaven, has disappeared from the latter play. Its fullest development was reached not in the war plays but in *The Knights*, and especially *The Birds*.

The Knights • *The Knights* and *The Birds* are quintessentially Athenian celebrations of a quality that only the Athenians (and not all of them at that) considered a virtue: *polupragmosunē*, "doing-muchness," or "having a finger in every pie." *The Knights* is an attack on the demagogue Cleon, whom Aristophanes accuses of pandering to the people's whims for his own profit. Cleon is defeated and replaced in the course of the play (which is one protracted agon) by a man who outdoes him in pandering—a Sausage-Seller, whose qualifications for the role of demagogue are low birth, an ear-splitting voice, and the ways of the streetwise. Cleon and the Sausage-Seller compete to satisfy the appetite of Demos, "the people" personified.

Although ostensibly Demos's slaves, the two panderers hold the purse strings, and what finally recommends the Sausage-Seller to Demos is the fact that he holds nothing back for himself. At the play's end, the Sausage-Seller rejuvenates his master (by "cooking" him, as Medea promised to do for the aged King Pelias), bringing back the sober and responsible Demos of the Persian War era. This miracle, however, lacks the dramatic power of his unrestrained pandering contest with Cleon. To judge from the parabasis, the poet's nostalgia is not so much for the sobriety of the old Athens as for its unchallenged supremacy.

The Birds • Aristophanes' ultimate power-fantasy is *The Birds*. Two Athenians, Pisthetairos and Euelpides, leave their city and go to live with the birds, because, they say, Athens has become unlivable. They proceed to found a new city in the sky (Nephelokokkugia, or "Cloudcuckooland"), which outdoes even imperial Athens in *polupragmosunē*. With the birds' help, they build a wall between heaven and earth that keeps the smoke of burnt offerings from reaching the gods; reduced to starvation, the gods are forced to yield Basileia, a female personification of kingship, to Pisthetairos.

The controlling metaphor in this play is flight, which confers not only freedom from the ordinary constraints of the human condition but also vast power—the power of one who surveys the world from a great height, the better to administer it. It is the divine power of Zeus, in short, for Pisthetairos is not content merely to become a bird; he must become a god and king of the gods. *The Birds* is the most fully realized of Aristophanes' power-fantasies, both in its dramatic coherence and in the beauty of its lyrics. It is also the one that leaves the "real world" most completely behind. Regardless of whether Aristophanes intended it as a commentary on the Sicilian expedition (which had been launched the previous year), it conveys perfectly the boundless Athenian audacity behind the expedition.

The Clouds • *The Clouds*, although a relatively early play, deserves to be considered with the later plays for several reasons. In the first place, it ends not with the apotheosis of the hero but with an act of violence bred of his frustration. At the same time, it places greater emphasis on the portrayal and interaction of the characters, a trait associated with the later plays (*The Frogs, Ecclesiazusae, Plutus*). The text of *The Clouds* that has survived is unfortunately not the text that was staged; it is a revision, though an incomplete one. In the revised parabasis, Aristophanes claims that he considers *The Clouds* his best play to date; he insists particularly on its subtlety and originality. Scholar Grene has suggested that he is referring to "the psychological study of human personality," which looms larger in this than in the other early plays. Though it lacks consistency and dramatic unity (perhaps because of the incomplete revision), the play features an unusually realistic hero—indeed, a sort of antihero. His name is Strepsiades (which means, roughly, "Twister"), and he is of humble country stock, like Dikaiopolis and Trygaios; unlike them, however, he is genuinely corrupt.

In order to get out of paying the debts his son has incurred, Strepsiades enrolls at the Thinkery, presided over by Socrates, who is here made to represent all the dubious achievements of the "new learning" (the sophistic movement of the fifth century B.C.E.). Strepsiades himself is too thick-witted to learn what Socrates has to teach, however, so he persuades his son Pheidippides to take the course—and thereby gets his comeuppance, for Pheidippides uses the specious reasoning he learns to justify not only defaulting on debts but also beating his parents. Strepsiades gets his revenge—by burning down the Thinkery, an act of desperation, not an assertion of comic possibility like Dikaiopolis's truce or the Sausage-Seller's trouncing of Cleon. In this play, Aristophanes came to grips with a knotty problem that has not lost its contemporary flavor: the interaction of character and values in the educational process. Perhaps because of this very complexity, the resolution, as it stands, lacks the comic release of most of Aristophanes' finales.

Ecclesiazusae • In this respect, *The Clouds* resembles *Ecclesiazusae*, one of Aristophanes' two surviving fourth century B.C.E. plays. Though it lacks the wit and subtlety of *The Clouds, Ecclesiazusae* shares its realistic, not to say pessimistic, perspective. *Ecclesiazusae* is also a kind of anti-*Lysistrata*, for it sets up a utopia under the leadership of women but then severely undercuts it by dramatizing the chaos that results. The women's edicts are either unenforceable (when ordered to surrender their goods to the community, some citizens simply withhold them) or profoundly unnatural (the young and beautiful are forced to gratify the sexual desires of the old and ugly). The sense of realism and disenchantment is strengthened by a drastic reduction in the role of the chorus (resulting in a dearth of lyric passages) and by a more concentrated plot. The old Aristophanes can be detected, though, in the antiphilosophical stances of the play.

Though the idea of pooling goods and sexual partners is attributed to the heroine, Praxagora, it is likely to have been the brainchild of a sophist or philosopher. Plato was its most famous exponent, but his *Politeia* (388-368 B.C.E.; *Republic*, 1701) came later (unless an early version of it was already in circulation in 392). Whatever its source, the idea belongs, in Aristophanes' view, to that class of abstractions ridiculed in *The Clouds* for the discomfort they cause to all but the few clever enough to manipulate them. It has been suggested that in contrast with the early plays, in which the old heroes are rejuvenated and the clock turned back to a more vigorous age, the late plays merely complete the work of destruction already in progress. According to this view, the rule of women is symbolic of the dissolution of the polity and the victory of the private over the political sphere. It is certain that politics disappeared entirely from New Comedy, the forerunner of the romance and of most modern comedy, in which the private sphere fills the foreground.

The Frogs • *The Frogs* is the last surviving work of Old Comedy and perhaps the greatest. It was produced in 405, shortly after the deaths of Sophocles and Euripides and just before the Athenian defeat at Aegospotami, which ended the Peloponnesian War. The hero is Dionysus, divine patron of the theater, who undertakes a trip to Hades because he can find no good tragedians aboveground. His idea is to bring back Euripides, but once below, he finds himself called on to judge between Euripides and Aeschylus, who are contending for the "chair of tragedy."

In the end, Dionysus declares Aeschylus the winner and brings *him* back to Athens. There are two choruses: one of frogs, who engage in a shouting match with Dionysus as he rows across the Stygian lake in Charon's boat, and one of Initiates to the Eleusinian Mysteries, whose life in the underworld is a joyous one of choral song and torchlight revels. The Initiates represent a kind of ideal community, warning away all who would engage in sedition or accept bribes, but they are also a true comic chorus, full of insults and bawdy jokes. This harmonizes perfectly with their dramatic identity as initiates, for the mysteries blended fertility cult with eschatological promises, and the ceremonies included the hurling of bawdy taunts.

The agon consists of the dramatic contest between the two tragedians, including hilarious parodies of each man's style and culminating in the actual weighing of their verses on a scale. Much has been made of the fact that Dionysus bases his final decision on the two men's political advice to the city. As in the finale of *The Knights*, however, the emphasis is not so much on the actual content of the advice as on the evocation of a time—that of Aeschylus's prime—when Athens was the unchallenged leader of Greece. Despite the play's premise, that the best poets are all in Hades, there is surprisingly little black comedy. The choral lyrics radiate hope (albeit an eschatological hope), and the spirit of emulation proper to Aristophanes' early plays enlivens *The Frogs* from first to last. In addition to the agon proper, there is not only a shouting match between Dionysus and the frogs but also a whipping contest between Dionysus and his slave Xanthias (to determine which of them is the god).

Aristophanes is aware, as always, of the dramatic competition in which he is himself a contestant and pulls out all the stops—just as he depicts Aeschylus and Euripides doing—in order to win. At the same time, however, there is a poignant emphasis on the need for reconciliation among the city's various factions if Athens is to survive. Therefore, the parabasis, sung by the chorus of Initiates, pleads not for Aristophanes' victory but for a general amnesty permitting exiled citizens to return. Though Aristophanes delights in competition to the very end, he recognizes that if the terms of competition are not adhered to, the city cannot stand. For later readers of *The Frogs*, the play's poignancy is increased by hindsight: Athens did fall, never to regain the eminence it enjoyed in Aeschylus's day. The fact that he chose Initiates for his chorus suggests that Aristophanes had an intimation of this and that he realized the dramatic art of Athens need not share the city's political fate—precisely because the "solutions" it offered were not political but poetic and self-sustaining visions.

Bibliography

Bowie, A. M. *Aristophanes: Myth, Ritual, and Comedy.* New York: Cambridge University Press, 1993. Bowie uses anthropological techniques in comparing Aristophanes' plays with Greek myths and rituals with similar story lines in an attempt to discover how the original audiences would have responded to the plays. Includes bibliography and index.

Harvey, David, and John Wilkins, eds. *The Rivals of Aristophanes: Studies in Athenian Old Comedy.* London: Duckworth and the Classical Press of Wales, 2000. Twenty-eight essays on the other comic poets of Athenian Old Comedy, based on the fragments and citations that survive. Includes bibliography.

Lada-Richards, Ismene. *Initiating Dionysus: Ritual and Theatre in Aristophanes' "Frogs."* New York: Oxford University Press, 1999. The author uses literary and anthropological approaches in looking at how a member of Greek society would have viewed the play and Dionysus as a dramatic figure. Includes bibliography and indexes.

MacDowell, Douglas M. *Aristophanes and Athens: An Introduction to the Plays.* New York: Oxford University Press, 1995. MacDowell provides an introduction to Aristophanes' plays, including information about Athens and the political climate, essential to understanding some of the allusions in Aristophanes' works. Includes bibliography and index.

Russo, Carlo Ferdinando. *Aristophanes: An Author for the Stage.* New York: Routledge, 1994. Russo examines Aristophanes' dramatic technique in a work that is both scholarly and lively. Includes bibliography and index.

Taaffe, Laurne K. *Aristophanes and Women.* New York: Routledge, 1993. Taaffe examines the portrayal of women in Aristophanes' plays, focusing on *Lysistrata, Thesmophoriazusae,* and *Ecclesiazusae.* Includes bibliography and index.

Lillian Doherty

Sir Alan Ayckbourn

Born: Hampstead, London, England; April 12, 1939

Principal drama • *The Square Cat*, pr. 1959 (as Roland Allen); *Love After All*, pr. 1959 (as Roland Allen); *Mr. Whatnot*, pr. 1963 (revised version pr. 1964); *Relatively Speaking*, pr. 1967, pb. 1968 (originally as *Meet My Father*, pr. 1965); *Ernie's Incredible Illucinations*, pb. 1969, pr. 1971 (for children); *How the Other Half Loves*, pr. 1969, pb. 1972; *Time and Time Again*, pr. 1971, pb. 1973; *Absurd Person Singular*, pr. 1972, pb. 1974; *The Norman Conquests*, pr. 1973, pb. 1975 (includes *Table Manners*, *Living Together*, and *Round and Round the Garden*); *Absent Friends*, pr. 1974, pb. 1975; *Confusions*, pr. 1974, pb. 1977 (five one-acts); *Bedroom Farce*, pr. 1975, pb. 1977; *Just Between Ourselves*, pr. 1976, pb. 1978; *Ten Times Table*, pr. 1977, pb. 1978; *Joking Apart*, pr. 1978, pb. 1979; *Men on Women on Men*, pr. 1978 (lyrics; music by Paul Todd); *Sisterly Feelings*, pr. 1979, pb. 1981; *Taking Steps*, pr. 1979, pb. 1981; *Suburban Strains*, pr. 1980, pb. 1982 (music by Todd); *Season's Greetings*, pr. 1980, pb. 1982; *Way Upstream*, pr. 1981, pb. 1983; *Me, Myself, and I*, pr. 1981, pb. 1989 (music by Todd); *Intimate Exchanges*, pr. 1982, pb. 1985; *A Chorus of Disapproval*, pr. 1984, pb. 1985; *Woman in Mind*, pr. 1985, pb. 1986; *A Small Family Business*, pr., pb. 1987; *Henceforward*, pr. 1987, pb. 1988; *Mr. A's Amazing Maze Plays*, pr. 1988, pb. 1989 (for children); *Man of the Moment*, pr. 1988, pb. 1990; *Invisible Friends*, pr. 1989, pb. 1991; *The Revengers' Comedies*, pr. 1989, pb. 1991; *Body Language*, pr. 1990, pb. 2001; *This Is Where He Came In*, pr. 1990, pb. 1995 (for children); *Wildest Dreams*, pr. 1991, pb. 1993; *My Very Own Story*, pr. 1991, pb. 1995 (for children); *Dreams from a Summer House*, pr. 1992, pb. 1997 (music by John Pattison); *Time of My Life*, pr. 1992, pb. 1993; *Communicating Doors*, pr. 1994, pb. 1995; *Haunting Julia*, pr. 1994; *The Musical Jigsaw Play*, pr. 1994 (for children); *Plays*, pb. 1995-1998 (2 volumes); *A Word from Our Sponsor*, pr. 1995, pb. 1998 (music by Pattison); *By Jeeves*, pr. 1996 (music by Andrew Lloyd Webber); *The Champion of Paribanou*, pr. 1996, pb. 1998 (for children); *Things We Do for Love*, pr. 1997, pb. 1998; *The Boy Who Fell into a Book*, pr. 1998, pb. 2000 (for children); *Comic Potential*, pr. 1998, pb. 1999; *Gizmo*, pr. 1998, pb. 1999; *"House" and "Garden,"* pr., pb. 2000

Other literary forms • Alan Ayckbourn is known primarily for his plays.

Achievements • A farceur of contemporary suburbia, Alan Ayckbourn enjoys distinction not only as a prolific writer of entertaining, well-made plays during a stage revolution when the *pièce bien faite* was out of fashion but also as a dramatist who, beginning in 1959, has averaged one play a year, claiming to have surpassed even William Shakespeare in the sheer quantity of plays written by the early 1990's. His early reputation as a commercial dramatist, however, changed with the times and the development of his own style and themes, so that he has enjoyed productions of his plays even at the prestigious National Theatre in London. A critic of contemporary society's greed, he has increasingly honed his farce into black comedy, earning for it the label of "theater of embarrassment." In 1987 Ayckbourn was awarded a royal honor as Commander of the British Empire, and in 1997 he was knighted for services to the theater.

In 1992 he was appointed Cameron Mackintosh professor of contemporary theater at St. Catherine's College, Oxford. Among other awards he has received are the Montblanc de la Culture Award for Europe and the Writers' Guild of Great Britain Lifetime Achievement Award. He has received several honorary degrees, and his work has been translated into more than forty languages.

Biography • Alan Ayckbourn was born in Hampstead, London, on April 12, 1939, to Horace and Irene Worley Ayckbourn, his father the first violinist with the London Symphony Orchestra and his mother a novelist and short-story writer for popular women's magazines. In 1943, when he was five, his parents were divorced and his mother married Cecil Pye, a manager for Barclays Bank. Winning a Barclays Bank scholarship, Ayckbourn attended Haileybury School in Hertfordshire, where, during the next five years, he became interested in drama, touring in Holland as Peter in *Romeo and Juliet* and in the United States and Canada as Macduff in *Macbeth*.

Thus began Ayckbourn's lifelong affair with the theater. He left school with "A" levels in English and history and, at seventeen, joined Sir Donald Wolfit's company at the Edinburgh Festival as acting assistant stage manager. He also worked in summer theater at Leatherhead and then at Scarborough's Studio Theatre (under Stephen Joseph, son of actress Hermione Ferdinanda Gingold), writing plays even as he was initiated into the production rites of professional theater.

In 1959, Ayckbourn married actress Christine Roland, had a son (Steven Paul), and saw two of his plays (*The Square Cat* and *Love After All*) produced in Scarborough under the pseudonym of Roland Allen. In 1962, his second son, Nicholas Phillip, was born, and in 1964, Ayckbourn's *Mr. Whatnot* opened at the Arts Theatre in London. Thereafter, he has averaged writing at least one play per year, and he is wont to talk fondly of providing amusement for bored surburbanite vacationers on rainy Scarborough days.

Ayckbourn's early days in the theater included acting in roles such as Vladimir in Samuel Beckett's *En attendant Godot* (pb. 1952, pr. 1953; *Waiting for Godot*, pb. 1954) and Stanley in Harold Pinter's *The Birthday Party* (pr. 1958, pb. 1960). He was founder-member and associate director of Victoria Theatre in Stoke on Trent, produced dramas on the British Broadcasting Corporation's radio, in Leeds, and, after Stephen Joseph's death in 1967, returned to Scarborough in 1970. After several name changes, the Victoria Theatre became the Stephen Joseph Theatre-in-the-Round in 1996, in tribute to Ayckbourn's mentor. It became also Ayckbourn's tryout home before openings in theaters in and around London and all over the world.

In the United States, the Alley Theatre in Houston, the Arena Stage in Washington, and the Manhattan Theater Club in New York, among others, became homes for Ayckbourn's plays. Having succeeded in small English theaters such as The Arts, The Roundhouse, and The Richmond Orange Tree, and later in commercial houses in the West End, Ayckbourn's *Bedroom Farce* reached the Royal National Theatre, where both his plays and his directorship (1986) have long enjoyed a liaison. In the best of all possible theater worlds—the provincial, fringe, West End commercial, Royal National, and international theaters producing his plays—Ayckbourn not only has survived the early critical attacks for writing the commercially profitable well-made play but also has continued writing in a long career that has no contemporary equal in quantity and consistency of experimentation. With more than fifty plays, Ayckbourn has continued to be more prolific than any of the new playwrights since the stage revolution began in 1956 with John Osborne's *Look Back in Anger* (pr. 1956, pb. 1957).

His marriage to Roland led to separation and divorce some years later. In 1997 he married Heather Stoney. He has continued to live in Scarborough, Yorkshire.

Analysis • With labels flourishing during the new era in drama (Osborne's angry theater, Beckett's Theater of the Absurd, Pinter's comedy of menace, Arnold Wesker's kitchen-sink drama), Alan Ayckbourn, too, has been honored with his own label, the comedy of embarrassment, based on the increasingly black comedy in his later farces. The term derives from the unease of audiences as their laughter is deflected by the intrusion of realities underlying that hilarity. For example, the accidental murders in *A Small Family Business* and *Man of the Moment* obtrude through the farce, giving it a hollow ring. This jarring union of farce and tragedy, alien to standard farce expectations, in fact, is subtly present even in early comedies such as *How the Other Half Loves*, markedly so in *A Chorus of Disapproval*, and shatteringly so in *A Small Family Business* and *Man of the Moment.* Ayckbourn has become the hilarious tragedian of contemporary life, not unlike Ben Jonson, whose seventeenth century farces about greed seem ancestors to Ayckbourn's.

Ayckbourn met the charges of early critics who faulted him for his commercially viable formula plays, commenting that one "cannot begin to shatter theatrical conventions or break golden rules until he is reasonably sure in himself what they are and how they were arrived at." The rules to which Ayckbourn is referring are the time-honored ones practiced by Greeks and Romans, Shakespeare, Jonson, Molière, George Bernard Shaw, and Oscar Wilde.

With the acknowledged influence of William Congreve, Wilde, Georges Feydeau, Anton Chekhov, Noël Coward, Terence Rattigan, J. B. Priestley, and Pinter, Ayckbourn has forged a style of old and new that has given his plays their unique quality. Using the farce conventions of his predecessors, he has experimented with the mechanics of traditional plotting by challenging its limits and extending its boundaries. One of his most noticeable changes in farce techniques is his avoidance of the linear movement of the plot and his replacing it with a sense of indefiniteness. The outcome is a circular movement, resulting in a play structure that is more akin to the static quality of Chekhov's plots than to the active one of Wilde's and Shaw's plays. His disarrangement of linear plot lines creates the illusion of a standard farce, deceiving the audience in its usual comic expectations. His technique is partly explained by the tripling, sometimes quadrupling, of the number of potentially comic couples or comic situations in the conventional farce. The standard use of the double takes what seems a quantum leap in Ayckbourn's farces.

The tripling extends to the overall architecture of plays, a number of them taking the form of trilogies. In *The Norman Conquests*, each of the three plays treats the same character and situations, one being the offstage action of what happens onstage in another. The order of performance of the three plays, thus, is of little consequence, for each is essentially repetitious of the other two. The chief difference among them is their locale: One occurs in the dining room, the second in the living room, and the third in the garden. The difference is diversionary, suggesting a traditional plot movement where there really is none.

Ayckbourn's trilogy *Sisterly Feelings* goes even further in its structural inventiveness, with each play's conclusion in a given performance being determined arbitrarily by a member of the cast. Still another sometimes confusing plot invention is Ayckbourn's use of the same stage space at the same time by two or more different sets of characters (frequently couples), most prominently illustrated in *How the Other Half Loves, Bedroom*

Farce, and *Taking Steps*. The single most famous of these scenes, in *How the Other Half Loves*, involves two different dinner parties by two different middle-class couples (one having achieved social status and the other desperately trying to do so) seated at the same table, their only common element a third couple who are the guests at both dinners.

Ayckbourn's ingenious plotting strategies provide him ample room to comment on his favorite theme: a satire on the foibles of individuals functioning in suburbia, his chosen slice of middle-class society. His satire has its brief, unrelieved grim moments as in *A Small Family Business* and *Henceforeward*, plays in which the families' children become victims of the pervasive greed of individuals and their society and are helpless to extricate themselves. The artificially happy ending of a farce is replaced by a realistically sober ending in which the comic surfaces of the plot are maintained, even as they cannot disguise the underlying tragic realities. Thus the play stylistically satisfies the farce's requirement for a happy ending while substantively changing the genre to an ironic farce at its best and a black comedy at its most pessimistic. It is appropriate that the title of one of Ayckbourn's late plays, *The Revengers' Comedies*, derives from Cyril Tourneur's seventeenth century title *The Revenger's Tragedy* (pr. 1606-1607, pb. 1607), with the obvious parallel of the earlier era with Thatcherite England of the 1980's.

The traditional purpose of comedy has been to reveal and thereby correct the vices of the society that it portrays by exposing them (usually with a *deus ex machina* ending), thereby bringing about correction of behavior in that society. The exposure involves stereotypical characters whose mechanical behavior engenders laughter. Mere exposure is the punishment for the perpetrator of the vice, either reform or prison frequently being the result of that exposure. The vices of the age have no such corrective results in Ayckbourn's farces.

In his exposure of rampant acquisitiveness, however, Ayckbourn does realize half of the farceur's aim. At the same time, he admits to an unease about the corrective results of prevailing farces. Of the Thatcherite regime he says, "It's no coincidence that you hardly ever see members of the present Government in the theatre. . . . The arts and gentle, civilized living are rapidly being downgraded for the fast buck. It has a narrowing effect. It creates an uncaringness."

The traditional purpose of tragedy has been to cleanse the body politic of its moral stain and to affirm life through increased self-knowledge on the part of the hero, a process in which guilty and innocent alike suffer. As realistic rather than stereotypical characters who embody the values of their respective societies, characters evoke, according to Aristotelian precepts, pity and fear in the polis even as they endure individual punishments and rewards. There is no such individual or collective affirmation in Ayckbourn's plays. Again, the darker elements only continue in their nonresolution, in character-generated farces, such as Jack McCracken of *A Small Family Business* and Douglas Beechey of *Man of the Moment*. Societally, business and mass-media corrupters conspire in their lack of awareness of the morality or immorality of their actions. Individually and collectively, characters continue in a context in which punishment and rewards in a moral sense do not exist.

Ayckbourn regards *Absurd Person Singular* with its three Christmas Eve celebrations as his first "offstage action" play, one in which two socially aspiring couples land in the thick of adversities of the most successful couple. The offstage importance increases with every play, with further inability on the part of the characters to extricate themselves from their adversities. For example, the celebratory tableaulike ending to *A*

Small Family Business coexists with a tableau of the young daughter in her drug-induced pain in the bathroom. John Peter describes an Ayckbourn play as "a requiem scored for screams and laughter."

As a dark farceur par excellence of contemporary suburbia, as an ongoing re-inventor of farce technique, and as the most prolific of a huge number of new drama-tists in the second half of the twentieth century, Ayckbourn continues to be a force on the world stage.

Relatively Speaking • Ayckbourn's first London success, *Relatively Speaking*, illus-trates his roots in the traditional mechanics of the well-made farce, such as abundant coincidences, well-timed exits and entrances, complicated romantic intrigues, central misunderstandings, quid pro quos, secrets known to the audience but not to the char-acters, and the crucial use of an object to progress the plot. At the same time, Ayck-bourn rejects the suspense-creating, teeter-totter action, the big revelatory scene, and the ending that neatly ties together the loose ends of the plot. Instead, as a keen ob-server and creator of character, he treats familial and marital situations whose prob-lems are revealed rather than resolved. The results are Chekhov-like revelations of states of being, contained within the guise of farce and an increasingly bitter satire on the moral bankruptcy of contemporary society. Deceptively embodied in the local, his farce is ultimately universal in its depiction of human foibles that know no bounds of time or place.

With echoes of the exploits of Oscar Wilde's Jack and Ernest in *The Importance of Be-ing Earnest* (pr. 1895, pb. 1899), *Relatively Speaking*, a four-character play, involves a young unmarried couple who set off for the country, each for secret reasons withheld from the other. Ginny wishes to retrieve letters from her former lover (and employer) to put a definite end to that affair. Unbeknown to her, Greg, her current lover, suspi-cious because of the flowers and chocolates cluttering Ginny's flat and the address he notices on her cigarette pack (like the cigarette case in Wilde's play), follows her on a different train. Ginny's lie about a visit to her "parents" begins a series of deceptions multiplied at breakneck speed, deceptions that stretch out to include an older couple, Philip and his wife, Sheila. A *sine qua non* of any farce, the seemingly unstoppable pil-ing up of deceptions, misunderstandings, and coincidences is absurd, one of the most comical being Greg's misinterpretation of Sheila's truthful insistence that she is not Ginny's mother. To Greg, Sheila is merely eluding potential embarrassment at having to reveal the illegitimacy of Ginny's birth.

Like all farceurs, Ayckbourn bases his suspense on secrets known to only some of the characters and on not having all characters on the stage at the same time until the play's end. Consequently, all characters act on the basis of only a partial knowledge of things. While observing this convention, Ayckbourn ignores the artificial disclosure scene (also known as the big scene, obligatory scene, or *scène à faire*) in which all secrets are revealed, all misunderstandings cleared up, and a happy ending contrived. For even as Ginny and Philip depart happily, neither Greg nor Philip is fully apprised of what has happened, the former of Philip's deceptive vacation plans having included Ginny and the latter of Sheila's untruthful claims to having a lover. Thus the turning point in the conventional farce (two of the most famous occurring in Richard Brinsley Sheridan's *The School for Scandal*, pr. 1777, pb. 1780, and Wilde's *The Importance of Being Earnest*) gives way even in Ayckbourn's early farces to a Chekhovian technique of the undramatic.

How the Other Half Loves • In *How the Other Half Loves*, Ayckbourn takes his technique one step further, this time in the use of stage space in a simultaneous depiction of two separate dinner parties. He superimposes the dinner party of one upwardly mobile couple (the Fosters) on that of a more affluent couple (the Phillipses) so that both couples are hosts to the same dinner guests (the Featherstones). In an eye-defying sequence of movements, the audience witnesses the two couples preparing for their guests in the same stage space, the distinctions between the relative affluence of the aspiring sets of hosts made clear only by a change in a few minor furnishings, such as pillows. The hilarious scene in which two separate dinner parties at two separate times are staged at one table is Ayckbourn's most inventive climactic scene. Their common guest, Mr. Featherstone, is the victim simultaneously of Teresa Phillips's thrown soup (intended for her husband) and the leaking upstairs toilet at the Fosters' home. Unwitting victim of the accidental physical high jinks of his hosts, Mr. Featherstone is victim in another sense, for although the fortunes of the Phillipses and the Fosters seem to be put to rights at the end of the play, the Featherstones—clearly the couple to be impressed—reveal their own marital problems, foreboding, ironically, similar problems for their younger, aspiring hosts.

Time and Time Again • Up to *Time and Time Again*, Ayckbourn's inventions focused on plots and staging areas. About this play, however, Ayckbourn speaks of "upsetting the balance," an upsetting involving the nature of his main character. Normally the driving force in the plot, the protagonist, Leonard, is upsettingly passive. According to Ayckbourn, he "attracts people who have an irresistible impulse to push him in one direction, but he slides out of the push." Some audiences, Ayckbourn continues, are "angered by this type," while "others get concerned." Hence, Ayckbourn himself supplies yet another basis for the label applied to him as a writer of the theater of embarrassment.

Leonard's "sliding" in the play is his refusal to be drawn into the banalities of middle-class social lunches and teas. He has developed his own system of quiet resistance. At one point, he relates the story of a telling of a tale from his former marriage. A schoolteacher at the time, Leonard arrives home one day to find his wife sampling homemade wine with a male friend. Unable or unwilling to react, Leonard spends the evening in the local jail, regaling the officers with his story and retelling it to every fresh batch of police officers as they arrive for duty. Leonard is the first of a series of Ayckbourn's passive heroes, the most humorous being Norman of *The Norman Conquests*; the most sympathetically satiric, Guy Jones in *A Chorus of Disapproval*; and the most devastating, Douglas Beechey in *Man of the Moment*.

There is an aggressive element in Leonard's passivity as he forces others to respond to his lack of involvement. From his school days, he tells yet another story of having developed a system of quoting a line or two of poetry, an "infallible system to fool all headmasters and school inspectors." He continues this pattern of behavior even as an adult. Bored by the others and interested by Leonard's erratic behavior, Joan, his current interest, joins Leonard in his game. In the meantime, Graham, a husband also attracted to Joan, pushes Peter, another admirer of Joan mistaken by Graham as her lover, into a physical fight. Leonard, as a result of the mistake, goes scot-free. The play ends with Leonard eventually leaving Joan (as he earlier had left his wife and her lover to entertain the local police officers) and walking off compatibly with Peter to the playing field, Graham and Peter still laboring under their misunderstanding.

Absurd Person Singular • Another Ayckbourn technique becomes more apparent with every play: his inventive use of the room. As character becomes more important than plot, Ayckbourn utilizes the room (frequently the kitchen) as a microscope under which he examines contemporary middle-class behavior in all of its acquisitiveness and sexual rituals. The kitchen, its appliances emblems of materialistic greed, is an appropriate setting for his examination.

In his *Absurd Person Singular*, structured loosely as three one-act plays, three couples celebrate Christmas Eve in three successive years in three different homes, the kitchen winding up as the room in which most of the action takes place. In the first act, the first host-couple, lowest on the social rung, aspire to the social status of their guests. In the second act, the hosts have to some extent realized their social aims. In act 3, the hosts, having played the social-status game longer than their guests, have long since been in a state of total noncommunication, a direction toward which the other two couples seem to be heading. The final scene of act 3 finds all three couples crowding the kitchen, each person in a wild frenzy of attending to chores such as replacing a light bulb, completely ignoring the suicide attempt of their hostess, with her head in the gas oven. The three couples are a variation on those in *How the Other Half Loves*.

The Norman Conquests • Rooms continue to be the means of Ayckbourn's microscopic examination of suburban rituals in *The Norman Conquests*. Here, Ayckbourn locates the similar actions in three different places: the dining room in *Table Manners*, the living room in *Living Together*, and the garden in *Round and Round the Garden*. The family consists of Annie, who is single and the caretaker of their sick mother, her married sister Ruth, and her married brother Reg (and the spouses of the latter two). All convene in the family's country home to provide some relief for Annie. Norman, Ruth's husband, enjoys hilariously romantic encounters with the women in each location of the three plays.

Like Leonard of *Time and Time Again*, Norman attracts female attention and finds himself in situations not of his making. A Chekhovian immobility asserts itself in Annie's abortive plans for a "dirty weekend" with Norman in East Grinstead. There is a sixth character, an outsider in the person of a slow-witted local veterinarian, played in the original stage production with exquisitely hilarious dullness by Michael Gambon, who would later become a regular actor in Ayckbourn's plays. He is a foil to Norman, whose sexual attractiveness and agility drive the women to respond to him. Each of the three plays is complete in itself, and the order in which they are performed (or seen) is more or less immaterial to the audience's understanding of each play because the action in each does not essentially depend on that in the other two and because the actions in all three are essentially the same, their different "rooms" creating different perspectives on the same situation.

Taking Steps and **Bedroom Farce** • Two plays, *Taking Steps* and *Bedroom Farce*, revert to Ayckbourn's reliance on hectic physical stage business as in *How the Other Half Loves*. The action of *Taking Steps* occurs on three different floors of an old Victorian house, but one stage space is used to represent all three floors of the house. Hence the actors must take a variety of steps in imitation of stair climbing. Similarly, in *Bedroom Farce*, one stage area is occupied by three large beds to represent three different bedrooms. The potential audience confusions as to who is doing what in whose bed and the risk of actors in making false steps as they maneuver their way through time and space create suspense and keep the play's pace lively. At times, Ayckbourn's risk taking with physical matters seems its own excuse for being, an entertaining ploy to avoid the greater risk of banality potentially inherent in his repetitive marital and extramarital situations.

Season's Greetings • In the plays of the 1960's and 1970's, Ayckbourn's ingenious strategies of plot, space, and character dominate, and laughter governs the plays' moods. In the 1980's, however, the hilarity, although remaining intact to the end of the play, is mixed with increasing audience uncertainty—to laugh or not to laugh. For example, in *Season's Greetings*, a stranger (a writer with only one book to his credit) becomes the romantic object of attention of the females. A guest of the single sister at a Christmas family gathering, he is a later version of the outsider, Leonard, in *Time and Time Again*. When the women of the household (including his hostess, the unmarried sister) are attracted to him, an angry husband shoots and almost kills him. The intrusion on farce of a potential disaster changes the nature of the laughter into the kind produced by Chekhov's Uncle Vanya, whose shot at his rival misfires.

Chekhov-like also in his use of a family gathering as the central event of a play, Ayckbourn has commented on that event as unimportant. It is, rather, "the response to the dinner party, not the dinner party itself." He spoke to author Bernard Dukore of the inevitable line in that response: "Wasn't that a boring dinner party?" In that line and as a consequence of it, revelations occur, not only of the problems of those couples who have succeeded but also of the pending fate of those who have not yet arrived but are on the same path. An attractive outsider acts as a catalyst to reveal the Chekhovian inner states of being that lie beneath the politely banal surfaces.

A Chorus of Disapproval • The outsider in *A Chorus of Disapproval* is Guy Jones, a lonely bachelor drawn into a provincial production of John Gay's *The Beggar's Opera* (pr., pb. 1728), when the leading role is suddenly vacated. A fuller version of dull Tom in *The Norman Conquests*, he rises to the occasion, though untalented and inexperienced, and becomes the hero not only of the production but also of the women who thrust themselves on him as a result of dissatisfactions in their own marriages. He is the means by which they respond to the emptiness of their suburban lives.

A Small Family Business, Henceforward, and **Man of the Moment** • In three later plays—*A Small Family Business, Henceforward,* and *Man of the Moment*—the farce is increasingly ironic in Ayckbourn's progressive shift to emphasize the emotional and moral bankruptcy of middle-class family life in Thatcherite England of the 1980's. In all three, outside forces exert pressures on family situations, pressures that the family finds difficult or impossible to control.

In *A Small Family Business*, the pressure is money, involving a family furniture business in which greed corrupts completely, simultaneously involving a hilariously stereotyped, Mafia-like quintet of Italian brothers. In *Henceforward*, a gang-infested neighborhood is a refuge for a divorced composer of electronic music, who contests his wife for custody of their daughter. In a stunning move, Ayckbourn deploys a female robot, the composer's means of assuring the social worker of the presence of a maternal influence in his daughter's life. Ayckbourn compounds this bit of theatricality with the appearance of the teen daughter in full regalia as a member of one of the neighborhood gangs. In *Man of the Moment*, the theatricality takes the form of an overweight woman who accidentally kills a most repulsive character when she steps on him rather than saving him, as was her intention. Individual greed and corruption, although present, are given societal approval in the impunity and impersonality with which a television crew exploits personal tragedy in the name of a good news story. Both business and television interests conspire in a cover-up of the real story.

In these three plays, the laughter caused by coincidences and central misunderstandings is still there, but now the plays are darkened by their context of a pervasive societal hypocrisy. The problems are no longer those of innocently human complications but of socially accepted amorality. In *A Small Family Business,* the last person with any scruples, Jack, the new head of the business, cannot extricate himself from its corruption. The gang-infested neighborhood of *Henceforward* and the moral vacuum of the mass media in *Man of the Moment* remain. Ayckbourn provides no artificial resolutions to the problems, only a microscopic examination of them. Amid the farcical humor that is sustained to the end in two of the plays, two teenagers, as a result of their being ignored because of other family problems, become innocent victims, one a drug addict and the other a gang member. In the third play, an adult innocent, dull and passive Douglas Beechey, is a subject for both hilarity and tragedy, as he is made into a mass-media hero through no attempt on his part. He belongs to a long gallery of Ayckbourn characters who have their roots in the early outsider characters such as Tom in *The Norman Conquests.*

Despite widening his settings, for example to the Costa del Sol in southern Spain in *Man of the Moment,* to ethnic restaurants, in *Time of My Life,* even to imaginary landscapes, as in *The Revengers' Comedies* and futuristic households, as in *Henceforward,* Ayckbourn's themes and theatricality have developed naturally. He has never lost sight of the little man and his desire for self-fulfillment in domesticity, even though evil may lurk abroad.

Other major works

SCREENPLAY: *A Chorus of Disapproval,* 1989 (adaptation of his play).
TELEPLAY: *Service Not Included,* 1974.

Bibliography

Allen, Paul. *Alan Ayckbourn: Grinning at the Edge.* New York: Continuum, 2002. A biography that looks at the playwright's life and works. Based on more than twenty years of interviews with Ayckbourn and of his friends and acquaintances. Photographs. Index.

Billington, Michael. *Alan Ayckbourn.* New York: St. Martin's Press, 1990. A chronological analysis by a leading critic and scholar of Ayckbourn's plays, from his earliest unpublished works to *The Revengers' Comedies.*

Dukore, Bernard. *Alan Ayckbourn: A Casebook.* New York: Garland, 1992. A compilation of lively, analytical articles on Ayckbourn's plays in terms of their stylistic and thematic characteristics, as well as their effectiveness onstage. Includes an interview with Ayckbourn, a complete chronology, and an extensive bibliography.

Holt, Michael. *Alan Ayckbourn.* Plymouth, England: Northcote House, 1999. One of the British Council's "Writers and their Works" series, it is a sensible introduction. It contains a biography, bibliography, and commentary on the plays up to *Things We Do for Love.*

Kalson, Albert E. *Laughter in the Dark: The Plays of Alan Ayckbourn.* Cranbury, N.J.: Associated University Press for Fairleigh Dickinson University Press, 1993. The first chapter is biographical, then aspects of Ayckbourn's theater are explored, including chapters on technique; men's and women's roles; and moral, social, and political aspects. There is a separate chapter on *Absent Friends*. The best full study of the dramatist.

Page, Malcolm. *File on Ayckbourn*. London: Methuen Drama, 1989. A compilation of biographical information, production and publication data, synopses and comments on each play, interview excerpts, and a bibliography.

Watson, Ian. *Conversations with Ayckbourn*. Rev. ed. London: Faber and Faber, 1988. Unified into what seems to be an autobiography, Ayckbourn's comments range over the achievements of his entire career. Includes useful play synopses and chronology.

White, Sidney Howard. *Alan Ayckbourn*. Boston: Twayne, 1984. A chronological discussion of Ayckbourn's plays, tracing the dramatist's progress from farce to plays of character up to 1972. Includes a chronology, a bibliography, and an index.

Susan Rusinko,
updated by David Barratt

Amiri Baraka

LeRoi Jones

Born: Newark, New Jersey; October 7, 1934

Principal drama • *The Baptism*, pr. 1964, pb. 1966; *Dutchman*, pr., pb. 1964; *The Slave*, pr., pb. 1964; *The Toilet*, pr., pb. 1964; *Experimental Death Unit #1*, pr. 1965, pb. 1969; *Jello*, pr. 1965, pb. 1970; *A Black Mass*, pr. 1966, pb. 1969; *Arm Yourself, or Harm Yourself*, pr., pb. 1967; *Great Goodness of Life (A Coon Show)*, pr. 1967, pb. 1969; *Madheart*, pr. 1967, pb. 1969; *Slave Ship: A Historical Pageant*, pr., pb. 1967; *The Death of Malcolm X*, pb. 1969; *Bloodrites*, pr. 1970, pb. 1971; *Junkies Are Full of (SHHH...)*, pr. 1970, pb. 1971; *A Recent Killing*, pr. 1973; *S-1*, pr. 1976, pb. 1978; *The Motion of History*, pr. 1977, pb. 1978; *The Sidney Poet Heroical*, pb. 1979 (originally as *Sidnee Poet Heroical*, pr. 1975); *What Was the Relationship of the Lone Ranger to the Means of Production?*, pr., pb. 1979; *At the Dim'cracker Convention*, pr. 1980; *Weimar*, pr. 1981; *Money: A Jazz Opera*, pr. 1982; *Primitive World: An Anti-Nuclear Jazz Musical*, pr. 1984, pb. 1997; *The Life and Life of Bumpy Johnson*, pr. 1991; *General Hag's Skeezag*, pb. 1992; *Meeting Lillie*, pr. 1993; *The Election Machine Warehouse*, pr. 1996, pb. 1997

Other literary forms • Amiri Baraka is an exceptionally versatile literary figure, equally well known for his poetry, drama, and essays. In addition, he has written short stories, collected in *Tales* (1967), and an experimental novel, *The System of Dante's Hell* (1965), which includes numerous poetic and dramatic passages. Baraka's early volumes of poetry *Preface to a Twenty Volume Suicide Note* (1961) and *The Dead Lecturer* (1964) derive from his period of involvement with the New York City avant-garde. Other volumes, such as *Black Magic: Sabotage, Target Study, Black Art—Collected Poetry, 1961-1967* (1969) and *It's Nation Time* (1970), reflect his intense involvement with Black Nationalist politics. Later volumes, such as *Hard Facts* (1975) and *Reggae or Not!* (1981), reflect his developing movement to a leftist political position and have generally failed to appeal to either his avant-garde or his Black Nationalist audience. Baraka's critical and political prose has been collected in *Home: Social Essays* (1966), *Raise Race Rays Raze: Essays Since 1965* (1971), *Selected Plays and Prose* (1979), and *Daggers and Javelins: Essays* (1984). *The Autobiography of LeRoi Jones/Amiri Baraka* was published in 1984.

Achievements • One of the most politically controversial playwrights of the 1960's, Amiri Baraka is best known for his brilliant early play *Dutchman* and for his contribution to the development of a community-based black nationalist theater. Throughout his career, he has sought dramatic forms for expressing the consciousness of those alienated from the psychological, economic, and racial mainstream of American society. Even though no consensus exists concerning the success of his experiments, particularly those with ritualistic forms for political drama, his challenge to the aesthetic preconceptions of the American mainstream and the inspiration he has provided younger black playwrights such as Ed Bullins and Ron Milner guarantee his place in the history of American drama.

Already well known as an avant-garde poet, Baraka, then LeRoi Jones, first rose to prominence in the theatrical world with the 1964 productions of *The Baptism*, *Dutchman*, *The Slave*, and *The Toilet*, which established him as a major Off-Broadway presence. Shortly after winning the Obie Award for *Dutchman*, however, Baraka broke his ties with the white avant-garde to concentrate on the creation of a militant African American theater. As his mainstream reputation declined, he gained recognition as a leading voice of the Black Arts movement, ultimately assuming a position of public political visibility matched by only a handful of American literary figures.

Baraka's many awards and honors include the Longview Best Essay of the Year award (1961) for his essay "Cuba Libre"; the John Whitney Foundation fellowship for poetry and fiction (1962); the Obie Award for Best American Off-Broadway Play of 1964 for *Dutchman*; a Guggenheim Fellowship (1965-1966); second prize in the First World Festival of Negro Arts (1966) for his play *The Slave*; a National Endowment for the Arts grant (1966); an honorary doctorate from Malcolm X College in Chicago (1972); a Rockefeller Foundation Fellowship in drama (1981); a National Endowment for the Arts poetry award (1981); a New Jersey Council for the Arts award (1982); the American Book Award (established by the Before Columbus Foundation), for *Confirmation: An Anthology of African-American Women*; a PEN-Faulkner Award (1989); the Langston Hughes Medal (1989) for outstanding contributions to literature; Italy's Ferroni Award and Foreign Poet Award (1993); and the Playwright's Award from the Black Drama Festival of Winston-Salem, North Carolina, in 1997.

Biography • Everett LeRoi Jones, who took the name Amiri Baraka in 1967, was born into a black middle-class family in Newark, New Jersey. An excellent student whose parents encouraged his intellectual interests, Jones was graduated from Howard University of Washington, D.C., in 1954, at the age of nineteen. After spending two years in the United States Air Force, primarily in Puerto Rico, he moved to Greenwich Village, where he embarked on his literary career in 1957. During the early stage of his career, Jones associated closely with numerous white avant-garde poets, including Robert Creeley, Allen Ginsberg, Robert Duncan, and Dianne DiPrima, and, with DiPrima, he founded the American Theatre for Poets in 1961.

Baraka married Hettie Cohen, a white woman with whom he edited the magazine *Yugen* from 1958 to 1963, and he established himself as an important young poet, critic, and editor. Among the many magazines to which he contributed was the jazz journal *Downbeat*, where he first developed the interest in African American musical culture that helped shape his theatrical "rituals." The political interests that were to dominate Jones's later work were unmistakably present as early as 1960, when he toured Cuba with a group of black intellectuals. This experience sparked his perception of the United States as a corrupt bourgeois society and seems particularly significant in relation to his subsequent socialist stance. Jones's growing political interest influenced his first produced plays, including the Obie Award-winning *Dutchman*, which anticipated the first major transformation of Jones's life.

Separating from Hettie Cohen and severing ties with his white associates, Jones moved from Greenwich Village to Harlem in 1965. Turning his attention to direct action within the black community, he founded the Black Arts Theatre and School in Harlem and, following his return to his native city in 1966, the Spirit House in Newark. After marrying a black woman, Sylvia Robinson (Amina Baraka), in 1966, Jones adopted a new name, "Amiri" (which means "prince") "Baraka" ("blessed one"), to which he added the honorary title "Imamu" ("spiritual leader"). Over the next half-dozen years, Baraka helped found and develop organizations such as the Black Community Development and Defense Organization, the Congress of African Peoples (convened in Atlanta in 1970), and the National Black Political Convention (convened in Gary, Indiana, in 1972). As a leading spokesperson of the Black Arts movement, Baraka provided personal and artistic support for young black poets and playwrights, including Larry Neal, Ed Bullins, Marvin X, and Ron Milner. During the Newark riots of 1967, Baraka was arrested for unlawful possession of firearms. Although convicted and given the maximum sentence after the judge read the jury his poem "Black People!" as an example of incitement to riot, Baraka was later cleared on appeal.

Baraka supported Ken Gibson's campaign to become the first black mayor of Newark in 1970, but later broke with him over what he perceived as the Gibson administration's bourgeois values. This disillusionment with black politics within

(Library of Congress)

the American system and Baraka's attendance at the Sixth Pan-African Conference at Dar es Salaam in 1974 precipitated the next stage of his political evolution. Although he did not abandon his commitment to confronting the special problems of African Americans in the United States, Baraka began interpreting these problems within the framework of an overarching "Marxist-Leninist-Mao Zedong" philosophy. In conjunction with this second transformation, Baraka dropped the title "Imamu" and changed the name of his Newark publishing firm from "Jihad" to "People's War." He undertook visiting professorships at Yale and George Washington universities before accepting a more permanent position at the State University of New York at Stony Brook.

In 1979, Baraka was arrested during a dispute with his wife; he wrote *The Autobiography of LeRoi Jones* while serving the resulting sentence at a halfway house in Harlem. In 1990, he was involved in a widely publicized dispute with Rutgers University officials who had denied him tenure; he compared the school's faculty to the Ku Klux Klan and the Nazi Party. Though such controversies perhaps exacerbated the difficulty Baraka experienced in finding publishers for his socialist writings, he remained an important voice in the literary world and the African American community. After teaching for twenty years in the Department of African Studies at State University of New York-Stony Brook, Baraka retired from his position in 1999.

Analysis • Working with forms ranging from the morality play to avant-garde expressionism, Amiri Baraka throughout his career sought to create dramatic rituals expressing the intensity of the physical and psychological violence that dominates his vision of American culture. From his early plays on "universal" alienation through his Black Nationalist celebrations to his multimedia proletarian pageants, Baraka has focused on a variety of sacrificial victims as his central dramatic presences. Some of these victims remain passive scapegoats who allow a corrupt and vicious system to dictate their fate. Others assume the role of heroic martyr in the cause of community consciousness. Yet a third type of victim is the doomed oppressor whose death marks the transformation of the martyr's consciousness into a ritual action designed to free the community from continuing passive victimization.

The dominant type in Baraka's early plays, the passive scapegoats unaware of their participation in ritual actions, condemn themselves and their communities to blind repetition of destructive patterns. Their apparent mastery of the forms of European American cultural literacy simply obscures the fact of their ignorance of the underlying reality of oppression. Responding to this ironic situation, Baraka's Black Nationalist plays emphasize the new forms of consciousness, their roots in Africa rather than Europe, needed to free the African American community from the historical and psychological forces that enforce such blind repetition. Inverting the traditional moral symbolism of European American culture, Baraka creates rituals that substitute symbolically white scapegoats for the symbolically black victims of his earlier works. These rituals frequently reject the image of salvation through self-sacrifice (seen as a technique for the pacification of the black masses), insisting instead that only an active struggle can break the cycle of oppression.

Because the rituals of Baraka's Black Nationalist plays frequently culminate in violence directed against whites, or symbolically white members of the black bourgeois, or aspects of the individual black psyche, numerous critics have attacked him for perpetuating the violence and racism he ostensibly criticizes. These critics frequently condemn him for oversimplifying reality, citing his movement from psychologically complex ironic forms to much more explicit allegorical modes in his later drama; the most insistent simply dismiss his post-*Dutchman* plays as strident propaganda, lacking all aesthetic and moral merit.

Basing their critiques firmly on European American aesthetic assumptions, such critics in fact overlook the central importance of Baraka's changing sense of his audience. Repudiating the largely white avant-garde audience that applauded his early work, Baraka turned almost exclusively to an African American audience more aware of the storefront preacher and popular music groups such as the Temptations than of August Strindberg and Edward Albee. In adopting a style of performance in accord with this cultural perception, Baraka assumed a didactic voice intended to focus attention on immediate issues of survival and community or class defense.

The Baptism • First produced in leading New York theaters such as St. Mark's Playhouse (*The Slave* and *The Toilet*), the Cherry Lane Theatre (*Dutchman*), and the Writers' Stage Theatre (*The Baptism*), Baraka's early plays clearly reflect both his developing concern with issues of survival and his fascination with European American avant-garde traditions. *The Baptism*, in particular, draws on the conventions of expressionist theater to comment on the absurdity of contemporary American ideas of salvation, which in fact simply mask a larger scheme of victimization. Identified only as symbolic types, Baraka's characters speak a surreal mixture of street language and theological argot. While the slang references link them to the social reality familiar to the audience, their actions are dictated by the sudden shifts and thematic ambiguities characteristic of works such as Strindberg's *Ett drömspel* (pb. 1902; *A Dream Play*, 1912) and the "Circe" chapter of James Joyce's *Ulysses* (1922).

The play's central character, named simply "the Boy," resembles a traditional Christ figure struggling to come to terms with his vocation. Baraka treats his protagonist with a mixture of irony and empathy, focusing on the ambiguous roles of the spirit and the flesh in relation to salvation. Pressured by the Minister to deny his body and by the cynical Homosexual to immerse himself in the profane as a path to the truly sacred, the Boy vacillates. At times he claims divine status; at times he insists, "I am only flesh." The chorus of Women, at once holy virgins and temple prostitutes, reinforces his confusion. Shortly after identifying him as "the Son of God," they refer to him as the "Chief Religious jelly roll of the universe." Given these irreconcilable roles, which he is expected to fulfill, the Boy's destiny as scapegoat and martyr seems inevitable; the dramatic tension revolves around the question of who will victimize him and why. Baraka uses a sequence of conflicting views of the Boy's role, each of which momentarily dominates his self-image, to heighten this tension.

Responding to the Homosexual's insistence that "the devil is a part of creation like an ash tray or senator," the Boy first confesses his past sins and demands baptism. When the Women respond by elevating him to the status of "Son of God/ Son of Man," he explicitly rejects all claim to spiritual purity. The ambiguous masquerade culminates in an attack on the Boy, who is accused of using his spiritual status to seduce women who "wanted to be virgins of the Lord." Supported only by the Homosexual, the Boy defends himself against the Women and the Minister, who clamor for his sacrifice, ostensibly as punishment for his sins. Insisting that "there will be no second crucifixion," the Boy slays his antagonists with a phallic sword, which he interprets as the embodiment of spiritual glory. For a brief moment, the figures of Christ as scapegoat and Christ as avenger seem reconciled in a baptism of fire.

Baraka undercuts this moment of equilibrium almost immediately. Having escaped martyrdom at the hands of the mob (ironically, itself victimized), the Boy confronts the Messenger, who wears a motorcycle jacket embellished with a gold crown and the words "The Man." In Baraka's dream allegory, the Man can represent the Roman/ American legal system or be a symbol for God the Father, both powers that severely limit the Boy's control over events. The Boy's first reaction to the Messenger is to reclaim his superior spiritual status, insisting that he has "brought love to many people" and calling on his "Father" for compassion. Rejecting these pleas, the Messenger indicates that "the Man's destroying the whole works tonight." The Boy responds defiantly: "Neither God nor man shall force me to leave. I was sent here to save man and I'll not leave until I do." The allegory suggests several different levels of interpretation: social, psychological, and symbolic.

The Boy rejects his responsibility to concrete individuals (the mob he kills, the Man) in order to save an abstract entity (the mob as an ideal man). Ultimately, he claims his right to the martyr's death, which he killed the mob in order to avoid, by repudiating the martyr's submission to a higher power. Losing patience with the Boy's rhetoric, the Messenger responds not by killing him but by knocking him out and dragging him offstage. His attitude of boredom effectively deflates the allegorical seriousness of the Boy's defiance, a deflation reinforced by the Homosexual's concluding comment that the scene resembles "some really uninteresting kind of orgy."

The Baptism's treatment of the interlocking themes of sacrifice, ritual, and victimization emphasizes their inherent ambiguity and suggests the impossibility of moral action in a culture that confuses God with the leader of a motorcycle gang. The encompassing irony of the Christ figure sacrificing his congregation to ensure universal destruction recalls T. S. Eliot's treatment of myth in *The Waste Land* (1922) and his essay "Ulysses: Myth and Order." Eliot's use of classical allusions and mythic analogies to underscore the triviality of modern life clearly anticipates Baraka's ironic vision of Christian ritual. Baraka's baptism initiates the Boy into absurdity rather than responsibility. If any sins have been washed away, they are resurrected immediately in pointless ritual violence and immature rhetoric. Although he does not develop the theme explicitly in *The Baptism*, Baraka suggests that there is an underlying philosophical corruption in European American culture, in this case derived from Christianity's tendency to divorce flesh from spirit. Increasingly, this philosophical corruption takes the center of Baraka's dramatic presentation of Western civilization.

Dutchman • Widely recognized as Baraka's greatest work in any genre, *Dutchman* combines the irony of his avant-garde period with the emotional power and social insight of his later work. Clay, a young black man with a highly developed sense of self, occupies a central position in the play analogous to that of the Boy in *The Baptism*. The central dramatic action of the play involves Clay's confrontation with a young white woman, Lula, who may in fact be seen as an aspect of Clay's own self-awareness. In both thematic emphasis and dramatic structure, *Dutchman* parallels Edward Albee's *The Zoo Story* (pr., pb. 1959). Both plays focus on a clash between characters from divergent social and philosophical backgrounds, both comment on the internal divisions of individuals in American society, and both culminate in acts of violence that are at once realistic and symbolic.

What sets *Dutchman* apart, however, is its intricate exploration of the psychology that leads Clay to a symbolic rebellion that ironically guarantees his real victimization. Clay *thinks* he exists as an autonomous individual struggling for existential awareness. Baraka implies, however, that this European American conception of self simply enforces Clay's preordained role as ritual scapegoat. As the Everyman figure his name suggests, Clay represents all individuals trapped by self-deception and social pressure. As a black man in a racist culture, he shares the more specific problem of those whose self-consciousness has been determined by white definitions.

The stage directions for *Dutchman* emphasize the link between Clay's situation and the decline of European American culture, describing the subway car where the action transpires as "the flying underbelly of the city . . . heaped in modern myth." Lula enters eating an apple, evoking the myth of the Fall. Together, these allusions contribute a literary dimension to the foreboding atmosphere surrounding the extended conversation that leads to Clay's sacrifice at the hands of Lula and the subway riders, mostly white but some black. Throughout, Lula maintains clear awareness of her symbolic and political intentions, while Clay remains effectively blind. Lula's role demands simply that she maintain the interest of the black man until it is convenient to kill him.

Meanwhile, Clay believes he can somehow occupy a position of detachment or spiritual superiority. Changing approach frequently, Lula plays the roles of temptress, intellectual, psychologist, and racist. Clay responds variously to these gambits, sometimes with amusement, ultimately with anger and contempt. Consistently, however, he fails to recognize the genocidal reality underlying Lula's masquerade, unwittingly assuming his preordained role in the controlling ritual of black destruction. Much like the legendary ghost ship for which it was named, the *Dutchman*, Baraka implies, will continue to sail so long as blacks allow the white world to control the premises of the racial debate.

This rigged debate reflects Baraka's reassessment of his universalist beliefs and his movement toward Black Nationalism. Clay resembles the early LeRoi Jones in many ways: Both are articulate natives of New Jersey with aspirations to avant-garde artistic success. *Dutchman* implies that both are subject to fantasies about the amount of meaningful success possible for them in the realm of European American culture. Lula alternately reduces Clay to a "well-known type" and condemns him for rejecting his roots and embracing "a tradition you ought to feel oppressed by." During the first act, Clay stays "cool" until Lula sarcastically declares him the "Black Baudelaire" and follows with the repeated phrase "My Christ. My Christ." Suddenly shifting emphasis, she immediately denies his Christ-like stature and insists, "You're a murderer," compressing the two major attributes of the Boy in *The Baptism*, this time with a specifically social resonance. The sudden shift disrupts Clay's balance.

Ironically restating and simplifying the thesis of Ralph Ellison's universalist novel *Invisible Man* (1922), Lula concludes the opening act with an ironic resolution to "pretend the people cannot see you . . . that you are free of your own history. And I am free of my history." The rapid movement from Clay as Christ and murderer—standard black roles in the fantasy life of white America—to the *pretense* of his freedom underscores the inevitability of his victimization, an inevitability clearly dictated by the historical forces controlling Lula, forces that Clay steadfastly refuses to recognize.

Clay's lack of awareness blinds him to the fact that the subway car, occupied only by himself and Lula during act 1, fills up with people during act 2. Continuing to manipulate Clay through rapid shifts of focus, Lula diverts his attention from the context, first by fantasizing a sexual affair with him and then by ridiculing him as an "escaped nigger" with absurd pretensions to cultural whiteness. Abandoning his cool perspective for the first time, Clay angrily takes "control" of the conversation. His powerful soliloquy establishes his superior understanding of his interaction with Lula, but only in the theoretical terms of European American academic discourse. Admitting his hatred for whites, Clay claims a deep affinity with the explosive anger lying beneath the humorous surface of the work of the great black musicians Bessie Smith and Charlie Parker. Ridiculing Lula's interpretation of his psychological makeup, Clay warns her that whites should beware of preaching "rationalism" to blacks, since the best cure for the black neurosis would be the random murder of whites.

After this demonstration of his superior, and highly rational, awareness, Clay turns to go. He dismisses Lula with contempt, saying, "we won't be acting out that little pageant you outlined before." Immediately thereafter, Lula kills him. The murder is in fact the final act of the real pageant, the ritual of black sacrifice. Seen from Lula's perspective, the entire conversation amounts to an extended assault on Clay's awareness of the basic necessities of survival. Seen from Baraka's viewpoint, the heightened racial awareness of Clay's final speech is simply an illusion, worthless if divorced from action. Clay's unwilling participation in the pageant of white mythology reveals the futility of all attempts to respond to white culture on its own terms. Regarded in this light, Baraka's subsequent movement away from the theoretical avant-garde and from European American modes of psychological analysis seems inevitable.

Black Nationalist plays • Baraka's Black Nationalist plays, many of them written for community theater groups such as Spirit House Movers and the San Francisco State College Black Arts Alliance, occasionally employ specific avant-garde techniques. His earlier works take the techniques "seriously," but even his most experimental nationalist plays, such as *Experimental Death Unit #1*, clearly attempt to subvert the values implied by the European American aesthetic. Determined to communicate with his community through its own idiom, Baraka sought new forms in the African American aesthetic embodied in dance and music, African chants, experimental jazz, rhythm and blues, and reggae.

Particularly when its is performed in predominantly black contexts, Baraka's work in this idiom creates an emotional intensity difficult to describe in standard academic terms, an atmosphere often extremely uncomfortable for white viewers. Even while embracing and exploiting the aesthetic potential of the idiom, however, Baraka attempts to purify and transform it. Repudiating his earlier vision of universal alienation and victimization, Baraka no longer sympathizes with, or even tolerates, passive scapegoats such as Clay and the Boy. He does not, however, remove the victim from the center of his drama. Rather, he emphasizes two new types of victims in his nationalist rituals: the clearly heroic African American martyr in *Great Goodness of Life (A Coon Show)* and *The Death of Malcolm X*, and the whitewashed black and overthrown white oppressor in *Madheart* and *Slave Ship*, portrayed as deserving their death.

Madheart • *Madheart* and *Great Goodness of Life (A Coon Show)* employ different constellations of these figures to criticize the failure of the black community to purge its consciousness of European American values. Like *A Black Mass*, *Madheart* borrows the image of the "white devil" from the theology of the Nation of Islam (sometimes referred to inaccurately as the "Black Muslims") to account for the fallen condition of black awareness.

Beginning with a confrontation between allegorical characters identified as Black Man and Devil Lady, *Madheart* focuses on the Devil Lady's influence over the Black Man's Mother and Sister, whose red and blonde wigs indicate the extent of their corruption. Aided by the supportive Black Woman, Black Man rejects and sacrifices the Devil Lady, symbolically repudiating white culture. Mother and Sister, however, refuse to participate in the ritual of purification. Sister loses consciousness, believing that the death of the Devil Lady is also her own death. Lamenting over her daughter, Mother calls on white "saints" such as Tony Bennett, Ludwig van Beethoven, and Batman for deliverance.

Clinging to their belief in whiteness, Mother and a revived Sister descend to the level of slobbering animals. Motivated by love rather than hatred, Black Man turns a firehose on them as the play ends. His concluding speech echoes Baraka's basic attitude toward his suffering community: "This stuff can't go on. They'll die or help us, be black or white and dead. I'll save them or kill them." To avoid being sacrificed like Clay, Baraka implies, the African American community must repudiate its internal whiteness. The elimination of the white "devil," far from being an end in itself, is simply a preliminary step toward the purification of the black self-image.

Great Goodness of Life (A Coon Show) • Extending this critique of the internalization of white corruption, *Great Goodness of Life (A Coon Show)*, with its title ironic at several levels, focuses on the trial of Court Royal, a middle-aged black man accused of unspecified crimes. An offstage voice, supported by a sequence of increasingly respectable-looking Ku Klux Klan figures, echoes Lula in *Dutchman*, claiming that Court Royal has been harboring a murderer. Although Court Royal interprets the claim in concrete terms, the voice seeks primarily to bring about his repudiation of his black identity. Manipulating his fear of personal loss, the voice forces Court to preside over the ritual murder of a black martyr whose body is carried onstage to the accompaniment of projected slides showing martyrs such as Malcolm X and Patrice Lumumba.

Ordering the disposal of the corpse, the voice says: "Conceal the body in a stone. And sink the stone deep under the ocean. Call the newspapers and give the official history. Make sure his voice is in that stone too." In fact, the primary aim of the voice is to silence the African American cultural tradition by encouraging individuals to see their own situations as divorced from that of their community. Despite Court Royal's dim awareness that the "body" is that of a collective figure, the voice forces him to deny his sense that "there are many faces." After Court Royal acquiesces to this European American vision of individualism, the voice declares him "free," stipulating only that he "perform the rite." The rite is the execution of the "body."

Assuring Court Royal that the murderer is already dead, the voice nevertheless demands that he actively contribute to the destruction of the African American tradition by sacrificing the "murderer" within. To distract Court Royal from the genocidal reality of his act, the voice delivers an intricate statement on the nature of ritual action. Court, caught in the trap of European American rhetoric, ironically assumes the role of the white God and executes his symbolic son; the young black man cries out "Papa" as he dies. His soul "washed white as snow," Court merely returns to his night-out bowling.

His voice sunk beneath the sea, Court can only echo the white voice that commands his passive acceptance of European American rituals. Where Clay was killed by white society directly, the martyr in *Great Goodness of Life (A Coon Show)* is killed by white society acting indirectly through the timorous and self-deluded black bourgeois. Ritual murder metamorphoses into ritual suicide. Baraka clearly intimates the need for new rituals that will be capable of presenting new alternatives not under the control of the white voice.

Slave Ship • *Slave Ship*, Baraka's most convincing and theatrically effective Black Nationalist play, develops both the form and the content of these rituals. Thematically, the play places the perceptions of *Madheart* and *Great Goodness of Life (A Coon Show)* in a broader historical perspective. Beginning in West Africa and progressing through the American Civil War, Baraka traces the evolution of African American culture, stressing the recurring scenes of betrayal in which traitors, frequently preachers, curry favor with their white masters by selling out their people. Such repeated betrayals, coupled with scenes of white violence against blacks, create a tension that is released only with the sudden ritual killing of the white voice and the black traitor. This sacrifice emphasizes Baraka's demand for an uncompromising response to the forces, inside and outside the community, responsible for centuries of black misery.

The real power of *Slave Ship*, however, stems from its performance style, which combines lighting, music, and at times even smell, to create an encompassing atmosphere of oppression that gives way to an even more overwhelming celebration. The sound of white laughter and black singing and moaning surrounds the recurring visual images that link the historical vignettes. A drumbeat reasserts itself at moments of tension and seeming despair, suggesting the saving presence of the African heritage. The drum, joined by a jazz saxophone as the black community rises to break its chains, initiates the celebratory chant: "When we gonna rise up, brother/ When we gonna rise above the sun/ When we gonna take our own place, brother/ Like the world had just begun?" Superimposed on the continuing background moaning, the chant inspires a communal dance that combines African and African American styles.

Invoking the choreography of the "Miracles/Temptations dancing line," Baraka calls the dance the "Boogalooyoruba," compressing historical past and present in a ritual designed to create a brighter future. Following the climactic sacrifice, the severed heads of black traitor and white oppressor are cast down on the stage. Given ideal context and performance, the dancing of the Boogalooyoruba will then spread through the audience. *Slave Ship* thus exemplifies African American ritual drama of the 1960's; merging aesthetic performance and political statement, it marks the culmination of Baraka's Black Nationalist work.

Plays of the 1970's and 1980's • Baraka's later plays express the Marxist-Leninist-Mao Zedong philosophy he embraced in the mid-1970's. Gauging the success of monumental dramas such as *The Motion of History* and *The Sidney Poet Heroical* is difficult, in part because they are rarely performed, in larger part because of a generally hostile political climate. The texts of the plays reflect Baraka's continuing interest in multimedia performance styles, incorporating a great deal of musical and cinematic material. Both plays comprise numerous brief scenes revealing the action of historical forces, primarily economic in *The Motion of History* and primarily racial in *The Sidney Poet Heroical.*

Both plays also present images of martyr-heroes and oppressor-scapegoats. On the page, however, both appear programmatic and somewhat naïvely ideological. The climaxes, for example, feature mass meetings intended to inspire the audience to political commitment, a technique anticipated in proletarian dramas of the 1930's such as Clifford Odets's *Waiting for Lefty* (pr., pb. 1935). The cries "Long live socialist revolution" and "Victory to Black People! Victory to all oppressed people!" that conclude *The Motion of History* and *The Sidney Poet Heroical* obviously require both a sensitive production and a politically sympathetic audience to work their desired effect. In the political climate of the late 1970's and 1980's, neither element was common, and Baraka's plays of this period could be considered closet dramas.

Primitive World • In his 1984 *Primitive World: An Anti-Nuclear Jazz Musical,* Baraka presents the money gods as the arch-fiends. Displeased at the audacity of the humans—and especially, the poor—to "want things," these money gods decide to put an end to human history. Speaking of the "grim moral" of his play, Baraka said, "we seem to be more endangered by greed and selfishness than we are by the weapons we have created to destroy each other." In this play, as in his earlier work, Baraka attempts to exorcise the demons and the demonic element within each human being that seem bent on nothing so much as the destruction of humanity—and, ultimately, of humankind.

In his speech on "Poetry and the Public Sphere" at the 1997 Conference on Contemporary Poetry, Baraka addressed more generally the recurrent theme of his work: "it is this wailing, this defiance, this resistance, this joy in the overwhelming of evil by good, that is at the base of our poetic traditions, our history, our continuing lives."

In his 1969 poem "Black Art," the poet asks that his poem "clean out the world for virtue and love"; and, bidding his poem scream, he cries, "Let Black People understand/ that they are the lovers and the sons/ of lovers and warriors and sons/ of warriors Are poems & poets &/ all the loveliness here in the world." In his still earlier drama *A Black Mass,* his black priest Tanzil speaks of reaching "back to warmth and feelings, to the human mind, and compassion. And ris[ing] again, back on up the scale, reaching again for the sphere of spheres, back to original reason. To where we always were." The exorcism of the demon oppressor in *A Black Mass* is not left to the imagination/intellect of the viewer as it is in *Primitive World*. The narrator of *A Black Mass* speaks to the audience of the need for diligence in the seeking out and in the destruction of the evil that the priests have let loose on the world in their experiment-gone-wrong—in their creation of the "soulless [white] monster." The oppressors in neither play recognize or employ the reason and the compassion possible to the occupants of this "sphere of spheres."

Later Plays • When "White people. . . made [him] famous" for *Dutchman*, Baraka felt that they were making it possible for him to "continue [the] tradition" passed on to him by *his* people:

> I don't know if y'all still have that in your homes. . . . I can't speak on that, but I know that is what we as writers have to do, continue that tradition. The only way I can see that tradition being extended is through the role and function of the writer in the community.

It is not surprising that, while he was praised by such prominent African American authors as James Baldwin, Toni Morrison, Sonia Sanchez, Nikki Giovanni, Ntozake Shange, and Maya Angelou, the admittedly vengeful nature of much of his art did not afford him a sustained popularity with mainstream audiences and he found himself unable to make a living as a writer. According to Baraka, his 1982 *Money: A Jazz Opera* was even "banned in France by the United States" because it was considered anti-American.

Baraka's 1990's plays *The Life and Life of Bumpy Johnson* and *Meeting Lillie* were somewhat less strident and, perhaps as a result, somewhat better received by mainstream critics.

Addressing a group of aspiring writers in 1998, Baraka spoke of his being readied by his parents and his grandmother for his life's work as out-of-the-mainstream writer and activist:

> It was like you had been doctored on by masters. . . . Every night at dinner, they'd be running it. . . . They would be telling you the history of the South, the history of Black people, the history of Black music and you would be sitting there. . . . My grandmother would tell me all the time about this Black boy they accused of raping this woman and they cut off his genitals and stuffed them in his mouth and then made all the Black women come there and watch. . . . Why would your grandmother tell you that story? . . . Oh, you still know the story, you still got it in your mind sixty years later. . . . Well, that's why she told it to you.

Baraka in his body of work strives to exorcise soullessness and to restore loveliness and humanity to humankind. Twentieth century African Americans, from Nobel Prize-winning author to factory worker, were influenced by the man who abandoned the title but not the role of "imamu"—spiritual leader. It remains to be seen whether the twenty-first century mainstream can overlook Baraka's and its own subjectivity in order that it may benefit, as well, from the spirit of his work.

Other major works

LONG FICTION: *The System of Dante's Hell*, 1965.

SHORT FICTION: *Tales*, 1967; *The Fiction of LeRoi Jones/Amiri Baraka*, 2000.

POETRY: *Spring and So forth*, 1960; *Preface to a Twenty Volume Suicide Note*, 1961; *The Dead Lecturer*, 1964; *Black Art*, 1966; *A Poem for Black Hearts*, 1967; *Black Magic: Sabotage,*

Target Study, *Black Art—Collected Poetry, 1961-1967,* 1969; *It's Nation Time,* 1970; *In Our Terribleness: Some Elements and Meaning in Black Style,* 1970 (with Fundi [Billy Abernathy]); *Spirit Reach,* 1972; *Afrikan Revolution,* 1973; *Hard Facts,* 1975; *Selected Poetry of Amiri Baraka/LeRoi Jones,* 1979; *Reggae or Not!,* 1981; *Transbluesency: The Selected Poems of Amiri Baraka,* 1995; *Wise, Why's, Y's,* 1995; *Funklore: New Poems, 1984-1995,* 1996.

NONFICTION: *Blues People: Negro Music in White America,* 1963; *Home: Social Essays,* 1966; *Raise Race Rays Raze: Essays Since 1965,* 1971; *The New Nationalism,* 1972; *The Autobiography of LeRoi Jones/Amiri Baraka,* 1984, revised 1997; *Daggers and Javelins: Essays,* 1984; *The Music: Reflections on Jazz and Blues,* 1987 (with Amina Baraka).

EDITED TEXTS: *The Moderns: New Fiction in America,* 1963; *Black Fire: An Anthology of Afro-American Writing,* 1968 (with Larry Neal); *African Congress: A Documentary of the First Modern Pan-African Congress,* 1972; *Confirmation: An Anthology of African-American Women,* 1983 (with Amina Baraka).

MISCELLANEOUS: *Selected Plays and Prose,* 1979; *The LeRoi Jones/Amiri Baraka Reader,* 1991.

Bibliography

Benston, Kimberly W., ed. *Imamu Amiri Baraka (LeRoi Jones): A Collection of Critical Essays.* Englewood Cliffs, N.J.: Prentice-Hall, 1978. A whole section, titled "Black Labs of the Heart," examines Baraka's drama in six essays on *Dutchman, The Slave, The Toilet, Great Goodness of Life (A Coon Show), Madheart,* and *Slave Ship.* "Baraka's theatre is one of deliverance, inexorably oriented toward liberation through confrontation," says Benston in her introduction. Contains a bibliography.

Brown, Lloyd W. *Amiri Baraka.* Boston: Twayne, 1980. Separating Baraka's literary output by major genre, Brown covers drama last, beginning with Mao Zedong's influence on the socialist perspective of such plays as *The Motion of History* and *S-1.* Even in Baraka's four early plays—*The Baptism, The Toilet, Dutchman,* and *The Slave*—Brown sees not an advocacy of revolution but "a highly effective analysis of American society" before his political views find an ideology. *Slave Ship* is a successful "ritual drama," Brown notes. Chronology, bibliography, index.

Gwynne, James B., ed. *Amiri Baraka: The Kaleidoscopic Torch.* Harlem, N.Y.: Steppingstones Press, 1985. This collection of essays hails Baraka as torchbearer: "He opened tightly guarded doors for not only Blacks but poor whites as well, and of course, Native Americans, Latinos, and Asian Americans" (Maurice Kenny); "Baraka . . . stands with Wheatley, Douglass, Dunbar, Hughes, Hurston, Wright, and Ellison as one of the eight figures . . . who have significantly affected the course of African American literary culture" (Arnold Rampersad).

Harris, William J. *The Poetry and Poetics of Amiri Baraka: The Jazz Aesthetic.* Columbia: University of Missouri Press, 1985. In his study, Harris shows that "throughout his career, even during the . . . Marxist stage, [Baraka] has used the jazz aesthetic process to create a new black art from the artistic and conceptual innovations of the twentieth-century avant-garde." A late chapter discusses Baraka's significance to and influence on African American artists. Includes selected bibliography and index.

Hudson, Theodore R. *From LeRoi Jones to Amiri Baraka: The Literary Works.* Durham, N.C.: Duke University Press, 1973. The last chapter, "Not the Weak Hamlets," deals with Baraka's almost single-handed invention of black theater and his theory of the drama as "a device for [political] edification and motivation." Hudson states that six plays produced in 1964 and an Obie Award established Baraka as "the subject of serious critical consideration by the American theatre establishment." Index and bibliography.

Lacey, Henry C. *To Raise, Destroy, and Create: The Poetry, Drama, and Fiction of Imamu Amiri Baraka (LeRoi Jones)*. Troy, N.Y.: Whitston, 1981. Unlike other studies, which separate the works by genres, this volume divides Baraka's life into a Beat period, a transition, and a rebirth symbolized by taking on a new name. Also discusses Baraka's dramatic work in context with his writing in other genres. Supplemented by an index and a list of Baraka's works.

Reilly, Charlie, ed. *Conversations with Amiri Baraka*. Jackson: University Press of Mississippi, 1994. In the text's introduction, the editor prepares the reader for the telling of the story—"much of it told for the first time"—of "the acclaimed author who walked back into the ghetto to support his people and who never looked back." Includes chronology and index.

Sollors, Werner. *Amiri Baraka/LeRoi Jones: The Quest for a "Populist Modernism."* New York: Columbia University Press, 1978. Three chapters of this study deal with Baraka's drama. "From Off-Bowery to Off Broadway" provides a close study of *The Baptism* and *The Toilet; Dutchman* gets a whole chapter to itself. Good photograph section of production stills. Bibliography and index.

Watts, Jerry Gafio. *Amiri Baraka: The Politics and Art of a Black Intellectual*. New York: New York University Press, 2001. A critical appraisal of Baraka from his early Beat poetry and on. Watts argues that Baraka's artistry declined as he became more politically active, though he considers Baraka an important poet and lens through which African American political history can be viewed.

Craig Werner,
updated by Thomas J. Taylor,
Robert McClenaghan, and Judith K. Taylor

Pierre-Augustin Caron de Beaumarchais

Pierre-Augustin Caron

Born: Paris, France; January 24, 1732
Died: Paris, France; May 18, 1799

Principal drama • *Eugénie*, pr., pb. 1767 (*The School of Rakes*, 1795); *Les Deux Amis: Ou, Le Négociant de Lyon*, pr., pb. 1770 (*The Two Friends: Or, The Liverpool Merchant*, 1800); *Le Barbier de Séville: Ou, La Précaution inutile*, pr., pb. 1775 (*The Barber of Seville: Or, The Useless Precaution*, 1776); *La Folle Journée: Ou, Le Mariage de Figaro*, wr. 1775-1778, pr. 1784, pb. 1785 (*The Marriage of Figaro*, 1784); *Tarare*, pr., pb. 1787 (libretto; music by Antonio Salieri); *L'Autre Tartuffe: Ou, La Mère coupable*, pr. 1792, pb. 1797 (*Frailty and Hypocrisy*, 1804); *Théâtre*, pb. 1966

Other literary forms • Pierre-Augustin Caron de Beaumarchais is known as a literary figure only for his plays, which were the only fictional works he published during his lifetime. Although he also wrote poetry, some of which was published posthumously, none of it proved to be of enduring value. His early, unpublished works for the theater were in the form of short curtain raisers or sidewalk shows, which the French call *parades*, some of which have also been posthumously published. Beaumarchais also published *mémoires*, or legal arguments, to defend his own position in several notorious lawsuits in which he was involved, and wrote prefaces for all but one of his plays, which describe the theoretical basis of his dramaturgy and exemplify his work as a critic. A considerable amount of Beaumarchais's correspondence has also been published, most of it merely of documentary value but some of it marked by a passion for ideas and a sparkling of style that elevate it to the status of literature.

Achievements • Pierre-Augustin Caron de Beaumarchais is that rarity among literary figures: a famous writer who also has solid achievements to his credit in other, nonliterary, domains. For example, at the age of only twenty-one, Beaumarchais invented a new mechanical device for pocket watches that permitted the construction of small, flat timepieces in place of the bulky, spherical ones then current. The invention made him famous in the scientific community, earned for him the title of "Watchmaker to the King," and assured the prosperity of his father's watchmaking business for years to come.

Later, when he was in his forties, Beaumarchais made significant contributions to the French monarch as a diplomat on foreign missions, his most notable achievement being his creation of a shipping company that helped the American colonists arm themselves during the American Revolution. Beaumarchais managed to supply the arms without implicating the French crown, earning the gratitude of his own government and a permanent niche in U.S. history as well. During that same period, Beaumarchais, by then a published playwright, was instrumental in founding the Société des Auteurs and was elected its first president, thus assuring for himself a place of honor in the history of playwriting as a profession in France.

Even taken together, however, all of Beaumarchais's extraliterary achievements are not the equal of his achievement as the author of the finest French comedy of the eighteenth century, *The Marriage of Figaro*, and as the creator of the modern, postclassical theater in France. This theater managed to take many liberties with the rigid rules of classical tradition without losing any of the aesthetic and philosophical power inherent in the nature of drama. Beaumarchais's greatest achievement was accomplished by example: He demonstrated how a play could be freed of the constraints of a prescribed form and yet be a work of art.

Biography • An ambitious activist by nature, Pierre-Augustin Caron de Beaumarchais, born Pierre-Augustin Caron, led a far more eventful life than is customary for a man of letters. The ups and downs of his often agitated existence, however, were seldom directly related to the literary life, resulting rather from his determined pursuit of wealth, preferment, and pleasure, from his involvement in legal wrangles, and, most honorably, from Beaumarchais's disinterested struggles against injustice.

The son of a watchmaker, Beaumarchais was apprenticed at an early age to his father's craft and mastered it so thoroughly that, when only twenty-one, he worked out a solution to one of the craft's most difficult problems in mechanics: the contrivance of a radically simplified escapement, the device that transfers the energy of a watch's spring to the network of interlocking wheels that make up its movement. The naïve young watchmaker made the mistake of showing his device to an older colleague, who promptly published a description of it as his own invention. The younger Caron complained to the Academy of Sciences, won public vindication and recognition thereby, and from that notoriety was able to establish himself as a personage of consequence at the court of Louis XV, even becoming music teacher to the king's daughters.

Thus launched into the social whirl, Beaumarchais went on to a series of other activities and enterprises over the next fifteen years, increasing his fortune and prestige, while marrying and acquiring the title that enabled him to call himself Caron de Beaumarchais. In those years, he continued to encounter envy and injustice and continued to fight against those evils with courage and energy, at the same time learning valuable lessons about the human heart.

Those lessons came to fruition when Beaumarchais began his career as a playwright in 1767, at the age of thirty-five, with a tearful family drama about a young and innocent girl seduced and deceived by an aristocrat. The play, *The School of Rakes* (*Eugénie* in the original French, after its heroine-victim), enjoyed only a brief and modest success with the public. With characteristic determination, Beaumarchais tried for public success in the theater three years later, with his second play *The Two Friends*, which fared even worse with the public and was withdrawn after a very few performances. Beaumarchais was disappointed in the public failure to understand his theme of the virtues of the merchant class but was still undeterred from his theatrical ambitions.

Meanwhile, Beaumarchais found himself embroiled in a lawsuit over an inheritance and discovered that the judge in the case had been corrupted. Again injustice brought out his best, and he turned the evil to his own advantage by publishing a brilliant *mémoire* in which he revealed the judge's corrupt dealings, thereby winning public support and acclaim. Eventually he even won his lawsuit, though it took four more years. Meanwhile, he had his first unalloyed success in the theater in 1775 with his Molièresque comedy, *The Barber of Seville*, in which the public delighted. A year later, aided by secret government funding, Beaumarchais found himself energetically assisting the American rebels in their war against the British by procuring and shipping armaments to them, having recruited a veritable fleet of ships for the purpose, from all over Europe.

Beaumarchais attained the pinnacle of his career even while engaged with his enterprise to aid the Americans. He had written a sequel to *The Barber of Seville*, called *The Marriage of Figaro*, which was ready for production in 1778 but was denied permission for public performance, by decree of the royal censor, because some of its themes struck the censor as disrespectful toward the ruling aristocracy. Not until 1784 were the objections overcome, but when the play was finally performed, it proved to be Beaumarchais's greatest triumph and one of the most successful plays of the entire century. Because the play was thought by some to be frankly revolutionary in its implications, Beaumarchais found himself in relatively good standing with the revolutionary government when it took over a few years later.

This success, Beaumarchais's last play, *Frailty and Hypocrisy*, a rather solemn sequel to *The Marriage of Figaro*, was coolly received by the public in 1792 when it was first presented. Moreover, the envy and injustice that had dogged his entire life soon emerged again, in his relations with the revolutionary government. Falsely accused of counter-revolutionary activity, he was forced into exile for several years, and all his property was confiscated. In failing health, Beaumarchais was permitted to return to Paris in 1796; he died of a stroke in the spring of 1799.

Analysis • Perhaps because he was already in his middle thirties when his literary career began, Pierre-Augustin Caron de Beaumarchais showed little of the ambitious originality or inventiveness of youth in his plays—most of his plots and character-types were quite consciously derived from the work of others—but he exhibited, from the first, an exceptional understanding of the real world, which he approached with high moral seriousness. Whether somber or lighthearted in tone, whether contemporary or historical in setting, whether traditional or modern in form, the plays of Beaumarchais are all, without exception, centrally concerned with some abuse or injustice in his own society.

It is true that all of Beaumarchais's plays, even the most somber, end happily and may in that sense be called romantic comedies; yet each play, including the most cheerfully frivolous of them, has an underlying seriousness of theme which is unmistakable. Although he quickly mastered the trick of entertaining the sophisticated Paris public, Beaumarchais never allowed his moralist's impulse to be obscured by theatrical technique. In his art as in his life, he remained always the passionate and vocal opponent of injustice and fraud: His open advocacy of moral positions was perhaps his most distinctive trait as a playwright.

Through two of his plays, *The Barber of Seville* and *The Marriage of Figaro*, Beaumarchais redefined the art of theatrical comedy in France, making moral seriousness an acceptable main ingredient of the genre, and gave future generations one of the great character-types in literature with the invention of Figaro. He has had a significant and durable influence on all subsequent theatrical writing in France.

The School of Rakes • Beaumarchais's outspoken advocacy of moral positions was already fully in evidence with his very first play, *The School of Rakes*. The focus of the play is a crisis in the life of a young and innocent English lady, Eugénie, who believes herself to be married to a prominent aristocrat, Lord Clarendon, only to learn, by chance, that her "husband" is about to marry someone else. The announcement of that impending marriage reveals to Eugénie that she has been deceived by Lord Clarendon, who staged a false wedding ceremony with the complicity of servants and friends in order to make her his mistress. To make her sense of shame truly complete, Eugénie finds herself newly pregnant just when the crushing truth of her plight emerges. The result is a crisis of despair, followed by a tense confrontation scene with Lord Clarendon as the play's dramatic climax.

The play ends with a genuine marriage between a contrite Lord Clarendon and a forgiving Eugénie, but Beaumarchais's thrust is plain: His purpose is to attack the immoral cynicism of the powerful nobility, who prey on the innocence of decent young ladies. Surprisingly modern in its viewpoint, *The School of Rakes* is a protest against high society's double standard of sexual morality.

The theme of the social victimization of women was probably "borrowed" by Beaumarchais from Denis Diderot's novel *La Religieuse* (1796; *The Nun*, 1797), which had been written in 1760 and had made the subject popular. Beaumarchais openly claimed Diderot as his inspiration for the form of his play, at any rate, noting in his preface that he admired Diderot's invention of a new theatrical genre called *le drame sérieux*—a play neither tragic nor comic but occupying the intermediate ground between the two.

It was that middle ground Beaumarchais sought to occupy with *The School of Rakes*, portraying scenes of great emotional anguish arising out of common human events, rather than events of heroic dimension, and showing the amusing side of human behavior as well, without employing the devices of excess and exaggeration that make up classic comedy. For Diderot, and for his admirer Beaumarchais, the new order of theater, *le drame sérieux*, was to be above all human, and therefore touching, rather than awe-inspiring as the classic theater had been, because it dealt with human behavior at its extreme limits.

The Two Friends • These theories of Diderot were even more fully put into practice in Beaumarchais's second play, *The Two Friends*—more fully because, whereas *The School of Rakes* had concerned privileged members of the English aristocracy, albeit with very ordinary problems of human relationships, *The Two Friends* concerns members of the urban middle class, men engaged in commerce and finance, and a drama of bankruptcy and the sense of honor in the world of business. Diderot had advocated a focus on middle-class values in order to make the theater accessible to an increasingly middle-class audience—Diderot's preferred term was *le drame bourgeois*—but it proved difficult, after all, to find themes of compellingly high drama among the daily passions of the bourgeoisie.

Diderot himself never wrote a successful play, in spite of the persuasiveness of his theory about the imperatives of a truly modern theater, and Beaumarchais had the worst disaster of his career with the play in which Diderot's theories were most faithfully followed. *The Two Friends* failed both with the public and with the critics and had to be withdrawn after a few performances in 1770. With characteristic resilience, however, Beaumarchais abandoned *le drame sérieux*, devised a play with a more frankly comic action reminiscent of Molière, and in early 1775 was represented on the Paris stage with his first genuine success, the play that made him famous, *The Barber of Seville*.

The Barber of Seville • The basic plot of *The Barber of Seville* derives from the ancient traditions of farce, and had its most notably successful incarnation, before Beaumarchais, in Molière's witty comedy *L'École des femmes* (1662; *The School for Wives*, 1732). The ingredients of the plot are simple. An apparently innocent young girl is the ward of a tyrannical older man who keeps her strictly isolated from the company of potential young suitors because he intends to marry her himself. In spite of the guardian's vigilance, however, the not-so-innocent young girl finds a way to make contact with a suitable young man and so defeat the guardian's evil scheme.

Beaumarchais's distinctive contribution to this ancient plot is the invention of a clever and resourceful character of the servant class—Figaro—who conducts the intrigue by which the young suitor successfully wins the girl. Moreover, as one might expect, the playwright found in the simple comic plot an underlying serious theme to which he proposed to give some prominence: the abuse of the powers of guardianship and the consequent oppression of women.

Perhaps because he feared that such criticism of the social customs of his day might run afoul of the royal censor, Beaumarchais decided to set his play in the Spain of the seventeenth century rather than in the Paris of the eighteenth. To mask the seriousness of his theme, he adopted a tone of cheerful cynicism that pervaded all the dialogue and characterized the attitudes and actions of all the principal players. This tone is precisely established in the very first scene, in which Count Almaviva, in disguise, waits in a Seville street to catch a glimpse of Rosine at her window and sees coming toward him his former valet, Figaro, now a barber and general handyman for anyone who will pay him.

The dialogue that ensues is witty, disrespectful, even impudent, but always lighthearted. For example, when the Count reminds Figaro that, as a servant, he had been rather a bad lot, lazy and careless about his responsibilities, Figaro immediately replies: "Yes, my lord, but only in comparison to what is demanded of servant. . . . Considering the virtues expected of a domestic, does Your Excellence know very many Masters who have the qualifications to be Valets?"

Not only is the tone for the whole play set by this witty dialogue, but also the work of exposition is skillfully accomplished; in short order, the reader learns why the Count has followed Rosine from Madrid to Seville, why Doctor Bartholo is keeping her so carefully sequestered, and how Figaro can use his position as barber to the Bartholo household to arrange for the Count to have a private talk with Rosine. The scene that follows completes the exposition, showing Rosine in hostile conversation with Dr. Bartholo, while contriving to drop a written message from her window to the Count in the street below without allowing her guardian to grasp what is happening. As Figaro laughingly remarks of Rosine's maneuver: "If you want to bring out the skill of even the most innocent young girl, you have only to imprison her." The rest of the play, which is constructed in four acts, simply treats the audience to the step-by-step working out of the conspiracy among Count Almaviva, Rosine, and Figaro adumbrated in the two expository scenes that begin the play.

Such a simple plot, in which Dr. Bartholo's selfish designs are thwarted and Count Almaviva wins the hand of Rosine, has the great virtue of giving the play constant clarity of direction and aesthetically satisfying unity of action, but it carries the concomitant risk of boring the audience: The outcome is predictable from the opening moments. Beaumarchais uses two devices to overcome this predictability and intensify the sense of dramatic excitement as the action unfolds. First, he tightens the time frame by having Bartholo learn, early in the second act, from Rosine's music teacher Don Bazile, that Count Almaviva is in Seville, disguised and determined to make contact with Rosine. This news causes Bartholo to make hasty arrangements to marry his ward the very next day, leaving the conspirators only a few hours in which to achieve their goal.

Beaumarchais contrives a series of incidents, in the plays' second, third, and fourth acts, in which Rosine, the Count, Figaro, or all three together find themselves in danger of having their plan found out by Bartholo. Each such scene causes the tension to mount until the danger passes, at the same time forestalling any tendency on the spectator's part to become bored, since the outcome is thus repeatedly put in doubt.

It is, however, probably not the plot so much as the characters that attract and hold the interest of spectators and readers alike. Almaviva's insouciance and Rosine's native shrewdness make them an engaging couple, and their common enemy, Bartholo, is so absurdly self-centered and so maliciously jealous as a guardian that it affords the audience a positive pleasure to see his villainous intentions circumvented. The frank cynicism of Don Bazile, always ready to serve the highest bidder, is well calculated to amuse, and nowhere more so than in his brilliant and memorable speech, in the second act, explaining the virtues of calumny as the best weapon available against one's enemies.

The finest creation in the play, however, is unquestionably the character of Figaro, with his ready wit and indomitable good humor, his resourcefulness and amoral pleasure in every kind of intrigue, and above all his impudence in the face of power and his generous capacity for indignation against injustice. Nothing contributed more to the popular success of *The Barber of Seville* than the invention of this novel personality, so appealingly *sympathique* to the middle-class theater audiences of the 1770's. Beaumarchais understood, instinctively, the source of his sudden popularity, as he demonstrated by producing, almost immediately, a sequel to *The Barber of Seville* in which Figaro was even more prominently the main character. This was the sparkling masterpiece, *The Marriage of Figaro*, universally regarded as the crown jewel of Beaumarchais's theater.

The Marriage of Figaro • Having successfully slipped his rather strong social criticism in *The Barber of Seville* past the censor by burying it unobtrusively beneath a barrage of witty and irreverent dialogue, Beaumarchais set out, with perhaps understandable overconfidence, to make his sequel a much more explicit attack on the injustices of his time. By 1778, he was ready to present his new play, but the royal censor found it unacceptable. It took Beaumarchais six full years to overcome all the official objections and to see his new play, at last, on the boards. When it was finally performed, in 1784, it was to enthusiastic acclaim, both from the public and from the critics—not only Beaumarchais's greatest success but also probably the most successful work of the century in the theater.

The plot of *The Marriage of Figaro* is as intricate and convoluted as that of *The Barber of Seville* is simple and unilinear. It is true that, despite the complex interweaving of plots and subplots, the action of *The Marriage of Figaro* takes place within the space of a single day—but it is, as the subtitle in the original French indicates, a "mad day," full of unexpected twists and turns, arrivals and departures, disguises and deceptions, all of which transform Count Almaviva's palace into a daylong carnival.

However complicated, the action is nevertheless coherently organized around one central event that lends a certain unity to the whole: the promised marriage of Figaro, now in the full-time service of Almaviva as valet and concierge, to Suzanne, first chambermaid of the former Rosine, now Countess Almaviva. What complicates the plot is that the impending marriage faces threats from several quarters: Almaviva himself, who has granted permission for the marriage, is nevertheless scheming to seduce Suzanne and make her his convenient in-house mistress, using the threat to refuse permission for the wedding if Suzanne will not cooperate; Marceline, the former mistress of Dr. Bartholo, is bent on forcing Figaro to live up to a promise he made her in writing to marry her if he failed to repay a loan by a specific date; and the Countess, suffering in the role of abandoned wife, seeks to thwart her husband's efforts to seduce Suzanne, which in turn angers Almaviva and makes him prone to go back on his promise to Figaro.

Further complexities are added by the intersecting subplots involving the adolescent page, Chérubin, and the gardener's adolescent daughter, Fanchette; the old affair between Bartholo and Marceline, which turns out to have had surprising consequences when it is revealed that Figaro is their long-lost son; and the active plotting of the Countess, who suddenly decides to play an inopportune trick on her husband in an effort to win back his love.

This multiplicity of events imparts to the play a magical air of movement, merriment, and surprise that keeps the reader constantly amused and attentive, as though observing the action of a new and complicated mechanical toy. It is this interlocking of so many diverse elements that has led some critics to see, in the structure of *The Marriage of Figaro*, the influence of Beaumarchais's training as a watchmaker. Certainly that intricate structure has much to do with the enchantment that the play produces in its audiences. When well staged, *The Marriage of Figaro* is a delightful kaleidoscopic spectacle.

The multiplicity of the action is matched by the variety of the comic devices used, the many rather daring shifts in tone from scene to scene, and the dizzyingly numerous reversals in fortune; the advantage seems to lie now with Figaro, now with the Count, over the matter of who will have his way. *The Marriage of Figaro* is a play that is constantly in motion: Not only are the actors required to move about a lot physically, but also they are required to exhibit a wide gamut of changing moods and emotions, and to time their entrances, exits, dialogue, and gestures with exceptional precision. Nothing is more distinctive about this play—especially in contrast to *The Barber of Seville*—than the breakneck pace at which it must be performed. There is nothing very original about the individual scenes, for as always with Beaumarchais, the dramatic ideas are quite derivative, but the intricate meshing of so many different types of scenes, without any loss of coherence or unity, is a tour de force of inventive ingenuity, the result of which was a style of comic theater that had never been seen before in France.

The Marriage of Figaro, however, is much more than a triumph of theatrical technique. For all its artificiality, which is obtrusive and undeniable, the play still manages to be memorably alive, by virtue both of the underlying truth of certain of its characters and situations and of the major themes to which it gives powerful expression. An unforgettable example of truth in characterization is the figure of Chérubin, who makes a kind of poetry out of the impulses of puberty, feeling impelled by instincts he does not understand to be constantly in the female presence and comporting himself with the strangest mixture of mischievous playfulness and exaggerated sentiment. Chérubin is not so much a realistic as an imaginative portrait of an adolescent, simultaneously child and man.

Among the situations that delicately evoke emotions in the play is the daring moment, early in act 2, in which the Countess and Suzanne are trying out their scheme to disguise Chérubin as a girl so that he can be part of the wedding celebration, instead of going off to join a regiment as the Count has ordered. The situation is farcical in nature, but Beaumarchais is able to display a remarkable interplay of sensibilities as the two women react, each in a different way, to the ambiguous sexuality of the embarrassed adolescent.

The most pervasive of the play's principal themes is that represented by the struggle between Figaro and the Count, which epitomizes the eternal clash between figures of authority and privilege and the common individual longing for dignity. The nature of that clash and its basic injustice are memorably articulated by Figaro in his famous monologue of act 5, in which he complains that all the Count had to do to have so much wealth, prestige, and power was "to give himself the trouble to be born." Such words were daringly provocative to the Paris audiences of 1784, among whom the mood of revolution against aristocratic authority was already close to the surface. A second important theme is that of the systematic oppression of women, evident in the way the Count treats both the Countess and Suzanne, and the way Bartholo and Figaro deal with Marceline's wish to be legally married.

Again the theme is strikingly articulated in the famous words of Marceline in act 3, which read even today as a very enlightened manifesto of women's rights. One might add that the theme of injustice is broached in a variety of forms in the play, but nowhere more pointedly than in the trial scenes of act 3, in which Beaumarchais brings off a hilarious satire of the legal system of the time. It seems inescapable that the true greatness and originality of *The Marriage of Figaro* must, in the final analysis, be defined as an extraordinary blend of technical energy in comic style and moral passion powerfully expressed. It is difficult to find its equal in that special combination of qualities.

Tarare and **Frailty and Hypocrisy** • Beaumarchais himself never again reached such heights in his career. The libretto he composed for the opera *Tarare*, a few years after *The Marriage of Figaro*, was excessively simplistic and sentimental in plot, and written in flat and unimaginative verse. Poetry was not one of his talents.

When Beaumarchais tried to revive his flagging popularity among the new postrevolutionary audiences, he turned to the material that had brought him success in the past and composed a sequel to *The Marriage of Figaro*, entitled *Frailty and Hypocrisy*, which was performed in 1792. The comic verve was gone, however, and the characters of Figaro, Suzanne, Almaviva, and the Countess had all lost their youthful sparkle; the play seemed a self-righteous sermon on the need for compassion between spouses for the sins of youth. There was little in that final play of Beaumarchais's career to suggest the skillful theatrical technician of twenty years earlier. Only the passions of the committed moralist and the determined enemy of injustice were still in evidence, poignant reminders of past glory. Though *Frailty and Hypocrisy* was poorly received in 1792, it is interesting to note that a revival of the play in 1797 had a great success, and certainly eased the sorrow of Beaumarchais's painful last years. Nevertheless, the reputation he left behind was a major one.

Other major works
NONFICTION: *Mémoires*, 1773-1774.

Bibliography
Dunkley, John. *Beaumarchais: "Le Barbier de Séville."* Critical Guides to French Texts 86. London: Grant and Cutler, 1991. A critical appraisal of Beaumarchais's *The Barber of Seville*. Includes a bibliography.

Grendel, Frédéric. *Beaumarchais: The Man Who Was Figaro.* New York: T. Y. Crowell, 1977. An examination of the life and work of Beaumarchais. Includes a bibliography and index.

Howarth, W. D. *Beaumarchais and the Theatre.* New York: Routledge, 1995. Howarth examines six of Beaumarchais's plays and their reception by audiences, placing them within the context of pre-revolutionary France. He traces the dramatist's legacy in nineteenth century vaudeville and twentieth century comic drama. Includes a bibliography and index.

Niklaus, Robert. *Beaumarchias: "Le Mariage de Figaro."* Critical Guides to French Texts 21. London: Grant and Cutler, 1995. Niklaus provides a critical examination of Beaumarchais's *The Marriage of Figaro.* Includes a bibliography

Sungolowsky, Joseph. *Beaumarchais.* New York: Twayne, 1974. A basic biography of Beaumarchais, along with criticism and interpretation of his works. Includes a bibliography.

Murray Sachs

Samuel Beckett

Born: Foxrock, Ireland; April 13, 1906
Died: Paris, France; December 22, 1989

Principal drama • *En attendant Godot,* pb. 1952, pr. 1953 (*Waiting for Godot,* 1954); *"Fin de partie," Suivi de "Acte sans paroles,"* pr., pb. 1957 (music by John Beckett; *"Endgame: A Play in One Act," Followed by "Act Without Words: A Mime for One Player,"* 1958); *Krapp's Last Tape,* pr., pb. 1958 (one act), revised pb. 1992; *Act Without Words II,* pr., pb. 1960 (one-act mime); *Happy Days,* pr., pb. 1961; *Play,* pr., pb. 1963 (English translation, 1964); *Come and Go: Dramaticule,* pr., pb. 1965 (one scene; English translation, 1967); *Not I,* pr. 1972, pb. 1973; *That Time,* pr., pb. 1976; *Footfalls,* pr., pb. 1976; *Ends and Odds,* pb. 1976; *A Piece of Monologue,* pr., pb. 1979; *Rockaby,* pr., pb. 1981; *Ohio Impromptu,* pr., pb. 1981; *Catastrophe,* pr. 1982, pb. 1983; *Company,* pr. 1983; *Collected Shorter Plays,* pb. 1984

Other literary forms • Samuel Beckett worked in literary forms other than drama. Although his radio plays, film script, and teleplays may be viewed as dramas that differ only in their use of various media, they nevertheless indicate his versatile and experimental approach to literary form. In prose fiction, he wrote both novels and short stories. The trilogy of novels, *Molloy* (1951; English translation, 1955), *Malone meurt* (1951; *Malone Dies,* 1956), and *L'Innommable* (1953; *The Unnamable,* 1958), written in French between 1947 and 1949, constitutes a major accomplishment in the genre. These works, like the earlier novel *Murphy* (1938), developed a monologue style of unique tone, with which Beckett had first begun to experiment in his short stories, collected as *More Pricks than Kicks* (1934).

Beckett's first published literary work, however, was a poem on time and René Descartes, *Whoroscope* (1930), which won for him a prize; this work was followed by a collection of poems entitled *Echo's Bones and Other Precipitates* (1935). Beckett also turned to translations of Spanish poetry with Octavio Paz's *An Anthology of Mexican Poetry* in 1958. In addition, he distinguished himself with his several translations of his own work, from English into French (such as *Murphy*) and French into English (such as *Malone meurt*); Beckett continued this practice throughout his career as dramatist, notably with *En attendant Godot,* which he translated into *Waiting for Godot,* and *Fin de partie,* which he translated into *Endgame.*

Achievements • Samuel Beckett is famous for his fiction and drama, which he wrote both in French and in English. *Waiting for Godot* established the Irish Beckett as a unique writer because he elected the French language as his primary means of composition and English as his secondary one. The success of *Endgame* and *Krapp's Last Tape,* as well as his trilogy of French novels, led to Trinity College's awarding Beckett an honorary doctorate in 1959. Beckett also explored radio, cinema, and television for his art. So conscious was he of style that people disappeared into mere voices, mere echoes, and his plays could be called, as one was, ironically, simply *Play,* performed in 1963 at about the same time as his screenplay, *Film,* was being made. In 1961, Beckett received the International Publishers' Prize with Jorge Luis Borges, and in 1970, he was awarded the Nobel Prize in Literature for artistic achievements that define the ironic stance of modern reactions to an increasingly meaningless existence.

Biography • Samuel Barclay Beckett was born at Foxrock, near Dublin, Ireland, on April 13, 1906, the second son of Mary and William Beckett. In 1920, he was sent to Portora Royal School, Enniskillen, and in 1923, he proceeded to Trinity College, Dublin, to study Italian and French. After receiving his B.A. degree in 1927, he went to Belfast as a French tutor, then to the École Normale Supérieure in Paris as a lecturer for two years, a period during which he became acquainted with James Joyce. Beckett then became lecturer in French at Trinity College and studied for his M.A. After two years, he left for Germany and returned to Paris in 1932. Doing odd jobs and writing when he could, he traveled to London, through France and Germany. This trip led to two publications: *More Pricks than Kicks* in 1934 and *Echo's Bones and Other Precipitates* in 1935. Meanwhile, he had inherited an annuity after his father's death in 1933, allowing him to concentrate on his writing.

In 1937, Beckett returned again to Paris, where he began to write in French. At the same time, he was preoccupied with the English text of his first novel, *Murphy*, which was published in 1938, the same year that he was stabbed on a Paris street and nearly died. He recovered, however, and established himself in an apartment where he would live throughout World War II and long after, at 6, rue des Favorites. There, he began, with Alfred Péron, to translate *Murphy* into French. His friendship with Péron, however, was doomed by the war, which began while Beckett was visiting his mother in Dublin.

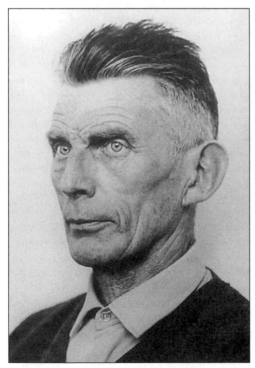

(© The Nobel Foundation)

Nevertheless, Beckett returned to Paris, where he joined the French Resistance. Most of his colleagues, including Péron, disappeared, and Beckett himself barely escaped capture by the Nazis in 1942, when he fled to Free France with Suzanne Deschevaux-Dumesnil, whom he married in 1961. While in Free France, he worked on a farm for two years and began his novel *Watt* (1953). After the war, in 1945, Beckett began a remarkable period of five years during which he wrote most of his important fiction and drama. His fame began, though, with productions of *Waiting for Godot* in French in 1953 and in English in 1955, followed by productions of *Endgame* in French in 1957 and in English in 1958.

Meanwhile, other plays were produced, including his radio dramas *All That Fall* and *Embers*, broadcast by the British Broadcasting Corporation in 1957 and 1959, respectively. These productions complemented the mimes that Beckett prepared for the stage at about the same time, beginning with *Act Without Words*, which was produced on a double bill with *Endgame*, and continuing with variations to the end of Beckett's career with *Nacht und Träume* in 1983. He also prepared the script for a motion picture, *Film*, with Buster Keaton in the leading role, filmed in New York in 1964. After *Endgame*, Beckett composed two important stage plays, *Krapp's Last Tape* first produced in 1958, and *Happy Days*, in 1961. Radio and television, however, were his favorite media. From 1959, with *Embers*, and 1966, with *Eh Joe*, to the time of his death in 1989, Beckett devoted much of his talent to numerous radio and television works, testing the limits of audience understanding.

Analysis • The dramatic works of Samuel Beckett reflect the evolution of his interests in various means of artistic expression, as he composed plays for stage, radio, cinema, and television. In his stage plays, he parodies traditional dramatic action and borrows the techniques used in other modes of entertainment. His themes are not constant, but they are grimly developed through a steady mood of ironic laughter if not outright sarcasm. Like the character "O" who runs from the camera's eye ("E") in *Film*, Beckett's art finds its form in a flight from conventional expectations and traditional observations. What seems meaningless and absurd is shown to be the only meaning possible in a universe where the human experience of consciousness (as subject) seems trapped by a nature and body (as object) without consciousness. Laughter is an intellectual triumph over material absurdity, and self-denial is self-affirmation. Beckett's plays are made of such paradoxes.

Whether it is in the nameless characters in *Play*, the lone and aging Krapp awaiting imminent death in *Krapp's Last Tape*, the pathetic Winnie sinking in her grave in *Happy Days*, the dying family in the masochistic *Endgame*, the monotonous life of waiting of Estragon and Vladimir in *Waiting for Godot*, or the down-and-outers in other dramatic works, Beckett demonstrates a preference for passive characters who attempt to make sense of an increasingly absurd existence and who struggle to survive in a universe that lacks love and meaningful relationships.

As a critic, a transitional thinker, an innovator, and a postmodernist who probed the human condition and sensed the absurdity of the modern world, Beckett tried to link art and life into unusual theatrical images in order to etch human beings' inner world and the human experience of consciousness. Even though his vision of life and the human predicament is discouraging, his plays are rich with clownish characters, slapstick humor, word games, irony, and sarcasm, allowing laughter to triumph over material absurdity.

Beckett is best known as the author of four intriguingly powerful stage plays; *Waiting for Godot, Endgame, Krapp's Last Tape*, and *Happy Days*. His later work has begun to receive critical attention, particularly those plays that focus on women, such as *Play* and especially *Not I*. With his first stunningly successful stage play, however, there is not a woman to be seen. Only two tramps, two strangely united male travelers, and a boy are on the stage of *Waiting for Godot*.

Waiting for Godot • In this play, Beckett established his major tone of comic despair, with his characters resigned to waiting for something to happen that never happens. He also created his major dramatic style out of vaudevillian and silent-film skits by clownish characters who are determined to endure without understanding why they must. In two acts that mirror each other in language and action, *Waiting for Godot* mocks audience desire for significant form and visionary comprehension of human experience. The two protagonists are tramps by the name of Estragon (called Gogo) and

Vladimir (called Didi). They seem doomed to repeat forever the experiences played out in the two acts, as they wait for the arrival of a mysterious person known to them only as Godot. This Godot never does arrive. Instead, a lordly fellow named Pozzo appears in the first act, leading his servant Lucky by a rope; in the second act, these two reappear, though Pozzo is now blind and Lucky is dumb.

The spareness of plot and scarcity of characters are reinforced by the stark setting. Only a tree (leafless in act 1, bearing a few leaves in act 2) and a lonely country road mark the location of this play's action through a day of trivial concerns by the two tramps. The interruption by Pozzo and Lucky of their monotonous life of waiting is dramatic, but it is drained of its significance by the incomprehension of the characters who participate in it. The dialogue of the four characters is, in its variety, a counterpoint to the monotony of the slapstick action: The tramps talk in short, quick bursts of verbal response to each other, Pozzo exclaims himself in bombastic rhetoric, and Lucky overflows once in a stream-of-consciousness monologue called "thinking." When they reappear in act 2, Pozzo's pomposity has been deflated into whining, and Lucky cannot speak at all. Thus does this play illustrate Beckett's intense concern for the nature and function of language itself in a world where there is so little worth communicating.

At the end of each act, Vladimir and Estragon threaten to separate, to leave—but in each act, they do not move as the curtain descends on them. The two tramps play word games to pass the time, and they entertain themselves with strategies for suicide, but they cannot kill themselves. Waiting is a part of their fate. Each act ends with the arrival of a boy to announce that Godot will not arrive this evening, but that he will come another time. The boy's claim that he is not the same boy who appeared in the first act, that he tends sheep and that the other boy is his brother, a goatherd, constitutes allusions hinting at some religious mystery in the identity of Godot, the god who will separate sheep from goats on the day of judgment. If Didi and Gogo are denied their meeting with Godot, they are no less heroic for their waiting.

Endgame • *Endgame* is one act of waiting also, not for an arrival but rather for a departure. The servant of this play, called Clov, threatens to leave his master, Hamm, when a boy is sighted through one of the two windows in the room, or "shelter," that makes the setting for this play's action. The curtain drops without a definite commitment by Clov to move outside, and the boy is never seen by anyone except Clov. The title refers to the last phase of a game of chess, and two of the four characters move as if they were pieces in such a game. Hamm is unable to leave his chair, and Clov is unable to sit; Hamm orders Clov about, and Clov moves Hamm around. A blind ruler of his household, Hamm is a modern King Lear, blind and helpless to tend to his bodily needs. He wants his painkiller, and Clov tells him it is depleted. Hamm wants the ultimate painkiller of death but that seems elusive as well. Both Hamm and Clov wait for the end of the game of life, as all life outside their room seems at an end, except for the mysterious arrival of the boy.

On the stage are two other characters, Nagg and Nell, Hamm's parents. They have lost their legs in an accident and are as immobile as their son. They are kept by Hamm inside ash bins, pathetically reminiscing about their lives until the mother, Nell, dies and Nagg is sealed in his bin by Clov on orders from Hamm. Family values are far from the traditional ones of conventional domestic plots. Hamm tortures his father, or what remains of him, and Nagg torments his son exactly as he did when Hamm was a child. There is some remnant of affection in this play, though, just as there was in *Waiting for Godot*. The emotional tie between Gogo and Didi is repeated between

Hamm and Clov, whose past binds them together even while they express a wish to separate. There is also a tie of romance holding the two parents together, though they cannot now reach each other for a kiss, and one of their most romantic adventures led to their helplessness—they lost their legs in a bicycle accident.

This play hints, through various allusions, at a meaning that transcends its apparent lack of meaning. Hamm is both an acting ham and a Prince Hamlet, calling attention to his role as a mockery of art in a meaningless universe; Hamm is also a piece of meat spiced by Clov in a world where human dignity no longer exists. The words and postures of both Hamm and Clov sometimes suggest that they are parodies of Christ on the Cross (where flesh is hammered with nails, puns on the names of the four characters), but there is no salvation for anyone in this play's world, unless it is to be in the boy waiting, perhaps contemplating his navel, beside a rock outside.

Hamm is anxious for all life to end, even including that of a louse, so that the absurdity of human consciousness will cease. That boy outside is a threat, and so Hamm wants his life. Will life go on despite Hamm and evolve again, or will it finally wind down into nothingness? The play does not provide a clear sign of the answer as it concludes: Hamm replaces a bloody handkerchief over his blind eyes, and Clov, dressed as if for traveling, stands immobile watching the last pathetic moves of his master. Pathos is not the essence, however, of *Endgame*, though it may threaten to become so, as in the relationship of the tramps in *Waiting for Godot*. At the point of revealing a depth of passion that might pass for pathos, Beckett's plays pull back and laugh at the pointlessness of the possibility. Everything falls into nothing, everything dies, everything comes to a stop, though not quite, and that is the wild absurdity of it all.

Krapp's Last Tape • If the drama of entropy cannot quite come to a complete stop, that is not the fault of desire for it. In *Krapp's Last Tape*, where an ingenious use of recording tapes creates a dimension of time always present in its absence, the protagonist (and only character onstage) listens to recordings of his own voice from many years past, especially one when he was thirty-nine years old, some thirty years before.

Krapp's wait for death, for an end to entropy, is supported by his ironic dismissal of all that was meaningful at the time that he recorded the most important events of his life. In the present time of the play, Krapp is about to record the fact that the sound of the word "spool" is important, but he is drawn back to listen again and again to his recording of thirty years ago, when he described a lovemaking scene on a boat. His lust has declined, but his hunger for bananas and his thirst for wine have not, as he records his last tape.

Krapp's sense of himself, however, is threatened by the fragmented voices from his past; indeed, there is no continuous identity in this character, whose self-recording is a figure for the author's work itself. There is an irony of similarity here, for Beckett's own work may be reflected by the "plot" of *Krapp's Last Tape*. Voices are separated from the body, memories are mixed by mechanical forms, and the self is a stranger to itself. The drama of this discovery is in the encounter of one self with another, of silence yielding to voice, and voice subsiding into silence. These features increasingly preoccupied Beckett, as he moved his wit more and more into the regions of radio (all sound and voice) and mimes (no sound or voice).

Happy Days • More pathetic than all is the situation of Winnie in *Happy Days*. Entropy is visually represented by the intensifying imprisonment of Winnie, who appears in act 1 buried in a mound up to her waist and then, in act 2, up to her neck; she has become increasingly immobilized, and through it all she maintains her view of life as one of "happy days." She is happily stupid or courageously optimistic as she recounts her life's pleasures against the background of an unresponsive husband, Willie. At the end, dressed fit to kill, Willie calls his wife "Win" and seems prepared to shoot her with a pistol that she cannot seize for herself. She may be happy because she expects now to end it all with her death at last.

Winnie's immobility is unchosen, and her waiting is absurdly imposed by the earth itself. As a ridiculous version of the earth-mother, Winnie is the opposite of her lethargic though "free" husband, and so she reflects the social condition of all women as well as the exploitation of that condition by men. *Happy Days*, like *Krapp's Last Tape*, develops through monologue rather than dialogue, though in both plays the possibility for dialogue is kept alive for the sake of its ironic futility.

Play • The futility of dialogue, of communication, even perhaps of drama itself seems to direct the shape of the play called *Play*, which appears to have three characters who talk to one another, but in fact has three characters who talk without regard for, or awareness of, one another. The ash bins of Nell and Nagg in *Endgame* have become three gray urns in *Play*, and these contain the three characters—rather, they contain the heads of three characters who stare straight ahead, as if at the audience, but in fact only into a fiercely interrogating spotlight. Their predicament, like that of Winnie in *Happy Days*, is more frustrating for communication and self-dignity than that of Winnie or Nell and Nagg, whose memories are functional for some modicum of dialogue with another who shares those memories with them. The nameless characters of *Play* are two women and one man, once involved in a shabby conventional love tryst of a married couple and "another woman."

The drama of *Play* is a hell of isolation, regrets, emotional ignorance, and intellectual darkness. The play proceeds from a chorus of three voices in counterpoint, interrupted reminiscences without self-understanding, and a concluding chorus that repeats the opening, as if about to begin again. The urns are funereal wombs for talking heads. The emptiness of meaning from the lives of these characters is the utmost meaning they can express, and their lack of relationship is a judgment by the play on the failure of relationships in modern life generally. As in other Beckett plays of this period, the women of *Play* have a particularly painful message to deliver: Love and marriage do not exist as real possibilities for meaning for anyone anymore, especially for women, who have depended on them far more than men. The refusal to accept this predicament without a protest is dramatized in *Not I*, a play in which an apparently female character is divided between a Mouth of denial and an Auditor of silent protest. Here, Beckett has combined mime with radiolike monologue, and he has done it through a sexual pun on "ad-libbing."

All That Fall • To his achievements in stage plays, Beckett added successful accomplishments in radio and television drama, as well as one interesting script for motion pictures, *Film*. The radio plays of note are *All That Fall* and *Embers*; the teleplay deserving attention is *Eh Joe*. Communication, its failure or its emptiness, is a common theme running through Beckett's writing, and his experiments in various modes of artistic expression illustrate his search for success in communication. Radio was a challenging medium, using voice and other sounds to create imaginative shapes for audiences. *All That Fall* uses the muttering voice of an overweight old woman, Mrs. (Maddy) Rooney, making her way to a train station to meet her blind husband, Mr. (Dan) Rooney; her innermost thoughts and feelings are easily expressed in this medium, as are the concerns of those she meets along her way.

Like Beckett's other women, Mrs. Rooney has little to report that is fulfilling in her marriage; indeed, she mourns the loss of her one child, a daughter who would have been forty had she lived. Mrs. Rooney's real character is in her voice, not in her body; she can feel her self through her peculiar choice of words and sentence arrangements. This attention to vocabulary reveals Beckett's profound interest in the power of language as shaped and shaping sound. Of lesser interest is the terrible deed that lies at the center of this play's plot, the death of a child beneath the wheels of a train. Whether Mr. Rooney killed the child or not is less important than whether the audience can be moved by the mere articulation of sound to feel the horror of such a life-denying deed. *All That Fall* takes its title from a biblical verse that praises the power of a deity who protects "all that fall." The Rooneys hoot at this notion, though the child that fell beneath the train may, for all they can know, be better off than all those who, like the Rooneys, merely endure as they slowly decay with the rest of the universe.

Embers and **Eh Joe** • Like them, the narrating speaker of *Embers*, Henry, endures through a failing nature, but he uses language to explain rather than affirm failure and death. Like the waves of the sea beside which he sits while he speaks, Henry returns again and again to the same scenes of his life, trying to make them acceptable, especially his father's death and his wife's love. They are not yet coherent for him because they were experiences of futility rather than fulfillment, and so he goes on telling his story, revising as he composes, and composing as he speaks. Henry's regrets are motives for his narratives, and in *Eh Joe*, Joe's refusal to feel regret is a motive for the teleplay. As the television camera moves, like an interrogator or conscience, for an ultimate close-up of Joe's face, a voice interrupts, or propels, the camera's movement to tell a tale of suicide by a woman condemning Joe.

Film • This technique is similar to that of *Film*, in which a male figure (played by Buster Keaton) fails to avoid self-perception, self-condemnation. In the movement of the film's narrative, the male figure is an Object ("O") for the subject of the camera's Eye ("E"); the whole action is a movement by the object of avoidance of becoming a subject. The drama of the story ends with the failure of avoidance. Art exists because of the duality narrated by the action of the film, and when the duality approaches unity, as self recognizes itself, the art ends and the object fades into a rocking subject. All that man the object, or the male figure, seems to be is an attempt to escape his consciousness of himself, including his destruction of photographs (apparently of himself) from his past. Ironically, however, in that final desperate attempt to remove images of himself, he is most fully brought to recognize himself as a subject.

The destructive deed turns out to be a constructive act, as if Beckett's film were commenting on the nature of his own art as a successful communication about failures of communication, an integration of disintegrating forms, and a discovery of meaning in meaninglessness.

Other major works

LONG FICTION: *Murphy*, 1938; *Molloy*, 1951 (English translation, 1955); *Malone meurt*, 1951 (*Malone Dies*, 1956); *L'Innommable*, 1953 (*The Unnamable*, 1958); *Watt*, 1953; *Comment c'est*, 1961 (*How It Is*, 1964); *Mercier et Camier*, 1970 (*Mercier and Camier*, 1974); *Le Dépeupleur*, 1971 (*The Lost Ones*, 1972); *Company*, 1980; *Mal vu mal dit*, 1981 (*Ill Seen Ill Said*, 1981); *Worstward Ho*, 1983.

SHORT FICTION: *More Pricks than Kicks,* 1934; *Nouvelles et textes pour rien,* 1955 (*Stories and Texts for Nothing,* 1967); *No's Knife: Collected Shorter Prose, 1947-1966,* 1967; *First Love and Other Shorts,* 1974; *Pour finir encore et autres foirades,* 1976 (*Fizzles,* 1976).

POETRY: *Whoroscope,* 1930; *Echo's Bones and Other Precipitates,* 1935; *Poems in English,* 1961; *Collected Poems in English and French,* 1977.

SCREENPLAY: *Film,* 1965.

TELEPLAYS: *Eh Joe,* 1966 (*Dis Joe,* 1967); *Tryst,* 1976; *Shades,* 1977; *Quad,* 1981.

RADIO PLAYS: *All That Fall,* 1957, revised 1968; *Embers,* 1959; *Words and Music,* 1962 (music by John Beckett); *Cascando,* 1963 (music by Marcel Mihalovici).

NONFICTION: *Proust,* 1931.

TRANSLATION: *An Anthology of Mexican Poetry,* 1958 (Octavio Paz, editor).

MISCELLANEOUS: *I Can't Go On, I'll Go On: A Selection from Samuel Beckett's Work,* 1976 (Richard Seaver, editor).

Bibliography

Acheson, James. *Samuel Beckett's Artistic Theory and Practice: Criticism, Drama, and Early Fiction.* New York: St. Martin's Press, 1997. An examination of Beckett's literary viewpoint as it expressed itself in his drama and early fiction. Bibliography and index.

Birkett, Jennifer, and Kate Ince, eds. *Samuel Beckett.* New York: Longman, 2000. A collection of criticism of Beckett's works. Bibliography and index.

Essif, Les. *Empty Figure on an Empty Stage: The Theatre of Samuel Beckett and His Generation.* Drama and Performance Studies 13. Bloomington: Indiana University Press, 2001. A look at the criticism of Beckett's theatrical works over time. Bibliography and index.

Kim, Hwa Soon. *The Counterpoint of Hope, Obsession, and Desire for Death in Five Plays by Samuel Beckett.* New York: Peter Lang, 1996. An analysis of several psychological aspects present in Beckett's plays, including death and obsession. Bibliography and index.

Knowlson, James. *Damned to Fame: The Life of Samuel Beckett.* New York: Simon & Schuster, 1996. Knowlson retraces the personal development and literary evolution of Beckett, known to many as a creator of unique worlds inhabited by solitary individuals imprisoned in a world devoid of coherent communication. Bibliography and index.

McMullan, Anna. *Theatre on Trial: Samuel Beckett's Later Drama.* New York: Routledge, 1993. An examination of the later plays created by Beckett. Bibliography and index.

Oppenheim, Lois, ed. *Directing Beckett.* Ann Arbor: University of Michigan Press, 1994. This study examines the production and direction of Beckett plays. Bibliography and index.

Pattie, David. *The Complete Critical Guide to Samuel Beckett.* New York: Routledge, 2000. A reference volume that combines biographical information with critical analysis of Beckett's literary works. Bibliography and index.

Pilling, John, ed. *The Cambridge Companion to Beckett.* New York: Cambridge University Press, 1994. A comprehensive reference work that provides considerable information about the life and works of Beckett. Bibliography and indexes.

Worth, Katharine. *Samuel Beckett's Theatre: Life Journeys.* New York: Clarendon Press, 1999. A look at the production history and psychological aspects of Beckett's plays. Bibliography and index.

Richard D. McGhee

Brendan Behan

Born: Dublin, Ireland; February 9, 1923
Died: Dublin, Ireland; March 20, 1964

Principal drama • *Gretna Green*, pr. 1947; *The Quare Fellow*, pr. 1954, pb. 1956 (translation and revision of his Gaelic play "Casadh Súgáin Eile," wr. 1946); *The Big House*, pr. 1957 (radio play), pr. 1958 (staged), pb. 1961; *An Giall*, pr. 1958, pb. 1981 (in Gaelic); *The Hostage*, pr., pb. 1958 (translation and revision of *An Giall*); *Richard's Cork Leg*, pr. 1972, pb. 1973 (begun 1960, completed posthumously by Alan Simpson, 1964); *The Complete Plays*, pb. 1978

Other literary forms • Brendan Behan's literary reputation rests on the merits of three works: *The Quare Fellow* and *The Hostage*, his dramatic masterpieces, and *The Borstal Boy* (1958), his autobiography, published in England by Hutchinson and in the United States by Alfred A. Knopf. The two plays were performed several times before their publication, and the performance rights are still retained by the Theatre Workshop in East London. *The Borstal Boy*, set in 1931-1941, is an autobiographical narrative of Behan's adolescent years in prison.

Several Behan stories included in *The Borstal Boy* appeared initially in literary magazines and journals. *Brendan Behan's Island: An Irish Sketchbook* (1962) was intended by Behan to be similar in tone and structure to John Millington Synge's *The Aran Islands* (1907), but it does not stand up to this literary comparison. Unable to write for extended periods of time in his later years, Behan began taping his stories and subsequently had them edited by his publishing guardian angel and friend, Rae Jeffs. *Brendan Behan's Island, Hold Your Hour and Have Another* (1963), *Brendan Behan's New York* (1964), and *Confessions of an Irish Rebel* (1965) are all edited results of taping sessions. *The Scarperer* (1964) was published in book form the year Behan died but had been published first as a series in *The Irish Times*, in 1953, under the pseudonym "Emmet Street."

Several of Behan's works were published posthumously. Among these are *Confessions of an Irish Rebel, Moving Out* (1952), *A Garden Party* (1952), and *Richard's Cork Leg*, the latter of which was begun by Behan in 1960 and ultimately completed by Alan Simpson.

In addition to his plays and books, Behan contributed scores of short stories and poems on a variety of subjects to journals and newspapers throughout his life. He was as renowned for his balladeering as he was for his writings, and he composed the songs for his plays. A recording entitled *Brendan Behan Sings Irish Folksongs and Ballads*, produced by Spoken Arts, provides insight into Behan's passionate personality.

Achievements • Brendan Behan has been called the most important postwar Irish writer by contemporary Irish, English, and American critics. His works represent an extraordinary mixture of Irish romance, history, patriotism, and racism. All his works reflect, in some measure, the Irish Republican Army's efforts to rid Northern Ireland of the English. Paradoxically, his major literary successes came first in England, and though productions of *The Quare Fellow* and *The Hostage* met with moderate success in the United States, his most receptive audience was always in London.

Stylistically, Behan has been compared to Jonathan Swift, James Joyce, Synge, and Sean O'Casey. His treatment of the Irish in his plays and stories is simultaneously warm and biting. Clearly a social critic, Behan's writings indict law, religion, Ireland, England, and the absurdity of politics. His literary career spans barely twenty years, though the most productive of these amount to less than a decade. His first story, "I Become a Borstal Boy," was published in June, 1942, after which he regularly contributed nationalistic essays, stories, and poems to various Irish periodicals, including organs of the Irish Republican Army (IRA) such as *Fianna: The Voice of Young Ireland* and the *Wolfe Tone Weekly*.

Behan's most productive years (1953-1959) were marked by the production of both *The Quare Fellow* and *The Hostage* and the publication of *The Borstal Boy*. During these years, Behan's fame began to wane, and his creative talent floundered in a sea of alcohol.

Behan wrote principally of a world of men, yet ironically it was his association with two women that accounted for much of his artistic success. Joan Littlewood, director and manager of the Theatre Workshop at the Theatre Royal, Stratford East, London, directed *The Quare Fellow* in 1956 and catapulted Behan into the international limelight. Her production of *The Hostage* in 1958 earned for Behan equally high praise. His friend Jeffs can be credited with virtually all Behan's productivity during his final years. The publicity manager for Hutchinson's Publishing Company, she was "assigned" the obstreperous Behan in 1957. From 1957 to 1964, Jeffs's formidable task included following Behan from pub to pub, trailing and assisting him on his trips from England to the United States to Ireland, all the while making sure he was writing or taping his work, to be edited later. Ultimately, she performed her task as a labor of love, serving as friend and confidante to both Behan and his wife, Beatrice. Without Jeffs's tenacity, Behan's literary career would have ended in 1957 in an alcoholic stupor.

In his final years, Behan became a drunken caricature of himself. The early works evidence the true spark of genius that carried him through the years of honor to the dark years plagued by alcoholism and self-doubt. It is to these early works that one must turn to capture the real genius embodied in the literature of this twentieth century Irish phenomenon.

Biography • Brendan Behan was born February 9, 1923, in Dublin, Ireland, the first child of Stephen and Kathleen (Kearney) Behan, though his mother had two sons by a previous marriage. Born into a family with radical political leanings, Behan was reared on a double dose of IRA propaganda and Roman Catholicism. The radical Left was part of his genetic makeup. His grandmother and a grandfather were jailed for their roles in the revolution, the former for illegal possession of explosives when she was seventy years old and the latter for his part in the murder of Lord Cavendish. Both of Behan's parents fought in the Irish Revolution and in the Troubles. Ultimately jailed for his participation in the violence, Behan's father saw his son for the first time through prison bars.

Behan was a precocious child whose reverence for writers was spawned by his father's readings of Samuel Pepys, Charles Dickens, Émile Zola, George Bernard Shaw, and various polemical treatises to his children. By Behan's own account, his home was filled with reading, song, and revolution. Juxtaposed to this violent heritage was

Behan's conservative religious training. He attended schools run by the Sisters of Charity of St. Vincent de Paul, where he was a favorite, and another operated by the Irish Christian Brothers, where he found himself in constant disfavor.

Behan's militant disposition surfaced early, when at the age of nine he joined the Fianna Éireann, the junior wing of the IRA. He spent most of his early adult years in prison. After being arrested in Liverpool at the age of sixteen for participating in IRA bombings in England, Behan spent three years in the Borstal, the English correctional institution for juvenile delinquents. Released in 1941 and deported to Ireland, Behan was again incarcerated the following year for shooting at a police officer. He had served four years of a fourteen-year sentence when he was released in 1946. Additional stays in jail followed throughout his life.

The worldview projected in Behan's works recalls the environment in which he matured, one dominated by a radical family and by his prison experience. Cradled in the romance of revolution, Behan was cultured in a more traditional sense. Kathleen and Stephen Behan reared their children with a love for music and literature. Nurtured with a reverential attitude toward Kathleen's brother Peadar Kearney, a noted composer who wrote the Irish national anthem, the Behan children learned his marches and ballads in a home continuously filled with music. According to Colbert Kearney, Behan's precociousness as a child was largely attributable to the education he received at home.

Behan's father instilled in him a deep-seated respect for Irish writers and rhetoricians. He learned to read at an early age and was fond of memorizing speeches by Irish patriots such as Robert Emmet. Not as readily discernible in Behan's work is the influence of his strict upbringing in Roman Catholicism. Behan had a love-hate relationship with the Church, and often his works condemn religion. Yet one of his most bitter disappointments came when he was excommunicated while serving time in prison. Some critics believe that this was a crisis in Behan's life from which he never recovered.

Behan began writing while in prison, and his first story, "I Become a Borstal Boy," was published in *The Bell* in 1942. The plays, poems, and short stories written during his prison terms are all autobiographical. The years from 1946 to 1956 were the most ambitious of his career. For a time he lived in Paris, but he was eventually drawn back to Ireland, where he worked as a housepainter and freelance journalist. During this hiatus from serious encounters with the law, he married Beatrice Salkeld, daughter of the noted Irish artist Cecil Salkeld. Behan's major break came when Alan Simpson agreed to produce *The Quare Fellow* at the Pike Theatre in Dublin in 1954.

The play met with critical acclaim, but, to Behan's disappointment, the more prestigious Irish theaters such as the Abbey refused to stage it. This rejection spurred in Behan an overwhelming desire to be accepted as an artist in his own country. *The Quare Fellow* was noticed by Joan Littlewood, whose 1956 London production made Behan an international sensation. He followed this success with another play, *An Giall*, which he wrote in Gaelic and later translated as *The Hostage*. Littlewood's subsequent production of *The Hostage* proved an even greater success than *The Quare Fellow*.

Critics proclaimed Behan a literary genius, but he was destroyed by his success. His notorious interruptions of his plays with drunken speeches shouted from his seat in the audience and his intoxication during interviews for the British Broadcasting Corporation enhanced the "bad boy" image he so carefully cultivated, but ultimately it killed him. The most tragic repercussion of his alcoholism proved to be his inability to sit and write for an extended period of time. *The Hostage* was Behan's last good work. When his writing sojourns to Ibiza, his favorite retreat, and the United States and Canada produced little, he resorted to taping sessions to meet his publication contracts.

By 1960, after two major breakdowns as well as intermittent stays in hospitals to dry out, Behan was a shell of his former robust personality. Riding on his reputation of acknowledged artistry, he found himself incapable of writing, which led him to drink even more. Behan died March 20, 1964, at the age of forty-one. Several of his edited works published after his death created a brief, cultish interest in the man and his writing, but this adulation soon passed. What remains is the recognition that Behan was one of the finest twentieth century Irish writers. His talent will be recognized long after his colorful reputation has faded.

Analysis • To understand Brendan Behan's work, one must first recognize the underlying Behan legend, which is built on paradox. Frank O'Connor, writing in the *Sunday Independent* (Dublin), said of Behan that "under his turbulent exterior there was quite clearly the soul of an altar boy." Behan was a kind, gentle man who acted violently. He was insecure and feared publicity yet perpetrated outrageous stunts to capture attention. He wrote of reasonableness and absurdity in the world yet persisted in his personal irrationality. Behan was saint and sinner, moralist and profligate, and this dichotomy is carried over into his works. Even his overriding thematic consideration, a politically divided Ireland, is complex. Gordon Wickstrom believes Behan writes of three Irelands: the Ireland of contemporary, illegal Republican fanaticism, dedicated to the destruction of everything English; the Ireland of glorious memory of the Troubles and Easter Week, needing no justification beyond the private experience of valor and sacrifice; and Ireland as it actually exists, complete with police attacks, sirens, bloodbaths, and terror.

The principal themes in Behan's works are culled from his close association with the Irish Republican Army: death, freedom, and the absurdity of humanity's impermanence in a hostile world. Behan's major plays, *The Quare Fellow* and *The Hostage*, examine these themes through the eyes of a prisoner, a character-type that figures prominently in Behan's works. As his life stands as a series of paradoxes, so, too, does his style. Behan fills his works with unsavory gallows humor and swings erratically between comedy and tragedy in a decidedly Brechtian manner. Yet the early works are tightly structured and astonishingly poetic.

Songs incorporated into Behan's plays serve as lyric Gaelic laments but can quickly turn into obscene ditties. Behan's use of vernacular and the overwhelming sense of freedom in the lines contribute to the impressive strength of his writing. An unlikely coupling of naturalism and absurdism is characteristic of his best work. His characters are drawn from the lower classes, with Irish nationalism, bordering on racism, binding them together. Ironically, Behan's genteel audiences find it easy to empathize with his murderers, prostitutes, homosexuals, and radicals, perhaps because the sordid individuals in Behan's plays and stories are presented with a depth of compassion and understanding usually reserved for more noble literary characters.

Behan's prison years had a profound influence on him. During these stultifying periods, he became preoccupied with the two themes that dominate his works: death and freedom. In the cells and work yards of the Borstal and Mountjoy prisons, Behan mentally cataloged information about individuals, human nature, and the absurdity of the world and its systems. The examination of conflicts between gentleness and violence, a trademark of Behan's work, stems directly from his own divided nature as much as his early background. Major characters such as Dunlavin and the Warder in *The Quare*

Fellow, Monsewer and Williams in *The Hostage*, or the prisoner in *The Borstal Boy* reflect various facets of his personality.

The Quare Fellow • In November, 1954, *The Quare Fellow* was labeled "a powerful piece of propaganda" by A. J. Leventhal, writing in *Dublin Magazine*. This assessment of Behan's first literary and theatrical success holds true for all his works. Though his plays do not strictly adhere to agitation-propaganda techniques used by earlier European playwrights, Behan's works are obviously propagandistic. *The Quare Fellow*, the most structured of his plays, examines the issue of capital punishment. Set in a prison, *The Quare Fellow* is a series of episodes in which the prison community prepares for the execution of the unseen titular character.

Tension is deftly established on two levels: the friction maintained in the relationship between prisoners and warders and the more insidious anxiety, hidden beneath the prattle and routine of the prison, that eats at the souls of both warders and prisoners as the moment of execution draws near. Every character waits in dread for the final moment, when a man will die. Their empathetic response to ritualized, state-supported death reinforces the horror felt by the audience. The prison serves as Behan's microcosm of the world in which primal struggles of life and death as well as social struggles of promotion, acceptance, pretense, and charity are all in evidence.

The Quare Fellow opens with the singing of a man in solitary confinement, trying to keep his sanity. His haunting lament, floating over the prison grounds, becomes almost a dirge as the play progresses. The plot is moved by the institution's preparations for the day of execution. Each character fears the approach of the hour of death and manifests his uneasiness in a different way. The prisoners attempt a forced jauntiness and irreverence but are unable to call the condemned man by his Christian name, preferring instead to force on him anonymity, calling him only "the quare fellow." As the climax approaches and the moment of death is imminent, a prisoner cynically announces the offstage procession to the gallows as though it were the start of a horse race: "We're off, in this order: The Governor, The Chief, two screws Regan and Crimmin, the quare fellow between them." Yet this comic diversion is incapable of diluting the dramatic effect of the climax when the clock strikes the hour and the prisoners wail, howl, and roar in primal lamentation, as the trap drops and the quare fellow hangs.

The hero of the play, the quare fellow, never appears onstage. Dunlavin, a crusty, experienced prisoner, and Regan, a compassionate warder, are the principal characters. This den of thieves and murderers has its own order, a social hierarchy based on criminal offenses and experience. Sex offenders are ostracized by the prison community, and Dunlavin bemoans his misfortune at having one placed in the cell next to his. The sex offender, for his part, is appalled that he must live among murderers and takes to quoting Thomas Carlyle.

Religion is brutally satirized in *The Quare Fellow*. The hypocritical representative from the Department of Justice is dubbed "Holy Healey" by the inmates, who paste religious pictures on their walls to curry favor during his visits. Dunlavin's friend and neighbor in the cellblock comments on the importance of the Bible to prisoners, stating, "Many's the time the Bible was a consolation to a fellow all alone in the old cell," not for its spiritual comfort, but because prisoners rolled mattress bits within its pages and smoked them. Dunlavin, in turn, recounts how in his first twelve months he smoked his way halfway through Genesis. The executioner, referred to imperially as "Himself," cannot face his job in a sober state and must be accompanied by a teetotaling, Bible-quoting, hymn-singing assistant to see him to his appointed rounds.

The incongruity of this misallied pair is obvious as Jenkinson, the assistant, sings a hymn while the hangman audibly calculates the weight of the condemned man and the height of the drop needed to kill him.

Behan's vision of the value of life and the awesome power of death is painted in masterful strokes throughout *The Quare Fellow*. The dignity of humankind, the worth of an individual life, and the inhumanity of a system devised for correctional purposes are powerfully juxtaposed in this play. The 1954 Pike Theatre production of *The Quare Fellow* was well received, but it was Joan Littlewood's direction in 1956 that made it a modern classic. Although the play has been criticized as being melodramatic, Behan mixes well-developed characters with stereotypes and caricatures to provide diverse opportunities for commentary on various levels. *The Quare Fellow* is not wholly a tragedy, nor is it merely black comedy. It is an unnatural two-backed beast that violently gives birth to Behan's pessimistic worldview.

The Hostage • The music-hall atmosphere of *The Hostage* differs radically from the sterile environment of *The Quare Fellow*. From the opening jig, danced by two prostitutes and two homosexuals, to the rousing chorus, sung by the corpse, Behan jars his audience with the unexpected. Like Bertolt Brecht's *Die Dreigroschenoper* (pr. 1928; *The Threepenny Opera*, 1949), *The Hostage* is populated by a cast of societal misfits. Brechtian influences can be noticed in the play's structure as well. *The Hostage*, according to Richard A. Duprey in *The Critic*, is an indictment of law, religion, home, country, human decency, art, and even death. What is espoused within its tenuous structure is IRA radicalism, but even this cannot escape Behan's satiric barbs. The IRA officer in the play is outraged by the shoddy accommodations—a brothel—afforded him and his political prisoner, while Pat, manager of the "brockel" and a veteran of the Easter Rebellion and the Troubles, denounces the new IRA soldiers as "white-faced loons with their trench coats, berets and teetotal badges."

Thematically, *The Hostage* compares with Behan's other major works in that the protagonist is a prisoner. Leslie Williams has committed no crime except that he is an English soldier in Ireland. Taken as a hostage by IRA reactionaries, Williams is offered in trade for a jailed Irish youth sentenced to hang. The IRA cause is felt most strongly in this play, and Behan's nationalistic biases are given ample voice in the songs about the Easter Rebellion, Monsewer's senile ravings about the days of glorious conflict, and Pat's diatribes against modern Ireland. Hidden beneath the brash, gaudy, and colorful language of the play, such weighty underpinnings emerge in flashes of seriousness.

A mélange of dramatic styles pushes the plot through a series of vignettes, comedy routines, and song-and-dance numbers. Songs, jokes, and malapropisms abound in this very political play. Individually, the characters lack depth and are only one step removed from the stereotyped clowns of burlesque houses. Collectively, they champion traditional Irish Republicanism while at the same time denouncing the absurdity of its violent contemporary manifestations. This is a play about the Republican cause; it is also a play about the value of life. Leslie Williams is an apolitical character who dies needlessly, an injustice that Behan adroitly condemns. Life and death in Behan's work are never equal forces; life always triumphs. He breaks the serious mood of his final scene, in which Williams's death is disclosed, by having the corpse jump up and sing, "The bells of hell go ting a ling a ling for you but not for me. . . ."

The original Gaelic-language version of the play, *An Giall*, was a much more serious play than the version presented in the internationally acclaimed 1958 London production. The seminal version had but ten characters, whereas *The Hostage* has fifteen.

Writer Colbert Kearney notes that *An Giall* is essentially a naturalistic tragedy, while *The Hostage* is a musical extravaganza. Certainly, the latter tolerates a greater degree of bawdiness than the original. Critics charged that Joan Littlewood's company substantially altered *An Giall* while in production for *The Hostage*, yet this was partially Behan's fault. During 1957 and 1958, he was committed to two projects: translating *An Giall* into *The Hostage* for Littlewood and finishing *The Borstal Boy*.

Behan became preoccupied with the publicity and lavish promotion given *The Borstal Boy* and neglected his commitments to Littlewood. Consequently, parts of *The Hostage* grew out of the improvisations of the Theatre Workshop and, though sanctioned by Behan, changed the play significantly from the original work. Scholar Ulick O'Connor believes several of the non sequitur scenes in *The Hostage* were invented by Littlewood and do not reflect Behan's hand in the revision. Nevertheless, the production was a hit. *The Hostage* was selected to represent Great Britain at the prestigious Théâtre des Nations festival in 1959, and it moved to the fashionable Wyndham Theatre on London's West End. Productions of Behan's plays opened in Dublin, New York, Paris, and Berlin.

The Hostage proved to be Behan's last theatrical success. His reputation sustained him as an artist for the next six years, but his talent abandoned him. He began another play, *Richard's Cork Leg*, but it remained unfinished at his death. *The Hostage* is not as neatly structured as *The Quare Fellow*, though Behan's genius for dialogue and *mise en scène* pervades the work. Behan—patriot, nationalist, and racist—is plainly seen in *The Hostage*, yet his persona, so dominant in his plays, turns to reveal Behan the humanitarian in equally sharp focus. Behan's works, like the man, are paradoxical. His legend lives on, supported by contemporary interest in Behan the revolutionary and artist.

Other major works

LONG FICTION: *The Scarperer*, 1953 (serial), 1964 (book; as Emmet Street); *The Dubbalin Man*, 1954-1956 (serial), 1997 (book).

SHORT FICTION: *After the Wake*, 1981.

RADIO PLAYS: *A Garden Party*, 1952; *Moving Out*, 1952.

NONFICTION: *The Borstal Boy*, 1958; *Brendan Behan's Island: An Irish Sketchbook*, 1962; *Hold Your Hour and Have Another*, 1963; *Brendan Behan's New York*, 1964; *Confessions of an Irish Rebel*, 1965; *The Letters of Brendan Behan*, 1992 (E. H. Mikhail, editor).

MISCELLANEOUS: *Poems and Stories*, 1978; *Poems and a Play in Irish*, 1981 (includes the play *An Giall*).

Bibliography

Behan, Brian, with Aubrey Dillon-Malone. *The Brother Behan.* Dublin: Ashfield Press, 1998. The brother of Brendan Behan writes of their lives and his brother's work.

Behan, Kathleen. *Mother of All the Behans: The Autobiography of Kathleen Behan as Told to Brian Behan.* 1984. Reprint. Dublin: Poolbeg, 1994. The mother of the dramatist and revolutionary describes her life and her family.

De Búrca, Séamus. *Brendan Behan: A Memoir.* 1971. Reprint. Dublin: P. J. Bourke, 1985. A memoir-style biography of the famous dramatist, covering his life and works.

Mikhail, E. H., ed. *Brendan Behan: Interviews and Recollections.* 2 vols. Totowa, N.J.: Barnes and Noble Books, 1982. A collection of extracts from published memoirs and interviews given by those who knew Behan. Contains fifty-one items in volume 1 and fifty-five in volume 2. Mikhail's introduction insightfully compares Behan and Oscar Wilde.

O'Sullivan, Michael. *Brendan Behan: A Life.* Boulder, Colo.: Roberts Rinehart, 1999. A biography of Behan that examines his life and works. Bibliography and index.

Witoszek, Walentyna. "The Funeral Comedy of Brendan Behan." *Études irlandaises* 11 (December, 1988): 83-91. Witoszek discusses the puzzling presence of laughter in Behan's writings in which execution is imminent. Though Death is the "central character" in all Behan's plays, there is also an orgiastic atmosphere of carnival madness, which is analyzed in terms of ritual, the Irish image of the laughing death, and Mikhail Bakhtin's theories of the carnivalesque.

Susan Duffy,
updated by William Hutchings

Eric Bogosian

Born: Woburn, Massachusetts; April 24, 1953

Principal drama • *Careful Movement,* pr. 1977; *Slavery,* pr. 1977; *Garden,* pr. 1978; *Heaven, Heaven, Heaven,* pr. 1978; *The Ricky Paul Show,* pr. 1979; *Sheer Heaven,* pr. 1980; *That Girl,* pr. 1981; *The New World,* pr. 1981; *Men Inside,* pr. 1981, pb. 1994; *Voices of America,* pr. 1982, pb. 1994; *Advocate,* pr. 1983; *FunHouse,* pr. 1983, pb. 1994; *I Saw the Seven Angels,* pr. 1984; *Talk Radio,* pr. 1984, pb. 1988; *Drinking in America,* pr. 1986, pb. 1987; *Sex, Drugs, Rock and Roll,* pr., pb. 1990; *Scenes from the New World,* pb. 1993; *The Essential Bogosian,* pb. 1994; *Pounding Nails in the Floor with My Forehead,* pr., pb. 1994; *subUrbia,* pr. 1994, pb. 1995; *31 Ejaculations,* pr. 1996, pb. 2000; *Griller,* pr. 1998; *Bitter Sauce,* pr., pb. 1998; *Wake Up and Smell the Coffee,* pr. 2000, pb. 2001

Other literary forms • In addition to his prolific career as a playwright and creator of solo shows, Eric Bogosian has branched out into other written forms as well. *Notes from Underground* (1994), which takes its inspiration from Fyodor Dostoevski's *Zapiski iz podpolya* (1864; *Letters from the Underworld,* 1913; better known as *Notes from the Underground*), is a novella in journal form detailing an isolated man's attempts to connect with the outside world and his increasing tendency toward antisocial and sociopathic behavior. Bogosian also published a novel, *Mall* (2000), which focuses on the ways in which a shopping mall ties together the lives of a bizarre array of seemingly unrelated characters. The novel is part comedy and part crime thriller and contains much of the stinging social criticism found in his plays.

Bogosian also wrote introductions to two books: *Physiognomy: The Mark Seliger Photographs* (1999), a collection of celebrity photographs, and *How to Talk Dirty and Influence People* (1992), the autobiography of comedian Lenny Bruce, whose standup routines laced with social criticism are an obvious forerunner to much of Bogosian's work as a dramatist. In addition, Bogosian has also written screenplays for adaptations of his work including *Talk Radio* (1988), which he co-wrote with director Oliver Stone, *Sex, Drugs, Rock and Roll* (1991), and *subUrbia* (1996), as well as the pilot episode of the television program *High Incident* (1996).

Achievements • Eric Bogosian has been an active and versatile playwright since the late 1970's, crafting numerous short ensemble dramas and full-length plays, of which *Talk Radio* and *subUrbia,* which were both adapted to film, and *Griller* are the best known. However, Bogosian's greatest contribution to modern drama is his series of solo shows. These solo performance pieces—*Men Inside; FunHouse; Drinking in America; Sex, Drugs, Rock and Roll; Pounding Nails in the Floor with My Forehead;* and *Wake Up and Smell the Coffee*—consist of short monologues spoken by different characters and have led to three Obie awards. *Drinking in America* and *Pounding Nails in the Floor with My Forehead* each garnered the Obie Award for playwriting, and *Sex, Drugs, Rock and Roll* received a special citation. An outspoken supporter of the National Endowment for the Arts (NEA), Bogosian has received two NEA fellowships, and the film version of *Talk Radio* received the Silver Bear Award from the Berlin Film Festival.

Bogosian's work, more than that of most writers, has drawn particular praise for being "hip" by demonstrating a thorough understanding of contemporary culture and concerns. From his searing indictments of consumer culture to his satirical takes on morally compromised yuppies, drug pushers, Hollywood agents, and traditional tough guys, Bogosian has garnered a reputation as a devastating social critic with a biting, edgy, and oftentimes grim sense of humor.

Biography • Eric Bogosian grew up in the suburbs in Woburn, Massachusetts, participating in theater at his local high school and enrolling in the University of Chicago. He dropped out of college in 1973 and returned to Woburn, where he worked as an assistant manager at a clothing store in the local mall before transferring to the theater department at Oberlin College, from which he was graduated. In 1975 he moved to New York City and began pursuing a writing career. After arriving in New York, he immersed himself in the world of theater and performance art and began contributing ensemble plays by the end of the 1970's. To help make ends meet, he learned to capitalize on his talents as a performer by creating monologues that he could produce inexpensively. This work brought him to the attention of producer Joseph Papp, and Bogosian appeared in the producer's Shakespeare Festival in 1982. During the early 1980's, Bogosian continued to develop his solo work, completing his first two solo shows, and in 1984 he completed a version of his first full-length ensemble play, *Talk Radio*. He also began to land sporadic acting jobs on television in such programs as *Miami Vice* and *The Twilight Zone*.

In 1986 he completed a longer collection of monologues, *Drinking in America*, for which he received an Obie Award and which was subsequently shortened and filmed as part of a comedy special on Cinemax. A successful New York production of *Talk Radio* in 1987 led to Bogosian's collaboration with film director Oliver Stone. The two expanded on the original play by including background material and incorporating elements from the life of Alan Berg, a Colorado radio talk-show host who had been murdered. The resulting film, in which Bogosian also starred, received a good deal of attention and was honored at the Berlin Film Festival. Capitalizing on his rising visibility as a performer, Bogosian landed a leading role in Robert Altman's television adaptation of *The Caine Mutiny Court-Martial* (1988), and Bogosian's next solo show, *Sex, Drugs, Rock and Roll*, was filmed by director John McNaughton in 1991.

Bogosian continued making occasional acting appearances in television programs such as *Law and Order* and *The Larry Sanders Show* in the early 1990's, and in 1994 he published his first novella, *Notes from Underground*. In 1994 Bogosian was quite busy. Theatre Communications Group published his early solo work along with *Talk Radio* in an anthology, *The Essential Bogosian*; he completed another award-winning solo show, *Pounding Nails in the Floor with My Forehead*; and he wrote his second, full-length ensemble play, *subUrbia*. The next year he accepted a high-profile acting job as the villain in the action film *Under Siege 2* (1995), and in 1996 he wrote the screenplay for director Richard Linklater's adaptation of *subUrbia*. He remained busy during the remainder of the 1990's, acting in small roles in films such as Woody Allen's *Deconstructing Harry* (1997); writing another ensemble play, *Griller*; completing another solo show, *Wake Up and Smell the Coffee*; and publishing a novel, *Mall*. A New York resident, Bogosian is married to Jo Bonney, who has also directed several of his solo shows.

Analysis • Eric Bogosian's work as a performer has continued to flourish along with his writing career, and his sensibilities as an actor have heavily influenced his writing.

(AP/Wide World Photos)

Unlike playwrights, such as Arthur Miller, who strived to produce the well-made play, Bogosian creates character-driven works, often with little regard to formalities of plot and theme. He tries to produce an event or a happening with his plays, placing his emphasis on the performance over the text. Although this technique might seem to make his drama less accessible to literary analysis, it actually provides his work with its greatest sense of intellectual tension.

Rather than carefully formulating his productions, Bogosian lets his characters bring to the stage all of their many contradictions and paradoxes, often leaving the reader or viewer with an uneasy (and highly literary) sense of ambiguity. He does not ask simple questions and does not provide direct answers. Rather, he uses the theater as a means for self-expression, particularly in his solo shows, in which he can pursue whatever thoughts are plaguing him at the moment and he can speak to his audience, whom he frequently refers to as his "tribe."

Many of those "plaguing thoughts" involve generational issues and popular culture. He often explores the ways in which his generation has moved from idealism to materialism, particularly in *Sex, Drugs, Rock and Roll* and *Pounding Nails in the Floor with My Forehead*. His view of the United States is large, and in his solo shows as well as the ensemble play, *Scenes from the New World*, he depicts a cross-section of the United States, presenting what he often describes in interviews as the "archetypes" for people that he knows. Readers of Bogosian's plays are as likely to encounter winos, prostitutes, muggers, rednecks, and drug addicts as they are to find yuppies, Hollywood agents, rock stars, family men, and business executives. In fact, although one might be tempted to point to obvious theatrical and cultural predecessors such as Bertolt Brecht and Lenny Bruce in order to place Bogosian's drama in a literary context, his affinity for such a broad range of American characters as well as his ability to juggle contradictory ideologies and personalize all the material links him as closely to the American poet Walt Whitman as to any other playwrights or performers.

Talk Radio • Bogosian's first full-length ensemble play, *Talk Radio*, centers on the personality of Barry Champlain, a confrontational radio talk-show host, whose program, *Nighttalk*, is on the verge of being distributed nationally. The action takes place during one difficult night when Champlain wrestles with off-beat phone calls, pressures to change the show, and ultimately, a crisis of conscience. He begins to question whether going national is "selling out," and both the character, Champlain, and the writer, Bogosian, seem to question whether there is any artistic integrity in such a show at all. The play ponders whether such programs are public forums for exchanging important ideas or merely spectacle entertainments for passive listeners who derive their pleasure from hearing Champlain take on the various callers.

This play bears the hallmarks of much of the playwright's subsequent work in that it asks more questions than it answers and examines the relationship of a performer to his audience, a theme that runs as a subtext throughout much of Bogosian's solo work. *Talk Radio* amply demonstrates his penchant for being "ahead of the curve" in terms of trends in popular culture. With *Talk Radio*, Bogosian actually anticipates the arrival of such celebrity hosts as Howard Stern, but when the play was first completed in the mid-1980's, the notion of the blistering talk-show host had not yet emerged as a national phenomenon.

Sex, Drugs, Rock and Roll • In this collection of monologues, Bogosian presents another diverse array of characters, including a British rock star turned recovering drug addict, a Texas "stud" who boasts of his sexual prowess, and a cutthroat business executive. Some of the pieces are more inventive conceptually than his previous monologues, such as "Benefit," which features the rock star and establishes as its unseen context a television interview show. As he notes in his introduction, Bogosian, as a child of the 1970's, has very mixed feelings about sex, drugs, and rock and roll. For many people of his generation, "sex, drugs, rock and roll" was not merely a slogan, but actually a motto for living that defined a sense of nonconformity and rebellion, and thus, implied some vague sense of integrity. Yet, as his monologues detail, the sex, the drugs, and the rock and roll are, all three, suspect in that they have all contributed to disease, death, and debilitation for many of these characters. Bogosian's sense of contradiction and paradox is fully at work in this show as he manages to evoke the mixed feeling of a generation struggling to romanticize the values of its youth while simultaneously questioning the validity of those values.

subUrbia • Bogosian's second full-length ensemble play, *subUrbia*, focuses on a handful of young people, most in their early twenties, who spend their time hanging out behind a local 7-Eleven convenience store drinking beer, eating pizza, and discussing sex. The action focuses on one evening when an old friend of the group who has gained a small degree of fame as a member of a rock band returns home with his publicist. Although the play begins as a comedy, simultaneously reveling in and satirizing the various attitudes struck by the characters, it grows increasingly serious in tone with incidents of racism, threats of violence, betrayal, drug overdoses, and ultimately tragedy when one of the characters unexpectedly dies.

While Bogosian has suggested that the characters and events of the play emerged from his own experiences in the 1970's, the play speaks much more directly to the existentialist and nihilistic impulses of Generation X in the 1990's. Most of the characters struggle with a sense of aimlessness in which such time-killing activities as eating, drinking, and "hanging out," become an end unto themselves rather than the means to an end. The play also fits quite comfortably into the context of a mid-1990's comedy of manners, much like the television program *Seinfeld* (1990-1998) and films such as Quentin Tarantino's *Pulp Fiction* (1994) and Kevin Smith's *Clerks* (1994) in that it provides characters who are not particularly well educated or intellectually sophisticated with what is nevertheless a highly complex and, at times, elevated rhetorical style of speech, as these young people explore the deeper philosophical implications of how they see the world.

Pounding Nails in the Floor with My Forehead • This solo show demonstrates increasing ambition and experimentation in Bogosian's work. It begins with "America," in which a nameless speaker launches into an extreme attack against anyone and anything even purporting to be politically "liberal." He follows this disturbing opening monologue with a deliberately offensive one, spoken in black dialect, by a train conductor who claims to be spreading diseases to everyone, including audience members who may be sitting in a chair in which he has urinated or leaning against a wall where he has vomited.

After sufficiently numbing his audience, Bogosian then appears as "himself," attacking the audience for not applauding the previous monologue. By the end of this monologue, he winds up arguing with himself backstage about his image as an "angry" performer. This type of textual self-awareness, in which monologues segue smoothly from one to another and in which Bogosian directly draws his own character into the fray, is new to the solo shows and gives *Pounding Nails in the Floor with My Forehead* a greater sense of unity and development than its predecessors.

Other major works

LONG FICTION: *Mall,* 2000.

SCREENPLAYS: *Talk Radio,* 1988 (with Oliver Stone); *Sex, Drugs, Rock and Roll,* 1991; *subUrbia,* 1996.

TELEPLAY: *High Incident,* 1996.

MISCELLANEOUS: *Notes from Underground,* 1994 (novella and play).

Bibliography

Clements, Marcelle. "Eric Bogosian as the Man Who Won't Shut Up." *Esquire,* September, 1991, 184. This profile attempts to see the similarities between Bogosian in private and his public persona as evidenced in *Sex, Drugs, Rock and Roll.*

Handelman, David. "A Man Under the Influence." *Rolling Stone,* June 19, 1986, 49-51. Written during the period of Bogosian's solo show, *Drinking in America,* this article connects the performance to the playwright's feelings about the death of the comedian John Belushi.

Lacher, Irene. "Bogosian Says So Long to Solo Performances: The Older and Wiser Bad Boy of Monologuists Says He Is Moving on to New Projects." *Los Angeles Times,* February 6, 2002, p. F2. Bogosian discusses his years of doing monologues and expresses how his interests and focus have changed since he began. He suggests that he might stop doing solo shows and devote his attention to other works.

Shirley, Don. "At His *Worst.*" Review of *The Worst of Eric Bogosian. Los Angeles Times,* February 8, 2002, p. F21. A review of *The Worst of Eric Bogosian,* a monologue taken from Bogosian's *Wake Up and Smell the Coffee* and other solo performances. Shirley finds the show, in which Bogosian portrays a series of flawed men, including an obsequious actor at an audition and a randy drug dealer, to be a sort of "best of" compilation.

Thomas Gregory Carpenter

Bertolt Brecht

Born: Augsburg, Germany; February 10, 1898
Died: East Berlin, East Germany; August 14, 1956

Principal drama • *Baal,* wr. 1918, pb. 1922, pr. 1923 (English translation, 1963); *Trommeln in der Nacht,* wr. 1919-1920, pr., pb. 1922 (*Drums in the Night,* 1961); *Die Hochzeit,* wr. 1919, pr. 1926, pb. 1953 as *Die Keinbürgerhochzeit* (*The Wedding,* 1970); *Im Dickicht der Städte,* pr. 1923, pb. 1927 (*In the Jungle of Cities,* 1961); *Leben Eduards des Zweiten von England,* pr., pb. 1924 (with Lion Feuchtwanger; based on Christopher Marlowe's play *Edward II; Edward II,* 1966); *Mann ist Mann,* pr. 1926, pb. 1927 (*A Man's a Man,* 1961); *Die Dreigroschenoper,* pr. 1928, pb. 1929 (libretto; based on John Gay's play *The Beggar's Opera; The Threepenny Opera,* 1949); *Aufstieg und Fall der Stadt Mahagonny,* pb. 1929, pr. 1930 (libretto; *Rise and Fall of the City of Mahagonny,* 1957); *Das Badener Lehrstück vom Einverständnis,* pr. 1929, pb. 1930 (*The Didactic Play of Baden: On Consent,* 1960); *Happy End,* pr. 1929, pb. 1958 (libretto; lyrics with Elisabeth Hauptmann; English translation, 1972); *Der Ozeanflug,* pr., pb. 1929 (radio play; *The Flight of the Lindberghs,* 1930); *Die Ausnahme und die Regel,* wr. 1930, pb. 1937, pr. 1938 (*The Exception and the Rule,* 1954); *Der Jasager,* pr. 1930, pb. 1931 (based on the Japanese Nō play *Taniko; He Who Said Yes,* 1946); *Die Massnahme,* pr. 1930, pb. 1931 (libretto; *The Measures Taken,* 1960); *Die heilige Johanna der Schlachthöfe,* pb. 1931, pr. 1932 (radio play), pr. 1959 (staged; *St. Joan of the Stockyards,* 1956); *Der Neinsager,* pb. 1931 (*He Who Said No,* 1946); *Die Mutter,* pr., pb. 1932 (based on Maxim Gorky's novel *Mat; The Mother,* 1965); *Die Sieben Todsünden der Kleinbürger,* pr. 1933, pb. 1959 (cantata; *The Seven Deadly Sins,* 1961); *Die Horatier und die Kuriatier,* wr. 1934, pb. 1938, pr. 1958 (*The Horatians and the Curatians,* 1947); *Die Rundköpfe und die Spitzköpfe,* pr. 1935, pb. 1936 (based on William Shakespeare's play *Measure for Measure; The Roundheads and the Peakheads,* 1937); *Die Gewehre der Frau Carrar,* pr., pb. 1937 (*Señora Carrar's Rifles,* 1938); *Furcht und Elend des dritten Reiches,* pr. in French 1938, pr. in English 1945, pb. in German 1945 (*The Private Life of the Master Race,* 1944); *Leben des Galilei,* first version wr. 1938-1939, pr. 1943; second version wr. 1945-1947, third version pb. 1955 (*The Life of Galileo,* 1947, also known as *Galileo*); *Der gute Mensch von Sezuan,* wr. 1938-1940, pr. 1943, pb. 1953 (*The Good Woman of Setzuan,* 1948); *Das Verhör des Lukullus,* pr. 1940 (radio play), pb. 1940, pr. 1951 (staged; libretto; *The Trial of Lucullus,* 1943); *Herr Puntila und sein Knecht, Matti,* wr. 1940, pr. 1948, pb. 1951 (*Mr. Puntila and His Hired Man, Matti,* 1976); *Mutter Courage und ihre Kinder,* pr. 1941, pb. 1949 (based on Hans Jakob Christoffel von Grimmelshausen's *Der abenteuerliche Simplicissimus; Mother Courage and Her Children,* 1941); *Der aufhaltsame Aufstieg des Arturo Ui,* wr. 1941, pb. 1957, pr. 1958 (*The Resistible Rise of Arturo Ui,* 1972); *Die Gesichte der Simone Machard,* wr. 1941-1943, pb. 1956, pr. 1957 (with Feuchtwanger; *The Visions of Simone Machard,* 1961); *Schweyk im zweiten Weltkrieg,* wr. 1941-1943, pr. in Polish 1957, pb. 1957, pr. in German 1958 (based on Jaroslav Hašek's novel *Osudy dobrého vojáka Švejka ve světove války; Schweyk in the Second World War,* 1975); *Der kaukasische Kreidekreis,* wr. 1944-1945, pr. in English 1948, pb. 1949, pr. in German 1958 (based on Li Xingdao's play *The Circle of Chalk; The Caucasian Chalk Circle,* 1948); *Die Antigone des Sophokles,* pr., pb. 1948 (*Sophocles' Antigone,* 1990); *Die Tage der Commune,* wr. 1948-1949, pr. 1956, pb. 1957 (based on Nordahl Grieg's *Nederlaget; The Days of the

Commune, 1971); *Der Hofmeister,* pr. 1950, pb. 1951 (adaptation of Jacob Lenz's *Der Hofmeister, The Tutor,* 1972); *Turandot: Oder, Der Kongress der Weisswäscher,* wr. 1950-1954, pr. 1970; *Der Prozess der Jeanne d'Arc zu Rouen, 1431,* pr. 1952, pb. 1959 (based on Anna Seghers's radio play; *The Trial of Jeanne d'Arc at Rouen, 1431,* 1972); *Coriolan,* wr. 1952-1953, pb. 1959 (adaptation of William Shakespeare's play *Coriolanus; Coriolanus,* 1972); *Don Juan,* pr. 1953, pb. 1959 (based on Molière's play; English translation, 1972); *Pauken und Trompeten,* pb. 1956 (adaptation of George Farquhar's *The Recruiting Officer; Trumpets and Drums,* 1972)

Other literary forms • Bertolt Brecht experimented with several literary forms, and his output in all genres was considerable. He wrote novels, short fiction, nonfiction, and screenplays. His novel *Der Dreigroschenroman* (1934; *The Threepenny Novel*) was translated in 1937; his short fiction is collected in *Geschichten von Herrn Keuner* (1930, 1958; *Stories of Mr. Keuner,* 2001); and many of his essays appeared in his three-volume *Arbeitsjournal, 1938-1955* (1973; *Bertolt Brecht Journals,* 1993). *Kuhle Wampe* (1932; English translation, 1933) is an example of his fine work in film. An exhibit of Brecht's works, on display in his final residence, includes more than thirty dramatic works, about thirteen hundred poems and songs, three novels, numerous screenplays, and more than 150 works of nonfiction.

Achievements • Bertolt Brecht's influence on the contemporary theater—especially on the development of political drama—extends worldwide. In Germany, Austria, and Switzerland, his plays are the most frequently performed after William Shakespeare's. Translated into many languages, they are included in the repertoire of theater companies throughout both Western and Eastern Europe and the United States. Among the prizes that Brecht received for his works are the Kleist Prize in 1922, the East German National Prize in 1951, and the International Stalin Peace Prize in 1954. Brecht formed the Berliner Ensemble in 1949 and made it into one of the best acting companies in Europe. In 1954, Brecht's production of *Mother Courage and Her Children* was awarded first prize at the International Theater Festival in Paris. In the following year, his production of *The Caucasian Chalk Circle* received second prize at the same festival. These two productions contributed to Brecht's international reputation as a director as well as a playwright.

Biography • Bertolt Brecht was born in Augsburg in southern Germany on February 10, 1898. Between 1908 and 1917, Brecht attended Realgymnasium (high school) in his hometown, but he was almost expelled in 1916 for writing a pacifist essay (pacifism is a constant theme in his works). After leaving high school in 1917, he enrolled at the University of Munich to study medicine. In 1918, he was called for military service and worked as an orderly in the venereal disease ward of the Augsburg military hospital. After the war, he lived in Munich as a freelance writer. In 1922, he married Marianne Zoff but was later divorced from her in 1927. Brecht established himself in Berlin at the Deutsches Theater in 1924, where he worked under Max Reinhardt until 1926. That year marked the turning point in Brecht's career: He began studying Marxism and economics, and his subsequent conversion to Marxism decisively shaped his life and works. Brecht's contacts with Erwin Piscator's political theater at this time also had an impact on his dramatic theory.

As the Nazis gained power, Brecht found it increasingly difficult to have his works performed. The Nazis had long harbored resentment against Brecht. At the time of the Munich Putsch, Brecht was the fifth person on their list of people to be arrested because of his poem "Legende vom toten Soldaten" ("Legend of the Dead Soldier"), which tells how the kaiser has a dead soldier disinterred, declared fit, and sent off to the front again. In January, 1933, a performance of *The Measures Taken* in Erfurt was broken up by the police. On February 28, 1933, the day after the Reichstag fire, Brecht and his family (in 1929, he had married the actress Helene Weigel) fled from Germany. They went to Prague, Vienna, Lugano, and Paris, and finally settled in Denmark.

On May 10, 1933, Brecht's works were burned in Germany. During his exile, Brecht campaigned energetically against Fascism, contributed to anti-Fascist exile journals, wrote anti-Fascist works, and maintained close contacts with other exiles. In 1935, the Nazis revoked Brecht's German citizenship. In 1939, when Denmark became unsafe, Brecht and his family moved to Sweden. From there, they went to Finland, and in 1941, they fled to California by way of Moscow and Vladivostok, settling in Santa Monica, where they remained for six years. Brecht worked occasionally for the film industry, but the only project that was actually carried out was his script for *Hangmen Also Die* (1943), which he wrote in 1942. The film, which was directed by Fritz Lang, concerns the assassination of the notorious Nazi Reinhard Heydrich by the Resistance in Czechoslovakia. On October 30, 1947, Brecht was called before the House Committee on Un-American Activities. He managed to outsmart the committee, which exonerated him of pro-communist activities. The next day, Brecht left for Zurich.

In 1948, Brecht and his wife returned to East Berlin, where Brecht was put in charge of the Deutsches Theater. In the following year, he and his wife (considered one of the most effective interpreters of his work) formed the Berliner Ensemble with the help of generous subsidies from the state. Together they received Austrian citizenship in 1950. In 1954, the Berliner Ensemble moved to the Theater am Schiffbauerdamm. Brecht's last years in Berlin were devoted mostly to directing the Berliner Ensemble. He adapted plays for the ensemble and produced model stagings of his plays.

Although Brecht had an uneasy relationship with the East German government, which often criticized his plays for what it perceived to be formalism and pacifism, he did not take a public stand against the regime. In fact, during the worker uprising in June, 1953, Brecht refused to support the workers and sent a letter to Walter Ulbricht expressing his loyalty, an action that the playwright Günter Grass later criticized strongly in his play *Die Plebejer proben den Aufstand* (pr., pb. 1966; *The Plebeians Rehearse the Uprising*, 1966). Brecht died in East Berlin of a coronary thrombosis on August 14, 1956.

Analysis • Bertolt Brecht's early dramas are anarchic, nihilistic, and antibourgeois. In them, he glorifies antisocial outsiders such as adventurers, pirates, and prostitutes; the tone of these works is often cynical. In the years after his conversion to Marxism, Brecht wrote didactic plays, similar in many respects to late medieval morality plays, whose style is austere and functional. These plays were intended to be performed in schools and factories by nonprofessional actors. In his later plays, Brecht combined the vitality of his early period with his Marxist beliefs to create plays that are dramatically effective, socially committed, and peopled with realistic characters. To the end of his life, Brecht thought of the theater as both a place of entertainment and of learning. By making people aware of social abuses, he believed, literature can help make the world a better place; it can help bring the Marxist goal of a classless Utopia closer to realization.

Epic theater • Brecht is well known for his theories on epic theater. Although this concept did not originate with Brecht, he developed it into a revolutionary form of drama. (Toward the end of his life, Brecht wanted to change the name of his theater from "epic" to "dialectical," to stress the central role of argument in his plays.) Brecht summarizes his theories of epic theater in his notes to *Rise and Fall of the City of Mahagonny*; he later recapitulated and revised his theories in *Kleines Organon für das Theater* (1948; *A Little Organum for the Theater*, 1951) and in other theoretical writings.

In his notes to *Rise and Fall of the City of Mahagonny*, Brecht lists the differences he perceives between his epic theater and the Aristotelian (or dramatic) theater. Unlike dramatic theater, in which the tightly constructed plot creates suspense, epic theater uses loosely connected scenes that are set off against one another. The loose narrative structure helps to break the suspense and makes the audience focus on the course of the play, not on how the play will be resolved at the end. Brecht is extremely critical of dramatic theater: According to him, it is static; it shows universally human, that is, fixed and unchangeable, traits. Epic theater depicts the world as it changes and shows how it can be changed. It shows that human behavior can be altered. Therefore, epic theater should make people aware of social abuses and provoke them to change social evils.

Instead of activating its spectators, dramatic theater, in Brecht's view, numbs the audience by making it identify with the characters and become involved in the action. When spectators attend such plays, he remarks caustically, they hang up their brains with their coats. Brecht satirically describes the typical audience at a dramatic play, sunk into a peculiarly drugged state, wholly passive. Brecht comments that the worst gangster film shows more respect for its audience as thinking beings than does the conventional dramatic play. If people are to learn from the theater, they should be alert, rational, and socially concerned. Instead of identifying with the characters, they should remain critically aloof—certainly a necessary attitude if they are to come to grips with the ideas that Brecht presents. In his notes to *The Threepenny Opera*, Brecht expresses his wish to create a theater full of experts like those in sporting arenas. To prevent empathy, he says, theaters should allow people to smoke: He suggests that people who are puffing on cigars (Brecht himself was an inveterate cigar smoker) would be less easily carried away by events onstage.

Nevertheless, while epic theater stresses reason, it does not dispense with all emotions. In a discussion with playwright Friedrich Wolf in 1949, Brecht noted that his theater actually tries to reinforce certain emotions such as a sense of justice, the urge for freedom, and righteous anger. Although Brecht believed that the theater should teach, he stressed that it should be entertaining as well. This emphasis is apparent in his early theoretical writings such as in "Mehr guten Sport" (1926; "Emphasis on Sport"), but it becomes even more pronounced in later writings such as *A Little Organum for the Theater*, in which he notes that if the theater were turned into a purveyor of morality, it would run the risk of being debased. The function of epic theater is not to moralize but to observe and to entertain the "children of the scientific age."

Brecht uses many so-called alienation devices to prevent the audience from becoming involved in the action. *Verfremdung* (alienation) is a term that Brecht probably borrowed from Viktor Shklovsky, the leader of the Russian formalists. Alienation makes familiar things strange. In *A Little Organum for the Theater*, Brecht describes why alienation is important: Alienation effects are designed to free socially conditioned phenomena from the stamp of familiarity that protects them from being grasped. Brecht argues that when conditions have not been changed for a long time, they begin to seem impossible to change. One must therefore present the status quo in a new light in order to provoke understanding and change.

Brecht admired the Chinese theater, with its stylized acting, masks, and anti-illusionist staging; his theater is similarly anti-illusionist. Narrators, film projections, and titles comment on the action and break the suspense by indicating what is going to occur in each scene. Brecht stresses that the titles must include the social point of a particular scene. The songs that Brecht includes in his plays are not an integral part of the action, as in an opera; rather, they comment on the action. When a character is about to sing, he steps forward to the front of the stage and the lighting changes. The songs thus interrupt the course of the action and change the mood of the play. The music itself serves as an alienation device, featuring jazz rhythms and ballad forms that are not congruent with the stage action. In epic theater, the sources of lighting and scene changes are visible to the audience, and scenes are often played simultaneously to heighten the audience's awareness that it is watching a play.

The use of historical material also plays an important part in Brecht's epic theater. Brecht believed that the distancing effect of history (or geography) can make the audience more aware of the modern world: It can show that there are no universal values, that life is impermanent, that the world can be changed. Brecht notes that historical events are unique and transitory. The conduct of people in them is not fixed and universal; rather, it includes elements that have been or may be overtaken by the course of history, and it is subject to criticism from the viewpoint of the period immediately following. As a Marxist, Brecht believed in the ultimate goal of a classless Utopia, however far in the future it may be, and this belief made him optimistic about humankind's potential and about the possibility of changing society.

Brecht also focused attention on the most effective way of acting in epic theater. He rejected Konstantin Stanislavsky's method of having the actor identify with the character that he is portraying. Brecht likens the actor to a witness at an accident: The witness explains to passersby what has happened; he does not try to cast a spell but demonstrates; he alternates imitation and commentary and acts so that the bystanders can form an opinion about the accident. The actor should be a teacher; he should make the audience understand. Brecht writes that for a scene to qualify as epic, it must have socially practical significance. Through gestic acting, social attitudes can be conveyed.

Brecht's theater is realistic, although not in conventional terms. Realism, Brecht writes, lays bare society's causal network. The realistic writer shows that the dominant viewpoint is the viewpoint of the dominators; he writes from the standpoint of the class that has prepared the broadest solutions for the most pressing problems afflicting human society—that is, from the standpoint of the proletariat. Realism, as Brecht understands it, is a Marxist critique of society. His anti-illusionist theater depicts the social problems of his age. Brecht argues that literature should give the working masses a truthful representation of life.

Indeed, the notion that art should appeal to wide audiences, rather than solely to an intellectual elite, is central to Brecht's theater. For Brecht, to be popular means to be intelligible to the masses, which can be accomplished by taking over their forms of expression and enriching them. For this reason, Brecht uses folk sayings, parables, street ballads, and other folk forms in his plays. Brecht's plays also abound in biblical allusions—Martin Luther's German translation of the Bible, he confesses, was the single most important influence on his work; he admired Luther's vigorous prose.

Many of Brecht's plays were either stimulated by existing plays or parody them. Through his parodies of classical works, Brecht hoped to make his audience question middle-class values. Brecht did not believe that classical works were sacrosanct; he wanted to reshape classical works to make them relevant to present-day society, taking over verbatim what he thought was useful and then rewriting the remainder of the play. An example of such an adaptation is Shakespeare's *Coriolanus* (pr. c. 1607-1608), which Brecht changed from a personal tragedy to a history play that reflected the viewpoint of the common individual—a change of focus that he accomplished mostly by giving the plebeians a larger role.

Brecht's dramatic theories were not intended to be dogmatic. They evolved out of his practical work in the theater, and he constantly tested them, discarding them if they were not workable. This method was typical of Brecht's writing: He was always prepared to change, to adapt, to incorporate suggestions from others—even from stagehands—into his plays. The actual staging of his plays always made Brecht aware of changes that were needed to make his works dramatically effective.

Life of Galileo • Brecht's use of historical materials to illuminate contemporary problems is exemplified in one of his finest plays, *Life of Galileo*. When Brecht first became interested in Galileo, he was concerned about the fate of friends and comrades who remained in Nazi Germany and who nevertheless managed somehow to continue working. Brecht wrote three versions of the play: The first was written in 1938-1939; the second, which was an English version for the actor Charles Laughton, was written in 1945-1947; and the third was written in 1955-1956. The major difference is between the first and second versions, during which time Brecht's attitude toward Galileo changed. As in his other plays, Brecht uses many alienation devices to ensure that the audience does not identify with Galileo. He uses titles at the beginning of each scene to comment on the action. The plot is not tightly constructed. Instead, Brecht shows typical scenes in Galileo's life, beginning when Galileo is middle-aged and ending when he is an old man. Brecht's treatment of this celebrated historical figure (he sees Galileo as a pioneer of the scientific age) is intended to make his spectators see the modern world, their own world, from a critical perspective.

Like many of Brecht's characters, Galileo is a contradictory figure: He is a great scientist with a passion for the truth as well as a man with human frailties. Galileo cherishes the consolations of the flesh. He loves eating, drinking, and living a comfortable life, and he defends these habits by saying that he cannot help it if he gets his best ideas over a good meal and a bottle of wine. The pope later says that Galileo cannot refuse an old wine or a new thought. In *A Little Organum for the Theater*, Brecht remarks that Galileo thinks out of self-indulgence.

Galileo's love of good living contributes to his subsequent problems. At the beginning of the play, he is living in Venice, which pays its scientists badly but leaves them free to conduct research. To earn money, Galileo must take rich private pupils, most of whom are not intelligent. Ludovico, for example, only wants to learn about science because his mother thinks that such knowledge is necessary for conversation. Teaching such students takes away valuable time from Galileo's research. Because Galileo's request for money for his work has been refused (the Venice republic values only practical inventions), he tries to fool the government.

Ludovico tells Galileo about a new invention, a telescope, that he has seen in Holland, and Galileo then pretends that the device is his own invention. Members of the government of Venice are immediately interested in the telescope because of its military implications. Galileo soon forgets about the financial rewards for his "invention" because he suddenly grasps the value it will have for his own research in astronomy. Galileo decides to move to Florence, where scientists are better paid, but where, because of the Inquisition, he will not have the freedom to publish his findings.

Galileo is excited about the dawn of a new age that, he believes, his research will make possible. For centuries, people had believed that the Sun revolved around the earth; now Galileo can tell them the truth. His new cosmology will, however, have far-reaching social effects: It will destroy the old hierarchy of power. The old cosmology, as interpreted by the Church (which, in the play, represents authority in general), taught that people had to be satisfied with their destined places in society. The stars can no longer be used to justify some people exploiting others. Galileo predicts that astronomy will become the gossip of the marketplaces, and the sons of fishwives will pack the schools. To make his findings accessible to the common people, Galileo writes in the vernacular, not in the Latin of the elite. Because the Church recognized the revolutionary nature of Galileo's work, it banned his research.

In the first version of the play, Galileo is seen more positively than in the later versions. After he has recanted, he still manages to continue working. He outsmarts his inquisitors by pretending to be blind and works secretly on his major work, the *Discorsi*, which his disciple Andrea later smuggles out of the country under his coat: For Brecht, cunning is necessary for disseminating the truth in repressive societies. Through his cunning, Galileo has defended the truth and caused light to dawn in an era of superstition.

As Brecht was working on the second version of the play, the atom bomb was dropped on Hiroshima, and this event radically changed Brecht's attitude toward Galileo. He no longer viewed Galileo's recantation as a cunning plan to defend the truth but as a betrayal, as a shameful capitulation to reactionary forces. In his notes to the second version, Brecht describes Galileo as practicing his science secretly, like a vice, without any obligation to society. Instead of ushering in a new age, science has become allied with the forces of oppression. According to Brecht, Galileo's crime was the original sin of modern science. Out of a new astronomy that had revolutionary implications, he made a sharply limited special science, a pure science, and he was not concerned about the practical applications of his findings.

The atom bomb, Brecht notes, as a technical and social phenomenon, is the result of Galileo's social failings and his scientific accomplishment. In the second version of the play, when Andrea praises Galileo for deceiving those who perpetrated the Inquisition, Galileo denounces himself. He insists that he recanted only because he was afraid of physical pain (he was threatened with torture). Now, he says, he sees that he has betrayed his profession. He argues that in his day astronomy emerged into the marketplaces. If someone had stood and fought then, that stand could have had wide repercussions. Instead, Galileo surrendered his knowledge to the authorities—to use, or rather misuse, as they saw fit.

The revolutionary impact of Galileo's teachings is particularly evident in the carnival scene. In this scene, the ballad singer relates how Galileo's work will destroy the social hierarchy and free people. The last scene of the play, however, contrasts with the hope and excitement of the carnival scene and shows the consequences of Galileo's cowardice. Andrea is smuggling the *Discorsi* across the border. Some children are pointing to a house where they see a grotesque shadow that looks like a witch stirring something in a cauldron. They sing "Old Marina is a witch." Andrea lifts up a boy so that he can look through the window and see that the "witch" is only an old woman cooking porridge. He tries to teach him, as Galileo had taught Andrea, to rely on observation, not superstition. Nevertheless, superstition proves to be stronger; the boy cries out that Marina is a witch, even after he has seen her with his own eyes. This scene shows that the dark ages of superstition, which Galileo's science could have changed, will be difficult to overthrow. Galileo's recantation has delayed the dawn of a new age.

Mother Courage and Her Children • *Mother Courage and Her Children* also took its inspiration from contemporary events, seen from the perspective of history. Brecht finished this play in 1939 just before the outbreak of World War II. The play was loosely based on the seventeenth century novelist Hans Jakob Christoffel von Grimmelshausen's depiction of the Thirty Years' War, *Der abenteuerliche Simplicissimus* (1669; *The Adventurous Simplicissimus*, 1912). One of Grimmelshausen's characters is also called Courage, and Brecht takes from him Courage's name, her numerous husbands and lovers, and her business dealings. The play criticizes both war and business. Brecht meant to show that war is a continuation of business by other means and that it makes human virtues deadly; therefore, no sacrifice is too great to fight against war.

As her name indicates, the protagonist, Anna Fierling, is both mother and businesswoman. She is named Courage not because of an act of real courage but because she drove through the bombardment at Riga. She had to do this because she had fifty loaves of bread that she needed to sell quickly because they were becoming moldy. Mother Courage tries unsuccessfully to protect her three children, Eilif, Swiss Cheese, and Kattrin (each of whom has a different father), from the war, but her motherly instincts often conflict with her business instincts—her wagon, which is both a home and refuge for herself and her children, as well as her place of business, shows how inextricably her roles of businesswoman and mother are intertwined. Yet she does not always consider profit first. Toward the end of the play, when her fortunes are at a low point, she refuses the cook's offer to escape from the war to a small inn that he has inherited because he will not let her take her daughter Kattrin with her. In this case, Mother Courage acts against her own best interests.

One by one, Mother Courage loses her children. In the first scene, her oldest son, Eilif, is taken away by the recruiting officer, who tempts him with tales of the glory of war while Mother Courage's attention is diverted by the sergeant, who says that he wants to buy a buckle. When Swiss Cheese is arrested by the Roman Catholic soldiers, who try to make him surrender the regimental cash box entrusted to him by the Protestants, Mother Courage bargains to free him. She is willing to pawn her wagon, hoping to find the cash box and redeem it. After she discovers that Swiss Cheese has thrown it into the river, she is faced with a dilemma: How can she and Kattrin survive without the wagon? She is actually prepared to sacrifice her wagon, but she haggles too long, and Swiss Cheese is shot. When Eilif is arrested, she is away on business and cannot help him. Kattrin is sent into town to fetch supplies for her mother and is attacked on the way back. When Kattrin is killed, Mother Courage is away at the market, taking advantage of those who are fleeing and selling their possessions cheaply. In each of these cases, she loses her children because she is involved in business activities.

Although Brecht intends the audience to be critical of Mother Courage, she is still, in many respects, a sympathetic figure, despite her negative qualities. She is cunning and tenacious and has an earthy sense of humor. Throughout the play, she debunks heroism. When Eilif is praised by his commander for his heroic deed of stealing cattle, she boxes Eilif's ears: She tells him that he should have surrendered and not exposed himself to danger, as the peasants who owned the cattle were in the majority. Later, she argues that only poor commanders need to demand heroism of their men: Good commanders can manage without it. To survive in this world, she believes, one must be unobtrusive, not heroic. Mother Courage also sees clearly why the war is being fought. The commanders speak as though they are fighting for religion, but Mother Courage remarks that they are not so stupid; they are actually fighting only for profit.

Mother Courage's wagon symbolizes her waning fortunes: At the beginning of the play, the wagon looks prosperous and is pulled by Eilif and Swiss Cheese; at the end, it is dilapidated and pulled by Mother Courage alone. Brecht emphasizes that Mother Courage does not learn from her experiences. Only in the scene in which Kattrin is attacked does she curse the war. Usually, however, she is worried that the war could end when she has just bought supplies, which would bring about her financial ruin. After the Zurich premiere in 1941, Brecht changed parts of the play to make Mother Courage's disagreeable traits more emphatic, since the Zurich audience had seen her as a tragic figure who was simply trying to survive.

In a conversation with the playwright Friedrich Wolf, Brecht defended his portrayal of Mother Courage. (He had been criticized for depicting her as unable to learn from her mistakes.) Brecht told Wolf that he was a realist, that he was not convinced that people would learn from the war he saw coming when he was writing the play. He hoped, however, that the audience could learn from watching Mother Courage. According to Brecht, Mother Courage is free to choose whether to take part in the war, yet the scope of the war, which seems to fill the whole world, suggests that she really has no viable alternative—she can either wait for the war to reach her, or she can try to earn her living from it. There seems to be no place where she could be safe to lead a peaceful life.

The deaths of her children show that virtue is dangerous. The heroic Eilif is executed for stealing cattle and killing, deeds for which he was praised in wartime. Ironically, he is executed when the war has broken out again and when his action would again have been considered heroic, but the soldiers who execute him are unaware that the war is on again. Swiss Cheese is executed for his honesty in trying to save the cash box. Kattrin is killed because she is humane. Even though Kattrin is dumb, according to Brecht she should not be played as though she were an idiot. She is perfectly normal; it is the world that surrounds her that is abnormal. Kattrin desperately wants children but will never be able to marry because of the disfiguring scar that remains from her having been attacked. The war also made her dumb, since a soldier shoved something in her mouth when she was a child. Because of her motherliness, she is in constant danger.

In the scene in which "the stone begins to speak," soldiers are preparing to attack a town where people are asleep and unaware of danger. To save the children in the town, Kattrin takes a drum and climbs up onto a roof where she beats the drum loudly to alert the town to the danger. She is shot, but she saves the town. Her positive action is contrasted with the futile actions of the peasants, whose only thought is to pray to God for help.

Brecht did not choose World War I for his setting—he thought that the war was still too recent for an audience to observe the events on the stage dispassionately and to learn from the play. The Thirty Years' War was the most destructive war in German history before World War I; in his notes to the play, Brecht writes that this was the first large-scale war that capitalism had brought to Europe. Brecht was not interested in the history of "important" people such as kings, princes, and generals (no historical character appears on the stage) but in the perspective of the common person, whom history usually ignores. Throughout the play, Brecht satirizes those who are in charge of conducting the war. The commander Tilly, who is given a hero's funeral, actually died, Mother Courage says, because he lost his way in the mist and went to the front by mistake. Brecht also shows that victory and defeat for the commanders does not always mean victory and defeat for the common people—for example, Tilly's victory at Magdeburg costs Mother Courage four shirts.

In addition to the historical setting, Brecht used several other alienation devices in the play. The titles before each scene break the suspense and are intended to encourage a critical attitude in the audience. As in *The Life of Galileo*, the scenes are loosely connected and the time span is long (twelve years). Brecht includes songs to comment on the action: The song that Mother Courage sings at the beginning and at the end of the play is an ironic commentary on this war of "religion," while her "Song of the Great Capitulation" describes life as full of broken hopes and dreams.

The mood of the play is basically pessimistic. Even after she has lost her family, Mother Courage still believes in the war: Neither she nor anyone else has learned anything by the play's end. Instead, the war continues, people continue to be killed, and some (though not Mother Courage) make profits.

The Caucasian Chalk Circle • *The Caucasian Chalk Circle*, which was written in 1944-1945, was based on the story of Solomon in the Bible and on a thirteenth century Chinese drama by Li Xingdao, which was adapted as *Der Kreidekreis* by the playwright Klabund in 1925. As in his other plays, Brecht includes many alienation effects. The play consists of three stories: The first takes place in the twentieth century; the other two stories, those of Grusche and Azdak, take place in medieval Russian Georgia (Grusinia). Brecht also used a singer/narrator to comment on the play-within-a-play, and the actors wear masks.

The first scene takes place in Russian Georgia just after the defeat of Adolf Hitler. The owners of the land, a collective that raises goats, fled from Hitler's soldiers, while the neighboring collective stayed and fought. The members of this neighboring collective now want the land formerly used for goat-raising; they intend to grow fruit trees there and have designed an irrigation scheme for that purpose. The old owners, however, want the land returned to them. Together, the two collectives discuss the conflict peacefully and rationally and decide that the fruit growers should have the land. Goats can be raised anywhere, but only here is the topography of the land suitable for the irrigation plans. To celebrate this decision, the members of the fruit-growers' collective act the play of the chalk circle.

The first part of this play-within-a-play tells of the shrewd and good-hearted servant girl Grusche. In medieval Georgia, she works for the governor and his wife, who have an infant son Michel. At first, the mother seems to be overly solicitous about her child's welfare. She is worried when he coughs or is exposed to drafts, and she is always accompanied by two doctors. When the Revolution breaks out, however, she is so busy deciding which dresses she should take on her flight that she forgets to take her son. At first, Grusche is reluctant to take the baby—it is too dangerous to do so because the soldiers are seeking to kill him. As the singer says, however, she is overcome by the terrible temptation to goodness, and she flees with the child.

Through her work and sacrifice for the child, Grusche gradually becomes more and more a mother to him. In her flight from the soldiers with him, she faces danger and hardship. She seeks refuge in her brother's house, where she claims that the child is hers and invents a husband who is fighting in the war. When the husband does not arrive to fetch her, her brother's wife, a "pious" person (always a term of criticism in Brecht's works), begins to become suspicious that the child is illegitimate; she fears that Grusche will become the object of gossip and shame the family. Grusche's brother arranges a marriage for her with a supposedly dying man, but once the "deathly ill" man hears that the war is over, he revives—he had pretended to be ill to avoid fighting. For the sake of the child, Grusche is now tied to a disagreeable husband. When Grusche's fiancé, Simon, returns from the war, Grusche again claims that the child is hers, preferring Simon to believe that she has been unfaithful to him than have the soldiers take away the child.

The Grusche story is interrupted at this point, and the Azdak story is begun. Azdak is a sort of Lord of Misrule, one of Brecht's cunning rogues. During a time of revolution, he has unwittingly given refuge to a beggar, who turns out to be the fleeing grand duke. Through an improbable series of events, Azdak is made a judge. During his tenure, he proves to be corrupt, licentious, and contemptuous of the law, yet often he turns the law upside down to help the poor. In one case, Azdak acquits a doctor who has operated free of charge on a poor patient: Despite the doctor's professional incompetence (he operated on the wrong leg), his motives were good. In another case, a landlord brings an action against a stable boy for raping his daughter-in-law. Azdak takes one look at the voluptuous daughter-in-law and declares that the stable boy is innocent—he is the one who has been raped. Another case concerns a poor widow who is accused of receiving stolen goods. She claims that Saint Banditus has given her the goods. Azdak fines the rich farmers who brought the suit against her: They do not believe in miracles; they are impious. It must be a miracle, Azdak reasons, if the poor are helped. In these decisions, Azdak intentionally disregards the actual law in order to administer a rough justice that helps the poor.

The last part of the play brings together the Azdak and the Grusche stories in a trial scene in which both Grusche and the governor's wife claim to be the mother of the child (Brecht had a predilection for trial scenes because of the central role of argument in them). The governor's wife has assembled lawyers to fight for her child, and Grusche and Simon represent themselves. It turns out that the governor's wife is only interested in her child because of what he will inherit. Without him, she is poor. Azdak listens to the arguments on both sides, berates Simon and Grusche for not having money to bribe him, and, finally, draws a chalk circle on the floor. He puts Michel in the middle and orders the two women to hold the child by the hand. The real mother, he tells them, will have the strength to pull the child out of the circle. Both times, Grusche lets go for fear of hurting the child, while the real mother pulls him out of the circle with all her strength. In a reversal of the Solomon story, Azdak decides that Grusche should have the child because she, and not the real mother, actually cares for the child.

In his last action as judge, Azdak decides the case of an old couple who want a divorce. By "mistake" he divorces Grusche from her husband so that she can marry Simon, justifying his action by saying that because the old people have lived together for so long, they would be better to continue living together. Unlike most of Brecht's plays, this play-within-a-play ends happily. Grusche is reunited with Simon and keeps the child. To be a biological mother alone is not enough, according to Azdak; one must actually love and make sacrifices for a child, as Grusche has done.

In his notes to the play, Brecht mentioned that there is an American expression "sucker," and that this is what Grusche is when she takes the child: The more she does for the child, the more her own life is endangered. The biblical allusions in the Grusche story (the birth of Christ and the flight into Egypt, for example), together with Azdak's wise and humane judgments, indicate that a new age is dawning. Azdak's decision to give Grusche the child because she is good for him brings the play-within-a-play back to the peacefully resolved dispute in the first scene. In a similar manner, the fruit growers are given the land because they will make it more productive. The promise of a new age has been fulfilled in the first scene—a Socialist Utopia has been reached.

Other major works

LONG FICTION: *Der Dreigroschenroman,* 1934 (*The Threepenny Novel,* 1937, 1956); *Die Geschäfte des Herrn Julius Caesar,* 1956.

SHORT FICTION: *Geschichten von Herrn Keuner,* 1930, 1958 (*Stories of Mr. Keuner,* 2001); *Kalendergeschichten,* 1948 (*Tales from the Calendar,* 1961); *Me-ti: Buch der Wendungen,* 1965; *Prosa,* 1965 (5 volumes); *Collected Stories,* 1998.

POETRY: *Hauspostille,* 1927, 1951 (*Manual of Piety,* 1966); *Lieder, Gedichte, Chöre,* 1934 (*Songs, Poems, Choruses,* 1976); *Svendborger Gedichte,* 1939 (*Svendborg Poems,* 1976); *Selected Poems,* 1947; *Hundert Gedichte,* 1951 (*A Hundred Poems,* 1976); *Gedichte und Lieder,* 1956 (*Poems and Songs,* 1976); *Gedichte,* 1960-1965 (9 volumes); *Bertolt Brecht: Poems, 1913-1956,* 1976 (includes *Buckower Elegies*); *Bad Time for Poetry: 152 Poems and Songs,* 1995.

SCREENPLAYS: *Kuhle Wampe,* 1932 (English translation, 1933); *Hangmen Also Die,* 1943; *Das Lied der Ströme,* 1954; *Herr Puntila und sein Knecht, Matti,* 1955.

NONFICTION: *Der Messingkauf,* 1937-1951 (*The Messingkauf Dialogues,* 1965); *Kleines Organon für das Theater,* 1948 (*A Little Organum for the Theater,* 1951); *Schriften zum Theater,* 1963-1964 (7 volumes); *Brecht on Theatre,* 1964; *Arbeitsjournal, 1938-1955,* 1973 (3 volumes; *Bertolt Brecht Journals,* 1993); *Tagebucher, 1920-1922,* 1975 (*Diaries, 1920-1922,* 1979); *Letters,* 1990; *Brecht on Film and Radio,* 2000.

Bibliography

Bodek, Richard. *Proletarian Performance in Weimar Berlin: Agitprop, Chorus, and Brecht.* Columbia, S.C.: Camden House, 1997. A study of proletarian theater and agitprop theater in Berlin, with emphasis on Brecht.

Fuegi, John. *Brecht and Company: Sex, Politics, and the Making of the Modern Drama.* New York: Grove, 1994. Fuegi is a professor of comparative literature at the University of Maryland and founder of the International Brecht Society and has published two previous books on Brecht. According to Fuegi, his newest work, dealing at great length not only with Brecht but also with a wide circle of his associates and collaborators, is the result of twenty-five years of research.

Giles, Steve, and Rodney Livingstone, eds. *Bertolt Brecht: Centenary Essays.* Atlanta, Ga.: Rodopi, 1998. A collection of essays on Brecht written one hundred years after his birth. Bibliography.

Jameson, Fredric. *Brecht and Method.* New York: Verso, 1998. A major neo-Marxist literary theorist assesses the position of one of the twentieth century's central figures in dramatic literature as a modernist and postmodernist thinker.

Thomson, Peter. *Brecht: "Mother Courage and Her Children."* Plays in Production series. New York: Cambridge University Press, 1997. An examination of the stage history and dramatic production of *Mother Courage and Her Children,* the conclusion of which was written by Viv Gardner. Bibliography and index.

Thomson, Peter, and Glendyr Sacks, eds. *The Cambridge Companion to Brecht.* Cambridge Companions to Literature series. New York: Cambridge University Press, 1994. This extensive reference work contains a wealth of information on Brecht. Bibliography and index.

Willett, John. *Brecht in Context: Comparative Approaches.* Rev. ed. London: Methuen, 1998. A comparative analysis of the works of Brecht. Bibliography and index.

Jennifer Michaels

George Gordon, Lord Byron

Born: London, England; January 22, 1788
Died: Missolonghi, Greece; April 19, 1824

Principal drama • *Manfred*, pb. 1817, pr. 1834; *Marino Faliero, Doge of Venice*, pr., pb. 1821; *Sardanapalus: A Tragedy*, pb. 1821, pr. 1834; *The Two Foscari: A Tragedy*, pb. 1821, pr. 1837; *Cain: A Mystery*, pb. 1821 (with *Sardanapalus* and *The Two Foscari*); *Heaven and Earth*, pb. 1822 (fragment); *Werner: Or, The Inheritance*, pb. 1823, pr. 1830; *The Deformed Transformed*, pb. 1824 (fragment)

Other literary forms • George Gordon, Lord Byron, is considerably better known as a poet than as a dramatist, and the relative importance of the poetry is quickly evident in any review of Byron's literary career. His first book, *Fugitive Pieces*, was printed at his own expense in November of 1806, and though it consisted primarily of sentimental and mildly erotic verse, it also contained hints of the satiric wit that would be so important to Byron's later reputation. The volume is also notable for having inspired the first accusations that Byron lacked poetic chastity; at the urging of some of his friends, he withdrew the book from private circulation and replaced it with the more morally upright *Poems on Various Occasions*, printed in Newark in January of 1807 by John Ridge, who had also printed *Fugitive Pieces*.

In his first attempt at public recognition as a man of letters, Byron published *Hours of Idleness* in June of 1807. The volume shows the obvious influence of a number of Augustan and Romantic poets, but despite its largely derivative nature, it received several favorable early reviews. Fortunately for Byron's development as a poet, however, the praise was not universal, and subsequent critical attacks, notably by Henry Brougham of *The Edinburgh Review*, helped inspire the writing of Byron's first poetic triumph, *English Bards and Scotch Reviewers* (1809). In the tradition of Alexander Pope's *The Dunciad* (1728-1743) but written under the more direct influence of *Baviad* (1794) and *Maeviad* (1795), by William Gifford, *English Bards and Scotch Reviewers* is the earliest significant example of Byron's satiric genius. Three more satiric poems soon followed, but none of these—*Hints from Horace* (1811), *The Curse of Minerva* (1812), and *Waltz: An Apostrophic Hymn* (1813)—attracted as much admiring attention as *English Bards and Scotch Reviewers*.

During this same period, Byron was composing the poem with which he would be most closely associated during his lifetime and which would make him the most lionized literary figure of his day, *Childe Harold's Pilgrimage*, Cantos I-IV (1812-1818, 1819). The first two cantos of the poem, an imaginative meditation loosely based on two years of travel on the Continent, were published on March 10, 1812, and produced an immediate sensation. In his own words, Byron "awoke one morning and found myself famous." Cantos III and IV were greeted with equal excitement and confirmed the identification of Byron in the popular mind with his poem's gloomy protagonist.

In the meantime, Byron published a series of poetic tales that further exploited the knowledge derived from his Eastern travels and that continued the development of the Byronic hero, the brooding, titanic figure whose prototype within Byron's canon is Childe Harold. These tales include *The Giaour* (1813), *The Bride of Abydos* (1813), *The*

116

Corsair (1814), *Lara* (1814), *Parisina* (1816), and *The Siege of Corinth* (1816). Illustrative of the diversity of Byron's poetic output is the publication, during this same period, of *Hebrew Melodies Ancient and Modern* (1815), short lyrics based largely on passages from the Bible and accompanied by the music of Isaac Nathan. Although Byron lacked the lyric mastery of a number of his extraordinary contemporaries, he produced well-crafted lyrics throughout his literary career, none of which is more admired or more often quoted than the first poem of *Hebrew Melodies Ancient and Modern*, "She Walks in Beauty."

Also published in 1816 was "The Prisoner of Chillon," a dramatic monologue on the theme of human freedom, which Byron was inspired to write after a visit to the castle where François de Bonivard had been imprisoned during the sixteenth century. *The Lament of Tasso* (1817), written during the following year, is a less successful variation on the same theme and, more important, an early manifestation of Byron's fascination with the literature and history of Italy. This fascination is also seen in *The Prophecy of Dante* (1821), "Francesca of Rimini" (inspired by Canto V of Dante's *Inferno*), and the translation of Canto I of Luigi Pulci's *Morgante Maggiore* (1483), which were produced in the years 1819 and 1820.

The importance of Pulci to Byron's poetic career is immeasurable. Through *Whistlecraft* (1817-1818), by John Hookham Frere, Byron became indirectly acquainted with the casual, facetious manner of the *Morgante Maggiore* and adapted the Pulci/Frere style to his own purposes in his immensely successful tale of Venetian dalliance, *Beppo: A Venetian Story*. Written in 1817 and published in 1818, *Beppo* is the direct stylistic precursor of *Don Juan*, Cantos I-XVI (1819-1824, 1826), the seriocomic masterpiece whose composition occupied Byron at irregular intervals throughout the last six years of his life.

Although the final years of Byron's literary career are important primarily for the writing of *Don Juan*, several of Byron's other works deserve passing or prominent mention. *Mazeppa* (1819) is a verse tale in Byron's earlier manner that treats heavy-handedly a theme that the first cantos of *Don Juan* address with an adroit lightness: the disastrous consequences of an illicit love. *The Island* (1823) is a romantic tale inspired by William Bligh's account of the *Bounty* mutiny, a tale that possesses some affinities with the Haidée episode of *Don Juan*. The years from 1821 to 1823 produced three topical satires, *The Blues: A Literary Eclogue* (written in 1821 but first published in *The Liberal* in 1823), *The Vision of Judgment* (1822), and *The Age of Bronze* (1823), the second of which, a devastating response to Robert Southey's obsequious *A Vision of Judgment*, is one of Byron's undoubted masterworks.

Finally, no account of Byron's nondramatic writings would be com-

(Library of Congress)

plete without making reference to his correspondence, among the finest in the English language, which has been given its definitive form in Leslie A. Marchand's multivolume edition, *Byron's Letters and Journals* (1973-1982).

Achievements • In his *The Dramas of Lord Byron: A Critical Study* (1915), Samuel C. Chew, Jr., makes it abundantly clear that George Gordon, Lord Byron, was simultaneously fascinated with the theater and contemptuous of the accomplishments of contemporary dramatists. He was frequently to be found in the playhouses, especially during his days as a student and during the period immediately following his Eastern travels, and on at least two occasions, he acted, with considerable success, in amateur theatrical productions. His comments on the stage suggest, however, that he was appalled by the reliance of early nineteenth century playwrights on melodramatic sensationalism and visual spectacle.

Byron's letters mention the scarcity of fine plays, and his poetry castigates modern dramatists for their tastelessness. *English Bards and Scotch Reviewers*, for example, calls contemporary drama a "motley sight" and deplores the "degradation of our vaunted stage." It cries out to George Colman and Richard Cumberland to "awake!" and implores Richard Brinsley Sheridan, who had achieved a recent success with *Pizarro: A Tragedy in Five Acts* (pr. 1799), an adaptation of a play by August von Kotzebue, to "Abjure the mummery of the German schools" and instead to "reform the stage." It asks, in indignant mockery, "Shall sapient managers new scenes produce/ From Cherry, Skeffington, and Mother Goose?" and makes sneering reference to the extravagances of Matthew Gregory "Monk" Lewis's *The Castle Spectre* (pr. 1797). It suggests, on the whole, that the once glorious English theater is in woeful decline.

Despite Byron's sense of the theater's decay, or perhaps because of it, evidence exists, in epistolary references to destroyed manuscripts and in a surviving fragment or two of attempted drama, that, as early as 1813-1814, he had ambitions of becoming a playwright, but he had completed nothing for the stage when, in 1815, he was appointed a member of the Drury Lane Committee of Management. Although he found his committee work "really good fun," it did nothing to improve his opinion of the taste of contemporary dramatists and their audiences, and when he finally finished a dramatic work, it was not intended for popular presentation.

Like the rest of his completed drama, *Manfred* was written during Byron's final, self-imposed exile from England. Begun in Switzerland and finished in Venice, the play is psychosymbolic rather than realistic and may have been inspired, as any number of commentators have pointed out, by Byron's acquaintance with Johann Wolfgang von Goethe's *Faust: Eine Tragödie* (pb. 1808, pb. 1833; *The Tragedy of Faust*, 1823, 1828). Byron appears to have known of Goethe's masterpiece through translated passages in Madame de Staël's *De l'Allemagne* (1810) and through an extensive oral translation by Monk Lewis during a visit to the poet in August of 1816.

Considerable controversy has occurred, however, over the extent of *Faust*'s influence on *Manfred*, the consensus now being that *Faust* is simply one of many sources of the play's intricate materials, albeit an important one. Chew makes mention of Vicomte Françoise Auguste-René de Chateaubriand's *René* (1802, 1805; English translation, 1813), Goethe's *The Sorrows of Young Werther* (1774), Horace Walpole's *The Castle of Otranto* (1764) and *The Mysterious Mother* (1768), Samuel Taylor Coleridge's *Remorse* (1813), John Robert Maturin's *Bertram: Or, The Castle of St. Aldobrand* (1816), William Beckford's *Vathek* (1782), and Lewis's *The Monk* (1796) as other works with which *Manfred* has affinities and from which borrowings may have occurred. More important, however, *Manfred* is a cathartic projection of Byron's own troubled psyche, an attempt, which some critics have called Promethean rather than Faustian, to cope with the seemingly unconquerable presence of evil in the world, to deal with his frustrated aspirations toward an unattainable ideal, and, on a more mundane level, to come to terms with his confused feelings toward his half sister Augusta.

With respect to *Manfred*'s place in theatrical history, Malcolm Kelsall, in *The Byron Journal* (1978), has made an excellent case for grouping Byron's play both with *Faust* and with Henrik Ibsen's *Peer Gynt* (pb. 1867; English translation, 1892). Kelsall states that "the new kind of stage envisaged" in these plays

> is unfettered by any kind of limitation of place, and that assault, which is as much upon the conceived possibilities of stage allusion as upon unity of place, demands of the imagination that it supply constantly shifting visual correlatives for the inner turmoil of the hero's mind.

Byron's next play, *Marino Faliero, Doge of Venice*, is of an entirely different sort and ushers in a period in which Byron attempted to return to classical dramatic principles to produce plays whose themes are essentially political. He sought to counteract the undisciplined bombast and sprawling display of the drama with which he had become familiar in England by making use, without becoming anyone's slavish disciple, of theatrical techniques exploited by the ancient Greeks and Romans, the neoclassical French, and the contemporary Italians, notably Conte Vittorio Alfieri.

Because Byron did this during a time when his involvement in Italian political intrigue was beginning to develop, Byron's decision to center his play on Marino Faliero, the fourteenth century doge of Venice who was executed for conspiring to overthrow the oppressive aristocratic class to which he himself belonged, is hardly surprising. He wrote the play as a closet drama—to be read rather than staged—considering its classical regularity an impossible barrier to its popular success, and he was furious when he learned of Drury Lane's intention of producing it. As he summarized the matter in a journal entry of January 12, 1821, how could anything please contemporary English theatergoers that contained "nothing melodramatic—no surprises, no starts, nor trapdoors, nor opportunities 'for tossing of their heads and kicking their heels'—and no *love*—the grand ingredient of a modern play"?

In *Sardanapalus*, Byron extended his experimentation with classical regularity and continued his exploration of political themes while at the same time appealing in two particular ways to popular taste. The play's setting, ancient Nineveh, accorded well with popular interest in Eastern exoticism, an interest that Byron's own Eastern tales had intensified, and the devotion of the slave Myrrha to Nineveh's troubled ruler satisfied the public's desire to witness pure, selfless love.

The Two Foscari, the third of the classically constructed political plays, again makes use of Venice for its setting. Although generally considered to be less successful than the earlier of the Venetian dramas, *The Two Foscari* contains autobiographical elements, embodied in Jacopo Foscari, that give a certain fascination to the play. Jacopo, after a youth of aristocratic gaiety, has been unjustly exiled from his native land. He had been the boon companion of the city's most promising young men, had been admired for his athletic vigor, particularly in swimming, and had drawn the attention of the city's most beautiful young women. Then the powerful had intrigued against him, and his banishment had begun. Byron's contemporaries could hardly have missed the personal significance of this situation or have overlooked the note of defiant anguish in such an exchange as the following:

> GUARD: And can you so much love the soil which
>   hates you?
> JAC. FOS: The soil!—Oh no, it is the seed of the soil
> Which persecutes me; but my native earth
> Will take me as a mother to her arms.

Jacopo's persecution is carried out as an act of vengeance by an enemy of the Foscari family, an act that corrupts its perpetrator, but unlike Percy Bysshe Shelley's *The Cenci* (pb. 1819), whose theme is much the same, *The Two Foscari* is not effective theater.

Cain was published as part of a volume that also contained *Sardanapalus* and *The Two Foscari*, but it ought instead to be grouped with *Heaven and Earth*, which was written at about the same time but whose publication was delayed because of the controversy inspired by *Cain*. In *Cain* and *Heaven and Earth*, Byron returned to the style of *Manfred*, but he derived his materials from biblical lore and from previous literary treatments of these same stories. He called the plays "mysteries," a reference both to the medieval mystery plays and to the mystified response Byron was expecting from the general public. *Cain* is a reinterpretation of the tale of the primal murder, a reinterpretation in which Cain is clearly the superior of his brother Abel and kills his brother, as Chew observes, in an "instinctive assertion of freedom against the limitations of fate." *Heaven and Earth* is based on the passage in Genesis that states that "the sons of God saw the daughters of men that they were fair; and they took them wives of all which they chose." Its plot culminates in the nearly total destruction of the flood, a destruction so general and arbitrary that the play becomes, in Chew's summary, "a subtle attack on the justice of the Most High."

Werner was much more in keeping with the literary tastes of the time than Byron's other plays, a fact that can be at least partially explained by its having been begun in 1815, during the period of Byron's closest association with Drury Lane. A surprisingly faithful rendering of "The German's Tale" from Sophia and Harriet Lee's *The Canterbury Tales* (1797-1805), *Werner* centers on the title character and his perfidious son, Ulric, an ambitious villain of the deepest dye. Making no pretense of adhering to the classical unities, the play moves with gothic ponderousness toward its dark conclusion, in which Ulric is revealed to be the cold-blooded murderer of his own fiancée's father, Stralenheim, the one man who stood between Ulric's family and their return to hereditary wealth and power.

The Deformed Transformed is one of Byron's two dramatic fragments (the other being *Heaven and Earth*). As its prefatory "Advertisement" states, Byron based it on Joshua Pickersgill's novel *The Three Brothers* (1803) and on Goethe's *Faust*. Chew points out the autobiographical significance of Byron's adding lameness to the other deformities from which his central character, Arnold, escapes by dealing with the Devil, but the play's incompleteness and incoherence make it difficult to comment further on Byron's dramatic intention. The fragment was composed in 1822 and published in February of 1824 by John Hunt.

The history of Byron's plays in theatrical production appears largely to be a tale of creative misinterpretation in the twentieth century and commercial adaptation and exploitation in the nineteenth. Margaret Howell's 1974 account in *The Byron Journal* of Charles Kean's June 13, 1853, production of *Sardanapalus* is particularly instructive. Reduced from its full length of 2,835 lines to 1,563, the play was presented almost solely as spectacle and required the approval of the local fire inspectors, because of one of its more impressive effects, before it could be performed. The production seems to have embodied everything that most disgusted Byron about London theater.

Biography • Born in London, England, on January 22, 1788, George Gordon, Lord Byron, who, from birth suffered from a deformed foot, was the son of Captain John Byron, nicknamed "Mad Jack" because of his wild ways, and the former Catherine Gordon. On his mother's side, the poet claimed descent from James I of Scotland and on his father's, with less certainty, from Ernegis and Radulfus de Burun, estate owners in the days of William the Conqueror. Newstead Abbey, which the poet would inherit at age ten as the sixth Lord Byron, had been granted to Sir John Byron by King Henry VIII, though the title of lord was first held by General John Byron, follower of Charles I and Charles II, the latter of whom is said to have seduced the general's wife. The poet received the title on the death, in 1798, of his great-uncle, William Byron, nicknamed "the Wicked Lord."

Because the poet's grandfather, Admiral John Byron, himself something of a rake, had disinherited Mad Jack for his even greater irresponsibility and because his father, before his death at age thirty-six, had squandered nearly all the wealth of both of the heiresses he had married, the poet's earliest years were spent in genteel poverty in his mother's native Aberdeen, Scotland, where he attended Aberdeen Grammar School. During these years, he developed his lifelong interests in both athletics and reading and was imbued, under the influence of his nurse, Agnes Gray, and his Presbyterian instructors, with the sense of predestined evil that marked so much of his later life.

After coming into his inheritance in 1798, Byron and his mother moved to Nottinghamshire, the location of Newstead Abbey, in which the young lord proudly took up residence despite the warning of John Hanson, the family attorney, that the abbey was in such disrepair that it ought not to be lived in. During 1799, Byron's clubfoot was incompetently treated by a local quack physician, Dr. Lavender, and Byron was physically and sexually abused by his new nurse, May Gray, events that left the poet with permanent emotional scars. Later in the same year, Byron was taken to London to be treated by a more reputable physician. He was also placed in the Dulwich boarding school of Dr. Glennie, who was to prepare young Byron for admission to Harrow.

Byron entered Harrow in April of 1801, and despite an occasional period of haughty aloofness, he soon became a favorite of his schoolmates. Some of his most intense friendships dated from his Harrow days, friendships the intensity of which was probably an expression, as his biographers have pointed out, of his fundamentally bisexual nature. Nevertheless, the instances of Byron's overt amatory passion, especially early in his life, more often involved women than men. He had become infatuated with a cousin, Mary Duff, perhaps as early as age seven; had written his first love poetry for another cousin, Margaret Parker, at age twelve; and had fallen so deeply in love with Mary Chaworth during a hiatus in Nottinghamshire in 1803 that he at first refused to return to Harrow. Nevertheless, he did return, and after completing his course of studies, he enrolled in Trinity College, Cambridge, during the fall of 1805.

During his Cambridge days, Byron formed romantic attachments with two male friends, won acceptance by the university's liberal intellectual elite, kept a bear in his living quarters, and became thoroughly acquainted with the distractions of London, including the theater. He also assembled his first books of poetry, most notably *Hours of Idleness*, and, almost incidentally, earned a Cambridge master's degree, which was granted in July of 1808. After a short retirement to Newstead Abbey, during which he worked on *English Bards and Scotch Reviewers*, Byron left for London, where he became a member of the House of Lords on March 13, 1809, and where *English Bards and Scotch Reviewers* was anonymously published several days thereafter. The authorship of the scathing satire was soon discovered, and Byron had the satisfaction of being lauded for his poem by Gifford and others before his departure on July 2, 1809, for his Continental tour.

Traveling with John Cam Hobhouse and several retainers, Byron disembarked in Lisbon and made the journey to Seville and later to Cádiz by horseback. The frigate *Hyperion* then took them to Gibraltar, after which they sailed for Malta, where he managed a romantic interlude with the fascinating Mrs. Constance Spencer Smith. The brig *Spider* next delivered them to Patras and Prevesa in Greece, then ruled by the Turks, from which they set out for Janina, capital of the kingdom of the barbarous Ali Pasha, sovereign of western Greece and Albania and prototype of *Don Juan*'s piratical Lambro. Ali Pasha's court was located seventy-five miles away, in Tepelene, where Byron arrived on October 19, 1809, and where the colorful ruler flattered the young poet with an audience. The Tepelene adventure was one of the most memorable of Byron's memorable life, and when he returned to Janina, he began *Childe Harold's Pilgrimage* in an attempt to capture the poetic essence of his travels.

Following his perilous return to Patras by way of Missolonghi, where he was to die fifteen years later, Byron journeyed on to Athens, stopping first at Mount Parnassus and writing several stanzas to commemorate the event. In Athens itself, he and Hobhouse lived with the Macri family, whose twelve-year-old Theresa was immortalized by Byron as "the Maid of Athens." The two travelers explored the city and its historic surroundings from Christmas Day, 1809, through March 5, 1810. The sloop *Pylades* then carried them to Smyrna, where they took a side trip to Ephesus, after which they embarked for Constantinople aboard the frigate *Salsette*. On May 3, 1810, during a pause in the voyage, Byron swam the Hellespont from Sestos to Abydos, an accomplishment about which he would never tire of boasting.

Byron's stay in Constantinople brought him further invaluable knowledge of the decadent splendors of the East and also involved him in several petty disputes over matters of protocol, disputes in which Byron's aristocratic arrogance, one of his least attractive traits, came repulsively to the fore. Such matters appear to have been smoothed over, however, by the time Byron left Constantinople on July 14, 1810.

Hobhouse returned directly to England, but Byron spent the next several months in Greece, where he added to his sexual conquests, contracted a venereal disease, saved a young woman from threatened execution, and continued his exploration of a country for whose freedom he was eventually to offer up his life. On April 22, 1811, he sailed from Greece for Malta, where he temporarily renewed his affair with Mrs. Smith, and then returned home to England, stepping ashore on July 14, 1811.

Within a month of his landing, Byron's mother died, an event that caused him considerable distress despite the uneasy relationship that had long existed between them. The year also brought news of the deaths of three of Byron's closest friends. The poet dealt with his grief as best he could and continued preparations for the publication of *Childe Harold's Pilgrimage*, Cantos I and II. He also resumed his place in the House of Lords, delivering his maiden speech on February 27, 1812, an effective denunciation of a bill requiring the execution of frame breakers (workers who violently resisted the mechanization of the weaving trade). Byron delivered two more parliamentary speeches, on April 21, 1812, and June 1, 1813, but the sudden fame that *Childe Harold's*

Pilgrimage brought him after its appearance on March 10, 1812, drew his attention away from politics and changed his life forever.

The immediate effect of Byron's renown was that he became the most sought-after guest in London society and the most avidly pursued of handsome bachelors. In particular, Lady Caroline Lamb, despite being already married, descended on him with extraordinary enthusiasm. She found him "mad—bad—and dangerous to know," a description that might, with equal or greater justice, have been applied to Lady Caroline herself. Their tempestuous liaison occupied much of Byron's attention during the spring and summer of 1812 and involved indiscreet meetings, plans of elopement, threats of suicide, and a great deal of public scandal. Although they parted in September, to Byron's infinite relief, occasional storms broke out in the months thereafter.

During the years 1812 and 1813, Byron began the series of Oriental tales that would solidify his literary fame and involved himself in affairs with various other women, most peculiarly and most deeply with his half sister, Mrs. Augusta Leigh. He spent much of the summer of 1813 with Augusta, and Elizabeth Medora Leigh, born on April 15, 1814, has always been assumed to be the poet's daughter. Though Byron never publicly acknowledged her, various passages in his letters, especially those to his close confidante, Lady Melbourne, suggest his paternity.

Lady Melbourne's brilliant niece, Annabella Milbanke, also figured prominently in Byron's life during this period. Although he despised "bluestockings" (intellectual women), Byron was unaccountably drawn to Annabella, whose intelligence and wide reading distinguished her so completely from the impulsively romantic Lady Caroline and the passively maternal Augusta. Perhaps as a means of escaping the chaos of his unstable love life, Byron proposed to Milbanke on two occasions, in September of 1812 and again in September of 1813. Unfortunately for both of them, Byron's second proposal was accepted. After various delays, apparently involving visits to Augusta, Byron and Annabella Milbanke were married on January 2, 1815.

The several months of Byron's marriage were marked by continuing literary activity (especially work on the later Oriental tales and on *Hebrew Melodies Ancient and Modern*), by visits to and from Augusta, by Byron's association with the Drury Lane Committee of Management, and by fits of temper, related to the poet's marital and financial problems, which terrified both his wife and his half sister. The birth of the poet's only legitimate child, Augusta Ada Byron, in December of 1815, did nothing to improve the situation, and when mother and daughter left on January 5, 1816, for what was purportedly a temporary visit to Annabella's parents, the marriage was effectively at an end. By March of 1816, a separation had been agreed on, and Byron affixed his signature to the necessary legal documents on April 21, 1816. A week earlier, he had spoken for the last time to his beloved Augusta, and on April 25, still experiencing financial difficulties and being roundly denounced by the press for his marital problems, Byron left England forever.

Once more on the Continent, Byron visited the Waterloo battlefield, journeyed up the Rhine Valley, crossed into Switzerland, and began looking for accommodations near Lake Geneva. Along the lakeshore, he and his traveling companion, Dr. John Polidori, were approached by Claire Clairmont, who, as a result of an affair earlier in the spring, was pregnant with Byron's child. Clairmont was accompanied by her stepsister, Mary Godwin (later to become Mary Shelley), and Percy Bysshe Shelley. The poets soon became fast friends and by early June had established households very near each other and within two miles of Geneva. Their animated conversations deeply influenced the lives of both poets, with the inspiration of their contact communicating itself, on one particular evening, to two other members of the group. During a gathering at the Villa Diodati, where Byron had taken up residence, a challenge to compose ghost stories resulted in the eventual publication of Dr. Polidori's *The Vampyre* (1819), the first English vampire tale, and Mary Shelley's classic gothic novel, *Frankenstein* (1818). During the several weeks of his almost daily talks with Shelley, Byron himself wrote "The Prisoner of Chillon" and worked diligently on *Childe Harold's Pilgrimage*, Canto III.

Although Claire had at first kept her relationship with Byron a secret from Mary and Percy, they inevitably became aware of Claire's pregnancy, after which Percy and Claire approached Byron in an attempt to resolve matters. Because Byron did not feel the same affection for Claire that she felt for him, it was decided that they should not live together. It was further decided that the child should be cared for by Byron, with Claire being addressed as its aunt. The child, Allegra Byron, was born in Bath, England, on January 12, 1817, and died in Ravenna, Italy, on April 20, 1822.

John Cam Hobhouse arrived at the Villa Diodati with another of Byron's friends, Scrope Davies, on August 26, 1816, and following the departure for England of the Shelley household on August 29, the two toured the Alps with Byron and Polidori. Another tour, with Hobhouse only, began on September 17. Byron's combined impressions of the Alps helped inspire *Manfred*, whose composition was well advanced when the poet gave up the Villa Diodati on October 5 and journeyed with Hobhouse to Milan.

After a sojourn of less than a month in Milan, during which he met the Italian poet Vincenzo Monti and the French novelist Stendhal, rescued Polidori from an encounter with the local authorities, and came under the surveillance of the Austrian secret police, Byron left with Hobhouse for Venice, where they arrived on or about November 10. Hobhouse soon departed to see other areas of Italy, but Byron, having fallen in love with Venice and with Marianna Segati, his landlord's wife, settled in for an extended stay. In the several months of this first Venetian interlude, he completed *Manfred* and overindulged during the Carnival period.

On April 17, 1817, Byron set out, by way of Arqua, Ferrara, and Florence, for Rome, where Hobhouse showed him the local antiquities. He returned on May 28 with the completed *The Lament of Tasso* and with vivid impressions that would be incorporated in *Childe Harold's Pilgrimage*, Canto IV. Soon thereafter, he and Marianna established themselves at the Villa Foscarini in La Mira, outside Venice. There, Byron formed another liaison, this time with the beautiful Margarita Cogni; worked at what was to become the final canto of *Childe Harold's Pilgrimage*; and began the precursor of *Don Juan*, the charming *Beppo*. Late in 1817, he returned to Venice with the visiting Hobhouse and, on January 7, 1818, said goodbye to his friend after a last ride together. Byron entrusted Hobhouse with the manuscript of *Childe Harold's Pilgrimage*, Canto IV, whose publication in April brought the poet further literary fame during a time when his personal life had rendered him infamous.

In 1818, Byron's Venetian dissipations reached a level of obsessive frequency that threatened his health. Nevertheless, he continued to write, producing *Mazeppa* and Canto I of *Don Juan* and beginning Canto II. He was showing signs of physical exhaustion by April of 1819, when he became reacquainted with a woman whom he had casually encountered during the previous year. With this woman, the nineteen-year-old Countess Teresa Guiccioli, he was soon involved in one of the most long-lasting and passionate relationships of his life. In June, he followed her to Ravenna, in August to Bologna, and in September back to Venice, where they spent some of their time at Byron's quarters in the Palazzo Mocenigo and longer periods at the Villa Foscarini in La Mira. At the end of the year, when Teresa's husband cajoled her to return to Ravenna, Byron followed again.

The continuation of *Don Juan* had been one of Byron's primary literary projects in 1819, and further material was written in 1820. The year was significant for other reasons, too, including the writing of *Marino Faliero, Doge of Venice*, Byron's increasing entanglement in the revolutionary Carbonari movement, and Teresa's formal separation from Count Guiccioli. When the Carbonari movement collapsed in 1821 and Teresa's family was exiled from Ravenna, Byron accepted Shelley's invitation to move himself, his lover, and her banished relatives to Pisa, where Shelley had taken up residence. Despite this political and personal upheaval, Byron completed three plays during 1821 (*Sardanapalus, The Two Foscari*, and *Cain*) and wrote the magnificent *The Vision of Judgment*.

Byron became part of the Pisan Circle in November of 1821, and he remained a resident of the general Pisa area until September of 1822. These months witnessed the writing of much of *Don Juan*, which Byron had previously ceased composing on the request of Teresa and which he now resumed with her permission. The period also saw the beginnings of Byron's acquaintance with the colorful Edward John Trelawny and the less satisfactory relationship between Byron and the improvident Hunt family. Most sadly, however, these were the months in which Byron's daughter, Allegra, died in a convent at Ravenna and in which Shelley, with Edward Williams, was drowned off the Italian coast. What ultimately drove Byron from Tuscany, however, was the latest banishment of Teresa's family, this time to Genoa, where Byron joined them in late September.

In Genoa, Byron wrote his last Augustan satire, *The Age of Bronze*, and a romantic verse narrative, *The Island*, while continuing *Don Juan*. He also began making serious plans to leave for Greece, where a war of independence had recently broken out. After a traumatic parting with Teresa, he set sail from Italy aboard the *Hercules* in July of 1823, accompanied by Trelawny and Teresa's brother, Pietro Gamba. In early August, they reached Cephalonia, and in late December, they left for Missolonghi, where Byron arrived on January 4, 1824, to be greeted the next day by Prince Alexandros Mavrocordatos, the Greek military leader.

During the previous August, Byron had been taken ill after an excursion to Ithaca. At Missolonghi, on February 15, he became ill once again. His recovery was slow and was hampered by terrible weather, the disunity of the Greek leadership, and their constant demands that he supply them with money. After riding through a rainstorm on April 9, he experienced a relapse. His condition worsened during the following days, and after being bled by his physicians until his strength was gone, he died on April 19, 1824. His remains were returned to England, where they were denied burial in Westminster Abbey. Instead, he was interred on July 16, 1824, in Hucknall Torkard Church, near his ancestral home of Newstead Abbey.

Analysis • Although a number of George Gordon, Lord Byron's, plays are more easily approached as dramatic poetry than as theatrical drama, the political tragedies are readily accessible to dramatic analysis. His political tragedies are literary explorations of the relationship, in an unregenerate world, of the extraordinary individual to the state. They examine the place of the almost superhumanly proud and passionate man within corporate humanity. They express the fascination with the link between earthly power and individual freedom and fulfillment that manifested itself in Byron's first speech before Parliament and that would lead him, finally, to his death at Missolonghi. The following discussion centers on three such works, the classically constructed *Marino Faliero, Doge of Venice* and *Sardanapalus*, and the gothic, melodramatic *Werner*.

Werner • Of Byron's dramatic works, *Werner* most closely resembles the popular theater of his day. Despite being the last play that Byron completed, *Werner* is the earliest of the plays in terms of initial composition, having been begun during the year preceding Byron's final exile from England. Byron's fascination with the story on which the play is based dates from an even earlier period. As he explains in the play's preface, he had read "The German's Tale" from the Lees' *The Canterbury Tales* at about age fourteen, and it had "made a deep impression upon" him. It "may, indeed, be said to contain the germ of much that" he wrote thereafter, an admission that suggests the importance of the play within the Byron canon, despite the play's obvious literary deficiencies.

The play's title character embodies many of the traits of the Byronic hero and has much in common, too, with Byron's father, "Mad Jack" Byron. As the play begins, Werner is a poverty-stricken wanderer, who, like Mad Jack, has been driven out by his father because of various youthful excesses resulting from the indulgence of his overly passionate nature. Although a marriage that his father considered improvident was the immediate cause of this estrangement, Werner was guilty of other, unstated transgressions before this, transgressions that prepared the way for the final severing of the parental tie. Since then, Werner has been a proud exile, burdened by a sense of personal guilt and too familiar with the weaknesses of human nature to rely on other people for consolation. His love for Josephine, herself an exile, partially sustains him, but his realization that her sufferings are a product of his own foolish actions exacerbates his gloom.

The one embodiment of hope for Werner and Josephine is their son, Ulric, who has been reared by Werner's father, Count Siegendorf, after Werner's banishment. Ulric, however, possesses his father's passions without possessing the sense of honor that would prevent those passions from expressing themselves in hideous crimes. As the play begins, Ulric is missing from his grandfather's court, disturbing rumors are circulating concerning his possible whereabouts, and the nobleman Stralenheim, a distant relation, is poised to usurp the family inheritance in the event of Werner's father's death.

The play's elements of gothic melodrama are obvious from the opening of the first scene. The play begins at night during a violent thunderstorm, and act 1 is set in "The Hall of a decayed Palace" in a remote section of Silesia. The palace is honeycombed with secret passages, which receive considerable use during the course of the play's action. The Thirty Years' War has just ended, rendering the profession of soldier superfluous and lending glamour to professional thievery, that favorite occupation of many a Sturm und Drang hero-villain. Ulric, as we eventually discover, is himself the leader of a band of soldiers turned marauders.

Ulric, another avatar of Byronic heroism, is something of a superman, possessing traits that render him capable of great good and great evil. One of the play's characters, the poor but honorable Gabor, describes him as a man

> Of wonderful endowments:—birth and fortune,
> Youth, strength and beauty, almost superhuman,
> And courage as unrivall'd, were proclaim'd

> His by the public rumour; and his sway,
> Not only over his associates, but
> His judges, was attributed to witchcraft,
> Such was his influence.

Ulric's dual nature expresses itself most clearly in his treatment of the potential usurper, Stralenheim. When Ulric is unaware of Stralenheim's identity, he courageously rescues him from the floodwaters of the River Oder, but later, when he learns that Stralenheim is a threat to his family's wealth and power, he cold-bloodedly murders him. He then conceals his responsibility for the crime and hypocritically questions his father about his possible role in Stralenheim's death. Werner has compromised his honor by stealing gold coins from Stralenheim's room, a crime that suggests the family's moral weakness, but he is incapable of murder. Freed of restraint by one additional generation of moral decay, Ulric, by contrast, is capable of almost anything.

Because of Stralenheim's murder and the nearly simultaneous death of Werner's aged father, Werner becomes Count Siegendorf and Ulric his heir apparent. All goes well for a year, although Werner, troubled by his possession of the tainted gold and by the mysterious circumstances of his rise to power, is plagued by a guilty conscience. There are manifestations of guilt in Ulric's behavior, too, but that strength of will that allowed him to rescue Stralenheim from the flood and later to cut his throat sustains him through subsequent unsavory deeds. He continues his clandestine command of the marauders who threaten the fragile peace and accepts betrothal to the loving and innocent Ida, daughter of the murdered Stralenheim. The ultimate proof of Ulric's reprobate nature occurs when Gabor, who had witnessed the hideous crime and had been unjustly branded as its likely perpetrator, comes forward to accuse Ulric. In an attempt to silence this threat to everything he has striven to accomplish, Ulric sends his minions in pursuit of the innocent man, at the same time uttering a defiant confession of his guilt before the startled Ida, who immediately falls dead in shocked disbelief.

Werner deviates from classical restraint in both content and form. In addition to relying on melodramatic plot devices, *Werner* violates the unities of place and time, a major shift in location and period occurring between acts 3 and 4. *Marino Faliero, Doge of Venice* and *Sardanapalus*, on the other hand, are much more regular, with only slight changes in setting and time taking place from one scene to the next. Like *Werner*, however, both plays center on the consequences of having men of powerful but uncertain character in positions of responsibility.

Marino Faliero, Doge of Venice • The tenuous thread on which the plot of *Marino Faliero, Doge of Venice* hangs is the apparent historical fact that the title character, while he was doge of Venice, conspired against the tyrannous Venetian oligarchy partly because he found their rule unjust and, more important, because they failed to punish one of their number severely enough for a scrawled insult to the doge's wife. When Faliero discovers that Michel Steno is to receive one month of imprisonment instead of death for an unsavory comment inscribed on the ducal throne, he becomes furious, although his wife, Angiolina, counsels restraint. His rage is motivated by his disgust that the oligarchy, with its facelessly diffused and inflexibly selfish power, refuses, on the one hand, to recognize the rights of the common people and neglects, on the other, to show the deference due superior spirits. His rebelliousness (like Byron's own) is simultaneously an assertion of individual, proud will and a genuine concern for democratic principles. He detests the oppressive rule of the privileged few and joins a conspiracy against them, but he maintains an aristocratic haughtiness among the "common ruffians leagued to ruin states" with whom he throws in his lot.

Ultimately, his joining the conspirators is an expression of that irrepressible, restless pride that he shares with Byron's other heroes. He exhibits not simply the temporal pride of a Coriolanus but also the everlasting, self-assertive pride of a Lucifer. Indeed, his is

> the same sin that overthrew the angels,
> And of all sins most easily besets
> Mortals the nearest to the angelic nature:
> The vile are only vain: the great are proud.

In addition to treating, with considerable complexity, the frequently self-contradictory motivations of the rebel, *Marino Faliero, Doge of Venice* explores the moral ambiguities of instigating violent actions to achieve just ends. Like the French revolutionaries, the Venetian conspirators are about to sweep away the old order in a bath of blood, but one of their number, Bertram, refuses to abandon his humanity and warns an aristocratic friend that his life is in danger. The ironic result of this humane gesture is that the rebellion is discovered and the conspirators themselves, including the proud doge, are put to death. Victory belongs to those whose ruthlessness wins out over their compassion, and he who would be kind becomes a Judas.

Sardanapalus • In *Sardanapalus*, this conflict between humanity and harsh political reality is again examined. Sardanapalus is a lover of life whose mercy and whose desire for peace, love, and pleasure bring down a dynasty. As a descendant of Nimrod and the fierce Semiramis, he is expected to conduct the affairs of state by means of bloodshed and unrelenting conquest. Instead, he allies himself with the forces of vitality against those of death and thereby earns a reputation for weakness. He knows the harem and the banquet hall better than the battlefield and is judged effeminate because he prefers the paradisiacal celebration of life to the ruthless bloodletting of war and political persecution. Even when he knows that two of his most powerful subjects, the Chaldean Beleses and the Mede Arbaces, have plotted against him, he refuses to have them killed and thereby opens the way to successful rebellion. After merely banishing the two from Nineveh, he finds himself, during a symbolically appropriate banquet, beset by a usurping army.

Despite his seeming weakness, Sardanapalus, like Byron's other heroes, possesses unquenchable pride and courage. Assuming the weapons of the warrior but refusing to wear full armor, so that his soldiers will recognize and rally to him, he enters battle and temporarily staves off defeat. His lover, Myrrha, a character added to the play, significantly enough, at the suggestion of Teresa Guiccioli, shows an equally fierce courage, as do Sardanapalus's loyal troops, and for a time, victory seems possible. Still, the kingly worshiper of life is troubled in his dreams by the image of the worshiper of death, Semiramis, and there are dark forebodings of approaching catastrophe.

When it finally becomes clear that defeat is inevitable, Sardanapalus expresses regret that the fallen world in which he found himself was unwilling to accept the temporary renewal that he attempted to offer:

> I thought to have made mine inoffensive rule
> An era of sweet peace 'midst bloody annals,

A green spot amidst desert centuries,
On which the future would turn back and smile,
And cultivate, or sigh, when it could not
Recall Sardanapalus's golden reign.
I thought to have made my realm a paradise,
And every moon an epoch of new pleasures.

When the world refuses his great gift, he turns to the only paradisiacal sanctuary available in a universe of spiritual disorder. He unites himself with the one individual who most loves him. He has his last loyal subjects build a funeral pyre, symbolic of his and Myrrha's passion, and the lovers die amid its flames.

Other major works

POETRY: *Fugitive Pieces*, 1806; *Poems on Various Occasions*, 1807; *Hours of Idleness*, 1807; *Poems Original and Translated*, 1808; *English Bards and Scotch Reviewers*, 1809; *Hints from Horace*, 1811; *Childe Harold's Pilgrimage*, Cantos I-IV, 1812-1818, 1819 (the four cantos published together); *The Curse of Minerva*, 1812; *Waltz: An Apostrophic Hymn*, 1813; *The Giaour*, 1813; *The Bride of Abydos*, 1813; *The Corsair*, 1814; *Ode to Napoleon Buonaparte*, 1814; *Lara*, 1814; *Hebrew Melodies Ancient and Modern*, 1815; *The Siege of Corinth*, 1816; *Parisina*, 1816; *Poems*, 1816; *The Prisoner of Chillon, and Other Poems*, 1816; *Monody on the Death of the Right Honourable R. B. Sheridan*, 1816; *The Lament of Tasso*, 1817; *Beppo: A Venetian Story*, 1818; *Mazeppa*, 1819; *Don Juan*, Cantos I-XVI, 1819-1824, 1826 (the sixteen cantos published together); *The Prophecy of Dante*, 1821; *The Vision of Judgment*, 1822; *The Age of Bronze*, 1823; *The Island*, 1823; *The Complete Poetical Works of Byron*, 1980-1986 (5 volumes).

NONFICTION: *Letter to [John Murray] on the Rev. W. L. Bowles's Strictures on the Life and Writings of Pope*, 1821; "A Letter to the Editor of 'My Grandmother's Review,'" 1822; *The Blues: A Literary Eclogue*, 1823; *The Parliamentary Speeches of Lord Byron*, 1824; *Byron's Letters and Journals*, 1973-1982 (12 volumes; Leslie A. Marchand, editor).

Bibliography

Brewer, William D., ed. *Contemporary Studies on Lord Byron*. Lewiston, N.Y.: Edwin Mellen Press, 2001. A collection of essays on the works of Byron. Bibliography and index.

Chew, Samuel C., Jr. *The Dramas of Lord Byron: A Critical Study*. 1915. Reprint. New York: Russell and Russell, 1964. The first sustained analysis of Byron's plays, Chew's book is one of the best single introductory examinations of Byron's dramatic works and his career as a dramatist.

Foot, Michael. *The Politics of Paradise: A Vindication of Byron*. New York: Harper and Row, 1988. Foot's analysis of Byron's poetics as it relates to his dynamic life, which Foot divides into formative periods linked to Byron's place of residence, includes incisive analyses of *Cain*, *Manfred*, and *Sardanapalus*. The book also includes a pithy select bibliography that would serve as a good starting point for in-depth research on Byron. Also included are two appendices.

Franklin, Caroline. *Byron: A Literary Life*. New York: St. Martin's Press, 2000. A study of Byron's career, with some attention to the poet's neglected playwriting.

Garrett, Martin. *George Gordon, Lord Byron*. New York: Oxford University Press, 2000. A basic biography of the writer Byron that examines his life and works. Bibliography and index.

Gross, Jonathan David. *Byron: The Erotic Liberal.* Lanham, Md.: Rowman & Littlefield, 2001. A study of Byron that focuses on his political and social views. Bibliography and index.

Martin, Philip. *Byron: A Poet Before His Public.* Cambridge, England: Cambridge University Press, 1982. This fine biographical-historical analysis of Byron's plays, with chapters on *Manfred, Cain,* and *Sardanapalus,* places Byron's work within the context of his contemporaries of the second generation of Romantic poets. Bibliography.

Peters, Catherine. *Byron.* Stroud, Gloucestershire, England: Sutton, 2000. A concise biography of Byron that covers his life and works. Bibliography.

Robert H. O'Connor,
updated by Gregory W. Lanier

Pedro Calderón de la Barca

Born: Madrid, Spain; January 17, 1600
Died: Madrid, Spain; May 25, 1681

Principal drama • *Amor, honor y poder*, pr. 1623, pb. 1634; *El sitio de Breda*, pr. 1625, pb. 1636; *El príncipe constante*, pr. 1629, pb. 1636 (*The Constant Prince*, 1853); *La dama duende*, wr. 1629, pr., pb. 1936 (*The Phantom Lady*, 1664); *Casa con dos puertas, mala es de guardar*, wr. 1629, pr., pb. 1636 (*A House with Two Doors Is Difficult to Guard*, 1737); *Los cabellos de Absalón*, wr. c. 1634, pb. 1684 (*The Crown of Absalom*, 1993); *La devoción de la cruz*, pb. 1634, pr. 1643 (*The Devotion to the Cross*, 1832); *El gran teatro del mundo*, wr. 1635, pr. 1649, pb. 1677 (*The Great Theater of the World*, 1856); *El mayor encanto, amor*, pr. 1635, pb. 1637 (*Love, the Greatest Enchantment*, 1870); *La vida es sueño*, pr. 1635, pb. 1636 (*Life Is a Dream*, 1830); *El médico de su honra*, pb. 1637 (*The Surgeon of His Honor*, 1853); *A secreto agravio, secreta venganza*, pb. 1637 (*Secret Vengeance for Secret Insult*, 1961); *El mágico prodigioso*, pr. 1637, pb. 1663 (*The Wonder-Working Magician*, 1959); *El pintor de su deshonra*, wr. 1640-1642, pb. 1650 (*The Painter of His Dishonor*, 1853); *El alcalde de Zalamea*, pr. 1643, pb. 1651 (*The Mayor of Zalamea*, 1853); *La hija del aire, Parte I*, pr. 1653, pb. 1664 (*The Daughter of the Air, Part I*, 1831); *La hija del aire, Parte II*, pr. 1653, pb. 1664 (*The Daughter of the Air, Part II*, 1831); *El laurel de Apolo*, pr. 1659, pb. 1664; *La púrpura de la rosa*, pr. 1660, pb. 1664; *Hado y divisa de Leonido y Marfisa*, pr. 1680, pb. 1682

Other literary forms • Although Pedro Calderón de la Barca is remembered primarily as a verse dramatist, he is also noted for his lyric poetry, some of which was not incorporated into his plays. The sonnet was the most prevalent poetic form used by Calderón. The collection *Los sonetos de Calderón en sus obras dramáticas* (1974) contains his nondramatic sonnets, those included in his plays, and the one sonnet from his long poem, *Psalle et sile* (1711).

Achievements • Pedro Calderón de la Barca, whose death in 1681 marks the end of Spain's great period of literary and artistic excellence known as its Golden Age, is generally recognized as one of the most accomplished Spanish dramatists of all time. His plays differ from the plays of his predecessor Lope de Vega Carpio (the "father of Spanish theater") in several ways. Calderón's dramas are generally regarded as more polished than Lope de Vega's, and their complex structure contrasts with the seeming naturalness of Lope de Vega's works. Although Lope de Vega often seems primarily interested in capturing the essence of seventeenth century Spanish life, Calderón's dramas demonstrate the author's concern with more universal—and often abstract—questions of human existence. It is probably because of his more universal focus that Calderón's work has had a wider appeal than Lope de Vega's. *Life Is a Dream*, his most famous drama, ranks as one of the unquestioned masterpieces of world theater.

Calderón is particularly noted for his religious theater. He is the undisputed master of the *auto sacramental*—the one-act, allegorical, religious drama performed as part of Spain's celebration of Corpus Christi. This genre accounts for 74 of the 182 works included in the standard Spanish edition of his complete works, and many of his full-

131

length plays are also about religious topics. Surprisingly, even these works continue to enjoy a wide appeal in an age in which religious faith is declining. *The Devotion to the Cross*, for example, was much admired by the agnostic philosopher Albert Camus, who translated this play into French in 1953.

Biography • Pedro Calderón de la Barca was born in Madrid on January 17, 1600, to an aristocratic family. Little is known about his childhood. His mother died when Calderón was ten, and his father died five years later. Calderón was educated in the Jesuit Colegio Imperial in Madrid and later in the University of Alcalá de Henares and the University of Salamanca, where he prepared himself for the priesthood. He

(Library of Congress)

did not, however, embark immediately on an ecclesiastical career, but preferred instead to dedicate himself to literary pursuits, participating in various poetry contests in which he won some recognition—including praise on two occasions from Lope de Vega, who at the time was Spain's leading dramatist.

In 1623, Calderón's first datable play, *Amor, honor y poder* (love, honor, and power) was performed in Madrid. At approximately the same time, the poet embarked on a military career and may have participated in the surrender of Breda, which he dramatized in his play *El sitio de Breda* (the siege of Breda). For a time, he continued to involve himself with both the theater and the military. Following the death of Lope de Vega in 1635, Philip IV appointed Calderón court dramatist and director of the newly constructed and lavish court theater at Buen Retiro. In 1637, the king named him a knight in the Order of Santiago. In 1638, he fought against the French in the Battle of Fuenterrabía, and in 1640, he helped suppress a rebellion in Catalonia (northeastern Spain). Finally, in 1642, ill health—perhaps resulting from a wound received in battle—put an end to his military career.

Little is known of Calderón's personal life during these years, but his involvement in an altercation in 1629 affords a brief glimpse into a side of his personality not revealed by his military and artistic triumphs. In that year, one of his brothers was seriously wounded in a fight with an actor who took refuge in a Trinitarian convent, and Calderón was among the crowd that, with the legal authorities, forced its way into the convent and, when they were unable to find the man they were pursuing, subjected the nuns to insults and rough treatment. When the court chaplain, Hortensio Paravicino, later protested this conduct in a sermon, Calderón included in his play *The Constant Prince* a passage ridiculing the priest—lines that the authorities, acting on Paravicino's instigation, ultimately forced the dramatist to expunge.

Sometime after the end of his military career, Calderón became involved in a love affair and fathered an illegitimate son, Pedro José, whom he treated initially as his nephew. Following this affair and his mistress's death (perhaps as a result of it), he finally realized his ambition of becoming a priest and was ordained in 1651. In an ironic reversal of customary practice, he acknowledged after his ordination that his "nephew" was actually his son. For two years following his ordination, Calderón remained in Madrid. In 1653, he became chaplain of the Capilla de Reyes Nuevos in Toledo. During this time, he continued to provide plays for the court and also busied himself composing *autos sacramentales* for Madrid's annual celebration of Corpus Christi.

In 1663, Calderón returned to Madrid to become honorary chaplain to Philip IV, and for the rest of his life, he remained in that city, where he continued to write secular dramas for the court as well as the *autos sacramentales*. His last full-length play, *Hado y divisa de Leonido y Marfisa* (the destiny and design of Leonido and Marfisa), was written and performed before the court of Charles II in 1680. Calderón's death occurred a year later on May 25, 1681, while he was working on an *auto sacramental.* The circumstances of his death caused a friend to comment that Calderón had died singing "like a swan."

Analysis • Initially, Pedro Calderón de la Barca's theater seems most defined by its varied nature. The topics of his dramas are diverse, ranging from religious faith and revenge to mythological fantasy and marital fidelity. The tone of his works likewise varies from frivolity to gravity. In many respects, Calderón's theater continues to conform to the norms established by his predecessor Lope de Vega. Like Lope de Vega, he violates the classical sense of decorum by mixing humorous and tragic elements in the same play and by including in highly serious works a stock character known as the *gracioso* (funny one), usually a servant, whose lack of dignity provides occasion for laughter. Calderón also follows Lope de Vega's practice of disregarding the classical unities of time and place, which sought to limit a play's setting to a single place and decreed that its action should occur in a single day. Also, like Lope de Vega's, his plays are written in polymetric verse.

Calderón's cultured, baroque language, however, gives his plays a noticeably different tone from those of his predecessor. Because most of his plays were written for the court, he adopted a style designed to appeal to his educated audience. Thus, his characters often speak a highly complex language, rich in poetic conceits, parallelism, and classical allusions, which is intentionally artificial.

A recurrent theme in Calderón's plays is the confusion between reality and appearances. The theme is, like his style, characteristic of the baroque, and it had already been treated in various other literary works of the period, including Miguel de Cervantes's famous novel *El ingenioso hidalgo don Quixote de la Mancha* (1605, 1615; *The History of the Valorous and Wittie Knight-Errant, Don Quixote of the Mancha,* 1612-1620; better known as *Don Quixote de la Mancha,*1605, 1615). With Calderón, however, this theme is so consistently present that it could be considered a constant that gives unity to his diverse corpus.

Another characteristic of Calderonian drama is the author's insistence—rare in Spanish Golden Age theater—on carefully "finished" pieces. Often the originality of Calderón's plays lies in the polished form in which they are presented rather than in the material treated. More than any other Golden Age dramatist, he reworked material that had already been used, and he often succeeded in transforming a mediocre work into a quite memorable one.

The Constant Prince • One of Calderón's early plays, *The Constant Prince,* is already illustrative of much that is characteristic of his later work. *The Constant Prince* is a reworking of an earlier play attributed to Lope de Vega, *La fortuna adversa del Infante Don Fernando de Portugal* (n.d.; the adverse fortune of Prince Fernando of Portugal). Both plays dramatize the legendary faith of a historic Portuguese prince who, when captured by the Arabs, allegedly chose to die as a martyr rather than order the surrender of the Portuguese-held city of Ceuta in order to gain his freedom. The changes that Calderón made in Lope de Vega's treatment of this story—the reduction of the cast of characters from thirty-six to fourteen and the transformation of Prince Fernando from a pious weakling to a dynamic and determined fighter, for example—illustrate the author's concern to present the material in the most effective manner.

Calderón's most significant modification of the original play, however, is his introduction of the Moorish princess Fénix (Phoenix), the daughter of Fernando's captor, the King of Fez. By incorporating into the play a subplot dealing with Fénix's persistent love for the Arab general Muley in spite of her father's wish that she marry Tarudante, the King of Morocco, Calderón establishes a parallel between Fernando and her. Like him, she is constant—in her love for Muley. Moreover, the competition between Muley and Tarudante for the beautiful Fénix mirrors the competition between Fernando and the King of Fez for the city of Ceuta (whose name corresponds to the Hebrew word for "beauty"). These parallels allow Calderón to evoke poetically the question of the true nature of beauty. When, at the end of the play, Fénix is captured by the Portuguese and returned to her people (with the stipulation that she is to marry Muley) in exchange for Fernando's dead body, it is evident that Calderón, establishing a baroque contrast between appearance and reality, wishes to communicate that the beauty of Fernando's faith is more real than Fénix's physical beauty.

Nowhere is the contrast between Fernando and Fénix more evident than in a much-discussed scene toward the end of the second act in which the two of them recite to each other sonnets on the impermanence of flowers and of stars. Fénix, who had ordered Fernando to bring her a bouquet of flowers, is horrified by the thought that their beauty is only transitory. Fernando, on the other hand, can face even the knowledge that the stars (which at the time the play was written were believed to influence human destiny) are not permanent. Unlike Fénix, he has learned to penetrate beyond appearances. Thus, he is neither captivated nor disturbed by temporary things; he recognizes that both physical beauty and misfortune will become lost in eternity, which he believes to be ordered according to a divine plan. Thus, Calderón has used Fernando's constancy in order to teach a moral lesson concerning the Christian virtue of fortitude.

Cape and sword plays • The theme of appearance versus reality, which is handled seriously in *The Constant Prince*, is also present in *The Phantom Lady* and *A House with Two Doors Is Difficult to Guard*, two Calderonian plays typical of a genre referred to as *comedias de capa y espada*, or cape and sword plays. The name for this genre, which was seventeenth century Spain's equivalent of a situation comedy, derives from the costume worn by the actors playing the leading male roles. Cape and sword plays have complicated plots revolving around the courtship of one or more sets of middle-class youths who devise ingenious measures to overcome the obstacles to their love. The obstacles are usually presented by a domineering father or brother, anxious to protect the honor or reputation of a daughter or sister, and the young people frequently resort to disguises and other forms of deception, which often backfire with comic results. Duels are a frequent ingredient of these plays, but they never have grave consequences; cape and sword plays invariably have happy endings involving at least one wedding.

The Phantom Lady • *The Phantom Lady* dramatizes the ingenuity of Angela, a bright and attractive young widow, whose brothers Don Juan and Don Luis, in a desire to protect her reputation, have confined her first to their home and then—during the visit of Don Juan's friend Don Manuel—to her room. Because the room Don Manuel is occupying is next to her own, Angela makes use of a secret door (concealed by a glass cabinet) joining the two rooms to enter their guest's quarters and play pranks on him and frighten his servant, who believes she is a ghost. As he is unaware of her existence, Don Manuel is also puzzled by Angela, but he refuses to believe that she is a phantom and eventually follows her into her room, where the two of them are discovered by Don Luis. Following a duel, which Don Manuel wins (sparing Luis's life), everyone receives an explanation of what has been happening, and Don Manuel and Angela agree to be married.

The use of illusion in the play is obvious. As a result of deceits, disguises, false entrances, and so on, all the play's male characters remain utterly confused until the final scene. As is typical of many cape and sword plays, only the female characters—Angela and her cousin Beatriz—realize what is really happening. Also typical is that the would-be deceivers (the two brothers who conceal Angela's presence from their guest) are themselves the most deceived. This is especially true of Don Luis, who, on an occasion when Angela has left the house in disguise, follows her and endeavors to seduce her, believing that she is another woman.

A House with Two Doors Is Difficult to Guard • The stereotyped plots and characters of all cape and sword plays bear a certain resemblance to one another—though Calderón somehow manages to endow most of his with a fresh quality which makes them appealing long after his death. Thus, many of the elements of *The Phantom Lady*—the unknown entrance, disguises, a tyrannical brother, a mysterious and beautiful lady who appears and disappears—are also present in *A House with Two Doors Is Difficult to Guard*. In this play, the appearance-versus-reality theme is even more noticeable, as when Fénix, describing (in typically baroque language) to his friend Lisardo his first encounter with the beautiful Marcela in the gardens of Aranjuez, remarks on the difficulty of distinguishing her from the carved statues of nymphs in the garden's fountains.

The Surgeon of His Honor • Appearances produce tragic consequences in *The Surgeon of His Honor*, a play that dramatizes Don Gutierre Alfonso's murder of his wife, Mencía, because of his belief that she has been unfaithful. In the eyes of a modern audience, at least, Mencía seems to be an innocent victim of misfortune. At the beginning of the play, she is a happily married woman whose happiness is seriously threatened when a former suitor, Prince Enrique, is thrown from his horse (a typical occurrence in Golden Age drama with men who are unable to control their passions) and is brought to her house to recover. When he awakens and discovers his former fiancée, Mencía, Enrique—even after learning that she is now married—persists in efforts to resume his former relationship with her. That night, when her husband is absent, he bribes a servant to gain entry to her house.

Although she rejects all Enrique's advances, Mencía does commit various indiscretions. When her husband returns unexpectedly, for example, she conceals Enrique in her room and later arranges a diversion so that he may leave. In his hasty departure, however, Enrique leaves behind a dagger, which Gutierre discovers and which causes him to suspect his wife of infidelity. After gathering additional misleading evidence that convinces him of his wife's guilt, Gutierre arranges a bloody and startling denouement that is typical of the Senecan tragic style then popular in Spain: He engages a bloodletter, brings him to the house blindfolded, and orders him to bleed his wife to death.

The Surgeon of His Honor is thus typical of a peculiarly Spanish genre that is referred to informally as the wife-murder play. These plays have plots based on Spain's old and infamous honor code, which gave a husband (or father or brother) the legal and moral right to kill a wife (or daughter or sister) whose sexual misconduct had threatened the family's reputation. Although the plots of these plays resemble that of William Shakespeare's *Othello, the Moor of Venice* (pr. 1604), there are notable differences. In *The Surgeon of His Honor*, Gutierre—unlike Othello, who becomes aware of Desdemona's innocence and of his own blindness—remains convinced that what he did (though lamentable) was right, and the play concludes with the announcement of Gutierre's engagement to a former fiancée, an engagement arranged by King Pedro (Enrique's brother).

Because the king has been informed by the bloodletter (who surreptitiously left a bloody handprint by the door of Gutierre's house so that it could be identified) of all that has happened, the king's arrangement of a new marriage for Gutierre seems puzzling. Basing their interpretation of the play on this ending, critics assumed for many years that Calderón—and other Spanish authors of similar plays—actually approved of the bloody honor code that was the basis of their dramas. Recent Calderón scholars have become convinced that this is not the case. Various elements of the play—the bloody handprint by the door (recalling the biblical account of the Passover) and the crucifix hanging above Mencía's bed when her dead body is discovered—invite the audience to examine the play's plot in a religious context and to compare the sacrifice of the innocent Mencía to the sacrifice of the innocent Christ. In this light, it is clear that Calderón has wished to show his audience how easily one may be deceived by appearances. Thus he structured the play in a way that makes the viewer participate initially in Gutierre's error, but he provided enough evidence so that further reflection would correct this initial illusion.

The Great Theater of the World • Calderón's most famous *auto sacramental, The Great Theater of the World*, again emphasizes the theme of illusion. Based on the idea that, quite literally, "all the world's a stage," this play dramatizes the production of a play in which a theater manager (an allegorical representation of God) assembles a set of characters (a rich man, a king, a peasant, a poor man, Beauty, Discretion, and a child) in order to represent human life. Because the purpose of the *autos sacramentales* was to instruct the public concerning the meaning of the Eucharist, at the end of the play, the theater manager issues an invitation for some of the characters (those who have behaved appropriately) to join him at his table for a feast, but only after the audience has had ample opportunity to observe how easily some of the actors were seduced into confusing their fictional roles with reality.

The Devotion to the Cross • Often, Calderón's full-length plays also appear to be religious allegories. It has been suggested, for example, that one must view *The Devotion to the Cross* as an allegorical representation of the fall and redemption of humankind. The play dramatizes the fate of Eusebio, a child of unknown parents who has been reared by a shepherd and who refers to himself as "Eusebio of the Cross" because his only clue to his identity is a cross-shaped birthmark. Eusebio wins the affection of a wealthy girl, Julia, but Julia's brother Lisardo—resentful of his sister's lowly suitor—challenges Eusebio to a duel and is killed by him. Pursued by Julia's father, Curcio, Eusebio then becomes the leader of a band of outlaws. He behaves erratically, however, when he captures a priest and sees a book entitled *The Mystery of the Cross*, for he continues to be tormented by the mystery of his own origin and by the meaning of his birthmark. The mystery of his identity is resolved at the end of the play when he and the other characters discover that he is Julia's twin, Curcio's own son.

In a sense, all the principal characters of this play are as confused about their identities as is Eusebio. Like the actors of *The Great Theater of the World*, they have been trapped into playing illusory roles. In *The Devotion to the Cross*, the roles are antagonistic ones, which belie the characters' true identity as a family, and it is clear that Calderón believes that their dilemma is shared by humanity in general. He thus invites his audience to view Eusebio as a kind of Everyman—born into a confused world, uncertain of his identity. Protected by a shepherd (evoking Christ the Good Shepherd), he finally discovers the secret of his existence in the sign of the cross.

Life Is a Dream • Unanimously recognized as Calderón's outstanding masterpiece, *Life Is a Dream* is again an expression of the author's favorite theme of reality and illusion, and of the almost inescapable human tendency to confuse them. Set in Poland, the play dramatizes the destiny of Prince Segismundo, who is imprisoned in a forest by his father, King Basilio, immediately after his birth. Basilio is motivated to imprison his son because—as an astrologer—he has become convinced that Segismundo will become a tyrant who will conquer his father.

As is usually the case in drama, Basilio's very efforts to avoid a prophesied destiny actually cause the prophecy to be realized. Because he grows up isolated from humanity and surrounded only by animals, Segismundo quite naturally becomes a savage himself. Thus, when his father—wishing to test the accuracy of his astrological deductions before declaring his Russian nephew Astolfo heir to the Polish throne—has his son drugged, brought to the palace, and informed that he is King of Poland, Segismundo does indeed behave as a tyrant by seeking to violate an attractive woman and by throwing from the palace window a servant who gets in his way. Convinced of the accuracy of the prophecy, Basilio has Segismundo drugged again and returned to prison and proceeds with his plan to have Astolfo declared heir to the throne.

The people of Poland, however, are unwilling to accept a foreign king, and, discovering the location of Segismundo's prison, they proclaim him their leader in an insurrection against Basilio. The prophecy that Segismundo would conquer his father is thus fulfilled. Its fulfillment has a rather odd twist, however, since Segismundo—who was indeed a tyrant in his first visit to the palace—is now changed. He has been told by his jailer that all that happened to him in his father's court was only a dream, that one can never distinguish between dreams and reality, but that even in dreams one has the opportunity to do good. Having learned this lesson, he pardons his father and is thus prepared at the play's close to become a wise and benevolent ruler.

Initially, it may appear that Segismundo's conversion derives from an illusion, but Calderón makes it clear that this is not really the case. Segismundo, like Fernando of *The Constant Prince*, has seen through the illusion of life and has glimpsed the reality of eternity. The soliloquy in which he proclaims that life itself is a dream is an excellent example of Calderón's poetic talent at its finest. Probably the most famous soliloquy in the Spanish language, it is as well known in Hispanic countries as Hamlet's question of existence is in English-speaking ones.

Indeed, it is clear that, in Calderón's view, Segismundo is one of the few characters of the play who has freed himself from illusion. In the author's mind, the greatest illusion of which humans are capable is the belief that they may autonomously control their destiny. It was because Basilio was a victim of this illusion at the beginning of the play that he had Segismundo imprisoned, but in the course of the drama, he also learns the nature of reality and thus kneels before his son at the play's end to ask his forgiveness. Another character, the gracioso Clarín, is not so fortunate. He tries cynically to manipulate each situation for his own gain and, during the battle between Segismundo's and Basilio's forces, hides to protect himself from harm until it is over. Ironically, an arrow lands in the very spot where he is hiding and kills him, illustrating once again Calderón's conviction that those who cling to the illusory beauty of life are inviting destruction.

Secret Vengeance for Secret Insult • Like *The Surgeon of His Honor*, *Secret Vengeance for Secret Insult* dramatizes a husband's murder of his wife (and her suspected lover) in order to defend his honor, and the later play repeats many elements of the earlier one. Shortly before her wedding, Doña Leonor, like Mencía in *The Surgeon of His Honor*, is surprised by the sudden appearance of a former suitor, Don Luis. Like Mencía, she resists her former suitor's advances, but also like her, she makes the mistake of granting him an interview and is forced to hide him when her husband returns unexpectedly. Her husband, Don Lope, becomes suspicious and resolves to protect his honor by killing both Leonor and Luis. Because his goal is to protect his reputation and he believes that no one else suspects his wife's supposed infidelity, he arranges for both murders to look like accidents, but again recalling *The Surgeon of His Honor*, King Sebastián learns the true nature of what has happened and gives it his approval.

It is clear again, however, that Calderón does not endorse what his protagonist has done, and he communicates his disapproval to the audience by ironically undermining Don Lope's character. From the beginning of the play, he portrays Don Lope as an arrogantly self-centered individual who is blindly proud of his ability to control his destiny. When a friend, Don Juan, confides his sorrow at having been forced (in order to protect his honor) to kill a man who insulted a lady he was courting, Don Lope replies that Don Juan should be happy because there is no greater joy than having one's honor unstained.

When Don Juan is obliged to kill yet another man (who, aware of the earlier duel, refers to him as the "offended" rather than as the "avenged" party), Don Lope decides confidently to avoid such complications by making his own vengeance a secret one. With this same air of confidence, he prepares at the end of the play to embark with King Sebastián on an expedition against the Moors in Africa—an expedition that the seventeenth century audience knew had ended in disaster. Therefore, at the conclusion of the play, Don Lope is a fine example of a tragedy about to happen—of hubris before a fall—and the audience is fully aware that the same blind pride that led him to murder two people is now leading him to his own destruction.

The Mayor of Zalamea • *The Mayor of Zalamea*, which is considered by Calderón scholars to be second only to his *Life Is a Dream*, is in many ways an atypical Calderonian play. Because its protagonist, Pedro Crespo, is a wealthy peasant (unlike most of Calderón's principal characters, who are noble) and because the theme of the play is a peasant's right to defend his honor, this work bears a certain resemblance to Lope de Vega Carpio's famous "peasant plays" such as *Fuenteovejuna* (wr. 1611-1618, pb. 1619; *The Sheep Well,* 1936), *Peribáñez y el comendador de Ocaña* (wr. 1609-1612, pb. 1614, *Peribáñez,* 1936), and *El mejor alcalde, el rey* (wr. 1620-1623, pb. 1635; *The King, the Greatest Alcalde,* 1918); indeed, *The Mayor of Zalamea* is a reworking by Calderón of another play by the same name attributed to Lope de Vega.

Initially, the plot of this play may appear to contradict Calderón's implied criticism of the honor code in *The Surgeon of His Honor* and *Secret Vengeance for Secret Insult,* for *The Mayor of Zalamea* dramatizes Pedro Crespo's utilization of his authority as the newly elected Mayor of Zalamea to order the death of Don Alvaro, a captain who, when quartered in Crespo's house, abducted and raped Crespo's daughter Isabel. Moreover, Crespo's use of this authority is of questionable legality because, as the offended party, he can scarcely be considered an impartial judge, and because the offender is a nobleman. Nevertheless, Crespo is neither blind nor arrogant. He orders Don Alvaro's death reluctantly and only after first imploring him to marry Isabel in order to repair the damage done to the family's honor. He likewise shows compassion for his daughter. A typical Golden Age father might have felt constrained by the honor code to murder a dishonored daughter, and Isabel actually expects her father to do so. Crespo arranges instead, after his efforts to have her honorably married have failed, for her to enter a convent.

Even in this play, however, Calderón makes it clear that the honor code allows no occasion for rejoicing. At the end of the play, the widowed Crespo is bereft of both his children. Isabel is in a convent, and he has reluctantly given his consent for his only son, Juan, to join the military. Although he has been honored by King Pedro II, who exonerated his execution of Don Alvaro by naming Crespo mayor for life, he faces a lonely future filled with sad memories.

The Wonder-Working Magician • Because of its resemblance to the Faust legend, *The Wonder-Working Magician* has received considerable attention and praise—exciting, for example, the admiration of the English poet Percy Bysshe Shelley, who enthusiastically compared it to Johann Wolfgang von Goethe's famous treatment of the same legend. Calderón's play dramatizes the fourth century martyrdom of two saints.

The protagonist Cipriano (Saint Cyprian) is enamored of the young and beautiful Justina and, like Faust, signs a pact with the devil so that he may learn black magic in order to seduce her. Though he does acquire spectacular powers, they are unable to prevail against Justina's virtuous will, and Cipriano—after embracing a skeleton that he has mistaken for Justina—recognizes, like all Calderonian heroes, that the seemingly impressive powers of evil are an illusion. The play concludes as he and his beloved, united at last, suffer death as martyrs. Ironically, the devil, who initially approached Cipriano in order to distract him from his study of theology, has been an instrument in his martyrdom and salvation. The purposes of evil have been thwarted by the purposes of good.

Los cabellos de Absalón • Of all the Calderón plays based on his reworking of earlier material, the best-known is *Los cabellos de Absalón.* Its source, Tirso de Molina's *La venganza de Tamar* (wr. 1621, pb. 1634), dramatizes the biblical story of King David's daughter Tamar's rape by her half-brother Amnon and her brother Absalom's murder of Amnon in order to avenge her honor. Calderón's play condenses Tirso's into two acts (the second of which is an almost word-for-word copy of Tirso's act 3) and adds an original third act that dramatizes Absalom's own death when, in his revolt against his father, his hair becomes entangled in the low branches of a tree as he is riding through a forest.

Although Calderón's appropriation of Tirso's material may appear questionable in an age that has become accustomed to copyright laws, one should note that in the seventeenth century such practices were considered entirely legitimate. Indeed, it is quite possible that Calderón composed his play at the request of a theater manager who instructed him to write a new final act for Tirso's material.

Obviously, both dramatists found in the biblical account of David's tragic family an echo of the nefarious Spanish honor code, and both of them implicitly criticize this code by reminding their audiences that the vindication of honor may—as in the case of Absalom—be only a disguise for self-serving motives. Calderón's arrangement of the material to emphasize Absalom's hair (of which Absalom was so proud that he mistakenly understood a prophecy that he would be "elevated by his hair" to mean that his physical beauty would cause him to become king) is typical of the author's penchant for showing his villains captivated by illusion.

The Painter of His Dishonor • Calderón's last famous wife-murder play, *The Painter of His Dishonor*, is perhaps his best contribution to the genre. In its rapid action, which shifts from Italy to Spain and back again, the author achieves a perfect synthesis of the themes of illusion and revenge. Many elements of its plot are familiar from *The Surgeon of His Honor* and *Secret Vengeance for Secret Insult*. The young and beautiful Serafina consents to marry Juan Roca, an old artist who attempts vainly to capture her beauty on canvas, only because she believes her former suitor, Don Alvaro, has perished at sea; Alvaro returns and, ignoring Serafina's protests that she wishes to be faithful to her husband, abducts her and hides her in his father's country house near Naples.

The Prince of Naples, who has also been captivated by Serafina's beauty, discovers her presence and engages a traveling artist to paint her portrait. Ironically, the artist is Serafina's husband, who has returned to Italy to locate his wife and avenge his honor. In an action-packed final scene, Juan manages at last to capture his sleeping wife's likeness on canvas; when Serafina awakens, frightened by a dream in which she imagined her husband was killing her, she rushes for the first time to seek comfort in her abductor's arms. Alvaro and Serafina's embrace convinces Juan of his wife's guilt, and he rapidly fires two pistols, leaving both his wife and her suitor dead inside the "frame" provided by the windows that served as the standard background for the seventeenth century Spanish stage.

The painting motif that is the context for this drama suggests a number of conclusions. By emphasizing art's ambiguity, Calderón clearly suggests that Juan Roca has fallen victim to his own artistic imagination. At the same time, however, Serafina's own conduct seems equally ambiguous. While on the conscious level she remains faithful to her husband, it is clear that unconsciously she is indeed guilty of an adulterous love for Alvaro. Indeed, Serafina and Juan are similar in that both struggle in vain to exercise conscious control over a deeper self that is more real than their illusory social masks; both are examples of the inevitable human subjection to sin. Calderón's solution to this human dilemma, which is a basic theme of his work, is found in an *auto sacramental* also entitled *The Painter of His Dishonor*, in which the offended husband, Christ, pardons his wife, Human Nature, and fires instead on guilt and Lucifer.

Other major works

POETRY: *Psalle et sile*, 1741; *Poesías*, 1845; *Obra lírica*, 1943; *Sus mejores poesías*, 1954; *Poesías líricas en las obras dramáticas de Calderón*, 1964; *Los sonetos de Calderón en sus obras dramáticas*, 1974.

Bibliography

Acker, Thomas S. *The Baroque Vortex: Velázquez, Calderón, and Gracián Under Philip IV.* New York: Peter Lang, 2000. Acker compares and contrasts the works of Calderón, Diego Velázquez, and Baltasar Gracián y Morales, examining the baroque influence. Bibliography.

De Armas, Frederick A. *The Prince in the Tower: Perceptions of "La vida es sueño."* Cranbury, N.J.: Associated University Presses, 1993. Various perspectives on Calderón's *Life Is a Dream.* Bibliography and index.

Delgado Morales, Manuel, ed. *The Calderonian Stage: Body and Soul.* Lewisburg, Pa.: Bucknell University Press, 1997. An analysis of the staging and production of the dramas of Calderón. Bibliography and index.

Levin, Leslie. *Metaphors of Conversion in Seventeenth Century Spanish Drama.* Rochester, N.Y.: Tamesis, 1999. This study examines the concept of religion and conversion in the dramas of Calderón as well as those of Tirso de Molina. Bibliography and index.

Rupp, Stephen James. *Allegories of Kingship: Calderón and the Anti-Machiavellian Tradition.* University Park.: Pennsylvania State University Press, 1996. An examination of Calderón's portrayal of the monarchy in literature and of his political and social views. Bibliography and index.

Currie K. Thompson

Karel Čapek

Born: Malé Svatoňovice, Bohemia, Austro-Hungarian Empire
(now in Czech Republic); January 9, 1890
Died: Prague, Czechoslovakia (now Czech Republic); December 25, 1938

Principal drama • *Lásky hra osudná*, wr. 1910, pb. 1916, pr. 1930 (with Josef Čapek); *Loupežník*, pr., pb. 1920 (*The Robber*, 1931); *Ze života hmyzu*, pb. 1920, pr. 1922 (with Josef Čapek; *The Insect Play*, 1923; also known as *And So Infinituam: The Life of the Insects*, 1923); *Věc Makropulos*, pb. 1920, pr. 1922 (*The Macropulos Secret*, 1925); *R.U.R.: Rossum's Universal Robots*, pb. 1920, pr. 1921 (English translation, 1923); *Adam Stvořitel*, pr., pb. 1927 (with Josef Čapek; *Adam the Creator*, 1929); *Bílá nemoc*, pr., pb. 1937 (*Power and Glory*, 1938; also known as *The White Plague*, 1988); *Matka*, pr., pb. 1938 (*The Mother*, 1939)

Other literary forms • Karel Čapek was essentially a thinker who used a variety of forms to express his philosophical and political ruminations. Aside from his dramatic writing, Čapek's work falls into three categories: political and philosophical writing, tales, and novels. Among his political and philosophical publications are *Pragmatismus* (1918), a direct outgrowth of work he did in his doctoral program at Charles University. This was followed in 1920-1921 by *Musaion*, a collection of essays on modern art, in part an outgrowth of his doctoral dissertation, "Objective Methods in Aesthetics." In 1928, Čapek published the first of the three volumes of *Hovory s T. G. Masarykem* (*President Masaryk Tells His Story*, 1934; also as *Masaryk on Thought and Life*, 1938). This extensive work, completed in 1935, grew out of Čapek's close friendship with his former university professor, Tomas G. Masaryk, who served as Czechoslovakia's president from 1918 until 1935. Out of this same period appeared a closely related collection of essays, *O věcech obecných: Čili, Zóon politikon* (on public matters), published in 1932. A posthumous collection of essays *Veci kolemnás* (the things around us) was published in 1954.

Čapek, sometimes in collaboration with his brother Josef, liked to write tales and sketches, often of the fantastic. Many of these tales and sketches were collected and published, beginning with *Zářivé hlubiny* (1916; *The Luminous Depths*, 1916), *Boží muka* (1917; wayside crosses), and *Krakonošova zahrada* (1918; the garden of Krakonoš)—all these pieces written with Josef. In 1929, Čapek published on his own two collections of tales, *Povídky z jedné kapsy* (tales from one pocket) and *Povídky z druhé kapsy* (tales from the other pocket), translated into English and published together as *Tales from Two Pockets* in 1932.

Čapek's novels combine political philosophy with a strong sense of the fantastic. The first, *Továrna na absolutno*, appeared in 1922 and is variously known in English as *The Absolute at Large* (1927), *Factory for the Absolute*, and *Manufacture of the Absolute*. Čapek then began the ambitious project of writing a trilogy that consisted of *Hordubal* (1933; English translation, 1934), *Povětroň* (1934; *Meteor*, 1935), and *Obyčejný život* (1934; *An Ordinary Life*, 1936). These three novels, coming just as Adolf Hitler's ascendancy in Germany was being noted widely, led to Čapek's fifth novel, *Válka s mloky* (1936; *The War with the Newts*, 1937), which was openly anti-Fascist and specifically anti-Hitler. *První parta* (1937; *The First Rescue Party*, 1939) continued to develop the political philosophies found in the early novels.

142

Achievements • Karel Čapek is remembered today for his popularization of the word "robot," actually first used by his brother Josef in his short story "Opilec" (1917) and used by Karel in *R.U.R.: Rossum's Universal Robots*, which was first produced in Prague in January, 1921. The word is from the Czech *robota*, meaning compulsory service or work. Popularizing this word, however, was certainly not Čapek's most notable professional achievement. A deeply philosophical man, professionally trained as a philosopher, Čapek was the first Czech writer to attract a broad international audience for his works, particularly for his expressionist drama, which has been translated into many languages and has been performed all over the world.

A versatile intellectual, Čapek, during his years on the staff of *Lidové noviny*, the most influential Czech newspaper, demonstrated by the excellence of his writing that journalism can be an art. He wrote on a broad range of subjects, from Persian rugs to gardening to drama and art. Čapek was also an incisive political thinker who wrote stirring political essays, but his political sentiments achieve a more universal expression in his plays and novels, particularly in such plays as *R.U.R.*, *The Insect Play*, and *Power and Glory* and in the novels of his trilogy comprising *Hordubal*, *Meteor*, and *An Ordinary Life*. His novel most familiar to English-speaking audiences is *The War with the Newts*, which builds directly on much of the social criticism found in *R.U.R.* and in *The Insect Play* and which presents one of the earliest direct literary attacks on Hitler. His trilogy has attracted considerable interest for its manner of dealing with the infinite diversity of the human personality.

Čapek, who was deeply involved in the arts and in the cultural life of Prague, served from 1921 to 1923 as director of Prague's City Theatre, where he directed thirteen plays. He was less comfortable as a playwright than he was as a journalist or a novelist because he believed that in drama the author has too little control over his own product: The actors and the director, by imposing their own interpretations on a play, wrest from it much of the authorial control that writers in other genres are able to preserve. It was perhaps this feeling that led him to directing for a short period of time.

Čapek's own plays show a concern with the man in the street, with the face in the crowd. He was a champion of such people, and he wrote allegorically, particularly in *R.U.R.* and *The Insect Play*, about the relationship of such people to a modern, mechanized society. *The Insect Play* is particularly medieval in its conception, with each figure in the play representing some vice or virtue, clearly defined and unilaterally depicted. In a sense, this play was a prelude to the more fully expanded consideration of human personality that one finds in his later trilogy.

Čapek often wrote parody in his early work, attacking conventions indirectly but forcefully, taking the particular and turning it into an allegorical generalization, as he did even in his earliest play, *Lásky hra osudná* (the fateful game of love), written in collaboration with his brother, Josef, in 1910, though not staged until a decade and a half later, when a small company in Prague gave it a limited run. It was not given a professional performance until it was presented by Prague's National Theatre in 1930 along with a number of other short dramatic works by a variety of Czech playwrights.

Čapek, although not philosophically comfortable with the subjectivism of expressionism, used many of the conventions of expressionist drama in his writing. His staging was often expressionistic, as was his use of characters who performed like overgrown puppets, particularly the automatons of *R.U.R.* He also departed with considerable dexterity from his philosophical stance that literature should report on the basis of objective, virtually scientific observation rather than be subjective. Although he was a deliberate and indefatigable observer, as is made clear in his essays, he could not exclude from his writing the fruits of his own careful introspection.

From the time that Czechoslovakia was established as a separate political entity by the Treaty of Versailles in 1919, Čapek worked continually for the democratization of the country. Much influenced by Western culture, particularly that of France and England, Čapek believed firmly in representative government. His political views were much influenced by his extensive study of the pragmatism of William James during his days as a doctoral student at Charles University in Prague.

His close and early friendship with Tomas G. Masaryk grew steadily throughout Čapek's lifetime, and when Masaryk rose to the presidency of Czechoslovakia, he and Čapek were in weekly contact with each other. Through Masaryk, Čapek became an informal force in Czech politics and government. His political influence persisted until the end of his life, which was clearly shortened by his deep distress about Hitler's rise to power. It is speculated that Čapek's attack on Hitler in *The War with the Newts* was responsible for his not being awarded a Nobel Prize in Literature, for in the mid-1930's, Sweden was still trying to appease Hitler and was quite unwilling, presumably, to bring to Stockholm to receive the world's highest award in literature someone who had taken a political stand against the German tyrant.

Biography • Born on January 9, 1890, Karel Čapek was the youngest of three children. His sister, Helene, after whom a major character in *R.U.R.* is named, was born in 1886 and also became a writer. Josef, who was Karel's closest lifelong friend as well as his brother, was born in 1887. The Čapek family was living at that time in the idyllic country town of Malé Svatoňovice, close to what later became Czechoslovakia's border with Austria and Germany. The town, situated in the Krakonoše Mountains, was essentially bilingual, so that Čapek and his siblings grew up with equal fluency in German and Czech.

Čapek's father, Antonín, was a country doctor, but his interests encompassed a wide range of topics. Always intrigued by theater, he headed an amateur theatrical group in his town. He enjoyed painting, was a poet although he remained unpublished, and was an enthusiastic gardener who passed on this enthusiasm to both of his sons. Čapek's mother, Božena Čapková, was extremely cultivated, having a particular interest in the folklore of her area and in the music and tales that had grown out of this folklore. She told and read many tales to her children when they were very young, and she sang to them the songs of their region. The later work of both Čapek brothers reflects directly these early influences. Until his final days, Karel was more devoted to fairy tales than to any other form of literature, save, perhaps, mystery stories, to which he was addicted.

Božena Čapková was basically quite neurotic. Abused by her father, she quickly developed a resentment for and distrust of her husband. Their marriage was not a happy one. Her hypochondria manifested itself in an overconcern for the health of her children, particularly for the health of Karel, who was very small at birth and who suffered early from weak lungs, an affliction with which he lived throughout his life and which ultimately brought about his death in 1938.

Čapek was exposed to a broad range of people as he was growing up, partly because his father's patients came from all walks of life and levels of society and partly because his mother surrounded herself with the people who best knew the folklore of the region, the peasants who lived in the environs in which Čapek was reared.

The closeness that developed between Karel and his brother Josef is largely attributable to the fact that Josef was expected as a small child to look after his sickly brother.

The two were virtually inseparable until 1910, at which time Karel went to Berlin to study and Josef went to Paris. By this time, Karel had studied at the gymnasium in Brno in the province of Moravia for two years, from 1905 to 1907; had completed secondary school in Prague, where his father, by then retired from his medical practice, had come with his wife to live; and had spent one year, 1909-1910, as a student of philosophy at Charles University, where he presumably first came under the strong influence of Tomas G. Masaryk, also a philosopher.

When Karel went to Berlin and his brother to Paris, the collaboration of their early days was interrupted. *Lásky hra osudná* had been completed, but it was still to be eight years before the two brothers published *Krakonošova zahrada,* a collection of their earlier sketches, and twelve years before they were to engage in the thoroughgoing collaboration of which *The Insect Play* was the product.

Čapek, who had an early interest in the writing of H. G. Wells, now developed a considerable and deep interest in the pragmatic and earlier philosophy of William James. During the summer of 1911, which he spent in France with his brother Josef, Čapek began to expand his interest in art and in aesthetics. He was introduced to the writing of Henri Bergson, whose concept of the *élan vital* was to become fundamental in the conscious vitalism found in much of Čapek's important writing. It was probably this exposure to Bergson that led Čapek in 1915 to complete a doctoral dissertation in the area of aesthetics. The title of his study, "Objective Methods in Aesthetics," clearly indicates the direction in which his thought was moving and suggests his philosophical, if not his actual, approach to art. From this period of his life, also, comes the seminar paper on pragmatism that was to result in the publication of *Pragmatismus* in 1918.

Čapek's spinal problems persisted, so that when he had completed his formal education he had to find a means of livelihood that would not overtax him. He suffered agonizing pain, which he is said to have borne with stoicism. In 1916, he found employment, which was to last for less than a year, as tutor to the son of Count Vladimír Lažanský. The count, on whose estate in western Bohemia Čapek resided during the term of his employment, was quite democratic in his outlook, and Čapek found his brief respite in residence with the count and his family congenial.

In 1917, however, Čapek returned to Prague to become a journalist, working for *Národní listy,* where he rose to the position of literary and art editor before resigning in 1921 to become a journalist for *Lidové noviny.* His brother Josef also worked as a member of the paper's staff. This work in journalism exposed Čapek to a broad variety of writing experiences and served to make him a sure and versatile writer.

It was at about this time that Čapek met Olga Scheinpflugová, an actress, who in 1920 played understudy to the lead in the Prague production of his play *The Robber.* Although their romance blossomed, Čapek believed that his health was not good enough for him to contemplate marriage, and it was not until 1935 that he and Olga, who was twelve years his junior, were finally married.

Meanwhile, Karel and Josef built a double house sharing a common wall in Prague. They lived in the close proximity that this house provided them from 1925 until Karel's death in 1938. In this house, they gardened together, worked together on their artistic endeavors, and held constant discussions. The "Friday Circle," established by Čapek in 1924, met weekly at this house and attracted the leading artistic and political figures of Prague, including President Masaryk, to its discussions.

In 1925, Čapek was elected president of Prague's PEN Club, but his tenure was short-lived because he did not wish to speak as an official. He resigned, craving the freedom and independence to speak as an individual artist rather than as the chief representative of a large group of writers. Again, in 1935, Čapek was drawn into PEN when, at H. G. Wells's prodding, he agreed to succeed Wells as international president of the organization. Čapek, however, was unable to attend the annual meeting of the international society, which that year was held in Latin America, so he was not to serve.

Politically, Čapek was a liberal of the Masaryk variety, deploring fascism and finding the representational governments of Great Britain and the United States far preferable to communism. He tried to solidify the Czech people, overcoming his inherent shyness in order to reach the citizenry by radio. If he succeeded at all politically, it must be said that he did so more fully through the indirect methods found in his literature than through his direct attempts to persuade his countrymen. His support of the presidency of Edvard Beneš brought livid outcries from many a Czech, as did his attempts to bring about some sort of peaceful concord between the Czechs and the southern Germans in the mid-1930's.

As the Nazi sphere of influence grew, Čapek became increasingly disheartened. The Munich agreement in 1938 between Germany and Great Britain in a way dealt Čapek a death blow. His disillusionment was ever with him for the remaining months of his life. His lungs, always weak, became inflamed, and on Christmas Day, 1938, less than a year before the beginning of World War II, he died. When Nazi troops entered Prague less than three months after his death, his widow, Olga, destroyed all his papers because she feared that his correspondence might incriminate the people named in it. The Nazis, apparently unaware of Čapek's death, came to this house with a warrant for his arrest. They succeeded in arresting Josef, who spent the rest of his life in the concentration camp at Bergen-Belsen, where he died shortly before the war ended.

Analysis • Karel Čapek was concerned with the natural order of things, a theme that pervaded much of his work. His allegorical approach to expressionism linked his deep philosophical concerns to striking and often disturbing human situations. Artistically, politically, and socially, Čapek dealt with the human personality and with the fate of humankind. He attacked not only the conventions of the day but also human beings' general lack of awareness of their place in nature and in the continuum of events that demands their attention to foster the perpetuation of values and ideals as well as the survival of the human race itself.

Lásky hra osudná • *Lásky hra osudná*, Čapek's early dramatic collaboration with his brother Josef, is a one-act play that was not given a major premiere until twenty years after it was written, although it was produced by an amateur group in the mid-1920's. The play has neoclassical overtones, but only inasmuch as it establishes them to parody neoclassical form. The play is technically in the tradition of the *commedia dell'arte*, and it satirizes this tradition by its own artificial form. Each of the characters in the play is the clear representative of some single aspect of human character: Scaramouche, the obvious madman; Gilles, unwell and emotionally vulnerable, largely because of his own self-indulgence; Isabella, the agent of consternation, whose skirts are lifted by Brighella, thereby enflaming the emotions of the two rival suitors, Trivalin and Gilles. The two fight a duel over Isabella, thereby enabling the opportunistic Brighella to whisk Isabella away and to steal money from her rival suitors.

This is the stuff of which operas are made. The plot is thin and contrived. Still, the play is rescued from the banality that such a plot would suggest by the well-controlled wit of the brothers Čapek, who used the dialogue as a means of ridiculing and poking fun at the theater itself. Particularly engaging is a love scene in which Scaramouche announces that the theater is on fire, tacitly suggesting that the audience might flee and leave him alone with his ladylove, Isabella.

The play begins with a verse prologue that continues until Gilles interrupts in prose. He refuses to speak in verse, although reminded of his obligation to do so, and the play proceeds with an intermixture of versified dialogue and prose, as suits the satiric nature of the production. Although not a notable artistic achievement, this play shows two significant wits working harmoniously to produce a delightful entertainment with a cutting edge of irony throughout.

The Robber • Čapek's first full-length play, *The Robber*, was begun in Paris in 1911, when the author was visiting his brother for the summer. The play apparently passed through a number of distinct versions before it was finally produced by the Prague National Theatre in 1920. The drama moves from realism to Symbolism and back again; it also moves from prose to verse, often without adequate preparation. The story is an old one: Mimi is dominated by her overly protective parents, who already have lost one daughter to an elopement with a man who quickly abandoned her. The father, a stuffy professor, and his wife have to go away on a trip, but the father fortifies the house against intruders and leaves Mimi in the capable hands of their trusted erstwhile servant, Fanka.

The robber is a rather typical hero: His background is unknown; he appears on the scene briefly, bringing about significant changes in the action; and he disappears almost as suddenly as he appeared in the first place. As soon as the parents have left, he makes his move. While Mimi tells him of her troubles, his understanding of and sympathy for her plight lead the hapless Mimi to lose her heart to him. He responds by instigating a fight with Mimi's suitor, a local bumpkin, who, being quicker on the draw than the robber, wounds him. The injured interloper leaves Mimi, promising to return, and being only slightly wounded, he returns that very night, meeting Mimi, who tiptoes past the sleeping Fanka, outside into the moonlight. The parents, who have premonitions of trouble, hurry home unexpectedly and send the robber off.

Mimi's parents exact from her a promise that she will never speak to the robber again, but as soon as he returns in the morning, she violates her promise. In a scene that is almost slapstick, Fanka and the parents come out to try to drive the robber away from outside the fortified dwelling, but he slips past them and into the house, locks the door, and takes to the balcony, gun in hand, ready to fight to the death if necessary to defend Mimi's right to make her own decision about whom she will marry. By this time, Mimi is hopelessly in love with the robber, although there is no suggestion that he reciprocates this love.

After one false start, the professor and his cohorts retake the house and the robber runs off to escape injury at the hands of Fanka, who is shooting at him. He does not leave, however, until the audience learns that Mimi's parents suffered through eight years of courtship before they married and that Mimi's father, the professor, assumes that such deprivation and suffering are what love is all about. Mimi's mother, though, questions the wisdom of their having been forced to wait so long. Mimi's sister returns, her face covered with a veil, to tell Mimi her tale of being deceived by the man she loved.

Though the play is somewhat lacking in substance, it provided a pleasantly diverting evening for audiences. It presents essentially several faces of love and the contrast between youth and age in matters related to the heart. It attacks the question of the rights of the young over the rights of their elders and examines several sets of rights quite closely. The setting had about it certain gothic elements that were well suited to the romantic tone of the play.

The Insect Play • Čapek is often at his best dramatically when he is not writing about human beings, who often turn out to be unconvincing in his plays. In his collaboration with his brother Josef on *The Insect Play*, Čapek wrote a virtual medieval morality play. The insects are presented allegorically, and the whole action is unified by the tramp, who, in his role as stranger, serves the function of seer.

The play is divided into three acts, the first called "Butterflies," the second called "Creepers and Crawlers," and the last called "The Ants." Through these sets of characters, and through their notable characteristics, the brothers Čapek depicted a coherent and quite pessimistic view of human beings. Questions of family organization are central to each act, as are questions of greed, pride, vanity, and other deadly sins.

In the first act, two aging butterflies compete for the affections of the youthful poet, Felix, also a butterfly, who has the reputation of being a Lothario but who is really shy at heart. The butterflies, ethereal and lovely, are subject to the same whims as anyone else. They experience rivalry in love, and their actions are misinterpreted. They contrast sharply with the beetles in the next act, whose family exclusivity is limiting and ultimately cruel.

The natural order of things is presented without comment in the cricket scene, in which two crickets looking for shelter rejoice at finding the nest of another cricket who has fallen victim to a hungry bird that has gobbled him whole. Their good fortune is short-lived because they are barely installed in their new habitat before a cuckoo fly attacks and paralyzes them. The tramp ruminates on the cruelty and rapacity that he sees here. The cuckoo fly kills; the parasite eats the crickets and their larvae. In accord with Čapek's philosophy that drama should be objective rather than subjective, the authors present the facts of what has happened and leave the audience with these facts, although the tramp represents a subjective intrusion on the scene, somewhat in violation of Čapek's philosophy of objective realism in drama.

In *The Insect Play*, the brothers balance the actions of their three allegorical groups, using the tramp as a conscience, a representative of those who view the play. In the end, the tramp, begging for just a little more life, dies, his body left in a fen where slugs begin to feast on it. It finally is discovered by a woodcutter, and nearby, a group of schoolgirls on holiday, oblivious to the tramp's death, play in the lustrous sunshine. The natural order is irresistible. Life goes on, with all its cruelty and suffering.

R.U.R.: Rossum's Universal Robots • Čapek's reputation as a dramatist of international stature was assured by *R.U.R.: Rossum's Universal Robots*, first performed in Prague early in 1921. The play was rapidly translated into many European and some Oriental languages. Foreign productions were staged as far away as the United States and Japan.

The play is concerned with the fate of humankind in the face of mechanization. The robots produced by the Rossum factory look and feel like human beings. They can experience pain, because were they not able to, they would soon be destroyed accidentally. They have no souls, not because souls are not manufacturable but because to give them souls would increase their price tremendously. They are good servants because they cannot feel fear, hatred, love, and sorrow, emotions that weaken human beings and divert them from their tasks.

Čapek's concerns in *R.U.R.* are broadly human and neither focus on any one nation nor point an accusing finger at the industrialized world; neither is *R.U.R.* a nostalgic looking back to more simple times. Rather, it is a quite objective statement of many of the problems brought on by industrialization, exaggerated just enough to make it seem slightly fantastic, yet based sufficiently in truth that its central message is not lost on audiences.

At first, the robots seem a great convenience. Soon there is no need for anyone to work. Robots do all the tasks, having been developed so successfully that they can perform in specialized, highly advanced occupations as well as in the menial occupations to which the early robots were consigned. Robots can typewrite and converse, and they provide specialized information in conversational tones. They are ever obedient, yet they have the ability finally to make discriminating responses.

Ultimately, however, the human race is threatened, first because it begins not to reproduce and then because the robots rebel and threaten to conquer the humans. The only advantage the humans have when the attack comes is that the robots do not know how to reproduce, how to make more robots, and their typical life span is only thirty years. This bargaining chip is lost, however, because Helena has burned the papers in which Rossum details how robots are made. With this act, all hope is lost.

R.U.R. harks back to the suggestion in *The Insect Play* of the specialized function of all creatures. In seeing the robots going about their specialized duties, one thinks back to the ants, beetles, and butterflies of the earlier play. Čapek is dealing conceptually with the whole question of purpose—not human purpose alone, but the purpose of all life. In *R.U.R.*, Čapek the philosopher achieved an ideal harmony with Čapek the dramatist. The play is filled with philosophical portents, yet it is good theater. If it avoids preaching, it probably does so because Čapek employed literary techniques that he learned as a child listening to fairy tales.

The fact that Helena Glory, when she appears early in the play, cannot distinguish between robots and humans suggests that Čapek thought the dehumanization of humankind was already well advanced. He sensed distant, indistinct rumblings on the international scene that were to spring full-blown on the world when Hitler began to take over Eastern Europe. It is not surprising that Čapek died shortly before the Nazi invasion of his own country. In some ways, the macabre fantasies that his plays had presented were now being acted out in ways more horrible than he could ever have imagined they would be. His spirit broken by the certainty of impending conflict, Čapek could no longer face the struggle, and his health, never very robust, failed utterly.

By the end of the second act, the robots in *R.U.R.* have killed all the humans except for Alquist, a construction engineer who may be their only hope. Alquist tries to unlock the secret of making robots, but he cannot. Finally, it is suggested that he dissect living robots to see how they are put together. He has trouble doing this. He then notes that two of the robots who serve him, Primus and Helena, have fallen in love, a contention he confirms by suggesting that he dissect one of them, only to have the other volunteer to be dissected instead. Alquist gives the two his blessing, and presumably there is some distant hope that a new race will come into being.

The play is structurally interesting. Its prologue is comic, while the rest of the play is solidly dramatic in a serious sense. The main action is over by the end of the first act. The two succeeding acts are anticlimactic and need dramatic alternatives.

The Macropulos Secret • In *The Macropulos Secret,* first produced in Prague in November, 1922, Čapek created perhaps his most memorable character, Emilia Marty.

This protagonist is more than three hundred years old when the play opens, having been given a secret formula to ensure longevity by her father, physician to Emperor Rudolph II. This formula assures not only long life but also continuing youth, so that Emilia, who has now lived many lifetimes, all under different names, is not decrepit. She is merely bored at having been around too long. Life has lost all interest for her. The excitement is gone from it, and the audience is led to the inevitable conclusion that too long a life is far worse than death. Indeed, Čapek wrote, "A short life is better for mankind, for a long life would deprive man of his optimism."

As *The Macropulos Secret* develops, Emilia Marty tries to give the secret formula away. Various people want it, some for selfish and others for generous purposes. None, however, is to have it, because Kristina grabs the formula and burns it in a candle's flame, much as Helena in *R.U.R.* burns Rossum's formula for making robots.

Adam the Creator • In 1927, Karel and Josef Čapek again engaged in a collaboration, *Adam the Creator*, which, although promising dramatically, was not successful. The play's basic idea is an intriguing one. Adam, not pleased with the world as his God has made it, destroys it with the Cannon of Negation when humankind fails to listen to him. In his haste to do away with an unsatisfactory world, however, Adam has forgotten to include himself in the destruction, so that now he alone exists in a solipsistic state. God calls on Adam to rebuild the world he has destroyed, and he gives him a heap of dirt with which to accomplish his task.

Adam fails utterly to accomplish his deed and in desperation creates someone in his own likeness, Alter Ego. As similar as they first seem, the two are not compatible, and they quarrel bitterly and often. Alter Ego has an accountant's mentality. He wants his share of everything, including the Clay of Creation. When he and Adam set about remaking the world, Adam creates individuals, whereas Alter Ego creates nothing but hordes of undistinguished and undistinguishable beings, products of a mechanistic and materialistic mind. Alter Ego's creations are all the same; Adam's, on the other hand, are all different.

As might be predicted, the world that Adam and Alter Ego create is unbearable, and the two, now wholly discredited by their fellows, seek refuge in the hole from which the Clay of Creation originally came. Just a smidgen of earth remains in the hole. Alter Ego kicks it, and there being too little clay to make a whole man, the pile produces an unsightly dwarf, Zmeten, whose name means monster.

Adam and Alter Ego decide to destroy the world they have created, but Zmeten, who now has six children, will not hear of such a thing. He threatens them with their own Cannon of Negation, which he has now turned into a cookpot. As the play ends, a shrine marks the spot in which creation began, and the Cannon of Negation has been melted down and made into a bell. As the bell clangs, God speaks to Adam, who responds by saying that he will not tamper further with God's creation. In other words, he accepts things as they are, settling for the status quo.

The play leaves little cause for hope. In fact, it ends with the sort of encompassing ennui found in Emilia Marty in *The Macropulos Secret*, with the important difference that the people living in the world Adam and Alter Ego have created are mortal and are only serving a term. Nothing is perfect; life, rather than being good or bad, just is.

Power and Glory • *Power and Glory*, written in 1937, was openly anti-Nazi in its original form. The Nazis had already infiltrated the Czech hierarchy by that time, and they refused to allow the play to be produced until it was made antiseptic by their standards. The title of the play refers to a horrible disease that decimates people past forty years of age by eating away at their flesh. Significantly, it is those over forty who conduct, but do not actively fight in, wars.

A brilliant physician, appropriately named Galén, has come up with a cure for the dreaded scourge, but he withholds his secret formula, demanding that in return for it the world must agree to live peacefully. The world is not ready to meet such a demand until the dictator, who, like Hitler, is preparing for an offensive war, develops the disease and is mortally ill with it. He concedes to Dr. Galén's demands, but as Dr. Galén is rushing with his cure to the dictator's bedside, he is waylaid by the mob and killed. The pessimism of the play presages the utter futility that was building in Čapek and in many other European intellectuals in the years of Hitler's rise to power.

The Mother • Čapek's last play, which was his favorite, is an estimable one. *The Mother*, written in 1938, the year in which Čapek died, revolves around a mother, presented as the prototype of motherhood, who has stirred her five sons by telling them stories of their dead father's heroism in dying for his country. The father was the typical patriot, and the sons each represent a different category of person. One is a physician who loses his life in the practice of his profession. The twins are Petr, a liberal, and Kornel, a conservative, who fight in different armies in the same war and die on opposite sides. Another son is a pilot who dies while flying his plane to altitudes not previously reached. The youngest son, the only survivor, aspires to be a poet.

In the course of the play, each of the dead sons returns as a spirit and engages in dialogue with the mother. It is she who has made these youths, she who has shaped their values and ideals. Without her encomiums about the heroism of their father, her four dead sons might not have made the sacrifices they did and might still be alive. Her motherly love makes her wish that they were, and she cannot understand why they have sacrificed as each has. Having lost four sons, she first hides her youngest, trying to save him. Finally, however, she gives him a rifle and sends him off to fight. Čapek, never a pacifist, was not a warmonger either. The events through which he was living in Czechoslovakia in 1938 led him to the inevitable conclusion that under some sets of circumstances, people must fight.

Kornel and Petr seem like offshoots respectively of Alter Ego and Adam in *Adam the Creator*. Kornel, in rearranging a room, would keep everything as it had been, whereas Petr would arrange things as they should be. The mother represents the synthesis of these two opposing stands and would put things where they belong, where they can prosper.

Other major works

LONG FICTION: *Továrna na absolutno*, 1922 (*The Absolute at Large*, 1927); *Krakatit*, 1924 (English translation, 1925); *Hordubal*, 1933 (English translation, 1934); *Povětroň*, 1934 (*Meteor*, 1935); *Obyčejný život*, 1934 (*An Ordinary Life*, 1936); *Válka s mloky*, 1936 (*The War with the Newts*, 1937); *První parta*, 1937 (*The First Rescue Party*, 1939); *Život a dílo skladatele Foltýna*, 1939 (*The Cheat*, 1941).

SHORT FICTION: *Zářivé hlubiny*, 1916 (with Josef Čapek; *The Luminous Depths*, 1916); *Boží muka*, 1917; *Krakonošova zahrada*, 1918 (with Josef Čapek); *Trapné povídky*, 1921 (*Money and Other Stories*, 1929); *Povídky z jedné kapsy* and *Povídky z druhé kapsy*, 1929 (*Tales from Two Pockets*, 1932); *Devatero pohádek*, 1931 (*Fairy Tales*, 1933); *Kniha apokryfů*, 1946 (*Apocryphal Stories*, 1949).

NONFICTION: *Pragmatismus,* 1918; *Kritika slov,* 1920; *O nejbližších vecech,* 1920 (*Intimate Things,* 1935); *Musaion,* 1920-1921; *Italské listy,* 1923 (*Letters from Italy,* 1929); *Anglické listy,* 1924 (*Letters from England,* 1925); *Hovory s T. G. Masarykem,* 1928-1935 (3 volumes; *President Masaryk Tells His Story,* 1934; also as *Masaryk on Thought and Life,* 1938); *Zahradníkův rok,* 1929 (*The Gardener's Year,* 1931); *Výlet do Španěl,* 1930 (*Letters from Spain,* 1931); *Marsyas,* 1931 (*In Praise of Newspapers,* 1951); *O věcech obecných: Čili, Zóon politikon,* 1932; *Obrázky z Holandska,* 1932 (*Letters from Holland,* 1933); *Dášeňka,* 1933 (*Dashenka,* 1940); *Cesta na sever,* 1936 (*Travels in the North,* 1939); *Měl jsem psa a kočku,* 1939 (*I Had a Dog and a Cat,* 1940); *Obrázky z domova,* 1953; *Veci kolemnás,* 1954; *Poznámky o tvorbě,* 1959; *Viktor Dyk-S. K. Neumann-bratří Č.: Korespondence z let 1905-1918,* 1962.

TRANSLATION: *Francouzská poesie nové doby,* 1920 (of French poetry).

Bibliography

Bradbrook, Bohuslava R. *Karel Čapek: In Pursuit of Truth, Tolerance, and Trust.* Portland, Oreg.: Sussex Academic Press, 1998. A critical analysis of the works of Čapek. Bibliography and index.

Makin, Michael, and Jindrich Toman, eds. *On Karel Čapek: A Michigan Slavic Colloquium.* Ann Arbor: Michigan Slavic Publications, 1992. A group of papers presented at a colloquium on Čapek. Bibliography.

Pynsent, R. B., ed. *Karel Matel Čapek-Chod: Proceedings of a Symposium Held at the School of Slavonic and East European Studies 18-20 September, 1984.* London: The School, 1985. A collection of papers presented at a symposium on Čapek. Index.

Schubert, Peter Z. *The Narratives of Čapek and Cexov: A Typological Comparison of the Authors' World Views.* Bethesda, Md.: International Scholars Publications, 1997. A comparison of the philosophical views of Čapek and Anton Chekhov as expressed in their works. Bibliography and index.

R. Baird Shuman

Anton Chekhov

Born: Taganrog, Russia; January 29, 1860
Died: Badenweiler, Germany; July 15, 1904

Principal drama • *Platonov*, wr. 1878-1881, pb. 1923 (English translation, 1930); *Ivanov*, pr., pb. 1887, revised pr. 1889 (English translation, 1912); *Medved*, pr., pb. 1888 (*A Bear*, 1909); *Predlozheniye*, pb. 1889, pr. 1890 (*A Marriage Proposal*, 1914); *Leshy*, pr. 1889 (*The Wood Demon*, 1925); *Svadba*, pb. 1889, pr. 1890 (*The Wedding*, 1916); *Yubiley*, pb. 1892 (*The Jubilee*, 1916); *Chayka*, pr. 1896, pb. 1897, revised pr. 1898, pb. 1904 (*The Seagull*, 1909); *Dyadya Vanya*, pb. 1897, pr. 1899 (based on his play *The Wood Demon*; *Uncle Vanya*, 1914); *Tri sestry*, pr., pb. 1901, revised pb. 1904 (*The Three Sisters*, 1920); *Vishnyovy sad*, pr., pb. 1904 (*The Cherry Orchard*, 1908); *The Plays of Chekhov*, pb. 1923-1924 (2 volumes); *Nine Plays*, pb. 1959

Other literary forms • Within the ten-volume edition of his works published in 1901, Anton Chekhov included 240 of the hundreds of stories he had written for dozens of newspapers and magazines. Many of these stories were collected and published in hardcover form as Chekhov progressed in his career: *Pystrye rasskazy* (1886; motley stories), *Nevinnye rechi* (1887; innocent tales), *V sumerkakh* (1887; in the twilight), and *Rasskazy* (1888; stories). Some of his most famous stories are "Gore" ("Sorrow"), "Toska" ("Misery"), "Step'" ("The Steppe"), "Skuchnaya isoriya" ("A Dreary Story"), "Palata No. 6" ("Ward No. 6"), "Chorny monakh" ("The Black Monk"), "Tri goda" ("Three Years"), "Muzhiki" ("Peasants"), "Kryzhovnik" ("Gooseberries"), "Dushechka" ("The Darling"), "Dama s sobachkoi" ("The Lady with the Dog"), and "Nevesta" ("The Betrothed"). In addition, Chekhov wrote a work of reportage on conditions on the island penal colony of Sakhalin: *Ostrov Sakhalin* (1893-1894).

Achievements • Anton Chekhov began writing as a means of earning an income, and in doing so he built up a large audience for his comic tales, which he wrote at a rate of more than one per week. At the same time, he attracted the attention and approval of a broad range of writers and critics. As his career progressed and his literary efforts grew more serious, his appeal never wavered, and his popularity and reputation continued to grow as he expanded into drama. In 1900, he became one of the first ten literary members of the Russian Academy of Sciences, inducted at the same time as Leo Tolstoy, and during his life he influenced many younger writers, including Maxim Gorky. Since his death, his reputation has grown steadily, and now he is universally recognized as one of the founders of modern drama and one of the greatest of short-story writers.

Biography • Anton Pavlovich Chekhov was born in the provincial town of Taganrog, Russia, on January 29, 1860. The grandson of a serf, Chekhov was the third of seven children. Chekhov said of his early days, "There was no childhood in my childhood," largely because of his father, Pavel, who frequently forced Chekhov to tend the family's unheated food and hardware store until late at night. Chekhov's father beat his children and taught them how to cheat customers, yet he was in his own eyes a religious man. He forced his children into a religious choir that rehearsed frequently and sang at various churches. Chekhov disliked these duties. It is not surprising that in later life he was not a religious man, that he spent his life trying to "burn the slave" out of himself and become a man of culture, and that he became convinced that work was useless unless it improved humankind's lot.

Chekhov's home life was disrupted in 1876 when his father's business went into bankruptcy and his father fled to Moscow to escape debtors' prison. His mother sold the house, took the younger children, and joined her husband. Chekhov stayed behind to finish his schooling and became, at sixteen, the main support of the family, providing income by tutoring. He finished school in 1879, rejoined his family, and tried to provide material and moral support, lecturing at times on the need to avoid lies, affirm human worth, and be fair, all values that would be of great importance in his later work.

In Moscow, Chekhov studied medicine and supported the family by writing stories in humorous magazines under the name Antosha Chekhonte. His first story was published in 1880 in the magazine *Strekoza* (dragonfly), and in 1881, he finished his first full-length play, *Platonov*, though it was not performed or published in his lifetime. In October of 1882, he met Nicolai Leikin, the owner of the weekly magazine *Oskolki* (fragments); they became friends, and soon scarcely a week went by without a Chekhov story appearing in the magazine. These early ventures saw him through medical school, and in 1884, Chekhov finished his medical studies and took up practice. By December 10 of that year, however, Chekhov became ill, coughing up blood, his first attack of tuberculosis, the disease that would kill him twenty years later. For the rest of his life, no year would go by without similar attacks.

Chekhov recovered rapidly and managed to ignore the implications of his symptoms, resuming his normal life. In December, 1885, he accompanied Leikin to St. Petersburg, the literary center of Russia at the time, meeting Aleksei Suvorin, owner of the powerful daily newspaper *Novoye vremya* (new times), and Dimitry Grigorovich, a noted novelist. After his return to Moscow, he received a letter from Grigorovich urging him to respect his talent and write seriously; Chekhov responded that Grigorovich's letter was "like a thunderbolt," making him believe in his talent for the first time. Suvorin also wrote, inviting Chekhov to contribute to *Novoye vremya*. Chekhov accepted, beginning a long relationship with the newspaper and with Suvorin.

In 1887, Chekhov completed the full-length play *Ivanov*, which was a popular success. In 1888, he experimented with longer prose forms and produced the much-acclaimed novella "The Steppe"; he was also awarded the Pushkin Prize for the best literary work of the year for his

(Library of Congress)

collection of stories *V sumerkakh*. In drama, he achieved financial success with two popular one-act comedies, *A Bear* and *A Marriage Proposal*.

In June, 1889, Chekhov's brother Nicolai died of tuberculosis as Chekhov tended him, and late in the year, his full-length play *The Wood Demon*, at first rejected as "too tedious," was finally performed but was an almost complete failure. Chekhov began to doubt his dramatic ability, and, except for the one-act comedy *The Jubilee*, he abandoned drama until 1896. Indeed, Chekhov underwent a crisis of self-examination in 1889, doubting his literary and medical abilities and even his own worth.

Until this time, Chekhov's writing had been extraordinarily fluent. He wrote quickly, and almost everything he wrote was successful. Critics had begun to complain, however, that he had no purpose, no aim, and Chekhov was troubled with the same thought. Tolstoy's moral philosophy, advocating an ascetic search for self-perfection, influenced him for a time. In 1890, Chekhov startled his friends but lifted himself out of what he described as a "spiritual stagnation" by undertaking a long and arduous trip to the prison colony of Sakhalin, located on an island off the eastern coast of Russia, to make study of conditions there. It may be that this trip crystallized Chekhov's belief that a person must not be content merely to see everything; he must also do something about what he sees.

There is ample evidence of Chekhov's activity after he returned from Sakhalin. In 1891, a famine year, he devoted himself to collecting food and money for starving farmers. In 1892, he bought Melikhovo, an estate of 675 neglected acres, and poured his efforts into planting, pruning, and improving. He planted thousands of trees, including an apple and a cherry orchard. At Melikhovo, he led medical efforts to forestall threatened cholera epidemics. He also took on the tasks of constructing rural schools, stocking the Taganrog library, and providing constructive criticism for many aspiring writers, displaying the energy and purpose lacking in so many of his dramatic creations.

By 1896, Chekhov was again tempted by the theater, and *The Seagull* opened on October 17 of that year. *The Seagull* failed, and its author vowed never again to write drama. In 1898, however, Vladimir Nemirovich-Danchenko and Konstantin Stanislavsky created the Moscow Art Theater and received permission to use *The Seagull* in its repertory. The theater's first few productions failed, and by the time that the company was ready to stage *The Seagull*, it needed a success. The opening on December 17, 1898, exceeded everyone's hopes; it was an enormous success, and the theater adopted the seagull as its permanent emblem.

The success of *The Seagull* was shadowed by a deterioration in Chekhov's health. A severe pulmonary hemorrhage in 1897 forced him away from Moscow to temperate Nice, Italy, during the winter of 1897-1898, and in 1898, he settled outside Yalta and gave up the practice of medicine.

On October 26, 1899, the Moscow Art Theater performed the second of Chekhov's great plays, *Uncle Vanya*. This play was followed by *The Three Sisters* on January 31, 1901, and then by *The Cherry Orchard* on January 17, 1904. All three plays were only moderate successes at first but gained in favor as audiences and actors grew to understand them.

Chekhov met Olga Knipper, an actress, through the Moscow Art Theater. They were married on May 25, 1901, but most of their married life was spent apart, Olga's career demanding that she live in Moscow and Chekhov's health preventing him from living there except during the summer. Chekhov's belief in purposeful work made him content with this situation.

Throughout 1903 and 1904, Chekhov's health declined steadily, and in June of 1904, he went with Olga to a German health resort in Badenweiler. He seemed to respond to treatment at first, but he died early in the morning on July 15. He was buried a week later in Moscow.

Analysis • Anton Chekhov was talking about other writers when he said, "The best of them are realists and depict life as it is, but because every line they write is permeated, as with a juice, by a consciousness of an aim, you feel in addition to life as it is, also life as it should be, and it is that that delights you." These very qualities that Chekhov praises in other great writers are the qualities in his greatest plays, *The Seagull, Uncle Vanya, The Three Sisters*, and *The Cherry Orchard*, plays that continue to delight audiences throughout the world, though that delight is sometimes expressed in tears.

Chekhov has been called a depressing writer, one who bring tears to an audience's eyes, but he rejected that view adamantly, saying that he had never wanted tears:

> I wanted something else. I wanted to tell people honestly: "Look at yourselves. See how badly you live and how tiresome you are." The main thing is that people should understand this. When they do, they will surely create a new and better life for themselves.

Audiences will continue to be moved to tears by Chekhov's plays, but his words give his audience a way of understanding the main ingredients of his greatness. His powers of observation and his honesty permitted him to create characters readily recognizable as human, characters sharply individualized yet representative. He was convinced of the need for unceasing striving, a belief that pervaded his life and work; and he had a faith that the future would bring a better life for humankind.

Chekhov's exceptional powers of observation, no doubt sharpened by his scientific training, enabled him to bring to the stage living characters. This was the single guiding purpose of Chekhov's early writing, to show "life as it is." This purpose, however, could not sustain him for long, and especially after his crises in 1889 and his trip to Sakhalin in 1890, he came to believe that "A work of art should express a great idea." If Chekhov's plays can be said to have a great idea, it must be that human beings must work ceaselessly and that their labor must be accompanied by a faith in the usefulness of that work, a faith in the future. In all his best plays, the themes of work, faith, and purpose are present, and in all there is a stab of pain and pity at the recognition of how often humans are idle, how many there are who do no work, how many who work to no end, how few who possess faith, how difficult it is to persevere in one's faith, how often dreams are not fulfilled, and how transient is all human happiness. Chekhov's purpose, however, went beyond the pain of recognition. He hoped that when people recognized themselves in his characters, they would go on to "create a new and better life."

Chekhov did not begin his dramatic career with the happy mixture of observation, purpose, and knowledge of the stage that was to characterize his later work. His earliest play, untitled by Chekhov but commonly referred to as *Platonov*, is a long and rambling work, full of dramatic stereotypes and heightened, exaggerated scenes, with little of the flavor of his later works. His next full-length play, *Ivanov*, was staged and was a popular success, but Chekhov was not satisfied with it, for good reason. It, too, was stilted and did not in Chekhov's view reflect the truth about human life. By the end of the 1880's, Chekhov had already formed the opinion that "A play ought to be written in which people come and go, dine, talk of the weather, or play cards . . . because that is what happens in real life. Life on the stage should be as it really is and the people, too, should be as they are and not stilted."

Chekhov would need a new kind of drama to embody such perceptions, and he was not successful at creating it until 1896. His first attempt at a new drama, *The Wood Demon*, first performed in 1889, failed so badly that Chekhov turned away from drama for six years. During this time, he achieved fame for his fiction. As fame brought more money and therefore allowed him more time to work on each piece, he wrote longer and longer pieces, and so was gradually led back to full-length drama.

Ultimately, Chekhov found a way to fulfill his dream of capturing real life on the stage by rejecting the dramatic conventions of his time. Although the drama of his contemporaries focused on action, often melodramatic action, Chekhov's last plays are primarily works of inaction, works in which the needed action takes place offstage. Chekhov prevents the audience from being distracted by activity, focusing attention on the inner lives of his characters.

These inner lives are often both painful and ridiculous. It has long been a difficulty for critics that Chekhov called *The Seagull* and *The Cherry Orchard* comedies and insisted that they were not tragic. In truth, many of the characters in his plays are absurd: Their concerns are ridiculous, and the detached observer must confess that they are silly. It is a rare viewer, however, who can be detached about Chekhov's characters. The audience simultaneously recognizes the foolishness and the humanity of the characters, touched by the recognition of how real the characters' problems are to them, how impossible the characters find it to extricate themselves from their problems. Some of their dreams are absurd, but they do not know how to help themselves, and so their lives pass them by without teaching them how to live. Chekhov shows convincingly "what fools these mortals be," but the audience, being mortal, is moved to pity, not laughter.

The Seagull • *The Seagull* was partially inspired by events in Chekhov's life. Chekhov had for years known a woman named Lydia, or "Lika," Mizinova, who was apparently in love with him; he was seemingly less in love with her. They were very close, but Chekhov was not interested in marriage, and Lika turned her attention to another man, I. N. Potapenko, a married friend of Chekhov. The two had an affair that resulted in Lika's pregnancy and her abandonment by Potapenko. She went to Europe to deliver the baby, but the baby died soon after Lika's return to Russia. The episode no doubt disturbed Chekhov, and there is some indication that he felt a degree of guilt in the matter. Nina, a central character in the play and the only one who finds an answer for her life, is based on Lika, whose true experience provides the central theme of *The Seagull*.

The play opens at the country estate of Sorin, a retired justice. His sister, Arkadina, an actress, is making a visit to her brother's home with her lover, the writer Trigorin. Living with Sorin is Arkadina's twenty-five-year-old son, Konstantin Trepliov, who, as the play begins, is about to stage a play that he has written for the benefit of his mother and the other guests on the estate. The play features Nina, whom Trepliov loves. Also attending the performance are Dorn, a doctor; Medvedenko, a schoolmaster; Shamrayev, Sorin's bailiff; his wife, Polena, and their daughter Masha. Masha sets the tone of Chekhov's play with her first lines. When Medvedenko asks her why she always wears black, she replies that she is "in mourning for my life."

Medvedenko loves Masha and wants to marry her, but Masha feels nothing for him and loves Trepliov instead. In turn, Trepliov cares nothing for Masha and focuses all his dreams on Nina. As Trepliov's play gets under way, strain is plainly seen in the relationship between Arkadina and her son. Trepliov wants very much to impress his mother with the play, but she interrupts it several times with her comments. Arkadina claims that her son has no talent, but Dorn sees some power in the play, though he thinks it lacks a "definite idea." Nina complains that the play has no living characters, but the novice playwright defends himself by claiming that plays ought not to show things as they are, or as they ought to be, but rather as they appear to us in our dreams, an attitude that would get little sympathy from Chekhov.

Chekhov would certainly sympathize, however, with the most prevalent problem in the play: unrequited love. Trepliov yearns for the love of his mother but does not receive it, Nina becomes enamored of Trigorin and ends up running off to meet him in Moscow, and Arkadina also wants the love of Trigorin but must settle for dominance over him: He loves no one. Dorn comments on the situation at the end of act 1 with the lines, "How distraught they all are! And what a quantity of love about! . . . But what can I do, my child?" One can almost hear Chekhov directing these words to Lika Mizinova.

Acts 2 and 3 develop Nina's infatuation with Trigorin and the relationship between Arkadina and Trepliov. Nina is impressed by Trigorin's fame and occupation and thinks only of him. Trepliov sees that he has lost his mother to Trigorin and that he is losing Nina as well. He is wrought up enough to kill a seagull and present it to Nina, telling her that he will soon kill himself as well. Trigorin comes on the scene shortly after Trepliov leaves, and the scene gives him an idea for a story, as he tells Nina in a speech that foreshadows their future affair: "A young girl, like you, has lived beside a lake since childhood. She loves the lake as a seagull does . . . but a man comes along, sees her, and having nothing better to do, destroys her, just like this seagull here." This "idea" is of great symbolic importance because it is the first example of a perspective that will come up again and again in Chekhov: The greatest destruction is casual, ignorant, rooted in idleness. Nina understands nothing of the implications of the speech and, by the end of act 3, the affair is arranged.

Trepliov, true to his word, shoots himself but suffers only a grazed head. Nina is "casual" about the injury, and Arkadina, though maternal for a few moments, soon begins to argue with her son again.

In act 4, which opens two years later, Trigorin and Arkadina return to visit Sorin, who is ill. In the two-year interval, Masha has married Medvedenko in an attempt to put Trepliov out of her mind, and they now have a child but essentially nothing has changed: Medvedenko still spends all his time worrying, either about his daughter or about money, and Masha, still yearning for Trepliov, is cruel to her husband and has virtually abandoned her child. Trepliov has succeeded in publishing but has found no contentment. Nina, after running away with Trigorin, became pregnant. He abandoned her, she lost her child, and her acting career is floundering.

While the rest of the company go to a late supper, Nina comes on the scene, drawn by the news that Arkadina and Trigorin have returned. She converses with Trepliov, and clearly he still loves her. Of all the characters in the play, only Nina has changed. She has suffered greatly, but she has learned from her trials; as she tells Trepliov, "what really matters is not fame, or glamour . . . but knowing how to endure things." Nina then leaves to pursue her acting career in an obscure village; she still loves Trigorin, but that does not stop her from living. Trepliov, however, does not have Nina's faith. With the final realization that she is gone from his life and that his mother has no need of him, he has no use for himself, and he goes offstage and shoots himself. The rest of the characters, playing cards as they hear the shot, send Dorn out to investigate. They accept his explanation that the noise was just a bottle of ether exploding; as the curtain falls, Dorn takes Trigorin aside to give him the news of the shooting and to tell him to take Arkadina back to the city lest she find out. Thus the audience hears of the shooting as the card game continues, and really nothing is changed.

The play ends on the same note on which it began. If Masha started the play mourning her life, she has not stopped mourning during the two years of the play's action, and though she has a husband and a child, she cannot be said to live. Trepliov, too, has spent his time mourning rather than living, and if his death brings about no change, that is not surprising, for his death is no different from his life. Arkadina starts the play wrapped in her idleness, incapable of feeling or understanding her son's misery, and it is not at all surprising that she plays cards as he shoots himself. Change can be seen only in Nina, who has learned not to fear life, and who works toward a future goal with faith and dedication.

Uncle Vanya • The exact date of composition of *Uncle Vanya* is unknown, but it is known that it had been performed for some time in rural theaters before it was performed by the Moscow Art Theater. In fact, though Chekhov claimed that it was a totally new play, acts 2 and 3 are taken almost completely from his earlier failure, *The Wood Demon*. Although *Uncle Vanya* had its beginnings in *The Wood Demon*, it is in fact a very different play. While the earlier play was a failure, *Uncle Vanya* is a convincing, deeply moving work, perhaps Chekhov's most touching play.

Uncle Vanya is subtitled "Scenes from Country Life in Four Acts," and all the action of the play takes place on the estate of Serebryakov, who has recently come there to live with his young, beautiful second wife, Yelena, after retiring from his university position. Their arrival proves a disturbance to those who have been living on or about the estate, especially Sonya, Serebryakov's daughter; Vanya, Sonya's uncle, the brother of Serebryakov's first wife; and Astrov, a doctor who is Vanya's friend. Both Serebryakov and Yelena have a hand in the crisis.

Vanya and Sonya have devoted their lives to managing the estate, saving and scrimping to send every spare ruble to Serebryakov, thinking him talented, even brilliant. When he arrives on the estate, however, he is seen to be another sort of man. He suffers from gout, is perpetually in a bad mood, thinks of no one but himself, and disturbs the routine of the estate, staying up late at night writing and then not rising until late in the day. For Vanya, Serebryakov's arrival is even more disturbing; his routine and his illusions are shattered. He realizes that all of Serebryakov's work has been shallow, commonplace, and that his writing will not outlive him. Vanya believes he has lost his life and has worked for the last twenty-five years for nothing.

More disturbing yet is the presence of Yelena, for she is young, beautiful, and idle. She draws the attention of all who see her. Vanya falls in love with her, and his love is made more painful by his jealousy of Serebryakov. Astrov, hardworking and idealistic, has been a friend of the family for years and has paid monthly visits to the estate; his work as a doctor and his efforts to preserve the ecology of the region have exhausted him, and while his intelligence is still sharp, he complains that his feelings have become deadened, leaving him incapable of love. Even he, however, is susceptible to Yelena's charms, and before long he is ignoring his work and making daily visits to the estate. Sonya, a good-hearted, hardworking, but plain woman, has been cherishing a love for Astrov for some time, and it is agony for her to see him attracted to Yelena instead.

The crisis comes to a head when Serebryakov calls a family meeting, expresses his discontent with life on the estate, and presents his plan to sell the estate so that he can live more comfortably. Vanya goes into a rage because Serebryakov's plan would leave Vanya and Sonya homeless, and Serebryakov backs down from his plan, after which Vanya twice tries to shoot him, missing both times. He gives up in disgust, and the third act ends. In act 4, Serebryakov and Yelena return to the city, where they will be mailed money by Vanya and Sonya.

In short, things return to their original state, except that illusions have been stripped away. Vanya knows that his efforts have been wasted, and Sonya knows that her love for Astrov has been in vain. Astrov leaves also, and while he will return, his visits will be less frequent than before. In the final scene, Sonya and Vanya sit down to their work again, and while Vanya might not be able to endure on his own, Sonya's strength and faith in the future enable them to continue. In the long closing monologue, she voices her resolve to endure: "Well, what can we do? We must go on living. We shall go on living. . . . We shall live through a long, long succession of days and tedious evenings."

It is not difficult to see the resemblance between Sonya and Nina in *The Seagull*. Both possess what Chekhov called "iron in the blood," a strength that keeps them living and working, a strength born of faith in the future. There are also resemblances among other characters in the two plays. The idleness of Yelena and selfishness of Serebryakov have their parallels in Arkadina, Masha, and Trigorin. Indeed, the general atmosphere of the two plays is similar: Life is hard, and work and faith are needed to endure it well. Few have such faith, and thus, few are able to endure and still live vitally. As Vanya says, "When people have no real life, they live on their illusions."

In Astrov, the audience sees Chekhov's complex human vision. In many ways, Astrov is like Chekhov: He is a dedicated doctor and takes delight in the planting of trees. He suffers, however, for his efforts; they exhaust and deaden him, and his exhaustion threatens him with loss of faith and leaves him incapable of love. Yet he is a man of ideals, respected by all in the play except the self-centered Serebryakov. Yelena sees his excellence clearly and speaks movingly when she says, "He plants a tree and wonders what will come of it in a thousand years' time, and speculates on the future happiness of mankind. Such people are rare, and we must love them." The symbol of tree planting is particularly apt in communicating Chekhov's vision, for it is an act which yields no instant gratification. Astrov sees that the casual destruction of forests will create a dismal future, but deliberate efforts to restore them will bring hope for a better life.

In contrast, Yelena is an object of present beauty. She represents a human physical ideal, less than ideal in other ways. She does no work, has no thoughts of the future, and lives her life in idleness and boredom. Her threat is that she infects others with her ennui and self-indulgence. If there is no work for the future, Chekhov asks in this play, how is human life to improve?

The Three Sisters • Chekhov had always prided himself on the speed and ease with which he wrote, but *The Three Sisters* was different. Numerous letters testify to the difficulty with which the play progressed; it was pulled out of him slowly, no doubt a result in part of his declining health, but probably also because it is his most searching, introspective play. It looks long and deeply at its characters, and it is no accident that it is the only one of his major works that he referred to as a "drama." Chekhov might have claimed that *The Seagull* and *The Cherry Orchard* were comic in their vision, but in *The*

Three Sisters, his sympathy for the plight of his characters outweighs all other considerations: The play is a choral lament over the loss of life.

At the center of the chorus are the three Prozorov sisters: Olga, an unmarried teacher; Masha, married to Kuligin; and Irina, the youngest sister, who is twenty as the play begins. These characters are supplemented by a considerable supporting cast. Of greatest importance are Andrey, the brother of the three sisters; Vershinin, the battery commander of the military garrison in the provincial town where the sisters live; and Tuzenbakh, a lieutenant who is in love with Irina. Others are Chebutykin, an army doctor; Natalya, Andrey's fiancée and then his wife; Kuligin, a teacher; and Solyony, a suitor for Irina. Each of the characters takes on a life of his or her own, all come together in the complex harmony that makes the work so compelling.

The three sisters, though the details of their dreams are different, sing the same refrain: "To Moscow." Eleven years before the action of the play, the family lived in Moscow, and each of the sisters yearns for Moscow as the fulfillment of her dream. Olga thinks that she would be happy if she were married, and Masha thinks that she would be happy if she were not. Irina thinks that happiness lies in working, but when she goes out to work she resents it. Andrey thinks that he would be happy if he were a professor in Moscow, but he does nothing to realize that dream; he spends his time making picture frames and playing the violin.

The play's action spans four years, beginning on the celebration of Irina's name day, at which Vershinin, the new battery commander, presents himself. He is from Moscow and was a friend of the sisters' late father; the sisters immediately are interested in him. They envy his recent life in Moscow, though he claims to prefer the provincial town. Masha takes a special interest in him, and, though both are married, an affair develops as the play proceeds. Also in the first act, Andrey proposes to Natalya; they are married by the time act 2 begins, and by the play's end, they have two children, though by then, Natalya (not, like the other characters, part of the aristocracy, but rather a member of the rising middle class of Chekhov's time) is having an affair with the head of the local council and has virtually driven the Prozorovs from their home. Another love theme concerns Irina. Tuzenbakh is in love with her and remains devoted to her throughout the four-year span of the play. Irina gives him little encouragement, for he is not handsome, and she has always dreamed of meeting her husband in Moscow. Tuzenbakh has a dangerous rival in Solyony, an eccentric, morbid character who insults everyone but Irina and is determined that he will have "no happy rivals."

The dream of going to Moscow remains unfulfilled. As the play ends, Vershinin and his men are transferred to another city, ending his affair with Masha, who returns in misery to her spineless but kind husband. Irina, finally convinced that her dream of going to Moscow will never be realized, consents to marry Tuzenbakh, though she does not love him. Before they marry, however, Solyony kills Tuzenbakh in a duel, and Irina is left alone. Olga has gone through the play hoping for some change in her burdensome life, a husband perhaps, or a rest from the constant demands of her teaching, but no husband is forthcoming, and by the end of the play her teaching chores are multiplied, because she has been made headmistress. Andrey has spent four years regretting his marriage and dreaming of great academic triumphs in Moscow, yet by the play's end, he is reduced to baby-sitting while his wife entertains her lover. All the dreams of the sisters have been crushed, four years of life have been lost, and the play ends with the courageous but tragic spectacle of the sisters trying to cope, trying to live, though they suffer and do not know why. While Sonya in *Uncle Vanya* believes that the future will bring her rest, the three sisters try to believe that the future will bring them life.

Though the sisters arrive at no answers, the questions of happiness and the future are raised often in the play. These questions are debated by Vershinin and Tuzenbakh several times; the most important of the debates takes place in act 2, when Masha joins in. Vershinin poses the question, "What will life be like in two or three hundred years?" and leaves the floor open for speculation. Tuzenbakh responds that the superficial details of people's life will change, but their essential situation will not: ". . . man will be sighing much the same as before, 'Ah, how difficult life is.' And yet he will be afraid of death and as unwilling to die as he is nowadays." Vershinin's views are different; he believes that somewhere in the future "a new, happy life will appear." He believes that the present generation sacrifices happiness now so that future generations can be happy—indeed, that such altruism is the meaning of life—but Tuzenbakh denies that people know anything about meaning. At this point, Masha breaks in, claiming that "man must have faith, or he must look for faith. Otherwise, his life is empty, empty. . . . Either you know the reason why you are living, or else everything is nonsense."

In this debate lies all the suffering of humankind. Masha seeks to know why she exists, but who is to tell her? While she waits for an answer, life passes her by. Tuzenbakh denies that there is an answer or rather denies that there is any way to find the answer and so does not trouble himself overmuch with the question. Vershinin defines his own answer, his own explanation for his sufferings, one very similar to Chekhov's own beliefs, and it helps him to carry on. What makes the difference, Chekhov suggests, is faith in the future. Faith is belief without proof, and only such faith can enable a person to work with confidence for the future happiness of the race while recognizing its present misery. This was Chekhov's situation. He could see that most people were miserable and dissatisfied, that they frittered their lives away on trivial concerns, and so he postulated a movement toward perfection and tried with his plays to contribute to it. Though many around him did nothing, he viewed them more with pity than with disdain, as Tuzenbakh views Solyony: "I'm both sorry for him and annoyed, but I'm more sorry."

The Cherry Orchard • *The Cherry Orchard,* Chekhov's last play, caused considerable disagreement between Chekhov and Stanislavsky over questions of staging, for Chekhov contended that it was a comedy while Stanislavsky claimed it was a tragedy. One must feel sympathy for Stanislavsky, for, despite many farcical elements in the play, it moves the audience to a complex sadness rather than to laughter. Most of the characters, though silly, even hilariously so, fail to understand their lives, fail to live meaningfully, and therefore lose their lives. Still, Chekhov was at least partially right, for, in the character of Anya, who at seventeen is the youngest character in the play, the audience can see some hope for the future, for a new life beginning, as in the character of Nina in *The Seagull.*

The action of the play takes place on the estate of Madame Lyubov Ranevsky. She has been absent from her estate for some time, having run off to Paris with her lover to escape the grief she felt over the loss of her young son. She returns virtually penniless, confronted with the problem of what to do to save the estate and its beautiful cherry orchard. With her on the estate are her brother Gaev; Varya, her adopted daughter; Anya, her natural daughter; and their servants Sharlotta, Yepihodov, Dunyasha, Firs, and Yasha. This group is supplemented by Trofimov, a young student who keeps getting expelled from the university for his revolutionary views, and Lopakhin, a wealthy merchant and former peasant. As the action opens, the problem to be solved is how to pay all the money owed on the estate; this question remains unresolved throughout the play. Indeed, Lyubov and her clan seem incapable of any kind of action. She and her kind, like the Prozorovs, are a dying breed. Although they recognize the fact, they seem helpless to do anything about it. They are fast being replaced by the rising merchant class, Lopakhin and his kind, as the Prozorovs were gradually replaced by Natalya and her lover in *The Three Sisters*.

The play is full of comic touches: Yepihodov's shoes squeak, Trofimov falls down a flight of stairs (without hurting himself), Varya gives Lopakhin a swat on the head meant for Yepihodov, Lopakhin teases Varya, Gaev speaks nonsense and talks to bookcases, and Sharlotta gives demonstrations of parlor magic. The play is kept from farce, however, by Chekhov's delineation of character. The audience comes to know the characters too well to laugh at them, instead feeling a sense of profound pity for their pain and helplessness.

Only Lopakhin has a plan to "save" the estate, but his plan is to destroy the orchard, build little villas on the property, and rent them out, thus providing a steady income. He suggests this solution to Lyubov, but she has lived on the estate since she was a child; she loves the orchard and does not seriously consider Lopakhin's plan. Instead, the family debates grand schemes and hopes for aid from distant relations but proves incapable of taking any action. Lyubov has grown so used to squandering her money that she cannot stop, and during the play, she gives gold to a beggar, though Varya is forced to feed the servants nothing but soup. The audience waits for the inevitable to happen, as it does when the estate is sold at auction, bought by Lopakhin, who proceeds with his original plan. The final act shows the Ranevsky family leaving their beloved home with the sound of axes in the background as their cherry orchard becomes a thing of the past.

The play's plot is simple; there are no surprises. Chekhov brings forth the inner lives of his characters so that the audience can understand them, see their foolishness, and yet pity them. Gaev is an excellent example. He has deep feelings and the urge to express them, but no one wants to listen to him. No one protests when he speaks in meaningless billiard terms, but when he speaks what is really in his heart, everyone protests. Perhaps it would be better for Gaev to remain silent, as Anya suggests he should, for no one listens to him; he does not even listen to himself, for though he hears the "call" to work, he has never heeded it.

Therein lies the problem of the play: No one combines the qualities necessary for a meaningful life. Some, such as Varya and Lopakhin, are workers, and some—such as Trofimov, Lyubov, and Gaev—have beautiful ideas, but no one works in behalf of worthy ideas. Lopakhin labors only for money, without any vision of the future, so he is able to destroy the orchard without even recognizing what he is doing, what is being lost. Trofimov makes compelling speeches about the need for work, the need to build for the future, but he only listens to the sound of his voice; he does not work. Varya spends every moment working, caring for the estate, but she labors only so that she will not have time to lament her fate. She hates her work but cannot bear idle time, for when idle, she weeps. Lyubov herself has compelling ideas, centering on her love for the man in Paris and for the orchard, but she does not know what to do for the things she loves. She loves the cherry orchard and idly watches it pass from her hands.

Each of the characters speaks of his or her innermost anxieties, and yet each remains alone, for while they speak their anguish the others go about their lives, never

listening, caught up only in their own struggles. This failure to listen, this oblivious-
ness, is the most distinctive element of the play, for it isolates the characters from one
another and makes any individual effort fruitless.

The final image of the play is that of Firs, the oldest character, who is left behind,
forgotten by the family he has served all his life. Left alone after his years of service, he
comments to himself that "Life has slipped by as though I hadn't lived." The last
sounds of the play are the mournful sound of a breaking string and the sound of an ax
chopping down a tree in the orchard. Much that is beautiful goes to waste and is destroyed in this play, and the orchard stands as a symbol for all. It was beautiful, but it
had no purpose, and so it must be reduced to nothing. The same can be said of Lyubov,
Gaev, and others. The one bright spot is Anya, still young enough to put her life to
some purpose, as she plans to do as the play ends. She does not mourn the loss of the
orchard, for she plans to make all Russia her orchard, a plan of which Chekhov would
approve.

In this last play, Chekhov included a bit of dialogue that goes a long way toward explaining his purpose in writing for the theater. Lopakhin tells Lyubov that he went to
see a play (a conventional comedy) the day before that was very funny. Lyubov answers with a speech that could not have defended Chekhov's drama more eloquently:
"And most likely there was nothing funny in it. You shouldn't look at plays, you should
look at yourselves a little oftener. How gray your lives are. How much nonsense you
talk." That is why Chekhov has, and will continue to have, so secure a place in the
world of drama: He shows his audiences the triviality, the grayness of their lives, so
that they will change themselves, working with faith toward a greater future for humankind.

Other major works

SHORT FICTION: *Skazki Melpomeny*, 1884; *Pystrye rasskazy*, 1886; *Nevinnye rechi*, 1887;
V sumerkakh, 1887; *Rasskazy*, 1888; *The Tales of Tchehov*, 1916-1922 (13 volumes); *The Un-
discovered Chekhov: Forty-three New Stories*, 1999.

NONFICTION: *Ostrov Sakhalin*, 1893-1894; *Letters on the Short Story, the Drama, and
Other Literary Topics*, 1924; *The Selected Letters of Anton Chekhov*, 1955.

MISCELLANEOUS: *The Works of Anton Chekhov*, 1929; *Polnoye sobraniye sochineniy i pisem
A. P. Chekhova*, 1944-1951 (20 volumes); *The Portable Chekhov*, 1947; *The Oxford Chekhov*,
1964-1980 (9 volumes).

Bibliography

Allen, David. *Performing Chekhov*. New York: Routledge, 2000. A look at the production of Chekhov's dramatic works on the stage. Bibliography and index.

Bloom, Harold, ed. *Anton Chekhov*. Philadelphia, Pa.: Chelsea House, 1999. A critical
assessment of the literary works of Chekhov. Bibliography and index.

Callow, Philip. *Chekhov, the Hidden Ground: A Biography*. Chicago: Ivan R. Dee, 1998. A
biography of Chekhov that covers his life and works. Bibliography and index.

Gilman, Richard. *Chekhov's Plays: An Opening into Eternity*. New Haven, Conn.: Yale
University Press, 1995. A scholarly study of the dramas of Chekhov. Bibliography
and index.

Gottlieb, Vera, and Paul Allain, eds. *The Cambridge Companion to Chekhov*. New York:
Cambridge University Press, 2000. A guide to the life and works of the playwright.

Malcolm, Janet. *Reading Chekhov: A Critical Journey*. New York: Random House, 2001.
A critical analysis of the works of Chekhov. Bibliography.

Rayfield, Donald. *Anton Chekhov: A Life.* 1998. Reprint. Evanston, Ill.: Northwestern University Press, 2000. A detailed biography of Anton Chekhov including material about his relationship with various members of his family and his antecedents, his literary friendships, and the literary environment of prerevolutionary Russia. Index.
_____. *Understanding Chekhov: A Critical Study of Chekhov's Prose and Drama.* Madison: University of Wisconsin Press, 1999. A critical examination of the writings of Chekhov. Index.
Senelick, Laurence. *The Chekhov Theatre: A Century of the Plays in Performance.* New York: Cambridge University Press, 1997. A look at the stage history and production of Chekhov's works.

Hugh Short

Chikamatsu Monzaemon

Sugimori Nobumori

Born: Fukui, Echizen Province, Japan; 1653
Died: Sakai, Japan; January 6, 1725

Principal drama • *Yotsugi Soga*, pr. 1683, pb. 1896; *Shusse Kagekiyo*, pr. 1686, pb. 1890; *Semimaru*, pr. 1686 (English translation, 1978); *Sonezaki shinjū*, pr. 1703 (*The Love Suicides at Sonezaki*, 1961); *Yōmei Tennō Shokunin Kagami*, pr. 1705; *Horikawa nami no tsuzumi*, pr. 1706 (*The Drum of the Waves of Horikawa*, 1961); *Shinjū Kasaneizutsu*, pr. 1707; *Tamba Yosaku*, pr. 1708 (*Yosaku from Tamba*, 1961); *Shinjū Mannensō*, pr. 1708 (*The Love Suicides in the Women's Temple*, 1961); *Keisei Hangokō*, pr. 1708; *Meido no hikyaku*, pr. 1711 (*The Courier for Hell*, 1961); *Yugiri Awa no Naruto*, pr. 1712; *Kokusenya kassen*, pr. 1715 (*The Battles of Coxinga*, 1951); *Yari no Gonza*, pr. 1717 (*Gonza the Lancer*, 1961); *Nebiki no kadomatsu*, pr. 1718 (*The Uprooted Pine*, 1961); *Soga kaikeizan*, pr. 1718 (*The Soga Revenge*, 1929); *Heike nyogo no shima*, pr. 1719 (English translation, 1979); *Hakata Kojorō Namimakura*, pr. 1719 (*The Girl from Hakata: Or, Love at Sea*, 1961); *Futago sumidagawa*, pr. 1720 (*Twins at the Sumida River*, 1982); *Tsu no kuni meoto-ike*, pr. 1721 (*Lovers Pond in Settsu Province*, 1992); *Shinsu kawa-nakajima kassen*, pr. 1721 (*Battles at Kawa-nakajima*, 1992); *Shinjū ten no Amijima*, pr. 1721 (*The Love Suicides at Amijima*, 1953); *Onnagoroshi: Abura jigoku*, pr. 1721 (*The Woman-Killer and the Hell of Oil*, 1961); *Shuju Yoigoshin*, pr. 1722 (*Love Suicides on the Eve of the Koshin Festival*, 1992); *Kanhasshu tsunagi-uma*, pr. 1724 (*Tethered Steed and the Eight Provinces of Kanto*, 1992); *Major Plays of Chikamatsu*, pb. 1961; *Chikamatsu: Five Late Plays*, pb. 2001

Other literary forms • Chikamatsu Monzaemon is known primarily for his plays.

Achievements • Chikamatsu Monzaemon took the *jōruri* puppet theater, the leading popular theatrical form of his day, and through his own dramatic and poetic skill lifted a plebeian art form to the heights of serious drama. In this accomplishment, he brought changes to the theater of his age as significant as those achieved by Zeami Motokiyo in the medieval Nō theater several centuries earlier. The range of his writing, from political dramas on Chinese and Japanese themes to intimate stories about the domestic life of his contemporary society, has given him the nickname of the Japanese William Shakespeare. The two societies were sufficiently different that the appellation cannot hold; nevertheless, the comparison does suggest the power of Chikamatsu's theatrical creations to hold the attention of audiences down to the present day. Widely admired and often copied, Chikamatsu remains the most important figure in the Japanese theater from the seventeenth century to modern times, when his works have been adapted for the modern stage and for films as well with great success.

Biography • Despite Chikamatsu Monzaemon's enormous popularity, few details about his life are clear that do not relate directly to his theatrical activities. Born Sugimori Nobumori, his exact place and date of birth and death are still contested, and little is known of his early education, except from the internal evidence of the plays, which reveals his real familiarity with Chinese philosophical writings and Japanese Buddhist texts, as well as a love of Japanese classical prose and poetry. Chikamatsu began writing plays for both the puppet theater and then later for live actors (in Kabuki), but he spent the major part of his career working in the puppet theater, particularly at the Takemotoza in Osaka; a number of his great plays were written for that performing group. When his patron Takemoto Gidayū died in 1714, Chikamatsu, by then an experienced writer of sixty-one, decided to help the new head of the troupe to continue and, putting forth his best efforts, wrote a half dozen of his greatest plays in the next and final decade of his active life. The exact circumstances of his last years are unknown, and details about his domestic life are few and contradictory. What is known of the man is derived from his art.

Analysis • Although Western writers tend to use the world "play" or "drama" in describing the work of Chikamatsu Monzaemon, some explanation of the word *jōruri* will be helpful in understanding Chikamatsu's accomplishments, as well as his inevitable limitations. When Chikamatsu began his career, there were no troupes of live actors performing any kind of real dramatic spectacle. Rather, chanters of various sorts of stories, usually historical accounts of the Japanese medieval wars, considerably embellished, began to use musical accompaniment, simple puppets (worked by multiple handlers from below), and scenery to illustrate their accounts. The very name *jōruri*, which defines the genre, is taken from the name of one of those historical embellishments, a fictional princess who supposedly fell in love with Yoshitsune, the celebrated general who died during the civil wars in 1185 and who remained one of the great cultural heroes of the Japanese tradition.

During the period prior to Chikamatsu's ascendancy, various chanters (all of whom wrote their own texts) tried adapting certain features from the elegant medieval Nō theater in order to give their popular stories more shape and substance. When Takemoto Gidayū himself decided to commission the young Chikamatsu to compose a text for him to perform, a new tradition was begun, for up until that time, no "playwright" as such had ever been used. This new division of labor helped increase enormously the potential for literary expression.

Reading a translation of a Chikamatsu play, Westerners will find the structure of dialogue plus narrator relatively familiar, yet it must be remembered that in Chikamatsu's time, one performer chanted all the roles and created all the voices. This bravura aspect of the performance was an important consideration in the planning and organization of the texts and gives *jōruri* a resemblance to Western opera, where certain conventions are also embedded in the text. This is one limitation placed on Chikamatsu's art, and yet, on the whole, it was one with which he could live comfortably as he was in control of the script. Chikamatsu also experimented at various points in his career with writing for Kabuki actors, theatrical groups that had begun to perform dramas in the large cities.

Actors had a tendency to change Chikamatsu's lines, however, and so he returned to writing for the puppet theater and continued to do so for most of his career. The Kabuki theater, indeed, grew up in the shadow of the *jōruri* puppet theater and imitated its style in many important respects, including the stylization of physical movement. By the middle of the eighteenth century, the Kabuki had become more popular than the *jōruri*; efforts were made in the early nineteenth century to win back audiences to the puppet theater (by then called Bunraku), but the actor's theater continued in its ascendancy. By that time, the actors often performed Chikamatsu's dramas as though they had been written for them, but, in fact, virtually all of Chikamatsu's great works were composed for the puppet stage.

During the early years of his career, Chikamatsu tended to write dramas on historical themes, adapted from various chronicles or from medieval Nō dramas. In 1703, he wrote a play about contemporary life, *The Love Suicides at Sonezaki,* and after the success of that experiment, his writings began to encompass both styles.

Chikamatsu's audiences in his mature years were almost completely made up of the merchant class in Osaka, the center of protobourgeois culture in Japan during that period. Because of strict social class barriers imposed by the Tokugawa shoguns since shortly after 1600, the merchants were cut off from higher forms of culture, yet came to have the money, the leisure, and, eventually, the cultivation to pursue artistic interests and pastimes. Therefore, both types of plays written by Chikamatsu appealed greatly to them: The history plays (*jidaimono*) served as a means to teach them about the glories and complexities of the Japanese past, both in the court and in military circles, and the domestic dramas (*sewamono*) provided them with a powerful glimpse into the intimacies of the world that they themselves inhabited.

For modern audiences as well, these domestic dramas, which deal with the vicissitudes of the personal lives of the townspeople, still possess an emotional reality that is compelling. For all the differences between the urban society at the time of Chikamatsu and now, there are certain powerful similarities, which make the domestic dramas both appealing and poignant even today. In fact, Chikamatsu may have been the first major dramatist to make ordinary men and women, with all their foibles and weaknesses, the protagonists of tragic drama. A dramatist such as George Lillo in eighteenth century England attempted to do the same sort of thing in his play *The London Merchant: Or, The History of George Barnwell* (pr., pb. 1731), but it was not until much later that such characters were regularly portrayed in a sympathetic fashion on the European stage. For a modern reader, Chikamatsu may often seem closer to an Arthur Miller than to a Shakespeare.

As the historical dramas of Chikamatsu were always drawn from actual events in the past, so the domestic dramas, too, were taken from real events in Japanese society, often dramatized as soon after the fact as possible. In a special way, these domestic plays served as living newspapers, which presented accounts of lurid or sensational events adapted for their theatrical effectiveness. The attraction for the audience of such plays thus lay far less in the "plot" of the events portrayed, which they knew at least in outline, than in experiencing the art with which Chikamatsu reworked his material.

Much ink has been spilled over the question as to whether Chikamatsu was a "realist," in a contemporary sense of the world. The playwright himself put these questions to rest in an eloquent statement he made during the course of an interview that was published after his death. When asked about the need to create an art that would resemble reality closely, he replied that art and reality were not the same. Pure realism "does not take into account the real methods of art. Art is something which lies in the slender margin between the real and the unreal . . . and entertainment lies between the two." To a modern reader, it is clear that both the artifice of the puppets and the beauty of Chikamatsu's language (and here he most resembles Shakespeare) could lift the most banal, even sordid, "reality" to great heights of genuine pathos.

The Battles of Coxinga • Of the history plays, the only drama available in full translation is Chikamatsu's most successful effort, *The Battles of Coxinga,* first performed in

1715 and undoubtedly his most popular work. The play concerns the exploits of Coxinga, a famous hero in Japanese history who was involved in the battles surrounding the fall of the Ming Dynasty in China, about a century or so before the composition of the play. His exploits had become legendary, and the play contains a number of incidents from his complex career juxtaposed and embellished to make as brilliant a series of effects as possible. Read on the page, the text seems full of bombast and arbitrary confrontations, but seen in performance, *The Battles of Coxinga* provides a series of striking vignettes that exploit the possibilities of the puppet stage to their fullest. It has often been said that audiences were particularly excited by *The Battles of Coxinga* because it dealt with the exotic Chinese scenes at a time when, because of the policies of the Tokugawa shogunate, the Japanese themselves were no longer allowed to travel abroad. Whatever the reason, the scenes of China and Chinese life presented make up in color and fantasy what they may lack in historical veracity.

The play opens at the court of the Ming emperor in Nanking. He is portrayed as a weak man, surrounded by corrupt ministers; only one, Go Sankei, argues for justice, but he cannot stop the rout of the imperial forces by the enemy Tartars. The emperor is murdered. Go Sankei manages to escape with the empress, who is pregnant with the child who will carry on the imperial line; when she in turn is killed, he exchanges his own newborn child for hers, so that the imperial line may continue. Go Sankei then sends the imperial princess off on a boat so that she can escape the battle and, he hopes, reach Japan. This first act, like the rest of the play, is filled with devices that call to mind the most outrageous Jacobean tragedies: Eyes are gouged out; babies are torn from the womb. With actors, the effect would be merely grotesque; with puppets, the results seem larger than life and quite heroic.

In the second act, Coxinga (who is half Japanese and half Chinese) is quietly fishing and thinking on the fate of the Ming court, where his father had been a high-ranking minister. When the princess drifts to shore in her boat, Coxinga and his Japanese wife decide that he should travel to China to attempt to keep the Ming Dynasty from collapse. In this section of the play, Coxinga's speeches are a model of powerful eloquence, indeed, grandiloquence. The subsequent scenes contain a combination of battles and adventures, including a fight with a tiger that must have taxed the original producers considerably. Coxinga now begins to gather around him brave Chinese who wish to fight the Tartars as well.

In act 3, Coxinga meets his half sister, and after a complex series of maneuvers, he manages to win both her and her husband, a general, to his side. Again, the actions are, like the language employed, far larger than life. In act 4, Go Sankei, still attempting to escape the Tartar soldiers, leads the young imperial prince to a mystical mountain summit where the Nine Immortals of China look out over the destinies of the nation. Coxinga appears, and the two unite for a final victory, helped by the Immortals, who build a sort of rainbow bridge to help them escape from the attacking enemy. When the villainous soldiers rush across, the bridge dissolves and they are crushed below at the foot of the mountain. The final act of the play brings all the contending forces together. The evil minister is captured, and Coxinga and his allies are triumphant.

Described in such a fashion, the play may seem merely bombastic, but it possesses a beauty and excitement in the original that in some fashion may call to mind the effect of a play such as Christopher Marlowe's *Tamburlaine the Great* (pr. c. 1587). As noted above, the play is meant to be larger than life, both in its language and as a theatrical event. At the same time, even within this heroic framework, Chikamatsu manages moments of humor and whimsy that are on a wholly human scale. In terms of high entertainment, the play is unsurpassed. Indeed, Chikamatsu's formula for success—a mixture of the nationalistic, the exotic, and the poetic—is one that has succeeded in most cultures.

Other historical dramas • Most of Chikamatsu's other historical dramas deal with events in earlier Japanese history, with stories taken either from the world of the Heian court in the eleventh century or from the medieval war period that followed. Again, bombastic generals and sophisticated courtiers are brought to life in complicated plots that allow for a full range of fantasy in setting, action, and language. Some plays use earlier dramas and expand on them. A notable case in point is that of Chikamatsu's *Semimaru*, which uses the Nō drama of Zeami by the same title as a centerpiece and then extends the story backward and forward until a full evening of intrigue and adventure is created. Again the audience, doubtless familiar with the original drama, took pleasure less from the tale of the blind prince than from the variations that Chikamatsu played on a legend already known. Modern audiences often find these historical dramas somewhat unsatisfying because of their general and diffuse nature, in which plots and subplots often relate to each other in only the most general way. Then too, the cultural knowledge on the part of spectators that could bind these elements together has been lost, so that modern Japanese audiences are practically at as much of a loss as Western spectators or readers in catching the subtle implications of Chikamatsu's juxtapositions.

Domestic dramas • It is perhaps for reasons such as these that Chikamatsu's reputation has shifted from his historical to his domestic plays, which now have taken on new value. Original audiences could take much for granted in these plays. Now, because of Chikamatsu's faithful renderings of certain details of Tokugawa life and culture, modern viewers can savor the atmosphere of a quite different time through the means of these dramas, which, although often melodramatic and arbitrary in plot structure, contain the kind of elegant language and emotional commitment on the part of the author that make the situations powerfully touching.

The Love Suicides at Sonezaki • The first of the domestic plays, *The Love Suicides at Sonezaki*, was written twelve years before *The Battles of Coxinga*. The play was evidently written to serve as a kind of interlude for a longer historical drama, and in its three brief scenes, Chikamatsu portrayed a highly poetic version of the suicide of the two young lovers. In Tokubei, the shop attendant, Chikamatsu created what may be the first modern hero—weak, vacillating, yet capable of being aroused to righteous fury. He is in love with a courtesan from the licensed quarters, Ohatsu, who works in a teahouse, actually a kind of elegant brothel sanctioned by the Tokugawa authorities. Forced to part from her by the machinations of the evil Kuheiji, Tokubei decides to "show all Osaka the purity at the bottom of my heart," and the couple vow to commit suicide together.

The couple's parting moments in the teahouse, filled with little touches of realism provided by the minor servants and other characters, are nicely portrayed, and the final scene, when the lovers journey to their death at the Sonezaki Shrine, is one of the most sustained examples of lyric writing in the Japanese theater. Through the device of the narrator, Chikamatsu solves the problem that has plagued all writers of realistic theater who have sought for a way for characters of limited education and insight to speak with eloquence. The great poetry is here provided by the narrator, who takes the audience both inside the thoughts of the characters (who actually say very little) and then back into the realm of philosophical, in particular Buddhist, speculation. The death of the lovers is both touching and convincing. With this play, Chikamatsu successfully created a new genre of drama, and, at least in the final scene, achieved a standard of poetic excellence that he later equaled, but never surpassed.

As his career continued, Chikamatsu went on to develop the genre of the domestic play, adding new elements and more complex plots, so that, rather than serving as interludes during longer performances of historical dramas, the domestic plays came to stand as independent and complete works in themselves. Quite often the plays were written about incidents that took place in the licensed quarters, such as *The Uprooted Pine*, but others dealt with adultery, murder, and piracy, even life in a Buddhist monastery.

The Love Suicides at Amijima • Chikamatsu's greatest achievement in this genre, however, is surely his play *The Love Suicides at Amijima*, written in 1721, just at the end of his career. Performed countless times by puppet troupes and by Kabuki companies as well, the play has both been adapted for the modern stage and made the subject of a famous film. *The Love Suicides at Amijima* is often considered to be the greatest single work written for the traditional Japanese stage. Like Chikamatsu's first domestic play, *The Love Suicides at Sonezaki*, *The Love Suicides at Amijima* builds its complex plot on a simple story of a weak but good-hearted man who falls in love with a courtesan and decides to die with her. In the later play, however, which is in three acts, the playwright has provided a whole network of minor characters and situations that flesh out the action and render the outcome all the more moving and inevitable. As with the other plays of this sort, Chikamatsu based his drama on a series of actual events and evidently went to considerable trouble to learn certain details of the incident before composing his text.

The earlier play, *The Love Suicides at Sonezaki*, shows poetic excellence, but *The Love Suicides at Amijima* is graced as well with a certain elegiac tonality that can only be described as religious. Even the title itself in the original Japanese contains a hint of Buddhist salvation, since the place-name Amijima can be rendered as the "island of nets," a reference to the image that depicts Buddha catching the innocent and the sinful alike in his nets to haul them up to paradise.

In the first act, Jihei, the paper merchant, is in love with the courtesan Koharu, in defiance of his wife and her relatives. There is also a villain who vies for Koharu's affections, Tahei. Within this simple basic structure, Chikamatsu weaves a number of new elements to add emotional complexity. A mysterious samurai, who remonstrates with Jihei about his debauchery, later turns out to be his brother. Later, in the second act, Jihei learns that his wife, Osan, has been instrumental in attempting to separate him from Koharu, but in a stunning twist, he manages to persuade his wife to allow him to ransom Koharu to save her from the advances of Tahei. Jihei's parents-in-law suddenly arrive and, shocked by his behavior, decide to take their daughter Osan back home with them.

In the final act, Jihei decides to commit suicide with Koharu. He pays his debts and leads her away. As in *The Love Suicides at Sonezaki*, the language of this last act is particularly powerful. The lovers lament their fate, and, by implication, the power of the society that has forced them to part. Through the power of his language and imagery, Chikamatsu allows the pair to make a kind of transcendental spiritual pilgrimage to a realm where obligations can be cast aside, and where the two can live as Buddhist priest and nun, "to escape the inconstant world." As the priests at a nearby temple begin their chant at dawn, Jihei puts Koharu to death, then does away with himself. His body, washed out to sea, is picked up by the fishermen in their nets.

In terms of consistency of characterization and power of imagery, *The Love Suicides at Amijima* remains a superb example of the possibilities of *jōruri*. For a modern reader, the form certainly has limitations. Characters are seldom ambiguous, since the heads used for the puppets have fixed expressions which reveal the general nature of the character being portrayed. Then too, since the puppets are lifeless, the text prepared for the chanter must be strong, even strident, in order to make up for the lack of interior life in the dolls themselves. The social mores of the time, particularly those pertaining to the licensed quarters, are sufficiently removed from those of modern life to make the passions of the various characters seem overwrought and, occasionally, downright outlandish. Nevertheless, a play like *The Love Suicides at Amijima* still rings true, whatever the problems of historical distance, because of the power of Chikamatsu's language and his commitment to an understanding of what were, for him, situations of genuine dignity and pathos within the context of his own society.

Bibliography

Brazell, Karen, ed. *Traditional Japanese Theater: An Anthology of Plays.* New York: Columbia University Press, 1998. Includes one of Chikamatsu's love suicide plays as well as introductions describing the genre and the specific play.

Gerstle, C. Andrew. *Circles of Fantasy: Convention in the Plays of Chikamatsu.* Cambridge, Mass.: Harvard University Press, 1986. A study of the plays of Chikamatsu, focusing on literary conventions. Bibliography and index.

_____. "Heroic Honor: Chikamatsu and the Samurai Ideal." *Harvard Journal of Asiatic Studies* 57, no. 2 (December, 1997): 307-381. A look at the samurai in the play *Kanhasshu tsunagi-uma* (*Tethered Steed and the Eight Provinces of Kanto*).

Heine, Steve. "Tragedy and Salvation in the Floating World: Chikamatsu's Double Suicide Drama as Millenarian Discourse." *The Journal of Asian Studies* 53, no. 2 (May, 1994): 367. Chikamatsu's dramas are examined in the light of Buddhist and Confucian theology regarding double suicide.

Kominz, Laurence R. *Avatars of Vengeance: Japanese Drama and the Soga Literary Tradition.* Ann Arbor: Center for Japanese Studies, University of Michigan, 1995. An examination of the story of the Soga brothers' failed vendetta through its retelling in Nō, Kabuki, and Bunraku. Chikamatsu wrote thirteen plays about the Soga brothers.

Pringle, Patricia, ed. *An Interpretive Guide to Bunraku.* Honolulu: University of Hawaii at Manoa, 1992. Essays examine various aspects of the puppet theater, particularly Chikamatsu's *The Love Suicides at Sonezaki.*

Sakamoto, Edward. "The Ancient Artistry of Bunraku: A Japanese Puppet Theater Keeps a Four-Hundred-Year-Old Tradition Alive." *Los Angeles Times,* September 25, 1988, p. 3. An introduction to Bunraku and Chikamatsu written on the occasion of the Bunraku Puppet Theatre of Osaka performing one of Chikamatsu's works in Los Angeles.

Sasayama, Takashi, J. R. Mulryne, and Margaret Shewring, eds. *Shakespeare and the Japanese Stage.* New York: Cambridge University Press, 1999. Contains a comparison of Chikamatsu and William Shakespeare.

J. Thomas Rimer

Frank Chin

Born: Berkeley, California; February 25, 1940

Principal drama • *The Chickencoop Chinaman*, pr. 1972, pb. 1981; *The Year of the Dragon*, pr. 1974, pb. 1981

Other literary forms • In addition to his plays, Frank Chin has published a collection of short stories, the novels *Donald Duk* (1991) and *Gunga Din Highway* (1994), and numerous articles on Asian American literature and culture, some of which have been collected in *Bulletproof Bandits and Other Essays* (1998). He also co-edited a pioneering anthology of Asian American writing titled *Aiiieeeee! An Anthology of Asian American Writers* (1974), substantially revised in 1991 as *The Big Aiiieeeee!*

Achievements • Frank Chin is the first Chinese American playwright to have had serious drama produced on the New York stage (at the American Place Theater) and on national television (by the Public Broadcasting Service). Having come into prominence in the 1960's and 1970's, he represents the consciousness of Americans of Chinese descent—those born and reared in the United States, who thus have only tenuous ties to the language and culture of China.

In addition to his achievements as a playwright, Chin has garnered attention as an editor of Asian American literature, a fiction writer, and an essayist. His work has been recognized with many awards, among them the American Book Award for lifetime achievement, and several prizes and grants from organizations such as the Rockefeller Foundation, the American Place Theater (New York), and the National Endowment for the Arts.

Biography • Frank Chew Chin, Jr., was born a fifth-generation Californian of Chinese American parentage on February 25, 1940, in Berkeley, California, near Oakland, where his parents lived and worked. During World War II, his family sent him to the Sierras, where he was cared for by a retired vaudeville acrobat and a silent-film bit player. After the war, he rejoined his family and grew up in the Chinatowns of Oakland and San Francisco, attending Chinese as well as English schools. During these years, he identified closely with his father, who was prominent in Chinatown governance and who became the president of the Six Companies (roughly the Chinatown equivalent of being elected mayor). Chin was graduated from the University of California at Berkeley, where he won several prizes for fiction writing; during his student years, he undertook the adventure of traveling to Fidel Castro's Cuba. In 1961, he was awarded a fellowship at the Writers' Workshop at the University of Iowa.

After leaving Iowa, Chin spent some time with the Southern Pacific Railroad, becoming the first Chinese American to work as a brakeman on the rails laid by his forefathers. Chin left the railroad company to become a writer-producer for KING-TV in Seattle, and several of his shows were aired by the Public Broadcasting Service (PBS) and on *Sesame Street*.

Chin left Seattle to teach Asian American studies at San Francisco State University and the University of California, Davis. With a group of scholars, he organized the

173

(Corky Lee)

Combined Asian American Resources Project (CARP), which collected literary, documentary, and oral history materials now kept in the Bancroft Library of the University of California, Berkeley. CARP has since been responsible for the publication of key Asian American texts by the University of Washington Press. In 1972, Chin founded the Asian American Theater Workshop in San Francisco with the support of the American Conservatory Theater (where he has been a writer-in-residence).

In 1971, Chin married Kathleen Chang, daughter of a prominent intellectual Chinese family; the marriage ended in divorce after five years, and Chang later became haunted by visions that drove her to commit suicide in 1996 on the campus of the University of Pennsylvania. In the last decades of the twentieth century, Chin maintained his residence in the Los Angeles area (living with his third wife and third child), where he channeled his energies toward the writing of fiction, essays, and children's literature rather than drama. Meanwhile, his continuing research in Asian American folklore and history was supported by several grants (including a Rockefeller Fellowship at the University of California, Los Angeles) and bore fruit in several important exhibitions.

Analysis • It may be said that Frank Chin has pioneered in the field of Asian American literature. His daring and verbally exuberant theater has asserted the presence of the richly unique and deeply human complexities of Chinese American life, and his work has brought this presence to the attention of the American public. Chin has sometimes been considered the John Osborne—the "angry young man"—of his generation of Chinese Americans. His plays turn on themes of identity—anguished and indignant probings into ethnic identity, gender identity, and self-identity. In them, Chin mirrors the issues and realities of Chinese American life and history as lived in Chinatown ghettos; they seek to expose and explode generally held stereotypes of Chinese Americans as an emasculated model minority with a quaintly exotic culture.

Painful truths told with exuberant verbal pyrotechnics are trademarks of Chin's theater, and the characteristic gamut of his language ranges from black ghetto dialect to hipster talk to authentic Chinatown Cantonese (not Hollywood's "Charlie Chanese"). He has criticized the false myths and the deadening stereotypes of self and ethnicity held by Asians and whites alike. At a time when it was ripe and necessary to do so, Chin proclaimed and proved that there is such an entity as Asian American literature. American literary history must henceforth reckon with that claim if it is to be true to itself.

Since the initial mark made by his two plays written in the 1970's, Chin has not had any new plays published or staged. Chin has instead turned his very considerable creative literary energies toward writing novels, short fiction, juvenile literature, and essays of cultural criticism. Chin's turn away from drama is in part due to a disappointment that an authentic Asian American theater (as he sees it) has not emerged. When he wrote his first plays, he had hoped that a genuinely Asian American theater would come into being, a theater that would resemble Dublin's Abbey Theater of the early 1900's and that would nurture genuinely Asian American dramatic talents just as the Abbey nurtured a crop of distinctively Irish playwrights such as Sean O'Casey, John Millington Synge, and William Butler Yeats. Chin's two plays, nevertheless, are considered classics of Asian American literature, and they continue to be studied in the academy and to attract analytical commentary and debate. There have been many revivals of these plays, especially in Los Angeles and San Francisco.

Chin's plays center on a protagonist's confrontation with the problematics of identity. *The Chickencoop Chinaman* is the more experimental in technique, with an almost cinematic use of montage, flashbacks, symbolic stage sets, and surrealistic, dreamlike sequences. *The Year of the Dragon* is more conventional, a drama of family and psychological conflict set in a San Francisco Chinatown apartment.

The Chickencoop Chinaman · *The Chickencoop Chinaman* is a play that treats the theme of identity through dispelling stereotypes and myths. The play is divided into two acts. Each act has a scene in Limbo (a surreal transitional time-space located between realistic time-spaces), a sequence recollecting a past obsession with a mythic figure (for example, the miracle-working Helen Keller in act 1, the popular-culture hero the Lone Ranger in act 2), and scenes set in the realistic location of 1960's Pittsburgh, where the problem of the protagonist's identity is worked out.

The play's action centers on Tam Lum, a Chinese American filmmaker who is making a documentary about a black boxing champion named Ovaltine Jack Dancer, a boyhood idol with whom he once shared a moment of mystic brotherhood urinating in unison in a roadside bush. Tam comes to Pittsburgh from San Francisco in search of Dancer's father, Charley Popcorn, who was a quintessential formative figure for Dancer and who now runs a Pittsburgh theater. Allegorically, Tam's creation of a film about Dancer is an effort to express an identity for himself, and his search for Charley is his search for a father figure.

Before arriving in Pittsburgh, Tam is introduced in a Limbo scene on his airliner from San Francisco. The flight attendant is transformed into a Hong Kong Dream Girl clad in a drill team uniform and twirling a baton (hence an American dream girl, too). Indeed, the woman represents the American stereotype of Asian women—attractive, compliant, trained to give pleasure. Although Tam scoffs at the Hong Kong Dream

Girl's stereotypical identity, it becomes apparent that his own identity is problematic. For example, when asked what his mother tongue is, Tam can speak no Chinese, but instead begins speaking in tongues, using a startling array of American dialects. Tam also points out that Chinese American identity is not one ordained by nature; Chinese Americans are not born to an identity but must synthesize one out of the diverse experiences of living in crowded Chinatown tenements, metaphorical chicken coops. This opening sequence, then, poses the play's central theme: the problem of stereotyping and identity.

In Pittsburgh, Tam stays with a boyhood friend, a Japanese American dentist named "Blackjap" Kenji. Kenji's apartment in Pittsburgh's black ghetto, Oakland, ironically underlines the circularity of Tam's search (since the San Francisco Bay area has its Oakland, too), and its location within earshot of a railroad yard is a symbolic reminder of the Chinese American contribution to American history. Tam and Kenji, who grew up in the black ghetto of Oakland, California, talk in exuberant black dialect and express themselves by slapping skin; they have, to a great degree, adopted the style and expressiveness of a black identity.

Kenji's ménage includes Lee, a part-Chinese woman who is passing for white. She has a young son, Robbie, by a previous liaison or marriage. Lee has a love-hate relationship with men of color, men whom she collects and then uses her whiteness and sexuality to dominate and intimidate. Thus, Lee lives platonically and parasitically with Kenji, in fact reducing him to a sexless host.

During their reunion scene in act 1, Tam and Kenji reenact a past obsession that they had with the figure of Helen Keller, imitating and parodying her. This may seem pointlessly cruel until one realizes that, in Chin's play, Keller symbolizes the myth of the disadvantaged person who overcomes all handicaps and pulls herself up by her own bootstraps. In other words, she epitomizes what American society fondly thinks that every disadvantaged minority group can do for itself. When Tam and Kenji mock and demythologize the figure of Helen Keller, they are, in particular, rejecting the popular American myth that Asian Americans are a model minority capable of miracles of self-help.

Act 2 opens with another scene in which Tam and Kenji again recollect a mythic figure, this time the Lone Ranger. As a boy, Tam had fantasized that, behind his mask, the Lone Ranger was Chinese, and Tam had therefore identified with him as a heroic role model who represented the possibility that a Chinese American could become an idol of the American public. As Tam reenacts his past fantasy in his adulthood, however, he realizes that the Lone Ranger is a racist, as is clear in his treatment of Tonto, and that he is not by any means a Chinese. In fact, the Lone Ranger is an obese white man who sadistically shoots Tam in the hand (symbolically handicapping him physically), then lays on him the curse of being an honorary white (handicapping him psychologically with this false identity). This episode, then, demythologizes the private fantasies of any Chinese American who might believe that he can easily achieve heroic status in the American imagination; it also shows the wounding consequences of the Chinese American fantasy that they can be accepted as honorary whites.

Tam and Kenji then track down Charley Popcorn. They are crushed, however, when Charley reveals that he is not, in fact, Dancer's father—that Dancer had constructed a myth around his memories of their association. Thus Tam's search for a surrogate and idolized father figure in a black man ends in disillusionment.

Returning to the apartment, Tam and Kenji undergo another identity crisis, this time precipitated by Lee's former husband, Tom. His name suggests the stereotype of the subservient minority, "Uncle Tom," and he is the very model of the minority that has attained middle-class success. Tom has heard of Kenji's decent but sexless relationship with Lee and wants to take Lee and Robbie back. Yet, now Kenji authoritatively stands his ground, sends Robbie to bed, and asserts that he wants Lee to stay and that he will father children with her.

Tam, too, appears to recover from his shattering disillusionment with Charley. In the surrealistic penultimate scene, he is shown being borne to Kenji's apartment on Charley's back, and in this position, Tam recalls the unmanning events when his wife left him on his birthday. In the play's last scene, however, Tam makes a great effort and stumbles into Kenji's apartment carrying Charley on his back. This reversal of position symbolically denotes Tam's freedom from his past reliance on an identity borrowed from the blacks and a new determination to find the wherewithal for a future identity from sources within himself. He is thus able to keep his integrity despite the needling of Lee and the allurement of Tom's imitation whiteness. Just as Kenji and Lee are united in a new relationship, so Tam is shown coming to terms with an identity grounded on his own ethnicity. Before the curtain falls, Tam is shown in the kitchen unashamedly practicing the craft of his ethnic group *par excellence*. As he prepares the food, he reminisces about the Chinese American legend of the Iron Moonhunter, a mythic train that the Chinese railroaders supposedly created out of parts stolen from the railroad companies, and which wanders the West searching out the souls of dead Chinese to bear them home to their families. Chin seems to understand that people need myths, and in the end, his protagonist, disillusioned with the black myth that is unavailable to him and rejecting a white myth that he finds contemptible, shapes his own myth of identity in the heroism and craft of Chinese America.

The Year of the Dragon • Chin's second play, *The Year of the Dragon*, is more conventionally structured than its predecessor and was accorded a national audience in a television production on the Public Broadcasting Service's "PBS Theatre in America" in 1975. This play also treats the theme of identity, but it focuses more sharply and poignantly on the question of self-worth: the worth of an individual self to loved ones (family) and the worth of a minority ethnic group to the majority society (white-dominated America). Again, stereotypes form the chief factor that obscures individual worth and identity—stereotypes about family relationships, stereotypes about ethnicity. These thematic strands are worked out in the exposition of the many psychological conflicts and confrontations in the well-established Eng family of San Francisco's Chinatown.

The exposition, and exposé, of ethnic stereotypes is presented chiefly through two elements of the play: the family business of providing tours of Chinatown and the new Anglo son-in-law whom their daughter has brought from Boston. The family owns Eng's Chinatown Tour and Travel agency, and the eldest son, forty-year-old Fred, conducts tours of San Francisco's Chinatown. For the sake of business, however, Fred cannot show Chinatown as it really is; rather, he must pander to the stereotypes of Chinatown held by the American public—that it is an exotic place of delicious foods, mysterious (but safe) goings on, and incomprehensible (but happy) inhabitants composed of attractively available women, complaisant men, and harmonious families with above-average children. Fred knows that he is being false to himself and his people when he gives his happy tour-guide's spiel, and he mutters curses at his customers under his breath beneath his patter. In reality, Fred would like to tell the truths of Chinatown, which he sets down in short stories, but no one will publish his work. Through Fred's situation, then, Chin portrays the stifling effects of ethnic stereotypes.

The other element in the play that deals with ethnic stereotypes is presented through the character Ross, the Eng family's Boston-bred son-in-law on a honeymoon visit from the East. He is portrayed as a well-meaning but oafish Sinophile who has studied Chinese (although in a dialect different from the Eng family's), admires Chinese culture and customs, and thinks of Chinese Americans as the only minority group that does not dislike white dominance. Such stereotypes prevent him from seeing the Chinese American realities that trip him up constantly. His type of cultural voyeurism is subtly captured in the play's final scene, in which he is appointed photographer to take posed pictures of the Eng family. In this technically effective scene, Chin uses spatial form as adroitly as did Gustave Flaubert in the "agricultural fair" scene of *Madame Bovary* (1857; English translation, 1886). Through a kind of auditory montage, Chin creates an ironic counterpoint commenting on Ross's photography by interspersing the scene with the sounds and spiel of a tour guide describing a Chinese New Year's parade offstage. Just as the tourists are gawking at the Chinatown parade, so is Ross ogling his new Chinese American family.

In probing the stereotypes of familial relationships, Chin makes a painful but necessary criticism of stereotypes held by his own ethnic group. He also dispels the Charlie Chan-esque stereotype held by many Americans, that Chinese families are uniformly harmonious and hierarchical.

Much of the conflict in the family swirls around its patriarch, Pa Eng, who came to the United States in 1935 accompanied only by his infant son Fred, for he was forced to leave his wife in China because United States immigration laws excluded Chinese women from entering America. Pa Eng soon married a fifteen-year-old American-born Chinese girl (Ma Eng), who risked losing her American citizenship by marrying the man she loved (her citizenship was at risk not because she married a bigamist but because another American anti-Chinese law forbade American-born women to marry Chinese men on pain of forfeiting their citizenship). Ma Eng bore and reared two children, meanwhile pampering Pa Eng in his stereotypical Chinese view of the patriarch as a kind of semidivinity.

When the play opens, Pa Eng has prospered, to the point that he has been elected mayor of Chinatown. Yet he is now old and ill, and he believes that his days are numbered. He wants to die in the bosom of his family, so he has sent for his first wife (China Mama). This he has done without communicating his intent to his family. (In fact, throughout the play, the family members can hardly be said to communicate; they never bother to listen to what others have to say.) China Mama's arrival, as can be expected, precipitates several crises during which Pa Eng appears an inconsiderate, uncomprehending, ego-bound patriarch. He commands Ma Eng, who is unnerved by this presence in her household, either to relinquish her home or to be subservient to China Mama and begin teaching her English. It is in his relationship with Fred, however, that Pa Eng's authoritarian role becomes most apparent.

Pa Eng's patriarchal dominance and his Chinese values have acted as longstanding denials of Fred's identity and self-worth. Fred had aspired to be a writer, but his father scoffed at this: According to stereotypes he holds, if one is not a doctor or a lawyer, one is nothing at all. Pa Eng gives his mayoral speech to Ross to edit, not to Fred, who majored in English. Nevertheless, Fred is a dutiful son, nursing his father when he spits blood and even going through a daily ritual of accompanying him to the toilet and wiping him after a defecation, a viscerally affecting scene to stage. Fred has also sacrificed his own college career to work and provide for his sister's college expenses, but his father does not appreciate that, probably because his stereotypical values do not accord much importance to daughters. Fred also is aware that his younger brother, Johnny, is deteriorating into a gun-wielding Chinatown mobster and wants him to leave his environment and go to college in the East. This Johnny resists.

Fred knows that Johnny will go to college if Pa Eng orders him, but Pa Eng refuses. Instead, Pa Eng wants Fred to accompany him as he delivers his mayoral speech. In this speech, he plans to acknowledge Fred as his heir, but he will do it in such a way that Fred will always be fitted with the stereotypical identity of a Number One Son, a person who has no self-worth beyond that which derives from his father. This is unacceptable to Fred, who refuses to go with his father as long as he refuses to order Johnny to leave Chinatown. In attempting to impose his will on his son, Pa Eng resorts to violence and slaps him repeatedly. Yet the physical exertion is too much for the sick old man, and he dies in this pitiable moment of futile tyranny. Tragically, Pa Eng's death does not free Fred. The closing tableau of the play shows Fred being submerged by his milieu as he slips into the spiel of the Chinatown tour guide, and as the spotlight singles him out, Fred is shown dressed glaringly in white, the Chinese symbol of death.

Other major works

LONG FICTION: *Donald Duk*, 1991; *Gunga Din Highway*, 1994.

SHORT FICTION: *The Chinaman Pacific and Frisco R.R. Co.*, 1988.

TELEPLAYS: *S.R.T., Act Two*, 1966; *The Bel Canto Carols*, 1966; *A Man and His Music*, 1967; *Ed Sierer's New Zealand*, 1967; *Seafair Preview*, 1967; *The Year of the Ram*, 1967; *And Still Champion . . .* , 1967; *The Report*, 1967; *Mary*, 1969; *Rainlight Rainvision*, 1969; *Chinaman's Chance*, 1971.

NONFICTION: *Bulletproof Buddhists and Other Essays*, 1998.

EDITED TEXTS: *Aiiieeeee! An Anthology of Asian American Writers*, 1974 (with others; Asian American writing); *The Big Aiiieeeee!*, 1991.

Bibliography

Barnes, Clive. "Theater: Culture Study." *The New York Times*, June 3, 1974, p. 39. A balanced review of *The Year of the Dragon* in performance at the American Place Theater in New York City. Barnes notes that the play has "gaps" and "lacks energy at times" but is still "interesting." He praises the "absolutely fascinating . . . insights" that Chin provides while dispelling stereotypes about Chinese Americans, investigating Chinese American identity, and exploring generational differences.

Chua, C. L. "*The Year of the Dragon*, by Frank Chin." In *A Resource Guide to Asian American Literature*, edited by Sau-ling Wong and Stephen Sumida. New York: Modern Language Association, 2001. Intended for students and teachers, this essay provides an overview of the play, historical contexts, pedagogical suggestions, and intertextual linkages.

Kim, Elaine H. *Asian American Literature: An Introduction to the Writings and Their Social Context*. Philadelphia: Temple University Press, 1982. In chapter 6 of this essential and pioneering study of Asian American literature, Kim discusses Chin together with other writers of his generation. Kim's focus is on Chin's short fiction and *The Chickencoop Chinaman*. She analyzes the play as a forum for Chin's ideas on Chinese American culture, identity, and manhood, ideas that are darkened by a pervading sense of futility, decadence, and alienation. Kim also faults Chin for the use of "unbalanced" dialogue (that is, monologic lectures) and stereotyped women characters.

_____. "Frank Chin: The Chinatown Cowboy and His Backtalk." *Midwest Quarterly* 20 (Autumn, 1978): 78-91. This essay by the doyenne of Asian American literary critics is an earlier version of the previous bibliographic entry. The essay, however, is more acerbic than the book chapter; it finds that *The Chickencoop Chinaman* conveys "contempt for the Asian American identity" and portrays the "pathetic futility of the male protagonist."

Kroll, Jack. "Primary Color." *Newsweek*, June 19, 1972, 55. Extols *The Chickencoop Chinaman* as "the most interesting play of the American Place Theater" that year. Compares Chin with John Osborne and Chin's protagonist to Lenny Bruce, sees Chin's thematic concerns as his generation's search for identity, and characterizes Chin's language as "rogue poetry of deracination" enlivened by the "beat and brass, the runs and rim-shots of jazz."

Ling, Jinqi. *Narrating Nationalisms: Ideology and Form in Asian American Literature.* New York: Oxford University Press, 1998. This book devotes a complete chapter to the plays of Frank Chin, discussing their ethics and poetics. It also comments on issues of masculinity, the effects of commercialization, and the postmodern nature of Chin's theatrical art.

McDonald, Dorothy Ritsuko. Introduction to *"The Chickencoop Chinaman" and "The Year of the Dragon": Two Plays by Frank Chin.* Seattle: University of Washington Press, 1981. This extensive introduction provides information on Chin's background and his views on Chinese American history. Makes an intelligent thematic commentary on Chin's plays. Sees Chin's intent as attempting to dispel stereotypes about Chinese Americans and to recover mythic archetypes (such as Kwan Kung, patron deity of war and letters) to validate the Chinese American male. A valuable essay marred by some errors of detail.

Oliver, Edith. "Off Broadway." *The New Yorker* 48 (June 24, 1972): 46. An enthusiastic response to *The Chickencoop Chinaman* that hails its historical importance for bringing "the first news (theatrically speaking) of the Chinese Americans in our midst." Characterizes the play as "moving, funny, pain-filled, sarcastic, bitter, ironic . . . in a furious and dazzling eruption of verbal legerdemain." Notices a "few paltry things that are wrong" with it but finds that these "hardly matter," given the play's theatrical inventiveness.

Wong, Sau-ling. *Reading Asian American Literature: From Necessity to Extravagance.* Princeton, N.J.: Princeton University Press, 1993. Contains a brilliant chapter analyzing theme and imagery in Chin's drama.

Yin, Xiao-huang. *Chinese American Literature Since the 1850's.* Urbana: University of Illinois Press, 2000. This study contains a section dealing with the debate between Maxine Hong Kingston and Frank Chin when Chin had accused her of inauthenticity.

C. L. Chua

Caryl Churchill

Born: London, England; September 3, 1938

Principal drama • *Downstairs,* pr. 1958; *Easy Death,* pr. 1962; *Owners,* pr. 1972, pb. 1973; *Moving Clocks Go Slow,* pr. 1975; *Objections to Sex and Violence,* pr. 1975, pb. 1985; *Light Shining in Buckinghamshire,* pr. 1976, pb. 1978; *Vinegar Tom,* pr. 1976, pb. 1978; *Traps,* pr. 1977, pb. 1978; *Cloud Nine,* pr., pb. 1979; *Three More Sleepless Nights,* pr. 1980, pb. 1990; *Top Girls,* pr., pb. 1982; *Fen,* pr., pb. 1983; *Softcops,* pr., pb. 1984; *Plays: One,* pb. 1985; *A Mouthful of Birds,* pr., pb. 1986 (with David Lan); *Serious Money,* pr., pb. 1987; *Ice Cream,* pr., pb. 1989; *Hot Fudge,* pr. 1989, pb. 1990; *Mad Forest: A Play from Romania,* pr., pb. 1990; *Churchill Shorts: Short Plays,* pb. 1990; *Plays: Two,* pb. 1990; *Skriker,* pr. 1993; *Blue Heart,* pr., pb. 1997; *Hotel: In a Room Anything Can Happen,* pr., pb. 1997 (libretto). *This Is a Chair,* pr. 1997, pb. 1999; *Plays: Three,* pb. 1998; *Far Away,* pr. 2000, pb. 2001; *A Number,* pr., pb. 2002

Other literary forms • Although Caryl Churchill is known primarily as a playwright, her writing career actually began with radio plays in the early 1960's, when *The Ants* was broadcast in 1962. *The Ants* was followed by other radio plays, including *Lovesick* (1967), *Identical Twins* (1968), *Abortive* (1971), *Not, Not, Not, Not, Not Enough Oxygen* (1971), *Schreber's Nervous Illness* (1972), *Henry's Past* (1972), and *Perfect Happiness* (1973). Churchill has also written several teleplays: *The Judge's Wife* (1972), *Turkish Delight* (1974), *The After-Dinner Joke* (1978), *The Legion Hall Bombing* (1978), and *Crimes* (1981).

Achievements • Caryl Churchill is claimed by several political and artistic constituencies: She is hailed as a major voice for English socialists; is cited frequently by feminists; is the darling of proponents of workshops, or group construction, of plays; and is clearly a postmodern voice. Certainly, Churchill is each of these things, but, above all, she is a writer of the human presence and a champion of the individual choice. Her particular achievement is not to experiment but to experiment with a difference. Her unusual use of theatrical structure always aims to reveal the value of the eccentric individual over the concentricities of an exploitive social order. She is an established playwright whose work, though highly unusual in structure, is widely and well received in the English-speaking world, having been successfully produced both in London and in New York. Churchill won the Obie Award for best Off-Broadway play in 1982, 1983, and 1988. In 1988, she also won London's Society of West End Theatre Award.

Biography • Caryl Churchill was born in London, England, on September 3, 1938. She lived in Montreal, Canada, from 1948 to 1955, and there attended the Trafalgar School. From 1957 to 1960, she studied English literature at the University of Oxford and took her bachelor of arts degree from that institution in 1960. Her first dramatic works were produced at the University of Oxford, but many of her early plays remain unpublished. In 1961, she married David Harter; she is the mother of three sons. As his wife's career developed, Harter gave up his lucrative private law practice so that his wife could spend more time writing.

A prolific playwright, Churchill received her first professional stage production in

1972 when *Owners* was performed at the Royal Court Theatre. From that point on, she became closely associated with that theater. She has been a member of the Joint Stock Theatre Group, an organization dedicated to collective creation of theatrical work, and has worked with the Monstrous Regiment, a feminist theater union. Churchill has contributed frequently to the British Broadcasting Corporation's (BBC) radio and television broadcasts. In an incident now notorious, she and her director, David Lan, insisted that their names be left off the credits of the BBC's 1978 television production of *The Legion Hall Bombing* because the producers had censored the work. As her reputation spread, Churchill's works were brought to the United States and were staged by Joseph Papp in New York. She is a playwright of considerable international importance.

Analysis • Caryl Churchill has become well known for her willingness to experiment with dramatic structure. Her innovations in this regard are sometimes so startling and compelling that reviewers tend to focus on the novelty of her works to the exclusion of her ideas. Churchill, however, is a playwright of ideas, ideas that are often difficult and, despite her bold theatricality, surprisingly subtle and elusive. Her principal concern is with the issues attendant on the individual's struggle to emerge from the ensnarements of culture, class, economic systems, and the imperatives of the past. Each of these impediments to the development and happiness of the individual is explored in her works. Not surprisingly for a contemporary female writer, many times she makes use of female characters to explore such themes.

Churchill has openly proclaimed herself a feminist and a socialist. She is also emphatic in her position that the two are not one and the same. Indeed, her plays do not attempt to confound the two issues, although *Top Girls* does investigate the influence that capitalism can have on women and their willingness to forsake their humanity for economic gain. Churchill has examined with great sympathy, in works such as *Fen* and *Light Shining in Buckinghamshire*, the plight of the male, or of both genders, caught up in the destructiveness of inhuman economic forces. Churchill herself has argued that both issues are so important to her—the plight of women and the need for a socialist world—that she could not choose between them and would not have one problem alleviated without a concurrent solution to the other. In another sense, Churchill is interested in the greater issues of gender and the games of power played with gender at stake. Just so, she is equally committed to considering the individual and the power drained from that individual by the forces of modern economic and social systems.

Whatever her politics and philosophy, Churchill brings a fire and an energy, a special eye and ear, to the postmodern English drama. She is an inspiration to the feminist movement and to women intellectuals around the world. She remains a force crying out for the release of the individual of either gender from the oppressive imperatives of past practices and present expectations. To her art, she contributes an inventive mind and a willingness to invest great energies in wedding the play to the performance. She has continuously rejected linear structure and the use of the master narratives of socialist realism to present her themes. She has also rejected the Brechtean epic theater in favor of using "found objects," such as various couples in a hotel room or snatches of everyday speech, and re-contextualizing these found objects into new situations that emphasize new meanings. In this way she is much like the famous avant-garde artist Gaston Duchamp who made a fountain of a toilet bowl.

An important factor in Churchill's proclivity for structural experimentation is her long and close association with workshop groups, whose aim is the collective creation of theater pieces through the interaction of actors, writers, directors, choreographers, and other artists. Two such groups have been especially influential on Churchill's artistic development: The first is the Monstrous Regiment, a feminist theater union that helped Churchill create *Vinegar Tom*; the other is the Joint Stock Theatre Group, with whose help she fashioned several important works, including *Cloud Nine, Fen,* and *A Mouthful of Birds.*

The Joint Stock Theatre Group, with directors such as Max Stafford-Clark, Les Waters, and David Lan, and choreographer Ian Fink, operates with suggestions that come from any group member. For example, *Light Shining in Buckinghamshire,* Churchill's first venture with the group, began with a member's suggestion concerning the motives for the mass immigration of villagers in seventeenth century England. After the initial proposal of the idea, the group set out to research the topic, following it with a theatrical workshop in which the group improvised scenes based on that research. These workshop scenes were interrupted by a "writing gap" during which Churchill wrote the script. Rehearsals came next, with more group interaction and improvisation on the script.

Fen followed virtually the same process and was based on a suggestion to explore what it must have been like, in a rural English village, to have the social and agricultural habits of centuries suddenly overturned by the intrusion of modern capitalism, brought in the persona of a Japanese businessman who buys all the village's farmland. In another example, the group's director, Lan, was interested in the politics of possession, while Churchill was interested in the theme of women becoming violent and rebellious rather than submitting to their traditionally assigned, passive role. The Joint Stock Theatre Group went to work with these ideas, and *A Mouthful of Birds* was born. This creative method, which gives a privilege to experimentation and outright and frank theatricalism, seems to serve Churchill well.

Churchill also has a special relationship with London's Royal Court Theatre, where she was resident dramatist in 1974-1975 and where she has had many of her plays performed in the main playhouse and the experimental Upstairs Theatre. Churchill's radio and television works are often broadcast by the BBC, and her plays are frequently staged outside Great Britain, especially in the United States, where she was first introduced by Joseph Papp at the Public Theatre of New York City.

Churchill has also worked with educational institutions such as the Central School of Speech and Drama in London. She and school director Mark Wing-Davey took a group of ten graduate students to Bucharest, where they worked with students at the Romanian Institute of Theatre and Cinema on the creation of *Mad Forest.*

Woman as cultural concept • In four of her best-known works–*Cloud Nine, Top Girls, A Mouthful of Birds,* and *Vinegar Tom*—Churchill presents woman as a cultural concept and displays the power of that concept to submerge and smother the individual female. In *Cloud Nine,* a parallel is suggested between Western colonial oppression and Western sexual oppression. This oppression is seen first in the family organization and then in the power of the past to demand obligations from the present. Although her characters use geographical distance and literally run away from the past, no one in *Cloud Nine* can exorcise the ghosts of established practices and traditions.

Top Girls is a depiction of the exploitation of women by women, a technique well learned through generations of women being exploited by men. The play portrays a group of friends, all successful women in the fields of literature and the arts, who gather for a dinner to celebrate Marlene's promotion to an executive position in the

Top Girls employment agency. Viewers are introduced to scenes of Marlene's workplace and to her working-class sister and niece, Angie. In a painful end to *Top Girls*, Churchill reveals how one woman character is willing to sacrifice her very motherhood to maintain her position in the world of business, a world that the play shows to be created by and for men. Following a bitter argument between Marlene and her lower-class sister, it is also revealed that Marlene's "niece" is actually her illegitimate daughter.

The issues in *Top Girls* and *Cloud Nine*, however startlingly presented, are ones commonly addressed in modern culture, even if usually addressed with an attitude different from that of Churchill. *A Mouthful of Birds*, however, is altogether different, for it addresses the most sensitive and most taboo of all matters concerning women: sex and violence. Furthermore, in *A Mouthful of Birds*, Churchill turns the tables and considers sex and violence as perpetrated not by men on women but by women on men, thereby taking one more step into the forbidden matters of gender.

The theme of society's oppressed females is perhaps most powerfully presented in one of Churchill's earlier works, *Vinegar Tom*, a piece created especially for the Monstrous Regiment. *Vinegar Tom* is a play about witches, but there are no witches in it, only four women accused of being witches. Set in seventeenth century England, the play depicts four women accused by society of the vaguest of crimes: sorcery. Their only crime, however, has been to follow an individual impulse. Joan Nokes is simply poor and old, two conditions that are not supposed to happen simultaneously to Western women. Her daughter, Alice, understands sex as an individual matter and is inclined to enjoy a man if he suits her fancy. When Alice asserts her right to have an illegitimate child, she is labeled a "whore," since she is neither a virgin nor a wife. Betty, the play's third woman, is called a witch for refusing to marry the man picked out for her, and Susan, the fourth, is seen as a witch for choosing life over death: When put to the water test (witches float, the innocent sink), Susan elects to swim, thus saving herself but forcing society to find a way to kill her. All four women are emerging, strong-willed individuals whose only crime is to be themselves in an oppressive and conservative society. Because they will not carry out their assigned female roles, they are cast as witches and hanged as a logical consequence of their chosen lifestyles.

Unique dramatic structure • It is virtually impossible to discuss thematic issues in Churchill's work without simultaneously considering her special treatment of dramatic structure. Each of her pieces is a unique construction, innovatively assembled and using unconventional and highly theatrical devices. Furthermore, Churchill's plays remain compelling, mysterious, and, at the same time, refreshingly accessible.

Cloud Nine presents, in part 1, an English family living in colonial Africa. The father, Clive, though far from home, "serves the Queen." He is father not only to his children but to the natives as well. Churchill has a special device for underscoring this male-dominated world. She calls for Billy, Clive's wife and the mother of the children, to be played by a male. To reinforce her statement, Churchill asks that the black servant, Joshua, be played by a white performer. Thus both characters, despite the race and gender of the performers, become whatever the white father wishes them to be. When a lesbian nanny, Ellen, appears, homosexual orientation is suspected in the children and the "perfect" family is created.

Part 2 has additional surprises. The colonial family returns to England without the father. In England, the grown-up children seek to realize their separate identities, but the freedom to be fully choosing individuals still eludes them. They fret over not having the father to tell them what to do, and the traditions of the past weigh heavily on them, keeping them in their assigned roles. One of the daughters, Lin, a diminutive for Ellen, the lesbian nanny of part 1, had married to fulfill social expectations.

Now divorced and having custody of her child, Lin openly lives with a female lover. Even that important change in sexual orientation, however, is not sufficiently liberating, for as Lin remarks, she can change whom she sleeps with but she cannot change everything. In a wistful scene, she attempts to conjure up a goddess, one she knows will never materialize, begging the deity to give her the history she never had, make her the woman she cannot be. In *Cloud Nine*, Churchill reverses the traditional immigration pattern. Often parents settle in a new land but bring the past and its old ways with them; in *Cloud Nine*, however, the children flee their past by returning to the old land, but they are still smothered by ancient habits, expectations, and icons. This preoccupation with the ghosts and hauntings of the past, indeed with the very nature of time itself, is further explored by Churchill in the unusual pieces *Traps* and *Moving Clocks Go Slow*.

A recurring structural device in Churchill's dramaturgy is to have one actor play several roles. Most of her better-known works—*Serious Money*, *Top Girls*, *Light Shining in Buckinghamshire*, and *Cloud Nine*—make use of multiple role playing. Although the device may be considered merely idiomatic with her, Churchill usually has a point to make in employing multiple role playing. In *Serious Money*, for example, the actors are assigned a series of roles that may be summed up in a single universal type, so that one actor, for example, plays a stockbroker or a financier while another plays various women who pander their bodies or their souls to men of high finance.

Even more idiosyncratic in structure is the powerful *A Mouthful of Birds*, in which the stories of seven contemporary personas are interwoven with the ancient ritualistic events of Euripides' *Bakchai* (405 B.C.E.; *The Bacchae*, 1781). Dionysus, the Greek God of wine, appears throughout the piece dancing in a modern woman's petticoat. Amid ancient scenes of ecstasy and emotional and physical violence, the modern characters appear in their normal daily activities. They each present a monologue in which they attempt to explain why they have failed to meet their obligations. Secret and mysterious problems of possession emerge. The atmosphere of the play is charged with the sensuality of accepted violence, violence intermingled with the irresistible quality of sex. One woman character, for example, who is stereotypically squeamish about skinning a dead rabbit for supper, calmly tells her husband to go to the bathroom, where he will find their baby drowned. Churchill juxtaposes this modern violence against the culminating terror of *The Bacchae*, the gruesome moment when Agave, in a Dionysian ecstasy, tears apart the body of her son Pentheus.

Hotel represents yet another structural experimentation for Churchill. It is an opera, with music by Orlando Gough, set in eight identical hotel rooms superimposed together on stage, with actors playing multiple roles. A number of different couples occupy the rooms at one time or another, including a couple having an adulterous affair and another couple who are homosexual. A television set also figures as a major character. By doubling and tripling the actors in various roles, Churchill subtly emphasizes the commonality of human oppression and pain.

Typical of Churchill, the story is not linear, but rather occurs in fragments. The dialogue is also presented in fragments. As Churchill points out in the introduction to the play, she has constructed the work in the way we perceive opera in performance, especially classic opera in languages other than English. We hear snatches of dialogue, but the requirements of the music often overshadow the entire line. The use of fragmented dialogue and non-linear story development is also found in plays such as *This Is a*

Chair, where a series of domestic scenes is compared to events about the world through the use of placards naming each scene. Churchill's use of fragments of dialogue suggests that language can often fail as a means of communication, especially when those using language take little care in its employment. This suggestion is further emphasized in that the fragments are always realistic bits of everyday conversation used in a surrealistic manner.

Other major works

TELEPLAYS: *The Judge's Wife*, 1972; *Turkish Delight*, 1974; *The After-Dinner Joke*, 1978; *The Legion Hall Bombing*, 1978; *Crimes*, 1981.

RADIO PLAYS: *The Ants*, 1962; *Lovesick*, 1967; *Identical Twins*, 1968; *Abortive*, 1971; *Not, Not, Not, Not, Not Enough Oxygen*, 1971; *Schreber's Nervous Illness*, 1972; *Henry's Past*, 1972; *Perfect Happiness*, 1973.

TRANSLATION: *Thyestes*, 1994 (of Seneca).

Bibliography

Betsko, Kathleen, and Rachel Koenig, comps. *Interviews with Contemporary Playwrights.* New York: Beech Tree Books, 1987. In this provocative interview, the playwright discusses her concept of feminism and compares the London and New York productions of *Cloud Nine.*

Bigsby, C. W. E., ed. *Contemporary English Drama.* London: Edward Arnold, 1981. This collection of essays about the British theater provides a key to locating Churchill among her contemporaries. The essay by Christian W. Thomsen, "Three Socialist Playwrights: John McGrath, Caryl Churchill, Trevor Griffiths," is informative about contemporary socialist thought in England and the way in which it is revealed in the plays of Churchill and her peers.

Cousin, Geraldine. *Churchill, the Playwright.* London: Methuen Drama, 1989. An excellent general study of Churchill's drama. All the issues present in Churchill's work are examined as they are found in the plays themselves.

Fitzsimmons, Linda, comp. *File on Churchill.* London: Methuen Drama, 1989. This brief volume is a compilation of "file material" on Churchill, including lists of sources to consult, quotations from articles about the playwright, biographical data, production information, and reviews of productions. An excellent and dependable source book.

Kaysser, Helen, ed. *Feminism and the Theatre.* Basingstoke, England: Macmillan, 1988. As the title suggests, this volume is a collection of essays on feminists in theater, and includes an excellent essay on Churchill by a leading feminist critic in the United States, Sue Ellen Case. The volume is useful not only for the Case essay but also for aiding those interested in placing Churchill in the context of contemporary feminist thinking. It is also instructive in the uses of feminist thinking in Churchill's work.

Kieburzinka, Christine Olga. *Intertextual Loops in Modern Drama.* Madison, N.J.: Fairleigh Dickinson University Press, 2001. Contains excellent chapter on the construction of *Mad Forest*, revealing how Churchill cooperated with various workshop groups in the writing and structuring of her plays, in this case a group of students from London and Romania.

Randall, Phyllis, ed. *Caryl Churchill: A Casebook.* New York: Garland, 1989. A collection of essays pertaining to Churchill as a working dramatist.

August W. Staub

Jean Cocteau

Born: Maisons-Laffitte, France; July 5, 1889
Died: Milly-la-Forêt, France; October 11, 1963

Principal drama • *Antigone*, pr. 1922, pb. 1928 (libretto; English translation, 1961); *Orphée*, pr. 1926, pb. 1927 (*Orpheus*, 1933); *Oedipus-Rex*, pr. 1927, pb. 1928 (libretto; English translation, 1961); *La Voix humaine*, pr., pb. 1930 (*The Human Voice*, 1951); *La Machine infernale*, pr., pb. 1934 (*The Infernal Machine*, 1936); *L'École des veuves*, pr., pb. 1936; *Les Chevaliers de la table ronde*, pr., pb. 1937 (*The Knights of the Round Table*, 1955); *Les Parents terribles*, pr., pb. 1938 (*Intimate Relations*, 1952); *Les Monstres sacrés*, pr., pb. 1940 (*The Holy Terrors*, 1953); *La Machine à écrire*, pr., pb. 1941 (*The Typewriter*, 1948); *Renaud et Armide*, pr., pb. 1943; *L'Aigle à deux têtes*, pr., pb. 1946 (*The Eagle Has Two Heads*, 1946); *Bacchus*, pr. 1951, pb. 1952 (English translation, 1955); *Théâtre complet*, pb. 1957 (2 volumes); *Five Plays*, pb. 1961; *L'Impromptu du Palais-Royal*, pr., pb. 1962; *The Infernal Machine and Other Plays*, pb. 1964

Other literary forms • Jean Cocteau took considerable delight in working on the borderlines separating various literary genres and those traditionally dividing literature from the other arts. As a result, his artistic output is both extraordinary and difficult to classify. *Le Potomak* (1919), his first important work, moves freely among verse, prose, dialogue, and drawing. His novel *Les Enfants terribles* (1929; *Children of the Game*, 1955), generally considered to be his masterpiece, is as much autobiography as fiction. He wrote magnificent poems, such as *La Crucifixion* (1946), but he also insisted that his novels, his criticism, in fact, all his works, are poetry. Many of his works for the stage can be called drama in only the broadest sense of the term: An example of such works is the scandalous ballet scenario *Parade* (1917), created in collaboration with Eric Satie and Pablo Picasso, and performed by Sergei Diaghilev's Ballets Russes. In 1921, Cocteau collaborated with six composers of the group known as "Les Six" (they included Louis Durey, Arthur Honegger, Darius Milhaud, Germaine Tailleferre, Georges Auric, and Francis Poulenc) and the Swedish Ballet Company in creating *Les Mariés de la tour Eiffel* (1921; *The Wedding on the Eiffel Tower*, 1937), this time contributing to the choreography as well as the dialogue.

Cocteau created a number of original and highly regarded films, beginning with *La Sang d'un poète* (1930; *The Blood of a Poet*, 1932), and including, among others, *La Belle et la bête* (1946; *Beauty and the Beast*, 1947) and *Orphée* (1950; *Orpheus*, 1950). He also wrote many witty, incisive nonfiction works, often autobiographical in nature; *Opium: Journal d'une désintoxication* (1930; *Opium: Diary of a Cure*, 1932) and *La Belle et la bête: Journal d'un film* (1946; *Beauty and the Beast: Journal of a Film*, 1950) are examples of his work in this area. Much of his work was experimental and often designed to shock, to break new ground and redefine the old.

Achievements • Neal Oxenhandler eloquently sums up the current image of Jean Cocteau by entitling a study of the latter's theater *Scandal and Parade*: Only time and cautious scholarship will be able to reveal the worth of the artist and his work buried beneath the "scandal and parade." There can be little doubt that he was an important innovator on the stage. If one judges by what has frequently been the twentieth century artist's basis for self-evaluation—that is, if one judges Cocteau as experimenter and innovator—then one can consider him a leader in the arts of his time. That he reveals in his dramas dark corners of the human condition, particularly that of the twentieth century, is an aspect of his work that is too little understood. Because Cocteau was not a partisan, as were George Bernard Shaw or Bertolt Brecht, critics have too often overlooked the importance of his social and, in the broad sense, political worldview. Indeed, Cocteau shows throughout his best works the uncanny and incisive perception of an outsider.

Biography • It could be argued that Jean Maurice Eugène Clement Cocteau was born and bred to be an outsider. Reared by a family of stockbrokers, diplomats, and admirals, he was a product of the *grande bourgeoisie française*, neither entirely of the middle class nor entirely of the aristocracy. His parents, Georges and Eugénie Lecomte Cocteau, a couple who were no strangers to the arts, introduced Jean, his brother Paul, and his sister Marthe to music, theater, architecture, indeed, all the fine arts. Georges died when Jean was nine years old, and his mother, with whom he had a long and close relationship, had difficulty keeping the boy at the Petit Lycée Condorcet, where he was a poor student. Instead, Cocteau preferred to follow his own interests at home and to attend the theater regularly.

His birthplace, Maisons-Laffitte, allowed Cocteau easy access to Paris, where he involved himself in the various avant-garde movements that followed hard on one another in the early part of the twentieth century, finding comradeship in unconventional undertakings with fellow outsiders. His friends included such writers as Edmond Rostand, Catulle Mendès, Leon Daudet, Marcel Proust, and the Comtesse Anna de Noailles. By 1909, he had published his first book of poems, *La Lampe d'Aladin*.

Soon afterward, he met the director of the Ballets Russes, Sergei Diaghilev, a man who influenced Cocteau immensely, inspiring him to write a number of ballet scenarios. Diaghilev's remonstrance to "Astonish me!" is claimed to have set Cocteau on his lifelong aesthetic course to surprise and shock his audiences.

Cocteau's homosexuality was another factor that contributed to his outsider's perspective, placing him outside conventionality and impressing itself on his life, outlook, and art. He formed pivotal mentor-student-love relationships that would shape his artistic endeavors. His friendship with Raymond Radiguet, which had much to do with Cocteau's movement toward a more simple, classical style, and that with actor Jean Marais were two such important unions.

With the outbreak of World War I, Cocteau, rejected for active service because of his poor health, joined a civilian ambulance unit on the Belgian front. His experiences during this time formed the basis for his novel *Thomas l'imposteur* (1923; *Thomas the Impostor*, 1925), which was later made into a film. Toward the end of the war, Cocteau began his association with Pablo Picasso. Along with Satie and Diaghilev, they collaborated to create the ballet *Parade*, whose atonal music and radical set and costumes caused a sensation. (This production marked Cocteau's break with Igor Stravinsky, with whom he had been closely associated, and his alignment with Les Six.) With Radiguet's death in 1923 from typhoid fever, Cocteau, inconsolable, became addicted to opium yet continued his prodigious artistic production. During this period, *Orpheus* and *Oedipus-Rex*, an opera-oratorio, were produced.

In the 1930's, Cocteau turned his attention to film, creating a number of highly original works in that medium. The late 1930's marked the beginning of Cocteau's long collaboration with Jean Marais, during which he designed many roles especially for the young actor; the result was a series of masterpieces for screen and stage.

Cocteau took a pacifist stand during World War II, and his nonconformity during the German Occupation nearly cost him his life. Several of his stage works were banned for being "immoral," and he was beaten by members of a French Fascist group for refusing to salute their flag. Somewhat later, he braved official disapproval by testifying on behalf of criminal-turned-novelist Jean Genet. Cocteau continued to write, paint murals, direct films, design fabrics, and travel until 1953, when his health began to fail. In 1955, he was elected to the Académie Française and the Royal Belgian Academy. In 1956, he was awarded an honorary doctorate of letters from Oxford University. Cocteau died at Milly-la-Forêt, outside Paris, on October 11, 1963.

Analysis • Early in his career, during and after World War I, Jean Cocteau wrote scenarios for ballets and adaptations of Greek myths. His plays of the late 1920's and early 1930's were highly original and brought him much attention. Cocteau gave the Oedipus legend a lasting form in his opera-oratorio *Oedipus-Rex*, and *Antigone* bears historical significance beyond its considerable intrinsic merits. In the late 1930's and the 1940's, under the influence of Jean Marais, Cocteau turned to contemporary problems, creating taut psychological dramas in the style of Boulevard drama; *Intimate Relations* is the most highly regarded of these middle works. Cocteau's later plays reflect his interest in reaching back into the past for both subject and form. *Renaud et Armide* and *L'Impromptu du Palais-Royal* appeal, respectively, to Jean Racine and Molière for models. *The Eagle Has Two Heads* returns to the nineteenth century romantic melodrama for conventions and to the period's history for plot elements. *Bacchus* combines historical drama and the Erasmian colloquy to create a mood-picture of the early Reformation. In these plays of his final years, Cocteau created works of transcendent stature. Of these, *The Eagle Has Two Heads* is the most beautifully crafted and most often performed.

(National Archives)

Although it can be claimed that Cocteau's plays fall into distinct groups, or periods, the essential unity of all of Cocteau's plays must be noted. That he consistently chose a perverse or inverted vantage point, in order to astonish his audience with the unexpected, reflects the essential relation of his art to society. Cocteau added immensely to the arsenal of modern stage techniques; he had a keen ability to pick a subject to pieces and, in the process, demonstrate the absurdity of the whole. Always ready to draw out those elements that another playwright might have omitted, Cocteau, at his best, could also pare down to a minimum what was to be included.

In *Bacchus*, a dramatic masterpiece from Cocteau's late period, the playwright has a character speak a line that might be taken as a summation of the standard view of critics that he had produced too many works: "You speak too much to say one memorable word." Yet while it is true that Cocteau poured forth so many volumes of plays, as well as so many other works, brevity and conciseness are the hallmarks of the works just treated. Moreover, in these plays, Cocteau combines the quality of a subtle artist who elusively moves by indirection with that of the "astonisher" of the bourgeoisie—that of the social and political satirist completely without partisan dogma. Few twentieth century writers have succeeded in being scandalous to the extent of being persecuted, even beaten, and having their works banned, and yet without ever having taken a clear partisan position. In this trait Cocteau recalls an earlier French iconoclast: Voltaire succeeded in fighting the Church without being an atheist; Cocteau, in lambasting the establishment without being a Marxist.

Antigone • *Antigone* clearly demonstrates this capacity, at once, to draw out and to pare down the elements of the original drama, so much so that Sophocles would have found Cocteau's version, if not unrecognizable, at least, un-Sophoclean and un-Greek. The play was a significant contribution to the neoclassical movement in the arts of the 1920's. Igor Stravinsky and Les Six were setting forth the aesthetic of the pared-down and the streamlined in music. Picasso, who did the scenery for *Antigone*, was making thin-lined sketches of classical subjects; indeed, it is commonly believed that he adopted this style under the direct inspiration of Cocteau's own drawing style. Cocteau's thin single line in ink, which captures the essentials of form and meaning, graphically embodies, not only the style of Cocteau's neoclassical works, but also the aesthetic underlying all his works. In all the arts of this avant-garde neoclassicism, Greco-Roman subjects are used wherever possible; they are rendered, however, with a style and for a purpose that is modern. Sometimes a small touch in the dialogue of *Antigone*, more often, in the stage directions, makes it clear that the work is about modern France, indeed, about the modern experience.

Cocteau heavily underlines those elements in Creon the Tyrant that would be found in any twentieth century ruler. Like his modern counterparts, he lives in constant fear that the opposition is secretly plotting his downfall. Above all, Creon mistakenly believes that money is the wellspring of everyone's deeds. He even accuses the obviously irreproachable seer Tiresias of taking foreign bribes. Money, which is but one element among many in the work by Sophocles, is heavily underscored by Cocteau in his delineation of Creon. The supreme irony of Creon's tragedy is that his downfall results not from a group of paid subversives, motivated by worldly considerations of money and power; rather, he receives justice from someone who is inspired by moral sanctions.

Yet the agent of Creon's undoing has a further irony—it is a young woman, Antigone. When Antigone tells her sister that they must jointly act according to higher ethical demands and bury their brother in spite of Creon's law forbidding it, Ismene replies that she cannot, because women are helpless in the face of male power. Although Ismene proves unable to take action with her sister, she desires, in accordance with her conception of women, to partake of the martyr role that grows out of Antigone's act.

Female submission in the face of male domination is the essence of Creon's conception of political power in the largest sense. He says that disorder is his greatest fear and that nothing would strike at the primal basis of his order with more certainty than the revolt of the women. "City," "family," and even the army depend on keeping women in their place within the patriarchal structure, and consequently, nothing is more deadly than should it happen that "the anarchist is a woman." Creon puts the matter even more brutally to his son Haemon, saying that the city is but a wife to its leader. In a patriarchal structuring of both family and city, both a wife and the people must be kept subordinate to the male in power. Cocteau's choice of lines for Creon cuts even deeper: As he believes that money is the motivating force of those who resist power, so, too, does he believe that women are instruments of propagation and nothing more. Concerning Haemon's deep love for Antigone, his intended wife, Creon says that "he will find another womb." These elements are in Sophocles' play, but Cocteau has selected them out from other elements, brought them to the fore, and underscored them in a way that renders them modern.

Cocteau's *Antigone* was the first in a series of Greek dramas adapted by twentieth century French writers to shed light on the modern human situation—a series culminating in Jean Anouilh's *Antigone* (pr. 1944; English translation, 1946) and Jean-Paul Sartre's *Les Mouches* (pr., pb. 1943; *The Flies*, 1946). Cocteau constantly reminds the viewer through subtle touches in the *mise en scène* that he is viewing the present indirectly through the past. He instructs the actors to speak in very high-pitched voices as though they were reciting from a newspaper article. In another stage direction, he tells the actors playing the guards to stand on either side of Antigone and hold each end of a spear before her so that she will resemble a prisoner in a courtroom dock between two policemen.

Cocteau's *Antigone* represents the eternal spirit of disorder that eats away at the social structure on all levels—a structure that Cocteau finds inevitably repressive of the best in the human spirit. The fact that Antigone is a woman gives an added impact to the symbol: She has the capacity to deconstruct not only the obvious political system at the top but also the institution of the family. Cocteau's drama presents an outsider who gives her life to reveal the hypocrisy and rottenness of the social fabric. *Antigone*, although possibly influenced by the first wave of the feminist movement as it broke around Cocteau at the time he was writing the play, is not a tract for the stage as is George Bernard Shaw's *Mrs. Warren's Profession* (wr. 1893, pb. 1898), but it is still no less important socially or politically, and it is in some ways, perhaps, more profound.

Intimate Relations • In his second dramatic period, Cocteau set out to grapple with modern situations directly. *Intimate Relations* is the most highly valued and frequently performed of Cocteau's dramas about contemporary life. This play is most remarkable for its objective, detached view of the family as a structure of emotional relations and the neuroses stemming from them. One might term it a sociopolitical work even though, on the one hand, it avoids the underlying support of middle-class morality of the Boulevard dramas and the overt left-wing preachments of the *pièce a thèse*, on the other.

Although it could be argued that the family relations of the characters in *Intimate Relations* are unusual, the truths revealed in the play still have general relevance. Cocteau has structured the characters and their relations in what might be described as a pentangle: A mother inordinately loves a son, who loves a young woman, who was the mistress of the son's father, who, in his turn, is loved by the sister of his wife. Cocteau has made the family an unusual one for the purpose of making the dynamics of such a group all the more painfully apparent.

The two sisters, Yvonne, the wife, and Lèo, the unmarried sister, form the symbolic crux of the play. Lèo's presence has a certain ambiguity. It is she who saves Yvonne's life in act 1, but it is her series of attempts to salvage the family from shipwreck that leads to Yvonne being emotionally jettisoned from the family, resulting, then, in her suicide. At first, Lèo hatches a plot to separate the young couple (Madeleine and Michel); then, growing to like Madeleine, she hatches another plot to bring the young people back together again, thereby separating mother and son (Yvonne and Michel). Lèo's will to rule is a double-edged sword that saves and kills. The stage directions for *Intimate Relations* make clear the polarity between Lèo, on the one hand, and Yvonne and Madeleine, on the other: Cocteau observes that Yvonne's room represents chaos and Madeleine's, cosmos.

It is one of the beautiful subtleties of *Intimate Relations* that Cocteau does not make it emphatically apparent that his sympathies are with the figure of disorder, Yvonne. It is only by viewing *Intimate Relations* in the context of Cocteau's other plays that this attitude becomes clear. Antigone, the emblem of disorder, must die to bring tragic self-awareness to Creon, the emblem of order. Yvonne must also die a martyr's death. Yet, in *Intimate Relations*, the martyrdom has little effect because, at the play's end, a sinister order has been restored: Michel has found a new and more solid mother figure in Madeleine. This inevitability moves toward its tragic end in a real *coup de théâtre*.

The Eagle Has Two Heads • Equally exciting in dramatic structure is *The Eagle Has Two Heads*, which is perhaps the most theatrically viable of all the plays of Cocteau's last period, during which he experimented with past forms and conventions. Indeed, considered formalistically, this play is both a literary and a theatrical tour de force. Cocteau has compared the three-act structuring of this drama to a fugue: The first act, he says, is devoted to the queen; the second act, to Stanislas. In the last act, the two themes jointly culminate in a double suicide. This literary structure, however, had less a musical than a theatrical inspiration: Marais requested from Cocteau a play in which he could remain mute in the first act, have moments of ecstatic vocalizing in the second, and mime a melodramatic death in the third act. Cocteau set out to write an actor's play much like the singer's opera of the bel canto style and, then, to combine this style with elements of the romantic dramas of Victor Hugo. The miracle is that Cocteau succeeded in creating a complexly formulated, but no less moving, drama.

In essence, the play is a carefully concerted interchange between the queen and Stanislas, the would-be assassin, then her lover, and, finally, her assassin in fact. The first act is pervaded by the queen's monologues: The first of these is addressed to the imagined presence of her husband, an assassinated king; later, when Stanislas, the king's *Doppelgänger*, appears, she addresses him—mute as he is with exhaustion and defiance. From his appearance up to the finale of the play, however, Stanislas, and not the queen, is the motive force of the action—the poet-playwright, as it were. Indeed, in a moment of authorial reflexivity, Cocteau has the queen say that Stanislas has been the "author" of the three-act structure, "the drama." In act 1, he is the assassin who breaks into her stuffy existence like a romantic storm; in act 2, he inspires her to true queenship; finally, he poisons himself in order not to stand in the way of the queen's new will to power. The queen then becomes the author of her own destiny, paradoxically, by rejecting temporal power and by driving the poet mad with anger so that he will carry through with her assassination. Within the realm of the drama, then, the tragic finale is the queen's creation—in the end, she plays poet-playwright.

The play is also structured around symbols of contradiction and paradox. Ten years before the action of the play, the assassin of the king used a dagger concealed in a bouquet of flowers. In act 1, the queen saves the life of her own would-be assassin; but, in act 2, the assassin, paradoxically, brings her back to life, at least for a temporary respite, from the living death of her ten-year state of mourning for the king. The double-headed eagle of the title represents contradiction and tension; yet, as the queen says, if one of the heads is cut off, the eagle dies. By means of this emblem, Cocteau seems to be saying that contradiction is needed if the spirit of a ruler, of a poet, or of a lover is to soar beyond the mundane. As Stanislas, the poet and lover, tells the queen, he does not offer her banal "happiness," but rather a joint alliance—"an eagle with two heads." During a dangerous horseback ride she takes in the mountains, the queen comes to realize that without the tension of life and death, there can be no beauty, no poetry in living. Only by loving her would-be assassin does she become a ruling queen; only by ruling does she discover the tragic desperation of life; only by discovering this desperation does she prepare herself for death.

Few directors have ever shown the keen sense for the psychological aptness of *mise en scène* that Cocteau does in this play—particularly in act 1. This play draws heavily on the *Hamlet, Prince of Denmark* (pr. c. 1600-1601) archetype; the relationship between Stanislas, who looks like the dead king, and the queen corresponds to that between Hamlet and his mother. The queen even describes Stanislas's sudden appearance through the open windows with poetic images used in William Shakespeare's scenes involving the ghost of Hamlet's father. To add point to the subtext, Cocteau has Stanislas, in his newly acquired capacity as court reader, recite the scene between Hamlet and his mother, the queen. It is no surprise, then, that the first act of the play is to be staged exactly like the traditional bedroom setting for *Hamlet*—complete even to the portrait of the king on the wall (an important touch in productions of *Hamlet* into the twentieth century, when it was replaced by a miniature in a locket). The stage directions call for the queen to make her first entrance from beyond the portrait, which pivots around; Cocteau thereby creates a concise metaphor for the ten years of the queen's life of mourning before the time of the play.

The queen is a strange composite of Elizabeth of Austria, Ludwig II of Bavaria, and Queen Victoria. In creating the queen and her environment, Cocteau has admirably captured the sense of the hothouse atmosphere of *fin de siècle* Europe, the country waiting for a great war to cut through the oppressiveness of emperors, kings, and aristocrats. The queen, as much as Stanislas, is an anarchist. She is an amateur of storms: She speaks of lightning that will destroy her genealogical tree and of the storm that will scatter the leaves of the book of court etiquette; she calls on Stanislas to destroy—to be a storm. In the end, she (herself) must be the anarchistic agent of the queen's (her own) assassination: Thereby, she becomes Cocteau's most complete symbol of self-sacrifice in celebration of disorder.

Other major works

LONG FICTION: *Le Potomak*, 1919; *Le Grand Écart*, 1923 (*The Grand Écart*, 1925); *Thomas l'imposteur*, 1923 (*Thomas the Impostor*, 1925); *Le Livre blanc*, 1928 (*The White Paper*, 1957); *Les Enfants terribles*, 1929 (*Enfants Terribles*, 1930; also known as *Children of the Game*); *Le Fantôme de Marseille*, 1933; *La Fin du Potomak*, 1939.

POETRY: *La Lampe d'Aladin*, 1909; *Le Prince frivole*, 1910; *La Danse de Sophocle*, 1912; *Le Cap de Bonne-Espérance*, 1919; *L'Ode à Picasso*, 1919; *Poésies, 1917-1920*, 1920; *Escales*, 1920; *Discours du grand sommeil*, 1922; *Vocabulaire*, 1922; *Plain-Chant*, 1923; *Poésie, 1916-1923*, 1924; *Cri écrit*, 1925; *Prière mutilée*, 1925; *L'Ange Heurtebise*, 1925; *Opéra*, 1927; *Morceaux choisis*, 1932; *Mythologie*, 1934; *Allégories*, 1941; *Léone*, 1945; *Poèmes*, 1945; *La Crucifixion*, 1946; *Anthologie poétique*, 1951; *Le Chiffre sept*, 1952; *Appogiatures*, 1953;

Clair-obscur, 1954; *Poèmes, 1916-1955*, 1956; *Gondole des morts*, 1959; *Cérémonial espagnol du phénix*, 1961; *Le Requiem*, 1962.

SCREENPLAYS: *Le Sang d'un poète*, 1932 (*The Blood of a Poet*, 1949); *Le Baron fantôme*, 1943; *L'Éternel retour*, 1943 (*The Eternal Return*, 1948); *La Belle et la bête*, 1946 (*Beauty and the Beast*, 1947); *L'Aigle à deux têtes*, 1946; *Ruy Blas*, 1947; *Les Parents terribles*, 1948 (*Intimate Relations*, 1952); *Les Enfants terribles*, 1950; *Orphée*, 1950 (*Orpheus*, 1950); *Le Testament d'Orphée*, 1959 (*The Testament of Orpheus*, 1968); *Thomas l'Imposteur*, 1965.

BALLET SCENARIOS: *Le Dieu bleu*, 1912 (with Frédéric de Madrazo); *Parade*, 1917 (music by Erik Satie, scenery by Pablo Picasso); *Le Boeuf sur le toit*, 1920 (music by Darius Milhaud, scenery by Raoul Dufy); *Le Gendarme incompris*, 1921 (with Raymond Radiguet; music by Francis Poulenc); *Les Mariés de la tour Eiffel*, 1921 (music by Les Six; *The Wedding on the Eiffel Tower*, 1937); *Les Biches*, 1924 (music by Poulenc); *Les Fâcheux*, 1924 (music by George Auric); *Le Jeune Homme et la mort*, 1946 (music by Johann Sebastian Bach); *Phèdre*, 1950 (music by Auric).

NONFICTION: *Le Coq et l'Arlequin*, 1918 (*Cock and Harlequin*, 1921); *Le Secret professionnel*, 1922; *Lettre à Jacques Maritain*, 1926 (*Art and Faith*, 1948); *Le Rappel à l'ordre*, 1926 (*A Call to Order*, 1926); *Opium:Journal d'une désintoxication*, 1930 (*Opium: Diary of a Cure*, 1932); *Essai de la critique indirecte*, 1932 (*The Lais Mystery: An Essay of Indirect Criticism*, 1936); *Portraits-souvenir, 1900-1914*, 1935 (*Paris Album*, 1956); *La Belle et la bête: Journal d'un film*, 1946 (*Beauty and the Beast: Journal of a Film*, 1950); *La Difficulté d'être*, 1947 (*The Difficulty of Being*, 1966); *The Journals of Jean Cocteau*, 1956; *Poésie critique*, 1960.

TRANSLATION: *Roméo et Juliette*, 1926 (of William Shakespeare's play).

Bibliography

Griffith, Alison Guest. *Jean Cocteau and the Performing Arts*. Irvine, Calif.: Severin Wunderman Museum, 1992. This museum catalog includes critical analysis of Cocteau's work as well as information on his contribution to the performing arts. Bibliography.

Lowe, Romana. *The Fictional Female: Sacrificial Rituals and Spectacles of Writing in Baudelaire, Zola, and Cocteau*. New York: Peter Lang, 1997. Lowe compares and contrasts the works of Cocteau, Charles Baudelaire, and Émile Zola, especially their treatment of women. Bibliography and indexes.

Mauriès, Patrick. *Jean Cocteau*. London: Thames and Hudson, 1998. A biography of Cocteau that covers his life and works, including details of his work in films.

Saul, Julie, ed. *Jean Cocteau: The Mirror and the Mask: A Photo-Biography*. Boston: D. R. Godine, 1992. This compilation from an exhibit celebrating the one-hundred year anniversary of his birth, with an essay by Francis Steegmuller, provides insights into the life of Cocteau.

Tsakiridou, Cornelia A. *Reviewing "Orpheus": Essays on the Cinema and Art of Jean Cocteau*. Lewisburg, Pa.: Bucknell University Press, 1997. Although this work focuses on the screenplays and film work of Cocteau, it also sheds light on his dramatic works.

Rodney Farnsworth

William Congreve

Born: Bardsey, Yorkshire, England; January 24, 1670
Died: London, England; January 19, 1729

Principal drama • *The Old Bachelor*, pr., pb. 1693; *The Double-Dealer*, pr. 1693, pb. 1694; *Love for Love*, pr., pb. 1695; *The Mourning Bride*, pr., pb. 1697; *The Way of the World*, pr., pb. 1700; *The Judgement of Paris*, pr., pb. 1701 (masque); *Squire Trelooby*, pr., pb. 1704 (with Sir John Vanbrugh and William Walsh; adaptation of Molière's *Monsieur de Pourceaugnac*); *Semele*, pb. 1710 (libretto), pr. 1744 (modified version); *The Complete Plays of William Congreve*, pb. 1967 (Herbert Davis, editor)

Other literary forms • Although William Congreve is remembered today as a dramatist, his first publication was a novella, *Incognita: Or, Love and Duty Reconcil'd*, which appeared in 1692. He also published a translation of Juvenal's eleventh satire and commendatory verses "To Mr. Dryden on His Translation of Persius" in John Dryden's edition of *The Satires of Juvenal and Persius* (1693), as well as two songs and three odes in Charles Gildon's *Miscellany of Original Poems* (1692). Later, Congreve reprinted these odes, together with translations from Homer's *Iliad* (c. 750 B.C.E.; English translation, 1616), in *Examen Poeticum* (1693).

Congreve's other translations from the classics include Book III of Ovid's *Ars amatoria* (c. 2 B.C.E.; *Art of Love*, 1612) in 1709 and two stories from Ovid in the 1717 edition of *Ovid's Metamorphoses*. His original poetry was first collected with his other writings in *The Works of Mr. William Congreve* (1710) and frequently reprinted throughout the eighteenth century. After 1700, Congreve abandoned serious drama in favor of social and political interests, although he did write a masque and an opera after that date and collaborated with Sir John Vanbrugh and William Walsh on a farce. In response to Jeremy Collier's attacks on Restoration playwrights, Congreve wrote a short volume of dramatic criticism, *Amendments of Mr. Collier's False and Imperfect Citations* (1698). Congreve's letters have been edited by John C. Hodges and are available in *William Congreve: Letters and Documents* (1964).

Achievements • William Congreve's first play, *The Old Bachelor*, was an instant success; its initial run of fourteen days made it the most popular play since Thomas Otway's *Venice Preserved* (pr., pb. 1682). *The Double-Dealer* was not as instantly successful, but *Love for Love* was so popular that Congreve was made a manager of the theater. *The Mourning Bride* was still more successful; in 1699, Gildon said of the work that "this play had the greatest Success, not only of all Mr. Congreve's, but indeed of all the Plays that ever I can remember on the English Stage." Congreve's last comedy, *The Way of the World*, though now universally regarded as his best and arguably the best Restoration comedy as well, met with little support at the time, and its cool reception drove Congreve from serious drama.

Throughout the eighteenth century, Congreve's reputation remained high, both for his poetry and his plays. Edward Howard, in his *Essay upon Pastoral* (1695), said that Congreve possessed the talent of ten Vergils. Dryden, who equated Congreve to William Shakespeare on the stage, declared that in his translations from the *Iliad*, Congreve surpassed Homer in pathos. Alexander Pope's translation of the *Iliad* (1715-1720) was dedicated to Congreve, as were Sir Richard Steele's *Poetical Miscellanies* (1714) and his 1722 edition of Joseph Addison's *The Drummer: Or, The Haunted House.*

In the nineteenth century, Congreve's reputation declined, along with the public's regard for Restoration comedy in general, because of the sexual licentiousness depicted in the plays. With the twentieth century, however, came a reevaluation. When *The Way of the World* was revived at Cherry Lane Theatre in New York in 1924, it ran for 120 performances. That work and *Love for Love* remain among the most frequently acted of Restoration plays, and Congreve's other two comedies are also occasionally staged. Although Congreve's one tragedy has not worn as well, he may be today the most popular and most highly regarded English dramatist between William Shakespeare and George Bernard Shaw.

Biography • William Congreve was born on January 24, 1670, at Bardsey, Yorkshire, England. In 1674, his father, also named William, received a lieutenant's commission to serve in Ireland, and the family moved to the garrison of Youghal. In 1678, the elder William was transferred to Carrickfergus, another Irish port, and again, the family accompanied him. Congreve's knowledge of port life may have contributed to his depiction of the sailor, Ben, in *Love for Love*; Ben's use of nautical terms demonstrates the playwright's familiarity with this jargon. When the elder Congreve joined the regiment of the duke of Ormond at Kilkenny in 1681, his son was able to enroll in Kilkenny College, which was free to all families who served the duke. There, Congreve received his first formal education and his first exposure to the high society that gathered around the wealthy duke of Ormond.

After spending four and a half years at Kilkenny, Congreve entered Trinity College, Dublin (April 5, 1686), where he had the same tutor as Jonathan Swift, Saint George Ashe. The theater in Smock Alley, Dublin, was at this period being run by Joseph Ashbury, who, like Congreve's father, served under the duke of Ormond. Congreve may already have known Ashbury before coming to Trinity College, and Congreve's frequent absences from college on Saturday afternoons suggest that he was spending his time at the theater. Here, he would have seen a fine sampling of contemporary drama and could have begun to learn those dramatic conventions that he perfected in his own works.

In 1688, James II fled to Ireland. Perhaps fearing a massacre of Protestants in retaliation for their support of William of Orange against the Roman Catholic Stuart king, the Congreves left Ireland for their family home in England. Congreve went first to Staffordshire to visit his grandfather at Stretton Manor; there, he wrote a draft of *The Old Bachelor* before coming to London to enroll in the Middle Temple to study law. Congreve was not, however, an ideal law student. Like Steele's literary Templar in *The Spectator*, he frequented the Theatre Royal in nearby Drury Lane and Will's Coffee House rather than the Inns of Court.

At Will's, Dryden held literary court; by 1692, Congreve had become sufficiently friendly with the former laureate that he was asked to contribute a translation of Juvenal's eleventh satire to Dryden's forthcoming edition of the satires of Juvenal and Persius. Together with Arthur Manwayring and Thomas Southerne, Dryden was helpful to Congreve in revising *The Old Bachelor*. (In 1717, Congreve partially returned the favor, editing and writing an introduction to a posthumous edition of Dryden's *Dramatick Works*.) The play opened at the Theatre Royal in Drury Lane on March 9, 1693, with a brilliant cast, including Anne Bracegirdle as Araminta. Congreve was soon in love with Bracegirdle, who would play the heroine in each of his succeeding works and who may have been his mistress. In December, 1693, Congreve's second comedy, *The Double-Dealer*, was performed. Though Dryden praised it profusely, the play was not initially well received. After Queen Mary requested a special performance, however, its popularity increased.

Love for Love needed no royal sponsorship for its success. The first play to be performed in the restored Lincoln's Inn Fields Theatre (April 30, 1695), it ran for thirteen nights. Congreve was made one of the managers of the theater in return for a promise of a play a year, if his health permitted. Congreve needed two years to complete *The Mourning Bride*, which opened on February 27, 1697. The tragedy was worth the wait, for it was eminently successful. Three more years elapsed before Congreve's next play. Meanwhile, in 1698, Jeremy Collier attacked the Restoration stage in general, and Congreve in particular, for immorality. Congreve replied with his *Amendments of Mr. Collier's False and Imperfect Citations*. Between ill-health and the controversy with Collier, Congreve was unable to stage *The Way of the World* until March, 1700. Dryden recognized its genius, writing to Mrs. Steward on March 12, "Congreve's new play has had but moderate success, though it deserves much better." Coupled with Collier's attacks, the poor reception of *The Way of the World* persuaded Congreve to abandon serious drama, but he continued to write and remain interested in the theater.

On March 21, 1701, *The Judgement of Paris*, an elaborate masque, opened at Dorset Garden with Bracegirdle as Venus. With Vanbrugh and Walsh, Congreve adapted Molière's *Monsieur de Pourceaugnac* as *Squire Trelooby*, which was performed in March, 1704. He also wrote the libretto to an opera, *Semele*, which was not performed in his lifetime. For a brief time, too, Congreve, Vanbrugh, and Walsh managed a theater in the Haymarket.

Although Congreve held a variety of government posts throughout his life—the type of minor posts with which men of letters were often rewarded in that era—he did not have a lucrative position until 1705, when he was made a commissioner of wines, with an annual salary of two hundred pounds. Congreve was an ardent Whig, but he had so agreeable a personality that when the Tories came to power, Jonathan Swift and Lord Halifax (to whom Congreve had dedicated *The Double-Dealer*) intervened to help him retain this income. Dryden was not merely flattering when he wrote, "So much the sweetness of your manners move,/ We cannot envy you, because we love." Not until almost a decade later, when the Hanoverians came to power, did Congreve enjoy a substantial income, receiving the post of secretary of the Island of Jamaica. He discharged his duties by a deputy, continuing to lead a placid, retired life in London during the winter and in various country houses during the summer. As he wrote to Joseph Keally, "Ease and quiet is what I hunt after. If I have not ambition, I have other passions more easily gratified."

One passion was for Henrietta, duchess of Marlborough, whom he met in 1703. In 1722, Congreve went to Bath for his health, and Henrietta accompanied him, even though she was married to the son of Lord Treasurer Godolphin. The following year, when she gave birth to her second daughter, Mary, it was assumed that Congreve was the child's father. Henrietta was by his side when he died on January 19, 1729, and when she died four years later, she was buried near him in Westminster Abbey.

Analysis • William Congreve began writing some thirty years after the Restoration, yet his plays retain many of the concerns of those written in the 1660's and 1670's. Foremost among these concerns is what constitutes a gentleman; that is, how one should act in society. The seventeenth century, particularly after 1660, was very interested in this matter; some five hundred conduct books were published during the century, the majority of them after the Restoration.

The response that Congreve gives, which is identical to that of Sir George Etherege, William Wycherley, and other Restoration dramatists, may be summed up in a single word: wit. This wit encompasses far more than mere verbal facility. By the time Sir Richard Blackmore attacked wit as suitable "only to please with Jests at Dinner" ("A Satyr Against Wit," 1700), the term had lost much of its significance. For Congreve, Dryden's definition is more relevant than Blackmore's: "a propriety of thoughts and words"— and, he might have added, of conduct. As Rose Snider wrote in *Satire in the Comedies of Congreve, Sheridan,*

(Library of Congress)

Wilde, and Coward (1937), "Decorum (true wit) might be defined simply as a natural elegance of thought and conduct, based on respect for sound judgment, fidelity to nature, and a due regard for beauty."

What constitutes propriety and fidelity to nature is subject to varying interpretation. To the nineteenth century, Restoration comedy was at best "the Utopia of gallantry, where pleasure is duty, and the manners perfect freedom" (Charles Lamb, "On the Artificial Comedy of the Last Century"), at worst the height of immorality. Chastity was not a requirement for the late seventeenth century gentleman, though it was for the lady. Charles de Saint-Denis de Saint-Évremond expressed well the age's sexual ethics: "As for the Hatred of villainous Actions, it ought to continue so long as the World does, but give leave to Gentlemen of refin'd Palates to call that Pleasure, which gross and ill-bred People call Vice, and don't place your Virtue in old musty Notions which the primitive Mortals derived from their natural Savageness."

In keeping with this genial libertinism is a rejection of prudence, financial as well as sexual. Money is not to be saved but spent, and spent on pleasure. Business is rejected as an improper pursuit. In the first scene of *The Old Bachelor*, Congreve presents in the dialogue between Bellmour and Vainlove a catalog of unworthy occupations for the genteel and indicates that the proper pursuits are witty conversation and love.

To a certain extent, this hedonism was a reaction to the restraints imposed by the Puritan Protectorate. After the Restoration, playwrights, who had lost their occupation under Cromwell, continued to portray the final victory of Cavalier over Roundhead. The Puritan cleric is a standard butt of Restoration satire. So, too, is the "cit," the merchant—not only because he was likely to be a Dissenter rather than an Anglican but also because mercantile London supported Cromwell while in general the country squires remained loyal to the Crown. Those who suffered the most under the Protectorate, the Court party, took their revenge in their plays when they returned to power.

Restoration comedy does not, however, restrict itself to negatives, nor to rejecting conventional morality and ridiculing its followers. The Truewit is indeed a libertine and often a spendthrift and freethinker, but he espouses positive values that offset these signs of youthful exuberance. Bravery, for example, is highly prized. The wit will not tolerate an insult; a sign of wit is a willingness to defend one's honor. A character such as Captain Bluffe (in *The Old Bachelor*), who draws his sword only when all danger is past, or Fainall (in *The Way of the World*), who draws his sword on a woman, shows himself to be no true wit.

Urbanity is another attribute of the Truewit. He must be able to engage in brilliant repartee; his conversation must never be dull, vulgar, overly serious, or abstruse. A wit must never lose his temper, for reason should always control emotion. He must be aware of the latest fashions and observe them. Excesses in dress, manner, or speech are scorned, as are rusticity and bad taste. Because the wit must fit into polite society, the rustic is a butt of humor on the stage even though his political views probably harmonized with those of the playwrights who were mocking him.

Yet another virtue is intelligence, of which one outward sign is again brilliant conversation. A further indication is the ability to outsmart those who would thwart the wit's desires—generally comic villains who try to prevent his attaining a suitable wife and estate. Although these villains make a pretense of being clever and urbane, their speeches and action expose their flawed nature, which leads to their punishment at the end of the play.

Selflessness is also a Restoration ideal. Prodigality is not a vice but rather a manifestation of generosity. Fondlewife (*The Old Bachelor*) leaves his wife to secure five hundred pounds and is almost cuckolded during his absence. By contrast, Valentine (*Love for Love*) is willing to give money to a discarded mistress (though not to a creditor). When wits scheme, they are trying to secure what should rightfully be theirs; when fools and Witwouds plot, they are trying to secure what should belong to another. The latter are greedy and so are frustrated.

Restoration comedy is thus moral in its intent, punishing those who deviate from societal values and rewarding those who are faithful to those norms. These values are not Victorian, nor are they the values of religious fanatics, Puritans, or nonjurors such as Jeremy Collier—hence the repeated charges of immorality brought against Congreve and his contemporaries. In emphasizing intelligence, generosity, urbanity, and bravery, though, these dramatists were drawing on a tradition that went back to Aristotle's *Ethica Nicomachea* (335-323 B.C.E.; *Nicomachean Ethics*, 1797), and their view of comedy is Aristotle's as well. Defending himself against Collier, Congreve conceded that he portrayed vice on the stage, but he did so because comedy, according to Aristotle, depicts "the worst sort of people." It portrayed such people, Congreve continued, because "men are to be laugh'd out of their Vices in Comedy; the Business of Comedy is to delight, as well as to instruct: And as vicious People are made asham'd of their Follies or Faults, by seeing them expos'd in a ridiculous manner, so are good People at once both warn'd and diverted at their Expense." Collier and his successors did not find this response persuasive; they saw little to choose between Bellmour and Heartwell (*The Old Bachelor*) or between Mirabell and Fainall (*The Way of the World*). On the other hand, Congreve's appreciative audiences have always understood the important distinction.

At the same time that Congreve's plays are the artistic consummation of the traditions of Restoration comedy, they also reveal a breaking away from those traditions.

Though these plays accept societal norms, and though the hero and heroine must be able to conform to societal expectations, they recognize the flaws of society also. Instead of trying simply to blend into society, the true wits seek to establish a private world beyond it. They recognize that beneath the glittering costumes and language lurk hypocrisy and brutality. Marriages are more often made in countinghouses than in heaven; a wedding is often the beginning of a domestic tragedy rather than the end of a social comedy. Life does not always proceed smoothly, and even when it does, it leads to a loss of youth, beauty, and attractiveness. Congreve reaffirms the *carpe diem* spirit—eat, drink, and be merry—but he does not blink from the rest of the refrain— for tomorrow we die.

The sadness beneath the surface of Congreve's plays also derives from his refusal to dehumanize the targets of ridicule. Restoration comedy is social rather than psychological, and Congreve's plays are primarily concerned with how one should act in society. For the first time in the period, though, those who do not conform are not simply dismissed as fools. In fact, Pope wondered whether Congreve actually portrayed any fools, and in his dedication of *The Way of the World*, Congreve noted that audiences had difficulty distinguishing "betwixt the character of a Witwoud and a Truewit" in that work. Congreve probes beneath action to motivation to reveal what Heartwell, Fondlewife, Lord Plyant, and Lady Wishfort are thinking. These characters recognize their weaknesses; they are not merely two-dimensional types but three-dimensional people capable of suffering. By granting humanity to would-be wits and fools, Congreve was unconsciously moving away from the purely satiric toward sentimental comedy.

His one tragedy, which is actually a tragicomedy, similarly uses many of the conventions of the period while showing significant variations. The diction is inflated, as is typical of heroic tragedy. The action is remote in time and place, the characters of noble birth and larger than life, the conflict Hobbesian as rivals ruthlessly contend. Unlike earlier heroic tragedy, however, the resolution to the conflict comes not through a Leviathan, not through some divinely ordained ruler, but rather through a Glorious Revolution that overthrows unjust, though otherwise legitimate, authority in favor of a benign, popularly proclaimed monarch as exponents of power yield to advocates of love. The influence of John Locke and the deposition of James II echo in the play, especially when contrasted with Dryden's tragedies, which espouse the divine right of kings.

The Old Bachelor • Congreve may have begun *The Old Bachelor* as early as 1689, at the age of nineteen. Although Dryden proclaimed it the best first comedy he had ever seen, it shows in many ways evidence of being an apprentice piece. It is the only one of Congreve's comedies that lacks dramatic tension. There is no reason why Bellmour and Belinda could not marry in the first scene because there are no blocking characters to prevent the match. Another flaw is Congreve's ambiguous attitude toward Belinda. In the *dramatis personae*, he describes her as "an affected Lady," and in his *Amendments of Mr. Collier's False and Imperfect Citations*, he indicates that she is not intended to be admirable. Anne Bracegirdle, who always played the heroine in Congreve's works, took the role of Araminta; Belinda was played by Susanah Mountfort, who performed as the obviously foolish Lady Froth in *The Double-Dealer*. Because role and performer blended with each other in Restoration drama, audiences would expect that Belinda/ Mountfort was intended as a butt of ridicule for her affectation and that Araminta would be the ideal to be admired. Yet at the end of the piece, Belinda is rewarded with marriage, while Araminta remains single.

The Old Bachelor also suggests its author's youth in its close adherence to the conventions of Restoration drama. It is, for example, the only one of Congreve's comedies that has for its hero a practicing, rather than a reformed, rake. It introduces, somewhat gratuitously, standard butts of Restoration satire: a rustic boor (Sir Joseph Wittol), a pretender to valor who is in fact a coward (Captain Bluffe), a Puritan merchant (Fondlewife), and an old man who, according to the *dramatis personae*, while "pretending to slight Women, [is] secretly in love."

Aside from the treatment of Belinda, the play does show a sure hand in exposing these various pretenders and in providing suitable punishment for them. Sir Joseph Wittol is tricked out of one hundred pounds and married to Vainlove's discarded mistress. Captain Bluffe is shown to be aptly named; he is valorous only in the absence of danger. He is beaten and kicked by Sharper and married off to Silvia's maid, Lucy, who had been Setter's mistress. Heartwell, who pretends to misogyny and candor, is punished by being made to believe that he has married Silvia and then being informed that she is not as chaste as he had assumed. Though he is again unmarried, he is tormented and mocked for his folly. Fondlewife has married a woman too young and sprightly for his years; additionally, he devotes himself to business, which Bellmour calls "the rub of life [that] perverts our aim, casts off the bias, and leaves us wide and short of the intended mark." Fondlewife narrowly escapes cuckolding, and one senses that the escape is only temporary. As Vainlove notes, "If the spirit of cuckoldom be once raised up in a woman, the devil can't lay it, 'till she has done 't."

Congreve shows great skill in handling the dialogue. Bellmour and Belinda exemplify the witty couple of Restoration comedy; as is typical of duels between the witty man and woman, Belinda has the better of their exchanges. Vainlove and Araminta, too, engage in witty debate, and again the woman proves the wittier; in one dialogue, Araminta reduces Vainlove to a defeated "O madam!," at which point she dismisses the conversation—and her suitor—with a call for music. The men and women also engage in repartee among themselves, deftly leaping from one topic to another, devising fresh and apt similes, coining paradoxes, brilliantly sketching a character in a line. The play abounds in the sheer joy of words, as when Barnaby tells Fondlewife, "Comfort will send Tribulation hither." Restoration audiences attended comedies less for their plots than for their wit, and the success of *The Old Bachelor* shows that Congreve did not disappoint them in this regard.

While Congreve was offering largely conventional fare in his first comedy, even here one finds hints of sadness beneath the comic surface. John King McComb argues (in his essay "Congreve's *The Old Bachelor:* A Satiric Anatomy") that Bellmour, Vainlove, Heartwell, Fondlewife, and Spintext are stages in the rise and fall of the lover—from rake, to fop, to gull, and finally, to cuckold. The "cormorant in love," as Bellmour describes himself in the first scene, admits that "I must take up or I shall never hold out; flesh and blood cannot bear it always." Vainlove has been a cormorant in love, too, but now contents himself with arousing desire and leaving to others the task of satisfying it.

Heartwell, too, was a rake in his youth, but his passion has ebbed; unlike Vainlove, he no longer can excite women at those rare instances when he wishes to and so must attempt to purchase love. At the last stage are Fondlewife and Spintext; the latter never appears in the play but is mentioned as being a cuckold, while the audience sees Fondlewife first almost suffering the same fate and then refusing to believe the ocular proof. Bellmour, too, will age, Congreve seems to suggest; he will lose his looks and gaiety and perhaps be reduced to the state of a Heartwell or Fondlewife. The last speech of the play, which Congreve gives to Heartwell, projects such a fate for the youth.

Restoration satire is also muted in the play through the humanization of Heartwell and Fondlewife, both of whom show more sense than the typical comic butt. Heartwell's pretended aversion to "the drudgery of loving" must be exposed, since love is the chief concern of the Truewit and thus not to be slighted. Neither can pretense go unpunished. Yet Heartwell himself understands his dilemma as he is caught between reason and desire. Standing before Silvia's house he declares, "I will recover my reason, and begone." He is, however, fixed to the spot; his feet will not move: "I'm caught! There stands my north, and thither my needle points.—Now could I curse myself, yet cannot repent." After Heartwell is caught and exposed, Congreve does not mask his real anguish. In a speech reminiscent of Shylock's "Hath not a Jew eyes," Heartwell turns on his mockers: "How have I deserved this of you? any of ye?" Vainlove urges Bellmour to stop ridiculing Heartwell—"You vex him too much; 'tis all serious to him"—and Belinda agrees: "I begin to pity him myself."

Similarly, Fondlewife, Puritan, banker, old man that he is—and any one of these characteristics would suffice in itself to render him ridiculous in a Restoration comedy—has moments of self-knowledge that grant him a touch of humanity. When he discovers Bellmour with his wife, he, too, speaks with dignity. Though Bellmour kisses Laetitia's hand at the very moment she is being reconciled to her husband, Fondlewife's tears and professions of kindness take some of the edge off the satire. If one must choose between the world of Bellmour and that of Fondlewife, one will certainly prefer the former; even so, Congreve understands that with all its admirable qualities, its wit, grace, youth, and intelligence, that world, too, is not devoid of faults.

The Double-Dealer • Congreve's second play, *The Double-Dealer*, demonstrates much greater control over his material; it also contains a more fully developed negative portrayal of society. In *A Short View of the Profaneness and Immorality of the English Stage* (1698), Jeremy Collier noted, "There are but Four Ladys in this Play, and Three of the biggest of them are Whores. A Great Compliment to Quality to tell them there is not above a quarter of them Honest!" Despite Congreve's efforts to dismiss Collier's observation, Congreve does indeed indict the fashionable world, and his epigram from Horace—"Sometimes even comedy raises her voice"—suggests that he intended to go beyond the conventional butts of Restoration satire. Small wonder that fashionable society returned the favor with a cool reception of the piece.

Artistically, *The Double-Dealer* is much more coherent than *The Old Bachelor*. As Congreve wrote in the dedication, "I made the plot as strong as I could, because it was single; and I made it single, because I would avoid confusion." This single plot revolves around the love between Cynthia and Mellefont, who wish to marry, and the efforts of Maskwell and Lady Touchwood to prevent the match. The intrigues of these blocking figures, though conventional in comedies of the period, provide dramatic tension lacking in Congreve's earlier piece.

Congreve's handling of this central conflict, however, is less conventional. Typically, the Truewit defeats the Witwoud through his greater intelligence and so proves himself worthy of the witty heroine. When Mellefont proposes that he and Cynthia elope and thereby end the plotting and counterplotting, she rejects so simple a solution, demanding "a very evident demonstration of" her lover's wit. Until Maskwell overreaches and betrays himself, though, Mellefont is powerless to direct the action of the play; instead, he acts as Maskwell directs.

The conversation is not as sprightly as in Congreve's other plays or in Restoration comedy generally. Mellefont and Cynthia are too good-natured to take verbal advantage of the follies of those around them. While their benevolence makes them likable, it also tends to make them dull. They seem to anticipate the comedies of Steele rather than looking back to those of Etherege and Wycherley. Like Maskwell, the Witwouds are left to expose themselves: Lady Froth attempts a heroic poem on "Syllabub," for which Brisk provides inane commentary; Lord Froth claims that the height of wit is refraining from laughing at a joke, yet he laughs incessantly; Lady Plyant thinks herself a mistress of language but contrives such convoluted sentences that her lover, Careless, is driven to exclaim, "O Heavens, madam, you confound me!"

These Witwouds are as vain as they are foolish. In a telling piece of byplay, Lord Froth takes out a mirror to look at himself; Brisk takes it from him to admire himself. This sign of vanity is repeated when Lady Froth hands her husband a mirror, asking him to pretend it is her picture. Lord Froth becomes so enamored of the image he sees that his wife declares, "Nay, my lord, you shan't kiss it so much, I shall grow jealous, I vow now." Like false wit, vanity is left to mock itself.

Even sex, treated so cavalierly in other comedies of the period, is here largely a disruptive rather than a regenerative force. Each of the married women in the play is false to her husband. Lord Froth and Sir Paul Plyant are old and foolish and so "deserve" to be cuckolded, but the same cannot be said of Lord Touchwood. Lady Touchwood's passion for her nephew Mellefont threatens to upset Cynthia's marriage as well as her own and to subvert, through incest, proper familial relationships. Her passion for Maskwell, meanwhile, threatens to allow a member of the servant class to become a lord, as she contrives to have Maskwell supplant Mellefont as her husband's heir. The seriousness of this sexual promiscuity is manifest at the end of the play; Lady Touchwood is to be divorced and so lose her position in society.

Surrounded by vanity, infidelity, folly, and knavery, Cynthia has good reason to wonder whether she and Mellefont should continue to participate in the social charade. "'Tis an odd game we are going to play at; what think you of drawing stakes, and giving over in time?" she asks Mellefont. She understands that marriage is not a great improver: "I'm thinking, though marriage makes man and wife one flesh, it leaves them still two fools." The song that concludes this conversation with Mellefont warns of yet another threat: "Prithee, Cynthia, look behind you,/ Age and wrinkles will o'ertake you;/ Then, too late, desire will find you,/ When the power must forsake you." To become like her stepmother, Lady Plyant, or Mellefont's aunt, Lady Touchwood, may be the fate reserved for Cynthia.

The melancholy implicit in *The Old Bachelor* here rises to the surface. Mellefont remains cheerful, but his optimism seems misplaced. He has grossly misjudged Maskwell; he may be misjudging all of reality. Though the true lovers marry, and though Maskwell and Lady Touchwood are banished at the end of the play, Congreve had not yet found, as he did in his last play, a way to reconcile the private world of virtue with the public world of folly, sham, and pretense. Cynthia and Mellefont remain apart from society; they do not control their actions, nor do they appear much in the play. The implication is that one can preserve one's innocence only by avoiding the fashionable world. The play thus foreshadows the gloom of the Tory satirists as well as the sentimental comedy of the next age.

Love for Love • Congreve was stung by the cool reception of his bitingly satiric *The Double-Dealer*. Although he believed that satire is the aim of comedy, in his next play,

Love for Love, he disguised his attacks on fashionable society and offered a more traditional Restoration comedy. As he notes in the prologue: "We hope there's something that may please each taste." Much of the satire of *Love for Love* is confined to Valentine's mad scenes in the fourth act. By putting these comments into the mouth of a seeming madman, Congreve can be harsh without offending; it is as if he were stepping outside the world of the play to deliver these observations.

Valentine in his madness is utterly Juvenalian, railing against all aspects of the fashionable world. There is more truth than wit in such observations as, "Dost thou know what will happen to-morrow?—answer me not—for I will tell thee. Tomorrow, knaves will thrive through craft, and fools through fortune, and honesty will go as it did, frost-nipped in a summer suit." Scandal, Valentine's friend, is also harsh in his analysis of society: "I can shew you pride, folly, affection, wantonness, inconstancy, covetousness, dissimulation, malice, and ignorance, all in one piece. Then I can shew you lying, foppery, vanity, cowardice, bragging, lechery, impotence and ugliness in another piece; and yet one of these is a celebrated beauty, and t'other a professed beau." Beneath the surface, the way of the world is vicious and foul.

By the end of the play, though, Valentine abandons his feigned madness, and Scandal is willing to take a kinder view of the world than that expressed in the song: "He alone won't betray in whom none will confide;/ And the nymph may be chaste that has never been tried." Although society in *Love for Love* has its faults, these spring more from folly than from vice; the world here is closer to that of *The Old Bachelor* than to that of *The Double-Dealer*. There are no villains such as Maskwell or Lady Touchwood, no divorce, no banishment from society.

As in *The Old Bachelor*, there *is* considerable pretense that must be exposed and, to an extent, punished. Tattle pretends to be a great rake, a keeper of secrets, and a wit. Foresight pretends to be wise, to be able to foretell the future, and to be a suitable husband for a "young and sanguine" wife. Sir Sampson Legend pretends to be a good father and a fit husband for Angelica. Each of these pretenders is exposed and punished. Tattle is married off in secret to Mrs. Frail, a woman of the town. Fondlewife is cuckolded. Sir Sampson's plan to cheat his son of his inheritance and his fiancée is frustrated. These characters are Witwouds because they fail to adhere to the ideals of Restoration society. Sir Sampson is greedy; Foresight has failed to acquire wisdom with age; Tattle seeks a fortune rather than pleasure. They all want to be Truewits, but they are unable or unwilling to conform to the demands of wit.

Below them are Ben and Miss Prue, respectively a "sea-beast" and a "land monster." Neither has had the opportunity to learn good manners, Ben because he has spent his life at sea and Prue because she has been reared in the country rather than the town. They are no match for even the pretended wits. Tattle quickly seduces Prue; Mrs. Frail seduces Ben. Society has no place for these characters, who return to their element at the end of the play.

Above the fools and would-be wits are Valentine and Angelica. She is the typical Restoration witty lady, able to manipulate Foresight and Sir Sampson and control Valentine to attain her goal, which is a suitable marriage. Valentine has many of the characteristics of the wit—he is generous, he prefers pleasure to prudence, he is a clever conversationalist—but Angelica will not marry him until she is certain that he really is a proper husband.

At the beginning of the play, there is some question as to his suitability, not because he has been a rake, not because he has spent money recklessly—these are actually commendable activities—but because he has been trying to buy Angelica's love. Valentine's lavish entertaining has been to impress her; he seems to regard her as mercenary and must learn her true character. Having failed to purchase her with his wealth, Valentine next tries to shame her with his poverty; here, again, he fails. Then he tries to trick her into expressing her love by feigning to be mad. As a Truewit, Angelica is able to penetrate this disguise also. Only when Valentine abandons all of his tricks and agrees that Angelica should have free choice of a husband does she accept him. Marriage for her is a serious business; she must be certain she is not submitting to tyranny or being pursued solely for her large fortune.

The blocking figure in *Love for Love* is, then, Valentine himself, and the plot of the play concerns his learning how to interact in society. Ben and Miss Prue do not learn how to do so, in part because of their previous experiences, in part because their teachers are would-be instead of true wits, in part because they lack intelligence and so are easily deceived. Foresight, Tattle, and Sir Sampson fail to learn because their characters are flawed. Foresight thinks he will learn from astrology, while Sir Sampson and Tattle think so highly of themselves that they are not even aware that they need to be taught anything.

Congreve indicates in *Love for Love* that one must live within a society that is less than perfect but that one can do so pleasantly enough if one adheres to the ideals of Restoration comedy. The despair in *The Double-Dealer* yields here to a happier vision. Valentine and Angelica, unlike Mellefont and Cynthia, understand their society and have shown their ability to survive in it.

Because Congreve recognizes the limitations of the fashionable world, he is sympathetic to characters who do not quite fit in. Ben is not simply a butt of ridicule because he is an outsider. Whereas Tattle is punished with Mrs. Frail, Ben escapes that fate. Because he does not share society's viewpoint, Ben is also able to make some telling comments. He speaks his mind, shuns pretense, is generous, and understands that he will be happier at sea than in London. Prue, too, is honest; though she is Tattle's willing pupil, she does escape marrying him. The innocent fools suffer less than do the Witwouds.

With *Love for Love*, Congreve has found his true voice—a combination of satire, compassion, and wit. His hero and heroine understand both the attractions and faults of society and therefore are able to skate deftly on the surface of their world without succumbing to its folly, as Bellmour and Belinda may, or being overwhelmed by its viciousness, as Mellefont and Cynthia may be. It is a shorter step from *Love for Love* to *The Way of the World* than from *The Old Bachelor* to this comedy.

The Mourning Bride • Before making that step, however, Congreve turned to tragedy, though *The Mourning Bride* resembles Congreve's other plays, for, like the comedies, it explores the questions of how the individual should act in society and what constitutes a proper marriage. On the one hand are Zara and Manuel, who rely on royal birth and power. They believe that power can command even love; Manuel wants to compel his daughter to marry Garcia, the son of the king's favorite, and Zara seeks to force Osmyn to marry her. Manuel is therefore another version of Sir Sampson Legend, who would have his child act as he himself wishes, regardless of the child's desires. Zara is a tragic rendition of Lady Touchwood, who would rather murder the man she loves than see a rival marry him. Significantly, Elizabeth Barry played both Lady Touchwood and Zara. Zara and Manuel serve as blocking figures, much like Maskwell and Lady Touchwood, but with more power to do evil.

Contrasted to these two are Osmyn and Almeria. They, too, are of royal birth, but instead of using power to create love, they use love to get power. They are generous, brave, intelligent, like their comic counterparts. Like them, too, they are young, confronting a harsh world controlled by their elders. As in the comedies, the values of the young triumph, but in the process the villains are not simply exposed but, as befits a tragedy, killed. The true lovers wed; Zara and Manuel also "marry"—at the end of the play, Zara drinks to her love from a poisoned bowl, embraces him, and dies by his side exclaiming, "This to our mutual bliss when joined above." Like Tattle and Mrs. Frail, the unworthy characters are joined. The analogy is strengthened by the masked wedding each undergoes. Just as Tattle and Mrs. Frail do not recognize their partners until it is too late, so Zara believes she is dying beside Osmyn rather than Manuel.

The deposition of the old by the young marks a triumph of love over power. It also addresses the question of what constitutes legitimate power. The older generation believes that birth and rank alone are sufficient; Manuel and Zara sense no obligation to anyone but themselves. Theirs is the belief in the divine right of kings to govern wrongly. Osmyn and Almeria have a different view. Though of royal birth, Osmyn is elevated to the throne by the people, who rebel against Manuel's tyranny. Congreve, staunch Whig, is portraying the Glorious Revolution, in which the hereditary monarch, because he has abused his power, loses his crown to a more worthy, because more benevolent, successor.

The Way of the World • In the first scene of the fourth act of *The Way of the World*, Congreve directly addresses the issue of how two people can live harmoniously with each other while retaining personal autonomy and dignity on the one hand and remaining part of the social world on the other. This famous "Proviso" scene has a long theatrical history. A scene that first gained prominence in Honoré d'Urfé's *L'Astrée* (1607-1628, 1925; *Astrea*, 1657-1658), versions appear in four of Dryden's comedies–*The Wild Gallant* (pr. 1663), *Secret Love: Or, The Maiden Queen* (pr. 1667), *Marriage à la Mode* (pr. 1672, pb. 1673) and *Amphitryon: Or, The Two Socia's* (pr., pb. 1690)—in James Howard's *All Mistaken: Or, The Mad Couple* (pr. 1667), and Edward Ravenscroft's *The Careless Lovers* (pr. 1673) and *The Canterbury Guests* (pr. 1694).

As he did so often, Congreve used a well-established convention but invested it with new significance and luster. The proviso in *The Way of the World* is not only the wittiest of such scenes but also the most brilliantly integrated into the theme of the play. Indeed, the scene illuminates the plight of every witty heroine who had appeared on the Restoration stage and summarized the hopes and fears of all fashionable couples to that time.

Millamant does not want to "dwindle into a wife"; Mirabell does not want to "be beyond measure enlarged into a husband." She wishes to be "made sure of my will and pleasure"; he wants to be certain that his wife's liberty will not degenerate into license. In the Hobbesian world of self-love, rivalry, and conflicting passions, these two therefore devise a Lockean compact, creating a peaceful and reasonable accommodation between their individual and mutual needs. They will not act like other fashionable couples, "proud of one another the first week, and ashamed of one another ever after." They will act more like strangers in public, that they may act more like lovers in private. Millamant will remain autonomous in her sphere of the tea table, but she will not "encroach upon the men's prerogative." She will not sacrifice her health or natural beauty to fashion or whim; otherwise, she may dress as she likes. Together the lovers create a private world divorced from the follies and vices of the society around them while retaining the freedom to interact with that society when they must.

In contrast to this witty couple are Fainall and Marwood. As the names suggest, Fainall is a pretender to wit, and his consort, Marwood, seeks to mar the match between Mirabell and Millamant because of her love—and then hate—for Mirabell. She, too, is a pretender, a seeming prude who in fact is having an affair with Fainall. Whereas the witty couple seek to preserve their private world inviolate, Fainall and Marwood attempt to exploit private relationships. Fainall has married for money, not love, and once he has secured his wife's fortune, he intends to divorce her, marry Marwood, and flee society. Later, he and Marwood conspire to secure half of Millamant's and all of Lady Wishfort's estate by threatening to expose Mrs. Fainall's earlier affair with Mirabell, hoping that Lady Wishfort will pay to keep secret her daughter's indiscretion and prevent a public divorce.

On yet another level are Lady Wishfort, Petulant, and Witwoud, who have no private life at all. Lady Wishfort cannot smile because she will ruin her carefully applied makeup; the face she presents to society must not be disturbed by any unexpected emotion. All of her efforts are directed to appearing fashionable—hence her fear of Mrs. Fainall's exposure. Hence, too, her inflated rhetoric when she tries to impress the supposed Sir Rowland. Petulant wishes to appear the true Restoration wit and so hires women to ask for him at public places. He will even disguise himself and then "call for himself, wait for himself; nay, and what's more, not finding himself, sometimes [leave] a letter for himself."

Witwoud, as his name indicates, seeks to pass himself off as a wit but must rely on his memory rather than his invention to maintain a conversation. His cowardice or stupidity prevents his understanding an insult, and he mistakes "impudence and malice" for wit. He will not acknowledge his own brother because he believes it unfashionable to know one's own relations, thus surrendering private ties to public show. Sir Willful, Witwoud's half brother, is the typical rustic. Like Ben and Prue in *Love for Love*, he has no place in society. He withdraws from social interaction first by getting drunk and then by returning to his element, leaving the urban world entirely.

Congreve thus offers four ways of coping with the demands of society. One may flee completely, as Sir Willful does and as Marwood, Fainall, and Lady Wishfort talk of doing. Mirabell and Millamant could adopt this solution, too. If they elope, Millamant will retain half of her fortune, enough to allow the couple a comfortable life together, but they would lose the pleasures of the tea table, of the theater, of social intercourse—of all the benefits, in short, that society can offer. One can also submit one's personality completely to society and abandon any privacy (Petulant and Witwoud). One can use private life only to serve one's social ends (Fainall and Marwood), or one can find a suitable balance between them. Presented with these choices, Mirabell and Millamant wisely choose the last.

The question posed here is not only one of surfaces, of how best to enjoy life, although that element is important. Additionally, Congreve here explores differing ethical stances. The opening conversation between Mirabell and Fainall establishes the moral distinction between them. Fainall states, "I'd no more play with a man that slighted his ill fortune than I'd make love to a woman who undervalued the loss of her reputation." Mirabell replies, "You have a taste extremely delicate, and are for refining on your pleasures." Fainall's may be the wittier comment, but it is also the more malicious. True wit in *The Way of the World* embraces morality as well as intelligence. Mirabell does prove more intelligent than Fainall, outwitting him "by anticipation" just as he has cuckolded Fainall by anticipation. Even so, in their conversations the difference in cleverness is not as apparent as it is between Witwoud or Mirabell or Lady

Wishfort and Millamant. Congreve once more is moving toward sentimental comedy by creating an intelligent hero who is also sententious. He is foreshadowing Addison's attempt in the *Spectator* "to enliven Morality with Wit, and to temper Wit with Morality."

The tone is bittersweet—another anticipation of the next age. Like Belinda in Pope's *The Rape of the Lock* (1712, 1714), Millamant must grow up. Just as she cannot be a coquette forever, so Mirabell must put aside his rakish past. One has a sense of time's passing. Even amid the witty repartee of the proviso scene, Mirabell looks ahead to Millamant's pregnancy, and to the time beyond that when she will be tempted, as Lady Wishfort is now, to hide her wrinkles. Her maid will one day say to her what Foible tells her lady: "I warrant you, madam, a little art once made your picture like you; and now a little of the same art must make you like your picture."

With this new sense of the future coexists a new sense of the past, a sense that one's earlier actions have consequences. Valentine is able to dismiss a former mistress with a gift of money and to redeem his earlier extravagances through an inheritance and a good marriage. Mirabell is not so fortunate. His previous affair with Mrs. Fainall is not immoral—no one condemns Mirabell for it—but neither is it a trifle to be quickly forgotten. Because of that affair, Mrs. Fainall has had to marry a man she dislikes and who hates her; she is not merely asking for information when she inquires of Mirabell, "Why did you make me marry this man?" Nor has Mirabell escaped all consequences, for this affair gives Fainall the opportunity to seize half of Millamant's—and thus half of Mirabell's—estate.

The artificial world and golden dreams of *The Old Bachelor* have essentially vanished in *The Way of the World*. The form remains—the witty couple contending successfully against the Witwouds and the fools; the young struggling against the old; the flawed but brilliant urbane society opposing vulgarity and rusticity. Congreve has elevated this form to its highest point; there is no more lovable coquette than Millamant, no Restoration wit more in control of his milieu than Mirabell. Yet the substance, the sense of passing time, of the sadness of real life, is undermining the comedy of wit. Alexander Pope called Congreve *ultimus Romanorum* (the ultimate Roman). He is truly the greatest of the Restoration dramatists, but he is *ultimus* in its other sense as well—the last.

Other major works

LONG FICTION: *Incognita: Or, Love and Duty Reconcil'd,* 1692 (novella).

POETRY: "To Mr. Dryden on His Translation of Persius," 1693; *Poems upon Several Occasions,* 1710.

NONFICTION: *Amendments of Mr. Collier's False and Imperfect Citations,* 1698; *William Congreve: Letters and Documents,* 1964 (John C. Hodges, editor).

TRANSLATIONS: *Ovid's Art of Love, Book III,* 1709; *Ovid's Metamorphoses,* 1717 (with John Dryden and Joseph Addison).

MISCELLANEOUS: *Examen Poeticum,* 1693; *The Works of Mr. William Congreve,* 1710; *The Complete Works of William Congreve,* 1923, reprint 1964 (Montague Summers, editor; 4 volumes).

Bibliography

Bartlett, Laurence. *William Congreve: An Annotated Bibliography, 1978-1994.* Lanham, Md.: Scarecrow Press, 1996. A bibliography of works concerning Congreve. Index.

Hoffman, Arthur W. *Congreve's Comedies.* Victoria, B.C.: University of Victoria, 1993. A critical study of Congreve's comedic dramas. Bibliography.

Lindsay, Alexander, and Howard Erskine-Hill, eds. *William Congreve: The Critical Heritage.* New York: Routledge, 1989. These essays trace Congreve's critical reception from the immediate acclaim that greeted his first comedy to the emergence of modern academic criticism in the twentieth century. The editors include a generous selection of dramatic reviews, particularly from the eighteenth century, when all five of his plays were a standard part of the repertory. Bibliography.

Sieber, Anita. *Character Portrayal in Congreve's Comedies: "The Old Batchelor," "Love for Love," and "The Way of the World."* Lewiston, N.Y.: Edwin Mellen Press, 1996. An examination of the characters in three of Congreve's best-known comedies. Bibliography.

Thomas, David. *William Congreve.* New York: St. Martin's Press, 1992. A critical analysis of the works of Congreve, along with details of his life. Bibliography and index.

Young, Douglas M. *The Feminist Voices in Restoration Comedy: The Virtuous Women in the Play-worlds of Etherege, Wycherley, and Congreve.* Lanham, Md.: University Press of America, 1997. A look at female characters in the Restoration comedies of Congreve, George Etherege, and William Wycherley. Bibliography and index.

Joseph Rosenblum,
updated by Genevieve Slomski

Pierre Corneille

Born: Rouen, France; June 6, 1606
Died: Paris, France; September 30, 1684

Principal drama • *Mélite: Ou, Les Fausses Lettres*, pr. 1630, pb. 1633 (English translation, 1776); *Clitandre*, pr. 1631, pb. 1632; *La Veuve: Ou, Le Traîte trahi*, pr. 1631, pb. 1634; *La Galerie du palais: Ou, L'Amie rivale*, pr. 1632, pb. 1637; *La Suivante*, pr. 1633, pb. 1637; *La Place royale: Ou, L'Amoureux extravagant*, pr. 1634, pb. 1637; *Médée*, pr. 1635, pb. 1639; *L'Illusion comique*, pr. 1636, pb. 1639 (*The Illusion*, 1989); *Le Cid*, pr., pb. 1637 (*The Cid*, 1637); *Horace*, pr. 1640, pb. 1641 (English translation, 1656); *Cinna: Ou, La Clémence d'Auguste*, pr. 1640, pb. 1643 (*Cinna*, 1713); *Polyeucte*, pr. 1642, pb. 1643 (English translation, 1655); *La Mort de Pompée*, pr. 1643, pb. 1644 (*The Death of Pompey*, 1663); *Le Menteur*, pr. 1643, pb. 1644 (*The Liar*, 1671); *La Suite du menteur*, pr. 1644, pb. 1645; *Rodogune, princesse des Parthes*, pr. 1645, pb. 1647 (*Rodogune*, 1765); *Théodore, vierge et martyre*, pr. 1645, pb. 1646; *Héraclius*, pr., pb. 1647 (English translation, 1664); *Don Sanche d'Aragon*, pr. 1649, pb. 1650 (*The Conflict*, 1798); *Andromède*, pr., pb. 1650; *Nicomède*, pr., pb. 1651 (English translation, 1671); *Pertharite, roi des Lombards*, pr. 1651, pb. 1653; *Œdipe*, pr., pb. 1659; *La Toison d'or*, pr. 1660, pb. 1661; *Théâtre*, pb. 1660 (3 volumes); *Sertorius*, pr., pb. 1662 (English translation, 1960); *Sophonisbe*, pr., pb. 1663; *Othon*, pr. 1664, pb. 1665 (English translation, 1960); *Agésilas*, pr., pb. 1666; *Attila*, pr., pb. 1667 (English translation, 1960); *Tite et Bérénice*, pr. 1670, pb. 1671; *Pulchérie*, pr. 1672, pb. 1673 (English translation, 1960); *Suréna*, pr. 1674, pb. 1675 (English translation, 1960); *The Chief Plays of Corneille*, pb. 1952, 1956; *Moot Plays*, pb. 1960

Other literary forms • Although Pierre Corneille is known principally for his plays, he wrote a number of poems and at least one ballet libretto. Of his poetry there remain approximately one hundred pieces in French and a small number in Latin. Outside the theater, however, his best-known literary work is a long religious poem of thirteen thousand lines, the *Imitation de Jésus-Christ*, published in its entirety in 1656. A free translation of Saint Thomas à Kempis's Latin work, it enjoyed an immediate success; four editions were published in 1656 alone. Another adaptation of a Latin religious work into a lengthy French verse, *Office de la Sainte Vierge*, published in 1670, was a relative failure, for it was not reedited. To accompany a three-volume edition of his plays, Corneille published in 1660 a series of essays in which he formally presented his critical theories: three *Discours* and the *Examens* (one for each play). While some critics refer to Corneille's theory of drama as evidence that he misunderstood his own plays, the *Discours* and *Examens* can nevertheless be very helpful in understanding French classical theater. There exist twenty-four letters by Corneille, of little general interest.

Achievements • Generally hailed as the originator of French classical tragedy, Pierre Corneille is recognized as a master dramatist whose work founded a theater admired and envied by the rest of Europe throughout the seventeenth and eighteenth centuries. Ever the innovator, Corneille attempted many types of drama during his long career.

Although he is known mainly as a tragedian, his thirty-three plays include heroic comedy, comedy of manners, comedy of intrigue, sacred plays, machine plays, and ballet librettos. His career met with both dazzling success and abysmal failure. He was praised as the greatest French dramatist during the first half of his career, but the changing tastes of the Parisian audience and the popularity of Corneille's younger rival Jean Racine marred the latter part of his life. Although his later plays were for the most part critical and financial failures, recent critics have rehabilitated a number of these mature works.

Corneille's lasting influence on the French theater is perhaps his most noteworthy achievement. Most commentators agree that he fixed the genre of tragedy, separating it from its Greek origins and giving it an entirely new character. With Corneille, tragedy presents to its audience a precise moral and emotional conflict which is thoroughly analyzed and finally resolved through the interactions of a limited number of characters. Many have noted that Corneille's drama is not tragic in the Aristotelian sense. It was in essence a modern conception based not on the emotions of terror and pity but rather on admiration. Although destiny plays a role in Corneillian tragedy, the Greek tragic hero, a plaything of fate, becomes for Corneille a being confronted by an apparently irresolvable—and thus tragic—conflict, but who prevails, guided by an essential freedom enlightened by sound judgment and supported by will. Derived from tragicomedy, Corneille's tragedies, with the exception perhaps of his last play, *Suréna*, end on a note of hope and even joy. In general terms, it is a theater of optimism.

Biography • Pierre Corneille was born to a prosperous bourgeois family. His father and grandfather were lawyers in the parliament of Rouen, and, after studying Latin at the local Jesuit school (where he won prizes for Latin verse composition), Corneille took a law degree in 1624. In 1628, his parents bought for him a position as king's counselor in the Rouen office of the departments of waterways and forests and of the admiralty, posts that he conscientiously filled until 1650. Corneille lived for many years in Rouen, moving to Paris only in 1662 in order, perhaps, to satisfy a promise made to the French Academy on his election in 1647, which required that its members reside in Paris. His younger brother Thomas, also a popular dramatist, with whom Corneille had a long and close relationship, may also have influenced the decision to move to the capital. Corneille had six children with Marie de Lampérière, whom he married in 1641 and whose family background was similar to his own.

Corneille met with immediate success as a dramatist. His first play, the comedy *Mélite*, submitted to the famous actor Montdory while his theatrical troupe was performing in Rouen in 1629, was a triumph when Montdory performed it in Paris in the following year. Seven more plays (of which six were comedies) made Corneille a well-known young author when, in early 1637, probably the most significant play in the history of French drama, *The Cid*, scored an unheard of popular success. Historians have made much of the three-year silence following *The Cid* (pique at the critics who condemned the play? or pressing legal burdens in Rouen?), yet three more resounding successes followed: *Horace, Cinna,* and *Polyeucte.*

During the "Corneillian decade," the 1640's, Corneille consolidated his status as the premier French playwright. In 1651, the dismal failure of *Pertharite, roi des Lombards* precipitated a second "silence." From 1651 to 1656, Corneille devoted most of his time to the *Imitation de Jésus-Christ.* Finally, encouraged by the powerful financial secretary Nicolas Fouquet, Corneille returned to the theater with *Œdipe,* presented in 1659 to a

delighted Parisian audience. The remainder of his productions did not equal the popular acclaim of the earlier plays. Although he continued to write, Corneille's inability to
adapt to changing tastes most likely explains his decline. Almost unnoticed by the public, *Suréna*, produced in 1674, marks his definitive retirement. Corneille was considered passé, although the performance of six of his tragedies at Versailles in 1676 is evidence of the dramatist's continuing reputation.

Very little is known of Corneille's private life. Literary historians have emphasized,
however, the duality of his life. The creator of heroic and majestic characters designed
to elicit the public's admiration, a dramatist with worldwide fame, Corneille was apparently a good bourgeois family man, a minor magistrate who led an uneventful life.
Contemporary accounts indicate that he was a shy, retiring man who cut a very poor
figure in Parisian society. As a writer, nevertheless, Corneille was a proud man, very
conscious of his merit.

Analysis • The concept of the Corneillian hero, although it is somewhat misleading
because it tends to oversimplify a vast and varied body of plays, has fired the imagination of generations. Seen in purest form in the earlier plays, this hero, torn between
the dictates of duty, honor, and patriotism and the demands of love, achieves, through
the strength of reason and will, an absolute realization of self. Often surrounded by me-
diocrity or by relative values, the hero is concerned solely for his *gloire*, which might
be defined as an extreme form of aristocratic honor and self-respect, providing self-
definition. Love in the hero is not an irrational, all-consuming emotion but rather is
based on reason and respect for the beloved's merit, or *gloire*. It is not surprising that Pierre Corneille has historically enjoyed periods of popularity before and during wars:
His work has been the source of heroic inspiration and energy in France's spiritual heritage.

L'Illusion comique • Corneille's first eight plays, all but one of them comedies, combine obvious influences from contemporary drama with the playwright's search for
greater independence. The most remarkable of his early plays is *L'Illusion comique*,
which Corneille in 1660 called a "strange monster." It is clear that he wrote the play
without the slightest regard for the dramatic unities then being promulgated by literary
theorists. Called a Baroque drama because of its emphasis on illusion, instability, and
metamorphosis, the play is the culmination of Corneille's early period and contains an
effective apology of the theater, and, perhaps, of the career that Corneille had chosen
for himself.

Act 1 is a kind of prologue: Pridamant has spent years searching for his son
Clindor, who was alienated from his father ten years earlier. Having found no trace
of his son, Pridamant is brought by his friend Dorante to the grotto of the magician
Alcandre. With a sweep of his magic wand, Alcandre shows to Pridamant some of
his son's varied adventures during the last ten years. Thus, in act 2 a play-within-a-play
begins in which Clindor is valet to the cowardly military captain Matamore, a farcical
character who boasts of fantastic military and amorous exploits. Both men love
Isabelle, who in turn loves Clindor. Adraste, another rival for the love of Isabelle,
fights Clindor, who, though wounded, kills Adraste. Clindor is condemned to execution for murder. Isabelle's servant, Lyse, who is loved by Clindor's jailor, succeeds
in freeing Clindor. He, Lyse, and the beloved Isabelle flee. At the end of each act,
there is a brief return to the grotto, where Pridamant records his reactions to his
son's adventures. At the end of act 4, Pridamant breathes easily after his son's es-

cape, but Alcandre promises him more tense moments.

Suddenly, in act 5, a transformation in Alcandre's show occurs: Clindor, richly dressed, courts another woman. He has forsaken Isabelle, who, dressed as a princess, complains of Clindor's infidelities to Lyse. The jealous husband of the woman whom Clindor is courting, Prince Florilame, has Clindor killed and kidnaps Isabelle. Pridamant, who believes that he has witnessed the murder of his son, is inconsolable until Alcandre reveals yet another scene: Clindor, Isabelle, and the others are counting and dividing money. It turns out that they are actors, and the last scene was a fragment of a trag-

(Library of Congress)

edy that they had just performed. Pridamant, relieved but scandalized by the idea that his son has chosen such a "degrading" profession, is finally convinced by Alcandre's eloquent defense of the theater and of Clindor's honorable profession.

Built on levels of illusion, *L'Illusion comique* contains a play-within-a-play-*within*-a-play. The notion of theatricality is central to the play. The magician Alcandre takes on the role of director and author while Pridamant represents the dazzled and deceived audience. Within the levels of illusion, there is a hierarchy. On the lowest and least effective level, Matamore and his swashbuckling boasts create "illusions" that fool no one. On the highest level, Alcandre creates superbly effective, magical, supernatural illusions that occur in a secret place (the grotto) and are inaccessible to the vast majority of people. Between these two extremes lies the theater, a remarkable source of illusion accessible to all, a "magical" place presided over by "magicians"—actors, directors, and, above all, playwrights. *L'Illusion comique* reflects the generally high esteem in which the theater was held in the period. In 1641, a royal decree affirmed the dignity of the actor's profession; only toward the end of the century did the prestige of the stage begin to decline. The extraordinary renown of Corneille's next play attests the popularity of drama in the 1630's.

The Cid • For *The Cid*, by far his most successful and well-known play, Corneille drew his inspiration from a contemporary Spanish work, Guillén de Castro y Bellvís's *Las mocedades del Cid* (1621). It was necessary to adapt this long and diffuse foreign play to the tastes of the French audience. Corneille simplified and condensed, keeping the essential Romanesque theme of an aristocratic hero who accepts the tragic burden of opposing moral obligations and thus transcends the contingencies of the human condition.

The two major characters are Rodrigue and Chimène, who are betrothed at the beginning of the play. The rivalry between Rodrigue's aging father, Don Diègue, and

Don Gomès, father of Chimène, initiates the conflict. Furious after the king's appointment of Don Diègue as tutor to the prince, the younger Don Gomès slaps and thus mortally insults Rodrigue's father. Too old to avenge this affront, Don Diègue asks his son to preserve the family honor. Rodrigue must choose between his family and his love, and in a famous soliloquy (the "Stances du Cid," act 1 scene 6), decides to challenge the more experienced Don Gomès. In arriving at this decision, Rodrigue realizes that failure to uphold the family honor would inevitably result in the loss of Chimène because inaction would make him unworthy of her. Though steeped in emotion, the decision is thus both logical and necessary. In act 2, Rodrigue kills Don Gomès in a duel. The act's last scene stages a confrontation before the king between Chimène, who demands that her father's murderer be punished, and Don Diègue, who justifies his son's honorable action. Chimène thus undergoes a conflict similar to that of Rodrigue: She is torn between two passions, family honor and love, and she chooses honor.

Act 3 contains the poignant scene in which Rodrigue confronts Chimène, asking that she personally end his life and thereby avenge her father. This she cannot do: She demands that he leave her house yet gives him to understand that she loves him still. Her true feelings are expressed with marvelous economy in a famous line often cited as an example of Corneille's use of *litotes* (a figure of speech in which an affirmative is expressed by the negation of its contrary): "*Va, je ne te hais point*" ("Go, I do not hate you"). This emotional duel is said to have provoked great admiration and emotion in contemporary audiences. This scene of interior conflict accompanies an exterior threat: The infidel Moors are massing to attack the city of Seville. Exhorted again by his father, Rodrigue leads a force that, in the course of a nocturnal battle, defeats the Moors and saves the realm. Now a great hero, the right arm of the king, Rodrigue receives the title of le Cid, or Lord, from his vanquished foes. This turn of events obliges Chimène to assert an even greater force of will: For honor's sake, she must persist in seeking vengeance on the new and acclaimed hero of Spain. Although knowing that Chimène still loves Rodrigue, the king allows her to choose a champion. Don Sanche, rejected lover of Chimène, will uphold her cause in single combat with Rodrigue, after which Chimène will marry the victor.

In the last act, Rodrigue bids farewell to Chimène: He is resigned to his death. After the duel, Don Sanche enters the scene, and Chimène believes that he has triumphed. Cursing Don Sanche, she admits publicly her undying love for Rodrigue. The king reveals the truth: that Rodrigue had won, spared his adversary, and sent him to Chimène as messenger. Asking that she forgive Rodrigue, the king declares that a year's delay will temper Chimène's desire for revenge, after which she and Rodrigue will marry. During this time, Rodrigue will be able to accomplish greater exploits, thus increasing his *gloire* and making him even worthier of Chimène's noble hand.

The concept of rivalry informs the action of *The Cid*. The king's decision at the outset exacerbates the rivalry between the proud fathers. The inevitable conflict then falls on the children: Both Rodrigue and Chimène must equal the aristocratic resolve of the other. Products of a feudal ethic that places honor above all else, the young couple are heroic yet sensitive. Each suffers, yet neither's strength of will weakens. The seemingly irresolvable conflict is reconciled by the couple's submission to higher authority. The king, who has the last words in the play, imposes his will on a younger generation, which accepts the idea of monarchical order. Represented by the fathers, the less-sympathetic older generation exhibits the intransigent feudal mentality of kill or die.

Corneille's emphasis on youth, on young lovers who provoke the pity but above all the admiration of the audience, is a keystone in his drama. It is important to note that the play traces the development of Corneillian heroism in Rodrigue. An inexperienced young man at the opening of the play, albeit with much potential because of his illustrious blood, Rodrigue becomes the "Cid." There is an upward movement in which Rodrigue and Chimène are apotheosized. *The Cid* remains perhaps the best example of the ethical values of Corneillian drama: a noble idealism oriented toward the glorification of the passions and the self.

The huge popularity of *The Cid* touched off a debate famous in French literary history—"la querelle du *Cid.*" This quarrel is significant, reflecting a period in which the "baroque" and the "classical" styles were at odds. One of Corneille's major rivals, Georges de Scudéry, wrote in 1637 *Observations sur le Cid,* in which he condemned the choice of subject as being inappropriate in a genre whose subjects should have ancient sources; he also attacked Corneille's "plagiarism," the play's stylistic defects, and its inattention to the rules of drama. The last criticism is perhaps the most interesting. Scudéry declared that *The Cid*'s many plot elements could never occur within the prescribed twenty-four-hour time limit; the play's action is therefore not verisimilar.

The concept of *vraisemblance*—verisimilitude—was a fundamental tenet of the classical theoreticians. Scudéry also complained of the play's apparently unnecessary characters, in particular the Infante, the princess who also loves Rodrigue. Much emphasis was placed on act 1 scene 3, in which the overweening Don Gomès insults and slaps the older Don Diègue onstage. Critics condemned the incident as shocking: It violated the dictum of *bienséance*—decorum—a moral and social principle that required propriety of representation and satisfaction of the tastes and mores of the public.

The debate became so bitter that the powerful minister Cardinal Richelieu, wishing to establish the authority of the newly formed French Academy, ordered it to arbitrate the dispute. The *Sentiments de l'Académie sur Le Cid,* issued in October, 1637, praised the playwright yet confirmed Scudéry's criticisms concerning Corneille's neglect of the rules. Disturbed by the Academy's judgment, Corneille corrected certain verses condemned by his critics; not until the author's preface in the 1648 edition and in the play's *Examen,* published in 1660, did Corneille attempt detailed self-justification. At any rate, the public acclaim accorded the play must have mitigated Corneille's chagrin.

Horace • That Corneille was affected by academic criticism seems to be confirmed in his next play, *Horace,* first performed in 1640. After the depiction of Castilian honor, Corneille chose a subject taken from Roman history, thus apparently bowing to one of Scudéry's criticisms of *The Cid.* Although Corneille is still somewhat cramped by the unities of time, place, and action—there are many incidents and a complex plot structure in *Horace*—they are well observed, and many critics regard the play as the first true French classical tragedy.

The action opens on the eve of the decisive battle between Alba and Rome, two historically linked cities engaged in fratricidal war. These links are manifest in the play's major characters. The Roman hero Horace is married to Sabine, from Alba, while Horace's sister Camille is fiancée to Curiace, brother of Sabine. The atmosphere of foreboding before the battle yields to hope when, to limit bloodshed, Curiace announces the decision to allow three champions from each side to determine the war's outcome. This initial hope, however, is disappointed when Rome reveals its choice. Horace and his two brothers are designated to champion their city's cause. Fate strikes another blow when Alba reveals its choice: Curiace and his two brothers will defend Alba's honor and independence. An intimate conversation between Horace and Curiace, who are friends, discloses their characters. Horace demonstrates an inhuman resolve, renouncing all former ties of love and friendship, while Curiace tempers his patriotism with emotion and regret.

The two armies share Curiace's sentiments, for the play's fourth *coup de théâtre* offers renewed hope. Each side refuses to allow the two families to destroy each other, and a decision to consult the gods is made. Destiny is irresistible: The gods confirm the initial choice. Act 3 concludes with the outcome of the battle seemingly decided, for the news from the field of combat is that Horace's two brothers are dead and that he has fled. Another dramatic surprise ensues in act 4: A messenger reveals that Horace's flight was simply a ruse to separate his opponents, a trick that has given him the victory.

Despite the death of two sons, Horace's father is ecstatic at his news, while Camille, overcome with grief, curses both Rome and her brother when he returns, glorious, from the field. Provoked beyond endurance, Horace kills his sister. Act 5 presents the trial of Horace, presided over by King Tulle. Although Valère, who loved Camille, pleads passionately for swift and harsh punishment of the fratricide, Old Horace eloquently declares that his son's act was virtuous, for he punished a traitor, and that Horace should be permitted to continue to uphold the strength and honor of Rome. Tulle pronounces judgment: Horace will live to serve the state, but he must submit to an expiatory ceremony. Curiace and Camille will be interred in the same tomb.

Like *The Cid*, *Horace* presents a hero who overcomes an emotional conflict and accepts a painful obligation. His victory, like that of Rodrigue, accords him the status of national hero, but whereas Rodrigue's star continues to rise at the play's close, Horace's *gloire* is apparently overshadowed by his crime. For him, his act is reasonable. Just before dispatching his sister, he declares: "... *ma patience à la raison fait place*" ("my patience yields to reason"), yet his wife, Sabine, Valère, and Tulle consider it a brutal, inhuman act. Perhaps not a Corneillian ideal, Horace fails to maintain the balance of tender sentiments and an impulse to heroic action that Rodrigue attained. Critics hold divided opinions concerning Horace's culpability. The traditional view sees him as a "ferocious brute," an unrepentant fanatic. This judgment, however, ignores Corneille's idea, expressed in the third *Discours*, that Horace is indeed a hero. Under Horace's apparent insensitivity is a young man who suffers a cruel destiny. His barbarous yet necessary act reveals his strength of will.

As a Roman conscious of Rome's destiny, Horace believes that his act is patriotic and religious: He destroys an individual, his own sister, who has refused to accept the gods' decree of Roman supremacy. His blind acceptance of this fateful decree isolates him and thus constitutes a tragic situation *par excellence*. Despite differing interpretations of *Horace*, the Corneillian formula obtains in this play: a series of ordeals that the hero must overcome at the peril of his life, reputation, and personal happiness.

The political overtones of *Horace* should not be ignored. The play was produced in a time of an almost fratricidal war between France and Spain and was dedicated to Cardinal Richelieu. In addition, its themes corresponded to a governmental policy based on authority and national unity. Horace is the hero of a totalitarian regime at war. The play seems to acknowledge a political doctrine supporting unquestioned submission to the public interest in a time of national danger, a doctrine promulgated by Richelieu. Corneille's vision of Roman history is thus reflected in and supported by the political realities of 1640. A modern viewpoint has seen in *Horace* a powerful message: In a totalitarian state, in which total obedience is demanded, war dehumanizes. Horace, at the beginning of the play a sympathetic, humane young man, becomes, in his loyalty to the state, a fanatic who will destroy all dissenters.

Cinna • Corneille's interest in the political becomes more apparent in his next play, *Cinna*, produced also in 1640. A play of vengeance pursued and clemency achieved, *Cinna*, set in ancient Rome, pits the young couple Emilie and Cinna, in league with a coconspirator, Maxime, against the emperor Auguste. Emilie, whose father was murdered by Auguste, has promised to marry Cinna if he succeeds in assassinating the emperor. Just as Cinna and Emilie exult in the conspirators' well-conceived plans for the assassination set for the following day, Auguste summons Cinna and Maxime. This occurs at the end of act 1, thus creating great suspense, a trademark of Corneille's dramaturgy. Act 1 immediately reveals Auguste's purpose. Tired of maintaining his power, he asks for advice: Should he continue to rule or step down? Cinna, fearful of losing the opportunity to assassinate Auguste and thus lose Emilie, advises the emperor to keep his power, advice that dumbfounds Maxime, who had counseled the alternative.

After this fateful interview, Cinna confides to Maxime the true reason for the plot: It is merely a means by which he will win Emilie. Maxime, a secret lover of Emilie, is devastated, and he arranges for Auguste to discover the plot. Meanwhile, Cinna's initial resolution yields to doubt. He is torn between his love for Emilie and his rekindled loyalty to a trusting Auguste. However he acts, he will lose self-esteem, a major component of Corneillian *gloire*.

In act 4, Auguste learns of the conspiracy. He too is torn: Should he punish severely those whom he trusted, or—his political lassitude comes into play here—should he forgive? Auguste's wife, Livie, advises clemency. While clemency appears to be the most expedient political solution, Auguste vacillates, thus increasing suspense. Isolated and insecure, wishing to be free of the burden of rule yet conscious of his duty to Rome, Auguste grants forgiveness to the plotters. This heroic change from the murderous tyrant described in the beginning of the play to a magnanimous ruler effects a change in the others; it appears that the seemingly endless cycle of revenge and suppression has ended. Demonstrating his ability to overcome personal feelings of anger and revenge, Auguste, inspired by the gods, has abandoned a rule based on fear and founded a new order of justice and humanity.

Many commentators have seen in *Cinna* echoes of the political climate in France in 1640. Numerous plots had sprung up against Richelieu, who was consolidating the central authority of the crown against the threatened and powerful nobility. The play has been judged an appeal to both the Cardinal and the French people: National interest demanded a renunciation of revenge for past wrongs. To accomplish this, both sides must exercise the heroic restraint exemplified in the play. He who reigns must take the initiative. It would be wrong, however, to insist on this aspect of the play. Contemporary audiences appeared to have been moved more by the love of Cinna and Emilie than by Auguste's clemency. To see the play as a study of the motives and behavior of conspirators in general is perhaps a more valid political interpretation.

Polyeucte • Whereas *Horace* depicted monarchical Rome at the beginning of its ascent to world power, and *Cinna* treated a restless Rome under its first emperor, *Polyeucte*, Corneille's next play, focuses on Rome later in its history, when mystical Christianity began to make inroads into pagan Rome's supremacy. Here Corneille deals with the psychology of the early Christians, ready and willing to endure martyrdom for their faith. The drama is played out on three broad levels: sentimental and familial, political, and religious. Polyeucte, an Armenian prince, is married to Pauline, the daughter of the ambitious Roman governor of Armenia, Félix, who has forced this marriage for political ends. Polyeucte's friend Néarque has persuaded him to be baptized, but Polyeucte hesitates because of Pauline's protests.

In act 1 scene 3, Pauline reveals to her confidante a dream in which she has seen her husband killed among a group of Christians and in the presence of Sévère, a Roman hero whom she loved and whom she believes dead. The play thus opens with Pauline's fears of impending disaster made manifest in a dream. In the following scene, a key piece of information emerges: Sévère, very much alive, is on his way to Armenia to celebrate his recent victories; Pauline is extremely disturbed by this news.

Pauline and Polyeucte are each torn by an emotional conflict: Polyeucte's love for Pauline competes with his love for God, while Pauline's emotions are divided between Sévère and her husband. This rivalry produces not jealousy and revenge but rather sacrifice and ultimate reconciliation. In an interview with Sévère, Pauline recalls her love for him but affirms her fidelity to Polyeucte. During a public ceremony in honor of Sévère, the recently baptized Polyeucte has resolved to break the pagan idols, thereby demonstrating his new faith and assuring martyrdom. The effect of divine grace after his baptism explains this sudden transformation from the fearful and hesitant Polyeucte of act 1. Between acts 2 and 3, Polyeucte commits this daring act; unrepentant, he is immediately imprisoned, while Néarque is summarily executed by order of Félix.

There follows a series of entreaties to Polyeucte, who refuses to recant. Pauline's feelings for her husband grow as she realizes the strength of his will and his faith. Still somewhat hesitant when he thinks of his beloved Pauline, Polyeucte finally sacrifices his terrestrial love, entrusting Pauline to Sévère. Although Félix is torn between fear of Rome, whose policy is to put to death Christian dissidents, and his affection for his daughter, who implores her father to forgive Polyeucte, Polyeucte is, indeed, executed. Before his death, Polyeucte declared that he would "obtain" divine grace for Pauline and Félix when he sees God face to face. This wish is granted after his death: Pauline, then Félix, miraculously convert to Christianity at the end of the play. Sévère marvels at this sudden turnabout and promises to do his utmost to prevent further persecutions.

Polyeucte resembles the archetypal Corneillian hero: He undergoes and overcomes a series of ordeals in which friendship, love, and passion combat a higher ideal. He attains genuine apotheosis; his death not only has brought about the blessed conversion of his wife and father-in-law but also has benefited many other converts. This is confirmed by Sévère's reaction at the play's close. Polyeucte, however, does not aim for worldly glory as do Rodrigue, Horace, and Auguste. He strives for an otherworldly glory that far transcends the heroism of other plays. As in other plays, reconciliation and union reign at the end. On the sentimental level, the marriage of Polyeucte and Pauline, never truly united in life, has been transformed into a union divinely consecrated through Polyeucte's martyrdom. Politically, the conversion of Félix marks the end of the ancient pagan order and inaugurates the rise of the Christian era of the Roman Empire. Finally, on the religious level, divine grace has proven its efficacy; Polyeucte's militant faith will serve as an illustrious example to others.

The Death of Pompey • With *Polyeucte,* Corneille had reached the summit of his success. The tragedies written and produced between 1643 and 1651 bear witness to his ambition to produce plays that were at once innovative and entertaining. *The Death of Pompey,* in which Pompée does not appear (although Corneille called him the "principal actor), is a political play that opposes two sets of characters: César and Pompée's widow, Cornélie, who strive to be worthy of the heroic Pompée's memory; and the youthful Egyptian king Ptolomée and his Machiavellian advisers. Unlike the protagonists of earlier plays, however, no character here undergoes a heroic ascension.

The Liar • Also during the 1643 theatrical season, Corneille returned to comedy with *The Liar,* considered by some scholars a self-parody. A complex comedy of intrigue, *The Liar* presents Dorante, who, after confusing the names of two young ladies, finds himself in an amusing imbroglio. Parodic elements are occasionally quite specific: Dorante's father, Géronte, chiding his dishonest son in act 5 scene 3, for example, parodies Don Diègue challenging Rodrigue in act 1 scene 5 of *The Cid.* The liar's constant self-transformations also recall the heroic metamorphoses of the tragedies. Motivated no doubt by the success of the play, Corneille composed a sequel, *La Suite du menteur,* his last true comedy, presented in 1644.

Nicomède • Corneille's last great success before the failure of *Pertharite, roi des Lombards* and his subsequent retreat from the theater in the 1650's was *Nicomède.* After exploiting the Romanesque and the melodramatic in *Rodogune, Héraclius,* and *The Conflict,* Corneille returned to political and familial tragedy in *Nicomède.* Arisonoé, the stepmother of Nicomède, who is the son of King Prusias of Bithynia, plots to destroy her proud and courageous stepson. Encouraging Nicomède to defy the Roman conquerors of Bithynia, she hopes that Rome will kill him, leaving the throne empty for her own son, the docile Attale, whom the Romans favor as the next king.

Nicomède scorns the political machinations of his weak father and of Rome's ambassador, Flaminius, who use Laodice, loved by both Nicomède and Attale, as political blackmail. After Nicomède's arrest for refusing with disdain and contempt Prusias's ultimatum, Attale is named king, but he immediately realizes that the Romans will never permit him to marry Laodice. In a sudden turnabout, Attale, aided by a popular uprising in support of Nicomède, saves his half brother. Nicomède, ever generous and strong, returns the throne (which the populace wished for him) to Prusias. Touched by Nicomède's magnanimity, all are reconciled at the play's close.

Inasmuch as the hero in *Nicomède* suffers no true inner conflict, the play differs fundamentally from the earlier tragedies. The "happy" denouement does not project an optimistic vision of an ever more glorious future for the hero but suggests rather the political reality of a dominant Rome which has the power and the will to control the individual liberty so essential to Corneillian *gloire.* Personal choice is thus limited, for Nicomède succeeds only temporarily in safeguarding his own independence and that of the state. The last words in the play belong to the politically astute Prusias: "Let us ask the gods . . . for the friendship of the Romans."

Œdipe • Corneille ended his retirement in 1659 with *Œdipe,* a popular success, the subject of which had been suggested to the author by the influential finance minister Fouquet. There followed a series of plays that did not enjoy the success of the earlier works. It is apparent that Corneille's continued emphasis on the political and his appeal to the intellect did not meet with favor among a new generation of theatergoers who craved, according to a contemporary observer, only "sorrow and tears." Although Corneille attempted to respond to the public's changing tastes, his theater continued to depict large historical and political tableaux; they had become anachronisms.

Suréna • His last play, *Suréna*, met the same fate as most of the later plays. Recent critics have rehabilitated this unjustly ignored masterpiece. Eurydice, the daughter of the king of Armenia, is betrothed to Pacorus, the son of Orode, king of Parthis. Although she dutifully accepts this political engagement, she loves Suréna, a famous Parthian general who has defeated the Romans and who returns Eurydice's affection. Orode, fearful of Suréna's reputation and power, offers his daughter Mandane to Suréna in order to assure his loyalty. Suréna, having made a vow of fidelity to Eurydice, refuses to marry Mandane. In vain, Suréna attempts to conceal the true reason for his refusal. After discovering that Suréna loves Eurydice, Orode gives an ultimatum: Suréna will either marry Mandane or die. The unshakable Suréna refuses to yield despite the entreaties of his sister Palmis. Just as Eurydice has decided to prevail on Suréna as well, grave news arrives: He has been assassinated. On hearing the news, Eurydice collapses, dying of grief.

Some commentators have judged this play a substantial modification of Corneille's earlier heroic manner: They emphasize that Suréna sacrifices all to love, that he is indifferent to *gloire*, thus in a mold different from Rodrigue, and so on. Despite his assertion that worldly fame does not equal one moment of happiness, Suréna does, however, demonstrate a strength of character not unlike that of earlier Corneillian heroes. He affirms his essential liberty and individual rights by not submitting to Orode's ultimatum. Moreover, the political situation, in which a king feels threatened by a more noble subject, recalls other plays, most notably *Nicomède* and *Agésilas*. Like other Corneillian heroes, Suréna is the right arm of the king and a courageous warrior. That Eurydice—a princess—loves him bears witness to his inherent merit. Suréna elicits pity by his unjust death and admiration, the touchstone of Corneille's drama, by the grandeur of his resolve. Corneillian glory, for Suréna a "cold and vain eternity," is opposed to an inner freedom that provides protection against the vagaries of destiny. Suréna dies faithful to himself: He is perhaps the supreme expression of Corneillian psychology.

Other major works

NONFICTION: *Discours*, 1660; *Examens*, 1660.

TRANSLATIONS: *Imitation de Jésus-Christ*, 1656; *Office de la Sainte Vierge*, 1670.

Bibliography

Auchincloss, Louis. *La Gloire: The Roman Empire of Corneille and Racine.* Columbia: University of South Carolina Press, 1996. A study of the dramas of Corneille and Jean Racine that dealt with the Roman Empire.

Carlin, Claire L. *Pierre Corneille Revisited.* New York: Twayne, 1998. A basic biography of Corneille that examines his life and works. Bibliography and index.

_____. *Women Reading Corneille: Feminist Psychocriticisms of "Le Cid."* New York: Peter Lang, 2000. Corneille's *The Cid* from a feminist perspective. Bibliography and index.

Clarke, David. *Pierre Corneille: Poetics and Political Drama Under Louis XIII.* New York: Cambridge University Press, 1992. An examination of the political aspects of Corneille's dramatic works. Bibliography and index.

Goodkin, Richard E. *Birth Marks: The Tragedy of Primogeniture in Pierre Corneille, Thomas Corneille, and Jean Racine.* Philadelphia: University of Pennsylvania Press, 2000. A study of the tragedies of Pierre Corneille, Thomas Corneille, and Jean Racine with emphasis on primogeniture. Bibliography and index.

Longstaffe, Moya. *Metamorphoses of Passion and the Heroic in French Literature: Corneille, Stendhal, Claudel.* Lewiston, N.Y.: Edwin Mellen, 1999. An examination of the hero as portrayed in the works of Corneille, then Stendhal and Paul Claudel. Bibliography and index.

Lyons, John D. *The Tragedy of Origins: Pierre Corneille and Historical Perspective.* Stanford, Calif.: Stanford University Press, 1996. A look at history in the tragedies of Corneille. Bibliography and index.

Robert T. Corum, Jr.

Noël Coward

Born: Teddington, England; December 16, 1899
Died: Port Royal, Jamaica; March 26, 1973

Principal drama • *I'll Leave It to You*, pr. 1919, pb. 1920; *Sirocco*, wr. 1921, pr., pb. 1927; *The Better Half*, pr. 1922 (one act); *The Young Idea*, pr. 1922, pb. 1924; *London Calling*, pr. 1923 (music and lyrics by Noël Coward and Ronald Jeans); *Weatherwise*, wr. 1923, pb. 1931, pr. 1932; *Fallen Angels*, pb. 1924, pr. 1925; *The Rat Trap*, pb. 1924, pr. 1926; *The Vortex*, pr. 1924, pb. 1925; *Easy Virtue*, pr. 1925, pb. 1926; *Hay Fever*, pr., pb. 1925; *On with the Dance*, pr. 1925; *The Queen Was in the Parlour*, pr., pb. 1926; *This Was a Man*, pr., pb. 1926; *Home Chat*, pr., pb. 1927; *The Marquise*, pr., pb. 1927; *This Year of Grace!*, pr., pb. 1928 (musical); *Bitter Sweet*, pr., pb. 1929 (operetta); *Private Lives*, pr., pb. 1930; *Some Other Private Lives*, pr. 1930, pb. 1931 (one act); *Cavalcade*, pr. 1931, pb. 1932; *Post-Mortem*, pb. 1931; *Words and Music*, pr. 1932, pb. 1939 (musical); *Design for Living*, pr., pb. 1933; *Conversation Piece*, pr., pb. 1934; *Point Valaine*, pr., pb. 1936; *Tonight at 8:30*, pb. 1936 (3 volumes; a collective title for the following nine plays, which were designed to be presented in various combi- nations of three bills of three plays: *We Were Dancing*, pr. 1935; *The Astonished Heart*, pr. 1935; *Red Peppers*, pr. 1935; *Hands Across the Sea*, pr. 1935; *Fumed Oak*, pr. 1935; *Shadow Play*, pr. 1935; *Family Album*, pr. 1935; *Ways and Means*, pr. 1936; and *Still Life*, pr. 1936); *Operette*, pr., pb. 1938; *Set to Music*, pr. 1939, pb. 1940 (musical); *Blithe Spirit*, pr., pb. 1941; *Present Laughter*, pr. 1942, pb. 1943; *This Happy Breed*, pr. 1942, pb. 1943; *Sigh No More*, pr. 1945 (musical); *Pacific 1860*, pr. 1946, pb. 1958 (musical); *Peace in Our Time*, pr., pb. 1947; *Ace of Clubs*, pr. 1950, pb. 1962; *Island Fling*, pr. 1951, pb. 1956; *Relative Values*, pr. 1951, pb. 1952; *Quadrille*, pr., pb. 1952; *After the Ball*, pr., pb. 1954 (musical; based on Oscar Wilde's play *Lady Windermere's Fan*); *Nude with Violin*, pr. 1956, pb. 1957; *South Sea Bubble*, pr., pb. 1956; *Look After Lulu*, pr., pb. 1959; *Waiting in the Wings*, pr., pb. 1960; *High Spirits*, pr. 1961 (musical; based on his play *Blithe Spirit*); *Sail Away*, pr. 1961 (musical); *The Girl Who Came to Supper*, pr. 1963 (musical; based on Terence Rattigan's play *The Sleeping Prince*); *Suite in Three Keys: Come into the Garden Maude; Shadows of the Evening; A Song at Twilight*, pr., pb. 1966; *Cowardy Custard*, pr. 1972, pb. 1973 (also as *Cowardy Custard: The World of Noël Coward*); *Oh! Coward*, pr. 1972, pb. 1974 (also as *Oh Coward! A Musical Comedy Revue*); *Plays: One*, pb. 1979; *Plays: Two*, pb. 1979; *Plays: Three*, pb. 1979; *Plays: Four*, pb. 1979; *Plays: Five*, pb. 1983

Other literary forms • Noël Coward was an extraordinarily prolific playwright, lyricist, and composer, writing more than fifty plays and musicals during his lifetime. He did not limit his literary endeavors solely to drama but ventured into other genres as well. These diversions into the realm of fiction, nonfiction, and poetry proved equally successful for him. In addition to his plays, Coward wrote three novels (two unpublished), several collections of short stories, satires, a book of verse, and several autobiographical works, *Present Indicative* (1937), *Middle East Diary* (1944), and *Future Indefinite* (1954).

Coward's versatility is also apparent in his original scripts for five films, his screenplays and adaptations of his hit plays, and his several essays on the modern theater that

222

appeared in popular journals and in *The Times* of London and *The New York Times*. Like his plays, Coward's other works reveal his distinctive satiric style, sharp wit, and clever wordplay.

Achievements • In 1970, Noël Coward was knighted by Queen Elizabeth II for "services rendered to the arts." The succinct phrasing of this commendation is as understated as some of Coward's best dialogue, considering his long and brilliant career in the theater. Coward wrote plays specifically designed to entertain the popular audience and to provide an amusing evening in the theater. Few of his plays champion a cause or promote a social issue. His most noteworthy achievement came in the writing of scores of fashionable comedies, revues, and "operettes" that were resounding successes on the English, American, and Continental stages and continue to enjoy success today. For this insistence on writing light comedy, he received substantial criticism, and several of his works were brusquely dismissed as "fluff" by critics. These same plays, however, never wanted for an audience, even during the most turbulent, politically restless years.

Coward came to be associated with the 1920's in England in much the same way that F. Scott Fitzgerald was identified with the Jazz Age in the United States. Whereas Fitzgerald seriously examined the moral failings of his prosperous characters, however, Coward treated them lightly. His plays chronicle the foibles, fashions, and affairs of the English upper class and provide satirical vignettes of the social elite. Coward's life and work reflect the same urbane persona; indeed, he wrote his best parts for himself. Coward's world was that of the idle rich, of cocktails, repartee, and a tinge of modern decadence; this image was one he enjoyed and actively promoted until his death.

For all their popularity, most of Coward's plays are not memorable, save for *Private Lives, Blithe Spirit, Design for Living,* and possibly one or two others, yet his song lyrics have become part of the English cultural heritage. "Mad Dogs and Englishmen," from *Words and Music,* achieved immortality when its famous line "Mad dogs and Englishmen go out in the mid-day sun" was included in *The Oxford Dictionary of Quotations.*

Coward's reputation rests less on the literary merits of his works and more on the man, who as an accomplished actor, entertainer, and raconteur displayed enormous resilience during his five decades in the public eye. One of the obvious difficulties in producing a Coward play is finding actors who are able to han-

(Library of Congress)

dle the dialogue with the aplomb of "the master." What made Coward's plays successful was not so much a strong text, but virtuoso performances by Gertrude Lawrence, Jane Cowl, Alfred Lunt and Lynn Fontanne, and Coward himself. The public continues to be amused by his works in revivals, especially when performed by actors, such as Maggie Smith, who can transmit Coward's urbane humor to today's audiences.

Biography • Noël Pierce Coward was born December 16, 1899. He was the child of Arthur Sabin Coward and Violet Agnes Veitch, who married late in life after meeting in a church choir. Coward's family on his father's side was very talented musically. They helped nurture the natural virtuosity of the child, instilling in him a lifelong love of music.

Because his birthday was so close to Christmas, Coward always received one present to satisfy both occasions, but on December 16, his mother would take him to the theater as a special treat. He first attended a matinee at the age of four, never realizing he would spend the next seventy years of his life in service to the dramatic muse. As he grew older, he found these junkets to the theater more and more fascinating, and after returning home would rush to the piano and play by ear the songs from the production he had just seen.

Coward made his first public appearance, singing and accompanying himself on the piano, at a concert held at Miss Willington's School. Though obviously a very talented child, Coward's precocity did not carry over to his formal education. At best, his schooling was sporadic. For a time, he attended the Chapel Royal School at Clapham in hopes of becoming a member of the prestigious Chapel Royal Choir. Failing his audition as a choir member, he was taken from school and did not attend any educational institution for six months, at which time he was sent to school in London. He was ten years old.

Coward was an incorrigible, strong-willed child, given to tantrums when he did not get his way. These traits, inherited from both sides of his argumentative family, are evident in his characters, and each of his plays contains a rousing altercation scene. He was indulged by his mother, who became the stereotypical stage mother during his early years, and it was at his mother's insistence that he began attending Miss Janet Thomas's Dancing Academy in addition to his regular school in London. Soon, Miss Thomas's school usurped the position of importance held by traditional academic fare, and Coward became a child performer.

Coward's first professional engagement, and that which launched his long career, was on January 28, 1911, in a children's play, *The Goldfish*. After this appearance, he was sought after for children's roles by other professional theaters. He was featured in several productions with Sir Charles Hawtrey, a light comedian, whom Coward idolized and to whom he virtually apprenticed himself until he was twenty. It was from Hawtrey that Coward learned comic acting techniques and playwriting. He worked in everything from ballets to music halls and made it a point to study the more experienced performers to learn to "catch" the audience quickly. This skill was one he actively drew on in the writing of his plays.

At the tender age of twelve, Coward met one of the actresses who would help contribute to his overwhelming success, Gertrude Lawrence; she was then fifteen and a child performer as well. The occasional acting team of Coward and Lawrence would become synonymous with polished, sophisticated comedy during the 1920's, 1930's, and 1940's.

When he was fifteen, Coward was invited to stay at the country estate of Mrs. Astley Cooper. This stay, and subsequent visits, influenced his life markedly in two ways: He grew to know intimately the manners and mores of the upper class, and through Mrs. Cooper, he came to meet Gladys Calthrop, who was to become his lifelong friend and the designer for his productions.

Coward began his writing career when he was sixteen by writing songs and selling them for distribution. He turned his hand to playwriting when he was seventeen and found that he was very good at writing dialogue. Success came quite early to Coward. He was already accepted as an accomplished actor on the London stage when he began writing. By 1919, his play *I'll Leave It to You* was produced in the West End with Coward in the leading role. One of the idiosyncrasies of Coward's writing is that often he wrote "whacking good parts" for himself or for people he knew. Some of his best plays are essentially vehicles for his own talents or those of Gertrude Lawrence and later of the Lunts.

I'll Leave It to You met with moderate success, and Coward received great praise from critics for his playwriting abilities, although Sir Neville Cardus, writing in the *Manchester Guardian,* faulted the play for its narrow focus on the world of the idle rich. This criticism dogged Coward throughout his career.

Coward went to New York for the first time in 1921 and arrived virtually penniless. He sold three satires to *Vanity Fair* in order to support himself. Though he may have begun the 1920's in penury, Coward's position as the most popular playwright in the English theater became secure during this decade. In 1924, *The Vortex* was produced in London. Coward's most important serious play, *The Vortex* broke with English theatrical tradition in its choice of subject matter: drug addiction. This Ibsenesque approach to a problem created quite a sensation. It was hailed by many critics as an important play but also found dissenters who labeled it "filth" and "dustbin drama."

In late 1927, Coward purchased 139 acres in Kent called Goldenhurst Farm. This was the first residence he used as a retreat to escape the glitter of the stage. Eventually, he would own others in Jamaica, Paris, Geneva, and London. The years from 1928 to 1934 are regarded by many as Coward's "golden years." His string of successes during this period include some of his best and most famous plays and revues: *This Year of Grace!, Bitter Sweet, Private Lives, Cavalcade, Words and Music, Design for Living,* and *Conversation Piece.* According to Coward in a letter written to his mother, *Bitter Sweet* was the only show that played to capacity houses in New York during the stock market crash of 1929. By the 1930's, the opening of a Coward play in London was regularly attended by royalty and other prominent socialites.

Coward took his success and the responsibility of fame seriously. When asked to aid the Actors' Orphanage, he did so willingly and subsequently became president of the organization, a position he retained from 1934 to 1956.

After World War II, Coward fell from grace with many critics, who regarded him as being past his literary prime. The year 1949-1950 proved the lowest point in his career as he received poor reviews for his plays and scathing reviews for his film *The Astonished Heart.* The drama was changing during these restless years that would produce playwrights such as John Osborne, and Coward was momentarily out of step with the times. He turned to the writing of fiction and produced several short stories and his autobiographical work *Future Indefinite.*

By the late 1950's, audiences were once again in love with Coward. His plays, revues, and nightclub appearances were extremely successful. The critics, however, remained vitriolic, but their rancor failed to dim the enthusiasm of the general theatergoing public, who clamored for more Coward plays. In 1969, there was a seventieth birthday tribute to Coward in London that lasted a full week. On January 1, 1970, Coward's name appeared on the Queen's New Year's list as a Knight Bachelor, for services rendered to the arts. For the remaining years of his life, he was Sir Noël Coward. In the same year, he was awarded a special Tony Award by the American theater for Distinguished Achievement in the Theatre. In 1972, he received an honorary Doctor of Letters from the University of Sussex.

Coward died of a heart attack in Jamaica on March 26, 1973, bringing to an end a career of more than sixty years in the theater. The most lasting tribute awarded to Coward is the continued success that meets revivals of his plays and musicals. Coward created a mystique about himself during his lifetime, and this intangible quality of wit and sophistication has become part of the Coward legend, which has become a part of the colorful heritage of the theater.

Analysis • As a playwright, composer, lyricist, producer, director, author, and actor, Noël Coward spent his life entertaining the public. This he did with a flair, sophistication, and polish that are not readily found in current drama. He wrote farce, high comedy, domestic and patriotic melodramas, musical comedies, and revues. His plays were popular fare in England and the United States for years because Coward recognized that the "great public" for which he wrote his plays wanted, above all, to be entertained.

All of Coward's plays fall into easily recognizable stylized patterns. Essentially, Coward wrote modern comedies of manners that are as reflective of twentieth century mores and sentiments as their Restoration forebears were of those in the seventeenth century. For the most part, his plays are set in drawing rooms and usually have a couple involved in a love relationship as the central characters. He draws heavily on his theatrical background and populates his plays with theatrical and artistic characters. These temperamental personages allow Coward to involve them easily in the constant bickering and verbal fencing that came to be the trademarks of a Coward play. Each of his characters vies to get the upper hand over the others. Arguments are central to his work, and much of his humor relies on sophisticated insults. Coward's dialogue bitingly exposes hypocrites and the petty games played by the upper class; his plays parody Mayfair society mercilessly. Unfortunately, his plays involve little else. There is little motivation of character, less development of theme, and what thin remnant of plot remains is swept along in the incessant bantering of the characters. Robert Greacen, referring to *Fumed Oak*, remarked that "an observant foreigner might sit through the entire play . . . and simply hear people talking and believe that no action was taking place at all." Such statements apply to most of Coward's plays.

This criticism reveals both the strongest and the weakest aspects of Coward's theater. He was capable of writing brilliant, naturalistic dialogue with an astonishing economy. In spite of this enormous talent for writing dialogue, however, little happens in his plays to advance the plot. Most of his plays remain structurally flawed, relying heavily on the use of *deus ex machina* and coincidence for plot resolutions.

Thematically, Coward's comedies examine true love, adulterous affairs, and domestic upheavals. His more serious plays focus on a variety of topics, including drug addiction, infidelity, and patriotism. The few patriotic plays he attempted strongly support solid middle-class values and promote a stereotyped image of the stoical Englishman.

Though his works appear to have identifiable themes, they lack a thesis. Coward's plays realistically depict modern characters in absorbing situations, but the characters are not as fully developed as the situations in which they find themselves. Their motivations remain obscure. Even in the serious plays, his position on his subject is never clearly revealed. Most of his serious dramas fail because he never brings the moment to a crisis, and so his plays end anticlimactically. According to Milton Levin, Coward's plays "raise no questions, they provide few critical footholds, they simply ask to be praised for what they are, sparkling caprices."

Generally, the success of Coward's plays depended on the ability of the actors to carry his rapier-sharp dialogue. He freely admitted tailoring choice roles to his talents and those of his friends. Coward and Lawrence in *Private Lives*, Coward and the Lunts in *Design for Living*, Coward with Beatrice Lillie in *Blithe Spirit* mark legendary moments in theatrical history that cannot be replicated. When criticizing drama, one must consider the text in production. It is this consideration that elevates the relatively weak scripts of Coward's plays to modern classics.

Embodied in Coward is a theatrical trinity of actor, playwright, and producer. The inability to separate completely one from the other in studying his works contributes to the mystique that surrounds the man. Rarely are his works found in academic anthologies of the genre, but the imprint of his productions is still discernible in the theater today.

Coward was a highly developed product of the 1920's and the 1930's and of the social milieu he frequented, and, to a not inconsiderable extent, the current popularity of his work originates in the nostalgic hunger of contemporary audiences for an age more verbally sophisticated and carefree than their own. Nevertheless, at their best, Coward's plays continue to sparkle with their author's lively sense of wit, talent for dramatic dialogue and construction, and genius for the neat twist in dramatic action. These significant talents make Coward's theater instructive as well as delightful.

Design for Living • *Design for Living* was the end result of a plan by Coward, Alfred Lunt, and Lynn Fontanne to act in a play together, written specifically for them. They originally conceived of this idea in the early 1920's, and the gestation period required for Coward actually to write and produce the play lasted eleven years. *Design for Living* scrutinizes a free-spirited and occasionally painful *ménage à trois* comprising Gilda, an interior decorator, Otto, a painter, and Leo, a playwright. The most striking quality of the play is its completely amoral stance on marriage, fidelity, friendship, and sexual relations. Pangs of conscience are fleeting in these characters as their relationships as friends and lovers become apparent to one another and to the audience.

It is the amorality of the characters, rather than a perceived immorality, that has provoked criticism of this play. Coward forms no conclusions and passes no judgment: The play ends with the three characters embracing and laughing wildly on a sofa, and the audience is provided no clue as to how they should judge these amorous individuals. They are asked to watch and accept without being given a resolution to the plot. Most of the criticism directed at the production resulted from a misunderstanding of the title on the part of the critics. Coward intended his title to be ironic. It was taken to be an admonition that the Bohemian lifestyle depicted onstage was not merely acceptable but was actually preferable to conventional ways as a "design for living."

Design for Living was a vehicle for the formidable talents of Coward and the Lunts. The dialogue is quick and sharp as the three characters alternately pair off, argue, and reunite. The theme stressed most strongly in this play, and the one that offers its most redemptive qualities, is that of friendship. Gilda, Otto, and Leo value their mutual companionship, but their active libidos complicate their relationships. *Design for Living* was judged to be "unpleasant" by the critics, but it enjoyed a phenomenal success with audiences in England and the United States.

Private Lives • *Private Lives*, considered one of Coward's best plays, "leaves a lot to be desired," by the author's own admission. The protagonists, Amanda and Elyot, are divorced and meet again while both are honeymooning with their new spouses. Their former affection for each other is rekindled, and they abandon their unsuspecting spouses and escape to Paris. Here, they are reminded of what it was in their personalities that prompted them to seek a divorce. The scene is complicated by the arrival of the jilted spouses, who come seeking reconciliation, but who eventually are spurned as Amanda and Elyot, after arguing violently, leave together, presumably to lead a life of adversarial bliss.

Amanda and Elyot are interesting, fairly well-drawn characters; these roles were written with Lawrence and Coward in mind. The secondary characters, the spouses, Victor and Sibyl, are two-dimensional and only provide a surface off which to bounce the stinging repartee of the reunited couple. Coward himself has described *Private Lives* as a "reasonably well-constructed duologue for two performers with a couple of extra puppets thrown in to assist the plot and to provide contrast."

Other major works

LONG FICTION: *Pomp and Circumstance*, 1960.

SHORT FICTION: *Terribly Intimate Portraits*, 1922; *Chelsea Buns*, 1925; *Spangled Unicorn*, 1932; *To Step Aside*, 1939; *Star Quality: Six Stories*, 1951; *The Collected Short Stories*, 1962; *Pretty Polly Barlow and Other Stories*, 1964; *Bon Voyage and Other Stories*, 1967; *The Complete Stories of Noël Coward*, 1985.

POETRY: *Not Yet the Dodo*, 1967; *Noël Coward: Collected Verse*, 1984.

SCREENPLAYS: *Bitter Sweet*, 1933; *In Which We Serve*, 1942; *This Happy Breed*, 1944; *Blithe Spirit*, 1946; *Brief Encounter*, 1946; *The Astonished Heart*, 1949.

NONFICTION: *Present Indicative*, 1937; *Australia Visited*, 1941; *Middle East Diary*, 1944; *Future Indefinite*, 1954; *The Noël Coward Diaries*, 1982; *Autobiography*, 1986.

MISCELLANEOUS: *The Lyrics of Noël Coward*, 1965; *The Noël Coward Song Book*, 1980; *Out in the Midday Sun: The Paintings of Noël Coward*, 1988.

Bibliography
Briers, Richard. *Coward and Company.* London: Robson Books, 1987. A short, well-illustrated biography of the English actor, playwright, composer, director, producer, and bon vivant.

Castle, Terry. *Noël Coward and Radclyffe Hall: Kindred Spirits.* New York: Columbia University Press, 1996. Contains a comparison of Coward and Hall as well as of homosexuality and literature. Bibliography and index.

Citron, Stephen. *Noël and Cole: The Sophisticates.* New York: Oxford University Press, 1993. A comparison of Coward and Cole Porter as composers. Bibliography and index.

Fisher, Clive. *Noël Coward.* New York: St. Martin's Press, 1992. A biography of the multitalented Coward. Bibliography and index.

Hoare, Philip. *Noël Coward: A Biography.* New York: Simon and Schuster, 1996. A biography of the dramatist that covers his life and works. Bibliography and index.

Kaplan, Joel, and Sheila Stowell, eds. *Look Back in Pleasure: Noël Coward Reconsidered.* London: Methuen, 2000. A study of the dramatic works of Coward and his influence. Bibliography and index.

Levin, Milton. *Noël Coward.* Boston: Twayne, 1989. This short but updated biography of the playwright contains a useful bibliography.

Morella, Joe. *Genius and Lust: The Creative and Sexual Lives of Noël Coward and Cole Porter.* New York: Carroll and Graf, 1995. Morella compares and contrasts Coward and Porter, examining their works and lives. Index.

Susan Duffy,
updated by Peter C. Holloran

John Dryden

Born: Aldwinckle, England; August 19, 1631
Died: London, England; May 1, 1700

Principal drama • *The Wild Gallant,* pr. 1663, pb. 1669; *The Indian Queen,* pr. 1664, pb. 1665 (with Sir Robert Howard); *The Rival Ladies,* pr., pb. 1664; *The Indian Emperor: Or, The Conquest of Mexico by the Spaniards,* pr. 1665, pb. 1667; *Secret Love: Or, The Maiden Queen,* pr. 1667, pb. 1668; *Sir Martin Mar-All: Or, The Feign'd Innocence,* pr. 1667, pb. 1668 (adaptation of Molière's *L'Étourdi;* with William Cavendish, duke of Newcastle); *The Tempest: Or, The Enchanted Island,* pr. 1667, pb. 1670 (adaptation of William Shakespeare's play; with Sir William Davenant); *An Evening's Love: Or, The Mock Astrologer,* pr. 1668, pb. 1671 (adaptation of Thomas Corneille's *Le Feint Astrologue*); *Tyrannic Love: Or, The Royal Martyr,* pr. 1669, pb. 1670; *The Conquest of Granada by the Spaniards, Part I,* pr. 1670, pb. 1672; *The Conquest of Granada by the Spaniards, Part II,* pr. 1671, pb. 1672; *Marriage à la Mode,* pr. 1672, pb. 1673; *The Assignation: Or, Love in a Nunnery,* pr. 1672, pb. 1673; *Amboyna: Or, The Cruelties of the Dutch to the English Merchants,* pr., pb. 1673; *Aureng-Zebe,* pr. 1675, pb. 1676; *The State of Innocence, and Fall of Man,* pb. 1677 (libretto; dramatic version of John Milton's *Paradise Lost*); *All for Love: Or, The World Well Lost,* pr. 1677, pb. 1678; *The Kind Keeper: Or, Mr. Limberham,* pr. 1678, pb. 1680; *Oedipus,* pr. 1678, pb. 1679 (with Nathaniel Lee); *Troilus and Cressida: Or, Truth Found Too Late,* pr., pb. 1679; *The Spanish Friar: Or, The Double Discovery,* pr. 1680, pb. 1681; *The Duke of Guise,* pr. 1682, pb. 1683 (with Lee); *Albion and Albanius,* pr., pb. 1685 (libretto; music by Louis Grabu); *Don Sebastian, King of Portugal,* pr. 1689, pb. 1690; *Amphitryon: Or, the Two Socia's,* pr., pb. 1690; *King Arthur: Or, The British Worthy,* pr., pb. 1691 (libretto; music by Henry Purcell); *Cleomenes, the Spartan Hero,* pr., pb. 1692; *Love Triumphant: Or, Nature Will Prevail,* pr., pb. 1694; *The Secular Masque,* pr., pb. 1700 (masque); *Dramatick Works,* pb. 1717; *The Works of John Dryden,* pb. 1808 (18 volumes)

Other literary forms • If one follows the practice of literary historians and assigns John Milton to an earlier age, then John Dryden stands as the greatest literary artist in England between 1660 and 1700, a period sometimes designated "the Age of Dryden." In addition to his achievements in drama, he excelled in poetry, translation, and literary criticism. He wrote some two hundred original English poems over a period of more than forty years, including the best poetic satires of his age, memorable odes, and a variety of verse epistles, elegies, religious poems, panegyrics, and lyrics. His prologues and epilogues, attached to his dramas and those of his contemporaries, stand as the highest achievements in English in that minor poetic genre.

For every verse of original poetry Dryden wrote, he translated two from another poet. Moreover, he translated two long volumes of prose from French originals—in 1684, Louis Maimbourg's *Histoire de la Ligue* (1684) and, in 1688, Dominique Bouhours's *La Vie de Saint François Xavier* (1683)—and he had a hand in the five-volume translation of Plutarch's *Bioi paralleloi* (c. 105-115; *Parallel Lives,* 1579) published by Jacob Tonson in 1683. The translations were usually well received, especially the editions of Juvenal and Persius (1693) and Vergil (1697).

Dryden's literary criticism consists largely of prefaces and dedications published throughout his career and attached to other works. His only critical work that was published alone was *An Essay of Dramatic Poesy* (1668). As a critic, Dryden appears at his best when he evaluates an earlier poet or dramatist (Homer, Vergil, Ovid, Geoffrey Chaucer, William Shakespeare, Ben Jonson, John Fletcher), when he seeks to define a genre, or when he breaks new critical ground, as, for example, in providing definitions of "wit" or a theory of translation.

Achievements • In a period of just over thirty years (1663-1694), John Dryden wrote or coauthored twenty-eight plays, an output that made him the most prolific dramatist of his day. His amplitude remains even more remarkable when one considers the amount of poetry, criticism, and translation he produced during the same period. This prolific production is equaled by the variety of the plays: heroic plays, political plays, operas, heroic tragedies, comedies, and tragicomedies. In his prefaces and other prose works, Dryden commented at some length on the various types of plays, seeking to define and to clarify the dramatic forms in which he wrote.

Yet Dryden himself recognized that his dramas were not likely to wear well, and his literary reputation today rests largely on his poetry and criticism. The operas *King Arthur* and *The State of Innocence* (which was not produced during his lifetime) survive primarily in their lyrics. Like other operas of the time, they were somewhat primitive, judged by modern standards, with relatively little music—something more akin to the masque or to modern musical comedy than to grand opera. The heroic plays are too artificial to appeal to any but the most devoted scholars of the period, and Dryden's comedies and tragicomedies suffer in comparison with those of his contemporaries, Sir George Etherege, William Wycherley, and William Congreve, not to mention his predecessors in English drama. As an index to the taste of the Restoration, however, the plays remain valuable and instructive, reflecting the levels of achievement and prevalent values of dramatic art of the time. Further, a study of Dryden reveals much about both aesthetic and intellectual influences on the drama of his period and the development of the dramatic genres of his age.

Biography • John Dryden was the eldest of fourteen children in a landed family of modest means whose sympathies were Puritan on both sides. Little is known of his youth in Northamptonshire, for Dryden, seldom hesitant about expressing his opinions, was reticent about details of his personal life. At about age fifteen, he was enrolled in Westminster School, then under the headmastership of Dr. Richard Busby, a school notable for its production of poets and bishops. Having attained at Westminster a thorough grounding in Latin, he proceeded to Cambridge, taking the B.A. in 1654. After the death of his father brought him a modest inheritance in the form of rents from family land, Dryden left the university and settled in London.

Although little is known of Dryden's early years in London, he served briefly in Oliver Cromwell's government in a minor position and may have worked for the publisher Henry Herringman. He produced an elegy on the death of Cromwell, yet when Charles II ascended the throne, Dryden greeted the new ruler with a congratulatory poem, *Astraea Redux* (1660). After the Restoration, he turned his main interest to the drama, producing an insignificant comedy, *The Wild Gallant*, and collaborating with Sir Robert Howard on a heroic play, *The Indian Queen*. He married Lady Elizabeth Howard, Sir Robert's sister, a marriage that brought him a generous dowry and, eventually, three sons in whom he took pride.

Throughout his career, Dryden was no stranger to controversy, whether literary, political, or religious; in fact, he seemed all too eager to seize an occasion for polemics. In literature, he challenged Sir Robert Howard's views on drama, Thomas Rymer's on criticism, and the earl of Rochester's and Thomas Shadwell's on questions of literary merit and taste. After receiving encouragement from Charles II, Dryden entered the political controversy over succession to the throne with *Absalom and Achitophel* (part 1, 1681; part 2, with Nahum Tate, 1682). Later, he explained his religious views by attacking Deists, Roman Catholics, and Dissenters in *Religio Laici: Or, A Layman's Faith* (1682); then, he shifted his ground and defended Roman Catholicism in *The Hind and the Panther* (1687).

For a variety of reasons, Dryden was the most often assailed among major poets in his time, a fact attributable in some measure to envy. In an age when almost everyone prized his own wit, Dryden attained eminence without obviously possessing more of that quality than many others. Yet his willingness to plunge into controversy won him a host of enemies, and his changes of opinions and beliefs—literary, religious, political—made him vulnerable to criticism. Examining Dryden's changes of allegiance and point of view one by one, a biographer or critic can provide a logical explanation for each. This task is perhaps most difficult in literary criticism, where Dryden defended a position with enthusiasm only to abandon it later for another, which he advocated with an equal enthusiasm. To his contemporaries, some of his changes were to be explained by self-interest, and, rightly or wrongly, the charge of timeserving became a potent weapon in the hands of his critics.

In 1668, Dryden was appointed poet laureate, a position he held for twenty years, and he also signed a lucrative contract with the Theatre Royal to produce three new plays each year. Though he was unable to produce this stipulated number over the decade of the contract, he nevertheless received his share of theater revenues. During his term as laureate, he received a two-hundred-pound annual stipend, an amount that was later increased to three hundred pounds when he became historiographer royal, but irregularly paid. He was active as a dramatist throughout the 1670's, though he gradually turned his interest to poetic satire, beginning with *Mac Flecknoe: Or, A Satyre upon the True-Blew-Protestant Poet, T. S.* (1682).

With events surrounding the Popist Plot (1678) posing a threat to the government of Charles II, Dryden all but abandoned the theater, writing instead satires, translations, and then his religious poems. Initially, he carried the field for the king, but after the fall

of James II and the loss of his political cause, he also lost the laureateship and its accompanying pension.

During the final period of his life, 1688-1700, Dryden made a brief return to the theater, producing an additional five dramas, but he devoted most of his considerable energy and talent to translations of poetry, achieving success with his patrons and public.

Analysis • John Dryden was a prolific playwright, creating heroic plays, political
plays, operas, heroic tragedies, comedies, and tragicomedies; however, he is best remembered for his poetry and criticism, as many of his plays did not stand the test of
time.

Marriage à la Mode • Dryden's best comedy is generally considered to be *Marriage
à la Mode*. His others rely heavily on farcical situations and double entendre and, at
times, inept licentiousness that makes comedies such as *The Assignation* and *The Kind
Keeper* seem unnecessarily coarse even by the standards of his time. *Marriage à la Mode*
combines in its two distinct plot lines the conventions of the romantic tragicomedy and
the Restoration comedy of manners, a genre not fully established when Dryden produced his play.

The tragicomic plot involves the theme of succession, perhaps Dryden's most frequent dramatic theme after love and honor. Polydamas, having usurped the throne of
Sicily, discovers two young persons of gentle birth but unknown parentage who have
been living among fisher folk under the care of Hermogenes, a former courtier. When
Hermogenes tells the usurper that Leonidas is his son, born after his wife had fled from
him, the king accepts this as correct, even though Leonidas is actually the son of the
king he had deposed. When Polydamas insists that Leonidas marry the daughter of his
friend, Leonidas refuses because of his love for Palmyra, the girl with whom he had
been discovered. To frustrate this passion, Polydamas seeks to banish her, whereupon
Hermogenes declares that Palmyra is the king's daughter and claims Leonidas as his
own son, for he cannot risk revealing the truth about Leonidas, in reality the rightful
successor. Polydamas then seeks to have Palmyra marry his favorite, Argaleon, and
banishes Leonidas, later changing the sentence to death. Facing execution, Leonidas
manages to proclaim his right to the throne, to bring his captors over to his side, and to
oust Polydamas, whom he generously forgives as the father of his beloved Palmyra.

The tragicomic characteristics are all present—the unusual setting; the usurper; the
long-lost noble youth; the faithful servant; the idealization of romantic love, struggling
successfully against the odds and triumphing. To heighten the tone, Dryden uses blank
verse rather than prose and, in the most serious passages, employs rhymed heroic couplets. The tragicomic plot, in the manner of John Fletcher, reveals a significant debt to
Elizabethan and Jacobean tragicomedies.

Whereas in the main plot, the attitude toward love is idealistic, the subplot represents a sharp contrast in the value placed on both love and marriage. Dryden creates
two witty couples—Rhodophil and Doralice, Palamede and Melantha—the first pair
married and the second engaged by arrangement of their parents. Their attitudes toward marriage and love are as cynical and sophisticated as is standard in the comedy
of manners. Palamede hopes before marriage to carry off an affair with his friend
Rhodophil's wife, while Rhodophil hopes to make Melantha his mistress. They freely
satirize Puritans and country folk, and the prevailing attitude of society toward marriage is indicated by Rhodophil when he speaks of his wife, "Yet I loved her a whole
half year, double the natural term of any mistress; and I think, in my conscience, I

could have held out another quarter, but then the world began to laugh at me, and a certain shame, of being out of fashion, seized me."

Disguises, masked balls, and assignations keep Dryden's plot lively and suspenseful, though the couples' goals are never realized because all plans either are intercepted or go awry, and at the end, they part still friends. Throughout, the dialogue sparkles with repartee unequaled in any of Dryden's other plays. It includes Melantha's affected French expressions along with much double entendre and innuendo, yet it is never brutally licentious in tone, as is true of dialogue in comedies such as *The Kind Keeper*.

Though the two plots are loosely connected, Rhodophil does bring the newly found gentlefolk to the court, and both he and Palamede unite to support Leonidas in the final act. Further, the attitudes of parents who arrange marriages are condemned in both plot lines. For the most part, however, the plots occur in two separate worlds—the witty and sophisticated world of the comedy of manners and the idealistic and sentimental world of tragicomedy.

Heroic plays • During the period from 1663 to 1680, Dryden wrote, entirely or in part, twenty-one plays. His initial success came with his heroic plays from *The Indian Queen* to *Aureng-Zebe*, by which time the genre had almost run its course. The heroic play was influenced by a variety of sources, including the English dramas of John Fletcher, the French tragedies of Pierre Corneille, and the French poetic romances of Madeleine de Scudéry and Gautier de Costes de La Calprenède. The most prominent feature that set the genre apart from the usual tragedy was the dialogue in heroic couplets, attributed to the playwrights' efforts to please Charles II, who, it was said, had come to enjoy the rhymed French drama he saw during his years in exile. Dryden defended the artificiality of rhymed dialogue on the grounds that the plays dealt with conflicts and characters above the commonplace; thus, the stylistic elevation provided by rhyme was appropriate. The characters, however, engage in lengthy rhymed speeches, usually with two characters confronting each other, and the result has seemed in a later time excessively artificial.

The plays frequently employ spectacle, enhanced by songs, dances, and elaborate costumes. The settings are usually exotic rather than English, thus heightening their romantic appeal. *The Indian Queen* and *The Indian Emperor*, for example, are set in Mexico, whereas both parts of Dryden's *The Conquest of Granada by the Spaniards* are set in Spain. Warfare, conquest, and striving dominate the plays.

The characters belong to a set of types that include as the protagonist the love-honor hero, who finds himself involved in intrigues and power struggles that put those virtues to the test. Like the other characters, he does not change; the tests the characters encounter are intended to show the strength of their virtue or the depth of their depravity. The hero is surrounded by such Fletcherian types as the sentimental maiden, whom he loves; the evil woman, who shamelessly attempts to gain him for herself; the weak king, whom others are attempting to topple from the throne; the faithful friend; and an antagonist who is almost but not quite a Machiavellian villain motivated solely by ambition. The hero is sometimes fortunate and prevails over all of the obstacles he encounters; at other times, he dies without any success other than preserving his love and honor.

The romantic excesses of heroic plays were satirized by George Villiers, duke of Buckingham, in his burlesque *The Rehearsal* (pr., pb. 1672), which has as its major character John Bayes, a brilliant satiric depiction of Dryden. Villiers parodies many of the absurd and inflated lines of Dryden and others who wrote in the form, yet *The Rehearsal* failed to drive the heroic drama from the stage. The genre remained viable for nearly two decades, until the late 1670's, when the playwrights began shifting their efforts to a less flamboyant form of tragedy.

Aureng-Zebe • *Aureng-Zebe*, the last of Dryden's heroic plays, was judged by him to be his best, though in the prologue he announced that he had grown weary of rhyme, an indication of his imminent shift to blank verse as the appropriate meter for serious drama. By comparison to Dryden's earlier heroic dramas, *Aureng-Zebe* makes less use of song and dance and includes less rant and bombast, yet it clearly preserves the major elements of the genre.

Set in India at the time of the Mogul Empire, it derives events and characters from history, though Dryden freely alters the sources. The aging emperor, a stereotypical weak king, finds his throne challenged by several of his sons, the loyal Aureng-Zebe being an exception. Aureng-Zebe is depicted by his friend Arimant, governor of Agra, as "by no strong person swayed/ Except his love," a hero of unshakable loyalty who hopes that he will attain the hand of the captive queen Indamora for his support of the emperor.

While *Aureng-Zebe* is tame by earlier standards of the heroic play, echoes of the swashbuckling, superhuman hero remain. In armed conflict, the hero defeats two rebellious brothers, Darah being the first, "Darah from loyal Aureng-Zebe is fled,/ And forty thousand of his men lie dead." The threat represented by Morat, the ambitious villain of the play, is not so easily parried, for he has raised an immense force thus described by Abbas: "The neighb'ring plain with arms is coverd o'er;/ The vale an iron harvest seems to yield/ Of thick-sprung lances in a waving field." The hyperboles, typical of the genre, suggest the physical threat posed by Morat; his character also serves as a foil to that of Aureng-Zebe, for he does not properly control his passions. Primarily motivated by a desire for power, he also wishes to abandon his faithful wife, Melesinda, for Aureng-Zebe's beloved Indamora, who finds him repulsive. Further complications arise when the emperor falls passionately in love with Indamora, and the Empress Nourmahal, Aureng-Zebe's stepmother and the "evil woman" of the play, conceives a strong passion for her stepson. Confronted with news of his father's love for Indamora and his placing her under arrest, the hero accepts the challenge involving both his love and honor.

Aureng-Zebe finds himself threatened from many directions when he intercedes with the emperor and attempts to prevent the emperor's petulant imprisonment of Nourmahal. No sooner has the emperor seen Nourmahal taken away than he summons the rebellious Morat with the intent of making him his heir, all because of Aureng-Zebe's love for Indamora. Boldly entering unannounced, Aureng-Zebe attempts to end the alliance between the emperor and Morat by offering to disband his army if Morat will withdraw his forces from the city, leaving the emperor in control. Despite these peace-making efforts, the emperor orders Aureng-Zebe's arrest when he will not renounce his love for Indamora. When Indamora pleads for Morat to spare the life of Aureng-Zebe, he demands her love in exchange, which she curtly refuses. The alliance between the emperor and Morat is broken when the emperor learns of Morat's passion for Indamora. After Aureng-Zebe has been released through the efforts of Indamora and Arimant, Indamora finds great difficulty in convincing the jealous hero that she has remained faithful and has not betrayed him with Morat. Meanwhile, having lost the favor of the emperor, Morat rebels against him.

The outcome is obscured when Arimant, in a disguise that results in his being mistaken for Aureng-Zebe, is killed and Morat has to break off a long seductive speech to Indamora to quell an uprising. In the final battle, Aureng-Zebe leads the emperor's forces to victory, and Morat, mortally wounded, manages to prevent his mother from murdering Indamora. Her violent passion frustrated, Nourmahal poisons herself, and the Emperor grants Aureng-Zebe both the state and Indamora.

In *Aureng-Zebe*, the characters who retain their honor reap the rewards of both love and honor, whereas those who do not control their passions and ambition encounter misfortune. The abruptness and violence of passions are appropriately accompanied by abrupt and violent actions in the play. A major difference between good and evil characters becomes the measure of control over passions, not the violence of the passion itself. Dryden's characters, both the good and the bad, express themselves blatantly where sexual passions are concerned, a phenomenon not limited to the characters of the heroic plays.

All for Love • Of *All for Love*, his tragedy based on Shakespeare's earlier great work *Antony and Cleopatra* (pr. c. 1606-1607), Dryden himself commented that he had never written anything "for myself but *Antony and Cleopatra*." The drama reflects Dryden's vision of tragedy, sometimes designated by critics as "heroic tragedy" to indicate certain similarities to the heroic play. The chief among Dryden's works in the type include *Oedipus, Troilus and Cressida, Don Sebastian, King of Portugal* and *Cleomenes, the Spartan Hero*. Unlike the heroic plays, these are written in blank verse and their sources are Shakespearean or classical. They demonstrate fewer of the epic dimensions of the heroic play, and the heroes are more nearly realistic characters. Although Dryden succeeds more fully in presenting human emotions in these dramas, in part because the medium of blank verse is more suited to emotional expression, he achieves the effects of pathos and sentiment rather than pity and fear.

In *All for Love*, Dryden follows the dramatic unities of time, place, and action, which he regarded as ornaments of tragedy, though not indispensable. The hero, Antony, is presented on the final day of his life, which happens to be his birthday. Facing imminent defeat at the hands of Octavius, he encounters temptations to abandon the great passion of his life, Cleopatra, in order to prolong the contest or to minimize the consequences of the loss. Restrictions inherent in the dramatic unities result in characters that are not nearly so complex as those of the source, Shakespeare's *Antony and Cleopatra*. Cleopatra neither wavers in her devotion to Antony nor reflects at length on her role as queen, as she does in Shakespeare's tragedy. Dryden's Ventidius shares qualities drawn from Shakespeare's character of the same name but also from Shakespeare's Enobarbus, the devoted adviser who abandons Antony. Ventidius strives to deliver Antony from his passion for Cleopatra, while, at the same time, her servant Alexas is scheming with Cleopatra to keep Antony's devotion.

Caught in the struggle between love and duty, Antony appears a weak hero. Ventidius first offers Antony, then under attack by Octavius, the support of twelve legions if he will abandon Cleopatra, pointing to this as a necessary condition since the legionnaires refuse to come to Egypt and insist that Antony join them to assume command. Seizing on this chance for victory, Antony agrees, only to change his mind when he receives a parting gift, a bracelet, from Cleopatra, who unexpectedly arrives to put her gift on his arm.

Ventidius next arranges for Antony to make an honorable peace with Caesar, leaving him with limited power, if he will return to his wife Octavia. When Octavia appears with their two daughters, Antony is unable to withstand their pleas and agrees to return to her, dispatching Dolabella to deliver a farewell to Cleopatra. This episode reveals the flaws in Alexas's and Ventidius's calculations. Alexas reasons that Cleopatra may win Antony back by arousing his jealousy through Dolabella, whereas Ventidius assumes that jealousy will convince Antony that Cleopatra was worthless. Thus, both adversaries steer Antony in the same direction for different ends. The result is that Octavia becomes so distressed at Antony's obvious jealousy over their reports that she leaves him. In return for Antony's hostility and anger and after the loss of a battle at sea, Cleopatra sends word of her death, which Antony cannot bear. Following his self-inflicted mortal wound, he is taken to Cleopatra, whose death following his brings a sense of triumph.

Although scenes such as that between Antony and Octavia involve a generous amount of sentimentality, Dryden achieves in *All for Love* an intensity that is lacking in most of his plays, one whose emotional effects are not dissipated through digressions or loosely related subplots. The play reveals a tightly unified plot line in which characters' motives and actions are influenced primarily by strong romantic love.

Don Sebastian, King of Portugal • Dryden's tragedy *Don Sebastian, King of Portugal*, written after the Glorious Revolution, is his longest drama and, in the view of critics from Sir Walter Scott to Bruce King, his finest dramatic achievement. In the play's preface, Dryden acknowledges that the players cut more than twelve hundred lines from the acted version. Though the play's themes are universally appropriate for tragedy, it includes a closely related comic subplot, and it ends not with the death of the hero or heroine but with their retirement from the world of affairs. The play incorporates numerous qualities and dramatic techniques that Dryden employs elsewhere in his work and may be the most fruitful play to examine for clarifying his dramatic art.

The play is set in North Africa, where Don Sebastian, king of Portugal, and his allies have been defeated and captured after warring against the Moors. Sebastian's chief desire is to marry the woman he loves, Almeyda, Christian queen of Barbary, also held captive. This he manages to do after the emperor Muley-Moluch has given him a measure of freedom so that Sebastian can attempt to win Almeyda's hand for the emperor. Sebastian and Almeyda escape the emperor's retribution for their marriage, because he is slain in a rebellion, but they do not escape fate. In the final act, they learn from the old counselor Alvarez, who has just been freed from captivity, that they are half brother and sister, having had the same father. The incestuousness of their relationship, unknowing though it was, forces them to part, with each retiring to a separate religious house.

The Moors are portrayed throughout the play as riven by factions, the chief threat being the effort of the emperor's favorite, Benducar, to topple him from the throne, ostensibly in favor of the emperor's brother, Muley-Zeydan, but in reality for himself. In this attempt, he involves the populace, the religious leader Mufti Abdalla, and Dorax, a Christian who has turned against Sebastian and has joined the Moors. Dorax later joins Sebastian, after the fall of the emperor, to defeat the uprising and restore worthy leaders to their places. A comic subplot involves the efforts of the Christian captive Don Antonio to flee the household of the Mufti with his daughter Morayma and his treasure, in much the same way that Lorenzo and Jessica flee Shylock in Shakespeare's *The Merchant of Venice* (pr. 1604).

The exotic setting, the theme of heroic love, the stock characters, and the broils and warfare represent familiar themes and situations of Dryden's dramas. Occasionally, one also finds in the dramas some exceptional improbabilities. In this play, for example, Dorax, having lost the confidence of the Moors, is poisoned by two of them, Benducar and the Mufti, but survives because each poison neutralizes the effect of the other. Yet *Don Sebastian, King of Portugal* illustrates other characteristics of Dryden's dramatic art that are less obvious but more influential and significant: the theme of incest, actual or suppressed; anticlericalism; political satire and allusions; and scenes of reconciliation.

In *Don Sebastian, King of Portugal*, unwitting incest occurs between Sebastian and Almeyda after they are married, and such is their consternation when they discover they have violated the taboo that Sebastian believes suicide the only escape until Dorax dissuades him. The situation resembles somewhat that of Oedipus in the version of the old Greek drama that Dryden and Nathaniel Lee produced for the Restoration stage. It is as though love in Dryden is so exalted, wrought up to such a pitch, that introduction of the taboo acts to heighten it and make the plight of the lovers more poignant. In *Don Sebastian, King of Portugal*, the theme is counterbalanced by the story of Violante, who denied affection to the husband Sebastian had chosen for her and awaited for many years her beloved Dorax.

It is unclear why anticlericalism becomes such a prominent theme in the works of Dryden, though it seems plausible that his profound distrust and dislike of Puritan influence on political affairs may in part explain it. The Mufti represents the typical clergyman in Dryden, usually the object of satire in both the poems and the plays. He is ambitious, avaricious, sensual, officious, and usually hypocritical. The Mufti appears ridiculous in both political and personal affairs, becoming the object of humor and scorn. Dryden does not ridicule clergymen of the Church of England, but wherever he introduces a pagan, a Muslim, or a Roman Catholic religious figure, the character becomes the object of satire.

In its political theme, the play concerns betrayal and misappropriation of power. The emperor, having usurped the throne, discovers that he can trust no one, least of all Benducar, his closest adviser. Benducar incites the mob to rebellion, and they manage to defeat and kill the emperor, barbarously showing his head on a pike as that of a tyrant. Like a true Machiavellian, Benducar muses on the thesis that might makes right: "And I can sin but once to seize the throne; all after-acts are sanctified by power." Such passages as this in Dryden's plays, poems, and translations following the Glorious Revolution usually serve as oblique satire of the new monarchs, and his distrust of the judgment of the common people where political affairs are concerned is a recurring theme throughout his work.

A final characteristic of Dryden's theater is evident in act 4, scene 3, often considered the most successful scene of the play. It depicts the intense quarrel of the two friends, Dorax and Sebastian, and their reconciliation. Dryden may have based this scene on the quarrel of Brutus and Cassius in Shakespeare's *Julius Caesar* (pr. c. 1599-1600); similar scenes occur in other works of Dryden, notably in *Troilus and Cressida* and *Cleomenes, the Spartan Hero*. Although Dorax has fought on the side of the Moors, he defends and spares the life of Sebastian—so that he can kill him to exact his own revenge. He holds a powerful grudge because Sebastian did not adequately reward him for his prior service and awarded the hand of Violante to another courtier, Henriquez.

Facing an imminent fight to the death with Dorax, Sebastian explains that Henriquez had sought the hand of Violante first, that Henriquez had died defending Sebastian, and that Violante now waits for Dorax. Accepting Sebastian's explanation,

Dorax submits, is restored to favor, and promises that he will serve Sebastian as faithfully as Henriquez had done. In the final act, Dorax helps Sebastian bear manfully his sense of guilt and loss. Scenes of intense confrontation permit the dramatist to display a range of emotions in a brief space, as well as a heightening and diminution of passions. Dryden's ability to capture such a range of tones compensates to a degree for his lack of a greater gift as a dramatist—the ability to show growth and development of his characters.

Other major works

POETRY: *Heroic Stanzas*, 1659; *Astraea Redux*, 1660; "To My Lord Chancellor," 1662; *Prologues and Epilogues*, 1664-1700; *Annus Mirabilis*, 1667; *Absalom and Achitophel, Part I*, 1681; *Absalom and Achitophel, Part II*, 1682 (with Nahum Tate); *The Medall: A Satyre Against Sedition*, 1682; *Mac Flecknoe: Or, A Satyre upon the True-Blew-Protestant Poet, T. S.*, 1682; *Religio Laici: Or, A Layman's Faith*, 1682; *Threnodia Augustalis*, 1685; *The Hind and the Panther*, 1687; "A Song for St. Cecilia's Day," 1687; *Britannia Rediviva*, 1688; *Eleonora*, 1692; "To My Dear Friend Mr. Congreve," 1694; *Alexander's Feast: Or, The Power of Music, an Ode in Honor of St. Cecilia's Day*, 1697; "To My Honour'd Kinsman, John Driden," 1700.

NONFICTION: *Of Dramatic Poesie: An Essay*, 1668; "A Defence of *An Essay of Dramatic Poesy*," 1668; "Preface to *An Evening's Love: Or, The Mock Astrologer*," 1671; "Of Heroic Plays: An Essay," 1672; "The Author's Apology for Heroic Poetry and Poetic License," 1677; "Preface to *All for Love*," 1678; "The Grounds of Criticism in Tragedy," 1679; "Preface to *Sylvae*," 1685; *A Discourse Concerning the Original and Progress of Satire*, 1693; "Dedication of *Examen Poeticum*," 1693; "A Parallel of Poetry and Painting," 1695; "Dedication of the *Aeneis*," 1697; "Preface to *Fables Ancient and Modern*," 1700; "Heads of an Answer to Rymer," 1711.

TRANSLATIONS: *Ovid's Epistles*, 1680; *The History of the League*, 1684 (of Louis Maimbourg's *Histoire de la Ligue*); *The Life of St. Francis Xavier*, 1688 (of Dominique Bouhours's *La Vie de Saint François Xavier*); *The Satires of Juvenal and Persius*, 1693; *The Works of Vergil*, 1697.

Bibliography

Archer, John Michael. *Old Worlds: Egypt, Southwest Asia, India, and Russia in Early Modern English Writing*. Stanford, Calif.: Stanford University Press, 2001. Contains a scholarly examination of Dryden's *Aureng-Zebe*, along with Shakespeare's *Antony and Cleopatra* and the works of John Milton. Bibliography and index.

Bywaters, David. *Dryden in Revolutionary England*. Berkeley: University of California Press, 1991. This book describes the rhetorical stages by which Dryden, in his published works between 1687 and 1700, sought to define contemporary politics and to stake out for himself a tenable place within them. The study reveals much about the relationship between Dryden's politics, polemics, and art. Contains an epilogue and extensive notes.

Hammond, Paul. *John Dryden: A Literary Life*. New York: St. Martin's Press, 1991. This study of Dryden's life examines the texts that he produced and the relationship of these texts to the society they reflect. The work consists of chapters on different aspects of Dryden's works. They are arranged approximately chronologically to suggest the shape of his career and to explore his own developing sense of his role as the premier writer of Restoration England, both dominating and detached from the world in which he moved. Select bibliography and extensive notes.

Hammond, Paul, and David Hopkins, eds. *John Dryden: Tercentenary Essays.* Oxford, England: Oxford, 2000. A collection of twelve essays that place Dryden in the context of his time and suggest a more elevated place for the poet in literary history.

Owen, Susan J. *Restoration Theatre and Crisis.* New York: Clarendon Press, 1996. A look at theater in England in the seventeenth century, focusing on Dryden and Aphra Behn. Bibliography and index.

Winn, James Anderson. *John Dryden and His World.* New Haven, Conn.: Yale University Press, 1987. Examines the man, his work, and the world in which he lived. Considers the subtle relations linking this world's religious beliefs, its political alliances, and the literary styles it favored. Views Dryden's work as a product of his particular historical situation. Includes illustrations and appendices on Dryden's family history.

_____, ed. *Critical Essays on John Dryden.* New York: G. K. Hall, 1997. A collection of essays on the literary works of Dryden. Bibliography and index.

Stanley Archer,
updated by Genevieve Slomski

Christopher Durang

Born: Montclair, New Jersey; January 2, 1949

Principal drama • *The Greatest Musical Ever Sung*, pr. 1971; *The Nature and Purpose of the Universe*, wr. 1971, pr. 1975 (radio play), pr. 1979 (staged), pb. 1979; *Better Dead than Sorry*, pr. 1972 (libretto, music by Jack Feldman); *I Don't Generally Like Poetry but Have You Read "Trees"?*, pr. 1972 (with Albert Innaurato); *The Life Story of Mitzi Gaynor: Or, Gyp*, pr. 1973 (with Innaurato); *The Marriage of Bette and Boo*, pr. 1973, pb. 1976, revised pr. 1979, pb. 1985; *The Idiots Karamazov*, pr., pb. 1974, augmented pb. 1981 (with Innaurato, music by Feldman); *Titanic*, pr. 1974, pb. 1983; *Death Comes to Us All, Mary Agnes*, pr. 1975, pb. 1979; *When Dinah Shore Ruled the Earth*, pr. 1975 (with Wendy Wasserstein); *'dentity Crisis*, pr. 1975, pb. 1979; *Das Lusitania Songspiel*, pr. 1976 (with Sigourney Weaver, music by Mel Marvin and Jack Gaughan); *A History of the American Film*, pr. 1976, pb. 1978; *The Vietnamization of New Jersey (An American Tragedy)*, pr. 1976, pb. 1978; *Three Short Plays*, pb. 1979; *Sister Mary Ignatius Explains It All for You*, pr. 1979, pb. 1980; *The Actor's Nightmare*, pr., pb. 1981; *Beyond Therapy*, pr. 1981, pb. 1983; *Christopher Durang Explains It All for You*, pb. 1983; *Baby with the Bathwater*, pr., pb. 1983; *Sloth*, pr. 1985; *Laughing Wild*, pr. 1987, pb. 1988; *Naomi in the Living Rkoom*, pr. 1991, pb. 1998; *Media Amok*, pr. 1992; *Durang/Durang*, pr. 1994, pb. 1996 (6 short plays; *Mrs. Sorken, For Whom the Belle Tolls, A Stye of the Eye, Nina in the Morning, Wanda's Visit*, and *Business Lunch at the Russian Tea Room*); *Collected Works*, pb. 1995-1997 (2 volumes; volume 1, *Twenty-seven Short Plays*; volume 2, *Complete Full-length Plays, 1975-1995*); *Sex and Longing*, pr. 1996; *Betty's Summer Vacation*, pr. 1998, pb. 2000

Other literary forms • Although Christopher Durang is known primarily for his plays, he has written a screenplay, *Beyond Therapy* (1987).

Achievements • Christopher Durang belongs to a tradition of black humorists and fabulists who first emerged in the 1950's with the novelists Joseph Heller, Kurt Vonnegut, and Thomas Berger. His plays are ridiculous comedies that agitate the audience without propagating a particular political viewpoint, attacking every "great idea" of Western literature and philosophy merely because it is assailable. His writing centers on the enduring questions of human suffering and authority. His most popular play, *Sister Mary Ignatius Explains It All for You*, was hotly debated by theologians and theater critics alike and won an Obie Award as the best new Off-Broadway play of 1980.

Durang's other honors include grants from the Rockefeller Foundation and the Lecomte du Nuoy Foundation, fellowships from Guggenheim and the Columbia Broadcasting System, a Tony nomination for his musical *A History of the American Film*, the Sidney Kingsley Playwriting Award, and an Obie Award for distinguished playwriting for *Betty's Summer Vacation*. He co-chairs the playwriting program at the Julliard School in Manhattan. His work is characterized by energy and a sense of the ridiculous in life and art, sustained by anger and despair. The targets of his abusive wit are the sacred cows of contemporary American society: religion, family life, hero worship, law and order, and success.

Biography • Christopher Ferdinand Durang was born in Montclair, New Jersey, on January 2, 1949. A humorous autobiographical sketch is given in the introduction to his plays in *Christopher Durang Explains It All for You*, beginning with his conception and ending with the reviews of *Beyond Therapy*. His parents, Francis Ferdinand and Patricia Elizabeth Durang, were devout Roman Catholics who fought constantly until they were divorced, when Durang was still in grade school. Durang's interest in theater and playwriting became evident early in life. He wrote his first play while in the second grade in a Catholic elementary school. He subsequently attended a Catholic preparatory high school run by Benedictine priests. He continued to write plays, and though a fairly conservative and conventional student, he often inserted hints of sex for their shock effect. In high school, Durang was overcome with religious zeal and the desire to enter a monastery after graduation, but soon afterward he lost his faith and his interest in the Roman Catholic religion.

He attended Harvard University with the hope and expectation of discovering a more intellectual and less conservative dimension of Catholicism but was disappointed. In his second year at Harvard, he entered psychoanalysis with a priest. He became obsessed with motion pictures and neglected his academic studies. Although he had been a prodigious writer in high school, he wrote almost nothing in college until his senior year, when he wrote (as a form of therapy for his feeling of religious guilt) a musical-comedy version of the life of Christ called *The Greatest Musical Ever Sung*, which included such irreverent show-tune lampoons as "The Dove That Done Me Wrong" and "Everything's Coming up Moses." The play stirred up a local religious controversy but was well received by audiences, encouraging the young playwright to write more. His next effort, the ambitiously titled *The Nature and Purpose of the Universe*, was eventually produced in New York and, following Durang's graduation from Harvard in 1971, was submitted as part of his application to the Yale School of Drama.

At Yale, Durang met and worked with a number of actors and playwrights who were, along with him, to make their marks in the American theater. Among his classmates were Albert Innaurato (with whom Durang collaborated on several plays), Meryl Streep (who appeared in a Durang play in college), Wendy Wasserstein (with whom Durang wrote *When Dinah Shore Ruled the Earth*), and Sigourney Weaver (who appeared in several Durang plays in New York and with whom he wrote *Das Lusitania Songspiel*). His chief supporter at Yale and later in New York was Robert Brustein, who was dean of the drama school while Durang was enrolled there and artistic director of the Yale Repertory Theater. Durang received his M.F.A. in 1974 but remained in New Haven for an extra year, performing and writing at Yale, teaching drama at the Southern Connecticut College in New Haven, and working as a typist at the medical school.

Durang moved to New York in 1975. *Titanic*, which he wrote for a class at Yale, and *The Nature and Purpose of the Universe* were produced in Off-Broadway theaters. In 1976, his musical play *A History of the American Film* was produced in Waterford, Connecticut, as part of the Eugene O'Neill Playwrights Conference, and in 1977 it was produced simultaneously on both coasts at the Hartford Stage Company in Connecticut, the Mark Taper Forum in Los Angeles, California, and the Arena Stage in Washington, D.C. In 1978, the play opened on Broadway at the American National Theatre. The play's subsequent failure on Broadway precipitated a period of depression that climaxed with the death of Durang's mother in March, 1979. Watching his mother die of incurable bone cancer and reassessing his Catholic upbringing, Durang started writing the play on which his reputation as a playwright would be secured, *Sister Mary Ignatius Explains It All for You*.

The play was first produced in December, 1979, by Curt Dempster's Ensemble Studio Theatre in New York, along with one-act plays by David Mamet, Marsha Norman, and Tennessee Williams. Two years later, Andre Bishop's Playwrights Horizons produced the play Off-Broadway with two members of the original cast of six, along with Durang's *The Actor's Nightmare*, which he wrote as a curtain raiser. In 2000, the play was adapted for cable television under the title *Sister Mary Explains It All*, with Diane Keaton in the title role.

Sister Mary Ignatius Explains It All for You brought Durang to the public's attention, not only through the show's popularity but also through several battles against censorship when various Catholic organizations attempted to close down the play. The Phoenix Theatre commissioned Durang to write *Beyond Therapy*, which opened in 1981 and then, almost a year and a half later, was rewritten and produced on Broadway at the Brooks Atkinson Theater. Later, Durang revised and expanded two plays he originally wrote at Yale, *Baby with the Bathwater* and *The Marriage of Bette and Boo*, which also were produced in New York. A 1987 film version of *Beyond Therapy* directed by Robert Altman was a box-office failure, and Durang expressed his unhappiness with the experience. Nevertheless, he subsequently expressed his disenchantment with the New York theater scene and his intention to pursue work in film, which, he stated, offers more permanence and reaches a larger audience than live drama.

Analysis • Christopher Durang belongs to the postmodernist wave of American playwrights who emerged during the 1970's, including A. R. Gurney, Jr., Tina Howe, and Sam Shepard. These writers fused the experimental techniques of the structuralist theater experiments of the 1960's with the "traditional" domestic drama of the early twentieth century American realists, creating a new form of theater that is simultaneously naturalistic and self-consciously theatrical. Evolving as it did from collegiate travesties and comedy sketches, Durang's drama violates many of the established principles of the well-made play. However sloppily constructed and politically unsophisticated his plays may be, Durang's genius is to create comedies out of existential anger and to infuse them with energy, thought, and an unbounded sense of liberty.

Durang's plays are remarkable for their absurdist approach to the important questions of modern philosophy, for their hilarious disregard for social conventions and traditional sexual roles, and for their uncompromisingly bleak assessment of human politics and society. As early as the satirical travesties he produced in college, Durang's abiding themes have been suffering and paternalism. The cutting edge of his humor is his insistence on the commonplaceness of suffering in the world. His plays are populated by archetypal sadists and victims, and the comedy is usually cruel (as the audience is made to laugh at the exaggerated and grotesque misery of the characters) and nearly always violent; death, suicide, disaster, and murder are never too far away in typical Durang slapstick.

In a note accompanying the publication of *The Nature and Purpose of the Universe*, the writer explains that the violence of the play must appear simultaneously vicious and funny, demanding that performers make the audience sympathize with the victim and yet feel sufficiently "alienated" (in the sense of Bertolt Brecht's "alienation effect") from the theatrical action to be able to laugh at it. Presiding over the sufferers is a figure of authority, always coldly detached and frequently insane, who "explains" the suffering with banal truisms taken from philosophy, religion, and pop psychology, while in fact he or she acts as the instrument of the oppression and mindless malice.

Fear and insecurity are the principal components of Durang's comedy of paranoia.

While his plays are repeatedly criticized for not being positive and for not suggesting any remedy to the problem of human evil, they are in fact relentlessly moral, fueled by a profound sense of outrage at the crimes against human dignity. Like Eugène Ionesco, Joe Orton, and Lenny Bruce, Durang attempts to shock the audience out of its complacency through the use of vulgarity, blasphemy, violence, and other forms of extremism. If his endings seem less than perfectly conclusive, and if his characters seem to be no more than cartoons, still, underneath all the madcap and sophomoric nonsense is a serious and humane plea for tolerance, diversity, and individual liberty. The object of the writer's most satirical attacks is the incompetent guardian, a sometimes well-intentioned but always destructive figure of patriarchal authority who appears in many different guises: parent, husband, teacher, analyst, hero, nanny, doctor, author, and even deity. This figure embodies for Durang all the evil elements of human nature and social hierarchy.

The Idiots Karamazov • Durang's drama of the mid-1970's, the plays that grew out of his college exercises at Yale, is chiefly parodic and yet contains kernels of the preoccupation with suffering characteristic of his later works. *The Idiots Karamazov*, which he wrote with Innaurato, is a musical-comedy travesty of the great Russian novelists of suffering, Fyodor Dostoevski and Leo Tolstoy. The principal character, Constance Garnett, is the translator, an older woman who uses a wheelchair and is attended by a suicidal manservant, Ernest. In Durang and Innaurato's version of Dostoevski's *The Brothers Karamazov*, the holy innocent and idiot savant Alyosha becomes a pop music star, and the "Great Books," along with other academic pretensions to cultural importance, are thus trivialized as commodities in a money-and-glitter-oriented enterprise.

A History of the American Film • Durang ridiculed Hollywood and motion pictures in *A History of the American Film*, a 1976 musical that opened on Broadway in 1978. The five principal characters are caricatures based on familiar Hollywood types. Loretta (as in Loretta Young) is the long-suffering and lovingly innocent heroine. Jimmy (as in James Cagney) is the tough guy, part hoodlum and part romantic hero. Bette (as in Bette Davis) is the vamp, a vindictive but seductive figure who enjoys nothing more than making Loretta suffer. Hank (as in Henry Fonda) is the strong and silent all-American good guy, who eventually turns psychotic. Eve (as in Eve Arden) is the ever-present true friend, who covers up her own sexual frustration with dry witticisms and hard-boiled mottoes.

True to its title, the play satirizes the gamut of Hollywood kitsch, including jabs at *Birth of a Nation* (1915), *The Grapes of Wrath* (1940), *The Best Years of Our Lives* (1946), *Psycho* (1960), *Who's Afraid of Virginia Woolf?* (1966), and *Earthquake* (1974). On a deeper level, the play exposes the American film industry as a manufacturer of glamorous façades for real-life misery and fear.

The Vietnamization of New Jersey • In *The Vietnamization of New Jersey*, Durang takes on the legitimate theater itself. Using David Rabe's controversial Vietnam-era satire *Sticks and Bones* (pr. 1969, pb. 1972) as a starting place, Durang makes the social and political pretensions of "serious theater" seem silly, while castigating the various "isms" of contemporary culture: liberalism, consumerism, racism, militarism, and sexism. The play treats the horrors of war, mental illness, inflation, unemployment, and suicide with chilling comedy.

'dentity Crisis • In the late 1970's, when Durang wrote *'dentity Crisis, The Nature and Purpose of the Universe,* and the phenomenally successful *Sister Mary Ignatius Explains It All for You,* the playwright challenged the idea of authority or expertise itself. Inspired by R. D. Laing's controversial theories about schizophrenia, *'dentity Crisis* is an oddly moving comedy in one act and two scenes. The action centers on a young, depressed woman named Jane and her mother, Edith.

The play opens as Edith returns from the dry cleaner with Jane's bloodstained dress, which has been ruined after an unsuccessful suicide attempt. Despite the initial impression, it soon appears that Jane is the only character in the play who is "sane." Edith manufactures and discards versions of reality with breathless speed, and Robert, the other occupant of the house, manifests four distinct personalities, alternately Jane's brother, father, and grandfather, as well as the Count de Rochelay, a foreign suitor of the perversely promiscuous Edith.

Even Jane's psychoanalyst, Mr. Summers, is bizarrely inconsistent. In scene 1, the role is played by a man, and in scene 2, after a sex-change operation, by a woman (the actor who plays Mr. Summers in the first scene plays his wife in the second). Jane reveals the motive behind her suicide attempt in a poignant and surrealistic monologue concerning a production of *Peter Pan* she had seen as a girl. Life is not worth continuing, she says, if it only leads to death in the end. The play ends with the daughter's loss of her identity, but the audience's sympathy remains with her because it has entered her version of reality and regards the others as mad.

The Nature and Purpose of the Universe • The authoritative Mr. and Mrs. Summers in *'dentity Crisis* are remarkably similar to Ronald and Elaine May Alcott, the two "agents of God" who borrow various guises in *The Nature and Purpose of the Universe.* Like its glib title, the play pokes fun at those who would offer easy explanations of the mysteries of existence and evil. It is a play in thirteen "chapters," each chronicling a different aspect of the tragicomic downfall of the hapless Eleanor Mann.

Presiding over the events of the drama are Ronald and Elaine, who pretend to render meaningful the random catastrophes that they inflict on the Job-like Eleanor. Every now and then they enter the action of the play, purportedly to offer heavenly guidance and solace but actually to intensify the poor woman's suffering. Durang's comedy springs from the characters' absurdly cool responses to horror. When Eleanor is knocked to the kitchen floor and kicked by her drug-peddling son, her husband chides the boy, saying, "Donald, have a little patience with your mother." The play ends as, in a parody of Old Testament piety, Ronald and Elaine bind and gag Eleanor and sacrifice her to a distant and passively vicious God.

Sister Mary Ignatius Explains It All for You • Sister Mary Ignatius, teacher at Our Lady of Perpetual Sorrow and the menacingly maternal protagonist of *Sister Mary Ignatius Explains It All for You,* is the writer's classic realization of the banality and willful ignorance of human evil. The play falls into three sections. In the first, Sister Mary catechizes the audience on basic doctrines and practices of the Roman Catholic Church.

As Durang noted in several interviews, the humor of this section stems from the unexaggerated reportage of the irrational but devoutly held beliefs of certain Christians: the existence of Heaven, Hell, and Purgatory within the physical universe; the supernatural births of Jesus Christ and Mary; the efficacy of Christ's suffering and death on a cross; the exclusively procreative function of sex; and God's everlasting vengeance against wrongdoers such as Zsa Zsa Gabor, Brooke Shields, and David Bowie. Repeatedly, however, Sister Mary dodges the more interesting issue of God's responsibility for the existence of evil and suffering in the world.

The second section presents a Nativity play performed by four of Sister Mary's former students. More than anything else, the play demonstrates the triumph of dogma over narrative in traditional Christianity and portrays an absurdly abbreviated life of Christ. With only three characters, Mary, Joseph, and Misty the camel (two actors impersonate separate humps), and a doll as the infant Jesus, the play spans the time from the Immaculate Conception (of Mary) to the Ascension (of Jesus, Mary, Joseph, and Misty). The third section of the play involves the Nativity-scene actors' disclosure to Sister Mary of the courses their lives have taken after leaving Our Lady of Perpetual Sorrow.

Philomena (Misty's front end) has borne a daughter out of wedlock. Aloysius (Misty's back end) has become a suicidal alcoholic who regularly beats his wife. Gary (Joseph) has had homosexual relationships. Diane (Mary), whom Sister Mary especially detests, has had two abortions. Diane engineers the climactic confrontation in order to embarrass Sister Mary and then reveals her intention to kill her, much to the surprise of her three cohorts. Victorious in the end, Sister Mary whips out a gun and kills Diane; then, after assuring herself that he has made a recent confession of his sexual sins, she kills Gary as well. The play ends with a recitation of the catechism by Thomas, a boy currently enrolled in the parochial school.

Beyond Therapy • In the 1980's, Durang turned his attention to other kinds of oppression in society, specifically the normalization of sexuality and family relationships. In *Beyond Therapy*, he again attacks psychoanalysis from a Laingian perspective, portraying the analysts in the play as more bizarre versions of Mr. Summers and his wife in *'dentity Crisis*. Their clients are a heterosexual woman and a bisexual man who meet through an advertisement in the personals column of a newspaper. The complex relationship they form is played mainly for laughs, but the butt of most of the jokes is pop psychology, as well as the notion of anyone's being an expert about how other people ought to live their lives.

Baby with the Bathwater and **The Marriage of Bette and Boo** • Both *Baby with the Bathwater* and *The Marriage of Bette and Boo* have their origins in plays Durang wrote while in college and pertain to American family life. *Baby with the Bathwater* is a grim but humorous indictment of the science of child-rearing. Born as a boy but reared as a girl, Daisy, the baby of the title, is the victim of two inept parents and a manipulative nanny. In the last act he appears in his analyst's office wearing a dress, clearly suffering from a sexual identity crisis.

The Marriage of Bette and Boo takes the form of a college student's memories of his parents, both of whom are emotionally unbalanced and (for their son Matt, the narrator) unbalancing. The play is a parody of the family dramas of American dramatists Thornton Wilder and Eugene O'Neill. The mother, Bette, idolizes babies but is able to produce only one living descendant because her blood type is incompatible with her husband's. The several stillborn infants she produces she names after animal characters in Winnie the Pooh storybooks. The father, Boo, is an alcoholic whose life is a cycle of a reformation and backsliding. Though a comedy, the play touches on serious philosophical questions concerning God, suffering, death, the absurdity of life, and the meaning of love. It is also the most autobiographical of Durang's plays.

Later plays • In the late 1980's, tired of New York and the theater, Durang began touring as a cabaret act, Chris Durang and Dawne. He soon returned to the theater, however, with *Media Amok*, a satire on the sensationalism of television talk shows. *Durang/Durang* contained six sketches lampooning playwrights Tennessee Williams, Sam Shepard, and David Mamet, with titles such as *For Whom the Belle Tolls*. A more serious and disturbing play followed. *Sex and Longing* tells of Lulu, a nymphomaniac whose roommate is a sexually compulsive homosexual. Lulu is attacked by a serial killer; her savior, a fundamentalist preacher, first converts her, then later rapes her.

Betty's Summer Vacation begins as a comedic farce but soon spins out of control to an explosive ending. Betty is spending her vacation at a time-share by the beach with five bizarre strangers, one of whom is a serial killer. The American fascination with sensationalism on television is a theme again, with such targets as Fox network specials and coverage of the trials of Lorena Bobbit and O. J. Simpson.

Other major work
SCREENPLAY: *Beyond Therapy*, 1987.

Bibliography
Brustein, Robert. "The Crack in the Chimney: Reflections on Contemporary American Playwriting." *Theater* 9 (Spring, 1978): 21-29. A discussion of *The Vietnamization of New Jersey*, set against the more serious examination of the work of David Rabe, in *Sticks and Bones*.

Durang, Christopher. Introduction to *Christopher Durang Explains It All for You*. New York: Grove Weidenfeld, 1990. The introduction to this collection of six plays is a tongue-in-cheek autobiography, written in 1982, that includes anecdotes about playwriting classes under Howard Stein and Jules Feiffer and early psychiatric counseling.

_____. "Suspending Disbelief: An Interview with the Playwright by Himself." *American Theater* 16, no. 10 (December 1999): 37. A sardonic "interview" in which Durang discusses the writing of *Betty's Summer Vacation*, recurrent themes in his work, and future plans. Includes the full text of *Betty's Summer Vacation*.

Flippo, Chet. "Is Broadway Ready for Christopher Durang?" *New York* 15 (March 15, 1982): 40-43. "I was very depressed about how depressed I got," says Durang in this chatty, readable conversation. Discusses his early revues at Harvard University and cabaret pieces for the Yale School of Drama, his collaboration with Sigourney Weaver, and his development as a "fearless satirist."

Savran, David. *In Their Own Words: Contemporary American Playwrights*. New York: Theatre Communications Group, 1988. A brief overview is followed by a protracted interview, centering on biographical history, the development of *The Marriage of Bette and Boo*, and Durang's writing habits. Durang sees advantages to filmmaking (if the playwright's script is not desecrated as with *Beyond Therapy*), including reaching a larger audience and enjoying more permanence.

Weales, Gerald. "American Theater Watch, 1981-1982." *The Georgia Review* 36 (Fall, 1982): 517-526. Weales offers insightful comments on Durang's comic style, but he is not impressed by his structure or depth. Drawn from interviews in *The New York Times*, this article summarizes critics' first reactions to this new voice.

Joseph Marohl,
updated by Thomas J. Taylor and Irene Struthers Rush

Friedrich Dürrenmatt

Born: Konolfingen, Switzerland; January 5, 1921
Died: Neuchâtel, Switzerland; December 14, 1990

Principal drama • *Es steht geschrieben*, pr., pb. 1947 (revised as *Die Wiedertäufer*, pr., pb. 1967; *The Anabaptists*, 1967); *Der Blinde*, pr. 1948, pb. 1960; *Romulus der Grosse*, pr. 1949, second version pr. 1957, pb. 1958, third version pb. 1961 (*Romulus the Great*, 1961); *Die Ehe des Herrn Mississippi*, pr., pb. 1952, second version pb. 1957 (*The Marriage of Mr. Mississippi*, 1958); *Ein Engel kommt nach Babylon*, pr. 1953, pb. 1954, second version pb. 1957 (*An Angel Comes to Babylon*, 1962); *Herkulus und der Stall des Angias*, wr. 1954, pr., pb. 1959 (radio play), pr., pb. 1963 (staged; *Hercules and the Augean Stables*, 1966); *Der Besuch der alten Dame*, pr., pb. 1956 (*The Visit*, 1958); *Komödien I-III*, pb. 1957-1972 (3 volumes); *Frank der Fünfte: Opera einer Privatbank*, pr. 1959, pb. 1960 (libretto; music by Paul Burkhard); *Die Physiker*, pr., pb. 1962 (*The Physicists*, 1963); *Four Plays*, pb. 1964; *Der Meteor*, pr., pb. 1966 (*The Meteor*, 1966); *König Johann*, pr., pb. 1968 (adaptation of William Shakespeare's play *King John*); *Play Strindberg: Totentanz nach August Strindberg*, pr., pb. 1969 (adaptation of August Strindberg's play *The Dance of Death*; *Play Strindberg: The Dance of Death*, 1971); *Porträt eines Planeten*, pr. 1970, revised version pr., pb. 1971 (*Portrait of a Planet*, 1973); *Titus Andronicus*, pr., pb. 1970 (adaptation of Shakespeare's play); *Urfaust*, pr., pb. 1970 (adaptation of Johann Wolfgang von Goethe's play); *Der Mitmacher*, pr. 1973, pb. 1976 (*The Conformer*, 1975); *Die Frist*, pr., pb. 1977; *Achterloo*, pr., pb. 1983

Other literary forms • Friedrich Dürrenmatt was a versatile and prolific writer. In addition to his dramas, he wrote radio plays, stories, novels, detective novels, prose sketches, film scripts, and essays on dramatic theory and on a variety of literary, political, and social topics. He also adapted plays by William Shakespeare, Johann Wolfgang von Goethe, and Georg Büchner.

Achievements • Friedrich Dürrenmatt was the best-known dramatist writing in the German language of his day. In productions of German-language playwrights in West Germany, Austria, and Switzerland, his plays were consistently among the most frequently performed. They have also been widely translated and are a standard part of the repertoire in theaters in the United States and in the other countries of Western Europe. Dürrenmatt was awarded many prizes for his works, including the literature prize of the city of Bern in 1954, the Schiller Prize in 1959, and the Grillparzer Prize of the Austrian Academy of Sciences in 1968. He received honorary doctorates from Temple University, Philadelphia, in 1969, from the University of Nice in 1977, and from the Hebrew University in Jerusalem in 1977. A thirty-volume German-language edition of his works was published in 1980 by Diogenes in Zürich. Dürrenmatt helped to compile this edition, for which he also wrote new versions of some of his plays.

Biography • Friedrich Dürrenmatt was born in Konolfingen in the Canton of Bern, Switzerland, on January 5, 1921. His father, Reinhold, was a Protestant minister. In 1935, the family moved to Bern, where Dürrenmatt was graduated from the Humboldtianum (a high school) in 1941. In 1941 and 1942, Dürrenmatt studied philosophy, literature, and the natural sciences at the universities of Zürich and Bern, but he did not complete his studies. At this time, he wanted to be a painter, not a writer. During these years, Dürrenmatt read works by Franz Kafka (whose influence is evident in Dürrenmatt's early works) and Søren Kierkegaard. He said that his greatest literary experience was reading Aristophanes, whose comedies helped shape Dürrenmatt's own views of comedy. In 1946, Dürrenmatt moved to Basel; he married the actress Lotte Geissler in 1947. For a time, he tried to earn his living as a theater critic for the Bern newspaper *Die Nation* and later, between 1951 and 1953, for the *Zürcher Weltwoche*. In 1948, Dürrenmatt and his family moved to Ligerz on Lake Biel, where they stayed until 1952, when Dürrenmatt bought a house in Neuchâtel and settled there with his family. He died there on December 14, 1990.

Analysis • The world in Friedrich Dürrenmatt's plays is an enigma, peopled by executioners and victims, tyrants and the oppressed, and persecutors and the persecuted. It defies all rational attempts to change it and is dominated by accident and chance. Dürrenmatt believed that the world is indeed ruled by chance—a chance short circuit could launch the nuclear weapons that would destroy the world. The individual feels helpless: Those individuals in Dürrenmatt's works who do try to change the world are doomed to failure. Dürrenmatt was preoccupied with the question of justice (hence his fascination with the detective novel), but justice in his works is an unattainable, distant ideal.

Dürrenmatt believed that comedy is the only form of drama that can express adequately the situation of modern humanity; it alone can reproduce the formless contemporary world. Like his model, Aristophanes, Dürrenmatt was attracted to the social criticism inherent in the comic form. (Satire, he believed, is the only weapon that those in power fear.) In the essay *Theaterprobleme* (1955; *Problems of the Theater*, 1958), he writes that tragedy is no longer possible because it needs a fixed, moral order that does not exist today. In the modern world, tragedy is produced, in Dürrenmatt's view, by universal butchers and acted out by mincing machines. Tragedy presupposes acceptance of responsibility for guilt; without personal responsibility there can be no tragedy. Today, he said, people are no longer individually guilty; rather, they are collectively guilty. Dürrenmatt wrote, however, that the tragic is still possible within comedy; a comic plot for him was concluded only when it has taken the worst possible turn.

Through his comedies, Dürrenmatt lures the audience into confronting reality. He did not provide answers to the problems he depicted in the plays. Instead, he likened his role to that of a midwife—that is, he helps people find their own answers. In his comedies, Dürrenmatt emphasized *Einfälle* (ingenious plots). His plays are not intended to be faithful representations of reality. In all his plays, even when they are set in the past, the focus is on modern-day problems. Dürrenmatt believed that comedy creates the distance that enables people to view the present objectively. An essential part of his comedies is the grotesque. Dürrenmatt said that the logical contradiction of the grotesque makes the spectator laugh, while its ethical contradiction outrages him. He used the grotesque to portray the monstrous, the abyss concealed beneath the veneer of civilization.

Despite his gloomy view of the world, Dürrenmatt always stressed the importance of humor. His plays abound in grotesque and absurd situations, puns, slapstick, gags, verbal ingenuity, and parodies, all of which reflect his vital comic imagination. Humor, according to the playwright, does not mean to approve of the world, but rather to accept it for what it is, as something dubious, and not to despair; it means to accept this dubiousness and carry on.

In "Dramaturgische Überlegungen zu den *Wiedertäufern*" (1967; "Dramaturgical Considerations to *The Anabaptists*"), Dürrenmatt gives possible models of how the English antarctic explorer Robert Scott could be portrayed, and these models aptly summarize his theories of the drama. William Shakespeare, he said, would have shown Scott's downfall to be caused by a tragic flaw in his character. Ambition would have made him blind to the dangers of the region, and jealousy and betrayal by the other members of the expedition would have done the rest to bring about the catastrophe. Bertolt Brecht would have shown the expedition failing because of economic reasons and class thinking. An English education would have prevented Scott from making use of huskies, and in a style befitting his social class, he would have used ponies. Because of the higher cost of the ponies, he would have had to save on the rest of the equipment, which would have caused his downfall. Samuel Beckett would have concentrated only on the end. Changed into a block of ice, Scott would be sitting opposite other blocks of ice, talking without getting an answer from his comrades, not even sure whether he could be heard.

Another possibility, which Dürrenmatt would prefer, would be to show Scott buying provisions for the expedition. While putting the provisions into the cold storage chamber, he would be locked in accidentally, where he would freeze to death. Scott dying far from all help among the glaciers of the Antarctic is a tragic figure; Scott locked into a cold storage chamber through mishap and dying in the middle of a city only a few yards from a busy street is transformed into a comic figure. Dürrenmatt concluded that the worst possible turn that a story can take is the turn to comedy.

Although Dürrenmatt's comedies depict a world ruled by chance in which the individual is powerless, they are not utterly despairing. There are still courageous individuals such as Romulus and Graf Bodo von Übelohe-Zabernsee who try to change the world, even though they ultimately fail. As Dürrenmatt writes in *Problems of the Theater*, one has to accept the world for what it is and keep on living, refusing to give up. His vital comic imagination, evident in all his plays, alleviated his otherwise gloomy view of the world. In an interview with Horst Bienek in 1961, Dürrenmatt stressed the importance of humor in his plays; he said that he can be understood only from the point of view of humor taken seriously.

Common to most of Dürrenmatt's essays on dramatic theory is an emphasis on the practical problems of the theater. He was rarely satisfied with his plays, as the various versions of the plays demonstrate. Each time one of his plays was produced, he said, he saw new possibilities. Many of the problems he encountered in writing his plays could be solved only when he saw his play on the stage. Dürrenmatt protested against dramatic rules formulated by critics; such rules, he said, are of no use to the artist. He wanted his plays to be judged by their theatrical quality, not by how well they fit into some theory of drama.

Romulus the Great • Dürrenmatt's belief that the individual is powerless to change events is shown clearly in *Romulus the Great*, his first Swiss success, which had its premiere on April 25, 1949, in the Stadttheater in Basel. There are five versions of the play. The major change occurs in the second version and is kept in the remaining versions. In the first version, Romulus is portrayed as a cunning, successful politician who realizes his goals. In the subsequent versions, he is no longer victor but victim, a failed and tragic figure who sees that his life has been senseless.

The play depicts the destruction of the Roman Empire by the Germans. The time is the Ides of March, 476 c.e. (another change from the first version), by which Dürrenmatt parodies Shakespeare's *Julius Caesar* (pr. c. 1599-1600) and mocks heroic ideals. The action takes place on Romulus's chicken farm, a grotesque incongruity, because the spectator has entirely different expectations of what the Roman court should be like. Dürrenmatt employs the classical dramatic unities as an ironic contrast to the chaotic world of hens on the stage. The play is called an "unhistorical-historical comedy." The real Romulus was sixteen when he became emperor and was seventeen when he was forced to abdicate. Dürrenmatt's Romulus is an older man. The many anachronisms in the play—the capitalist Cäsar Rupf, for example, who manufactures trousers—show that Dürrenmatt is using the fall of the Roman Empire to analyze modern problems.

Initially, Romulus appears to be lazy and disagreeable. Instead of trying to defend his empire, he sits comfortably eating and drinking. His only concern appears to be the fate of his beloved chickens, whom he has named after different Roman emperors. Yet there are indications that he is not as foolish and despicable as he appears. When Cäsar Rupf demands his daughter Rea's hand as the price for saving Rome, Romulus is the only one who refuses to sell off his daughter in this way.

Romulus is also fully aware of the hopelessness of the situation. He deduces that the Germans will conquer Rome because the chicken named after the German leader Odoaker lays a lot of eggs. Only in the third act does Romulus appear as a wise man who is passionately concerned with justice and humaneness. He has become emperor of Rome only to liquidate his empire. His role, as he sees it, is to judge Rome: Rome has been tyrannical and brutal, and Romulus intends to punish it for its crimes by destroying it. His plan to punish Rome and thereby make the world more humane rests on a delusion: He assumes that the Germans are more humane than the Romans, yet the future ruler Theoderich is just as brutal as the Romans, if not more so. Odoaker, Theoderich's uncle (a man who, like Romulus, is a passionate chicken-raiser), did not come to conquer Rome but to surrender to Romulus in order to save the world from his nephew. Despite their well-intentioned plans, Romulus and Odoaker are helpless; they cannot prevent the rise of another brutal empire under Theoderich.

Most of the other characters are comic figures. They swear that they will fight to the last drop of blood, but they actually flee in haste once the Germans approach. The empress Julia speaks of heroism and sacrifice, but when she flees she is concerned only with saving the imperial dinner service. Her marriage to Romulus has been loveless, since they only married each other for political reasons, to become emperor and empress. Their daughter Rea draws her notions of heroism from the tragic roles she rehearses under the guidance of the actor Phylax, notions that are far removed from the real world.

The cynical art dealer Apollyon has no respect for art; for him it only means money. Cäsar Rupf parodies the political and economic power of the capitalist in the modern world (ironically, the capitalist, not the emperor, is called Caesar, an indication that the capitalist is the real power in the state). Zeno, the Byzantine emperor, is a would-be Machiavelli who has even intrigued against his own family. He is the only one who does not drown during the flight from the Germans: types such as Zeno, Dürrenmatt believed, are indestructible. Only Ämilian, Rea's fiancé, is not a comic figure. Ämilian is captured by the Germans and suffers from their brutality; Romulus sympathizes with him but thinks that his patriotism, heroism, and readiness to sacrifice himself for

Rome are senseless. Romulus is suspicious of all such concepts, since they can be so easily misused by the state to encourage people to commit crimes.

The play is a mixture of tragic and comic elements. The comic aspects include the setting, plot, and characterizations. Dürrenmatt also uses sight gags, such as the chickens that are always underfoot and the comical hiding places of the plotters who want to murder Romulus. Dürrenmatt's mixture of different levels of language—jargon, mercantile language, empty clichés, slang, and extremely formal diction—also has a comic effect. The tragic part of the play is the conclusion. With the best intentions in the world, Romulus has dedicated his life to trying to make the world more just and humane. He believes that he can change the course of history and is willing to sacrifice his own life for this illusion, yet the world under Theoderich will be just as repressive as the Roman Empire, if not more so. At the end, Romulus is not even allowed to die but is pensioned off, thus forced to live with the bitter realization that his whole life has been senseless.

The Marriage of Mr. Mississippi • In *The Marriage of Mr. Mississippi*, Dürrenmatt shows his distrust of all ideologies. The play, which had its premiere in the Münchner Kammer-spiele on March 26, 1952, contributed significantly to establishing Dürrenmatt's reputation in Germany. Like *Romulus the Great*, the play has gone through five versions, and it has also been filmed. The main difference between the first version and subsequent versions is that the earliest version is more surrealistic and contains more religious symbolism while the later versions are more political.

The play takes place in one room. Through one window, a southern landscape with a temple and a cypress tree can be seen; through the other, a northern landscape with a Gothic cathedral and an apple tree. This indicates that Western culture has not managed to synthesize its classical and Christian heritage. The room contains a hodgepodge of furniture from different periods and thereby parodies Western culture. The play (which is structured epically) is not divided into acts and scenes but is broken up by the monologues spoken by the protagonists, who step out of their roles and address the audience. Dürrenmatt uses many exaggerated alienation effects (the characters even step out of their roles to comment on their own behavior). These alienation effects contribute to the play's comic effect and also suggest a parody of Bertolt Brecht. The circular structure of the play (which actually begins with the last scene) indicates that nobody has learned anything—future ideologists will be just as fanatical as the present-day ones.

Three of the main characters represent particular ideologies. The state prosecutor Mississippi believes in absolute justice, which he thinks he has found in the law of Moses (he tries to reintroduce this law in the twentieth century). He is a fanatical reformer who in his search for justice has had 350 executions carried out. Because Mississippi's first wife committed adultery, he poisoned her—a just punishment, he believes, according to Mosaic law. He then sentences himself (as he says) to marry Anastasia, who has poisoned her husband, who was having an affair with Mississippi's wife. Through this loveless marriage, Mississippi hopes to change Anastasia for the better. To accomplish this, he forces her to attend executions. At the end of the play, he wants to know whether she has become a better person; his marriage to her would otherwise be senseless. Through her lie that she has been faithful to him, he is able to preserve his conviction that punishment improves people.

Like Mississippi, Saint-Claude is idealistic and fanatical. He wants to change the world through Marxism, but he is liquidated because his communism differs so radically from the party dogma. Like Mississippi, Saint-Claude believes that the end justifies the means—he does not even know how many people he has killed in his search for a better world.

The third ideologist is Graf Bodo von Übelohe-Zabernsee, who is a Christian. To help people, he has sacrificed his fortune and become a beggar. Although his goals of changing the world are praise-worthy, he is a laughable figure: Everything he tries to do fails. At the end of the play, he appears as Don Quixote, who fights senselessly, if courageously, against the windmills; he refuses, despite his failures, to give up his search for a better world.

In contrast to these ideologues, Anastasia and the politician Diego are pragmatic opportunists. Dürrenmatt said that Anastasia is supposed to symbolize the world. She has no morals or ideals, and she adapts easily to any situation. If it is to her advantage, she cold-bloodedly betrays her lovers. Through her, Dürrenmatt mocks the protagonists' attempts to change the world; like Anastasia, the world is impervious to change. Diego, who adeptly gains power during the play, is a cunning opportunist, like most of the politicians in Dürrenmatt's works.

Dürrenmatt's characteristic humor is especially evident in this play, which is filled with satiric depictions of murders and revolutions. The characters are exaggerated caricatures; through them, Dürrenmatt ridicules ideologies. In addition to the action, setting, and characterizations, Dürrenmatt employs other devices for comic effect. The language of the play is bombastic, and the betrayed husband is a staple of comedy. As in his other plays, Dürrenmatt delights here in using gags: A character jumps suddenly out of a grandfather clock; there is the frequent ritual of coffee drinking, and one never knows whether the coffee is poisoned. Sudden surprises, such as Mississippi's unexpected marriage proposal to Anastasia, also contribute to the comic effects.

Despite the comic elements, the atmosphere of the play is basically gloomy. At the end, Mississippi and Anastasia die (they have poisoned each other's coffee) and Saint-Claude is killed by the party. Yet they all rise up from the dead, and the play could start over again. As in *Romulus the Great* human life is depicted as a senseless, repetitive cycle that can never be changed.

The Visit • The central theme of *The Visit* is the problem of justice. Considered to be Dürrenmatt's masterpiece, *The Visit* had its premiere on January 29, 1956, at the Zürich Schauspielhaus. It is Dürrenmatt's most frequently performed play, and it established his reputation in the United States. *The Visit* takes place in the small town of Güllen (in Swiss dialect, *Güllen* means liquid manure); the time is the present. The town has stagnated economically: The local industries are ruined, the town is bankrupt, and the citizens live on welfare, while the neighboring towns are flourishing. The townspeople blame their misfortunes on Jews, Freemasons, communists—on anyone but themselves. Their town has a cultural heritage, they think, because Goethe stayed the night there, Johannes Brahms composed a quartet there, and Berthold Schwarz invented gunpowder there. For them, culture is merely a series of clichés.

As the play opens, the community is hoping that Claire Zachanassian, the richest woman on earth, who used to live in Güllen, will help them. The festivities to welcome her are, however, hypocritical. When she lived in the town forty-five years ago, they despised her; now their exaggerated praise of her is calculated to manipulate her into giving the town money. Her former lover Alfred Ill is designated to appeal discreetly for her charity; as a reward for this job, he will be made the next mayor. Because Claire comes early, the effects of the welcome are lost. The mayor's speech at the railroad station is drowned by the noise of the trains, and the choir has to be assembled hurriedly. At the dinner, the mayor's speech shows that he knows nothing whatsoever about Claire. Ill must keep on correcting him and, at the end of the speech, even Claire points out that he is wrong.

Claire is a grotesque figure whose right arm and left leg are prostheses to replace the limbs that she lost in accidents. Her retinue is equally grotesque: It consists of her butler; Toby and Roby, gumchewing gangsters whom she has saved from the electric chair; Koby and Loby, who are blind eunuchs; her seventh husband (she marries two more during the play); a black panther in a cage; a large amount of luggage; and a coffin. When she arrives, she asks strange and chilling questions: She asks the gymnast whether he has strangled anyone, the doctor whether he prepares death certificates, the policeman whether he can close his eyes, and the priest whether he consoles those who are condemned to death.

At the meal in her honor, Claire drops her bombshell: She will give five hundred million to the town and five hundred million to be divided evenly among the town's families, on one condition: Someone must kill Alfred Ill. She has come, she says, to buy justice. Forty-five years before, she was expecting Ill's child. Ill refused to acknowledge that he was the father; instead, he bribed two witnesses with schnapps to say that they had slept with her. Claire was forced to leave Güllen; she then became a prostitute, and her child died. Becoming a prostitute, however, made Claire rich because it was in the brothel that she met Zachanassian, a rich oilman. Ill did not want to marry Claire because she was poor; instead, he married Mathilde because she owned a store.

Claire's retinue consists, in part, of those connected with the paternity suit; the butler is the former judge, and Koby and Loby are the witnesses who committed perjury, whom she has relentlessly tracked down and then blinded and castrated. Claire is an emotional cripple whose life has been dedicated to revenge (the local teacher likens her to Medea). It turns out that Claire is responsible for the town's misfortunes: She has bought everything and let it stagnate. The mayor proudly refuses her money. He declares that the community is humane, that it is better to be poor than stained with blood. Claire knows better: She sits on her balcony and waits.

As she expects, the Gülleners cannot withstand temptation. All of them, including the leaders of the community to whom Ill vainly appeals for help, begin to spend freely and incur debts. They all buy yellow shoes; the policeman has a new gold tooth, the mayor a new typewriter; and even the priest has bought a new church bell. The priest tells Ill to flee so that he does not lead them into temptation. Even Ill's family joins in the spending spree: His wife buys a fur coat, his son a new car, and his daughter new clothes. His daughter also starts taking English and French lessons and plays tennis. The townspeople incur debts thoughtlessly, but as their debts mount, their attitude toward Ill changes. They no longer think of him as the most beloved member of the community, as they did when they thought he could persuade Claire to give the town money. Instead, they say that he is guilty of the crime and deserves punishment. When Claire's black panther escapes (Claire used to call Ill her panther), the citizens hunt and kill it, a foreshadowing of Ill's death.

Inevitably, they decide that Ill must die for the "well-being" of the community. A town meeting is called to decide Ill's fate. Before the meeting, the mayor tries to persuade Ill to commit suicide out of love for his community and thus spare the town the guilt of his death. Ill refuses. He says that he has been through hell, watching the debts of the community grow; if they had spared him this fear, he might have killed himself for them. On the surface, the town meeting seems a model of democracy (the press enthusiastically interprets it in that way). The teacher speaks of justice and honor; his noble words are used to mask the common agreement to kill Ill. At the end of the meeting, Ill is killed, presumably by the most muscular member of the gym club in the midst of the Gülleners. His death is termed a heart attack caused by the joy of learning about Claire's gift.

The Gülleners refuse to accept the fact that they killed Ill for money; instead, they see his death as just punishment for his earlier crime. The townspeople are not particularly evil—they had intended to protect Ill. As the teacher notes, however, the temptation was too great. The teacher himself tries hard to resist, yet he tells Ill that he feels himself turning into a murderer; his humanistic training cannot avert this. At the end, Claire has her revenge on the town whose citizens had looked on coldly when she was forced to leave in the midst of winter, forty-five years ago.

During the play, Alfred Ill grows in stature until he almost becomes a tragic figure. At the outset, he is not concerned in the least about his former treatment of Claire. When he is confronted with his past behavior, he begins to see that he was wrong. He gradually accepts his guilt and realizes that he has made Claire what she is. Dürrenmatt remarked that Ill becomes great through his death. He noted that Ill's death is both meaningful and meaningless: Meaningful, because Ill accepts his guilt and grows as a human being; meaningless, because it achieves no moral redemption for the community. In a tragedy by Sophocles, Dürrenmatt said, such a death would have saved the community from the plague. In Güllen, however, Ill's death marks the beginning of the plague—that is, of moral corruption.

Dürrenmatt called his play a tragic comedy. The comedy stems in part from the characters and their actions (the hypocritical welcome prepared for Claire, and the way in which the press misunderstands the town meeting, for example). Dürrenmatt mocked religious and cultural clichés. He satirized the manner in which language disguises meaning (the press thinks that the teacher's speech shows "moral greatness" when in reality the teacher is justifying Ill's murder). The "romantic" meeting of Claire and Ill in the forest parodies German romanticism (the townspeople play the part of trees, and the noise of the woodpecker is made by a citizen tapping on his pipe with a rusty key). Dürrenmatt's parody of the Greek chorus at the end shows his conviction that tragedy is no longer possible.

There are, however, tragic elements in the play. Ill's fate is tragic. He is made into a scapegoat and is sacrificed for money. Dürrenmatt depicts vividly the moral and spiritual corruption of a community in which everything, including "justice," can be bought. The Gülleners do not accept responsibility for Ill's death but enjoy their new wealth, undisturbed by a guilty conscience. In his notes to the play, Dürrenmatt stresses that the Gülleners are people like all of humankind, who would, he implies, act as they did.

Other major works

LONG FICTION: *Der Richter und sein Henker*, 1950 (*The Judge and His Hangman*, 1954); *Der Verdacht*, 1953 (*The Quarry*, 1961); *Grieche sucht Griechin*, 1955 (*Once a Greek . . .*, 1965); *Die Panne*, 1956 (*Traps*, 1960, pb. in England as *A Dangerous Game*); *Das Versprechen: Requiem auf den Kriminalroman*, 1958 (*The Pledge: Requiem for the Detective Novel*, 1959); *Der Sturz*, 1971; *Justiz*, 1985 (*The Execution of Justice*, 1989).

SHORT FICTION: *Die Stadt*, 1952; *Der Auftrag*, 1986 (*The Assignment*, 1988).

RADIO PLAYS: *Der Doppelgänger*, wr. 1946, 1961; *Der Prozess um des Esels Schatten*, wr. 1951, 1958 (based on Christoph Martin Wieland's *Die Abderiten*; *The Jackass*, 1960);

Stranitzky und der Nationalheld, 1952; *Das Unternehmen der Wega,* 1955; *Die Panne,* 1956 (adaptation of his novel; *The Deadly Game,* 1963); *Gesammelte Hörspiele,* 1961.

    NONFICTION: *Theaterprobleme,* 1955 (*Problems of the Theater,* 1958); *Theater-Schriften und Reden,* 1966 (*Writings on Theatre and Drama,* 1976).

    MISCELLANEOUS: *Stoffe I-III,* 1981; *Werkausgabe in 30 Bänden,* 1982 (30 volumes); *Plays and Essays,* 1982.

Bibliography

Arnold, Armin. *Friedrich Dürrenmatt.* New York: F. Ungar, 1972. A biography of Dürrenmatt, covering his life and works. Bibliography.

Chick, Edson M. *Dances of Death: Wedekind, Brecht, Dürrenmatt, and the Satiric Tradition.* Columbia, S.C.: Camden House, 1984. A study of satire in German drama, focusing on the works of Dürrenmatt, Bertolt Brecht, and Frank Wedekind. Bibliography and index.

Crockett, Roger A. *Understanding Friedrich Dürrenmatt.* Columbia: University of South Carolina Press, 1998. A biography and critical analysis of Dürrenmatt that includes analysis of his dramatic works. Bibliography and index.

Jenny, Urs. *Dürrenmatt: A Study of His Plays.* London: Eyre Methuen, 1978. A profile of the dramatist along with critical analyses of his plays. Index.

Tiusanen, Timo. *Dürrenmatt: A Study in Plays, Prose, Theory.* Princeton, N.J.: Princeton University Press, 1977. A critical study of the works and theory of Dürrenmatt. Bibliography and index.

Whitton, Kenneth S. *Dürrenmatt: Reinterpretation in Retrospect.* New York: St. Martin's Press, 1990. An examination of the works and life of Dürrenmatt. Bibliography and indexes.

_____. *The Theater of Friedrich Dürrenmatt: A Study in the Possibility of Freedom.* Atlantic Highlands, N.J.: Humanities Press, 1980. An analysis of the dramatic works of Dürrenmatt, with special emphasis on the subject of liberty. Bibliography and index.

Jennifer Michaels

T. S. Eliot

Born: St. Louis, Missouri; September 26, 1888
Died: London, England; January 4, 1965

Principal drama • *Sweeney Agonistes,* pb. 1932, pr. 1933 (fragment); *The Rock: A Pageant Play,* pr., pb. 1934; *Murder in the Cathedral,* pr., pb. 1935; *The Family Reunion,* pr., pb. 1939; *The Cocktail Party,* pr. 1949, pb. 1950; *The Confidential Clerk,* pr. 1953, pb. 1954; *The Elder Statesman,* pr. 1958, pb. 1959; *Collected Plays,* pb. 1962

Other literary forms • In addition to being a successful liturgical dramatist, T. S. Eliot was an editor, an essayist, and a poet of great distinction. He became assistant editor of *The Egoist* in 1917 and founded *The Criterion* in 1922, serving as editor of the latter from then until its demise in 1939. As an essayist, Eliot explored the place of modern literature with regard to tradition, discussed the relationship between literature and ethics, and emphasized the need for a modern idiom. Among his extremely influential collections of essays are *The Sacred Wood* (1920) and *After Strange Gods* (1934), both dealing with the individual's debt to tradition, the latter propounding a moral standpoint; *The Use of Poetry and the Use of Criticism* (1933); and *On Poetry and Poets* (1957). In *For Lancelot Andrewes* (1928) and *The Idea of a Christian Society* (1939), the impact of his 1927 confirmation in the Church of England on his life and letters is particularly evident.

Eliot's poetry has had a greater influence, not only in England and the United States but also in world literature, than that of any of his contemporaries. *Prufrock and Other Observations* (1917), *Poems* (1919; printed by Leonard and Virginia Woolf), and *The Waste Land* (1922) illustrate his growing despair over personal problems as well as modern social trends. *Ash Wednesday* (1930) and *Four Quartets* (1943), produced following his confirmation, are meditations concerning spiritual illumination. In *Old Possum's Book of Practical Cats* (1939), Eliot demonstrated his talent for writing comic verse with equal success. That work has been reprinted widely in many formats and even, in 1983, provided the basis for a Tony Award-winning musical, *Cats.*

Achievements • Any assessment of T. S. Eliot's achievements as a dramatist must be made in the light of his own comments about the relationship between past and present, between "tradition and the individual talent." For Eliot, a new work of art causes a rearrangement of the ideal, preexisting order. As Carol Smith points out, his comments about "historical perspective" are not innovative; what is new is his idea that the "given" order defines the artist, whose chief responsibility is to subsume his individual talent as part of the progress of literary history. Eliot's dramatic works are therefore "classical" in the altered sense of his attempting to employ a modern idiom in the service of the imperatives of history, both literary and religious.

One of Eliot's achievements was the presentation of liturgical drama on the modern stage to a commercial audience. His endeavor in this regard began with his writing both a pageant, *The Rock,* and a ritual drama, *Murder in the Cathedral,* for the limited audiences provided respectively by a benefit to promote church building in London and the Canterbury Festival, audiences preconditioned to dramas of redemption. (*Sweeney Agonistes,* an experimental fragment, was not produced until 1933.) With his later

257

plays, however, Eliot undertook the task of convincing secular audiences that traditional ideas about redemption were viable within a modern framework.

The Family Reunion, his first full-length experiment in turning drawing-room comedy into religious fable, was not immediately successful; as his close friend and adviser
Elliott Martin Browne reports, critics found the work mixed—the most negative reviews said that the play was characterized by "lifeless smoothness" and "difficulty" and
was guaranteed to leave the audience "vexed and exhausted." Some modern critics,
however, such as Eliot's biographer T. S. Matthews, find the play "extraordinary, . . .
far superior to his later, 'better made' plays." *The Cocktail Party,* on the other hand, was
better received; even those who wrote negative reviews acknowledged that the production bordered on greatness. Browne notes that similar comments were made about
The Confidential Clerk, although critical reception was influenced by the general belief
that Eliot's attempt "to combine the esoteric with the entertaining" was no longer innovative. *The Elder Statesman,* Browne believes, was overinterpreted by gossipmongers
intent on reading the play in the light of Eliot's marriage to his secretary, Valerie
Fletcher, the previous year.

Quite aside from their mixed commercial appeal, Eliot's plays illustrate his critical
theories not only about the connection between drama and poetry but also about the
failure of realistic theater. Eliot's Aristotelian viewpoint prompted him to criticize
modern drama for its lack of rhythm. For Eliot, poetry was more than a distraction,
more than an attempt to prettify dramatic diction. Never extrinsic to the action, poetry
provides an underlying musical pat-
tern that strengthens the audience's
response. The presence of such an
abstract pattern suggests, as Eliot
says in "Four Elizabethan Dramatists" (written in 1924), that the great
vice in English drama is realism, for
it detracts from the unity of the play.
As his large essay *Poetry and Drama*
(1951) makes clear, such unity is more
than a technical matter of form and
content, for the literary is hand-
maiden to the religious. Eliot's ideal
vision of verse drama is one in which
"a design of human action and of
words" is perpetuated in such a way
that the connection between the
everyday world and the universal
design is illustrated; such a drama,
Eliot believed, would provide the
proper feeling of "reconciliation"
to lead the audience to a spiritual
awakening.

Biography • Thomas Stearns Eliot
was born on September 26, 1888, in
St. Louis, Missouri. His celebrated
statement of his allegiances in *For*

(© The Nobel Foundation)

Lancelot Andrewes—"classicist in literature, royalist in politics, and Anglo-Catholic in religion"—ran counter to the family tradition of Unitarianism; his grandfather, William Greenleaf Eliot, descendant of a pastor of Boston's Old North Church, established the Unitarian Church of the Messiah in St. Louis. Eliot's father himself was a renegade, refusing the ministry for what was eventually the presidency of the Hydraulic-Press Brick Company. His mother, Charlotte Stearns, was a descendant of one of the judges in the Salem witch trials. An intellectual woman, Stearns began a career as a schoolteacher and eventually became active in children's causes.

As Matthews notes, the family saying "*Tace et fac* ('Shut up and get on with it')" suggests a household in which indulgence gave way to duty. As a child, Eliot was considered delicate but precocious. At Smith Academy, he took the Latin prize and excelled in English. Deemed too young at seventeen to enter Harvard, he was sent first to Milton Academy. At Harvard, he was conservative and studious. He became an editor of the *Advocate*, a literary magazine, but his decision to accelerate his undergraduate work to pursue a master's degree left him small leisure for friends, such as Conrad Aiken. Important influences during his college years included his discovery of Arthur Symons's *The Symbolist Movement in Literature* (1899), a book that led him to imitate the verse of Jules Laforgue; his love for Elizabethan drama; and, finally, his acquaintance with Irving Babbitt, the leader of the New Humanism, an anti-Romantic movement that stressed the ethical nature of experience. Certainly, Babbitt's influence led Eliot to spend one of his graduate years in France, where, resisting the attractive Bohemianism open to a writer of his talents, he decided to pursue a degree in philosophy at Harvard, where he came under the influence of Bertrand Russell.

The fellowship that Harvard awarded Eliot in 1914 proved to alter the course of his life. Enrolled in Merton College, at Oxford, he began his long friendship with Ezra Pound, under whose aegis Eliot published "The Love Song of J. Alfred Prufrock" in *Poetry* magazine in 1915. In England, Eliot met and married his first wife, Vivienne Haigh-Wood. Described as a beautiful and entrancing individual, she nevertheless suffered from a nervous disability that had devastating emotional effects. In increasing financial difficulty, Eliot worked as an usher at a boys' school, an employee at Lloyd's Bank, a freelance journalist, and an assistant editor of *The Egoist*.

Eliot enjoyed many fruitful friendships, among them those with Bertrand Russell, Virginia Woolf, and I. A. Richards. From 1921 to 1925, when he was publishing reviews in the *Times Literary Supplement*, Eliot's health deteriorated; the unforeseen result of an enforced vacation was *The Waste Land*. In 1922, he founded *The Criterion*, a literary quarterly that was sponsored financially by Lady Rothermere. After a long period of ill health and self-doubt, he joined the Anglican Church. His biographer suggests a number of reasons for the decision, including certain social and "aesthetic" attractions of this particular denomination, the authoritarian cast of the Church, and the long Church "pedigree" that satisfied Eliot's belief in the importance of tradition. His decision to become a British citizen followed soon thereafter, partly, Matthews believes, because Eliot felt that in the United States "the aristocratic tradition of culture was dead."

Eliot's 1932 return to his native land was, like his first journey away, a new start, for it began his separation from Vivienne, for whom he had become more nurse than husband. To be sure, the attempt to escape from her neurotic persecution made his middle years unhappy ones, years complicated further by the exigencies of World War II. Despite such distractions, however, these were the years in which Eliot began his career as a playwright.

Quite clearly, Eliot's religious conversion provided the themes not only for his poetry but also for his plays. Events in Eliot's personal life, including the death of his es-
tranged wife in 1947, are also reflected in his plays. Conceivably, his sense of alienation and guilt found its way into the portrait of Harry, the putative wife-killer in *The
Family Reunion*, as well as into the depiction of the dreary marriage faced by the
Chamberlaynes in *The Cocktail Party*. Other elements are identifiable, such as the figure of Agatha in *The Family Reunion*; the only one to understand Harry's spiritual
search thoroughly, Agatha is said to be based on Emily Hale, Eliot's longtime friend,
who had been a schoolmistress at Scripps College, Smith College, and Abbot Academy. Emily was as shocked by Eliot's second, clandestine, marriage as she was by his
first; at the age of sixty-nine, Eliot married Valerie Fletcher, his secretary.

Before the arrival of that emotional security, however, Eliot had achieved other triumphs. He was awarded the Nobel Prize in 1948, and, in the same year, received the
British Empire's Order of Merit. While he was drafting *The Cocktail Party*, he traveled
to Princeton, New Jersey, to accept a fellowship at the Institute for Advanced Study.
His last two plays—*The Confidential Clerk* and *The Elder Statesman*—were not as popular
as *The Cocktail Party*; they do, however, show an increasing understanding of the way in
which human relationships may be ameliorated. Indeed, in *The Elder Statesman*, the
love experienced by Monica and Charles seems a reflection of the happiness that Eliot
himself found with his second wife. For the first time in his dramatic writing, the possibility of redemption through human love is adequately broached. Indeed, for the first
time, human love seems a model of divine love rather than, as Celia observes in *The
Cocktail Party*, a distraction or a second-best choice.

On January 4, 1965, Eliot died in London. At his request, his ashes repose at East
Coker, the birthplace of his ancestors and the titular locale of one of the *Four Quartets*;
the memorial plaque in the Poets' Corner at Westminster Abbey was placed on January 4, 1967.

Analysis • T. S. Eliot's conservative dramaturgy is clearly expressed in his 1928 essay
"Dialogue on Dramatic Poetry" in which he suggests that "genuine drama" displays "a
tension between liturgy and realism." To be sure, Eliot differed sharply from the advocates of Ibsenite realism, maintaining throughout his career that untrammeled realism
operating outside the limitations of art did not produce classic harmony. In consequence, Eliot relied on a number of traditional forms, including the Mass and Greek
drama. On the other hand, he created new verse forms, convinced that traditional
forms such as Shakespearean blank verse would be inadequate to express modern experience. In *Sweeney Agonistes*, he made use of the rhythms of vaudeville, believing that
such robust entertainment contained the seeds of a popular drama of high artistic quality, comparable to the achievements of the great Elizabethan and Jacobean playwrights.

Modern religious drama, Eliot believed, "should be able to hold the interest, to
arouse the excitement, of people who are not religious." Redemption is the theme of
all of his plays, a theme explored on different levels. For example, Becket's understanding, in *Murder in the Cathedral*, that salvation is a willing submission to a larger pattern is developed and tempered in the later social comedies.

In almost all of his plays, Eliot presents characters on a continuum of spiritual understanding, including the martyr or saint figure, the "guardians" (the spiritual advisers), the common folk (capable of limited perception or at least of accommodation),
and the uncomprehending. In *The Family Reunion* and *The Cocktail Party*, respectively,

Harry and Celia experience a sense of having sinned and the desire to atone. Celia's illumination is also characterized by a sense of having failed another person. Her martyrdom is correspondingly more moving, not because it is graphically described, but because it seems inexorable.

In *The Confidential Clerk*, Colby, whose search for a human father parallels his desire for a divine one, experiences his éclaircissement as a private moment in a garden and works out his salvation as an organist. In the aforementioned plays, guardian figures abound. Agatha councils Harry to follow attendant Eumenides if he wishes to expiate the family curse; Julia, Alex, and Reilly not only show Celia the way to enlightenment but reinstate the Chamberlaynes' marriage; the retired valet Eggerson offers Colby a job as an organist and predicts his eventual entry into holy orders. Eliot's last play, *The Elder Statesman*, is the only one in which human love is an adequate guide to divine love; in that sense, Monica, in her affection for her fiancé and in her unwavering love for her father despite his faults, is a guardian figure.

A development in the characterization of the common people may be seen as well. Because of their foolishness or their attempt to dominate, all of Harry's relatives seem lost to perceptiveness, except, perhaps, for his Uncle Charles, who begins to feel "That there is something I *could* understand, if I were told it." A wider hope is held out in *The Cocktail Party*, for while not all may follow Celia's path, the Chamberlaynes learn to accept the "good life" that is available to them, and even Peter, in love with Celia, may learn to "see" through the same qualities that make him a film producer. Again, while Colby withdraws from the family circle, those who remain—no matter how superficially mismatched—engage in a communion characterized most of all by a desire to understand and to love. Finally, in *The Elder Statesman*, Eliot achieves a balance in his continuum of characters, for he presents the salvation of the Calvertons by love as well as the possibility that, through Monica, Michael might return to find his self-identity, while both Gomez and Mrs. Carghill become lost souls as they pursue their revenge.

Murder in the Cathedral • Although originally produced for the Canterbury Festival, *Murder in the Cathedral* has achieved the most lasting interest of all Eliot's plays. It is a psychological and historical exploration of martyrdom that speaks directly not only to current disputes about the interconnection between church and state but also to the ever-present contemporary threat of assassination. It is Eliot's most successful attempt to adapt verse forms to drama, particularly in the speeches of the Chorus, whose function, Eliot believed, was to interpret the action to the viewers and to strengthen the impact of the action by reflecting its effects. In the speeches of the Knights and Templers (characters doubled when the play is staged) as well, attitudes are mirrored by poetic cadence—a fine example of form following content. As Grover Smith notes, the title itself, while commercially attractive, is somewhat misleading, as were other possibilities Eliot considered, among them "The Archbishop Murder Case" and "Fear in the Way," for *Murder in the Cathedral* is less a whodunit than an attempt to startle the unimpassioned believer into percipience and the nonbeliever into understanding.

Like Eliot's first venture into ritualistic drama, *The Rock*, *Murder in the Cathedral* is based on an actual event, the martyrdom of Thomas à Becket in the year 1170 in the chapel of Saint Benedict in Canterbury Cathedral. Unlike *The Rock*, however, which is a spectacle play delineating the history of the Church, *Murder in the Cathedral* is focused on a dramatic event of great intensity. The play traces the spiritual education of Thomas, whose greatest temptation is self-aggrandizement; the education of the Chorus, who seek to escape both suffering and salvation; and the education of the Knights and the audience, whose worldliness implicates them jointly in the assassination.

Eliot's addition of a Fourth Tempter to Becket's "trial" in part 1 is crucial. The first three tempters are expected and easily rejected. The first, who offers sensual pleasures, resigns Becket to "the pleasures of [his] higher vices." One such vice is offered by the Second Tempter: "Temporal power, to build a good world," power that requires submission to secular law. Becket, who rejects this exercise in intelligent self-interest, also rejects the Third Tempter's offer of a coalition with the barons to overthrow the King; such an action would bestialize Becket, make him "a wolf among wolves."

The Fourth Tempter is, however, not so easily answered, for he brings the temptation of spiritual power through martyrdom. Counseling the archbishop to seek death, he offers as its rewards the joy of wielding power over eternal life and death, the adulation of the masses, the richness of heavenly grandeur, and, finally, the sweetness of revenge, for Becket will then be able to look down and see his "persecutors, in timeless torment."

For Becket, the only way to escape the damning effects of his own spiritual pride is to give up self-will so that he may become part of a larger pattern. As Grover Smith notes, the counsel that Becket gives to the Chorus (ironically quoted to him by the Fourth Tempter) has its roots in Aristotle's image of the still point—on a wheel, for exaample—as the source of action:

> You know and do not know, that acting is suffering,
> And suffering action. Neither does the actor suffer
> Nor the patient act. But both are fixed
> In an eternal action, an eternal patience
> To which all must consent that it may be willed
> And which all must suffer that they may will it,
> That the pattern may subsist, that the wheel may
>   turn and still
> Be forever still.

In theological terms, Eliot is suggesting that the nature of the relationship between action and suffering depends on the conception of God as the first mover, just as the still point is centered in the wheel. Becket, in willing martyrdom, has substituted his will for God's will. When he understands that he was doing the right deed for the wrong reason, he enters the ideal relationship between human beings and God—one of submission, of a person's consent to be an instrument. In that condition of bringing one's will into conformity with that of God, one paradoxically does not suffer, for one acts as an instrument; neither does one act, for one gives up will.

For the women whose barren lives are spent among small deeds, Becket becomes a new center; with their wills in conformity to his, they too become the instruments of God's will, even as the Knights are in the murder of Becket. For Grover Smith, whereas Becket's language is abstract and passionless, his decision hidden in difficult, paradoxical words, that of the women is overtly sensual; for Carol Smith, such language shows that the women have accepted their "Christian responsibility." The women's unwilling participation in the event is a violent disturbance of their willed attitude of noninterference; through Becket, they are touched not only by life but also by death. The key is in the homily delivered by Becket as an interlude in the play, a sermon in which he speaks of an attitude of mourning and rejoicing in martyrdom. Before his death, he warns the women that their joy will come only "when the figure of God's purpose is made complete"—when, in other words, they understand that his martyrdom is the answer to their despair.

The prose in which the Knights speak after the murder has taken place is to some critics jarring, but Eliot deliberately made it so; a far graver criticism is that it is either amusing, or misleading, insofar as the emphasis on the "contest . . . between brute power and resigned holiness" is shifted to an argument about Church and State. Jones disagrees; for him, the prose shakes the audience's sanctimonious complacency. The arguments offered by the Knights are familiar rationalizations. The Second Knight pleads disinterested duty as his reason for the murder, the Third that "violence is the only way in which social justice can be secured," and the Fourth that, since Becket's overweening egotism prompted the murder, the correct "verdict" is "Suicide while of Unsound Mind." The final words of the Chorus, spoken to a Te Deum in the background, serve as a corrective to any distorted view, for they, the "type of common man," not only accept responsibility for "the sin of the world" but also acknowledge that human consciousness is an affirmation of the ultimate design, of which they have willingly become a part.

The Family Reunion • Produced in March, 1939, *The Family Reunion* was considerably less successful than Eliot's first full-length play, partly because he was attempting to appeal to a secular audience; moreover, his evocation of the Aeschylean Eumenides—the Furies—as a group of well-dressed aunts and uncles and his deliberate blurring of the hero's motives and fate contribute to the weakness of the play. Various critics have traced the antecedents of *The Family Reunion*, including Henry James's "The Jolly Corner" (1908), William Shakespeare's *Hamlet, Prince of Denmark* (pr. c. 1600-1601), and Aeschylus's *Oresteia* (458 B.C.E.; English translation, 1777), sources discussed thoroughly by Grover Smith and David Jones. Eliot attempted to wed the classical and the modern, believing that poetry brought into the audience's world would help to heal social disintegration.

The two levels of the play—the realistic and the spiritual—are not always mutually illuminating. On the surface, the play depicts the homecoming of Harry, Lord Monchensey, to Wishwood, the family mansion that his mother, Amy, has maintained, unchanged, for his benefit. Harry, convinced that he murdered his wife a year ago, is unable to agree with the conventional wishes of his mother or of his featherheaded aunts, Ivy and Violet, or of his blundering uncles, Gerald and Charles. On another level, he arrives convinced that he is pursued by the Furies, only to learn from his Aunt Agatha that to *follow* the "bright angels" is the way to redemption through suffering.

The Family Reunion reflects Eliot's recurring preoccupation with original sin. Although Harry's own uncertainty about his responsibility for his wife's death may be unsettling to the audience, the point is surely that for Eliot the *fact* is irrelevant; what is important is that Harry (and Eliot, because of his own marital situation) feels guilty about the wish itself. Indeed, Harry seems to be burdened with a family curse that he must expiate. As Agatha tells him, his father wanted to murder Harry's mother but was prevented from doing so by Agatha, who loved him; Harry has lived to reenact his father's will. Harry's guilt thus is shifted to the larger framework of the *felix culpa*, or fortunate fall.

Again, Harry's character is so unappealing that to call him, as Agatha does, "the consciousness of your unhappy family,/ Its bird sent flying through the purgatorial fire," is not acceptable on the metaphoric level. His rudeness and abrupt repudiation of his mother (which leads to her death) conspire against the suggestion that he is to become a Christian mystic or saint—that, as Agatha says, he is destined for "broken stones/ That lie, fang up" or that, as he says, he is headed for "A stony sanctuary and a primitive altar" or "A care over lives of humble people."

The transformation of the Eumenides from "hounds of hell" to "bright angels" is justified not only by the *Oresteia* of Aeschylus but also by the idea, developed in *Murder in the Cathedral,* that suffering precedes atonement; on a psychological level, however, the idea poses problems. As the evocation of the watchful eyes possessed by both mother and wife, the Eumenides suggest a developing Oedipus complex; interpreted by Agatha as helpful guardians, they suggest a childish transference of affection to Agatha, an affection that is at once incestuous and spiritual. Mary, Harry's childhood sweetheart, simply presents the desired but now impossible fulfillment of human love. For Agatha, however, and eventually for Harry, the Eumenides posit a frontier beyond which all experience is private, save that it is a confrontation between the human spirit and the divine, a purgatorial confrontation under "the judicial sun/ Of the final eye."

In the final analysis, the play is not a triumph of comedy—or of tragedy. With Amy dead, Harry's father has ironically gotten his wish; Wishwood is to be ceded to Harry's brother John, about whom Harry says brutally, "A minor trouble like a concussion/ Cannot make very much difference to John." In the ritualistic chorus performed by Agatha and Mary at the end of the play, Eliot emphasizes the inexorability of the curse around which he has built his plot as well as the possibility of salvation. What is lacking is an explanation of the nature of expiation.

The Cocktail Party • First produced for the 1949 Edinburgh Festival, *The Cocktail Party* is, like *The Family Reunion,* an attempt to express modern concerns in the guise of ritualistic drama. In this case, however, Eliot depends on Euripides' *Alkēstis* (438 B.C.E.; *Alcestis,* 1781) as his classical antecedent, wisely eliminating the embodiment of the Furies that proved to be so dramatically disruptive. In one view, he effectively reproduced the sophisticated patois of cocktail-party chatter to distract his secular audience from the play's theological "underpattern." Some critics suggest that the comic approach was a deliberate attempt at a reversal in which "surfaces" become "depths" and the comic resolution an indication of divine order.

A number of this play's themes are taken from Eliot's earlier plays. There is a reunion, although not in the sense of Harry Monchensey's mythopoeic experience, for the Chamberlaynes literally as well as figuratively re-create their marriage; again, there is the figure of the mystic, this time, however, a more convincing one, in Celia; moreover, there is a guardian, Reilly, who achieves expressed validity in his role as a psychologist. Finally, and perhaps most important, there is a sense that spiritual illumination is not restricted, except in its intensity, to martyr figures.

Superficially, the plot is familiar drawing-room comedy, entailing a series of love affairs. Edward's wife, Lavinia, has inexplicably left him; Peter Quilpe, a filmmaker, is in love with Celia Coplestone, Edward's mistress, while Lavinia is in love with Peter. Comic relief is provided by the scatter-brained Julia Shuttlethwaite, the peripatetic Alexander MacColgie Gibbs, and Sir Henry Harcourt-Reilly, an enigmatic, gin-swilling psychologist. As in the well-made play, the plot revolves around a secret: Julia and Alex have conspired with Reilly to reinvigorate the Chamberlaynes' marriage, in an association called variously "the Christian conspiracy" or, as Jones puts it, "the Community of Christians."

The marital difficulties would be familiar to the audience, but not Eliot's interpretation of them. Having confused desire with affection in his attachment to Celia, Edward must face the fact that he is essentially unloving, whereas Lavinia is by nature unlovable: Thus, Eliot suggests, they are perfectly matched. In addition, Edward, who is indecisive, must learn to face the consequences of making a decision—in this case, the decision that Lavinia should return to him. What he realizes is that her return is tantamount to inviting the angel of destruction into his life.

Possessed by the belief that he is suffering "the death of the spirit," that he can live neither with the role Lavinia imposes on him nor without it, Edward goes to Reilly for help. The language that this counselor uses indicates his role of spiritual guardianship. He speaks of Edward's "long journey" but refuses to send him to his "sanatorium," for to do so would be to abandon him to the "devils" that feast on the "shadow of desires of desires." Instead, he brings him face to face with Lavinia to convince him that the unloving and the unlovable should make the best of a bad job—or, in terms of the blessing he administers, must "work out [their] salvation with diligence." Carol Smith's review of Christian mysticism as a background to the play makes clear that Reilly encourages the Chamberlaynes to follow the "Affirmative Way," in which "all created things are to be accepted in love as images of the Divine," rather than the "Negative Way," which is characterized by detachment from "the love of all things."

Reilly's interview with Celia is substantially different, for while she, like Edward, complains of an awareness of solitude, she focuses less on herself than on a perception that loneliness is the human condition and that communication is therefore illusory. She also complains, unlike Edward, of a sense of sin, of a feeling that she must atone for having failed "someone, or something, outside." She attributes her failure to a self-willed fantasy: In Edward, she loved only a figment of her imagination. Unlike Edward, she has had a vision of the Godhead, an ecstatic exaltation "of loving in the spirit." It is this vision that she chooses to follow, although Reilly emphasizes that it is an unknown way, a blind journey, a way to being "transhumanized," the "way of illumination." Her way, the "Negative Way" of mysticism, culminates in her crucifixion "very near an ant-hill" in the jungles of Kinkanja.

What Eliot offers in *The Cocktail Party* is a series of gradations of spiritual understanding, gradations that were not presented adequately in *The Family Reunion*. Celia's way of illumination is undoubtedly more believable because her developing perceptions are not expressed in sibylline pronouncements; likewise, the guardians are given authenticity by the comic role their very eccentricity engenders. The common way, represented by the Chamberlaynes, is not appealing but understandable, and, as Reilly says, "In a world of lunacy,/ Violence, stupidity, greed . . . it is a good life." Finally, Peter Quilpe, shocked by the news of Celia's death, comes to understand that he had been loving only the image he had created of her. As Grover Smith comments, "the kind of comedy Eliot devised has been compared generically by some critics to Dante's *Commedia*, for in it the characters either fulfill their greatest potentialities or else are set firmly on the way toward doing so."

The Confidential Clerk • In Eliot's sixth major play, *The Confidential Clerk*, the theme of redemption is again explored, this time through a dependence on Euripides' *Iōn* (c. 411 B.C.E.; *Ion*, 1781), a play that deals with hidden paternity. Eliot examines the sense of aloneness expressed so effectively by Celia, and the human penchant for recreating other individuals to conform with one's own desires. In addition, Eliot shows the path that a mystical vocation may take.

Denis Donoghue pertinently remarks that Eliot solved the "false tone" occasioned by Celia's death by shifting his terms: Illumination becomes Art, and the worldly way, Commerce, both terms that avoid doctrinal problems. Metaphorically, an escape into Art (illumination) becomes an escape into a garden, one in which real communication is possible. So it is for the musical Colby Simpkins, about whom Lucasta Angel, Sir Claude Mulhammer's illegitimate daughter, notes that he has his "own world." Taken in by Sir Claude as his presumptive son, Colby is immediately claimed by Lady Elizabeth Mulhammer, a fashionable reincarnation of Julia Shuttlethwaite, as the lost son of her former lover, a poet.

Each character imagines Colby in terms of personal wish-fulfillment. To Colby, the failed musician, Sir Claude reveals his early yearnings to be a sculptor and his decision to follow in the family business. For Sir Claude, the act of creation is "a world where the form is the reality" and an "escape into living" from an illusory world. Indeed, for Sir Claude, life is a constant compromise, just as it is for the Chamberlaynes, a constant coping with two worlds, neither of which offers perfect fulfillment. It is, as he says, a substitute for religion.

Despite this analogy, Colby is unwilling to accept Sir Claude as a father. Colby expresses his yearning for an ideal father in words that may be read for their religious connotation. He wishes, as he says, to have a father "Whom I had never known and wouldn't know now/ . . . whom I could get to know/ Only by report, by documents," a father, he continues, "whose life I could in some way perpetuate/ By being the person he would have liked to be." The analogues to Christ are unmistakable. The revelation that Colby is actually the son of Herbert Guzzard, a "disappointed musician," suggesting a harmony between the mystical and the commonplace that is seldom achieved in *The Family Reunion*, adds to the success of *The Confidential Clerk*.

Like Celia, Colby chooses a life of service, if one more prosaic than joining a nursing order and perishing in Kinkanja. He acknowledges his inheritance by becoming the organist at a small church (rather than continuing to live on Sir Claude's generosity, for Sir Claude is eager to think of Colby as one with whom he shared disillusionment); Eggerson, the retired confidential clerk—who, as Jones notes, was for Eliot "'the only *developed* Christian in the play'"—suggests that Colby will enter the ministry.

The play presents a succession of individuals who are reaching out after Colby, essentially as a way of gratifying their own expectations. It is only, however, when the audience knows the secret of Colby's birth that many of the early conversations make sense; consequently, the play is weak in its early acts. Despite this criticism, *The Confidential Clerk* offered Eliot's most convincing and optimistic treatment to that time of the possibility of human communion, pointing the way to his hopeful treatment of human love in his last play, *The Elder Statesman*. It seems less important that Lady Elizabeth's up-to-date spiritualism, her substitute for religion, fails her in her perception that Colby is her son than that she is willing to accept as her real offspring B. Kaghan, a brash, successful businessman, a diamond in the rough. Again, it seems less important that Sir Claude has lost his desired son than that, in the end, he emotionally accepts Lucasta as a daughter. Indeed, the note that Eliot strikes—that, as the Mulhammers say, they are "to try to understand our children" and that both Lucasta and B. Kaghan desire to "mean something" to their newfound parents—is exceptionally conciliatory and suggestive of greater amelioration in the "good life" than is posited in the earlier plays.

The Elder Statesman • Eliot's final play, *The Elder Statesman*, is an extension not only of the idea that one must come to terms with his past, just as Harry Monchensey and the Mulhammers attempt to do, but also that this is, indeed, the only way to redemption. Such atonement on the part of Lord Claverton is presented in words that are less mystical than prosaic; indeed, his past is populated by the blackmailers Federico Gomez, who seeks to capitalize on his knowledge that Lord Calverton had run over a dead man after a drinking party, and Mrs. Carghill, who, as the actress Maisie Montjoy, possesses incriminating love letters. Certainly Calverton's immediate problem—that of being a terminally ill, newly retired man of consequence, suffering from the loneliness of "sitting in an empty waiting room"—is one with which the audience can quickly identify.

As Jones points out, *The Elder Statesman* has a "naturalistic surface": The more plays Eliot wrote, the more muted the spiritual enlightenment became, so that eventually the social relationships became primary. Carol Smith, on the other hand, sees the play as a culmination of Eliot's development of the "dramatic fable" that serves as a "transparent mask" for permanent, religious meanings.

The corollary to Calverton's loneliness takes on sinister (and existential) connotations when it is present in Gomez, who has adopted a new name and a new country after a prison sentence. As he says, he has returned to face Lord Calverton in order to find the self he left behind. Gomez charges Calverton with "creating him," with engineering his tastes and altering his career. In revenge, he threatens to make others see Calverton for what he really is—a murderer and a hypocrite. Calverton, in fact, has created his own ghosts by dominating the lives of others. The lesson that he must take responsibility for meddling in others' lives is reinforced by his realization that he is no better than those he created.

Both Jones and Carol Smith point out that Calverton's and Gomez's careers parallel each other in that their ethical standards merely mirror the society of which they are a part and in that both have changed identities, the "statesman" Dick Ferry having adopted his wife's name for its impressiveness and the Oxford student having changed his name to blend into his new country. Gomez's desire to amalgamate his two personalities and his desire for revenge are satisfied when he meets Calverton's ne'er-do-well son Michael, to whom he offers the lure of easy money and a new identity. Gomez is, in short, reenacting Calverton's earlier role of tempter.

The other ghost that Calverton must face—Maisie Montjoy, known as Mrs. Carghill—has also been "created" by him. As his mistress, who sued him for breach of promise, she was irrevocably affected by his offer of and withdrawal of love. Indeed, their relationship is a parody of the fruitful, redeeming love that comes to Monica Calverton and Charles Hemington. Like Gomez, Mrs. Carghill has gone through a series of name changes reflecting a progressive confusion in identity. Like him, she resorts to blackmail to gain companionship, insisting on what Jones calls the "uncomfortable Christian conception of a man and a woman becoming the inseparable unity of 'one flesh,'" and like him, she seeks revenge by encouraging the weak-willed Michael to emigrate to South America.

The cure that Eliot proposes for Calverton's loneliness, for his series of facades, and for his discomfort with the past—love—also exorcises his ghosts by allowing him to face them. Accompanying that love is the relinquishment of power; understanding that Michael is a free agent, Calverton recognizes that he has been trying to dominate his son's choice of friends, lifestyle, and career. If Michael is a free agent, then Gomez and Carghill's revenge has lost its sting, because Calverton is no longer responsible for his son's actions.

The model for the cure is the love shared by Monica and Charles, a love that creates a new, viable personage out of the you and the me. Unlike the kind of false images projected by Calverton's desire to dominate, the new individual is created by a submission of wills, a voluntary merging of the selves. It is, in short, a model of divine love. Eliot thus points to an achievable salvation unspoiled by artificial dramatic techniques such as the evocation of the Eumenides or the awkward ritualistic libation in *The Cocktail Party.*

Although Jones notes that for one reviewer, at least, the language of the lovers is abstract and lacking in evocative details, Calverton's illumination is clearly expressed: As Calverton says, if an individual is willing to confess everything to even one person—willing, that is, to appear without his mask—"Then he loves that person, and his love will save him." Calverton further realizes that his wish to dominate his children arises not from love but from the desire to foist on them an image so that he "could believe in [his] own pretences." At peace with himself and with Monica, who has promised to remember Michael as he really is so that he may one day shed his mask and return to his real self, Calverton approaches death with serenity: "It is worth dying," he says, "to find out what life is."

Other major works

POETRY: "The Love Song of J. Alfred Prufrock," 1915; *Prufrock and Other Observations,* 1917; *Poems,* 1919; *Ara Vos Prec,* 1920; *The Waste Land,* 1922; *Poems, 1909-1925,* 1925; *Ash Wednesday,* 1930; *Triumphal March,* 1931; *Sweeney Agonistes,* 1932; *Words for Music,* 1934; *Collected Poems, 1909-1935,* 1936; *Old Possum's Book of Practical Cats,* 1939; *Four Quartets,* 1943; *The Cultivation of Christmas Trees,* 1954; *Collected Poems, 1909-1962,* 1963; *Poems Written in Early Youth,* 1967; *The Complete Poems and Plays,* 1969.

NONFICTION: *Ezra Pound: His Metric and Poetry,* 1917; *The Sacred Wood,* 1920; *Homage to John Dryden,* 1924; *Shakespeare and the Stoicism of Seneca,* 1927; *For Lancelot Andrewes,* 1928; *Dante,* 1929; *Thoughts After Lambeth,* 1931; *Charles Whibley: A Memoir,* 1931; *John Dryden: The Poet, the Dramatist, the Critic,* 1932; *Selected Essays,* 1932, new edition, 1950; *The Use of Poetry and the Use of Criticism,* 1933; *After Strange Gods,* 1934; *Elizabethan Essays,* 1934; *Essays Ancient and Modern,* 1936; *The Idea of a Christian Society,* 1939; *The Music of Poetry,* 1942; *The Classics and the Man of Letters,* 1942; *Notes Toward the Definition of Culture,* 1948; *Poetry and Drama,* 1951; *The Three Voices of Poetry,* 1953; *Religious Drama: Medieval and Modern,* 1954; *The Literature of Politics,* 1955; *The Frontiers of Criticism,* 1956; *On Poetry and Poets,* 1957; *Knowledge and Experience in the Philosophy of F. H. Bradley,* 1964; *To Criticize the Critic,* 1965; *The Letters of T. S. Eliot: Volume I, 1898-1922,* 1988.

Bibliography
Childs, Donald J. *From Philosophy to Poetry: T. S. Eliot's Study of Knowledge and Experience.* London: Athalone Press, 2001. Childs analyzes Eliot's literary works with emphasis on how he expressed his philosophy through his poetry. Bibliography and index.

Davidson, Harriet, ed. *T. S. Eliot.* New York: Longman, 1999. A collection of literary criticism regarding Eliot and his works. Bibliography and index.

Donoghue, Denis. *Words Alone: The Poet T. S. Eliot.* New Haven, Conn.: Yale University Press, 2000. Donoghue, having discovered Eliot's poetry in 1946 when he left his native Warrenpoint to attend University College in Dublin, writes autobiographically about the experience and offers a close reading of Eliot's major poems and essays.

Gordon, Lyndall. *T. S. Eliot: An Imperfect Life.* New York: W. W. Norton, 1999. A heavily revised and updated edition of the two-volume biography that made Gordon one of Eliot's most sensitive interpreters.

Habib, Rafey. *The Early T. S. Eliot and Western Philosophy.* New York: Cambridge University Press, 1999. A look at the philosophical beliefs held by Eliot and how they found their way into his literary works. Bibliography and index.

Jones, David E. *The Plays of T. S. Eliot.* Toronto: University of Toronto Press, 1960. This first book-length study to deal exclusively with Eliot's plays remains one of the best. In addition to separate sections on each of the plays, Jones includes general criticism relating them to Eliot's poetic and critical writings.

Malamud, Randy. *T. S. Eliot's Drama: A Research and Production Sourcebook.* New York: Greenwood Press, 1992. A close look at the production of Eliot's dramatic works. Bibliography and indexes.

_____. *Where the Words Are Valid: T. S. Eliot's Communities of Drama.* Westport, Conn.: Greenwood Press, 1994. A critical analysis and interpretation of Eliot's plays. Bibliography and index.

Moody, A. David, ed. *The Cambridge Companion to T. S. Eliot.* New York: Cambridge University Press, 1994. A comprehensive reference work dedicated to Eliot's life, work, and times. Bibliography and index.

Schuchard, Ronald. *Eliot's Dark Angel: Intersections of Life and Art.* New York: Oxford University Press, 1999. An analysis of Eliot's work from a psychological perspective. Bibliography and index.

Smith, Carol H. *T. S. Eliot's Dramatic Theory and Practice: From "Sweeney Agonistes" to "The Elder Statesman."* Princeton, N.J.: Princeton University Press, 1963. Unlike most studies of Eliot's drama, this book makes full use of Eliot's own statements on dramatic theory in his critical essays to help illuminate his own plays.

Patricia Marks,
updated by John R. Holmes

Euripides

Born: Phlya, Greece; c. 485 B.C.E.
Died: Macedonia, Greece; 406 B.C.E.

Principal drama • Of the 66 tragedies and 22 satyr plays Euripides wrote, the following survive: *Alkēstis*, 438 B.C.E. (*Alcestis*, 1781); *Mēdeia*, 431 B.C.E. (*Medea*, 1781); *Hērakleidai*, c. 430 B.C.E. (*The Children of Herakles*, 1781); *Hippolytos*, 428 B.C.E. (revision of an earlier play; *Hippolytus*, 1781); *Andromachē*, c. 426 B.C.E. (*Andromache*, 1782); *Heklabē*, 425 B.C.E. (*Hecuba*, 1782); *Hiketides*, c. 423 B.C.E. (*The Suppliants*, 1781); *Kyklōps*, c. 421 B.C.E. (*Cyclops*, 1782); *Hērakles*, c. 420 B.C.E. (*Heracles*, 1781); *Trōiades*, 415 B.C.E. (*The Trojan Women*, 1782); *Iphigeneiaē en Taurois*, c. 414 B.C.E. (*Iphigenia in Tauris*, 1782); *Ēlektra*, 413 B.C.E. (*Electra*, 1782); *Helenē*, 412 B.C.E. (*Helen*, 1782); *Iōn*, c. 411 B.C.E. (*Ion*, 1781); *Phoinissai*, 409 B.C.E. (*The Phoenician Women*, 1781); *Orestēs*, 408 B.C.E. (*Orestes*, 1782); *Bakchai*, 405 B.C.E. (*The Bacchae*, 1781); *Iphigeneiaē en Aulidi*, 405 B.C.E. (*Iphigenia in Aulis*, 1782)

Other literary forms • Like Aeschylus and Sophocles, Euripides wrote elegies and lyric poems, none of which has survived intact. The poet is said to have been commissioned by his fellow Athenians to write a funeral epitaph for the dead at Syracuse in 413 B.C.E., but the lines handed down in Plutarch's *Life of Nicias* (in *Bioi paralleloi*, c. 105-115 C.E.; *Parallel Lives*, 1579) are not usually accepted as Euripidean. Several lines exist of an epinician, or victory, ode said to have been dedicated by Euripides to the Athenian politician Alcibiades after an Olympic victory, but even in antiquity, this ode was attributed to others as well.

Achievements • The ancient *Bios Euripidou* (third century B.C.E.; life of Euripides) by Satyrus assigns to the playwright innovations in the following areas: prologues, scientific dissertations on nature, oratorical pieces, and recognitions. This vague statement requires considerable qualification. Although the extant plays show little of the interest in natural science suggested by the anonymous author of the *Life of Euripides* and confirmed by several fragments from lost plays, Euripides' dramatic application of set speeches and rhetorical devices is a common feature of his plays, as in the legal debate between Hecuba and Helen in *The Trojan Women*. These scientific and rhetorical features reveal Euripides' place in the intellectual mainstream of late fifth century B.C.E. Athens, a position that it is difficult for a modern reader to appreciate fully because so much of the existing nondramatic evidence is fragmentary. Euripides very well may have been the first tragedian to highlight these contemporary trends in his drama.

Euripides certainly did not invent anagnorisis, or recognition, which existed in Greek literature as early as Homer's *Odyssey* (c. 800 B.C.E.; English translation, 1616) and in drama as early as Aeschylus's *Choēphoroi* (458 B.C.E.; *Libation Bearers*, 1777), but Euripides uses these recognition scenes frequently and with a novelty and skill much admired by Aristotle in his *De poetica* (c. 334-323 B.C.E.; *Poetics*, 1705). Indeed, it is Euripides' focus on recognition and intrigue in his later dramas, such as *Ion*, *Helen*, and *Iphigenia in Tauris*, that has led him to be called a father of the New Greek Comedy of Menander in the late fourth century B.C.E. Although these recognition dramas were technically produced by Euripides as tragedies, they are not necessarily "tragic" in the modern sense, but are more "tragicomic" and have sometimes been labeled as *tyche* dramas, or dramas of "chance."

Alcestis deserves special mention. Technically not a tragedy, it is rather a pro-satyr play because it was produced in place of a satyr play. Euripides is known to have experimented with such pro-satyr plays several other times, and the pro-satyr play may have been a Euripidean innovation. Knowledge of the Greek satyr play tradition is generally scanty as Euripides' *Cyclops* is the only complete drama of this type to survive, along with significant papyrus fragments of two Sophoclean satyr plays, but two special features of satyr plays were known to have been choruses of satyrs and scenes of buffoonery. While *Alcestis* lacks the former, its links with the satyr play can be seen in the comic scene with Heracles. Euripides' *Alcestis* and his *tyche* dramas thus serve as a caution against making general statements about the genre of Greek "tragedy" or about "Euripidean tragedy" in particular. The definition of "tragedy" in fifth century B.C.E. Athens was clearly much broader than it is today.

The *Life of Euripides* notwithstanding, Euripides definitely did not invent the tragic prologue, which, by Aristotelian definition in *Poetics* was "that part of a tragedy which precedes the parodos or chorus's entrance song." Several extant plays of Aeschylus have such prologues, but Euripides, like Sophocles, added his own distinctive feature: a scene, often called expository, in which a character, usually a mortal but sometimes a god, identifies himself and outlines the characters and background of the plot. Every extant Euripidean tragedy has such an expository prologue, which cannot always be dismissed as a mere nondramatic playbill. The expositions spoken by gods (in *Alcestis*, *Hippolytus*, *The Trojan Women*, *Ion*, and *The Bacchae*) are particularly significant in that the dramatic events generally do not evolve exactly as predicted by the gods in the prologues. In each of these five prologues, the playwright makes his deity more or less misleading as to subsequent dramatic events. At the least, such "deceptive" prologues serve to create interest in the story without giving away the plot. At the same time, such prologues may reveal the gods' inability to control human action and to move it along their preordained plans.

The expository prologue has also been called an archaizing element in Euripidean drama, but too little is known of Greek tragedy in its infancy to say with certainty that such scenes were a common early feature. Euripides' plays, however, do exhibit several traits that could be labeled archaisms in that they can be traced back to Aeschylean elements. The dramas of Aeschylus, first produced in Euripides' youth and revived throughout his lifetime, seem to have been a particular source of dramatic inspiration to the younger playwright.

Euripidean imitation of Aeschylean techniques can be seen in several areas: Euripides' altar scenes, such as those in *The Suppliants* and *Ion*, may be based on similar scenes in such plays as Aeschylus's *Hiketides* (463 B.C.E.?; *The Suppliants*, 1777) and *Eumenides* (458 B.C.E.; English translation, 1777). Luring speeches, such as those in *Hecuba* and *Electra*, are probably derived from the carpet scene in Aeschylus's *Agamemnōn* (458 B.C.E.; *Agamemnon*, 1777). The pathetic ghost of Polydorus in *Hecuba* can be traced back to the ghosts in *Persai* (472 B.C.E.; *The Persians*, 1777) and *Eumenides*. The mad scene of *Heracles* may possibly be modeled on the last scene of *Libation Bearers*. Aeschylus's *Eumenides* and *The Suppliants* are the probable prototypes for Euripides' subsidiary choruses in *Hippolytus* and *The Suppliants*, and Euripides' *The Suppliants* is almost certainly following its predecessor in the use of the chorus as the main character. It has also been suggested that the model for the "bad women" of Euripides, such as

(Library of Congress)

Medea and Phaedra, was Aeschylus's Clytemnestra, and that Euripides' "unhappy women," such as Hecuba, were modeled on Aeschylus's Atossa.

Also like Aeschylus, Euripides was a master of stage machinery, including the *eccyclema*, a device used to show interiors, which Euripides employs in daring ways in *Alcestis*, *Hippolytus*, and other plays. For Euripides, however, stage machinery means especially the *mechane*, a crane used to swing an actor into the orchestra. Euripides has a *mechane*, which is the origin of the term *deus ex machina*, at the end of ten of his extant plays, almost always to enable a god to make an appearance and resolve dramatic difficulties. By contrast, the *mechane* is used in only one of Sophocles' surviving plays, *Philoktētēs* (409 B.C.E.; *Philoctetes*, 1729), and in none of Aeschylus's, except perhaps *Prometheus desmōtēs* (date unknown; *Prometheus Bound*, 1777). Euripides himself makes brilliant original use of the technique in *Medea*, in which it is Medea herself who escapes in a crane dramatically transformed into the magic chariot of the sun.

A final Aeschylean dramatic feature that is often linked with Euripides is the connected trilogy. T. B L. Webster is the most prominent proponent of this view, which has had remarkable tenacity despite meager evidence. The most that can be said about the possibility of Euripidean-connected trilogies is that neither of the most likely trilogic candidates, Euripides' production of 415 B.C.E. (including the lost *Alexander* and *Palamedes*, as well as the surviving *The Trojan Women*), often called his "Trojan Trilogy"; his production of c. 410-409 B.C.E. (*Antiope* and *Hypsipyle*, now lost, and *The Phoenician Women*), a "Theban Trilogy," appear to have been connected in the closely knit thematic and chronological way that is notable in the *Oresteia* (458 B.C.E.; English translation, 1777), Aeschylus's only surviving trilogy. It is possible that Euripides may have linked plays within a dramatic group through a sort of meaningful variation, but such connections do not necessarily make a trilogy. Like his contemporary, Sophocles, Euripides was an artistic master of the single play rather than of the connected trilogy.

Euripides was an acknowledged virtuoso of Greek tragic language in all its forms. In the iambic or spoken portions of his plays, his elaborate agons, or debates, and his carefully detailed messenger speeches, such as the famous report of Hippolytus's death in *Hippolytus* are particularly noteworthy. In the lyric, or sung, portions of his plays, Euripides was in the vanguard of the late fifth century B.C.E. trend toward more song by actors and less by the chorus alone. Thus, Euripidean plays tend to have more monodies, or solo songs by actors, and *kommoi*, or duets between the chorus and one or more actors, as well as fewer and shorter choral odes than in earlier tragedy. *Kommostic parodoi*, or choral entrance songs sung by both chorus and actor(s), are a special favorite of Euripides (as in *Medea* and *The Trojan Women*).

Under the influence of the contemporary poet Timotheus of Miletus, Euripides also moved in his later plays toward a New Lyric form marked especially by astrophic, or stanzaless, songs and *polymetria*, or the use of more than one meter in a single song (as in *Iphigenia in Tauris, Helen,* and *The Phoenician Women*). Late Euripidean tragedy only sporadically reflects another trend of New Lyric, that toward choral odes that are apparently unconnected to dramatic events. In general, even such a well-known Euripidean ode as the "Demeter Ode" (in *Helen*), which is difficult to relate to the plot, is not so much detached from the play as it is a more indirect, mythological exemplum of dramatic events.

New Lyric, connected, as it was, with a new school of emotional music, was an ideal medium for Euripides' dramatic art, which is preeminently a study of human psychology and emotion. The playwright, noted for his studies of the feminine psyche in such diverse characters as Alcestis, Medea, Phaedra, and Hecuba, created character studies filled with psychological insight. Unlike the Sophoclean hero, who never changes or loses his resolve, the Euripidean character is more unstable. Like Medea or Phaedra, the character may waver at length between several courses of action or, like Ion, who is transformed in the course of the action from a boy into a man, may exhibit significant growth of personality. The persona of Euripides often lacks that nobility of character that Aristotle believed to be essential to real tragedy, and which the seventeenth century French dramatist Jean Racine tried to restore in his imitation of Euripides' characters. Euripides' contemporary, Sophocles, demonstrated uncanny insight when he stated that he "made men as they ought to be; Euripides as they are."

Euripides' innovations in the mythical background to his plays are often the result of his realistic psychology as well as his desire for dramatic shock effect. His most noteworthy mythical changes are the marriage of Electra, the reversal of the traditional sequence of Heracles' madness and the hero's labors, and, probably, the murder of her own children by Medea. Euripides may also have been the inventor of scenes of voluntary self-sacrifice, of which the "Cassandra scene" of *The Trojan Women* is a noteworthy example. Other such scenes can be found in *Iphigenia in Aulis, The Children of Herakles, Hecuba,* and *The Phoenician Women*.

It is the rare Euripidean play that does not include at least one deity among its *dramatis personae*, but these divine appearances are generally restricted to the prologues and *exodoi*, or last scenes, and serve as a frame for the central, "human" part of the drama. Much has been read into Euripides' beliefs from the role of the gods in his plays, but it is also significant to note that the Euripidean gods serve an important dramatic function as causes of events independent of human motivation. In general, the gods place Euripides' psychological studies in their appropriate mythical background.

Biography • The manuscript tradition of Euripides contains an ancient *Life of Euripides*, clearly a composite of several sources, including Philochorus, a fourth century B.C.E. Attic historian, and Satyros, a third century Peripatetic biographer, fragments of whose own *Life of Euripides* exist on papyrus. Unfortunately, however, much of the ancient biographical tradition about Euripides is derived from ancient comedy, especially from that of Aristophanes, whose *Thesmophoriazousai* (411 B.C.E.; *Thesmophoriazusae,* 1837) and *Batrachoi* (405 B.C.E.; *The Frogs,* 1780) both contain caricatures of Euripides and who is therefore suspect as a historical source.

The problem of source reliability starts with Euripides' parentage. The comic tradition that Euripides' father, Mnesarchus (or Mnesarchides), was a shopkeeper and his mother, Clito, a greengrocer, is apparently contradicted by ancient statements that Euripides' mother belonged to a noble family and that Euripides himself was granted honors worthy of high rank, including those of dancing at Athens in the sacred dance to Delian Apollo and of being a fire bearer in another cult of Apollo. Euripides is said to have been born on the island of Salamis, but he was a member of the Athenian deme of Phlya, where he may have held a local priesthood of Zeus. His date of birth is variously given as either 485 or 480 B.C.E., the later date being based on the persistent ancient tradition that the playwright was born on Salamis on the very day of the battle in which Aeschylus may have fought and after which Sophocles as a youth is said to have danced in the victory celebration. Apparently, Euripides' ties with Salamis were strong, for he is said to have composed many of his plays in a solitary cave on the island.

The ancient *Life of Euripides* states that, as a youth, Euripides studied painting and was trained as an athlete because of a misinterpretation of an oracle stating that he would someday win "crowns in contests at Athens." Although Euripides may, as some sources suggest, have won some early athletic victories at Athens, his real victories were to be won in the dramatic competitions at Athens' Greater Dionysia.

Euripides is linked intellectually with many of the great thinkers of his day. The ancient *Life of Euripides* lists among his teachers Anaxagoras, whose doctrines can be seen in *Hippolytus, The Trojan Women,* and elsewhere; Protagoras, who is said to have read his treatise "On the Gods" in Euripides' house; the Sophist Prodicus; and even Socrates, who was at least fifteen years Euripides' junior and whom Aristophanes called a collaborator in Euripides' dramatic compositions. As a fifth century B.C.E. Athenian, Euripides certainly came in contact with all these men, but none of them is likely to have a formal student-teacher relationship with Euripides. The influence of the tragedian Aeschylus and the poet Timotheus on Euripides' dramatic development has already been mentioned. The poet may also have had some connections with the historian Thucydides. A memorial inscription dedicated to Euripides is ascribed to Thucydides, although it is sometimes attributed to Timotheus.

The story of Euripides' two unhappy marriages, first to Melito and then to a Choerile or Choerine, daughter of Mnesilochus, is too clearly entangled in comic tradition to be historical. According to the *Life of Euripides,* the second wife committed adultery with a certain Cephisophon, who is described both as a house slave and as a literary collaborator with Euripides. The playwright is said to have written his scandalous first *Hippolytus* in reaction to his wife's infidelity. Actually, both unhappy marriages and his traditional misogyny may be a comic exaggeration of Euripides' depiction of evil women in such plays as the first *Hippolytus* and *Medea.*

Euripides had three sons: Mnesarchides, a merchant; Mnesilochus, an actor; and Euripides the younger, a tragic poet who produced *Iphigenia in Aulis* and *The Bacchae* posthumously for his father.

Euripides appears to have led a very quiet life except for his dramatic career. The only public duty attributed to him, an ambassadorship to Syracuse, is generally discounted today. Euripides may have been friendly with the Athenian politician Alcibiades. An epinician ode to Alcibiades is perhaps attributable to the dramatist, and unmistakable strains of Athenian patriotism are notable in such plays as *Medea* and *The Suppliants,* in which the Athenian heroes Aegeus and Theseus are used as symbols of Athens's role as savior of the oppressed. On the other hand, intense hatred of war can be seen in such plays as *Hecuba* and *The Trojan Women,* and much of the exotic in late Euripidean plays such as *Helen* and *Iphigenia in Tauris* can be explained as dramatic escapism from the horrors of the Peloponnesian War. Criticism of the Athenian massacre of the Melians, described by Thucydides, can be read into Euripides' *The Trojan Women*, produced in 415 B.C.E., the year after the massacre. More specific political allusions have been sought in the extant corpus but are very difficult to document.

Euripides' first dramatic competition was in 455 B.C.E., when he placed with *Peliades*, now lost. He did not win a first prize until 442 or 441. In contrast to Sophocles' numerous dramatic victories, Euripides won first prize only five times (including one posthumous victory) out of twenty-two productions. Although Euripides' dramatic career began in 455, he produced very few plays in the next twenty-five years. Only six Euripidean productions are known before 431 B.C.E. The remaining sixteen productions fall in the period 431-406 B.C.E., roughly coinciding with the Peloponnesian War. In the last decade of the poet's life, 415-406 B.C.E., he competed every year but two.

In 438 B.C.E., Euripides placed second to Sophocles with a group composed of the lost tragedies *Cretan Women*, *Alcmaeon at Psophis*, and *Telephus* and the extant pro-satyr play *Alcestis*. Sometime in the period 437-432 B.C.E., Euripides produced a *Hippolytus*, later identified by the subtitle *Kalyptomenos*, or "veiled," to distinguish it from the extant play on the same theme, *Hippolytus Stephanophoros*, or "Hippolytus the wreath-bearer." Apparently, this first *Hippolytus*, now lost, received harsh criticism for its depiction of a scandalous Phaedra, who revealed her love to her stepson. In his revised *Hippolytus*, produced in 428 B.C.E., Euripides was more careful to preserve Phaedra's reputation and was awarded first prize over the tragedians Iophon, son of Sophocles, and Ion. *Medea*, produced in 431 B.C.E. with the lost *Philoctetes* and *Dictys*, was beaten by the works of both Euphorion, son of Aeschylus, and Sophocles. *Andromache*, while not firmly datable, is significant in that the play apparently was not performed at Athens, but the actual place of production is unknown. Euripides is said to have made several other productions outside Athens. In 415 B.C.E., Euripides came in second place to a certain Xenocles with his lost *Alexander* and *Palamedes* and the surviving *The Trojan Women*.

In 408 B.C.E., after the production of *Orestes* in Athens, the septuagenarian Euripides left his native city, never to return. The poet went first to Magnesia, where he received several honors, and then to Macedonia, to the court of Archelaus, whose patronage of the arts also attracted the tragic poet Agathon and Euripides' friend, the poet Timotheus. In Macedonia, Euripides produced *Archelaus*, now lost, which was a play about an ancestor of his royal host, and wrote the extant *Iphigenia in Aulis* and *The Bacchae* and the lost *Alcmaeon in Corinth*, which were produced posthumously in Athens by Euripides' son of the same name and which won first prize.

After Euripides' death in Macedonia in early 406, Sophocles dressed a chorus in mourning for his fellow tragedian at the *proagon*, or preview, to the Greater Dionysia of that year. That Euripides died by *sparagmos*—that is, by being torn apart either accidentally by Archelaus's hunting dogs or by women angered by the poet's depiction of their sex—must be dismissed as comic apocrypha because of the legend's similarity to the fate of Pentheus in *The Bacchae*.

The most disturbing result of all these biographical data tarnished by the comic tradition is the cloud that has enveloped Euripides' popularity in fifth century B.C.E. Athens. Like his contemporary, Socrates, Euripides was a favorite butt of comedy, both while he was alive (as in Aristophanes' *Thesmophoriazusae*) and after his death (as in Aristophanes' *The Frogs* of 405 B.C.E.), and according to the ancient *Life of Euripides*, this comic ridicule was so intense that it was the cause of Euripides' departure from Athens in 408 B.C.E. There are also several noncomic hints of Euripides' unpopularity:

the failure of the first *Hippolytus*, as well as the small number of first prizes that he won. On the other hand, this tradition of unpopularity may be the result of comic exaggeration misunderstood by later critics.

That Euripides was a prolific playwright, with sixteen productions in the last twenty-five years of his life, is itself strong evidence for sustained contemporary enthusiasm for his plays, as competition for permission to perform at the Greater Dionysia was stiff, and only three poets were chosen annually. There is also an attractive notice in Plutarch's *Life of Nicias* that some Athenian prisoners in Sicily were granted better treatment by their captors if they could recite Euripides' poetry, which was held in great esteem by the Sicilian Greeks. Nor must Euripides' sojourn in Macedonia be interpreted, as it is in the ancient *Life of Euripides*, as only a self-imposed exile from his Athenian critics. Rather, it may also be seen as the result of the attraction that royal patrons often held toward ancient Greek poets, including Anacreon and Ibycus to the court of the Samian tyrant Polycrates, Aeschylus and Pindar to the court of Hieron in Sicily, and Agathon and Timotheus to the court of Archelaus.

A more likely interpretation of the evidence is that Euripides' plays were often controversial in his lifetime because of their depiction of realistic characters in a traditional myth but were still generally admired for their dramatic and poetic force. As time passed, the sensationalism of Euripides' character development has worn off, and the poet has come to be admired for his masterful studies of human psychology, so that the funeral inscription written in Euripides' memory by either the historian Thucydides or the poet Timotheus is even more valid today than it was in the fifth century B.C.E.

> All Greece is the tomb of Euripides, whose bones rest
> In Macedonia where he met his end.
> His native city, Athens, is the Greece of Greece
> And he has earned much praise for the delights of his Muse.

Euripides' plays were certainly in demand after his death. Revivals of Euripidean plays occurred throughout the fourth century B.C.E. (a performance of *Orestes* is documented in 341 B.C.E.) and were a direct influence on the New Comedy of Menander (late fourth century B.C.E.) and, through Greek New Comedy, on Roman Comedy, including Plautus and Terence (second century B.C.E.). Enthusiasm for Euripides was maintained throughout antiquity, as is evidenced by the larger number of plays that survive and by the great number of papyrus fragments of Euripides that have been discovered in Egypt and that are second in quantity only to Homeric papyri. Adaptations of Euripidean plays include Seneca's *Phaedra* (c. 40-50 C.E.; English translation, 1581), modeled on Euripides' first *Hippolytus*; Racine's *Phèdre* (pr., pb. 1677; *Phaedra*, 1701), a seventeenth century version of *Hippolytus*; Eugene O'Neill's twentieth century version of *Mourning Becomes Electra* (pr., pb. 1931); and the contemporary Nigerian playwright Wole Soyinka's unique adaptation of *The Bacchae* (pr., pb. 1973), with its blending of Dionysus with the Yoruba deity Ogun.

Analysis • Euripides wrote eighty-eight dramas, including sixty-six tragedies and twenty-two satyr plays. Nineteen plays survive in the manuscript tradition, but one of these, the tragedy *Rhesus* (written sometime between 455 and 441 B.C.E.), is generally considered to be spurious. *Cyclops*, the only complete extant satyr play, is not precisely datable. In addition to the pro-satyr play *Alcestis*, seven tragedies are securely dated:

Medea, Hippolytus, The Trojan Women, Helen, Orestes, Iphigenia in Aulis, and *The Bacchae,* these last two produced posthumously. The other tragedies can be only approximately dated, based on metrical evidence and contemporary allusions. In addition, considerable fragments from lost plays survive on papyrus.

The large number of extant Euripidean plays (compared to only seven each for Aeschylus and Sophocles) is attributable to a combination of conscious selection and chance. When the Athenian orator Lycurgus established the texts of Aeschylus and Sophocles in the late fourth century B.C.E., he also made the first edition of Euripides, but not before numerous actors' interpolations had crept into the text. The number of plays contained in the Lycurgan edition is unknown, but only seventy-eight dramas, including four considered apocryphal by the editor, were included in the definitive Alexandrian edition by Aristophanes of Byzantium in the second century B.C.E. Another important edition was made by Didymus of Chalcedon in the first century B.C.E. Didymus's edition included scholia, or marginal notes, on which are based the scholia in the surviving manuscripts.

Sometime after the second century C.E., school anthologies were made of the plays of Aeschylus, Sophocles, and Euripides, but although only seven each were chosen for Aeschylus and Sophocles, Euripides' great popularity in antiquity caused ten plays to be included in his selection: *Hecuba, Orestes, The Phoenician Women, Hippolytus, Medea, Alcestis, Andromache, Rhesus, The Trojan Women,* and *The Bacchae.* Although this school group was narrowed in the Byzantine period to *Hecuba, Orestes,* and *The Phoenician Women,* all ten plays of the original selection reached the West in the fourteenth century, together with a group of nine other Euripidean plays, preserved by chance from an edition (perhaps that of Aristophanes) arranged alphabetically: *The Suppliants, Cyclops, The Children of Herakles, Heracles, Helen, Ion, Iphigenia in Tauris, Iphigenia in Aulis,* and *Electra.* The first printed edition of Euripides was the Aldine edition of Venice, 1503.

Although certain dramatic features, such as the expository prologue and the appearance of a god in the *mechane,* tend to recur in play after play of Euripides, the overall impression made by his corpus, when viewed as a whole, is one of remarkable diversity. Euripides is a poet of stark contradictions. A single production, such as *Hippolytus,* can display both bitter misogyny and a sensitive portrayal of a woman such as Phaedra. One play, such as *Medea,* may sink to the depths of tragedy; another, such as *Ion,* will float from those depths, buoyed on comic resolution. Certain plays, it is true, can be said to form subgroups, such as the so-called political plays, including *The Children of Herakles, The Suppliants,* and *Andromache,* or the *tyche* dramas *Ion, Helen,* and *Iphigenia in Tauris,* but the dramatic gulf that spans a career including *Alcestis, Hippolytus, Ion,* and *The Bacchae* cannot be easily bridged.

There are too few neat generalizations comparable to the Aeschylean concept of justice or the Sophoclean hero on which to establish a poetic or intellectual unity within the Euripidean corpus. Perhaps if as many plays of Aeschylus and Sophocles had survived, more variety would be found in those dramatists as well, but one has the impression after reading Euripides that for this playwright, at least, variety is almost an organizing feature. Most often, generalizations about Euripides have centered on his portrayal of the gods and his apparent disbelief in Greek deities and traditional myths, but then one is forced by *The Bacchae,* with its intense religious mood, either to see the play as an end-of-life palinode, a refutation of the earlier works, or to put aside the generalization entirely. Variety within the Euripidean corpus is caused, to a great extent, by the playwright's focus on the particular psychology of each character.

Like the Sophists of his age, who operated on an ethical system of amoral pragmatism, Euripides is a practical stage manager who is willing to thwart theatrical convention and traditional beliefs for dramatic effect. In general, the goal of Euripidean drama is not the development of a theological system or an ideal code of conduct, but rather the depiction of human emotions under strain. The dramas of Euripides are thus not really concerned with the gods or superheroes, but with ordinary people trying to deal, in their own personal ways, with real-life situations including love, jealousy, divorce, and death. This is the source of Euripides' diversity and of his appeal. His psychological studies, as diverse and as complex as the human mind itself, are at the heart of his plays, which fluctuate in form, mood, and tone to suit particular dramatic and psychological situations. Unlike Sophocles, who depicted people as they ought to be, Euripides depicted people as they are (according to Aristotle's *Poetics*). This Euripidean realism accounts for the differences among *Alcestis, Medea, Hippolytus, Ion, The Bacchae*, and his other plays. Euripidean tragedy is, above all, a drama of life itself.

Alcestis • In *Alcestis*, Euripides presents a study of the loyal, self-sacrificing wife. That Alcestis would die for her husband, Admetus, is easy to accept after Alcestis's touching and revealing speech in the second episode, but the character of Admetus is more difficult to understand and easier to condemn as selfish and self-centered. Interpretation of his character and of the play as a whole is widely debated, but Admetus's salvation, if it occurs at all, must be sought in *xenia*, the ancient Greek custom of guestfriendship. *Xenia* is Admetus's chief—and perhaps his only—virtue.

In the typically Euripidean expository prologue, the god Apollo explains how he will save Admetus's life because the latter was a good host to him while he, Apollo, was on earth, and, in the central portion of the fourth episode, Heracles is willing to get Alcestis back from Death because of the hospitality his friend Admetus has shown to him even at a time of deep mourning. The Third Choral Ode is filled with glowing praise for Admetus's *xenia*. On the other hand, Admetus comes off quite badly both in an agon with his father Pheres, in which the aged father explains his refusal to die for his selfish son, and in the exodos, in which Admetus accepts in marriage an unidentified woman from Heracles, despite his earlier promise to the dying Alcestis never to remarry, even before it becomes clear that the veiled woman might be Alcestis.

Perhaps some of this play's difficulty is attributable to its position as a pro-satyr play, a fact that helps explain the pathetic comedy of the drunken scene with Heracles and especially the tragicomic ambiguity of the exodos. Through it all, however, Euripides' depiction of Alcestis as a loving wife and mother is a constant on which the variables of Admetus's character and the play's denouement are based. Whether Admetus in the exodos is rewarded for his virtuous *xenia* or punished for his selfishness, neither could have occurred without the remarkable and loving selflessness of his wife. Euripides' emphasis on a human situation and human emotion is paramount.

Medea • *Medea* is one of the few extant plays of Euripides that function without the gods. Instead, Euripides has taken two superhuman figures from Greek mythology, Medea and Jason, and placed them in a very human situation: the breakdown of a marriage. Especially in their bitter agon in the second episode, Medea is clearly the wronged woman who has sacrificed everything for her husband and does not want the divorce, and Jason is shown to be heartless, calculating, and ambitious.

Euripides achieves his most brilliant dramatic stroke, however, by complicating his psychological study of Medea with an emphasis on the exotic side of her character. Not only is she depicted in her traditional role as a witch and as a foreigner and therefore a barbarian, but there is an implicit suggestion that Medea is also unnatural because of her love for Jason, because of her uncontrollable passion. Medea's emotional imbalance, caused by Jason's desertion, is therefore the heart of the play and leads inevitably to her murder of Jason's intended second wife and then of her own children, whose death, she realizes, will wound Jason more than would any other act of revenge.

Yet Medea is not completely unnatural; she is rather a woman caught between her jealous passion for Jason and her maternal instincts. That she does not lose all her sympathy by yielding in the end to her passion speaks highly of Euripides' character development of his heroine. The chorus is particularly significant in the play for this reason. From their arrival, the women of the chorus are sympathetic to Medea and convinced that she has been wronged by Jason. Their First Ode is a bitter condemnation of the perfidy of men toward women, and during Medea's intrigue, the chorus actually serve as Medea's confidante. The Fifth Choral Ode is about the sorrows of childbearing, and the chorus's last song is a terrified prayer to the Sun, Medea's grandfather, to stop Medea's unnatural act. The chorus members therefore are an important dramatic foil to Medea. As women, they are sympathetic to Medea, but they cannot understand or condone the murder of her own children. The chorus are a psychological scale by which Medea's passion is measured and found imbalanced.

Compared to the tragicomedy *Alcestis*, the dramatic effect of *Medea* can be nothing less than complete emotional exhaustion. In a memorable section of *Poetics*, Aristotle criticizes the emotional effect of *Medea* as *miaron*, moral revulsion, which inhibits the development of a true tragic feeling for Medea, who, fully conscious of the horrors of her act, murders her children. Yet this awareness that she is caught between Jason and her children is the emotional key to Medea's psychology and enables her to construe her act as both revenge against Jason and protection against further harm for her children. In *Medea*, Euripides has developed the illogical conclusions of a mind crazed by spurned love.

Hippolytus • Passion is also the subject of *Hippolytus*, but here, the heroine Phaedra struggles in vain to control her illicit love for her stepson Hippolytus. The gods play a much a greater role in this play. In the prologue, Aphrodite announces that she has caused Phaedra's love in vengeance against Hippolytus, who scorns her worship, and Artemis appears in the exodos to restore the good name of her dying devotee Hippolytus.

This drama, often praised for its structural and thematic balance between Aphrodite and Artemis, between Phaedra and Hippolytus, between passion and chastity, is another brilliant Euripidean study of emotional stress, of Phaedra striving desperately to maintain her good name, first by keeping secret her uncontrollable love and then by accusing Hippolytus of rape and committing suicide, and of Hippolytus, at first horrified when he learns of Phaedra's infatuation and then nobly faithful to his oaths of secrecy even when falsely accused of violating his stepmother. The tension between the two sides is maintained by well-developed hunting and sea imagery, which Euripides manipulates for meaningful character development. For example, Hippolytus's "untouched meadows" can be applied not only to nature and to the speaker's virtuous chastity but also to a sense of spiritual smugness, a holier-than-thou attitude against which Hippolytus is warned by his own servant. Phaedra's wish to "drink fresh water from a running spring" is a repressed sexual desire, especially when she couples this desire with one to "lie in the grassy meadow."

It would have been a useful guide for an interpretation of this play to know exactly how these characterizations of Hippolytus and Phaedra compared with those in Euripides' unsuccessful first version of the theme. How much less virtuous was the first Phaedra? Was the first Hippolytus as spiritually superior or as bitterly misogynistic? Satisfactory answers to these questions can probably never be found, however, and the extant *Hippolytus* must be interpreted on its own evidence. As such, *Hippolytus* can be seen to depict a passion that neither Phaedra nor Hippolytus is able to control. Both are engulfed in a powerful force, which, in this play at least, with its appearance of Aphrodite in the prologue, is more than human; it is divine.

The Second Choral Ode, poised dramatically between Phaedra's accidental confession of love to the nurse in the second episode and the nurse's disastrous conversation with Hippolytus in the third episode, is a lyric statement of love's power in which the chorus describe love's destructive force and add the stories of Deianira and Semele as mythological exempla. Although violent passions are the subjects of both *Medea* and *Hippolytus*, the former play is perhaps more devoted to the depiction of the horrible effects of Medea's passion. *Hippolytus* places more emphasis on the inevitability not only of Phaedra's love, which Euripides expresses in theological, mythological, and, above all, human terms, but also of Hippolytus's intractable, passionless nature, which is developed in the same powerful terms as Phaedra's. In *Hippolytus*, Euripides thus demonstrates an astute awareness of the complexities of human psychology.

Ion • *Ion* is one of several Euripidean dramas that revolve around anagnorisis, or recognition. This play, in fact, has two recognitions: a false recognition by Xuthus, king of Athens, that Ion is his son, and a true recognition by Creusa, Xuthus's wife, that Ion is really her son, conceived by the god Apollo and abandoned in infancy. Ion was reared as an orphan at Apollo's temple at Delphi, where the action of the drama takes place.

Although the major *dramatis personae* are all illustrious figures from the Athenian past, the events that they experience were not that extraordinary in fifth century B.C.E. Greece. Many Athenians would have gone to Delphi, as Xuthus and Creusa did, to consult the oracle and to visit Apollo's temple, which the chorus as sightseers describe in the parodos. The rituals preceding a request for a Delphic oracle would also have been familiar to Euripides' audience. Further, the reliability of Apollo's shrine as an oracular seat is an issue that haunts Ion and that very much concerned Euripides' contemporaries. Apollo's reputation in this play is especially tarnished by Creusa's claim that the god raped and then abandoned her to deal alone with an unwanted pregnancy. These concerns about Apollo are directed toward the character of Ion, whose idealistic view of Apollo at the beginning of the play is repeatedly challenged, first by Creusa's story of Apollo's rape and later by the story of his true identity.

The inevitable result of these intellectual challenges is Ion's transformation from a simpleminded boy into an intelligent, questioning adult. In the end, Ion accepts Apollo's story on trust, but this leap of faith, Ion's statement of implicit faith and trust in the god, can also be interpreted as ironic, as a cynical acceptance of his fate to be the son of Xuthus "by gift" and of Creusa "by Apollo." On an understanding of Ion's intent hinges the interpretation not only of Ion's character development but also an understanding of the play itself. On the one hand, if Ion is transformed into a skeptic, the play becomes a serious condemnation of Apollo. On the other hand, if Ion's belief in Apollo matures from childlike acceptance into the faith of an adult, the play is a more optimistic statement concerning the role of deity in human life. There is no answer to this ambiguity, just as there is none for the ambiguity of *Alcestis*.

It is perhaps significant that Athena's appearance in the *mechane* occurs, not at the very tense dramatic moment when Ion nearly kills Creusa without knowing that she is his real mother, but rather at the point when Ion turns to ask the truth of his identity from Apollo in an oracle. Athena prevents Ion from querying the oracle because Ion is searching for a direct answer to a question that cannot be answered directly. Rather, he must be content with the ambiguity of the situation, with the contradiction that he is the son both of Xuthus and of Apollo. The dramatic emphasis is thus on Ion's intellectual growth rather than on the veracity of Apollo.

The dramatic tone of *Ion* is in strong contrast to that of *Medea* or *Hippolytus*. The horrid deaths of the earlier plays are avoided in this drama. Both Creusa and Ion are brought in the play to the point of committing the crime of Oedipus—that of unwittingly killing a blood relation—but both murders are thwarted by the dramatic circumstances. This is a tragicomedy, a *tyche* drama, in which Euripides has approached the human situation and human psychology from a completely different, and less serious, direction.

The Bacchae • *The Bacchae* is, in several ways, Euripides' most unusual work. It is the only extant Greek tragedy based on a Dionysian story, despite the cultic association of Greek tragedy with that god. Unlike many of Euripides' works, *The Bacchae* displays a religious intensity that complicates any discussion of the gods in Euripides. Further, this religious fervor is most completely developed by the chorus of bacchants, who achieve in this play a dramatic centrality lacking in other choruses, even those, such as the chorus in Euripides' *The Suppliants*, which are meant to be main characters. Even more than Dionysus himself, who is one of the *dramatis personae*, his chorus of female followers project the meaning of the Dionysian religion and its complete psychological dependence on the god. The parodos is an especially vivid example of such Dionysiac ecstasy.

However, there are important points of intersection between *The Bacchae* and Euripides' earlier plays. Most notable are the expository prologue, spoken by Dionysus, with its deceptive features; the bawdy scene between Teiresias and Cadmus in the first episode; the vivid messenger speeches; and the appearance of Dionysus in the *mechane* in the exodos.

The Bacchae is not simply about Dionysus and his religion; it also concerns Pentheus, king of Thebes, and his opposition to the new religion. The conflict between Dionysus and Pentheus and the eventual death of Pentheus at the hands of the gods' followers make possible another superb Euripidean psychological study, this one of a human mind in deterioration. Dramatic events depict the progressive insanity of Pentheus, which, on a religious level, is imposed as a punishment for opposing Dionysus. On the level of imagery, the chorus emphasize Pentheus's irrationality by describing the king as a "wild beast" in the Second Choral Ode.

Bibliography

Allan, William. *The "Andromache" and Euripidean Tragedy*. Oxford, England: Oxford University Press, 2000. A thorough analysis of the play, which the author asserts deserves a greater degree of critical appreciation than it has received historically.

Bloom, Harold, ed. *Euripides*. Philadelphia: Chelsea House, 2001. Part of a series on dramatists meant for secondary school students, this book contains essays examining the work and life of Euripides. Includes a bibliography and index.

Croally, N. T. *Euripidean Polemic: The Trojan Women and the Function of Tragedy*. New York: Cambridge University Press, 1994. Croally argues that the function of Greek tragedy was didactic and that *The Trojan Women* educated by discussing Athenian ideology. He also looks at Euripides' relation with the Sophists.

Dunn, Francis M. *Tragedy's End: Closure and Innovation in Euripidean Drama.* New York: Oxford University Press, 1996. In this study of closure in Euripides' works, Dunn argues that the playwright's innovative endings opened up the form of tragedy although his artificial endings disallowed an authoritative reading of his plays.

Gounaridou, Kiki. *Euripides and "Alcestis": Speculations, Simulations, and Stories of Love in the Athenian Culture.* Lanham, Md.: University Press of America, 1998. Gounaridou examines the ambiguity and indeterminancy in *Alcestis*, analyzing about eighty scholarly attempts to interpret the play and adding her own interpretation.

Lloyd, Michael. *The Agon in Euripides.* New York: Oxford University Press, 1992. Lloyd examines the works of Euripides, focusing on the concept of agon.

Rabinowitz, Nancy Sorkin. *Anxiety Veiled: Euripides and the Traffic in Women.* Ithaca, N.Y.: Cornell University Press, 1993. Rabinowitz looks at the prominence of women in Euripides' plays and concludes that he was neither a misogynist nor a feminist. She sees him establishing male dominance while attributing strength to women.

Sullivan, Shirley Darcus. *Euripides' Use of Psychological Terminology.* Montreal: McGill-Queen's University Press, 2000. Sullivan uses psychology to dissect the works of Euripides.

Thomas J. Sienkewicz

George Farquhar

Born: Londonderry, Ireland; 1677 or 1678
Died: London, England; late May, 1707

Principal drama • *Love and a Bottle*, pr. 1698, pb. 1699; *The Constant Couple: Or, A Trip to the Jubilee*, pr. 1699, pb. 1700; *Sir Harry Wildair, Being the Sequel of a Trip to the Jubilee*, pr., pb. 1701; *The Inconstant: Or, The Way to Win Him*, pr., pb. 1702 (adaptation of John Fletcher's play *The Wild Goose Chase*); *The Twin Rivals*, pr. 1702, pb. 1703; *The Stage Coach*, pr., pb. 1704 (with Peter Anthony Motteux; adaptation of Jean de La Chapelle's play *Les Carosses d'Orléans*); *The Recruiting Officer*, pr., pb. 1706; *The Beaux' Stratagem*, pr., pb. 1707

Other literary forms • George Farquhar wrote a few short poems, one long occasional poem entitled *Barcellona* (1710), numerous prologues and epilogues for plays, a short novel called *The Adventures of Covent Garden* (1698), and one miscellany entitled *Love and Business* (1702), besides contributing letters to two other miscellanies.

Achievements • George Farquhar was one of the most popular dramatists at the end of the Restoration period. His success is illustrated by the number of prologues and epilogues he was asked to write for other plays and by his contributions to popular miscellanies such as *Familiar and Courtly Letters* (1700) and *Letters of Wit, Politicks, and Morality* (1701). The popularity of his plays with actors, particularly *The Beaux' Stratagem* and *The Recruiting Officer*, accounted in no small measure for their survival during the eighteenth century and has played a large part in their continued visibility in modern times.

Farquhar's skill in modifying typical Restoration themes and characters accounted for much of the success of his work. He reintroduced a significant degree of realism into drama and used topical issues for comic effect. Although classed among the Restoration playwrights, he stands somewhat apart from them in his craftsmanship and his philosophy of drama, showing greater variety of plot and depth of feeling. In his later work, he sought to reconcile the liberal sexual attitudes of early comedy of manners with the more severe, increasingly moralistic tone of the early eighteenth century. He thus produced a type of comedy that stands between the traditional Restoration comedy of wit and the later sentimental comedy.

The influence of Farquhar's approach to comedy is most apparent not in the work of succeeding dramatists (although Oliver Goldsmith reveals an indebtedness to Farquhar, particularly in *She Stoops to Conquer*, pr., pb. 1773), but in the novels of Henry Fielding, in both terms of sense of humor and breadth of social milieu. Oddly enough, Farquhar was to exert a considerable influence on the development of eighteenth century German drama, mainly as a result of Gotthold Ephraim Lessing's great enthusiasm for him. His continued influence on the history of German theater is displayed in the work of a major twentieth century dramatist, Bertolt Brecht.

Biography • Many traditions and legends have developed around the sparse facts known about the life of George Farquhar. The earliest documented evidence is contained in the records of Trinity College, which list him as entering in July, 1694, at the age of seventeen, establishing his year of birth as either 1677 or 1678. These records also note Londonderry, Ireland, as his place of birth, and Walker as the name of his previous teacher. Farquhar entered Trinity College, presumably to study for the Church, with a sizarship that entitled him to an allowance of bread and ale in return for serving duties. He won a scholarship less than a year after entering. This four pounds a year was suspended for a time, however, because of his riotous behavior at the Donnybrook Fair. Sometime after February, 1696, he left Trinity without taking a degree.

Not long after, Farquhar became an actor at the Smock Alley Theatre, the only theater in Dublin. His not particularly successful career as an actor ended after he wounded a fellow player in a duel scene, having forgotten to use a blunted foil. It was supposedly on the advice of his friend Robert Wilks, who was later to become one of the most popular actors on the London stage, that Farquhar went to London, probably in 1697, to write plays. *Love and a Bottle*, his first play, was produced at the Theatre Royal in Drury Lane in December, 1698. It reportedly ran for nine nights, a successful debut for the young playwright. That same month, a pamphlet entitled *The Adventures of Covent Garden* appeared anonymously. It has been attributed with some certainty to Farquhar on the basis of hints in the preface, the technique of the writer, and the fact that one of the poems appears in a later text, this time signed by Farquhar.

About a year later, again at Drury Lane, *The Constant Couple* was performed, which Farquhar later described as drawing some fifty audiences in a five-month period. Robert Wilks, who had probably joined the company at Farquhar's request, was immensely popular as Sir Harry, and another actor gained the lifelong nickname of "Jubilee Dicky" as a result of the play. Suddenly, Farquhar had become the most popular dramatist in London.

Between 1700 and 1703, three more plays appeared, all relatively unsuccessful: *Sir Harry Wildair*, a sequel to *The Constant Couple*; *The Inconstant*, an adaptation of John Fletcher's *The Wild Goose Chase* (pr. 1621, pb. 1652); and *The Twin Rivals*. Sometime between the fall of 1700 and the spring of 1702, a date earlier than the once-proposed 1704, Farquhar—in collaboration with Peter Anthony Motteux—adapted Jean de La Chapelle's *Les Carosses d'Orléans* into a farce entitled *The Stage Coach*. The authors probably did not make much money from it because one-act plays could not stand alone on a program. Adding to his increasing financial difficulties, Farquhar was married, probably in 1703, to Margaret Pemell, a widow by whom he was to have two daughters. Knowing that Farquhar needed money, Pemell tricked him into marriage by having rumors spread that she was an heiress.

During the period from 1704 to 1706, Farquhar did not stage any plays. In 1704, he received a lieutenancy from the earl of Orrery's Regiment of Foot, which was sent for service in Ireland. This commission assured him of a small yearly income of about fifty pounds. He was soon sent into western England on a recruiting campaign. In 1705, he wrote his poem *Barcellona* on the occasion of the taking of that city by the earl of Peterborough; the poem was not published until after his death. It was also in 1705, supposedly during a stay at the Raven Inn while recruiting at Shrewsbury, that *The Recruiting Officer* was written. In the spring of 1706, this play was an overwhelming success, first at Drury Lane, then at the Queen's Theatre when some of the Drury Lane players moved to the new rival company.

Despite this success, Farquhar still seems to have had financial difficulties. In the fall or winter of 1706, he sold his commission to pay his debts, reportedly after a promise by the duke of Ormonde that he would obtain for him another commission. This promise apparently came to nothing. In the meantime, Farquhar became ill. Wilks, seeking him out after an absence from the theater, advised him to write a new play and loaned him twenty guineas. The result was *The Beaux' Stratagem*, written in six weeks during his continued illness. The new play, produced in March, 1707, proved to be another success.

The register of St. Martin's in the Fields lists Farquhar's funeral, paid for by Wilks, on May 23, 1707, although his death must have occurred a few days earlier, rather than on the traditionally accepted date, that of the third performance of *The Beaux' Stratagem* in April. He may have died of tuberculosis.

Analysis • In general, past criticism of George Farquhar's plays has centered on two basic areas: finding possible autobiographical references in both characters and settings and comparing Farquhar's moral attitudes to those of previous Restoration dramatists. In fact, many critics view Farquhar as the harbinger of the eighteenth century sentimental comedy. Both these views fail to deal adequately with Farquhar's artistic development of comedy. Unlike the writers of previous Restoration drama and subsequent sentimental comedy, Farquhar presents a balanced view of humanity and an equal appeal to the intellect and the emotions. His notion of the proper function of comedy, as expressed in a letter entitled "A Discourse upon Comedy" from *Love and Business*, includes the responsibility to portray the times accurately. The playwright's diversions must be realistic if he is also to carry out his task of instruction. Following these ideas, Farquhar produced drama that rests at some point of balance between the earlier cynical, witty comedy of manners and the later melodramatic sentimental comedy. Thematic development, dramatic conflict, and sources of comedy in Farquhar's three most popular plays–*The Constant Couple*, *The Recruiting Officer*, and *The Beaux' Stratagem*—illustrate his philosophy of comedy.

In these three plays, the treatment of theme, dramatic conflict, and sources of comedy contributes to an increased realism. The stiff, artificial characters of early Restoration drama have no place in Farquhar's theater. The audience at the turn of the eighteenth century was mainly a middle-class audience with an awakening sense of social consciousness.

Farquhar opened the window to a blast of fresh air for English comedy. By placing his characters in the world of innkeepers, military recruits, and highwaymen, Farquhar directed attention to humor rather than wit, and, in so doing, broadened the scope for comedy. His plays may well be less sharp-tongued than those of the dramatists who preceded him, but his work displays a greater naturalness and a deeper sense of life. His is the more human view of the world.

The Constant Couple • *The Constant Couple* is characterized by a light, often farcical atmosphere centered on situational comedy that instructs both by positive and by negative example. The efforts of several of the characters to attend the Jubilee in Rome gave the play a topical flavor.

Farquhar's habit of sustaining dramatic tension by action rather than by dialogue is a primary characteristic of *The Constant Couple*. The main actions center on Lady Lurewell, Colonel Standard, Sir Harry Wildair, and Angelica Darling, whose names alone suggest positive and negative examples. Angelica virtuously rejects a hypocritical suitor in the beginning, quickly establishing her character. In revenge, this suitor, appropriately named Vizard, tells Sir Harry that Angelica is a prostitute. Sir Harry, who has followed Lady Lurewell from Europe in hopes of a conquest, makes several humorous attempts to solicit Angelica's services; the best he can do is to look foolish and to hum when he discovers his mistake.

Meanwhile, Lady Lurewell is involved in making all of her would-be lovers pay for the trickery of a man who seduced her at a young age. Her revenge takes the form of getting her suitors into foolish, farcical situations. Sir Harry finally abandons his wooing of Lady Lurewell to marry Angelica, and Standard is revealed as Lady Lurewell's seducer, who has been faithful to his previous engagement with her. All potentially sentimental situations, such as the reconciliation of Lady Lurewell and Standard, are short and factual rather than long and emotional.

Another aspect of *The Constant Couple* that is typical of Farquhar's plays is his modification of the usual Restoration characters. Sir Harry is not the stereotyped rake, cool and polished, living by his wit alone. Above all, he is good-natured and full of contradictions. He has been a good soldier, but he avoids a duel. He loves fashion as well as French phrases.

The Recruiting Officer • In *The Recruiting Officer*, typical Restoration characters and themes are similarly modified. The action centers on recruiting antics and the difficulties of the relationships of two couples: Plume and Silvia, and Worthy and Melinda. At the play's end, both couples plan to be married. This theme of marriage, a typical Restoration theme, is a common motif in the play, but marriage is no longer a loveless relationship with both parties finding pleasure in affairs. Much of the play is devoted to the growing companionship between Plume and Silvia. This marriage, unlike the marriages in earlier Restoration drama, is not for money alone.

Farquhar's characters are also modified from the previous extremes of the Restoration. Farquhar's fop figure, Brazen, who has hopes of marrying Melinda, represents a fragmentation of the usual Restoration fop. Brazen has none of the typical clothes and affectations of the Restoration fop and much less of the foolish gullibility. Farquhar instead takes the social qualities of a fop, exaggerates them, and fits them into a military atmosphere. Brazen's bragging, traditional for the fop, encompasses the world of battle and the world of the beau. The social memory and name-dropping tendency of a fop are exaggerated. It is precisely these characteristics of Brazen that leave him open to ridicule by other characters within the play.

The rake figure also undergoes modification in *The Recruiting Officer*. Plume asks the country girl, Rose, to his lodging not to debauch her but to get her to aid in his recruiting, his main area of manipulation. Plume has a definite share of kindness and good nature. He provides for the subsistence of his bastard and provides a husband for the mother. He releases the disguised Silvia from her enlistment because he values an obligation to her father above money. Plume's dialogue has its share of wit, but it also reveals his fundamentally kind nature.

Although wit is used to produce comedy in *The Recruiting Officer*, the dialogue also features puns, farce, and comical treatment of social issues. The greater use of the latter as one of the major sources of comedy distinguishes Farquhar from other Restoration dramatists. The recruiting issue underlies a large part of the comedy in *The Recruiting Officer* and often provides for major dramatic conflict. The light atmosphere is set in the prologue, when the action is foretold and ironically compared to heroic times. The recruiting tricks of Kite play on possibilities, however improbable, of military advancement and even on the superstitions of the people when he dons his fortune-telling disguise. Less gentle is the comedy of Plume's entering his bastard as a recruit and wanting no one in his company who can write or who is a gentleman.

The Beaux' Stratagem • In Farquhar's *The Beaux' Stratagem*, social issues and modification of traditional Restoration themes and characters again play a prominent role. *The Beaux' Stratagem* is regarded by most critics as Farquhar's finest achievement. Its great sense of naturalness, of fidelity to life, continues to make it a great favorite with actors and audiences alike. The action centers on Aimwell's courtship of Dorinda, first of all for her money but later for love. Archer, Aimwell's friend disguised as a servant, also courts Cherry, the innkeeper's daughter, and Mrs. Sullen, an unhappily married woman. In the meantime, a series of scenes alternates between the inn, whose owner is a highwayman, and the manor, in which a robbery and a midnight love scene occur.

Farquhar's use of the social issue of the recent war against France and the resulting anti-French sentiment pervades all levels of the play. In the inn, Frenchmen pay double the regular fee. Scrub, Mr. Sullen's servant, parodies the French, while Aimwell quips that he would not like a woman who was fond of a Frenchman. Count Bellair, Mrs. Sullen's suitor, and Foigard, Bellair's chaplain, both come in for a large portion of the anti-French comedy.

The concept of social equality also becomes a major source for comedy, including the financial inequality created by primogeniture. Gibbet, the highwayman, excuses himself because he is a younger brother. Aimwell initiates dramatic conflict because of his status as a younger brother. In *The Beaux' Stratagem*, Farquhar stresses the fact that class differences do not correspond to levels of virtue. He achieves this emphasis by showing the same goodness in Cherry and Lady Bountiful, and the same corruption in Boniface and Sullen. In the robbery scene, Archer himself is cleverly associated with the thieves by Mrs. Sullen's cry of "Thieves, Murder." The same fundamental human qualities are thus shown to exist both in the inn and in the country mansion.

As in *The Recruiting Officer*, the plot of *The Beaux' Stratagem* deals with a modified marriage theme. The subject of marriage is not discussed using the common gaming imagery of the earlier Restoration drama, and the only slave imagery is used to describe Mrs. Sullen's marriage. In this instance, the marriage conflict is a conflict between law and nature. Sullen lies with his wife because of the law, and the natural differences between them do not come within the bounds of divorce law. In the conclusion, however, the maxim of nature as the first lawgiver is upheld.

The roster of traditional figures, as in *The Recruiting Officer*, is again modified. Count Bellair in *The Beaux' Stratagem* is a different variety of fop. He is obviously less foolish than the traditional fop because Mrs. Sullen chooses the Count to be part of her manipulations. Bellair shows extraordinary intelligence, for a fop, in initiating his own manipulation to get into Mrs. Sullen's closet. In creating Count Bellair, Farquhar took one aspect of the traditional fop, the beau, and exaggerated it. Bellair functions exceedingly well in this role, but he is also ridiculed because of his French qualities and becomes emblematic of the deeper conflict of social ideas in Farquhar.

Other major works

SHORT FICTION: *The Adventures of Covent Garden*, 1698.

POETRY: *Barcellona*, 1710.

MISCELLANEOUS: *Love and Business*, 1702; *The Complete Works of George Farquhar*, 1930 (Charles Stonehill, editor); *The Works of George Farquhar*, 1988 (Shirley Strum Kenny, editor).

Bibliography

Bull, John. *Vanbrugh and Farquhar.* New York: St. Martin's Press, 1998. Bull compares and contrasts the comic dramatists Sir John Vanbrugh and George Farquhar. Includes bibliography and index.

James, Eugene Nelson. *The Development of George Farquhar as a Comic Dramatist.* The Hague: Mouton, 1972. After a brief introduction, "The Traditions in Farquhar Criticism," James marches through the plays a chapter at a time. *The Recruiting Officer* is judged "climactic" for its form, and *The Beaux' Stratagem* is the "fulfillment of a promise." Rich source notes.

Milhous, Judith, and Robert D. Hume. *Producible Interpretation: Eight English Plays, 1675-1707.* Carbondale: Southern Illinois University Press, 1985. "By 'producible interpretation' we mean a critical reading that a director could communicate to an audience in performance," the authors note. *The Beaux' Stratagem* is "an effective stage vehicle," and the authors devote twenty-seven pages to discussing possibilities of stage interpretation. An insightful essay.

Rothstein, Eric. *George Farquhar.* New York: Twayne, 1967. This volume in the Twayne series is an excellent introduction to and overview of both Farquhar's life and his work.

Stafford-Clark, Max. *Letters to George: The Account of a Rehearsal.* 1990. Reprint. London: N. Hern Books, 1997. These letters look at Farquhar's *Recruiting Officer* and the production of Farquhar's dramas. Includes bibliography.

Eril Barnett Hughes,
updated by Frank Day

Horton Foote

Born: Wharton, Texas; March 14, 1916

Principal drama • *Wharton Dance*, pr. 1939; *Texas Town*, pr. 1941; *Out of My House*, pr. 1942; *Only the Heart*, pr. 1942, pb. 1944; *Homecoming*, pr. 1944; *The Chase*, pr., pb. 1952; *The Trip to Bountiful*, pr. 1953, pb. 1954; *The Traveling Lady*, pr. 1954, pb. 1955; *Horton Foote: Three Plays*, pb. 1962; *Gone with the Wind*, pr. 1972 (based on Margaret Mitchell's novel); *The Orphans' Home*, pr. 1977-1997, pb. 1987-1988 (a cycle of nine plays); *Night Seasons*, pr. 1978, pb. 1993; *Harrison, Texas*, pr. 1985 (three one-act plays: *The One-Armed Man*, *The Prisoner's Song*, and *Blind Date*); *The Habitation of Dragons*, pr. 1988, pb. 1993; *Dividing the Estate*, pr. 1989; *Selected One-Act Plays of Horton Foote*, pb. 1989; *Four New Plays*, pb. 1993; *The Young Man from Atlanta*, pr., pb. 1995; *Laura Dennis*, pr. 1995, pb. 1996; *Collected Plays*, pb. 1996; *Getting Frankie Married—And Afterwards*, pb. 1998, pr. 2002; *"Getting Frankie Married—And Afterwards" and Other Plays*, pb. 1998; *The Last of the Thorntons*, pr., pb. 2000; *The Carpetbagger's Children*, pr. 2001

Other literary forms • Horton Foote's best-known works are the screenplays for such successful films as *To Kill a Mockingbird* (1962), *Tender Mercies* (1983), and *The Trip to Bountiful* (1985). Beginning in the early fifties, he also wrote numerous scripts for various television programs. His novel *The Chase* came out in 1956. In 1999, he published *Farewell: A Memoir of a Texas Childhood*, which was followed in 2001 by a sequel, *Beginnings: A Memoir*.

Achievements • Along with the Academy Awards he received for his screenplays of *To Kill a Mockingbird* and *Tender Mercies*, Horton Foote won a Pulitzer Prize for his play *The Young Man from Atlanta* (1995). He was also nominated for an Oscar for his screenplay of *The Trip to Bountiful* and received an Emmy in 1997 for his adaptation of the William Faulkner story *Old Man*. His work has received numerous other awards, and in 1996, Foote was named to the Theater Hall of Fame.

Biography • Albert Horton Foote, Jr., was born in Wharton, Texas, on March 14, 1916. His family had significant connections in Texas history, his great-great-grandfather having been the first elected lieutenant governor of Texas. While attending high school in Wharton, Foote developed an interest in drama and played parts in several school plays. He decided to study acting, and though the Depression was well under way, he was given enough assistance by members of his family to take classes at an acting school in Dallas, and a year later, his father sent him to California to study at the Pasadena Playhouse.

During his two years in Pasadena, Foote worked on his acting skills, and after seeing Eva Le Gallienne in a memorable performance of Henrik Ibsen's *Hedda Gabler* (pb. 1890; English translation, 1891), Foote resolved to pursue a career in the theater. After completing his second year in Pasadena, he accepted a friend's offer of summer work associated with a drama company in Martha's Vineyard, Massachusetts. After two months in Massachusetts, Foote moved to New York City, where he survived by getting occasional acting parts. A chance encounter with an old acquaintance led to his meeting Tamara Daykarhanova, Andrius Jilinsky, and Vera Soloviova, Russian exiles who taught acting, and from whom Foote began taking classes. Later, Foote joined several other students in forming the American Actors Company.

In 1939, Agnes de Mille suggested to Foote that he write a play. He wrote a one-act play titled *Gulf Storm*, which was produced as *Wharton Dance* by the American Actors Company and favorably reviewed by Robert Coleman. This production marks a significant milestone in the career of Foote, whose career as playwright was to last more than sixty years and to include, by his own estimate, some sixty plays. He continued to play various theatrical parts with the American Actors and wherever else he could find work, but as his desire to write plays grew, his desire to act in plays diminished. He had already realized that in writing drama he could combine the world of his own past with the cosmopolitan world of the theater, and it is significant that he went home to Wharton, Texas, to write his second play, *Texas Town*.

Shortly after the Japanese attack on Pearl Harbor in December, 1941, Foote's third play *Out of My House* was produced, and Foote prepared himself for the military draft. Somewhat to his shock, he was found by the medical examiners to have a hernia, which disqualified him. Foote found a job as a night-shift elevator attendant, which gave him time to write. His play *Only the Heart* was produced in both 1942 and 1943. While working as manager of a bookstore, he met his future wife, Lillian Vallish, and the two were married in 1945. Foote continued to write, and, in the year of his marriage, he moved to Washington, D.C., where he was a principal figure in the formation of a new acting school and theater company. While in Washington, Foote taught drama and directed four of his own new plays, and he directed plays by Ibsen, Federico García Lorca, and Tennessee Williams. By 1949, however, he came to realize that he preferred to write as he had done before going to Washington. As he explains in *Beginnings*, "I felt

(Marion Ettlinger)

I was a storyteller, and that I wanted to write plays simply and directly." In the fall of 1949, Horton and his wife returned to New York, where he found a position teaching at the American Theater Wing.

By this time, the development of television was producing new opportunities for actors and writers, and Foote's growing reputation led to his employment as writer for the new medium. He began writing for *The Gabby Hayes Show* in 1950 and soon was asked to write nine one-hour plays for television. He remained a writer of stage plays during this period. In 1956, he completed his first screenplay, an adaptation of Clinton Seeley's novel *Storm Fear*, and the film appeared that same year. Also in 1956, the Footes moved to Nyack, New York.

Although Foote remained busy in the 1950's, his next major career achievement was his successful screen adaptation of Harper Lee's novel *To Kill a Mockingbird* (1960), which had won a Pulitzer Prize. When the film was released in 1962, it won Oscars for both Foote and leading actor Gregory Peck.

In 1971, Foote's stage adaptation of Margaret Mitchell's novel *Gone with the Wind* (1936) was produced in London. By 1974, he had begun the composition of what would eventually be a nine-play cycle collectively titled *The Orphans' Home*. By the late 1970's, Foote was again fully engaged with the stage, and though he wrote two television adaptations of short stories by Flannery O'Connor ("The Displaced Person") and William Faulkner ("Barn Burning") during this time, he was also teaching, directing, and writing. In the early 1980's, his plays continued to be produced, and Foote won his second Academy Award for his screenplay of *Tender Mercies* (1983). His 1985 screenplay for *The Trip to Bountiful* was also nominated for an Oscar. Foote began producing independent films based on some of his earlier plays, with *1918* appearing in 1985, *On Valentine's Day* in 1986, and *Courtship* in 1987. In 1988, he directed *The Habitation of Dragons* in its first version, with his daughter Hallie and his son Horton, Jr., among the cast.

Foote remained productive and professionally active through the 1990's, despite the death in 1992 of his beloved wife. In 1995, he not only received a Pulitzer Prize for his play *The Young Man from Atlanta* but also was honored by Brigham Young University, which held a festival of his works.

In 1999, he published his first volume of memoirs, dealing mainly with his family's past, the local history of Wharton, Texas, and the events that led to his departure to Pasadena to study acting. The second volume, which describes his life in Pasadena, New York, and Washington, appeared in 2001. Also in 2001, Foote's play *The Carpetbagger's Children*, with Jean Stapleton, Hallie Foote, and Roberta Maxwell, had its world premiere in Houston, Texas.

Analysis • Like fellow southern fiction writers William Faulkner and Flannery O'Connor, Horton Foote derives much of his inspiration from his strong identification with a region he knew intimately. Also like Faulkner and O'Connor, Foote draws from his knowledge of local information a powerful sense of larger truths, particularly that of the human potential for spiritual nobility in the face of suffering. Unlike these authors, however, Foote does not allow the intensity of his perception to shape his art into the macabre, and he achieves his best effects with a certain lightness of touch that never reduces his work to triviality but instead magnifies the significance of casual things. Foote's mastery of the rhythms of conversation must be to some extent a product of his years of studying the art of acting, but many of those rhythms come from the endless conversations of his Wharton childhood. Because most of Foote's plays are set in Harrison, Texas, a fictional version of Wharton, the playwright's preoccupation with the past constitutes a significant element of his dramaturgic vision.

A descendant of families who had established themselves in Texas in the nineteenth century, Foote was thirteen when the Great Depression struck. His father, a diehard Democrat, became an ardent supporter of Franklin Roosevelt, who was one of the principal advocates of political reform. Thus Foote, who, given his ancestry, might have joined many of his fellow southerners in resisting change, saw in his father an example of openness to change. His experience in California and in New York also gave him a better sense of some of the less laudable aspects of southern life in the middle third of the century. Combined with this wider perspective, however, was an abiding sympathy for the ordinary people who live in a town whose economy is at the mercy of the notoriously unreliable cotton harvest. Always important to Foote is the relation of the individual to family, to the community, to hardship, and to death.

Only the Heart • Originally titled *Mamie Borden*, this play explores the relationships among the members of the Borden family. Mamie Borden, the central character, copes with life by controlling others, orchestrating a marriage for her daughter so as to maintain power over her. Mamie's machinations, however, only estrange Julia, who departs with her new spouse. Because Mamie's schemes of power have already alienated her husband, who has become unfaithful to her, Mamie finds herself finally isolated. This play bears an odd resemblance to Sophocles' *Antigonē* (441 B.C.E.; *Antigone*, 1729), if one considers the similarity of Mamie and Creon, each of whom allows a domineering spirit to annihilate the possible effect of good intentions. Foote's play, however, emphasizes the danger of dissociation of heart and mind in personal relationships.

The Trip to Bountiful • An early play that Foote later adapted for the screen, *The Trip to Bountiful* embodies many of the themes and qualities essential to his best writing. The main character is Mrs. Watts, who lives with her son and his wife in an apartment in Houston. Her son, Ludie, is a hangdog loser who loves his mother but is dominated by his selfish and rude wife, who only tolerates her mother-in-law's presence because of her pension check. Mrs. Watts's dream is to escape to her old home place at Bountiful, a few miles from Harrison. The dynamics of this household are disturbing. Mrs. Watts shows occasional ominous signs of losing mental clarity, suggesting that the days of her life (and pension check) are numbered. Ludie realizes that he needs to make more money, but his helplessness is not promising. He cannot even defend his mother from the abusive comments of his wife. Jessie Mae herself would like to see Ludie bring in more money, but she is generally satisfied with the situation because she controls the pension check once it arrives. Her complaints mainly have to do with the inconvenience of having Mrs. Watts around. She particularly dislikes Mrs. Watts's habit of singing hymns.

When Mrs. Watts, who has hidden the month's pension check away for the purpose, escapes on the bus to Harrison, she finds that the friend with whom she has planned to stay, and who was the last person living in Bountiful, has died. The sheriff arrives, having received word of Mrs. Watts's escape from her family, and, moved by her despair, eventually drives her to her old home, where they await the arrival of Ludie and Jessie Mae from Houston. When the two arrive in a car Ludie has borrowed from a friend, Mrs. Watts and her son reminisce privately in front of the house. At first Mrs. Watts is made desperate by the imminent prospect of returning to Houston, but as she looks into her son's agonized face she puts her own grief aside, telling him: "I've found my dignity and my strength." Calmly accepting Jessie Mae's new rules for her future behavior, Mrs. Watts quietly says good-bye to Bountiful and walks away.

In this final scene, a number of themes come together. Ludie (whose name suggests that he is something of a joke) is the last of the family, and the play strongly suggests that he and his wife are to have no children. The neglected old family home, it is noted, will soon fall into the river. Ludie's predicament, like that of the house and of his mother, results from the country's shift from a rural, agricultural economy to the industrial economy of the city, where car brakes squeal at all hours and country people have trouble sleeping. Yet compassion exists, and Mrs. Watts's love for her son is still such that she renounces her own claims to happiness to end his suffering. In addition, there is the compassion of the sheriff, and that of Thelma, the young woman with whom Mrs. Watts rides the bus from Houston to Harrison.

Despite the annihilation of Mrs. Watts's fantasy of a return to the past, the end of the play finds her with a new resolve that makes her more admirable than the confused and desperate person she was earlier in the play, and it can even be argued that Ludie, who has after all come up with the gumption to ask for a raise and to borrow a car, is showing signs of resolve, particularly when he speaks very firmly to Jessie Mae at the end of the play.

The Orphans' Home • This cycle of nine plays represents Foote's engagement of creative imagination with the specific history of his family and region. Resulting to some extent from his meditations on the deaths of his parents, this cycle of plays explores and develops various dimensions of the cycle of birth and death, elaborating, as always, the potential of personal relationships to fulfill or frustrate those involved in them. *Roots in a Parched Ground*, the first in the sequence, had been written before Foote decided to write the cycle, but the other plays were written in what seems to be an expanded variation of the early Athenian trilogy or the Shakespearian tetralogy.

Other major works

LONG FICTION: *The Chase*, 1956 (adptation of his play).

SCREENPLAYS: *Storm Fear*, 1956 (adaptation of Clinton Seeley's novel); *To Kill a Mockingbird*, 1962 (adaptation of Harper Lee's novel); *Tomorrow*, 1972 (adaptation of William Faulkner's short story); *Tender Mercies*, 1983; *The Trip to Bountiful*, 1985 (adaptation of his play); *Of Mice and Men*, 1992 (adaptation of John Steinbeck's novel).

TELEPLAY: *The Shape of the River*, 1960.

NONFICTION: *Farewell: A Memoir of a Texas Childhood*, 1999; *Beginnings: A Memoir*, 2001.

Bibliography

Briley, Rebecca. *You Can Go Home Again: The Focus on Family in the Works of Horton Foote*. New York: Peter Lang, 1993. Based on Briley's 1990 doctoral dissertation from the University of Kentucky, this study provides useful information about the importance of family in Foote's plays. However, Briley was not able to obtain access to some important resources that are now available, and her work, though helpful, suffers somewhat from excessive reiteration of her thesis.

Dawidziak, Mark. *Horton Foote's "The Shape of the River": The Lost Teleplay About Mark Twain with History and Analysis*. New York: Applause, 2003. Contains the complete script of Foote's 1960 teleplay about Mark Twain's last years, with extensive additional material about the production and Foote's television writing.

Moore, Barbara, and David G. Yellin, eds. *Horton Foote's Three Trips to Bountiful*. Dallas: Southern Methodist University Press, 1993. This work compares the alterations and revisions made in the successive versions of *The Trip to Bountiful* between the first 1953 version and the film version of 1985. Changes in the texts are set forth in a chart, and there is a useful bibliography.

Porter, Laurin R. "An Interview with Horton Foote." *Studies in American Drama, 1945-Present* 6, no. 2 (1991): 177-194. A 1988 interview with Foote, covering his tastes in literature, his development and training as actor and playwright, and the background of *The Orphans' Home* cycle. This interview gives the reader a good sense of Foote's conversational style, his humor, and his modesty.

Wood, Gerald C. *Horton Foote and the Theater of Intimacy.* Baton Rouge: Louisiana State University Press, 1999. Wood argues that Foote's dramas reflect his characters' struggles against fear, struggles that are often made victorious by the achievement of a personal intimacy made possible by a spiritual feminine presence. Well written and persuasive, this work also includes a splendid bibliographical appendix of materials for those working on Foote's plays, screenplays, and teleplays.

Wood, Gerald C., ed. *Horton Foote: A Casebook.* New York: Garland, 1998. Contains twelve articles by various critics, divided into three main categories: "Biographical/ Contextual Essays," "Perspectives on Style/Themes," and "The Signature Theater Series." Includes a chronology of Foote's life, a bibliography of his works, an annotated critical biography, and an index.

Robert W. Haynes

Brian Friel

Born: Killyclogher, near Omagh, Northern Ireland; January 9, 1929

Principal drama • *A Doubtful Paradise*, pr. 1959 (also pr. as *The Francophile*); *The Enemy Within*, pr. 1962, pb. 1979; *The Blind Mice*, pr. 1963; *Philadelphia, Here I Come!*, pr. 1964, pb. 1965; *The Loves of Cass Maguire*, pr. 1966, pb. 1967; *Lovers*, pr. 1967, pb. 1968; *Crystal and Fox*, pr. 1968, pb. 1970; *The Mundy Scheme*, pr. 1969, pb. 1970; *The Gentle Island*, pr. 1971, pb. 1973; *The Freedom of the City*, pr. 1973, pb. 1974; *Volunteers*, pr. 1975, pb. 1979; *Living Quarters*, pr. 1977, pb. 1978; *Faith Healer*, pr. 1979, pb. 1980; *Aristocrats*, pr. 1979, pb. 1980; *Translations*, pr. 1980, pb. 1981; *Three Sisters*, pr., pb. 1981 (adaptation of Anton Chekhov's play); *The Communication Cord*, pr. 1982, pb. 1983; *Selected Plays of Brian Friel*, pb. 1984; *Fathers and Sons*, pr., pb. 1987; *Making History*, pr. 1988, pb. 1989; *Dancing at Lughnasa*, pr., pb. 1990; *The London Vertigo*, pb. 1990, pr. 1992 (adaptation of Charles Macklin's play *The True Born Irishman*); *A Month in the Country: After Turgenev*, pr., pb. 1992; *Wonderful Tennessee*, pr., pb. 1993; *Molly Sweeney*, pr., pb. 1994; *Plays*, pb. 1996-1999 (2 volumes); *Give Me Your Answer, Do!*, pr., pb. 1997; *Uncle Vanya*, pr., pb. 1998 (adaptation of Chekhov's play); *The Yalta Game*, pr., pb. 2001 (adaptation of Chekhov's short story "The Lady with the Lapdog"); *Afterplay*, pr., pb. 2002; *The Bear*, pr., pb. 2002 (adaptation of Chekhov's play); *Three Plays After*, pb. 2002 (includes *The Yalta Game*, *The Bear*, and *Afterplay*)

Other literary forms • Brian Friel has published two collections of short stories, *The Saucer of Larks* (1962) and *The Gold in the Sea* (1966). Two selections from these works have appeared: *The Saucer of Larks: Stories of Ireland* (1969) and *Selected Stories* (1979), reprinted as *The Diviner* (1982). The short stories in these collections are gentle, well-turned tales of ordinary people caught, largely, in the coils of personal circumstances. They belong firmly in the tradition of pastoral frustration, to which the majority of modern Irish short stories belong. The narrative tone of Friel's stories is genial, quizzical, and often humorous, and it anticipates the affection and dignity that Friel's plays typically accord the common person.

Achievements • After a modest but assured beginning as short-story writer, Brian Friel has grown, thanks to his plays, into one of the most important figures in the cultural phenomenon that will surely come to be known as the Ulster Renaissance. Like many other artists from the North of Ireland, Friel has had his work deepened and darkened by the history of his native province, yet it is also true that his willingness to face that history and its web of cultural subtexts has thrown into bolder relief the innate humanity of all of his work, rendering it all the more estimable.

Throughout his plays, Friel has persistently exposed stereotype, cliché, and narrowness of various kinds. In their place, he has substituted joy, openness, and individuality, qualities that enhance the human lot and for which his birthplace has not been noted. A deep sense of division informs both his characters and his dramatic practice, yet acknowledgment of division is an avenue to sympathy, not a recipe for impairment. Emphasizing with increasing vigor, range, and sophistication the value of spontaneity and the necessity of love, Friel's work is a moving—and stirring—statement of human solidarity in a dark time.

This statement is constantly renewed by the author's formal innovations. Friel's technical brilliance, however, does not permit him to break faith with the heritage of twentieth century Irish drama: its attachment to a sense of locale, its concern for the common lot, and its resistance to institutionalized modes of thought. In fact, Friel makes these elements interrelate fruitfully and unexpectedly by subjecting them to the clear, unblinking light of his moral intelligence.

Historically and artistically, Friel's place as Ulster's most important dramatist ever and as one of Ireland's most significant modern dramatists is secure. Friel's achievements have been acknowledged with numerous drama awards on both sides of the Atlantic, and in 1981, *Translations* received the Ewart Biggs Memorial Prize, instituted to recognize outstanding contributions to Anglo-Irish understanding. In 1992, Friel's play *Dancing at Lughnasa* won a New York Drama Critics Circle Award for best play of the 1991-1992 theater season. Also in 1992, *Dancing at Lughnasa* received a Tony Award for best play in addition to two other Tony Awards: for featured actress (Brid Brennan) and for director (Patrick Mason).

The American staging of *Molly Sweeney* in 1996 received both the Outer Critics Circle Award and the Lucille Lortel Award for outstanding Off-Broadway play of the season.

Friel was elected to Aosdana, a national association of Irish artists, in 1982. He received an Honorary Doctorate of Literature from the National University of Ireland in 1983 and was elected to the Irish senate in 1987. The *Irish Times* awarded him its Lifetime Achievement Award in 1999 for his contributions Irish literature and theater. He is a member of the Irish Academy of Letters.

Biography • Order, industry, fixity, and quiet are the hallmarks of Brian Friel's life. He was born in Killyclogher, near Omagh, County Tyrone, Northern Ireland, on January 9, 1929, the son of a teacher. The family lived in Omagh for ten more years before moving to Derry, the second city of Ulster and the place that, along with its County Donegal hinterland, may be properly considered to be Friel's homeland.

Friel was educated at St. Columb's College, Derry, and at Maynooth, the Irish national seminary, where he was graduated in 1948, though it was not his intention to study for the priesthood. He attended St. Joseph's Teacher Training College, Belfast, from 1949 to 1950, and for the next ten years taught in various schools in Derry. In 1954, he married Anne Morrison, with whom he would have four daughters and a son.

During this period, Friel began to write in his spare time, and from the mid-1950's, he was a regular contributor of short stories to *The New Yorker*. During this period, he also turned to drama as a form, beginning with two radio plays, which were broadcast in 1958, and at the end of the 1950's, he branched out into staged drama.

In 1960, Friel resigned from teaching to devote himself to writing. The wisdom of that decision has been confirmed by the continuing string of international successes that has ensued. English and, particularly, American audiences have greeted his plays at least as enthusiastically as have Irish ones. Friel's rapid development as a playwright was decisively influenced by the celebrated director Tyrone Guthrie, at whose theater in Minneapolis Friel spent some months in 1968, in his words, "hanging around."

Beginning in 1980, a more public Friel has been in evidence as the moving spirit behind Field Day Productions, a theater company formed in collaboration, chiefly, with the actor Stephen Rea. Based in Derry, the company's objective is to renew the theatrical life of provincial Ireland by means of touring productions. Friel has also been instrumental in establishing Field Day Publications. This imprint has issued, most notably, an important series of pamphlets on Irish cultural matters by leading contemporary Irish poets and critics.

In 1991, the three-volume *The Field Day Anthology of Irish Writing*, edited by Seamus Deane, was published, extending and consolidating much of the range and interest of the Field Day pamphlet series and creating a landmark in the development of Ireland's conception of its literary culture. This publication coincided with the international success of Friel's play *Dancing at Lughnasa*, which played to packed theaters not only in Dublin but also in London's West End and on Broadway, and which brought its author a large number of theater awards. Friel resigned from Field Day in 1994. That same, year he debuted as a director with the premiere of *Molly Sweeney* at the Gate Theater in Dublin.

Since 1998, his work for the theater has been dominated by his treatments and interpretations of the stories and plays of Anton Chekhov, with whose work his own has been favorably compared. *Afterplay*, which debuted at the Gate Theatre in Dublin in 2002, is an original play based on an imagined meeting between characters from Chekhov's plays *Dyadya Vanya* (pb. 1897, pr. 1899; *Uncle Vanya*, 1914) and *Tri sestry* (pr., pb. 1901, revised pb. 1904; *The Three Sisters*, 1920), both of which Friel adapted.

Analysis • Brian Friel's dramatic output, wide-ranging in subject matter though it is, possesses a notable consistency of theme, tone, and attitude to the stage. Whether a Friel play's pretext is the mission of St. Columbia, Derry's patron saint, to the island of Iona in the sixth century (*The Enemy Within*), or the living room of decaying gentlefolk (*Aristocrats*), a hedge school in nineteenth century rural Ireland (*Translations*), or the encampment of a traveling show (*Crystal and Fox* or rather differently, *Faith Healer*), familiar themes recur. Their recurrence, however, is invariably fresh, given new life by the author's unfailing sympathy and the suppleness with which he shapes unexpected cultural nuances. Such flexibility and control may be seen as an expression of the author's essential good nature.

In Friel's plays, one can also see one of his work's most consistent traits, his daring use of theater itself. Friel's work shows a marked flair for dramaturgical experimentation, but the experiments themselves are exclusively in the service of broader human concerns, revealing how hollow yet how inevitable ritualized behavior can be, for example, or economically contrasting characters' public and private spaces. A consummate orchestrator of theatrical space and (as is increasingly evident from his later work) the possessor of a light, though commanding, touch with ensemble work, Friel's is preeminently a writer's theater rather than a director's or a star's.

Foremost among Friel's broad human preoccupations is love—its persistence, its betrayal, its challenge. Few of Friel's characters manage to rise fully to the challenge of loving adequately. Their inadequacy is transmitted from one play to another, like a cynosure of frailty. What is significant, however, is not success but the apparent inevitability of exposure to a sense of human limitation and imperfection. Love generates many other important Friel themes. The affection for common people—uneducated, shrewd street-folk—which is unsentimentally present in all of his plays, has a sympathetic loving kindness in it that his characters themselves generally decline to embody.

The destructiveness of family life, particularly the unhappy effects that parents may have on children—in Friel's world an unredeemable original sin—is also a feature of the author's preoccupation with love. Love likewise informs such concerns as fidelity to place and to cultural inheritance. A marked sharpness in attitude toward behavior that is determined by cultural institutions rather than by the vigor of the individual psyche is, again, motivated by Friel's concern with love. In fact, love has developed in Friel's work from being, in early plays, a matter of impossible romance, family bitterness, or sexual buoyancy to being the finely calibrated optic of a worldview. Friel's manipulation of the optic in later plays reveals love as a saving grace, not only personally but also culturally—and usually both, interdependently, offering at once the tolerance of charity and the zest of passion, a healing ethic and a moral force.

Philadelphia, Here I Come! • Yet division, symptomatic of love's failure, is very much in evidence in Friel's work. In *Philadelphia, Here I Come!*—his first and major international success—the dichotomy between self and world is given novel dramaturgical embodiment through the device of having two actors play different aspects of the protagonist, Gar O'Donnell: Public Gar and his alter ego, Private Gar. The world sees only the former, while the audience readily perceives that it is the latter who has the greater authenticity, by virtue of his ability to satirize Public's gaucherie and emotional timidity. (Gar O'Donnell is the most winning representative of the naïve, ardent youth, a type beloved of Friel, first seen as the novice in *The Enemy Within*.)

The action takes place on the night before, and early morning of, Gar's emigration to the United States, and consists less of a plot than of a tissue of what Friel in later plays calls "episodes." In effect, Gar's past life passes before him. The passage takes place in two dimensions—the public, by means of farewells, and the private, by means of Private's somewhat manic and mordantly witty analysis of that life's nugatory achievements. The only thing which will relieve life at home in Ballybeg of his abiding sense of depletion, as far as Gar is concerned, is an expression of affection by his father. It is never made; Gar is obliged to carry his incompleteness with him. In that case, staying or going becomes moot.

As in *The Enemy Within*, the conclusion is inconclusive. The difference is that in the earlier play, inconclusiveness was enacted in a condition; here, rather more satisfyingly, it is embodied in a character. *Philadelphia, Here I Come!* also benefits from having its cultural resonances localized, as well as having its treatment of division given clever dramatic form. This play launched Friel's mature playwriting career. It contains an affectionately critical characterization of restlessness and brio, as well as failed love and a lament for it, and longings for a fuller life and a fear of it.

Crystal and Fox • Friel's preoccupation with love, familial relations, and romance is offered in a delicate, bittersweet blend in *Crystal and Fox*, one of his most effective works. Crystal and Fox, a man-and-wife team, own a traveling show of no particular distinction. At first, audience response is poor, and Fox, in a typical fit of recklessness, fires some of the players. The company is now reduced to four, one of whom is Crystal's ailing and incompetent father, who is soon hospitalized.

The traveling show, for so long an expression of Fox's restlessness, now attains a stasis, a condition that makes Fox mean and destructive. All that can save the situation is the unwavering romantic attachment, tantamount to worship, that Crystal and Fox have for each other. Into their impoverished encampment comes Gabriel, their son. Gabriel has spent years in England, like Cass in *The Loves of Cass Maguire*, the victim of a family row. Now, however, all is forgiven, and Gabriel is seen as an embodiment of renewal. He soon tells Fox that he is on the run from the English police, having, in desperation, committed robbery with violence. This information is kept from Crystal until Gabriel is arrested before her eyes.

Crystal and Fox sell the show's remaining properties to help Gabriel, but en route to Gabriel's trial, Fox lies, telling Crystal that he informed on his son for the sake of the police reward. A demented Crystal leaves her husband, allowing the play to conclude with a statement from Fox about the motivation for his destructiveness. He wanted the whole of life to be reduced to one ardent form—namely, his romantic love of Crystal. Such a love, he believes, expresses the best in him. Everything else is tainted with contingency, incompleteness, and mortality. Yet the finality and totality of his love for Crystal is what prompts treachery and ruin.

The play is satisfying on a number of levels. Its spare language complements its essentially violent action. Friel's metaphoric use of playing and roles is deeply ingrained in the piece's fundamental texture. Bleakness and joy are communicated with great clarity and economy. The need for romance—the desire that there be something more to life than the mere role one plays in it—is boldly established and subjected to an impressively unsentimental critique. In all, *Crystal and Fox* is a fitting culmination of Friel's early phase. From this point onward, his work, while not forsaking love as a theme or the family setting as its representative focus, has engaged more public issues and has placed less emphasis on individual destiny than on collective experience, a departure that has meant the virtual elimination of the often stereotyped minor characters present in his early work.

The Freedom of the City • With *The Freedom of the City*, Friel began his major phase. Innovative dramaturgy, a marriage of private and public themes, and a major renovation of the part played by love in human affairs, all make this play a work of notable theatrical events.

The city in question is Derry, and the play is inspired by, though it does not mimic, the events of Bloody Sunday, January 30, 1972, when British forces killed thirteen civil rights demonstrators. Friel opens the play's action by having his three protagonists flee from the violent disruption by army and police of a banned civil rights demonstration. They seek refuge successfully in the mayor's parlor of the Guildhall (the ease with which they do so being one of the play's many ironies about "security"), and with nothing better to do, they have a party. They drink the mayor's liquor, smoke his cigars, dress up in ceremonial robes, and parody official ceremonies, including the conferring of the freedom of the city.

Skinner, the most restless, deprived, and anarchistically inclined of the threesome, does a minimal amount of damage to property, stabbing a city father's portrait with a ceremonial sword. His opposite is Michael, a clean-cut embodiment of civil rights aspirations, who, without skepticism, wants nothing more than a fair chance to better himself. Between them stands Lilly, a blowsy mother of eleven, who approves of Michael's respectability yet is stimulated by Skinner's vitality. Eventually, summoned by military bullhorn to emerge, the three (now thought of, thanks to rumor, as forty) emerge from the circumscribed freedom of their refuge, to be shot in cold blood on the Guildhall steps.

The play's action, however, is only one of its levels. It is surrounded by frameworks of judicial and intellectual evaluation. Thus, from the outset, the audience is privy to the findings of the court of inquiry, which examines and distorts the protagonists' actions and characters. The audience is also periodically subjected to an analysis of the culture of poverty voiced by an American sociologist. These two framing devices—

sophisticated revisions of an ironic use of omniscience, introduced in *Lovers* and used most tellingly in *Living Quarters*—help the audience appreciate the informal, living texture of the trio's activities, as it is that very quality that the processes of evaluation and formal discourse are unable to admit.

Perhaps the play is overloaded with framing devices. In addition to the two central ones mentioned, there are also two that derive from the trio's own cultural constituency, represented by the Roman Catholic Church and by a ballad singer. These two also distort what the characters embody. The aim to be comprehensive is no doubt laudable, and the resultant verbal range is an impressive feature of the play, but the ensuing emphasis on the distorting effects of objectification is overdone. At the same time, however, such an emphasis also draws attention to *The Freedom of the City* as a hymn to the theater, both in the value it implicitly locates in the spontaneous antics of the three victims and in the sense that the stage is large enough for spontaneity and formality to play opposite each other.

Volunteers • In *Volunteers*, Friel also uses an event and a set of issues from contemporary Irish history. The matter in question is the Wood Quay, Dublin, excavation, where, during groundbreaking for a new office block, invaluable remains of Viking Dublin were unearthed. Efforts to preserve the site on the part of local *bien-pensants* led to ugly clashes with the developers, the law, and Dublin's city fathers and also, ultimately, to frustrating defeat for the preservationists.

Out of this volatile material, Friel fashioned a marvelous play. His volunteers are jailed social activists of a not very well-defined variety; inasmuch as they have a social philosophy, it generally seems to speak in favor of a more abundant life. (The play's one ideologue, a student radical who is one of the supervisors, in the end lets down the volunteers rather seriously.) The play is set in a hole in the ground, and the action takes place on the last day of the dig, a closing date that has been peremptorily hurried forward and that will leave the work unfinished. When this state of affairs is brought to the attention of Keeney and his fellow volunteers, it increases the audience's appreciation of the magnitude of their contribution as well as exposes the sterility of orthodox socially instituted planning. Indeed, the spontaneous gesture of volunteering has placed Keeney and his mates in danger of their narrow-minded fellow prisoners. Those who give freely, it seems, will be regarded with the most suspicion.

This conclusion is reinforced by the attitude of George the foreman. Superior to the volunteers in social status alone, his inability to have anything other than a master-servant relationship with them expresses insufferable moral smugness on the part of one who watches but does not dirty his hands. The only figure with whom the volunteers can feel kinship is the skeleton they have disinterred and named Lief, and who seems to have been the victim of a ritual execution. Lief is the authentic representative of a past common to all in the play, a past that is only properly visible to the volunteers. Thus, Lief is to be cherished much more than the vase that George has assembled out of fragments rescued by the volunteers, and when one of them deliberately breaks the vase, the symbolic resonance is as great as that provided by their ceremonial reburial of Lief.

The volunteers, then, are those who come in closest contact with the texture of the past, its earthbound treasures and human blemishes—and this contact is all the more estimable for being freely given. Prisoners of the state, menaced by their own kind and by their masters, the volunteers give unlikely expression to *pietas*, which is in cultural terms what love is in personal affairs. Yet all this is communicated in anything but solemn terms; the breezy satire of *The Mundy Scheme* is here deepened and tightened almost beyond recognition. Finally, in Keeney, Friel has created a character who is in total command of himself and prepared to face whatever comes, a character whose abundant energies, verbal pyrotechnics, and keen mind equip him superbly to be the onstage director of what Seamus Heaney has memorably called "a masque of anarchy."

Translations • Friel's *Translations* is among his finest achievements, as well as being, both intellectually and culturally speaking, his most ambitious. Set in the 1830's among the Irish peasantry, it discourses wittily, economically, and profoundly on the clash between the English and the Irish cultures, on language and its imprecision, on violence and its distortions.

The play opens with young adult peasants entering the hedge school of Hugh O'Donnell for their evening class in Latin, Greek, and arithmetic. In itself, such a scene is replete with noteworthy cultural resonances, being both a far cry from the stage Irishman and a vivid introduction to contemporary peasant life, down to the aging "infant prodigy" in the background who relishes Homer in the original. Hugh's son, Manus, takes the class this particular evening, because of his father's inebriation. One of the students is Manus's sweetheart, ambitious Maire, who is anxious for a fuller life for both of them. She plans to emigrate to the United States, while Manus, to some extent his father's prisoner, possesses a fierce loyalty to the local native life he loves so well.

In a sense, Maire resembles Manus's brother, Owen. He, too, desires a wider arena for himself, as is clear from his entry into the schoolroom with two well-disposed British soldiers, Captain Lancey and Lieutenant Yolland. These two are members of a detachment of troops engaged in an ordinance survey of Ireland, an enterprise that has as one of its features the translation of Irish place names into English. Owen is employed in this work, under Yolland's supervision, and he is painfully aware of the offense against *pietas* constituted by the effective divorce of native tongue from native place that will inevitably result. His awareness is ironically contrasted with Yolland's onset of a vague, fashionable, romantic attachment to the locals, and Owen's situation is further underlined by the deft trick of showing that when the native characters speak among themselves, the soldiers do not understand them. In other words, at certain points, the audience must accept English to be Irish.

In the hope that the cultural conflict will not come to a head, Owen arranges for Yolland to attend a local dance. There, Yolland meets Maire, and despite linguistic barriers, hilarious at the time (Friel's flair for representing gaucherie is brilliantly displayed here), she seduces him. Having seen Maire home, however, Yolland is never seen again, and the play ends with peasant hegemony broken beyond repair by the threat of dire reprisal by Lancy, and by Manus's flight from the place whose main hope he was. The situation is left in the hands of Hugh, who is impotently eloquent about its linguistic implications, and Jimmy, the "infant prodigy," whom language has deluded to the extent of his announcing his impending marriage to Homer's *glaukopis Athene*.

The play's effectiveness is not solely derived from the novelty and richness of its cultural scenario: In addition, this scenario enabled Friel to marshal areas of interest that had hitherto existed separately in his works. Here one finds the intersection of public and personal history, the suffocation of love by unpromising family circumstances, the destructiveness and inevitability of passion, the author's devotion to the common people and to that sense of Ireland that Ballybeg connotes. The coalescence of these themes certainly makes *Translations*, in the words of the review in *The Times* of London, "a national classic." The play also sets the seal on Friel's reputation as the most resourceful, most engaging, and most serious voice in postwar Irish drama.

Dancing at Lughnasa • Friel's plays in the 1990's mark a return to the more intimate dramas of personal lives in conflict and private emotional turmoil that distinguish his early career. Political and social issues are not absent but usually appear as components of a backdrop that includes small-town life, extended families, occupational ambitions, and other ordinary influences on the personalities of his characters. Dominating the foregrounds of these plays are characters challenged by the circumstances of their lives, and ennobled by their ability to meets those challenges with courage and grace, if not success.

Dancing at Lughnasa is a quiet memory play set in 1936 in the home of the Mundy family two miles outside of the town of Ballybeg. Michael, its narrator, recalls a summer when he was seven years old, at home with his mother (who bore him out of wedlock), his three maiden aunts, and his uncle Jack, a clergyman recently returned home from missionary work in Africa for apparent health reasons. Virtually plotless, the play unfolds through exchanges and interactions between the Mundy sisters, each of whom plays a role in sustaining the family and endures the deprivations and hardships of life with stoic good nature. The sympathy and gentle bemusement Friel shows for common people is tinged with pathos because, as Michael reveals, within a year of the time of the play's events, the household will be irreparably sundered: His uncle will die, two of his aunts will seek employment in the city and become lost in its hopeless underclass, and he will never again see his loving but irresponsible father, who periodically returns to visit his mother. Unknown to any of the characters, this moment, no matter how bittersweet, is the last happy moment the Mundys will know as a complete family.

Dance is a recurring theme in the play, and Friel uses it as a central metaphor to give structure and significance to the play's events. The play takes place during the feast of the pagan god Lugh, which is celebrated in modern times with a harvest dance that the Mundy sisters used to attend but are now unable to because of their strained finances. In one of the play's most memorable moments, the women break into spirited spontaneous dancing to a traditional Celtic song on the radio, briefly expressing a passion and freedom that rarely manifests in the household. Michael's father is a dance teacher, and Michael sees the dance steps he and his mother share when they meet clandestinely as a ritual tantamount to a marriage ceremony. Dance even plays a role in Jack's missionary experiences: Recalling dance-based rituals he participated in during his years in Uganda, he arouses very strong suspicions that he was sent home because he had begun to "go native." No matter what form it takes in the play, dance evokes a simple, natural order that the characters are drawn to but allowed to enjoy only momentarily. The dance of their lives, as choreographed by Friel, is unpredictable and erratic, and puts them out of step with their world and each other.

Wonderful Tennessee • An implicit subtext of *Dancing at Lughnasa*—that happiness is either transient or ephemeral and must be lived in for the moment—is made explicit in *Wonderful Tennessee*. Like *Dancing at Lughnasa*, it is a nearly plotless play, centered around the interactions and relationships between six characters in a brief twenty-four-hour period. Also like *Dancing at Lughnasa*, it evokes a paradisiacal realm, compared with which the world the characters inhabit is fallen and compromised.

The six characters are three married couples celebrating the birthday of small-time entrepreneur Terry Martin, who has brought them to Ballybeg Pier to be ferried across to the island of Oelian Draiochta (which translates roughly as "island of mystery"). The island has a mystical history: It was a spectral island that appeared only once every seven years until sailors landed on it and dispelled its enchantment. Terry tells his party that he has bought the island sight unseen, based on cherished memories he has of it from a story his father told him in childhood. However, once their bus has departed, the six are unable to rouse the ferryman to take them across the water, and they are left to spend their time stranded on the shore, looking across at an island they cannot reach and can barely even see.

Typical of Friel's plays, the island symbolizes an ideal the characters live in hope for but cannot attain. The reality of their lives supports this. Private and group conversations reveal that each is wrestling with unhappiness. Terry's wife Berna knows that Terry preferred her sister Angela, and she feels guilty that she has not been able to bear him children. Angela's husband Frank is desperate to publish a book that he hopes will succeed financially and free him from his tedious job as a clerk. Terry's sister Trish is married to George, who is dying of cancer. Despite their hardships and disappointments, they manage to stay friends and muddle through, bearing out Berna's contention that "Maybe that's how most people manage to carry on—'about to be happy'; the real thing almost within grasp, just a step away . . . but there are periods—occasions— when just being alive is unbearable. . . ." The island is thus emblematic of their very lives, its idyllic aspect fleeting and intangible.

Although a work of theatrical realism, *Wonderful Tennessee* verges at some points on allegory. The ferryman is named Carlin, surely a play on Charon, who ferries souls to Hades in Greek mythology, and in the closing moments, the characters enact a farewell ritual that symbolically parallels pagan ceremonies rumored to have taken place on the island. Furthermore, the play calls for an intentionally ceremonial staging. It is punctuated at many points with snatches of popular song that the characters sing as a natural part of the festivities and also to express their feelings of the moment. The blending of song and dialogue, somewhat in the manner of classic Greek drama, suggest Friel's attempt to create a unique vocabulary for expressing the otherwise inarticulable, much as he did with dance in *Dancing at Lughnasa*. The challenging staging this requires did not meet with universal approval, however, and may have contributed to the play's premature closing on Broadway after a successful run in London. Nevertheless, *New York Times* theater critic Frank Rich praised the play as that rare theatrical experience that transported the audience, "however briefly, to that terrifying and hallowed place beyond words."

Molly Sweeney • In *Molly Sweeney*, Friel approaches the theme of fleeting happiness from a different angle. The title character is a woman who lives in as close to a state of joy as any of Friel's characters do. Molly has been blind since shortly after her birth, yet she does not feel handicapped or disabled. Her inability to see has sharpened her other senses to the point where she apprehends much of the world around her, albeit in a way vastly different from sighted people. An excellent swimmer, she feels pity for sighted people, because she thinks that seeing somehow qualifies the sense of total immersion in the activity that she experiences. Molly is drawn very much in the spirit of idealized characters evoked in Friel's other plays, who are vessels for a kind of mystic wisdom that transcends normal routes of expression.

All of this is stripped away from her when her husband Frank, a man whose zeal for self-improvement and noble causes exceeds his common sense, makes it his mission to restore Molly's sight. At his urging, Molly has eye surgery. The operation is a success, but the results are devastating. Wrenched from her familiar world into one of new and alien perceptions, she finds herself cut off from the comfort and peace she knew. Unable to return to the world of blindness, she retreats into "blindsight," a psychological blindness that leaves her in a world her physician describes as "neither sighted nor unsighted, somewhere she hoped was beyond disappointment; somewhere, she hoped, without expectation."

The play is very much about the difference between "seeing and understanding," as one character describes it, and it is staged with its the three characters—Molly, Frank, and the ophthalmologist, Mr. Rice—posed at different spaces onstage, reciting their parts in monologues that intersect though they themselves never interact with one another. This novel approach to staging reinforces the sense that the characters talk without communicating, and see without understanding one another. It is yet another example of Friel's continuing efforts to experiment and seek inventive dramaturgic vehicles suitable to both the form and content of his plays.

Molly Sweeney's blend of introspective drama, compassionate characterization, and provocative staging is characteristic of Friel's plays throughout the 1990's, which treat the personal struggles of characters in emotionally challenging situations with the same gravity and grace as his more politically conscious stage work of the 1970's and 1980's. Though Friel continues to evolve as a playwright, he remains a champion of the common person who bears up with dignity under the burden of a world indifferent to his or her right to happiness.

Other major works

SHORT FICTION: *The Saucer of Larks*, 1962; *The Gold in the Sea*, 1966; *The Saucer of Larks: Stories of Ireland*, 1969; *Selected Stories*, 1979 (reprinted as *The Diviner*, 1982).

RADIO PLAYS: *A Sort of Freedom*, 1958; *To This Hard House*, 1958.

NONFICTION: *Brian Friel: Essays, Diaries, Interviews, 1964-1999*, 1999 (Christopher Murray, editor); *Brian Friel in Conversation*, 2000 (Paul Delaney, editor).

Bibliography

Dantanus, Ulf. *Brian Friel: A Study.* London: Faber and Faber, 1988. A condensation and updating of the author's *Brian Friel: The Growth of an Irish Dramatist* (1985), which discusses Friel's career up to, and including, the production of *Fathers and Sons*. Through close readings of Friel's work, Dantanus focuses on the broad cultural and social issues that arise from it.

Kerwin, William, ed. *Brian Friel: A Casebook.* New York: Garland, 1997. A selection of essays by leading critics covering most of Friel's major plays, providing a variety of critical perspectives on themes that range from Friel's use of history, myth, religion, comedy, and language to his depiction of women.

McGrath, F. C. *Brian Friel's (Post)Colonial Drama: Language, Illusion, and Politics.* Syracuse, N.Y.: Syracuse University Press, 1999. An accessible study by one of Friel's more ambitious critics that views him working in the same tradition as Oscar Wilde, William Butler Yeats, Sean O'Casey, and other authors who blend historical and factual and personal memoir to a create a new national mythology that breaks with that of Ireland's colonial past.

Murray, Christopher. *Brian Friel: Essays, Diaries, Interviews, 1964-1999.* London: Faber and Faber, 1999. Chronologically ordered culling of Friel's own thoughts on the playwright's craft and specific works. Includes his seminal autobiographical essay, "The Theatre of Hope and Despair."

O'Brien, George. *Brian Friel.* Boston: Twayne, 1989. An introductory survey of Friel's stories and plays up to *Making History.* The primary emphasis is on the character and quality of Friel's artistic vision. Surveys the whole of the Friel canon, including the early, unpublished stage and radio plays. Contains an extensive bibliography.

O'Connor, Ulick. *Brian Friel: Crisis and Commitment.* Dublin: Elo, 1989. A pamphlet by a well-known playwright and biographer. Addresses the problems of the writer's social and cultural responsibilities in times of civic crisis, using as its focus the work of Friel in the context of the crisis of authority in Northern Ireland.

Pine, Richard. *Brian Friel and Ireland's Drama.* London: Routledge, 1990. The most comprehensive, intellectually sophisticated, and theoretically ambitious reading of Friel's output up to and including *Dancing at Lughnasa.* Numerous stimulating and challenging connections are made between Friel and other Irish and international dramatists, and Friel is used as a means of focusing on the status and significance of drama in contemporary Irish culture.

George O'Brien,
updated by Stefan Dziemianowicz

Max Frisch

Born: Zurich, Switzerland; May 15, 1911
Died: Zurich, Switzerland; April 4, 1991

Principal drama • *Nun singen sie wieder: Versuch eines Requiems*, pr. 1945, pb. 1946 (*Now They Sing Again*, 1972); *Santa Cruz*, pr. 1946, pb. 1947; *Die chinesische Mauer*, pr. 1946, pb. 1947, second version pr., pb. 1955, third version pr. 1965, fourth version pr. 1972 (*The Chinese Wall*, 1961); *Als der Krieg zu Ende war*, pr., pb. 1949 (*When the War Was Over*, 1967); *Graf Öderland*, pr., pb. 1951, second version pr. 1956, third version pr. 1961 (*Count Oederland*, 1962); *Don Juan: Oder, Die Liebe zur Geometrie*, pr., pb. 1953 (*Don Juan: Or, The Love of Geometry*, 1967); *Biedermann und die Brandstifter*, pr. 1953 (radio play), pr., pb. 1958 (staged; *The Firebugs*, 1959, also as *The Fire Raisers*, 1962); *Die grosse Wut des Philipp Hotz*, pr., pb. 1958 (*The Great Fury of Philip Hotz*, 1962); *Andorra*, pr., pb. 1961 (English translation, 1963); *Three Plays*, pb. 1962; *Biografie*, pb. 1967, pr. 1968 (*Biography*, 1969); *Three Plays*, pb. 1967; *Four Plays*, pb. 1969; *Triptychon: Drei szenische Bilder*, pb. 1978, pr. 1979 in French, pr. 1981 in German (*Triptych*, 1981); *Jonas und sein Veteran*, pr., pb. 1989; *Three Plays*, pb. 1992

Other literary forms • Max Frisch was a versatile writer whose reputation was founded on both his dramas and his novels. He also wrote diaries, radio plays, short stories, film scenarios, and essays. His essays include discussions of literature, drama, society, architecture, town planning, and travel. There is a six-volume German edition of his works up to 1976, published by Suhrkamp in Frankfurt.

Achievements • In West Germany, Austria, and Switzerland, Max Frisch's dramas are consistently among the most frequently performed works by German-language playwrights. They are also regularly performed in other European countries and in the United States. Frisch's international reputation was established in 1954 with the publication of the novel *Stiller* (*I'm Not Stiller*, 1958), which is still considered his most important work. In 1951, Frisch received a Rockefeller grant to study in the United States. He was awarded numerous prizes for his works. These include the Georg Büchner Prize, the literature prize of the city of Zurich in 1958, and the prize of the city of Jerusalem and the Schiller Prize in 1965. His works have been translated into most European languages and are often best-sellers.

Biography • Max Frisch was born in Zurich on May 15, 1911, the son of a self-made architect. After attending gymnasium in Zurich between 1924 and 1930, he began studying German literature at the university of Zurich in 1931, at which time he also heard lectures on art history, philosophy, law, and theology. When his father died in 1933, Frisch had to leave the university to earn a living. He became a freelance journalist and wrote for such newspapers as the *Neue Zürcher Zeitung*. In 1933, Frisch traveled to Prague, Budapest, Dalmatia, Istanbul, and Greece, experiences that he used in his first novel, *Jürg Reinhart* (1934). In 1936, thanks to the financial support of a friend, Frisch began studying architecture at the Institute of Technology in Zurich; he was awarded his diploma in 1941. Between 1939 and 1945, Frisch had to serve periodically in the

Swiss army. In 1942, Frisch opened his own architect's office in Zurich. The highlight of his architectural career was winning a competition to build an open-air swimming pool in the Zurich suburb of Letzigraben, a project that was completed in 1949. In 1948, Frisch became acquainted with Bertolt Brecht, whose theories were to have an important impact on his dramas.

Frisch, an inveterate traveler, wrote in *Tagebuch, 1946-1949* (1950; *Sketchbook, 1946-1949*, 1977) that a man travels for two reasons: to meet people who do not think that they know him once and for all, and to experience once again what is possible in life. Frisch traveled extensively in Europe and the United States and visited the Middle East, Mexico, Cuba, the Soviet Union, Japan, and China. His experiences in the United States were reflected especially in the novels *I'm Not Stiller* and *Homo Faber* (1957), and in the novella *Montauk* (1975). After 1954, when he gave up his architect's office, Frisch earned his living as a writer. After living in Rome between 1960 and 1965, Frisch returned to live in Tessin, Switzerland.

Analysis • Max Frisch's admiration for the playwright Bertolt Brecht was an important stimulus in formulating his own dramatic theories. Frisch disagreed with Brecht's theories in several ways. Unlike Brecht, Frisch was skeptical that the theater can bring about social and political change, but he did believe that it can change a person's relationship to the world—it can make him more aware of himself and of the society in which he lives. Frisch was convinced of the power of the theater. In *Sketchbook, 1946-1949*, Frisch related how he was once sitting unobserved in an empty theater. He saw a workman come onto the stage and grumble. Then an actress walked across the stage and greeted the workman briefly. Because this very humdrum scene took place on the stage, its impact was greater than it would have been in ordinary life. To illustrate how the theater functions, Frisch used the analogy of an empty picture frame. If it is hung on the wall, it focuses a person's attention on the wall for the first time and forces him to see it. Like the picture frame, the box stage focuses a person's attention; it points out and demonstrates. Ordinary events are turned into exemplary ones on the stage.

Unlike Brecht, Frisch did not believe that the real world can be portrayed effectively on the stage; the stage can only show models of experience. In an early essay titled "Theater ohne Illusion" (1948; theater without illusion), Frisch praises Thornton Wilder for discarding realistic theater and stressing the theatrical again. According to Frisch, the theater should never try to create the illusion that it is real life on the stage. For this reason, Frisch used many alienation effects to break the suspense and to prevent the audience from thinking that it is seeing a "slice of life."

In addition, Frisch, unlike Brecht, had no ideology to impart to his audience. His function as a dramatist, he said, is to raise questions, not provide answers. Frisch wanted to make people more aware, to provoke them into finding their own solutions to the problems that he depicted. An example of such provocation can be found in *The Firebugs* when Biedermann steps out of his role and addresses the members of the audience directly, asking them what they would have done in his place.

Although Frisch was not convinced that the theater can bring about social change, he nevertheless thought that the author has a responsibility to address social and political questions. In an interview with Horst Bienek in 1961, Frisch criticized the Theater of the Absurd. If he were a dictator, he said, he would allow only the plays of Eugène Ionesco to be performed. Because such plays are fun to watch, they make the audience forget political conditions in the real world outside the theater. Frisch's dramas focus mostly on personal questions, but some address social problems such as anti-Semitism and prejudice (*Andorra*) and the moral weakness of the middle class (*The Firebugs*). Yet even in those works that deal mostly with the individual, Frisch still criticizes modern society, especially for its hypocrisy and for the limits it places on the individual.

In most of Frisch's dramas, the quest for identity is a central theme. Frisch believed that most people either invent roles for themselves or else have roles imposed on them by others. Such role-playing prevents people from growing and realizing their potential as human beings—the role reduces them to fixed and known entities, a theme that Frisch develops in particular in *Andorra* and *Don Juan: Or, the Love of Geometry*. Frisch shows how difficult it is to escape from roles. Because society wants to preserve the status quo, it is hostile to any notion of change; it expects people to conform to certain socially acceptable roles that consist for the most part of deadening routine. Frisch portrays those who conform to society without any struggle as smug and self-righteous (a good example of such a character is Biedermann in *The Firebugs*). Most of Frisch's protagonists fight for the freedom to be themselves, but the social restrictions they confront are often so overwhelming that they are forced to capitulate.

Don Juan • *Don Juan* had its premiere on May 5, 1953, at the Zurich Schauspielhaus and at the Berlin Schillertheater. Don Juan appears in Frisch's works for the first time in the play *The Chinese Wall*, where he protests against his literary portrayal as a seducer. In the play named for him, Don Juan is the polar opposite of the legendary Don Juan. Far from being the seducer, he is actually the seduced. The first three acts show how Don Juan is forced into the role of seducer; the last two, how, like Stiller in the novel *I'm Not Stiller*, he tries to escape from the image that people have formed of him.

To those familiar with the legend, the picture of Don Juan as the play opens is startling. Don Juan's father, Tenorio, is worried about his son because, at the age of twenty, he avoids women. To try to remedy this, Tenorio sends Don Juan to a brothel; while there, however, Don Juan plays chess. Frisch's Don Juan is an intellectual who loves geometry because it is clear, exact, and "manly." Like Walter Faber in the novel *Homo Faber*, he distrusts feelings because they are too unpredictable and chaotic. Don Juan's love of geometry is, however, responsible for his present involvement with Donna Anna. When he is sent to measure the walls of the enemy stronghold in Córdoba, he returns unharmed with the information, is named hero of Córdoba, and is given Donna Anna as his bride. Don Gonzalo, the commander, does not realize that Don Juan has used simple geometry to arrive at the measurements and has not exposed himself to danger.

The play opens on the night before Don Juan is to marry Donna Anna. The erotic festivities of this night stem from a pagan custom that the Christians have adopted. In the original custom, everyone was supposed to wear a mask. Through the power of love, the bride and groom could find each other despite the masks they were wearing. Because there were so many instances of mistaken identity, the custom was changed. Now the bride and groom do not wear masks because love can obviously err. Don Juan is drawn into the stifling eroticism of this night and sleeps with Donna Anna. He does not know that she is his bride because he has not met her before.

Don Juan's experiences on this night make him suspicious of love. When he suddenly realizes at the wedding ceremony that he has slept with Donna Anna, he refuses to marry her. He cannot promise to be faithful to her because he thinks that people are interchangeable when the biological urge to mate is aroused. The cries of the peacock seeking a mate, which are a motif in the first part, stress this biological nature of love. Like most of Frisch's intellectuals, Don Juan is basically self-centered. In fact, he holds a grudge against heaven for separating people into two sexes; he protests that the individual alone lacks wholeness.

It is not surprising that Don Juan repudiates love, because the society that surrounds him treats love cynically. Celestina, the brothel owner, turns the prostitute Miranda away because she has fallen in love with Don Juan: Such "sentimentality," Celestina believes, is bad for business. Don Gonzalo and Donna Elvira, the parents of Donna Anna, supposedly have a model marriage, yet Donna Elvira thinks nothing of deceiving her husband by sleeping with Don Juan. When the captured Arab prince tells Don Gonzalo to take and enjoy his harem, Don Gonzalo curses the seventeen years of faithful marriage that prevent him from enjoying the proffered sensual delights. The only positive concept of love is held, ironically, by the prostitute Miranda, whose love for Don Juan remains constant.

Don Juan's refusal to marry Donna Anna and the subsequent events give rise to his reputation as a seducer. To help him escape from the family that is thirsting for revenge, Donna Elvira gives Don Juan refuge in her room, where she seduces him. From her, Don Juan goes to Donna Inez. He is curious to see whether she will sleep with him even though she is engaged to his friend Don Roderigo. When she does, this seems to confirm his belief that love is indiscriminate and merely biological. At the end of act 3, Don Juan is surrounded by people whose deaths he has unwittingly caused: His father dies of a heart attack because of his son's behavior, Donna Anna drowns herself because of Don Juan's rejection, Don Roderigo kills himself because Don Juan has slept with his fiancé, and Don Juan unintentionally kills Don Gonzalo with his sword.

The fourth act takes place thirteen years later and depicts Don Juan's descent into Hell, famous from the legend—but with a new twist. It is no longer an example of divine retribution but is actually staged by Don Juan himself to escape from his role as a seducer and from his financial problems. Don Juan seeks to persuade the bishop that his "descent into Hell" will provide the Church with proof of divine justice; the husbands of the seduced wives will have their revenge; and finally, youth will not be corrupted by following Don Juan's example as a seducer. In return, Don Juan wants the Church to give him a cell in a monastery in which he can devote his time to his beloved geometry.

Don Juan invites thirteen of the women he has seduced to witness the event, and arranges for Celestina to play the part of Don Gonzalo's statue, which comes to life to punish him. Before the company arrives, Miranda, now the widow of the Duke of Ronda, offers Don Juan refuge in her castle, which he abruptly refuses. Don Juan's plan goes awry because the bishop turns out to be a disguised husband in search of revenge. Even though he reveals Don Juan's deception, the legend proves stronger than the truth—nobody believes that Don Juan has not been taken off to Hell. In the intermezzo that follows this act, Celestina tries to tell Donna Elvira (who is now a nun) about the role she played in the "descent into Hell," but Donna Elvira prefers to believe in "miracles."

In the last act, Don Juan has been forced to accept Miranda's offer of refuge and has married her. He is sitting at the table, waiting for her to come. Outside the castle, his literary legend is being created on the stage. He is a virtual prisoner in the castle because, after his spectacular "descent into Hell," he cannot return to the world. To return as a husband would also make him the laughingstock of everyone. Yet the intellectual Don Juan who despised love is beginning to love Miranda (he confesses that he misses her when she is away). Before, Don Juan could not reconcile love and intellectual pursuits. When he was drawn into erotic adventures, he felt as if he were a piece of nature while he wanted to be an intellectual; he thought that heaven scorned him as a man of the spirit. He had not treated women as individuals but as members of the female sex; his affairs with them were unimportant episodes.

At the end of the play, Don Juan is beginning to grasp that a relationship with a woman can be meaningful and through it he can gain the wholeness that, as an individual, he lacks. When Miranda breaks the news to him that she is expecting his child, she tells him that she does not expect him to be pleased at first, but she is convinced that he will be pleased about it in the future. The play ends with a question mark: It is not clear whether the relationship will continue to grow or whether it will deteriorate into the dullness of everyday routine that Don Juan fears.

Throughout the play, Frisch shows how damaging preconceived images are to the individual. In contrast to the legend in which Don Juan appears as a fixed entity, Frisch shows him evolving from a naïve twenty-year-old, to a bored seducer, to a husband, and finally to a father-to-be (in the legend, Don Juan is never a father). Don Juan fights against his reputation, which does not fit him in the least. In the notes that follow the play, Frisch claims that Don Juan is more related to Icarus and Faust than to Casanova; despite his reputation, Don Juan, like Icarus and Faust, is a man of the spirit who thirsts for knowledge.

The Firebugs • *The Firebugs* had its premiere on March 29, 1958, at the Zurich Schauspielhaus. A prose sketch titled "Burlesque" that appears in *Sketchbook, 1946-1949*, right after Frisch has mentioned the fall of the Beneš government in Czechoslovakia in 1948, forms the basic plot for the later play. The sketch tells how a stranger comes to a man's house. The man wants to win the stranger's friendship to demonstrate how humane he is. He gives the stranger shelter, storage for his gasoline, and even the matches with which the stranger and his friend incinerate him. Frisch developed this into a radio play in 1953 and finally into *The Firebugs*, in which the satire is sharper. The play was intended to share a theatrical evening with a companion play that Friedrich Dürrenmatt was to write. Later, Frisch added an epilogue to fill out the theatrical evening, but the epilogue does not add anything important to the play.

Frisch is sharply critical of the middle class and capitalism in this play. The protagonist, Biedermann, is an Everyman of the middle class (the name implies a philistine; a respectable, unimaginative bourgeois). Biedermann has become rich by manufacturing a worthless hair tonic—as he tells his wife Babette, his customers might just as well put their own urine on their scalps for all the good his hair tonic does. Unlike most of Frisch's protagonists, Biedermann does not question his identity but is smugly satisfied with himself. Above all, he wants to enjoy his rest and well-being. His appearance of bonhomie, however, serves to mask an inner ruthlessness.

As the play opens, Biedermann is sitting comfortably at home reading about arsonists in the newspapers. He proclaims that they should all be hanged. Although he has been forewarned, he still lets Schmitz stay in his attic because he wants to appear humane. His humaneness is, however, a facade, as his treatment of his former employee Knechtling demonstrates. Because Knechtling (who has invented the hair tonic) wants to share in its profits, Biedermann fires him. When Knechtling comes to ask for help for his sick wife and three children, Biedermann refuses to see him and callously says that he should put his head in the gas oven—which he subsequently does. Biedermann is morally responsible for Knechtling's death because he has driven him to suicide.

The reign of terror in Biedermann's house grows. Because Biedermann is afraid of Schmitz, he asks his wife to turn him out the next morning. Schmitz's accomplice, the former waiter Eisenring, arrives, and together they bring barrels of gasoline into the attic at night. Biedermann again is too cowardly to throw them out. In fact, when the policeman arrives with the news of Knechtling's suicide, Biedermann tells him that the barrels contain hair tonic—he is afraid to tell the truth because Schmitz has heard him say that Knechtling should gas himself. To win the friendship of the arsonists—and thus (he hopes) be spared—Biedermann prepares a festive meal for them. He even gives them the matches with which they start the fire. Although he knows that they are arsonists, he deliberately closes his eyes because he is afraid of them.

The arsonists are adept at manipulating Biedermann. When Schmitz, a former heavyweight wrestler, arrives, he first alludes to his strength, in that way intimidating Biedermann. Then he flatters him by telling him how humane he is. Schmitz later manipulates Babette by telling her stories of his disadvantaged childhood. In this way, he arouses her compassion so that she will not have the heart to throw him out. Later, Eisenring describes how the arsonists use language to disguise their intentions. One disguise is joking about their intentions; another is using sentimentality (for example, when Schmitz describes his childhood); but the best disguise of all is telling the truth because nobody believes it.

The arsonists do not hide the fact that they are arsonists. They tell Biedermann that the barrels contain gasoline and that they have chosen his house because of its strategic location—when his house burns, the whole town will go up in flames. Yet Biedermann insists on thinking that they are joking. It is not exactly clear why the arsonists want to burn down the town. Their accomplice, Dr. Phil, who has joined them because he wants a revolution, claims that they set fires merely for the love of setting fires, and he leaves them because they do not have a political reason for their actions. They could represent anarchy or the principle of evil (in the epilogue, the arsonists are the devils in Hell). Yet they also administer justice by punishing Biedermann for Knechtling's death.

On one level, the play seems to allude to certain political events in the twentieth century. The original prose sketch could allude to the takeover of the Beneš government by the communists because it appears in *Sketchbook, 1946-1949* right after Frisch has mentioned this. There are also allusions to the rise of Nazism—like the arsonists, Adolf Hitler never concealed his intentions, as is shown in his autobiography *Mein Kampf* (1925-1926). Yet, it is a mistake to think that the play applies to a specific event. Frisch was concerned about the vulnerability of middle-class democracy to terrorism because of its inner weakness and moral corruption.

Frisch himself noted that this play in particular was influenced by Bertolt Brecht, an influence that is most evident in the form. The six scenes are broken up by a chorus of firemen that comments on the situation, interprets the action, and warns of danger. The chorus is, however, helpless to avert the catastrophe—firemen can only put out fires, not prevent them. Another Brechtian device is the lack of suspense. From the outset, it is clear to everyone (except Biedermann) that the strangers are arsonists. The attention of the audience is thus focused not on how the play will end but on how Biedermann causes his own destruction. In the play, Frisch parodies the dramas of fate; what happens to Biedermann is not fate (as he would like to believe) but could have been avoided.

Frisch called his parable a "morality play without a moral," an indication of Frisch's belief that people cannot be taught. Like Brecht's Mother Courage, Biedermann does not learn from his experiences. This is especially evident in the epilogue, which takes place in Hell. Hell here is on strike because Heaven has pardoned too many criminals, in particular those who have obeyed orders to kill while they were in uniform (an allusion to the Nazi war trials).

Biedermann refuses to believe that he is in Hell. He protests that he has always obeyed the Ten Commandments. To the end, Biedermann is convinced that his only failing was that he was too good-natured; he refuses to see that he acted wrongly. He even demands restitution for his damaged property. Because of the strike in Hell, Biedermann and Babette are saved. As the play closes, there is a vision of a new town arising out of the ashes of the old, but the chorus suggests that people have already forgotten the lesson of how the old town burned. Like Biedermann, people do not learn from their experiences, a pessimistic conclusion about the middle class.

Andorra • *Andorra* had its premiere in November, 1961, at the Zurich Schauspielhaus. Like *The Firebugs*, the plot is derived from a prose sketch, written in 1946, in *Sketchbook, 1946-1949*. The sketch, titled "The Andorran Jew," tells of a young man who everyone thinks is Jewish. Some criticize him for his supposedly Jewish traits, while others admire him for these same qualities. When he is killed, it turns out that he was an Andorran like the others. After this sketch, Frisch quotes the commandment "Thou shalt make no graven image." In *Andorra*, Frisch shows how the protagonist Andri becomes a Jew simply by being told that he is Jewish.

The action takes place in the fictional country of Andorra (Frisch stated emphatically that he was not alluding to the tiny country in the Pyrenees). Frisch intended the play to be a model: Such events, he believed, could happen anywhere. The characters are two-dimensional because Frisch was not interested in them as people but only in their attitudes to Andri. The Andorrans are convinced that their country is a model of all human virtues—it is a haven of peace, freedom, and human rights. To be an Andorran, they think, means to be moral and humane. As the image of whitewashing shows, their moral superiority is only a facade. When there is a storm, the whitewash is washed off the church, showing the red earth beneath. As the soldier comments, this makes the church look as if a pig has been slaughtered close by, an image that indicates that the virtuous appearance of the Andorrans masks brutality.

Although nobody knows it, Andri is in fact an Andorran, the illegitimate son of the teacher Can and a woman from the neighboring country of the Blacks. Instead of telling the truth, Can told everyone that he had rescued a Jewish child from the savage anti-Semitism of the Blacks, and wins praise for this "courageous" act. The Andorrans' treatment of Andri shows, however, that they cannot tolerate anyone who they think is different. The cabinetmaker is unwilling to take Andri as an apprentice; he thinks Andri should become a salesperson instead because he cares only for money. Later, the cabinetmaker assumes that the faulty chair is Andri's, and the other apprentice (whose chair it is) lets Andri take the blame. The soldier accuses Andri of cowardice, a supposedly Jewish trait. The doctor criticizes the Jews because they are ambitious. Yet these are traits of the Andorrans themselves. The cabinetmaker demands an exorbitant price for Andri's apprenticeship; the doctor is overly ambitious; and when the Blacks invade, the soldier gives up without a fight.

At first, Andri desperately tries to be an Andorran, but when this fails, the priest persuades him to accept the fact that he is different. When Can finally tells Andri the truth about his origins, Andri refuses to believe him; he thinks that it is only a pretext to prevent him from marrying Barblin, Can's daughter (his half-sister), whom he loves. When Andri's mother, who inexplicably comes to see him for the first time, is killed, the innkeeper, himself the culprit, accuses Andri of the crime. Because he is different, he is made the scapegoat. Andri's acceptance of his "Jewishness" causes his death. When the Blacks invade, everyone has to walk barefoot over the square, their heads covered by black cloths—a grotesque scene. Although Andri is in no way different from the others, the Jew Inspector selects him as a Jew, and Andri is taken away and murdered. Can, who belatedly has tried to tell the truth about Andri, hangs himself in remorse. As the play ends, Barblin is whitewashing—a futile gesture because the guilt of the community can only be covered up, not erased.

Like Biedermann, most of the characters do not learn from their experiences. After some of the scenes, the characters who are responsible for Andri's fate step forward to the witness box and try to justify their behavior. With the exception of the priest, no one accepts any responsibility for Andri's death; each proclaims his innocence and no one feels remorse. Despite Andri's death, the Andorrans' prejudice against people who are different is as strong as ever.

These plays (which are among his most successful) are typical of Frisch's concerns. Frisch protested against the roles that people assume, either by choice or because they are forced into assuming them because such roles limit people's potential to lead fulfilling lives. In most of his works, Frisch examined the consequences to the individual of such role-playing. In *Andorra*, however, he shows that people form preconceived images not only of individuals but also of different groups of people and of nationalities, which leads to prejudice and racism. Frisch pessimistically concludes that most people do not learn from their experiences. In a society consisting of conformists, Frisch's protagonists vainly try to free themselves from their imprisoning roles. Such failure causes their progressive alienation from society, family, and friends—and ultimately from themselves.

Other major works

LONG FICTION: *Jürg Reinhart*, 1934; *J'adore ce qui me brûle: Oder, Die Schwierigen*, 1943; *Stiller*, 1954 (*I'm Not Stiller*, 1958); *Homo Faber*, 1957 (*Homo Faber: A Report*, 1959); *Mein Name sei Gantenbein*, 1964 (*A Wilderness of Mirrors*, 1965); *Montauk*, 1975 (English translation, 1976); *Der Mensch erscheint im Holozän*, 1979 (*Man in the Holocene*, 1980); *Blaubart*, 1982 (*Bluebeard*, 1983).

SHORT FICTION: *Bin: Oder, Die Reise nach Peking*, 1945; *Wilhelm Tell für die Schule*, 1971.

NONFICTION: *Tagebuch, 1946-1949*, 1950 (*Sketchbook, 1946-1949*, 1977); *Tagebuch, 1966-1971*, 1972 (*Sketchbook, 1966-1971*, 1974); *Dienstbüchlein*, 1974; *Der Briefwechsel: Max Frisch, Uwe Johnson, 1964-1983*, 1999; *Die Briefwechsel mit Carl Jacob Burckhardt und Max Frisch*, 2000.

MISCELLANEOUS: *Gesammelte Werke in zeitlicher Folge*, 1976 (6 volumes); *Novels, Plays, Essays*, 1989.

Bibliography

Butler, Michael. *The Novels of Max Frisch*. London: Macmillan, 1985. Provides criticism and interpretations of Frisch's works up to the mid-1970's. Index and bibliography.

Köpke, Wulf. *Understanding Max Frisch*. Understanding Modern European and Latin American Literature series. Columbia: University of South Carolina Press, 1991. Explores the themes and dramatic approaches of Frisch. Bibliography and index

Lob, Ladislaus. "'Insanity in the Darkness': Anti-Semitic Stereotypes and Jewish Identity in Max Frisch's *Andorra* and Arthur Miller's *Focus*." *Modern Language Review* 92 (July, 1997): 545-558. Compares the depiction of the plight of Jews in a hostile environment in both playwrights' works.

Pickar, Gertrud Bauer. *The Dramatic Works of Max Frisch.* New York: Peter Lang, 1977. Explores themes and approaches of Frisch's plays. Bibliography.

Probst, Gerhard F., and Jay F. Bodine, eds. *Perspectives on Max Frisch.* Lexington: University Press of Kentucky, 1982. Offers criticism and interpretations of Frisch's life and works. Bibliography.

Reschke, Claus. *Life as a Man: Contemporary Male-Female Relationships in the Novels of Max Frisch.* New York: Peter Lang, 1990. Examines the psychology of gender roles in Frisch's works.

Weisstein, Ulrich. *Max Frisch.* New York: Twayne, 1967. Provides biographical discussion of Frisch and interpretations of his works.

White, Alfred D. *Max Frisch, the Reluctant Modernist.* Lewiston, N.Y.: Edwin Mellen Press, 1995. Offers a biography and criticism of Frisch's life and works.

Yang, Peter. *Play is Play: Theatrical Illusion in "The Chinese Wall" by Frisch and Other "Epic" Plays by Brecht, Wilder, Hazelton, and Li.* Lanham, Md.: University Press of America, 2000. Discusses dramatic techniques of Frisch and his contemporaries. Bibliography and index.

Jennifer Michaels

Athol Fugard

Born: Middelburg, South Africa; June 11, 1932

Principal drama • *No-Good Friday*, pr. 1958, pb. 1977; *Nongogo*, pr. 1959, pb. 1977; *The Blood Knot*, pr. 1961, pb. 1963; *People Are Living There*, wr. 1962, pr. 1968, pb. 1969; *Hello and Goodbye*, pr. 1965, pb. 1966; *The Coat: An Acting Exercise from Serpent Players of New Brighton*, pr., pb. 1967 (with Serpent Players); *The Occupation*, pb. 1968 (one act); *Ten One-Act Plays*, pb. 1968 (Cosmo Pieterse, editor); *Boesman and Lena*, pr., pb. 1969; *Friday's Bread on Monday*, pr. 1970 (with Serpent Players); *Orestes: An Experiment in Theatre as Described in a Letter to an American Friend*, pr. 1971, pb. 1978; *Statements After an Arrest Under the Immorality Act*, pr. 1972, pb. 1974; *Sizwe Bansi Is Dead*, pr. 1972, pb. 1973 (with John Kani and Winston Ntshona); *The Island*, pr. 1973, pb. 1974 (with Kani and Ntshona); *Three Port Elizabeth Plays*, pb. 1974 (includes *The Blood Knot, Hello and Goodbye*, and *Boesman and Lena*; revised pb. 2000 includes *"MASTER HAROLD" . . . and the Boys*); *Dimetos*, pr. 1975, pb. 1977; *A Lesson from Aloes*, pr. 1978, pb. 1981; *The Drummer*, pr. 1980 (improvisation); *"MASTER HAROLD" . . . and the Boys*, pr., pb. 1982; *The Road to Mecca*, pr. 1984, pb. 1985; *A Place with the Pigs*, pr. 1987, pb. 1988; *My Children! My Africa!*, pr., pb. 1990; *Blood Knot and Other Plays*, pb. 1991; *Playland*, pr., pb. 1992; *My Life*, pr. 1994, pb. 1996; *Valley Song*, pr. 1995, pb. 1996; *The Captain's Tiger*, pr., pb. 1997; *Plays: One*, pb. 1998; *Sorrows and Rejoicings*, pr., pb. 2001

Other literary forms • Although Athol Fugard has written in a variety of literary forms, he is known primarily for his plays. *Tsotsi*, a long-lost novel written between 1959 and 1960 and abandoned until its publication in 1979, displays characterization, graphic language, and sardonic humor that foreshadow much in Fugard's later drama. Of Fugard's screenplays–*The Occupation* (1964), *Boesman and Lena* (1973), *The Guest* (1977), and *Marigolds in August* (1982)—the last three, under the superb direction of Ross Devenish, have been filmed and released. A post-apartheid version of *Boesman and Lena* starring Danny Glover and Angela Bassett was released in 2000. Fugard also wrote *Mille Miglia* (1968), a television script for the British Broadcasting Corporation, which explores in flashback the relationship between race drivers Stirling Moss and Denis Jenkinson, who won the last Italian one-thousand-mile race in 1955, and their preparations for the race.

Fugard's *Notebooks, 1960-1977* (1983) testify to the breadth of the influences on him and his influence on others. The notebook entries reflect his political engagement as well as his practical concerns as a dramatist. His *Cousins: A Memoir* (1994) relates the playwright's early-life experiences with two influential relatives: his older cousins Johnnie and Garth. Johnnie's love of music and performance and Garth's adventurous wanderlust were important elements in shaping Fugard's personality.

Achievements • Athol Fugard—playwright, director, and actor—is South Africa's most widely produced dramatist abroad. His plays, though rooted in one nation, have earned international acclaim. Fugard meticulously details life in a remote corner of the globe yet raises compelling issues of general interest. Using social realism, linear plot development, and naturalistic language graced by metaphor and symbol, Fugard has forged an impressive body of work for the theater, ranging from full-length plays to improvisational exercises. Theatrically sparse, with small casts and little, if any, reliance on elaborate sets, costumes, or props, Fugard's plays have been read easily on radio and adapted frequently for television and film. On December 4, 1984, Fugard received the Commonwealth Award for Distinction in Dramatic Arts, an award which he shared with Stephen Sondheim.

Fugard's distinction as a playwright is inseparable from his contributions to and influences on South African theater, as well as on the Yale Repertory Theatre. He has radically affected both the practice and purpose of serious drama in his native land. His interpretation of his world, his use of "poor theater" for its maximum effect, and his dedication to his actors, both black and white, have earned for him a critical respect accorded few modern playwrights.

Early in his career, Fugard chose to be a witness against what he called a "conspiracy of silence" about South Africa's apartheid legislation. Fugard considers theater to be no more—and no less—than a civilizing influence, one that may sensitize, provoke, or anger. He deplores the label "political playwright." He believes that if a playwright tells a story, a good one, the larger implications will take care of themselves. Because they are set in South Africa, Fugard's plays cannot ignore apartheid, but Fugard's plays are not agitprop. Critics and actors alike commend Fugard's craft, especially his attention to what he calls "carnal reality" and his ability to develop resonant images that merit repeated readings or performances.

Fugard's plays—and his actors—have been honored often. *The New York Times* voted *The Blood Knot* Best Play of the 1964 season. Fugard was elected Man of the Year in the Arts in South Africa in 1969. *Boesman and Lena* received an Obie Award for Distinguished Foreign Play from the *Village Voice* in 1971. Janet Suzman won the London *Evening Standard* Award for Best Actress in 1973 for her portrayal of Hester Smit in Fugard's *Hello and Goodbye. Sizwe Bansi Is Dead,* devised by Fugard with actors John Kani and Winston Ntshona, was chosen Play of the Year in 1974 by the London Theatre Critics. Kani and Ntshona went on to share Tony Awards for Best Acting in the 1974-1975 New York season for *The Island,* another Fugard play devised with their help.

In 1975, Fugard was commissioned by the Edinburgh Festival to write a new play, *Dimetos,* and in 1980 the Actors Theatre of Louisville (Kentucky) commissioned an improvisational work, *The Drummer.* (These works, along with *Mille Miglia,* a 1968 British Broadcasting Corporation television play, are not set in South Africa.) *A Lesson from Aloes* was awarded the New York Drama Critics Circle Award for Best New Play of the 1980-1981 season, while *"MASTER HAROLD" . . . and the Boys* won both the Drama Desk Award and the Outer Critics Circle Award for Best Play of 1982, as well as a Tony Award for Zakes Mokae as Outstanding Featured Actor and the *Evening Standard* Award for Best Play of 1983. The play also won South Africa's largest cash award for theater: the AA Mutual Life/Vita Award for Best New South African Play, 1983-1984. In 1986, Fugard was also the recipient of the Drama League Award, and the New York Drama Critics Circle Award and Helen Hayes Award for Direction followed in 1988 and 1990, respectively.

Fugard has been given honorary doctorates by three South African universities: the University of Natal, Durban, in 1981; Rhodes University, Grahamstown, 1983; and the University of Cape Town, in 1984. Yale University in 1983 and Georgetown University in 1984 also honored Fugard with doctorates.

Fugard is also a gifted director who exhibited a wide range of his interests through the plays he chose to direct at The Rehearsal Room in Johannesburg in the late 1950's and to stage with the Serpent Players in New Brighton from 1963 to 1973, including Harold Pinter's *The Dumb Waiter* (pr. 1960) in Johannesburg and Niccolò Machiavelli's *La mandragola* (pr. c. 1519; *The Mandrake*, 1911), Sophocles' *Antigonē* (441 B.C.E.; *Antigone*, 1729), and August Strindberg's *Fadren* (pr., pb. 1887; *The Father*, 1899) in New Brighton. Fugard's talents as an actor have enabled him to perform in many of his own plays when they were first staged.

Biography • Harold Athol Lannigan Fugard (pronounced *fewgard*) was born June 11, 1932, in Middelburg, a town in the Great Karoo, a semidesert region of Cape Province, South Africa. The son of an Anglo-Irish father and an Afrikaner mother, Fu-

(Richard Corman)

gard is an ethnic hybrid. English is his first language, but because of his mother's dominant personality, Afrikaner culture profoundly affected him. Fugard simultaneously honors and excoriates his Afrikaner roots. The two major abstractions of Fugard's work—love and truth—he saw fleshed out as he grew up in Port Elizabeth, a multiracial, industrial, windswept town on the eastern Cape to which his family moved when he was three.

Fugard's father lost a leg in a shipboard accident as a child, and in spite of successfully leading a series of jazz bands, he retired early, when Fugard was young, to a life of unemployment and alcoholism. Fugard's ambivalent feelings about his father color much of his work, especially *Hello and Goodbye* and *"MASTER HAROLD"... and the Boys*. His mother supported the family, first by running a boardinghouse, the Jubilee Hotel, and then by operating the St. George's Park Tea Room, the scene of *"MASTER HAROLD"... and the Boys*. Early in life, Fugard thus learned about failed expectations, a major theme in his work, and about hard times.

As a schoolboy, Fugard, then known as Hally, shunned his peers and spent his free time with his mother's waiters, Sam Semela and Willie Malopo. (These men appear in *"MASTER HAROLD"... and the Boys* under their real names.) Sam, in particular, though middle-aged, became Fugard's friend and the most influential adult in his life. Fugard looked up to Sam as a man in the fullest sense of that word; while Sam taught Fugard about being a man, Fugard shared his schoolroom experiences and books with him. For some inexplicable reason, one day Fugard insulted Sam; he did not expiate his guilt for this act until he wrote *"MASTER HAROLD"... and the Boys*. In real life, Sam Semela forgave Fugard almost immediately, and they remained friends until Sam died in 1983, shortly before the play in his honor opened in Johannesburg.

Fugard studied philosophy at the University of Cape Town from 1950 to 1953, but he quit immediately before his final examinations to hitchhike through Africa with a poet friend, deciding that the academic life was not for him. From 1953 to 1955, he traveled around the world on a merchant ship on which he was the only white crew member. He was married in 1956 to Sheila Meiring, who introduced him to the theater. When they moved to Johannesburg in 1958, Fugard was employed for three months as a clerk in the Fordsburg Native Commissioner's Court; then he began working with amateur black actors in Sophiatown, then Johannesburg's black ghetto. He also worked as a stage manager for the National Theatre Organization before he and his wife went to England and Europe in 1959.

The Fugards returned to South Africa in 1960, and the initial production of *The Blood Knot* in 1961 and its six-month tour around South Africa were crucial to Fugard's development as a playwright. In 1962, Fugard instigated a boycott of South Africa's segregated theaters by British playwrights, but by 1967 he had decided that even in such compromising circumstances, voices were preferable to silence.

Fugard visited the United States briefly in 1964 and returned to England in 1966; both trips involved productions of *The Blood Knot*. The South African government withdrew his passport from 1967 to 1971. From 1963 to 1974, he directed and produced European plays as well as collaborating on indigenous South African material with the New Brighton actors known as the Serpent Players; many of these actors were arrested between 1965 and 1967. Since 1977, Fugard's reputation has been such that he divides his time between South Africa and the rest of the globe: the United States, Europe, Asia, and India. The United States, however, is the only place he could live, he claims, if he could not live in South Africa.

Fugard has singled out several early incidents in his life as being of particular importance. For example, he said that his experience as a sailor cured him of any racial prejudice he might have had. His wife's prodding him into helping her establish a theater workshop in Cape Town, the Circle Players, in 1956 and 1957 led to the evolution of his lean, one-room dramaturgy. The move to Johannesburg and his work in the Commissioner's Court caused him to see the worst of apartheid legislation; there, an African was sent to jail every two minutes. Fugard turned this ugly nightmare to dramatic use when he devised *Sizwe Bansi Is Dead* with actors John Kani and Winston Ntshona in 1972; the play is an exposé of the passbook law, which required every African over sixteen to carry an identity book that restricted both his employment opportunities and his movements inside South Africa.

The rejection of Fugard's scripts by the Royal Court Theatre in London in 1960, the hand-to-mouth existence the Fugards shared there, and Fugard's sense of isolation from his roots convinced him that he was a regional writer. Before the Fugards' return to South Africa in 1960, in response to the Sharpeville Massacre, they helped form—with Tone Brulin, David Herbert, and Clive Farrell—the short-lived New Africa Group, dedicated to the staging of original South African plays in Europe. Fugard played Okkie, the Greek who tries to pass for white, in Herbert's *A Kakamas Greek* (pr. 1960), which was set in the Karoo, Fugard's birthplace. This production won the Best Entry Award at the Festival of Avant-garde Theatre in Brussels in 1960 and toured thereafter in the Flemish part of Belgium, Holland, and Germany—performed in English. The question of racial identify in *A Kakamas Greek* also haunts Fugard's first critical success, *The Blood Knot*.

While he was writing, in solitude, *The Blood Knot, People Are Living There, Hello and Goodbye,* and *Boesman and Lena*, which detail claustrophobic relationships, Fugard was also experimenting with adapting European plays to South African life and with improvising from the raw material of his actors' lives. *The Coat* in 1967 and *Orestes* in 1971, which actress Yvonne Bryceland considers "the most important single thing" in Fugard's career, are examples of improvisations from life.

The "Statements" plays (*Statements After an Arrest Under the Immorality Act, Sizwe Bansi Is Dead*, and *The Island*), which secured Fugard's reputation outside South Africa, also evolved from collaborative theater. These plays together constitute Fugard's most outspoken indictment of apartheid. An early version of *Statements After an Arrest Under the Immorality Act* was the inaugural production in 1972 of The Space, an "open" theater in Cape Town that evaded audience segregation rulings. *Sizwe Bansi Is Dead* was next, followed by an early version of *The Island* in 1973. These two plays did not exist in written form until Fugard and actors Kani and Ntshona were safely in London, later in 1973, for the South African Season at the Royal Court Theatre. In 1977 and 1978, Kani and Ntshona performed *Sizwe Bansi Is Dead* and *The Island* in Johannesburg at the Market Theatre, an "open" venue.

In 1974, after Fugard's success in London, *Three Port Elizabeth Plays*—including *The Blood Knot, Hello and Goodbye*, and *Boesman and Lena*—was published by Oxford University Press, with a detailed introduction by Fugard of excerpts from his notebooks. This introduction, combined with that to *Statements After an Arrest Under the Immorality Act*, constituted the clearest summary of Fugard's aesthetics—as well as a biographical gloss on his plays—before 1984, when *Notebooks, 1960-1977* appeared. In 1978, the "Statements" plays were performed and published in German; in 1979, *The Island* was translated and performed in French, and *Boesman and Lena* was translated and presented in Afrikaans in Cape Town.

Fugard returned to solo composition when *Dimetos* was commissioned by the Edinburgh Festival in 1975, but in spite of rewriting and a cast headed by Paul Scofield for the London West End run in 1976, *Dimetos* failed with critics and audiences alike. Its poetic allegory and nonregional setting are atypical of Fugard, yet the play remains one of his favorites. Like *Statements After an Arrest Under the Immorality Act*, another play that Fugard cherishes, *Dimetos* attempts to use prose musically and frequently becomes too elliptical and ambiguous.

Between 1978 and 1984, Fugard produced three major plays: *A Lesson from Aloes*, *"MASTER HAROLD"*. . . *and the Boys*, and *The Road to Mecca*. Fugard's tenure at Yale, with which these plays are associated, began in January, 1980, and he later bought a house in rural New York State so that he could continue his hobby of birdwatching when he was not at the Yale Repertory Theatre.

Fugard's plays are frequently revived and produced and have become staples of nonprofit professional theater in the United States and Great Britain. Fugard has continued to direct his own plays, both in the commercial British and in the nonprofit professional American theaters, such as his production of *My Children! My Africa!*, which enjoyed several venues, including the Lyttelton Theatre in London, the Perry Street Theatre in New York, the Yale Repertory Theatre in New Haven, Connecticut, and the La Jolla Playhouse in California. He also continued to act in his own plays on occasion, starring in *A Lesson from Aloes* in Los Angeles in 1991.

Throughout the 1990's Fugard continued his multifarious participation in live theatre through acting and directing as well as writing. After *Playland* in 1992, Fugard directed and acted in the 1995 and 1996 productions of *Valley Song*. Most extraordinarily, Fugard played two characters in *Valley Song*, the white Author and black grandfather (Jonkers), and specified that in future productions only one actor could continue to play both parts. In 2001 and 2002 Fugard directed his *Sorrows and Rejoicings*, first at the

McCarter Theatre in Princeton, New Jersey, then in Cape Town, South Africa, and finally Off-Broadway.

Analysis • Athol Fugard's plays satisfy a major criterion of good drama: the creation of vivid, lifelike characters. His characterization is immature in his early plays, *No-Good Friday* and *Nongogo*—with their black-ghetto gangsters, hustlers, musicians, whores, pimps, dreamers, and even a white priest—but these stereotypes foreshadow such fully developed characters in the 1960's plays as the half brothers in *The Blood Knot*, the landlady in *People Are Living There*, the siblings in *Hello and Goodbye*, and the destitute couple Boesman and Lena, in the play of that title. In the 1970's, Fugard created such powerful characters as the miscegenational lovers in *Statements After an Arrest Under the Immorality Act*, the urban and country blacks in *Sizwe Bansi Is Dead*, the prisoners in *The Island*, and the isolated Anglo-Afrikaner couple and their "colored" friend in *A Lesson from Aloes*. In his later plays, Fugard presents two black waiters and a teenage schoolboy (*"MASTER HAROLD"... and the Boys*) and an elderly, reclusive sculptor, her young friend, and a local pastor (*The Road to Mecca*). Fugard's characters, who seem so specific and concrete as to personify South Africa, are at the same time universal in their humanity.

Most of these characters do little or nothing except validate their existence through words that cry out to be heard. Their language ranges from the harshly naturalistic to the eloquently poetic; their rhythms are acutely South African, yet they cross linguistic barriers. Fugard's *Notebooks, 1960-1977* records the South African images from which his plays come: two brothers in a shack; a landlady who stays in her nightclothes for a whole day; a woman arriving with a suitcase and a man on crutches; a couple with their worldly possessions on their backs; six police photographs of two naked lovers; a self-confident black with a cigarette in one hand, a pipe in the other; two prisoners putting sand into wheelbarrows; and a lonely man studying an aloe plant. Program notes for *"MASTER HAROLD"... and the Boys* and *The Road to Mecca* provide images of ballroom dancing and a magical room of light and color. From such images, Fugard has crafted works of art as solid as steel, as fragile as china. Sturdy yet delicate, his plays wear well—the ultimate tribute to a master artist.

Fugard has long acknowledged his debt to Albert Camus and Samuel Beckett. In Camus, he found a kindred spirit for his worldview and his role as an artist; in Beckett, he found a dramaturgy of maximum import with minimum theatrical outlay. Confined to one room or space, two or three characters recollect, recriminate, role-play, and resign themselves to their existence in a world without meaning and with little hope for change. They delude themselves with false hopes and dreams, amuse themselves with games to pass the time; such nobility as they possess comes in the fleeting, lucid moments when they acknowledge their condition—and their dependence on each other. As does Camus, Fugard opts for a "courageous pessimism" born of the clear-sighted recognition of modern human beings' plight—trapped in a world as capricious as Ariadne's web and as mazelike as the Cretan Minotaur's labyrinth.

In his 1957 Nobel address at the University of Uppsala, Camus said, "To create today is to live dangerously"; he continued, "The suffering of mankind is such a vast subject that it seems no one could touch it unless he was like Keats so sensitive . . . that he could have touched pain itself with his hands." In an interview with Barrie Hough in 1977, prompted by *The Guest*, Fugard's film about Eugène Marais, Fugard commented that "one of the major Marais statements was that all living, survival, is grounded on pain. . . . It's really a theme that has gone through all my work; it's the string that holds all the beads together to make a necklace." Fugard has touched pain in his plays, as much as he has touched love and truth. He revels in the palpable, the tangible. In the realities of daily living—sore feet, tired bodies, arthritic hands, mounting stress, and cruel insults—Fugard reminds people that they are the sum of their pain. The whole is greater than the sum of its parts, but their interdependence is undeniable. Fugard forces us to recognize this interdependence preeminently in *The Blood Knot, Boesman and Lena, The Island, A Lesson from Aloes,* and *"MASTER HAROLD"... and the Boys,* the most representative of his plays, as well as in *The Road to Mecca.*

The Blood Knot and **Boesman and Lena** • The two plays that began and ended Fugard's work in the 1960's, *The Blood Knot* and *Boesman and Lena,* illustrate his talent for full-bodied characterization, as well as his progression toward structural sparseness and multileveled, resonant language. The half brothers of *The Blood Knot,* bound inextricably in a union of opposites, reveal themselves completely in a long play of seven scenes that builds to a harrowing climax.

The Nomadic outcasts and mixed breeds, or "Coloreds," Boesman and Lena, hover on the edge of life and death in what appears to be a cyclic pattern of eviction, of breaking and making camp, of Boesman's beating Lena, and of Lena's manic search for her identity, in two acts that are half as long as *The Blood Knot.* However, unlike Beckett's tramps in *En attendant Godot* (pb. 1952, pr. 1953; *Waiting for Godot,* 1954), whose essence is not to change, Fugard's characters do change in the course of the play. Superficially, more happens in *The Blood Knot*'s shanty over a much longer period of time than the one cold evening under the stars of *Boesman and Lena,* but the latter's reduction in plot and stage business results in a thematic and symbolic complexity that allows for greater character revelation as well as greater character development.

In both plays, two characters diametrically opposite in temperament and goals explode in words and acts when confined in a small space. Such conflicts are the heart of Fugard's drama, beginning with *The Blood Knot.* Morris, the light-skinned brother, suffers from agoraphobia—fear of open spaces—after wandering ten years trying to pass for white, while Zach, the dark-skinned brother, has suffered from claustrophobia ever since Morris returned to minister to him by ordering his life.

In his notebook entry on the brothers, Fugard wrote, "Morris, if anything, hates himself. Zach hates the world that has decided his blackness must be punished. . . . Morris is the better equipped mentally for this last fight—also, weakened by thought and sympathy. Zach has the physical strength and impetus of hate. Zach wins." The tyrannical alarm clock that regulates the brothers' lives rings just in time to keep Zach's violence at bay. When Zach asks Morris for an explanation of why their game of black-white domination has gone awry, Morris responds, "I'll keep the clock winded, don't worry. One thing I'm certain is sure, it's a good thing we got the game. It will pass the time. Because we got a lot left, you know! Almost a whole life . . . stretching ahead. . . . I'm not too worried at all. . . . I mean, other men get by without a future. In fact, I think there's quite a lot of people getting by without futures these days."

Condemned at birth to have no future, the brothers reconstructed a brief childhood reprieve in which they took an imaginary, wild, car ride—stopped only by a flock of butterflies—chased donkeys in the veld, climbed trees, teased girls, stole fruit, and caught birds. In contrast, the humor of their adult games is sardonic and menacing, their laughter double-edged. They are two particular South African brothers, yet avatars of Cain and Abel.

Like Morris and Zach, Boesman and Lena are locked in an intimate love-hate relationship as mates—one they have fallen into years before the play opens, and one that

Lena chooses to reassert as the play ends, in spite of her open rebellion throughout. Motifs that recall *The Blood Knot*'s birds, donkeys, and aimless walking recur in the later play, while staccato, contrapuntal speeches are interleaved with poetic mono- logues in both. Lena's frenzied songs and dances on the mud flats parallel the brothers' childhood games, but the violence talked about in *The Blood Knot* actually happens in *Boesman and Lena*. Lena's bruises are real, and the old African whom she befriends dies before dawn. He literally becomes the white man's refuse that Boesman has said he and Lena are, and because they cannot dispose of him, they must resume walking.

Although she threatens to remain behind, Lena prepares to follow Boesman; in re- sponse, he tells her the correct sequence of their journeys, which she had so desper- ately tried to get straight throughout the play—as if that knowledge would explain how she got where she is. "It doesn't explain anything," she says, but her parting shot, "I'm alive, Boesman. There's daylights left in me," is believable because she has demon- strated repeatedly her will to live.

Suicide is out of the question for Boesman and Lena. As absurd as their existence is, they endure it; they even tried to perpetuate it, but only one of Lena's babies was born alive, and it lived only six months. In recounting her past to the old African, who can- not understand her language any more than Boesman and Lena can understand his, Lena defines pain: "Pain? Yes! . . . One night it was longer than a small piece of candle and then as big as darkness. Somewhere else a donkey looked at it. . . . Pain is a candle *entjie* [end] and a donkey's face."

Such metaphoric language typifies Fugard, as it does Beckett. Moreover, both have been accused of writing plays of despair or bitter comedy. Fugard defends Beckett against such charges, as many critics defend Fugard. Fugard finds Beckett's humor, combined with his love and compassion for humanity's "absurd and bruised carnal- ity," positive and life-affirming; describing Beckett's humor to his wife, Fugard once said, "Smile, and then wipe the blood off your mouth." *Boesman and Lena* is Fugard's most pessimistic play, in mood and theme, but it is not morbid or maudlin; it is his most profound response to the world as he sees it, a world in which endurance and sur- vival alone may be the only card human beings hold in a stacked deck.

The Island • In *The Island*, collaborative and improvisational in origin, Fugard ex- perimented with the theories of Polish director Jerzy Grotowski, as he did in the un- published *Friday's Bread on Monday*, in 1970, and *Orestes*, whose 1971 performance is de- scribed only in a letter. *The Island* is a tribute to actors' theater, but once written, it has stood on its own merits as a strong play for actors other than John Kani and Winston Ntshona, Fugard's original performers and collaborators. It reads as well as it plays. Unified structurally and centrally focused, it demonstrates Fugard's mastery of the one-act form. Its companion piece, *Sizwe Bansi Is Dead*, another virtuoso play for ac- tors, comes closer to a stream-of-consciousness novella than to a drama built on the classical unities of time, space, and action that Fugard observes in *Boesman and Lena* and his three subsequent critical successes. Yet Fugard has always practiced what he calls "actors' theater."

As early as 1962, Fugard defined the pure theater experience: "the actor and the stage, the actor *on* the stage. Around him is space, to be filled and defined by move- ment and gesture; around him is also a silence to be filled with meaning. . . ." The ac- tor, space, and silence—Fugard continued exploring these dramatic requisites after a reading of Grotowski's *Towards a Poor Theatre* (1969) that validated the use of the actor as a creator, not simply as an interpreter.

The Island could not have been written without Kani and Ntshona's experiences as South African blacks or without what they and Fugard knew of the Serpent Players, who had been sent to Robben Island, South Africa's hard-labor, maximum-security prison primarily as political prisoners; some returned to tell their stories. (Kani and Ntshona were never imprisoned on Robben Island, though they were arrested in 1976 before a performance of *Sizwe Bansi Is Dead* and imprisoned briefly until an international actors' protest secured their release.) Fugard credits Grotowski with giving him the courage to "write directly into . . . space and silence via the actor," using the basic device of "challenge and response"; he also credits Brian Astbury, the founder of The Space in Cape Town, for his "vision and tenacity of purpose" in providing the venue for the "Statements" plays.

The Island, like *The Blood Knot* and *Boesman and Lena*, features two characters who are polar opposites in every sense. John and Winston (both the actors' actual names and the names of the characters) wrestle with fundamental questions of identity and purpose. The play opens and closes with the two convicts miming the futile labor of putting sand into wheelbarrows, pushing a barrow to where the other has been digging, and emptying the sand into that hole; the piles of sand therefore remain the same. A whistle blows, and the prisoners mime being handcuffed together and shackled at the ankles before the whistle blows again to send them off on a torturous three-legged run. They do not run fast enough to avoid being beaten. Bruised and bleeding, they collapse in their cell before uttering a word.

After the prisoners nurse their wounds and curse their sadistic warder, John gives a news broadcast and weather report: "Black domination was chased by White domination. . . . Conditions locally remain unchanged—thunderstorms with the possibility of cold showers and rain. Elsewhere, fine and warm!" Soon, John begins to rehearse *Antigone* for a prison show. Winston does not want to play a woman, and his reluctance to appear as such is comic until the very end, when his identification with Antigone becomes complete. Condemned to life in prison, he faces the audience and cries, "Brothers and Sisters of the Land! I go now to my last journey"; he tears off his wig and confronts them with, "I go now to my living death, because I honoured those things to which honour belongs." (John had been sentenced for burning his passbook in front of a police station.)

The Island is more, however, than an anguished cry of defiance. Like all of Fugard's plays, it focuses on close human relationships; John and Winston are linked in a bond almost as indissoluble as that of Morris and Zach or Boesman and Lena—almost, because midway through the play, John discovers that he will be free in three months, while Winston must remain for life. Before receiving that news, they talked on an imaginary telephone to their friends in New Brighton, another funny game of the many that Fugard's characters play; after John's news, Winston re-creates John's release and welcome home. Ultimately, Winston recovers from his agony and, like Antigone, comes to terms with his fate. *The Island* is as compelling as Fugard's earlier plays because, once again, its particulars are transcended in a work of universal significance, a study of humanity's inhumanity to humanity and people's capacity to endure entrapment through a joy in embracing ideals—regardless of their consequences.

A Lesson from Aloes • In *A Lesson from Aloes*, isolation, neurosis, and exile are the cost that Fugard's characters must pay for their fidelity to the ideals of love and friendship; there is little laughter here. The three characters are Fugard's first attempt to portray his own kind: literate, well-meaning South Africans caught in their government's crackdown on dissent in 1963, which led many to flee the country. Every Fugard play can be seen as an exploration of the effects of public policy on individual lives, but *A Lesson from Aloes* is Fugard's most quietly anguished portrait of this phenomenon.

Aloes are thorny, spiky, succulents that survive without much water in very harsh environments. Piet Bezuidenhout, a middle-aged Afrikaner, once an active member of an antiapartheid group that was silenced by the police, grows aloes in his back garden. Identifying them by name is his chief pleasure, other than reciting English poetry. Piet's English-speaking wife, back home after a stay in the Fort English mental home, and his "colored" friend and former comrade, Steve Daniels—preparing to leave South Africa on a one-way exit permit and just out of jail for breaking his banning order—are the other characters in this subtle but searing study of personal desolation. All three characters have internalized the shocks their world has given them.

The first act opens with Piet trying to identify a rare aloe; this leads to a revelation of the bitterness that mars his relationship with Gladys. For her part, Gladys cannot forget the police seizure of her personal diaries during a raid prompted by Piet's political involvement; Piet broodingly wonders why his old friends suspect him of being an informer. Tension builds as Piet and Gladys await the arrival of the Daniels' family for a farewell celebration. When Steve does arrive, in the second act—without his family and a bit drunk—the party fails miserably.

Playing a very nasty game, Gladys tells Steve that Piet had informed on him, but then she withdraws the charge. Piet refuses, however, to say anything: "Hell, Steve, you know why. If you could have believed it, there was no point in denying it." Apparently reconciled with Piet, Steve leaves. Gladys decides to return to the hospital, and Piet is left alone with his unidentified aloe. In spite of its explicit title and insistent metaphor, *A Lesson from Aloes* is not didactic. There are no clear-cut answers and few, if any, happy endings in Fugard's plays. Like Piet, Fugard cultivates a private garden with unidentifiable species.

"MASTER HAROLD" . . . and the Boys • In *"MASTER HAROLD" . . . and the Boys*, Fugard returned to the humor associated with his earlier plays to underscore the point that personal choice and action define a life worth living. Set still further back in Fugard's past than *A Lesson from Aloes*, and his most autobiographical play, *"MASTER HAROLD" . . . and the Boys* takes place in a Port Elizabeth tearoom one rainy afternoon in 1950. A long one-act play—too long perhaps—it opens with two black waiters, Sam and Willie, joking and practicing ballroom dancing for a contest two weeks away. Both men will compete if Willie can appease the partner whom he has recently beaten for not getting the quickstep right. Sam hits on an ingenious solution for Willie's future practice sessions: "Give her a handicap. . . . Give her a ten-second start and then let Count Basie go. Then I put my money on her. Hot favorite in the Ballroom Stakes: Hilda Samuels ridden by Willie Malopo."

As Sam demonstrates his superior skills, Hally, the teenage son of the tearoom owner, enters and applauds. Hally's long friendship with the waiters—especially with Sam—is soon apparent, but Hally is tense because of his father's imminent release from the hospital. Hally loves but is ashamed of his crippled, bigoted, alcoholic father and looks to Sam as a role model instead. Fugard lovingly re-creates Hally's camaraderie with the waiters; he focuses particularly on a kite that Sam made for Hally from scrap materials—a kite that miraculously flew. Nevertheless, Hally's "second family" cannot stand up against the demons of his first. These malign forces are unleashed in the play's climax, when Hally insists that the "boys" call him "Master Harold," tells them a crude racial joke, and, when Sam responds, spits in his face. Sam almost literally turns the other cheek, but Hally is too wracked with guilt to apologize. He leaves, and the curtain falls on the two waiters dancing once again—after Willie has used what was to be his bus fare home to start up the jukebox.

A play about growing up and the real meaning of family as much as it is about racism, *"MASTER HAROLD" . . . and the Boys* is at once exhilarating, sobering, exuberant, and wrenching. Like all of Fugard's plays, it relies on resonant language; here, the governing metaphor is that of life as a ballroom dance, which leads Sam to dream of a world without accidents or collisions if people and nations can only get the steps right.

The game that Hally and Sam play to identify "men of magnitude" who have benefited all humankind leads to some provocative choices by Hally—Charles Darwin, Leo Tolstoy, Socrates, Karl Marx, and Friedrich Nietzsche among others; Sam's choices are Abraham Lincoln, William Shakespeare, Jesus Christ, and Sir Alexander Fleming. Sam's poor-looking kite becomes the most splendid thing Hally has ever seen aloft, and the bench to which Sam ties it when he has to return to work becomes the "Whites Only" bench of Sam's final words to Hally: "If you're not careful . . . Master Harold . . . you're going to be sitting up there by yourself for a long time to come, and there won't be a kite up in the sky. . . . I reckon there's one thing you know. You don't have to sit up there by yourself. You know what that bench means now, and you can leave it any time you choose. All you've got to do is stand up and walk away from it." Avoiding sentimentality in a play that revels in sentiment is Fugard's rare achievement here; *"MASTER HAROLD" . . . and the Boys* is a masterwork from a master craftsperson.

The Road to Mecca • Fugard's experiments as a dramatist have been within the confines of social naturalism or realism. His modes are representational rather than expressionist or surreal; his plots are convincing; his language is often poetic but rarely abstruse, colloquial but rarely vulgar. In short, Fugard is not an innovator but a conservator: He emulates the best of his predecessors, but he translates their voices and techniques into his own uniquely South African vision. Over the years—a quarter of a century—he has become inimitable, and no more so than in *The Road to Mecca*. A three-character play, like *"MASTER HAROLD" . . . and the Boys*, *The Road to Mecca* is one of Fugard's most daring experiments.

The play is set in the autumn of 1974, and all three of its characters are white: two proud Afrikaners who live in New Bethesda (a village in the Great Karoo) and an equally proud young English-speaking schoolteacher from Cape Town. The plot is essentially uncomplicated. The young woman, Elsa Barlow, drives eight hundred miles for an overnight visit with her old friend, Miss Helen—a reclusive sculptor whom the local pastor, Marius Byleveld, wants to put in a nursing home for her own security. In the first act, the two women slowly reestablish their long-standing friendship, but Marius arrives at the opening of the second act and begins to undermine Miss Helen's confidence in her ability to cope and to create.

Elsa briefly adopts Marius's point of view when he tells her that Miss Helen almost set her house on fire earlier. Finally, in a moving reverie about the purpose of her Mecca, Miss Helen becomes courageous enough to dismiss Marius and assert her right to live with the danger of her creative impulses. Disheartened by his failure to convert Helen—and to make her love him—Marius leaves. The play ends with the women trusting each other once again.

Although this plot is fairly conventional, Fugard's choice of characters, the importance of the set, and the focus on the self-realization of the artist mark this play as a genuine advance for Fugard, a widening of his range. Although women and their concerns crop up obliquely in other Fugard plays—especially in *People Are Living There* and *Boesman and Lena*–*The Road to Mecca* is Fugard's first attempt to fill space with two women talking, arguing, and nurturing each other. It is also the first time Fugard has dramatized the necessary isolation of the artist. Fugard's epigraph for *The Road to Mecca* is an Emily Dickinson poem: "The soul selects her own society/ Then shuts the door./ On her divine majority/ Obtrude no more." An extended metaphor for the artist's vision—its genesis and its consequences–*The Road to Mecca* may also be read as a parable about pain, the pain of loving and not being loved.

Apartheid is only the subtext of the play, but Fugard's initial title was "My English Name Is Patience." These are the words of the young, barefoot Afrikaner woman whom Elsa befriends en route to Helen's house. This absent character pervades *The Road to Mecca* from beginning to end—like so many of Fugard's striking offstage presences, whose silences become virtually audible. What all of these silent characters share is a need for love.

Near the end of *The Road to Mecca*, candles flicker in mirrors and cast light on the walls—a stunning witness to Fugard's belief that the "candle burns brighter because the night is dark" and an answer to his question, "Would the making of meaning be so moving without the eternal threat of chaos and nothingness?" Miss Helen's laboriously crafted garden of statues—all manner of animals, camels, wise men, mermaids, and earth goddesses pointing East—did exist, at the home of the real Helen, Helen Niemand, in New Bethesda, South Africa.

Created over a remarkable twenty years of Helen's life, from age fifty to seventy, by a small, slight woman using broken bits of glass and hand-mixed cement, the statues are mute witnesses to her courage, integrity, and imagination. Thought mad by her myopic neighbors, she persevered alone. In her life and work, Fugard found the perfect fusion of symbol and referent, fiction and fact. All artists try to give meaning to matter, form to the formless, but only rarely does an artist give meaning to beauty, truth, love, and trust in so magical a form as *The Road to Mecca*.

Playland • The first play Fugard wrote after the fall of apartheid takes place one month before the fall. Ironically titled, *Playland* concerns a dramatic encounter between a black night watchman (Martinus) and a white South African (Gideon) at an itinerant carnival on New Years Eve, 1989. Gideon's drunken bragging about killing blacks in a border war motivates Martinus's confession to killing a white man who was trying to rape a servant, Martinus's fiancé.

The difficulty of forgiveness is a major theme in *Playland*. Lurking beneath their stunning confessions are two angry, guilt-ridden characters both on the verge of violence and in search of expiation for their sins. In fact, Gideon's fear and self-loathing almost provoke Martinus into retributive violence against him, culminating in Gideon's exhortation, "Forgive me or kill me." Also Martinus's search to exorcise his own guilt is magnified because he would have to forgive the rapist that he killed as well as himself. The playland itself is an ironic symbol not of "play" but of escape from reality and denial of truth. Also the nonworking carnival ride, flickering lights, and Gideon's broken car are all emblems of national disrepair. Like South Africa's Truth and Reconciliation Commission to follow, Gideon and Martinus are microcosmic representations of two factions of a country that must listen to each other, rage, forgive, and choose to work together for the good of all, a reflection of Fugard's optimism about his new country's future.

My Life • *My Life*, Fugard's next work, is more a performance piece than a scripted play. Fugard chose diary entries from five different South African young women and wove the threads into performance art. His intent was to share the varied and similar hopes, dreams, and perceptions of the younger generation. *My Life* celebrates racial diversity, uniformity of visions, and South Africa's future.

Valley Song • Another play that blurs color lines is *Valley Song*. Here the main character is the Author, who speaks directly to the audience; even more unusual is that Fugard stipulates in the printed script that the same actor who plays the Author also play the role of a black farmer, Abraam Jonkers. This positive, forward-thinking play celebrates the limitless possibilities for South Africa's youth. For *Valley Song*, Fugard returns to the setting of *The Road to Mecca*, the fertile valley of the Karoo, which is ripe for the rebirth of a country and its peoples. In *Valley Song*, the classic generation gap is typified by seventeen-year-old Veronica's dreams of leaving the rural area for the big city while her seventy-year-old *oupa* (grandfather) is afraid of youthful rebellion and wants Veronica to continue to stay with him. The image of pumpkin seeds permeates the play—the celebration of nurtured growth. The play ends happily on a note of salvation, survival, and harmony.

The Captain's Tiger • In *The Captain's Tiger*, the young writer protagonist is running from a miserable childhood, trying to find his authorial voice while heading from Africa to Japan on a tramp steamer in 1952. The young author deals with his conflicted feelings for his mother by striving, in vain, to rewrite his mother's painful life into the happier life she should have had. *The Captain's Tiger* revealed a new post-apartheid Fugard who clearly feels free to explore more personal issues.

Sorrows and Rejoicings • The Off-Broadway production of Fugard's *Sorrows and Rejoicings* opened in February, 2002. When the play begins, South African writer Dawid Olivier is already dead. In flashback we discover that Dawid had chosen the creative suicide of political exile to England when threatened with jail for his activist views. Present at the funeral are Dawid's white British wife and angry eighteen-year-old daughter, his black former lover, and his own spirit. Fugard has said of this aptly titled play, "It is both a sorrowing for the pain of my country and the rejoicings of what it is becoming."

Other major works
LONG FICTION: *Tsotsi*, 1979.

SCREENPLAYS: *The Occupation*, 1964; *Boesman and Lena*, 1973; *The Guest*, 1977; *Marigolds in August*, 1982.

TELEPLAY: *Mille Miglia*, 1968.

NONFICTION: "The Gift of Freedom," in *At the Royal Court: Twenty-five Years of the English Stage Company*, 1981 (Richard Findlater, editor); *Notebooks, 1960-1977*, 1983; *Cousins: A Memoir*, 1994.

Bibliography
Benson, Mary. *Athol Fugard and Barney Simon: Bare Stage, a Few Props, Great Theatre.*

Randburg, South Africa: Ravan Press, 1997. Benson relates her friendship with South Africa's two major playwrights and extraordinary insights into their lives and works

———. "Keeping an Appointment with the Future: The Theatre of Athol Fugard." *Theatre Quarterly* 7, no. 28 (1977): 77-86. A personal biography regarding Fugard's wife and daughter, his early career struggles, and his aesthetic debts to Jerzy Grotowski, Albert Camus, and others. Benson's interview is followed by some comments on acting by and about Fugard. The entire issue is devoted to South African theater.

Fugard, Athol. "Athol Fugard's South Africa: The Playwright Reveals Himself to a Fellow Writer." Interview by André Brink. *World Press Review* 37 (July, 1990): 36-39. Excerpted from the Cape Town periodical *Leadership*, Brink discusses Fugard's "commitment to the search for meaning" in a warm interview following the opening of *My Children! My Africa!* Fugard states that he regrets the time he must spend away from Africa, where his energies belong.

Gray, Stephen. *Southern African Literature: An Introduction.* New York: Barnes and Noble Books, 1979. A strong discussion of *Boesman and Lena*, "seen by more South African audiences than any other South African play," in its stage or film versions. Gray interprets the play as a "rewording of the myth" of Hottentot Eve: "The play is ultimately more about the strains of the marriage bond between her and her husband than the colour problem which aggravates it."

Vandenbroucke, Russell. *Truths the Hand Can Touch: The Theatre of Athol Fugard.* New York: Theatre Communications Group, 1985. A full study of the playwright's life, work, and philosophies. Contains introductory material on South Africa and a concluding chapter on influences, crosscurrents, language, style, and critical reputation. Appendices offer the full text of *The Drummer*, an essay on *Dimetos*, and a production chronology. Bibliography and index.

Walder, Dennis. *Athol Fugard.* New York: Grove Press, 1985. A general survey and appreciation of Fugard's work up to *"MASTER HAROLD"... and the Boys.* Walder says, Fugard's plays speak "not only of the South African dimension of man's inhumanity to man, but also of the secret pain we all inflict upon each other in the private recesses of our closest relationships." Plates and index, but no chronology.

Wetheim, Albert. *The Dramatic Art of Athol Fugard: From South Africa to the World.* Bloomington: Indiana University Press, 2000. Wertheim explores Fugard's life and work in such great detail as to make this a vital resource.

Nancy Kearns,
updated by Thomas J. Taylor
and Howard A. Kerner

Federico García Lorca

Born: Fuentevaqueros, Spain; June 5, 1898
Died: Víznar, Spain; August 19, 1936

Principal drama • *El maleficio de la mariposa*, pr. 1920, pb. 1957 (*The Butterfly's Evil Spell*, 1963); *Mariana Pineda*, pr. 1927, pb. 1928 (English translation, 1950); *Los títeres de Cachiporra: La tragicomedia de don Cristóbal y la señá Rosita*, wr. 1928, pr. 1937, pb. 1949 (*The Tragicomedy of Don Cristóbal and Doña Rosita*, 1955); *El paseo de Buster Keaton*, pb. 1928 (*Buster Keaton's Promenade*, 1957); *La doncella, el marinero, y el estudiante*, pb. 1928 (*The Virgin, the Sailor, and the Student*, 1957); *Quimera*, wr. 1928, pb. 1938 (*Chimera*, 1944); *El público*, wr. 1930, pb. 1976 (fragment; *The Audience*, 1958); *La zapatera prodigiosa*, pr. 1930, pb. 1938 (*The Shoemaker's Prodigious Wife*, 1941); *Así que pasen cinco años*, wr. 1931, pb. 1937, pr. in English 1945, pr. in Spanish 1954 (*When Five Years Pass*, 1941); *El amor de don Perlimplín con Belisa en su jardín*, pr. 1933, pb. 1938 (*The Love of Don Perlimplín for Belisa in His Garden*, 1941); *Bodas de sangre*, pr. 1933, pb. 1935 (*Blood Wedding*, 1939); *Yerma*, pr. 1934, pb. 1937 (English translation, 1941); *Doña Rosita la soltera: O, El lenguaje de las flores*, pr. 1935, pb. 1938 (*Doña Rosita the Spinster: Or, The Language of the Flowers*, 1941); *El retablillo de don Cristóbal*, pr. 1935, pb. 1938 (*In the Frame of Don Cristóbal*, 1944); *La casa de Bernarda Alba*, wr. 1936, pr., pb. 1945 (*The House of Bernarda Alba*, 1947)

Other literary forms • It may be argued with some justification that Federico García Lorca is best remembered as a poet. Although recognition for his poetry came first, García Lorca did divide his creative energies almost equally between the two genres, concentrating on poetry during the 1920's and devoting himself more single-mindedly in the 1930's to the theater. His first collection, *Libro de poemas*, appeared in 1921, and between 1921 and 1924 García Lorca continued work on *Poema del cante jondo* (1931; *Poem of the Gypsy Seguidilla*, 1967), *Primeras canciones* (1936), and *Canciones*, 1921-1924 (1927; *Songs*, 1976)—all of which attest his considerable knowledge of Andalusian folklore and a genuine musical flair.

García Lorca's reputation soared after the 1928 publication of *Romancero gitano, 1924-1927* (*The Gypsy Ballads of García Lorca*, 1951, 1953), an ambitious attempt at recapturing tradition to express it in a modern idiom. The Gypsy is cast as a contemporary victim, a natural being at odds with an inflexible, repressive society, in powerful and compelling images of frustration, loss, and death. García Lorca's fusion of personal and universal symbolism was almost too successful; critics disseminated rather too freely the facile "myth of the Gypsy" with García Lorca as its poet. This brought the angry riposte that the Gypsy was only one manifestation of the persecution of minorities.

Other victims of persecution included the black and the homosexual, and both figured prominently in García Lorca's next collection, *Poeta en Nueva York* (*Poet in New York*, 1940, 1955), written in 1929-1930 but published posthumously in 1940. Visiting the United States in 1929, García Lorca had been appalled by what he saw of Depression-era New York, finding there an anonymous, transient, and brutally violent society with no unifying mythology or collective dream. His denunciations of the alienation, pain, and spiritual desolation inflicted by the ruthless inhumanity of modern technology found expression in nightmarish, surrealistic images of the entrapment and destruction of natural forces.

If García Lorca wrote less poetry after *Poet in New York*, anguish and inner torment characterize the difficult and often obscure metaphors of the poems of *Diván del Tamarit*, (*The Divan at the Tamarit*, 1944), posthumously collected and published in 1940. A notable exception is the elegy of 1935, *Llanto por Ignacio Sánchez Mejías* (*Lament for the Death of a Bullfighter*, 1937, 1939), which, classical in form, moves in four parts from shock and horror by way of ritualized lament and tranquil meditation to a philosophical funeral oration.

Less important than either his poetry or drama, but often a more explicit source of many recurring themes and images, is García Lorca's prose, particularly *Impresiones y paisajes* (1918). The most complete collection of his poetic prose and other more ephemeral writings, such as letters, lectures, and interviews, may be found in *Obras completas* (1973). Throughout his life, García Lorca displayed remarkable talents for music and drawing, and the piano arrangements of his own and traditional poetry and the sketches which accompany, and sometimes explain, his poems and letters are well worth consulting.

Achievements • In the decades since his death, Federico García Lorca has become something of a cult figure (particularly outside his native country, where the stylized image of Spain found in his poetry and plays has romantic appeal). His work has been widely translated, inspiring writers, composers, choreographers, painters, and filmmakers; critical studies, moreover, abound, and as a result, García Lorca's name is now probably as familiar as that of Miguel de Cervantes. Much of this fame comes from a personal myth inspired equally by memories of García Lorca's undeniably charismatic presence and the tragic circumstances of his untimely death. Proper assessment is therefore not easy.

At odds with the myth of García Lorca's quintessential Spanishness is the degree to which his stagecraft, both as dramatist and as director, belongs to broader European cultural currents. His constantly reiterated goal of the renovation of the Spanish theater was a vision entirely harmonious with the technical advances of luminaries such as Edward Gordon Craig, Max Reinhardt, and Konstantin Stanislavsky. Unlike them, he undertook the enterprise at a time when his national theater was sunk in the stagnation of unrelieved superficiality, and his achievement of a modern style is all the more creditable.

In collaboration with stage-director Rivas Cherif and actress Margarita Xirgu, García Lorca brought new techniques from Paris to the staging of his own plays. Not content with winning over the theatergoing public of the capital, García Lorca's five-year stint as codirector with Eduardo Ugarte of the "university theater," La Barraca, brought the same modern techniques to the Spanish classics performed throughout Spain. His energy, ingenuity, and experience revolutionized theatrical style in the 1930's, redeeming, albeit only briefly, the national theater from a creaking nineteenth century realism.

As a dramatist, García Lorca promised much; his death cut off a brilliant future. Plays such as *The Audience* and *When Five Years Pass* are truly innovative, with elements that foreshadow the experimental theater of Samuel Beckett, Jean Genet, and Eugène Ionesco. Even García Lorca's dramas firmly rooted in the Spanish context have a universal quality. By baring the human soul, he communicated the many facets of humanity's contact with the primitive, instinctual forces of the natural work in dynamic dramatic language stripped of all superficiality. The culmination comes in *The House of Bernarda Alba*, García Lorca's revival of the idea of tragedy for modern times. What new challenges and experiments he had in mind are, unfortunately, lost forever. Bernarda Alba's final imposition of silence was all too prophetic. Only since the 1970's, some forty years after García Lorca's death, have Spanish dramatists begun to grapple with the many innovations he envisioned so clearly.

Biography • Federico García Lorca was born in 1898 in a small Andalusian village about fifteen miles from Granada. His father was a prosperous landowner and his mother a sometime teacher. All four of their children grew up in comfortable circumstances with the advantages of a good formal education and the prolonged leisure to pursue the delights of music and literature. Indeed, García Lorca's interest in the theater was apparent from a very early age in the puppet-theater shows that he designed and directed to entertain the household. In 1909, the family moved to Granada, where García Lorca went to school and attended university. The move was significant: The rich and varied cultural life there fired the young García Lorca's ambition to write, while the city itself provided him with the subject matter of some of his most important works. Moreover, at the conservatory in Granada, García Lorca's considerable musical ability brought him to the attention of Manuel de Falla. Their long friendship and occasional professional collaboration was based on a mutual interest in traditional Spanish music and folklore.

In 1919, García Lorca left for Madrid and began a ten-year stay at the Residencia de Estudiantes that proved of great consequence to his artistic career. There, García Lorca kept company with the senior Spanish residents, Juan Ramón Jiménez, Gregorio Martínez Sierra, Antonio Machado; made friends with Salvador Dalí and Luis Buñuel; and enjoyed the frequent visits of famous European contemporaries of the stature of H. G. Wells, François Mauriac, Igor Stravinsky, Paul Valéry, and Albert Einstein. Above all, García Lorca found at the Residencia an audience that listened with intellectual acuity and sensitive appreciation to recitals of his poetry, plays, and music in what was, for him, a period of steady output and growing recognition.

About this time, however, he fell prey to deep depression, and, by the summer of 1929, either sentimental or psychological reasons connected with his homosexuality led García Lorca to leave Spain for the United States. He registered at Columbia University to study English but soon abandoned the course. His difficulties with the language and sense of isolation in an alien culture only increased his depression, and it was with great relief that he left New York in the spring of 1930 for Cuba. García Lorca's visit to Havana brought him fame and a sense of well-being, and when he returned to Spain later that year, he embarked on the most creative and productive period of his life.

The political climate in Spain had changed radically with the fall of the dictatorship of Primo de Rivera in 1930 and the election to power of a Republican government in 1931. In this liberal atmosphere, the arts flourished, and it is no coincidence that during these years García Lorca directed with such signal success the traveling-student theater group known as La Barraca. In the performance of plays of the Golden Age in the towns and villages of Spain, García Lorca set about the renovation of the Spanish theater that he would carry through into his own work. This fame as director, playwright, and poet led to a highly successful visit, in 1935, to Buenos Aires, which marked the high point of his career as the most celebrated dramatist in the Hispanic world.

By July, 1936, civil war was inevitable. As the hostilities began, García Lorca returned to Granada—ill-advisedly, as it happened, since the city came under military rule almost immediately and, worse still, suffered a reign of terror in which political opponents and innocent victims alike were assassinated. García Lorca's well-known friendships with pro-Republican supporters and his involvement with the Republican-funded La Barraca made him an obvious political target; his reputation as a homosexual and his flamboyant success as a writer made him an easy mark for prejudice and envy. In constant fear for his life, García Lorca finally took refuge in the home of Luis Rosales, a fellow poet whose family's political sympathies were with the Nationalist cause. García Lorca was, nevertheless, arrested there on August 16, held for a short time, and then shot either late on the night of August 18 or early the next morning.

Analysis • Most of Federico García Lorca's dramas were written when he was in growing command of his art. Intense creativity, however, meant little time for literary theorizing, and García Lorca's views on his own work and its part in the projected renovation of the Spanish theater must be sought in the plays themselves and the various interviews he gave. His vision was at once lucid and surprisingly socialist for an otherwise apolitical writer: "I have given myself over to drama which permits more direct contact with the masses."

García Lorca saw the theater as a vocation requiring personal sacrifice from the dramatist to ensure not commercial success but a real identification with his people. Only half-jokingly "speaking as a true socialist" did García Lorca think the theater should be a "barometer," marking the moral ascendancy or decadence of a nation. Thus finely attuned, the theater would act as a natural conscience, and its themes in Spain of the twentieth century would inevitably treat "a religious and socioeconomic problem." Far from seeking out the exotic, García Lorca advocated a return to the classical norms of tragedy. If he also insisted that poetry and theater were inextricably linked, his poetic drama was to be neither cultish nor middlebrow ersatz, but would live naturally onstage, since "the theater is poetry taken from books and made human." In less than ten years, García Lorca's own dramatic style moved from a quasiromantic sensitivity to a classical starkness. He utilized his poetic talent to develop symbols and re-create popular traditions that effectively emphasized his view of the omnipresence of the tragic in human life.

There is a tendency to restrict critical analysis of García Lorca's theater to the elaboration of the monolithic themes that recur throughout his works. Those most frequently identified are impossible love, frustrated love, separation, and the opposition between desire and reality. Such an approach, however, tends to fragment and compartmentalize without doing justice to the superb theatricality of García Lorca's dramas. By peopling his plays with characters who are "horribly tragic and bound to our life and times," García Lorca managed to communicate to his audience the true passions of men and women, facilitating catharsis in the best tradition of the theater.

Francisco Ruiz Ramón rightly argues that García Lorca's canon derives from a basic "dramatic situation" rather than from any single theme, that his dramatic universe springs from the essential conflict between the principles of authority and freedom. This conflict is repeated and elaborated in every play and provides the dramatic structure that in every case has a concatenation of poetic symbols or themes (such as earth, water, moon, horse, bull, blood, and knife) and dramatic incarnations (examples of order, tradition, reality, and collective conscience that oppose those of instinct, desire,

imagination, and individuality). Quite deliberately, García Lorca chose to present poetic drama on the modern Spanish stage; coincidentally, his is very much according to
the theories of William Butler Yeats and T. S. Eliot, though with more conspicuous success in the practice than either of those two. Any exploration of the range of moral, socioeconomic, telluric, sentimental, or psychological problems encompassed by his poetic theater must take into account this radical decision. With García Lorca, nineteenth
century realism in Spanish stagecraft gives way to a more fluid and dynamic concept of
dramatic action to which dialogue, language, song, dance, movement, and scenery all
make vital contributions.

García Lorca's theater was experimental and controversial, in keeping with his purpose of putting onstage "themes and problems that people are afraid to face." In his
chosen context of the dramatic conflict between authority and personal freedom, his
own untimely death was the greatest tragedy of all.

The Butterfly's Evil Spell • There is an obvious thematic connection between
García Lorca's first play, *The Butterfly's Evil Spell*, and, notably, poems such as "Los
encuentros de un caracol aventurero," "Canción otoñal," and "Balada triste," from his
first collection, *Libro de poemas*. Romantic in theme but influenced by the subtle symbolism of the early poetry of Juan Ramón Jiménez, both the poems and the play tell of
love, illusion, frustration, and death; a new force breaks through the tranquillity of the
old order, leaving senses and soul perturbed. The play dramatizes in lyric form the
confusion caused in the daily life of a community of insects by the eruption of love
which is mortal. The hero of this miniature tragedy, the cockroach poet Curianito,
breaks with the logic, conventions, and strictures of his codified world by falling in
love with "a vision which was far removed from his life," a dying butterfly that has
fallen to the ground. Precisely his atypical condition of poet makes Curianito seek
union with the butterfly, which is at once the incarnation of an unrealizable ideal and
the victim of the desire to attain that ideal. Through the impossible love between
Curianito and the butterfly, García Lorca dramatizes the subtle relationship between
aspiration and goal and the inevitable frustration of both as deviance in an otherwise
ordered world.

The essential dramatic situation of all García Lorca's theater is present even in this
early effort. The dramatic structure derives from the clash between the norm and the
ideal worked out onstage by archetypal characters (who will reappear in the later
plays) such as the mother (Doña Curiana), the spinster (Curianita Silvia), the doomed
lovers (Curianito and the butterfly), and the tyrannical voice of public opinion emanat-
ing from the chorus of neighbors and onlookers (beetles and worms).

With encouragement from Gregorio Martínez Sierra, *The Butterfly's Evil Spell* was
performed at the Teatro Eslava, in Madrid, on March 22, 1920. Despite García Lorca's
pious hope, expressed in the prologue, that his audience would appreciate this lesson
from the natural world, the public had little interest in a play ostensibly about beetles
and worms. Accustomed to the drawing-room plays of the commercial theater, they
booed it mercilessly off the stage. Bitterly disillusioned, García Lorca learned the hard
way that the Spanish theatergoing public still needed to be educated in the modern
techniques so successful in Prague and Paris.

Mariana Pineda • Seven years elapsed before García Lorca ventured back to the
commercial stage, and to a resounding triumph. *Mariana Pineda* was performed in
June, 1927, at the Teatro Goya, in Barcelona, by Margarita Xirgu's company, with

scenery designed by Salvador Dalí and under García Lorca's own direction. It premiered that October at the Teatro Fontalba, in Madrid.

In part, García Lorca's success was a matter of felicitous timing. *Mariana Pineda* was a legendary figure of Granada, and her contribution to the republican opposition to Ferdinand VII had contemporary relevance for a twentieth century audience living under Primo de Rivera's dictatorship. Probably this currency was rather more political than García Lorca intended; he had seized on the poetic possibilities of the historical facts. Certainly, García Lorca's second dramatic production was less esoteric than the first. His starting point was the ballad about Mariana Pineda sung in Granada's streets; this was developed into a total spectacle by expert staging and intuitive choreography. Such a combination, with the added appeal of topicality, assured the play a successful run.

On its simplest level, the play is a romantic love story full of passion and sacrifice. Mariana's association with the liberals of Granada is explained by her love for one of them, Pedro de Sotomayor, but both her love and the cause are doomed. Pedro escapes, leaving Mariana to face Pedrosa, the king's representative, and certain death. The play moves through moments of great lyricism, notably the meeting between Mariana and Pedro in act 2, and Mariana's tragic view of love in the final moments of the play. Good use is made of poetic symbolism both in a traditional visual fashion (for example, the red lettering on the banner and the children's game, which combine to suggest spilled blood and death, or the conflict between good and evil reflected in the use of white and black in the scene sets and costumes) and in novel poetic interludes or portents of disaster when García Lorca interjects a *romance* extraneous to the plot but integral to the play's thematic unity (for example, Amparo's retelling of the bullfight in act 1 or Mariana's lullaby of the tragic fate of Duke Lucena in act 2).

From the first, love dominates the scene, and there is a growing sense of individuals caught helplessly in their own passion and in the affairs of others: Mariana in her love for Pedro, Fernando in his love for Mariana, Mariana and Pedro in their hatred for Pedrosa, who himself hates Pedro and desires Mariana.

Mariana, the first fully realized character in García Lorca's theater, is also the first in a long succession of society's victims, but she never acts from purely political motives. This realization leads the spectator or reader to the second level of the play's action: a dramatic situation in which love and liberty become identical. García Lorca's heroine learns that individual liberty and society are mutually exclusive, that any attempt at personal freedom is doomed to failure and death.

The Tragicomedy of Don Cristóbal and Doña Rosita • García Lorca's early romanticism was one reaction against realism onstage; a return to the puppet theater of his youth, with its frantic pace, cross-purposes, and knockabout action, was another. His two puppet plays, *The Tragicomedy of Don Cristóbal and Doña Rosita* and *In the Frame of Don Cristóbal*, are, in effect, two versions of the same story, the second version being the more stylized.

In *The Tragicomedy of Don Cristóbal and Doña Rosita*, the theme of love in conflict with parental obligation is treated with dramatic vigor: The father sells his daughter Rosita to Don Cristóbal, a rich man known for his lechery and cruelty. In this broadly comic farce, however, the fact that Rosita and her true love Cocoliche kiss in front of the cuckolded husband is enough to make Don Cristóbal fume and die, literally, *ha estallado*. Again, the dramatic situation exposes the power that feeds on fear, lies, and covetousness and argues in favor of the authenticity of the individual who escapes societal conventions.

In the Frame of Don Cristóbal • In his *In the Frame of Don Cristóbal*, García Lorca shows some of the innovative technique that distinguishes the more ambitious *The Audience* by beginning the farce with a *prólogo hablado* in which Director and Poet turn the original story inside out. Don Cristóbal, by definition evil, now turns out to be good at the heart and forced by society to play an evil role, and Rosita has the truly insatiable sexual appetite. By replacing the lyric with the grotesque, García Lorca followed closely the *esperpentos* of Ramón María del Valle-Inclán and, as the Director notes, a whole tradition from "the Gallician 'Bululu,' Monsieur Guignol from Paris, and Bergamo's Signor Harlequin." How significant was this return to "the very essence of the theater" in order to give the theater new life is better seen in García Lorca's two farces for people, *The Shoemaker's Prodigious Wife* and *The Love of Don Perlimplín for Belisa in His Garden.*

The Shoemaker's Prodigious Wife • García Lorca started work on *The Shoemaker's Prodigious Wife* in 1926, but he did not finish the play until 1930. It was performed publicly first on December 24, 1930, at the Teatro Español with Margarita Xirgu in the leading role, Rivas Cherif as director, and costumes designed by Pablo Picasso; García Lorca subsequently revised and expanded the play into the version known today, which was premiered by Lola Membrives and her company on November 30, 1933, in Buenos Aires and on March 18, 1935, at the Teatro Coliseo in Madrid.

The play was a huge success; its similarities to the highly stylized forms of ballet and operetta were noted and parallels were drawn with Manuel de Falla's adaptation of *El sombrero de tres picos* (1874). Theater critics appreciated García Lorca's blend of dialogue, poetry, and song, pointing out how he had captured the essence of Andalusian speech rhythms. The protagonist was considered a tour de force; a modern version of the unhappily married wife who, however unhappy her condition, consistently rejects all suitors, she is one more in a distinguished literary lineage that dates back to the earliest Spanish ballads.

García Lorca, himself, however, insisted on the universality of the Shoemaker's Wife and increasingly emphasized the poetic element of her struggle. In interviews held in 1933, he explained that "the Shoemaker's Wife is not any woman in particular but all women" and, moreover, that "every spectator has a Shoemaker's Wife beating in his breast." He conceived this "poetic example of the human soul" to portray the violence of the clash between fantasy and reality:

> The poetic creature which the author has dressed as a shoemaker's wife with the grace of a refrain or simple ballad, lives and sparkles everywhere, and the public should not be surprised if she appears violent or assumes a bitter tone, for she is continually in conflict, she struggles against the reality which surrounds her and she struggles against fantasy when this becomes visible reality.

Violence is certainly the main characteristic of the Shoemaker's Wife; the play opens and closes with her sharp retorts: "Be silent, tattle tongue" and "Be quiet, chinwags." The whole of act 1 is rooted in violent antipathy: that of the Shoemaker's Wife toward her neighbors and toward her husband, which never diminishes. Although García Lorca provides some details about the conditions of this mismarriage (its basis in her poverty and his loneliness, the considerable differences in age and outlook) and its difficult circumstances (the harmful gossip and ill will of the neighbors), these motivations are not sufficient in themselves to account for such a violent attitude.

In a novel interpretation somewhat out of line with usual criticism, Ruiz Ramón makes much of García Lorca's own avowed intention to dramatize "a myth of our pure unsatisfied illusion." Thus, the anger of the Shoemaker's Wife derives from frustration at the extent to which reality limits not only her individual dreams or desires but also her whole way of being. Her husband's physical presence confines her very self; absent, he is absorbed into that fanciful self and so remembered with nostalgic affection; on his return, as he discloses his true identity, he again triggers her angry verbal abuse.

In *Mariana Pineda*, García Lorca depicts the incarnation of liberty as an ideal; in contrast, *The Shoemaker's Prodigious Wife* shows much more directly how personal liberty is attacked and endangered on a daily basis. The only nonthreatening presence is that of the child, "a compendium of tenderness and a symbol of that which is germinating and yet has long before it blossoms"; otherwise, the alienation of the Shoemaker's Wife is complete. This violence done to the self by the other takes on tragic proportions in *Yerma*. Here (in *The Shoemaker's Prodigious Wife*), humor and the comic spirit are ascendant.

Act 2 is a particularly good example of the comic treatment of integrity as reputation and public opinion and integrity as the self inviolate. The Shoemaker's Wife repulses Don Mirlo, the mayor, and others but is subject to increased vilification by the neighbors; she pursues her own dream reality, but this is shattered on the return of her husband. Hence, the gap widens between individual honor and societal norms. Precisely those forces that overwhelm the characters in the later play are at least superficially contained here: The couple agree on a modus vivendi in order to confront, together, the villagers' malicious tongues. The self joins with the other, but one may well ask oneself at what cost.

The Love of Don Perlimplín for Belisa in His Garden • This pattern of the antagonistic couple as protagonists appears once more in farce in *The Love of Don Perlimplín for Belisa in His Garden*, in which a marriage is contracted between two incompatible partners: the fifty-year-old Perlimplín, inexperienced in love, and the young and nubile Belisa, who dreams, half naked on her balcony, of her lovers. The characterization goes beyond caricature; in this farcical treatment of the juxtaposition of youth and age, sensuality and frustration, there is a certain element of pathos.

The comic action of the wedding night that brings the discovery of the delights of love to Perlimplín (and makes him a five-time cuckold) turns to tragedy as he plans the conquest of his wife by becoming the embodiment of her vision of love, an illusion brilliant and alluring, but one whose death is implicit in its creation. In such a paradox, García Lorca strips certain elements of farce (disguise and mistaken identity) of their comic effect and moves nearer to the innovative cryptodramas *The Audience* and *When Five Years Pass*, in which the techniques of farce are used for different and more subtle ends.

Innovative plays • During his stay at the Residencia de Estudiantes, García Lorca enjoyed close friendships with Dalí and Buñuel, which were to have an obvious effect on his work. Increasingly as the 1920's wore on, García Lorca's theater became more experimental; Surrealism, cinematic techniques, and E. Gordon Craig's theories of stagecraft permeated this most avant-garde phase of his drama, which belongs roughly to the years from 1929 to 1931 and has much in common with his contemporaneous New York poems.

García Lorca, wise from his initial bad experience with the commercial theater, had few illusions about his more innovative plays, calling them "irrepresentables." *The Audience* and *When Five Years Pass* were coldly received even by García Lorca's most intimate friends. Quite rightly, García Lorca considered that the frank treatment of homosexuality and the violence in *The Audience* placed it far beyond the grasp of the average audience of its time. Only the minority experimental theater clubs might have been persuaded to stage this kind of drama, and in 1936 there were plans (which came to nothing) for a performance of *When Five Years Pass* by Pura Ucelay's group, the Club Anfistora. If public taste and attitudes were not then ready, García Lorca knew that "the impossible plays contain my true intention." Time would confirm his opinion: In 1972, students at the University of Texas claimed *The Audience* for their own with great excitement, while in 1978, when *When Five Years Pass* finally reached the Spanish stage, it was hailed as García Lorca's most original contribution to the national theater.

The Audience • The Spanish title of *The Audience*, *El público*, stark and clinical, is, like its sets and most of its dialogue, a mystery designed to make one reflect on the meaning of love and life. As spectators, the audience observes the stage action, but, just as the play is the image of life, so the audience recognizes the masks and attitudes assumed by the actors as its own. There is, finally, no separation between actors and audience, between the episodes and incidents onstage and in life. R. Martínez Nadal's reconstruction of the incomplete text (1978) includes perhaps the most powerful and direct statement by García Lorca on the function of the theater: "My characters . . . burn the curtain and die in the presence of the public. . . . One must destroy the theatre or live in it!"

The audience of *The Audience* witnesses the process of self-discovery by the stage characters, who put on and take off their masks in a frenzied search for identity. They discuss the nature of the drama and participate in their own drama. By the offstage performance of *Romeo and Juliet*, the play-within-the-play, life is brought to the issues of homosexual love, the frustration of love by death, the treachery of appearances, and the shifting nature of all reality. For the spectators of this action onstage, the issues assume a living form; the characters are reflections of the public, and the audience of them. Boundaries and demarcations are dissolved and become, instead, an infinity of mirror images. In its intellectual range and daring use of technique and dialogue, *The Audience* is a startlingly "modern" play, certainly of the caliber of the experimental theater of Samuel Beckett, Jean Genet, or Eugène Ionesco written some twenty years later.

When Five Years Pass • *When Five Years Pass* was completed in 1931, barely a year after *The Audience*. Despite its difficulty, which stems from the same arbitrary radicalism and almost perversely individual symbolism of all experimental theater, it is less obscure and less shocking in theme and dialogue. Unambiguously, the title and subtitle, "A Legend of Time Passing in Three Acts and Five Scenes," point to the central issue, but the composition is a musical one whereby García Lorca has dramatized in a series of fugues the tragedy of time passing for people, who are always at counterpoint, desiring the impossible and destroying what they have.

Once again the characters are facets of the individual or the personification of differing attitudes toward a certain fact. El Amigo, Amigo 2° and El Viejo correspond to different facets of El Joven; their varying opinions on time passing are his at different moments in his life. They reflect the opinions and experience of the audience as well, for the play is an image which projects humanity's common concerns with time, love, and death.

Blood Wedding • *The Audience* and *When Five Years Pass* are García Lorca's dramas on the lives of men; too frank and disturbing for their time, they never enjoyed the acclaim given to his dramas on the lives of women. The premiere of *Blood Wedding* on March 8, 1933, at the Teatro Beatriz in Madrid, with García Lorca directing Josefina Díaz de Artigas and her company, and its enthusiastic reception by both critics and public, marked the beginning of the final and most successful phase of García Lorca's dramatic career both within Spain and abroad. The play was translated into French by Marcel Auclair and Jean Provost and was performed in English in New York in 1935; most important, its run in Buenos Aires, with Lola Membrives in the leading role, led to García Lorca's wildly successful tour of the River Plate Republics and the beginning of the myth that continued into the twenty-first century.

Blood Wedding and Lola Membrives' revivals of *Mariana Pineda* and *The Shoemaker's Prodigious Wife* made García Lorca famous, financially independent, and sure of his ability as dramatist and director. From a technical point of view, *Blood Wedding* reflects García Lorca's decision to set aside experimental theater in favor of another kind of experiment, equally audacious in its way: "We must go back to writing tragedy. We are compelled to do so by our theatrical tradition. There will be time later for comedies and farces. Meanwhile I want to give the theater tragedies."

Not conceived as a single offering, *Blood Wedding* was to be the first part of "a dramatic trilogy of the Spanish land." In 1933, García Lorca admitted that, if he was working hard on the second with its theme of the barren wife, "the third is maturing deep inside me. It will be called *La destrucción de Sodoma*"; despite García Lorca's assurances early in 1935 that this tragedy, also known as *Las hijas de Loth*, was "almost finished" and "very advanced," no version survives. Martínez Nadal again provides the only details available concerning the "magnificent theme" whose very title García Lorca conceded was "grave and compromising": "Jehovah destroys the city because of the sin of Sodom and the result is the sin of incest. What a lesson against the decrees of Justice! And the two sins, what a manifestation of the power of sex!"

While it is difficult to talk of structural unity when one of the three parts is missing, García Lorca did insist, first, that he was writing a trilogy and, second, that his tragedies were according to the classical model, "with four principal characters and chorus, as tragedies are meant to be." García Lorca probably intended a modern version of the ancient Greek trilogies; the common theme was the illustration of the power of sexual energy in conflict with established societal norms and conventions. In *Blood Wedding*, in an attempt to circumvent the passionate love between Leonardo and the Novia, a marriage is arranged that ends in the death of the only two surviving male members of the feuding families; in *Yerma*, the passionate desire for maternity destroys its only hope of fulfillment. All tragedies in the trilogy were to present a struggle to the death between the two opposing principles of authority and personal freedom. The conflict is a constant in García Lorca's work, but his revival of the classical form converts it into a spectacle of great theatricality.

Much has been made of the Aristotelian pattern of *Blood Wedding*. Catharsis is possible because the characters who suffer are closely related. The catastrophe that overtakes both the Mother and the Bride may be attributed to their error, the Mother's in her unforgiving hatred of the Félix family, which results in the death of her own son, and the Bride's in marrying a man she does not love. Because the Mother brings about her son's death, thereby thwarting her own desire to see her family grow and prosper, there is reversal of intention and, because she finally listens to the Bride's story, recognition. The final solitude and pain of both the Mother and the Bride awaken pity and terror in the audience. The figures of Moon and Death provide the supernatural intervention in human life, and woodcutters and neighbors supply the chorus.

The classical pattern gives style to the original source of the play, a short newspaper account in *El defensor de Granada*. The real incident and the play's action are identical, but García Lorca removed the concrete beings to an unreal world, converting them into forces whose incentives are beyond human control. This conversion of the personal to the generic is marked by the integration of poetry and drama.

With great dramatic economy, García Lorca built a logical construct: On the axis of action, the Novia and Leonardo are placed in jealous rivalry for family and personal reasons, while on the axis of passivity the respective parents arrange a marriage in which economic factors (money and land to be joined) and animal-like sexuality ("My son will cover her well. He's of good seed" and "My daughter is wide-hipped and your son is strong") outweigh any consideration of the Novia. The dramatic situation takes shape in the theme of passion first repressed and then triumphant: The Novia cannot resist Leonardo, the "pull of the sea," "the head toss of a mule," or force, which drives her to destruction. The power of sexual passion overthrows the proposed order (the marriage designed to lead to economic and moral prosperity) and justice, in that society demands retribution (persecution of the lovers), which leads to death: "On their appointed day, between two and three,/ these two men killed each other for love." The Luna-(Muerte)-Mendiga scene thus symbolizes the fatal relationship between the tragedy's two themes.

Yerma • This same conflict may be seen in *Yerma*, if one accepts García Lorca's own definition of the tragedy's theme: "*Yerma* will be the tragedy of the sterile woman." It is the only theme worked out in a *poema trágico* that deals with one character's continuous development. As the action begins, Yerma has been married for two years and twenty days; by the end of act 1, three years; and from act 2 until the end of the drama, five years. This concept of time passing is fundamental; it marks the movement from anxiety to desperation as Yerma suffers a gamut of emotions until she finally accepts her sterility. The entire action centers on Yerma because the other characters—Juan, Victor, Dolores, and the Vieja—derive their dramatic life from interaction with Yerma, and the chorus of washerwomen and neighbors merely provides a dramatic representation of conflicting views (her sterility or her husband's).

As Yerma begins the process of indicting her husband in order not to accept the truth about herself, the opposition between Yerma and Juan increases: He becomes the symbol of society's values, she a humiliated exception to nature's rule of fecundity. Again, as in *Blood Wedding*, at the height of the action, realism is displaced by poetic fantasy. As Yerma resists the truth, so the real world loses its reality for her until, in desperation, she seeks fecundity in magic.

When Yerma does accept her sterility during the *romería*, the dramatic situation is again conflictive. By killing Juan, Yerma takes possession of her inner life, but, like the Novia, she is "dead" to society; by her act of will, she is the author of her own sterility rather than the victim society would make of her. By engineering her own destiny, she destroys forever her own dream. The principle of authority is again set against that of personal freedom; sexual power is manifest in the overthrow of the natural order. The fecundity for which Yerma yearns but which she is denied becomes a destructive, not a creative, force, truly a "scandal" worthy of García Lorca's proposed trilogy.

Doña Rosita the Spinster • *Yerma* followed *Blood Wedding* in quick succession: The premiere took place at the Teatro Español, Madrid, on December 29, 1934, performed by Margarita Xirgu and her company and directed by Rivas Cherif. García Lorca did not, however, capitalize on its success and finish the trilogy. Instead, on December 13, 1935, he offered *Doña Rosita the Spinster: Or, The Language of the Flowers*, with Xirgu again in the leading role and again under Cherif's direction, to the Teatro Palacio Principal in Barcelona.

According to García Lorca, *Doña Rosita the Spinster* was conceived in 1924, when José Moreno Villa told him of the *rosa mutabile*. This became the central image for the passing of time in a play in which costumes, scenery, and dialogue change in minute detail with each act in order to recapture "the life, peaceful on the outside yet seething within, of a Granadine virgin who gradually becomes that being at once grotesque and moving which is the spinster in Spain." Gradually a difference is made between "real" time and the "inner" time of Rosita, who waits without hope for her fiancé's return. Like the Shoemaker's Wife, her self stays inviolate only while separate from the others. In act 2, Rosita explains to her aunt how easily she could divorce herself from the aging process, which occurs only through the eyes of others. Her tragedy is not the betrayal of her love but the destruction of her personal dream that she is loved.

In García Lorca's dramatic universe, other people, by their presence and their comments, pose a grave threat to the individual self's inner life. At first sight, Rosita is a banal heroine, one whose fussy gentility makes her pathetic self-sacrifice slightly ridiculous; she is, in fact, an excellent study in repression, revealing "the drama of Spanish vulgarity, of Spanish prurience, of the desire for enjoyment that women must suppress deep down in their febrile beings."

The House of Bernarda Alba • García Lorca never completed his projected trilogy, but shortly before his death he gave a private reading of *The House of Bernarda Alba*, the synthesis of his Spanish rural tragedies. His best work, it was an exciting shift away from poetic drama in favor of social realism. Its first public performance was by Xirgu and her company in Buenos Aires in 1945; it was not performed in Spain until January 10, 1964.

Like *Blood Wedding*, the play's inspiration was real enough: The original Doña Bernarda kept a tyrannical watch over her unmarried daughters in the house next door to that owned by García Lorca's parents in the small village of Valderrubio. Indeed, nothing is invented here except the story in García Lorca's attempt at *un documental fotográfico* on women's lives in rural Spain. The most violent conflict in García Lorca's theater between the principles of authority and personal freedom unfolds in a closed space whose dimensions are physical (Bernarda's house is variously described as a barracks, a prison, and a convent) and metaphorical (Bernarda's first and last words impose silence). Authority here is the exercise of power to further a moral and social order based on public opinion, the *qué diran*. From the first, Bernarda, defined as cruel, cold, and tyrannical, is seen as the incarnation of that authority.

Bernarda's instinct for absolute power denies anyone personal liberty and, finally, negates reality itself. In opposition to this instinct for power, personal freedom translates into an equally basic instinct: sex. In a conflict lacking human or rational moments, Bernarda and the members of her household are isolated from the world and from one another. The only solution is the destruction of one or another of the conflicting forces. Madness or suicide provides the only way out of this closed world; both are extreme, neither is successful. María Josefa eludes Bernarda's locks and bolts only in her fanciful ramblings; Adela's final rebellion questions Bernarda's authority, but Bernarda's word is final: "The youngest daughter of Bernarda Alba died a virgin. Did you hear me? Silence, silence, I said. Silence!"

Other major works

POETRY: *Libro de poemas,* 1921; *Canciones, 1921-1924,* 1927 (*Songs,* 1976); *Romancero gitano, 1924-1927,* 1928 (*The Gypsy Ballads of García Lorca,* 1951, 1953); *Poema del cante jondo,* 1931 (*Poem of the Gypsy Seguidilla,* 1967); *Llanto por Ignacio Sánchez Mejías,* 1935 (*Lament for the Death of a Bullfighter,* 1937, 1939); *Primeras canciones,* 1936; *Poeta en Nueva York,* 1940 (*Poet in New York,* 1940, 1955); *Diván del Tamarit,* 1940 (*The Divan at the Tamarit,* 1944).

NONFICTION: *Impresiones y paisajes,* 1918.

MISCELLANEOUS: *Obras completas,* 1938-1946 (8 volumes); *Obras completas,* 1954, 1960; *Obras completas,* 1973.

Bibliography

Cueto, Ronald. *Souls in Anguish: Religion and Spirituality in Lorca's Theatre.* Leeds, England: Trinity and All Saints, 1994. A look at the function of religion and spirituality in the plays of García Lorca. Bibliography.

Kiosses, James T. *The Dynamics of the Imagery in the Theater of Federico García Lorca.* Lanham, Md.: University Press of America, 1999. Kiosses examines the symbolism and imagery in the dramatic works of García Lorca. Bibliography and index.

Newton, Candelas. *Understanding Federico García Lorca.* Columbia: University of South Carolina Press, 1995. Newton's analysis of the life and works of García Lorca contains chapters on his major plays and his lesser-known plays. Bibliography and index.

Smith, Paul Julian. *The Theatre of García Lorca: Text, Performance, Psychoanalysis.* New York: Cambridge University Press, 1998. A critical analysis of the works of García Lorca that focuses on his plays, particularly their stage history. Bibliography and index.

Soufas, C. Christopher. *Audience and Authority in the Modernist Theater of Federico García Lorca.* Tuscaloosa: University of Alabama Press, 1996. Soufas examines García Lorca's dramatic works with reference to audience and authority. Bibliography and index.

Stainton, Leslie. *Lorca: A Dream of Life.* New York: Farrar, Straus, Giroux, 1999. A basic biography of García Lorca that examines his life and works. Bibliography and index.

Wright, Sarah. *The Trickster-Function in the Theatre of García Lorca.* Rochester, N.Y.: Tamesis, 2000. An examination of the role of the trickster in the dramatic works of García Lorca. Bibliography and index.

K. M. Sibbald

Jean Genet

Born: Paris, France; December 19, 1910
Died: Paris, France; April 15, 1986

Principal drama • *Les Bonnes*, pr. 1947, pb. 1948, revised pr., pb. 1954 (*The Maids*, 1954); *Splendid's*, wr. 1948, pb. 1993 (English translation, 1995); *Haute Surveillance*, pr., pb. 1949, definitive edition pb. 1963 (*Deathwatch*, 1954); *Le Balcon*, pb. 1956, pr. 1957 (in English), pr. 1960 (in French), revised pb. 1962 (*The Balcony*, 1957); *Les Nègres: Clownerie*, pb. 1958, pr. 1959 (*The Blacks: A Clown Show*, 1960); *Les Paravents*, pr., pb. 1961 (*The Screens*, 1962)

Other literary forms • Jean Genet's literary career began with a small group of lyric poems, highly personal in subject matter, the first of which was the 1942 work "Le Condamné à mort" ("The Man Condemned to Death"). Collected in *Poèmes* (1948), their quality has been a matter of much debate. Genet has written four novels, *Notre-Dame des Fleurs* (1944, 1951; *Our Lady of the Flowers*, 1949), *Miracle de la rose* (1946, 1951; *Miracle of the Rose*, 1966), *Pompes funèbres* (1947, 1953; *Funeral Rites*, 1968), and *Querelle de Brest* (1947, 1953; *Querelle of Brest*, 1966). His autobiographical work, *Journal du voleur* (*The Thief's Journal*, 1954) appeared in its original version in 1948 (only four hundred copies were printed), with a revised and expurgated version appearing in 1949.

Genet's so-called autobiography is perhaps more allegorical than factual, yet it remains the only available source on Genet's early adult years. Genet's ballet scenario, *Adame miroir*, with music by Darius Milhaud, was performed by the Ballets Roland Petit in 1946. His nonfiction includes essays on the philosophy of art, the most important being the 1957 "L'Atelier d'Alberto Giacometti" ("Giacometti's Studio") and the 1958 "Le Funambule" ("The Funambulists"); essays on dramatic theory, the most important of these being "Lettre à Pauvert sur les Bonnes," an open letter to the publisher Jean-Jacques Pauvert in 1954 concerning *The Maids* and including the letters to Roger Blin concerning the production of *The Screens* (collected as *Letters to Roger Blin*, 1969); and a series of sociopolitical broadsheets, including pamphlets in defense of the Black Panthers and the Palestinian liberation movement. His four-volume *Œuvres complètes* appeared in 1952.

Achievements • Despite Jean Genet's comparatively small output of only five published plays, which includes two one-act plays, he, along with Samuel Beckett and Eugène Ionesco, ranks as one of the major innovators in the French theater during that period (between 1945 and 1965) that witnessed the triumph of "the absurd" and led to the transformation of the whole concept of drama in the West.

The drama of this period, which includes that of Jean Tardieu and the earlier works of Fernando Arrabal and of Armand Gatti, is frequently defined as "absurdist" or as "neo-Surrealist." Neither term can be applied strictly to Genet, whose ancestry is to be sought much more profitably among the Symbolists of the beginning of the century and who appears to have been as unfamiliar with Antonin Artaud as with Bertolt Brecht until about 1954. Setting aside a precise debt to Jean-Paul Sartre, Genet seems to have evolved most of his fundamental dramatic theories, as opposed to his theatrical techniques, quite independently of his contemporaries. Thus, his drama is far more original than the works of, for example, Arthur Adamov or Jean Vauthier.

Genet was reared as a Roman Catholic, and behind his theater lies a mystic's vision of the world. Everything that exists, exists simultaneously in two dimensions: that of "pure materiality," which is purposeless, meaningless, and in the fullest sense absurd, and that of an ideal transcendence, which is the domain of "purified significance," independent of any need to be confined by reality, the domain of absolutes, of "angels" and of "miracles."

Neither of these dimensions, experienced alone, is tolerable. Pure materiality is existentially nauseating in its unjustifiable and arbitrary contingency; pure transcendence is unbearable, in that it is quite literally inhuman. Miracles are "unclean" (*immonde*, a key pun in Genet's philosophy, meaning both "not of this world" and "unspeakably filthy"). Truth, or "poetry," begins at the meeting point at which pure materiality is enhanced by the apprehension of a significance beyond and at which transcendence is humanized by being chained to some aspect of brutal and sordid reality.

Abstruse as this may sound, this theory constitutes the basis of Genet's theater. At the root of all theater, Genet declared in his letter to the publisher Pauvert, lies the ceremony, or ritual, of the Mass. In this ritual celebration, the real and the transcendental coincide absolutely. The celebrant priest is both an ordinary human being and the officiating Servant of God. The Blessed Host is both a nondescript and rather tasteless bit of wafer and the Body of Christ. No disguise, no illusion, no sleight of hand is necessary. It is the strength of faith in the communicant that will bring about the transformation of one dimension into another. To Genet, in this fundamental sense, all theater is religious: It is, or should be, an experience as intense as that of a personal communication with the beyond.

Because audiences in this century are rarely imbued with that degree of fervor in their religious beliefs sufficient to transmute reality into symbol, Genet had to find alternative sources of emotional commitment capable of effecting the transformation. He made use of three sources: sexuality (deviant in particular), politics of the extremist variety, and racial confrontation, together with a minor but effective adjunct (in *The Balcony*), which is blasphemy. None of these is used for its own sake, but rather for its efficiency as a theatrical device—for the sake of its effect on the emotions and the psyche of the audience. Genet's theater is a theater of hatred, summoned up for its pure emotional intensity, its ability to involve an audience so immediately and personally in the issues concerned that they will transmute the actors into symbols, with no need of illusion, costume, or any of the props of a naturalistic theater. If the supreme poetic experience is

Jean Genet in 1963 (Library of Congress)

that which transmutes "real" into "*sur*-real" without abandoning the plane of everyday reality, then a play that commits the audience to a hatred of the actors that is so intense that they forget that they are in a theater is the supreme poetic experience.

Thus, by a roundabout route, Genet comes to link hands with the absurdists, with the neo-Surrealists, and with all the other leaders of the revolt against naturalism in the theater. His characters are never stable with the stability of day-to-day existence. They exchange identities, as in *The Maids*, they wear masks, as in *The Blacks*—yet the masks are invariably ill-fitting, half-revealing the "real" actor hidden behind them. They work out their Utopian fantasies in looking-glass brothels beneath the menace of a looking-glass revolution, as in *The Balcony*. On the other hand, they engender an atmosphere of violence and of commitment totally foreign to the politically tranquil metaphysical despair of Beckett or Ionesco. In this, they herald the later confrontationist theater of the 1970's and 1980's, that of Roger Planchon and of Ariane Mnouchkine.

To write a play, *The Screens*, at the time Genet did, about the war in Algeria, with the Algerian revolutionaries as heroes and the French occupying forces as obscenely ludicrous, was an act of supreme political courage or one of senseless foolhardiness, or else of calculated nihilism. Or, perhaps it was an act that embodied Genet's dramatic philosophy in its most perfect form: a play calculated to raise the emotions of its Parisian audience to such a pitch that the transmutation of reality into symbol would operate of its own accord, and the supreme poetic communication between dramatist and audience would be achieved with the barest minimum of naturalistic subterfuge.

A final constituent of Genet's achievement lies in his dramatic language. In translation, this is difficult to recapture because it involves dramatic poetry of the highest order; yet its subjects and situations, even given the most liberal interpretation, must be classed as unpoetic. In early reviews of his plays, the epithet "hysterical" recurred constantly. Like Paul Claudel, Genet is a master of a certain kind of impassioned rhetoric that is rare in the French tradition; however, he applies it to situations where it is, to put it mildly, unexpected. His black prostitutes and his destitute Arab riffraff "speak with the tongues of men and of angels"; his squashed-cabbage-leaf domestics have inherited the poetry of Juliet and Cordelia. It is shocking and yet it is right, this "sudden gift of tongues," as Tardieu expressed it, "loaned unexpectedly to the eternally tongue-tied." As with all truly great dramatists, Genet's ultimate achievement lies in the fact that he is a poet.

Biography • Jean Genet has often been compared to his late-medieval predecessor, the thief and poet François Villon. That Genet was a thief is undeniable; the interest and the mystery lie in how he became transmuted into a poet.

Little is known with certainty about Genet's early life because for both literary and personal reasons, he took pains to transmute the events of his life into his "legend." Born on December 19, 1910, in a public maternity ward in the rue d'Assas in Paris, the child of a prostitute, Gabrielle Genet, and an unknown father, Genet was adopted by the Assistance Publique (the national foundling society) and sent off to foster parents in the hill country of Le Morvan, between Dijon and Nevers. There, he took to petty thievery and, by the age of ten, was branded irrevocably as a thief.

By Genet's early teens, he was confined to a reformatory for juvenile criminals at Mettray, a few miles north of Tours, where he was subjected to homosexual seductions and assaults. Details about the next ten years of his life are scarce; one way or another, he became a male prostitute, a pickpocket, a shoplifter, and a remarkably unskilled burglar. He traveled from place to place, eventually making his way to Spain and then

to North Africa, where he developed a sense of kinship with the Arab victims of coloni-
zation that would later emerge in *The Screens*. Yet he also, during this period, had become an assiduous autodidact who, when once arrested for stealing a volume of the poetry of Paul Verlaine, was more concerned with the quality of the verse than with the
commercial value of the book.

In Genet's life, these two strains, criminality and poetry, seem to have run together
in comfortable harness for twelve years or more. When he was sixteen, according to
one source, he worked as guide and companion to a blind poet, René de Buxeuil, from
whom he learned at least the rudiments of French prosody (and perhaps the principles
of Maurrassian Fascism). Some years later, in 1936 or 1937, Genet deserted the
Bataillons d'Afrique (the notorious Bat' d'Af'—the punitive division of the French
Army in North Africa) after striking an officer and stealing his suitcases, illegally cross-
ing frontiers in Central Europe, and running a racket in questionable currency. During
the same period, however, he also taught French literature to the daughter of a leading
gynecologist in Brno, Moravia, and wrote her long letters in which explications of Arthur Rimbaud's "Le Bateau ivre" ("The Drunken Boat") alternate with laments for the
fall of Léon Blum's Front Populaire in June, 1937.

It is unknown which arrest and what cause led him to the prison of Fresnes in 1942.
It is certain that it was during this detention that he wrote his first published poem,
"The Man Condemned to Death," and drafted his first novel, *Our Lady of the Flowers*.
According to the legend, he wrote the work on stolen sugar bags. When the first version was discovered and confiscated by a warder, he simply began all over again. In
prison, Genet met a visitor, Olga Barbezat, whose husband, Marc Barbezat, a publisher, could count among his friends Jean Cocteau and Simone de Beauvoir. Genet's
manuscripts began to circulate, and Cocteau pronounced them works of genius. A
year later, Genet had been released and arrested yet again. On this occasion, among
the witnesses in court for the defense appeared Cocteau himself, who declared publicly that he considered Genet to be "the greatest writer in France."

Genet, for his part, continued his dual career as brilliant writer (poet, novelist, and,
later, dramatist) and incompetent burglar. By the end of World War II, Genet had met
Jean-Paul Sartre and members of his circle. In 1946, he had met theater director Louis
Jouvet, a close friend of Sartre, and had shown him the manuscript of a four-act tragedy, *The Maids*. On Jouvet's advice, Genet condensed it to a one-act version. In April,
1947, Jouvet staged it at the Théâtre de l'Athénée, in an ironically conceived double
bill with Jean Giraudoux's *L'Apollon de Bellac* (1942; *The Apollo of Bellac*, 1954).

In 1948, Genet was arrested again and on this occasion was menaced with "perpetual preventive detention." The circumstances surrounding this final appearance of
Genet the criminal are, as usual, obscure. In all events, Genet now had powerful
friends. On July 16, 1948, the influential newspaper *Combat* addressed an open letter,
signed by Sartre, Cocteau, and the literary editors of the paper, Maurice Nadeau and
Maurice Saillet, to the president of the Republic, "imploring his clemency on behalf of
a very great poet." The president, Vincent Auriol, was persuaded, and he granted a
pardon. Thereafter, Genet was merely a writer. "I don't steal the way I used to," he told
an interviewer for *Playboy* in April, 1964, nearly two decades later, "but I continue to
steal, in the sense that I continue to be dishonest with regard to society, which pretends
that I am not."

This comment reflects how Genet saw the situation at the time of *The Screens*, his
clearest gesture of defiance against all that is held most sacred in the French bourgeois
tradition. Since that time, society has triumphed. It is the supreme irony of Genet's ca-

reer that the poet who used his poetry to defy society is condemned, not to be out-lawed, but to be adulated by that very society he had sought to challenge and to offend. It would seem to have been in reaction to this adulation that, during the 1960's and 1970's, Genet publicly allied himself with those whose defiance of society was much more effective than his own: the Black Panthers and the Palestinian terrorists.

During the latter part of his career, Genet occasionally sought to prevent the pro-duction of his own plays; yet, at the same time, he continued to oversee the publication of his complete works. Something of this paradox, and this dilemma, can be intuited from the closing scenes of *The Screens*: Except for a small scattering of short political di-atribes, Genet was silent following the writing of that play. In him, the romantic arche-type of the "poet misunderstood" has been transformed into a new, but nevertheless tragic equivalent: the subversive poet who is understood only too well by those whom he did not credit with the intelligence or the goodwill to understand him.

On April 15, 1986, Genet died alone in the Paris hotel room that had been his resi-dence for several years.

Analysis • Although Jean Genet's productive period as a dramatist covers a compara-tively short period, his inspiration ranges much more widely. His aestheticism, his con-cept of the drama as a quasi-mystical experience relating the human to the transcen-dental by way of the ambiguity of symbols, his uncompromising anarchism, his richly exuberant sensuality—all these link him directly with the enthusiasms of the *fin de siècle*, and clearly he would have felt as much spiritual affinity with Oscar Wilde and Aubrey Beardsley as with Joris-Karl Huysmans and Joséphin Péladan.

Genet's subject matter is rigorously contemporary. The problems he explores are those of the post-Hiroshima world, a world of tormented consciences and inverted val-ues, of racism and revolution, of flamboyant sexuality and puritanical indoctrination. At the same time, recalling that he was creating his drama in the comparatively calm epoch of "the absurd," with its emphasis on the ludicrous condition of humankind as viewed by the cold, ironic eye of indifferent eternity, his drama, in the violence of its revolt against the status quo, clearly anticipates that of the younger generation, a gen-eration that still lay ahead of him. Genet was writing his drama in the decade of the An-gry Young Men; however, while the causes of their anger are largely forgotten, those of Genet—a man who had much more to be angry about—are beginning only now to be appreciated.

Genet's five published plays fall into two distinct groups. The two earlier one-act dramas, *The Maids* and *Deathwatch*, have the economy of means, the tautness of con-struction, the close interdependence of characters, and the concentration within the rigid discipline of the three unities (time, place, and action) that are characteristic of all that is best in French classical and neoclassical theater. Their model and inspiration is almost certainly Sartre's most effective play, *Huis clos* (1944; *No Exit*, 1946). Both, moreover, are fundamentally addressed to the intellect of the spectator. By contrast, the three later plays, *The Balcony*, *The Blacks*, and *The Screens*, depend at least as much on visual effects as on language. The three are broad, flamboyant canvases of loosely re-lated episodes, panoramic rather than conventionally dramatic in structure, or rather (to use the term favored by Brecht, whose influence can be detected at every point), "epic."

Deathwatch • *Deathwatch* was the first play that Genet wrote, although not the first to be produced; it is also the most directly autobiographical. The character of Lefranc is clearly a self-portrait of the playwright, representing an alternative direction that his life might have taken. The play evokes the prison world of Fresnes and Fontevrault, as they are described in his novel *Miracle of the Rose*. Dominating this world by the aura of his invisible presence is Snowball, a condemned murderer incarcerated somewhere in his death cell on some remote upper story.

The French title for the play, *Haute Surveillance*, is one of Genet's more ingenious ambiguities, resuming in itself the significance of the action on three different levels. If *haute surveillance* is the technical name for the peculiarly sadistic form of detention that French criminal law had prescribed for its condemned prisoners awaiting execution, the term also suggests the watch kept from above by Snowball, in his transcendental state of "death in life," over the rest of the prison and all its myriad inmates. At the same time, and most important of all, it suggests the watch kept by God, who, from the high mansions of Heaven, looks down on the tragedies of humankind and makes or mars (generally mars in Genet's world) his destiny.

Onstage, three men are confined in a cell that is open to the audience: Lefranc, a burglar, shortly due to be released; Maurice, a delinquent who, had he been only a few months younger, would probably have been packed off to Mettray; and Green-Eyes, another murderer, but one who, unlike Snowball, is awaiting trial and is still not condemned. Between these three men, with only rare interruptions from a warder, the entire action takes place in one cell and in the course of a single afternoon.

In the "normal" world, there is a hierarchy of virtue having, at its summit, the saint, the man or woman who, having pushed the totality of human experience beyond the limits of endurance, has come face to face with God. In the prison, there is a similar hierarchy, not so much of evil, as of its metaphysical equivalent, transgression. He who has transgressed beyond this limit is imbued with the same mystic aura of sanctity; he sheds the same brilliant transcendental light (or darkness) over more common mortals, as does the saint. Just as the seeker after virtue may calculate by what act of self-destroying asceticism and sacrifice he may aspire to sanctity, and yet, by the very fact of having calculated, forever exclude himself from the ranks of the elect, so may a sneak thief ponder the steps that would lead to the ineffable summit of transgression, and yet, by having pondered, condemn himself for all eternity to the lowly status of failed transgressor.

This is the theme, and the action, of *Deathwatch*. At the very bottom of the hierarchy is Lefranc, the most insignificant of criminals, because, while he has violated the laws of bourgeois society, he has left intact the major taboos of humanity. Next comes Maurice, who, although still young, already possesses the flintiness, the inhumanity that promises great crimes in the future. Then comes Green-Eyes, the murderer, who has violated the most sacred of all taboos, that which decrees the sanctity of human life. Finally, at the summit, stands Snowball, in whom the cycle of crime and punishment (Genet at this stage owes much to Fyodor Dostoevski), of transgression and retribution, is complete. The range extends from petty lawbreaking to absolute evil.

The immediate problem of the play is whether an essentially passive character, such as Lefranc (or such as Genet himself), having accepted the fact that the absolute, in his own case, can never be an absolute good and therefore must necessarily be an absolute evil, is capable of achieving this negative transcendence. The outcome is failure. Deliberately and gratuitously, Lefranc strangles the helpless Maurice, while Green-Eyes looks on, smiling sardonically; Lefranc then turns to Green-Eyes, believing that at last he has escaped his ignominious destiny and has earned his place among the elite. Green-Eyes, however, rejects him out of hand, and Lefranc discovers that it is not sufficient merely to be a murderer to shatter the walls that guard the transcendence of the spirit. His gratuitous crime is but one more failure added to the list of failures that constitute his life. He achieves his solitude, but it is Genet's own solitude of degradation, not Snowball's solitude of glory. The other path is closed to him forever.

Alone among the critics who saw the play at its first performance, François Mauriac grasped the work's implications; Mauriac described *Deathwatch* as a modern reevocation of the doctrines of Calvinism (or, in a French context, of Jansenism): a statement of the futility of the individual against the predestined patterns ordained by God since the moment of the Creation. The Grace of God alone, and not the will of humankind, however well intentioned, determines the ultimate value of the act. From Lefranc, the Gift of Efficient Grace was withheld, and so, in the end, his only reward is a contemptuous "Bastard!" from Green-Eyes. All appearances to the contrary, *Deathwatch* embodies a theological proposition in a modern context.

The Maids • Genet's second play, *The Maids* (his first play to be performed), is based on a real-life murder trial of 1933, in which two sisters, Christine and Léa Papin, were convicted of having murdered their mistress. *The Maids* contributed almost as much as Beckett's *En attendant Godot* (pb. 1952, pr. 1953; *Waiting for Godot*, 1954) to exciting an international interest in the new French theater.

The sisters Christine and Léa have become the sisters Claire and Solange; their names alone, with suggestions of light and darkness, of sun and of angels, suffice to lift them out of the domain of sordid reality and to elevate them to the very center of Genet's mythology. From the very first line of the dialogue, however, this secondary symbolism is supplemented by another, which is rooted in the nature of the drama itself: The simultaneous awareness, for the audience, of illusion and reality is presented so that the two opposites, far from either merging or canceling each other, subsist together in all their irreconcilable hostility, each a dynamic and irreducible force in its own right. As the curtain rises, Claire and Solange, within the general context of dramatic illusion, possess a degree of reality as maids. Within this general context, however, they create a domain of secondary illusion, a play within a play. Claire plays the part of Madame, a deliberately faulty illusion in her grotesque and borrowed dresses, with her gruesomely padded body that parodies Madame's sexual attributes, whereas Solange, perfectly disguised as Solange, plays the part of Claire.

Thus, all reality is reduced to appearance, and all appearance to the status of a game. In terms of Genet's dualist metaphysic, the confrontation of two incompatible dimensions, the two symbols play an essential part: that of the mirror and that of the double. The "real" is both itself as well as its transcendental reflection. Therefore, when Solange plays the part and takes on the character of Claire, the real Claire addresses the pseudo-Claire as "Claire," even when she herself has temporarily slipped back out of her stage character as Madame and resumed her own reality as herself.

The complexity of this doubling is further increased by Solange, who also slips back and forth from her role as Claire (in which case she is the maid, insulting and working herself up to a fury of hatred and vengeance against the mistress) to her reality as Solange. "In reality," Solange is jealous of her sister and accuses her of having alienated the affections of her (Solange's) lover, the Milkman. On both levels, reality and game, the hatred alone remains identical, but the transition from one level to another frequently takes place within a single speech, so that the dualities Claire/Solange and real-Claire/pseudo-Claire merge into each other and produce the fourfold mirror reflection of a single identity.

Nightly, in their ritual-sacrificial game of exchanged identities, Claire and Solange ceremonially enact the murder of Madame. As always in Genet's work, the contents of the dream spill over into waking life, for there is a real Madame, and the maids have planned her real murder, with a poison dissolved into her evening potion of lime tea. The plan, however, goes wrong. Madame has a lover, Monsieur, whom Claire has denounced to the police for some nameless felony, having first manufactured sufficient evidence to ensure that he will be convicted. The police are hesitant, and, just before Madame returns home, a telephone call informs the maids that Monsieur has been released on bail.

Certain now that their treachery will be discovered, the maids realize not only that their dream of murdering Madame must become a reality if they are to escape the consequences of their denunciation but also that it must be realized immediately. Madame returns, the poison is ready, but then Claire and Solange, human beings who have betrayed another human being, are in their turn betrayed by the active malevolence of the inanimate world. The whole of the ritual is on the point of discovery when Claire reveals that it was Monsieur who had telephoned. Delirious with excitement, Madame rushes off to meet him, leaving her lime tea untasted; Claire and Solange remain alone once more, their dream of murder having evaporated, with one final sacrificial ritual for their only consolation.

For the last time, they go through their exchange of identities. This time, Solange dresses as Madame but, by her words and gestures, acts the part of Claire the maid, while Claire remains dressed as Claire (or perhaps Solange), but acts the part of Madame. As the curtain falls, it is Claire/Madame who shifts even this "reality" out of time into eternity by herself drinking the lime tea. Thus, truth and falsehood become forever indistinguishable in the wordlessness of death. The poison was intended for Madame; Claire is Madame and, now that she can no longer speak her name, will remain so for all eternity.

This extraordinary play, with its perfect one-act structure, its overwhelming dramatic tension, and its density of thought and symbolism, is rightly considered one of the masterpieces of the contemporary theater. It is a play about masks and doubles, about the evanescence of identity It is also, marginally, a play about social injustice. In the plays that follow, this secondary preoccupation emerges ever more menacingly.

The Balcony • *The Balcony,* the first of Genet's plays in the Brechtian-epic (as opposed to the Sartrian-classical) tradition, was perhaps the most controversial of those that he had so far published. The very term "Brechtian" implies a degree of social commitment, and indeed the play shows the symbolic representatives of a threatened bourgeoisie (a Bishop, a General, a Judge, a Chief of Police) acting out in merciless caricature their erotic-masochistic fantasies in a luxurious Second-Empire brothel ("The Balcony"), while the hostile forces of the Revolution are actively engaged in occupying every point of vantage in the city.

In Genet's own introduction to the play, he denied most emphatically that it represents a satire or a parody of anything, calling it merely "the glorification of the Image and the Reflection." He was furious when, in the world premiere of the play at the Arts Theatre Club in London, the director, Peter Zadek, portrayed the Queen as a caricature of the British monarchy. In an interview granted only a few days later, however, he declared that "my starting-point was Spain, Franco's Spain; and the revolutionary who castrated himself was the symbol of all Republicans who have acknowledged their defeat."

The Balcony epitomizes the problems of interpretation arising when a dramatist uses social or political themes for both asocial and apolitical purposes. On the realistic level, both reactionaries and revolutionaries are equally unacceptable to Genet's ideal of "pure poetry," for both represent the disciplined forces of anti-individualism that are repugnant to him. The difference is that the first group represents a society that has already excluded him, whereas the second group represents a movement from which he would rather exclude himself. He is strongly attracted by the archaic mysticism of reaction yet is repelled by the individuals who incarnate it. On the other hand, he is on the whole attracted by individual revolutionaries yet disgusted by their materialistic ambitions and disciplinarian methods.

In *The Balcony*, Genet reveals himself as an anarchist of the most classical variety. He has defined his own intrinsic attitude again and again. He is not in revolt against any particular society; he has simply opted out of all societies, which position, in the long run, presents him with a far more difficult attitude to sustain. Genet diligently abstracts his heroes from their social context, shows them as negative, individualistic, and concerned only with sanctity and with transcendental absolutes. With equal diligence, the audience replaces them where they came from and persists in interpreting them as positive heroes or victims in a relative social or political setting. The essence of Genet's dilemma as a dramatist consists in that although he refuses to create a socialist theater, inevitably his negative revolt will be interpreted as some sort of socialism.

These are the ambiguities that plague *The Balcony* and that make of it at once the most successful and at the same time the least convincing of Genet's dramas. *The Balcony* is another of his symbolic-suggestive titles. As the throne (Heaven, altar, or condemned cell) from which an isolated consciousness looks down on humanity and bears away the weight of its sins, the Balcony is a brothel of a special type. It is a microcosm, a mirror reflection of the real world, in which all appearances become reality. It provides costumes, props, accessories, and endless mirrors; each customer acts out, in an erotic ritual of pure appearances, the part in which he or she would like to see himself. Inside the elaborate decor of these tiny closed worlds of absolute illusion, prostitutes and customers together enact the rituals of make-believe.

Two realities lie behind all this aesthetic sublimation: the Revolution and, less obtrusive but more significant, a "theory of functions." In the last analysis (this is the essence of the play), both establishment and revolution emerge as "functions" of each other. If a judge exists, he exists only as a function of a potential criminal: Were there no criminals, there would be no judges. Similarly, were there no bourgeoisie, there would be no revolution. The proletariat depends on the bourgeoisie for its very definition, its very existence. The one is the mirror reflection of the other; as always in Genet, the reflection is more real than the image. (Once the Queen is dead, and Madame Irma, the "Madame" of the Brothel, "plays" the Queen, the "real" revolution is crushed immediately.)

By destroying the establishment, the Revolution destroys its own identity, which was defined and given existence by its function, which was that of opposing the establishment. Similarly, the Chief of Police (the most enigmatic figure in the play) is defined as the opponent of the Revolution. In annihilating the Revolution, he destroys his own function and thus annihilates himself, leaving himself only the brothel as an ultimate refuge, with his quest for his own mausoleum, whereby he might perpetuate his own nonfunctional existence as a myth.

The Balcony is the most complex of Genet's plays, the most ambiguous, and yet one of the most impressive. In a social situation, a person is what he or she is seen to be by others. This other-created self is given substance by the individual's appearance—his or her uniform, robes, vestments. These props are the power symbols that constitute the person's essence, yet power is defined by the object over which that power may be exercised. Remove that object, and both the power and the symbol of power, hence the identity, evaporate into nothingness. A "function" must function; where there is no context in which functioning is possible, the power is thrown back on itself. To be, the image can only contemplate its own reflection in the mirror. Therefore, in a sense, the first four mirror scenes of *The Balcony* should also recur at the end.

Had the play been written by Beckett, this might have happened. As it is, there are suggestions: "In a little while, I'll have to start all over again," says Madame Irma in her concluding monologue, "put all the lights on again . . . dress up . . . distribute roles again . . . assume my own." Basically, the structure of Genet's later plays is too Brechtian-linear to allow this type of cyclical conclusion to be fully developed. *The Balcony* is a transitional play, and the experimental audacities of its form are not quite adequate to express the sophistication of its content.

If Genet, together with many of his contemporaries, refused absolutely to commit himself to any ideology of the Left, this was for literary as well as for political reasons. To the poet, the most repulsive feature of the established Left was its reliance on platitudes and slogans. It needed the freakish genius of a Vladimir Mayakovsky to transmute slogans into poetry. For the rest, it is the seemingly irrevocable mission of the Left to crush poetry into slogans.

The Blacks • Genet's reply to this, both in *The Blacks* and in *The Screens*, was to reverse the accepted order of moral values accorded to either side in his confrontation of ideological opposites, thus giving the conventional platitudes a startling and shocking originality when bestowed on the right side for the wrong reason or on the wrong side for the right reason. In the drama of the political platitude (as in the melodrama, from which such drama springs), there are heroes and villains; the revolutionary heroes are good, while the reactionary villains are bad. In Genet's variant, the revolutionary "heroes" are bad (degraded, murderous, and treacherous), while the reactionary "villains" are good (beautiful, idealistic, and constructive).

The structure of *The Blacks* is that of a total theater—that is, of a theater employing all the media that contribute to the dramatic impact of the spectacle. It uses music, dance, rhythm, and ritual; contrasts masks and faces, illusion and reality; and employs different levels, exploiting a multiplicity of stage dimensions (Antonin Artaud's "poetry in space"). It borrows its techniques from the jazz band and the jam session, from the church service and from the music hall, from the circus, and even, in the episodes of orchestrated laughter, from the stylized, cadenced mockery of the Aristophanic chorus.

In such a context, the chief function and dramatic value of language is realized as a medium of incantation. This play has more in common with music than with normal drama, wherein representation has given way to abstraction. The aim of convincing an audience, assumed to be intellectual, has been replaced by that of rousing it to a state of mystical or hysterical delirium, using means that the high priest shares with the demagogue and the jazz trumpeter, with the snake charmer. The final effectiveness of the piece lies in the fact that it is by no means devoid of ideas. The dialectic is there, but it is conveyed by implication rather than by statement.

The Blacks has little or no coherent story. Rather, it has a theme (the theme of black and white) and a structure that gradually reveals itself as having significance on different and unsuspected levels. The actors are black actors. They are introduced as a group of blacks with ordinary, everyday backgrounds—cook, sewing maid, medical student, prostitute—but have now come together to produce an entertainment, a "clown-show."

Meanwhile, entombed on the stage in a white-draped, flower-covered catafalque lies the corpse of a murdered white woman. Around this, a further dimension of illusion is developed: the rhythms, rituals, and ceremonies of hatred and violence. Observing this, high up in their gallery, sit five blacks masked as whites: the Queen, the Missionary, the Governor, the Judge, and the Valet, providing yet a further dimension, an audience for the clownery of the others. What precisely is this audience? For the actors below them on the stage, the court both is and is not an audience. It watches them, listens to them, applauds them, yet it is composed of actors acting as an audience, an unreal mirror reflection of the "real" audience in the pit and stalls facing them. It is also a chorus and, in symbolic form, the enemy.

So the play develops for more than half its length, working out permutations and combinations with the elusive material of dimensions, of plays within plays and audiences within audiences, until suddenly, with the dramatic entry of Ville-de-Saint-Nazaire, the whole delicate structure collapses with the revelation of still another dimension: a play outside the play. Ville-de-Saint-Nazaire is not concerned with any dream of village love or of ritually murdered whites. He is a real political agitator (but what, at this point, is "real"?) who has been attending a secret meeting "just up the street outside the theater," at which not a white but another black has been condemned to execution for having betrayed the clandestine Society for Black Rights.

Meanwhile, all the others—actors, audience, true or false, black whites, and white blacks—disintegrate into dreams. The whole evening's clownery was merely a deliberate diversion (as Archibald warned from the beginning), a smoke screen to keep the audience's attention fixed while the executive committee got on with its job. The white court strips off its masks, the others strip off their personalities, and for an instant, they are any group of real blacks having an urgent political discussion. The former Valet, that erstwhile masked caricature of the bourgeois intellectual or artist in capitalist society, is now revealed as the cell leader, whose orders are obeyed instantly and without question. Eventually, he commands his combat section to take up their parts again and to resume the act; thus the audience is back in the dimensions of illusion. The victory, however, lies with Genet.

In the closing scenes, when the audience knows that all is merely a "clown-show," the hard, political play outside the play moves even further from reality than the actors portraying actors of the play itself. In yet another dimension, there is more reality— immediate political reality this time—in the notion of an armed and organized Direct Action Committee for Negro Rights than there is in ritualistic dances about the imaginary catafalque of an imaginary murdered white. Which is real and which is illusion? Compared with *The Blacks*, Luigi Pirandello's experiments with the same problem seem almost childish. Ultimately, since there must be an end, the whole masked court of whites makes its way reluctantly toward the "infernal regions," enveloped in a rain of muddled colonialistic platitudes. There is neither triumph nor fear on either side. What must be, must be. For the blacks, their victory over the whites is scarcely worth a comment; it is all in the day's work. Their real problems lie elsewhere.

In this play, masks reveal even more than they hide of the reality beneath. Among these, for the blacks, the most disquieting is the mask of language. These blacks, for all their blackness, are speaking with the language of the whites, not even Creole or *petit-*

nègre (pidgin French), but the purest, most classical language of the Princesse de Clèves. The face masks can be removed easily enough, the language mask, never. Thus, when Village makes love to Vertu, he makes love to her in white language, and his black love for a black girl is transmuted into a white love for a white girl and thus becomes, even in its purest poetry, a pure falsehood. The Judge, the Governor, and the Missionary are gone, but the language remains: the irremovable trace of servitude imposed by a benevolent paternalism. In the final analysis, the black imitates more than the white: He imitates the very language that condemns his imitation. Such is the conclusion of *The Blacks* and the ultimate tragedy of colonialism.

The Screens • Written in 1959-1960, at the climax of France's catastrophic conflict with Algerian nationalism, it was inconceivable that *The Screens*, a play that ridiculed French patriotism and that caricatured as ludicrous buffoons conscript members of the French Army on active service, should be performed in Paris—or indeed anywhere within metropolitan France. Fragmented versions in translation were presented in Berlin and in London; the true world premiere was given in Stockholm in Swedish. Only some four years after the war had concluded had the accompanying emotions subsided sufficiently to allow a tentative, carefully spaced run at the Théâtre National de l'Odéon in Paris; even then, there were "incidents."

Insofar as Brecht must be considered a major influence on Genet's later drama, *The Screens* is the most purely Brechtian of all his plays. Explicit argument is reduced to a minimum, and traditional psychology has dwindled to the vanishing point. Instead, the dramatic effect is created by a series of brilliant visual images, stylized and simplified almost to the point of primitivism, by violence, slogans, caricature, deliberate vulgarity, and by the overwhelming impression of hatred that remains in the atmosphere long after the actors of each individual scene have vanished. Most of the more obsessive themes and problems of Genet's earlier dramas are present but are now reduced to their visual equivalent, acted out in front of the four levels of screens on the stage, on which the performers roughly chalk in a symbolic decor as required (a technique derived from cabaret shows of the period). Beneath this camouflage of primitivism, parody, and purely dramatic spectacle, traces of ideas reveal that Genet's complex vision of the world has by no means ceased to evolve.

The "hero" of the drama is Saïd, the most abject, cowardly, debased, and unlovable of all the *fellahin*, and the "heroines" are Warda and Malika, the ritualistically costumed and painted whores of the brothel. The "villains" are, on the one hand, the European colonists and the French Army of Occupation; on the other hand, and rather more ambiguously, they are the Arab militant insurgents, armed and disciplined, the very mirror reflection of the European occupiers whom they are driving back into the sea. In this respect, but only in this respect, *The Screens* recapitulates the argument of *The Blacks*; to maintain their identity in the face of the power of the white peoples, the oppressed of the Third World must assimilate the technology and master the efficiency of the Europeans and, in so doing, destroy forever the authentic heritage of those whom they are seeking to defend. It is a dilemma from which there is no escape, one of the profoundest tragedies of the modern world.

Beneath the conflict of French and Arabs that forms the obvious subject of the play lies a much profounder and, for Genet, more immediately relevant conflict: that between anarchy and organization. If the main division of the characters is into white and brown, there is also a secondary division that cuts right across the first. On the one hand are anarchists, the reversers of conventional values so dear to Genet's heart—

Saïd; his mother; Leïla, his wife; Kadidja; and Ommu—and on the other, the orthodox forces of political reality. These include not only the colonials and the *Légionnaires* but also the disciplined Arab combatants themselves, who, in the final moments of the play, execute Saïd and, in so doing, relegate Genet's dreams to where they belong: to the world of poetry, which, in political terms, is the world of acquiescent nonfunction, the world of death.

When the audience first meets Saïd, he is on his way to his wedding, accompanied by his mother. Like that of Genet himself, Saïd's authenticity resides in his abjection. He plunges downward into "sanctity" through his experiences of degradation and of evil. Leïla, his bride (the Arabic word means "night"), has only one outstanding individual characteristic: her ugliness. She is "the ugliest woman in the next town and all the towns around." Progressively her ugliness becomes, for herself, for Saïd, and for his mother, the symbol of a total negativity, a total rejection of "accepted" values, aesthetic or otherwise. Meanwhile, Saïd progresses through ever more categoric stages of negation. From an outcast he becomes a thief; from a thief, a jailbird; from a jailbird, a traitor. His treachery is his final negation of positive values because he is betraying not only his own but also his creator's committed cause; however, it is all so useless.

As had happened with the prostitute Chantal in *The Balcony*, the Revolution seizes on Saïd's image and elevates it into that of a hero. It transforms him into a symbol of himself, thus condemning him to the dimension of death and of unreality, even while he is yet alive. Just as Genet himself had been transformed from a criminal into the Poet (and thus transmuted from an ignominious life into a glorious death while alive), so Saïd is transmuted from his rebellious and abject self into a Glorious Cause. Death, after that, is a relief.

The death of Saïd, however, is no solution to Genet's own problem; it merely places Genet himself in the position of having to abandon either politics or poetry, having failed successively, through *The Balcony*, *The Blacks*, and *The Screens*, in his attempt to reconcile the two. "Certain truths are not applicable, otherwise they'd die," says Ommu toward the end of *The Screens*. "They mustn't die, but live through the songs they've become." Poetry, in fact, is one thing, and politics, another. One is life, and the other is death. The only question is, which is which? Such is the insoluble problem left hanging in the air at the end of *The Screens*. "It's dead we want you, *dead*," says Ommu to Saïd. "That's leaving me dead alive," replies Saïd. After the writing of *The Screens*, Genet, caught finally in the trap of politics, would appear to have existed "dead alive."

Other major works

LONG FICTION: *Notre-Dame des Fleurs*, 1944, 1951 (*Our Lady of the Flowers*, 1949); *Miracle de la rose*, 1946, 1951 (*Miracle of the Rose*, 1966); *Pompes funèbres*, 1947, 1953 (*Funeral Rites*, 1968); *Querelle de Brest*, 1947, 1953 (*Querelle of Brest*, 1966).

POETRY: *Poèmes*, 1948; *Treasures of the Night: The Collected Poems of Jean Genet*, 1980.

NONFICTION: *Journal du voleur*, 1948, 1949 (*The Thief's Journal*, 1954); *Lettres à Roger Blin*, 1966 (*Letters to Roger Blin*, 1969).

MISCELLANEOUS: *Œuvres complètes*, 1952 (4 volumes).

Bibliography

Dobrez, L. A. C. *The Existential and Its Exits: Literary and Philosophical Perspectives on the Works of Beckett, Ionesco, Genet, and Pinter.* New York: St. Martin's Press, 1986. Dobrez examines existentialism in the works of Genet as well as those of Samuel Beckett, Eugène Ionesco, and Harold Pinter. Contains index.

Hauptman, Robert. *The Pathological Vision: Jean Genet, Louis-Ferdinand Céline, and Tennessee Williams.* American University Studies series. New York: Peter Lang, 1984. Hauptman examines ethics, specifically the presence of evil, in the works of Genet, Céline, and Williams. Contains bibliography.

Knapp, Bettina Liebowitz. *Jean Genet.* Boston: Twayne, 1989. Knapp looks at Genet's life and analyzes and interprets his works. Includes bibliography and index.

Plunka, Gene A. *The Rites of Passage of Jean Genet: The Art and Aesthetics of Risk Taking.* London: Associated University Presses, 1992. This analysis of Genet and his works focuses on the psychology of risk taking. Includes bibliography and index.

Read, Barbara and Ian Birchall, eds. *Fowers and Revolution: A Collection of Writings on Jean Genet.* London: Middlesex University Press, 1997. This collection of essays examines the life and criticizes and interprets the works of Genet. Includes index.

Sartre, Jean-Paul. *Saint-Genet, Actor and Martyr.* 1963. Reprint. New York: Pantheon Books, 1983. The French writer Sartre's biography of Genet. Includes bibliography.

Stewart, Harry E., and Rob Roy McGregor. *Jean Genet: From Fascism to Nihilism.* New York: P. Lang, 1993. The authors examine how fascism, nihilism, and other political currents affected the writings of Genet.

White, Edmund. *Genet: A Biography.* New York: Random House, 1994. A look at the life of the French writer. Includes bibliography and index.

Richard N. Coe

W. S. Gilbert

Born: London, England; November 18, 1836
Died: Harrow Weald, England; May 29, 1911

Principal drama • *Ruy Blas*, pb. 1866 (in *Warne's Christmas Annual*); *Dulcamara: Or, The Little Duck and the Great Quack*, pr., pb. 1866 (based on Gaetano Donizetti's opera *L'elisir d'amore*); *Allow Me to Explain*, pr. 1867; *Highly Improbable*, pr. 1867; *Harlequin Cock Robin and Jenny Wren: Or, Fortunatus and the Water of Life, the Three Bears, the Three Gifts, the Three Wishes, and the Little Man Who Woo'd the Little Maid*, pr., pb. 1867; *The Merry Zingara: Or, The Tipsy Gipsy and the Pipsy Wipsy*, pr., pb. 1868; *Robert the Devil: Or, The Nun, the Dun, and the Son of a Gun*, pr., pb. 1868; *No Cards*, pr. 1869, pb. 1901 (libretto; music by Lionel Elliott); *The Pretty Druidess: Or, The Mother, the Maid, and the Mistletoe Bough*, pr., pb. 1869; *An Old Score*, pr., pb. 1869; *Ages Ago: A Ghost Story*, pr., pb. 1869 (libretto; music by Frederick Clay); *The Princess*, pr., pb. 1870; *The Gentleman in Black*, pr. 1870 (libretto; music by Frederick Clay); *The Palace of Truth*, pr., pb. 1870; *A Medical Man*, pb. 1870, pr. 1872; *Randall's Thumb*, pr. 1871, pb. 1872; *A Sensation Novel*, pr. 1871, pb. 1912 (libretto; music by Florian Pascal); *Pygmalion and Galatea*, pr. 1871, pb. 1872; *Thespis: Or, The Gods Grown Old*, pr., pb. 1871 (libretto; music by Sir Arthur Sullivan); *The Brigands*, pb. 1871, pr. 1889 (libretto; music by Jacques Offenbach); *On Guard*, pr., pb. 1872; *Happy Arcadia*, pr., pb. 1872 (libretto; music by Frederick Clay); *The Wicked World*, pr., pb. 1873; *The Happy Land*, pr., pb. 1873 (as F. Tomline, with Gilbert A' Beckett); *The Realm of Joy*, pr. 1873; *The Wedding March*, pr. 1873, pb. 1879 (adaptation of Eugène Labiche's *Le Chapeau de paille d'Italie*); *Charity*, pr. 1874; *Ought We to Visit Her?*, pr. 1874 (with Annie Edwards); *Committed for Trial*, pr. 1874, pb. 1930 (adaptation of Henri Meilhac and Ludovic Halévy's *Le Réveillon*, later revised as *On Bail*); *Topsy Turveydom*, pr. 1874, pb. 1931; *Sweethearts*, pr. 1874, pb. 1878; *Trial by Jury*, pr., pb. 1875 (libretto; music by Sullivan); *Tom Cobb: Or, Fortune's Toy*, pr. 1875, pb. 1880; *Eyes and No Eyes: Or, The Art of Seeing*, pr. 1875, pb. 1896 (libretto; music by Pascal); *Broken Hearts*, pr. 1875, pb. 1881; *Princess Toto*, pr., pb. 1876 (libretto; music by Frederick Clay); *Dan'l Bruce, Blacksmith*, pr., pb. 1876; *Original Plays*, pb. 1876-1911 (4 volumes); *On Bail*, pr. 1877, pb. 1881 (revision of *Committed for Trial*); *Engaged*, pr., pb. 1877; *The Sorcerer*, pr., pb. 1877 (libretto; music by Sullivan); *The Ne'er-do-Weel*, pr., pb. 1878; *H.M.S. Pinafore: Or, The Lass That Loved a Sailor*, pr., pb. 1878 (libretto; music by Sullivan); *Gretchen*, pr., pb. 1879; *The Pirates of Penzance: Or, The Slave of Duty*, pr. 1879, pb. 1880 (libretto; music by Sullivan); *Patience: Or, Bunthorne's Bride*, pr., pb. 1881 (libretto; music by Sullivan); *Foggerty's Fairy*, pr., pb. 1881; *Iolanthe: Or, The Peer and the Peri*, pr., pb. 1882 (libretto; music by Sullivan); *Comedy and Tragedy*, pr. 1884, pb. 1896; *Princess Ida: Or, Castle Adamant*, pr., pb. 1884 (libretto; music by Sullivan); *The Mikado: Or, The Town of Titipu*, pr., pb. 1885 (libretto; music by Sullivan); *Ruddigore: Or, The Witch's Curse*, pr., pb. 1887 (libretto; music by Sullivan); *The Yeomen of the Guard: Or, The Merryman and His Maid*, pr., pb. 1888 (libretto; music by Sullivan); *Brantinghame Hall*, pr., pb. 1888; *The Gondoliers: Or, The King of Barataria*, pr., pb. 1889 (libretto; music by Sullivan); *Rosencrantz and Guildenstern*, pr. 1891, pb. 1893; *The Mountebanks*, pr., pb. 1892 (libretto; music by Alfred Cellier); *Haste to the Wedding*, pr., pb. 1892 (libretto; music by George Grossmith); *Utopia, Limited: Or, The Flowers of Progress*, pr., pb. 1893 (libretto; music by Sullivan); *His Excellency*, pr., pb. 1894 (libretto; music by Osmond Carr); *The Grand Duke: Or, The Statutory Duel*, pr., pb. 1896 (libretto; music by Sullivan); *The Fortune Hunter*, pr., pb. 1897; *Fallen Fairies*, pr., pb. 1909 (with Edward German); *The Hooligan*, pr., pb. 1911; *Gilbert Before Sullivan: Six Comic Plays*, pb. 1967 (Jane Stedman, editor); *Plays*, pb. 1982 (George Rowell, editor)

Other literary forms • Apart from his writing for the theater, W. S. Gilbert's principal literary accomplishment is *The Bab Ballads* (1869), whimsical verses that he illustrated himself. Originally published in comic journals such as *Fun* and *Punch*, they are generally regarded as the well from which Gilbert drew many of the songs and situations of his comic operas.

Achievements • The comic operas of W. S. Gilbert and Sir Arthur Sullivan are the product of one of the most successful collaborations in theatrical history, for while other teams of librettist and composer have achieved comparable distinction, in no other pair have the talents so complemented each other. Both chafed at the fact that their more serious accomplishments were less well regarded, and both tried, without great success, to work with other collaborators. Gilbert's whimsy and legalistic paradoxes would have been little more than quaint if they had not been humanized by Sullivan's melodies, and Sullivan's choral and orchestral virtuosity and his propensity to parody found their focus in Gilbert's preposterous plots.

Gilbert and Sullivan's initial collaborations took place over a span of six years, during which they were engaged in other artistic enterprises as well. With the composition of *H.M.S. Pinafore*, however, they began a decade of enormous popularity, with virtually one new opera a year, each with a measure of uniqueness yet all derived from a recognizable formula. Although the later operas are somewhat more musically complex and more extravagantly plotted, these advances are less the consequence of artistic maturity than of technical confidence. Gilbert's not too serious social criticism, his tongue-twisting lyrics, and his gentle spoofs of romantic conventions appealed to a middle-class audience that had only recently been persuaded that the theater might be a respectable institution after all. The two operas Gilbert and Sullivan produced after the great breach that lasted from 1889 to 1893 are not sufficiently inferior to the others as to account for their unpopularity. The vogue of Gilbert and Sullivan had not ended, for the earlier operas continued to be revived. It is more likely that the collaborators had produced enough operas to keep their public happy.

For almost a century, these operas have remained favorites on both sides of the Atlantic, kept alive largely by the D'Oyly Carte Opera Company, holders of the copyright, from whose elaborately stylized and insistently Victorian productions other professional and amateur renditions have been derived. Although changes in the company's finances forced its closure in 1982, interest in the operas was not noticeably diminished, with both Joseph Papp's 1980 revival and the 1983 film version of *The Pirates of Penzance* being well received. Continued interest in Gilbert and Sullivan was evidenced by the release of *Topsy-Turvy*, a 1999 feature film on their collaboration by British filmmaker Mike Leigh.

Biography • William Schwenck Gilbert was born at 17 Southampton Street, Strand, London, on November 18, 1836, the son of a fairly well-to-do naval surgeon, who turned to a literary career at about the same time as young William did. At the age of two, while on holiday with his parents in Italy, Gilbert was kidnapped from his nurse and ransomed for twenty-five pounds. He later claimed to have a perfect recollection of the incident. At any rate, his plots frequently hinge on the removal of infants from their real parents.

Educated at Boulogne, France, and Great Ealing School, he then attended King's College, London, hoping to obtain a commission in the Royal Artillery. The sudden end of the Crimean War made a military career less appealing, and he obtained, by competitive examination, a clerkship in the Education Department of the Privy Council Office, a post he occupied from 1857 to 1862. Coming into an unexpected sum of money, Gilbert was able to free himself from that "ill-organised and ill-governed office." Having already entered the Inner Temple, Gilbert was called to the Bar in 1863. He did not thrive as a barrister, however, earning no more than seventy-five pounds in his first two years of practice. He never wholly abandoned either his military or his legal aspirations, for he held a commission in the Fifth West Yorkshire Militia, the Royal Aberdeen Highlanders, and, from 1893, was a justice of the peace for the county of Middlesex.

Gilbert's career as a writer had been launched as early as 1857, when he accepted a commission to translate a French song for a theater program. His first play to be produced, *Dulcamara*, a travesty based on Gaetano Donizetti's opera *L'elisir d'amore* (1832), was followed in succeeding years by similar treatments of operas by Donizetti, Vincenzo Bellini, Giacomo Meyerbeer, and others. In 1867, Gilbert was confident enough of his abilities to marry Lucy Blois Turner, a woman fourteen years his junior. Despite the example of the tempestuous marriage of Gilberts' parents, his own irascibility, and his almost total absorption in his work, the union appears to have been a happy one.

The 1860's were also the years of the composition of *The Bab Ballads.* In 1869, he became a contributor of short comic plays for the German Reed's Royal Gallery of Illustration, which provided a kind of family en-

(Library of Congress)

tertainment mixing song with improbable fable, presented without the elaborate trappings of the stage. He also began writing full-length comedies, such as *The Palace of Truth*, *Pygmalion and Galatea*, and *Broken Hearts*, whose plots involve the intervention of fairies or other supernatural agencies in human affairs.

The first meeting of Gilbert and Sullivan took place at the Gallery of Illustration and was brought about through a common friend. Though each knew the work of the other, it was another two years before Gilbert proposed that Sullivan set to music the draft of *Thespis* (the musical score has since been lost). Neither appears to have taken this first collaboration very seriously, and four years were to elapse before they worked together on another opera, a curtain raiser prodded into being by Richard D'Oyly Carte, then the manager of the Royalty Theatre, in the Soho district of London. The extraordinary success of this piece, *Trial by Jury*, prompted D'Oyly Carte to lease the Opéra Comique as the home of the Comedy Opera Company and to commission a third opera, *The Sorcerer*.

One success followed another. To frustrate theatrical piracy, a continuing problem as the popularity of their work increased, the premiere of *The Pirates of Penzance* took place in New York. By 1881, the trio of Gilbert, Sullivan, and D'Oyly Carte had opened their own theater, the Savoy, the first in the world to be illuminated by electric light. All their subsequent operas were produced here. That two men so temperamentally different—Gilbert, robust and litigious, and Sullivan, frail and affable—should have collaborated at all is more remarkable than that their association became strained during the decade of their greatest artistic and commercial success. Each considered that he was being asked to yield too much to the other. These differences were precipitated by the famous "carpet breach."

Believing that D'Oyly Carte had wrongly charged the theater's new carpeting as a cost of production of *The Gondoliers*, rather than as one of building maintenance, and that Sullivan and he were thereby aggrieved, Gilbert insisted on an immediate renegotiation of the agreement among them. When D'Oyly Carte demurred and Sullivan proved insufficiently vigorous in his support of Gilbert's demands, Gilbert became furious and actually took legal action against both of them. Although a compromise was eventually worked out, and two more operas followed the reconciliation, the heyday of the team of Gilbert and Sullivan was over.

Gilbert continued to be active with other collaborators in the 1890's, and he reverted as well to the fairy comedies of his pre-Sullivan days. Gout and other ailments, however, compelled him to lead a life of greater retirement. In 1907, some twenty-four years after Sullivan had received a similar honor, Gilbert was knighted for services to the theater—as a playwright rather than with the more prestigious designation he had craved, that of dramatist. Though rancor figured significantly in Gilbert's life, his death was gallant. Diving to rescue a young woman swimming in the lake on his estate, Sir William suffered a fatal heart attack on May 29, 1911.

Analysis • Alone among the comic versifiers of his age—Lewis Carroll, Edward Lear, C. S. Calverley, Richard Barham, and others—W. S. Gilbert succeeded in converting comic verse to comic song, thereby transcending whimsy. For this, he certainly owes much to Sullivan. Yet in how many operas, comic or grand, does the work of the lyricist or librettist count for much? Gilbert has earned classic status not because he is timeless and universal, but because even after a century, he can impose a Victorian sensibility on his audience.

Gilbert has occasionally been called "the English Aristophanes"; however extravagant that designation, it may serve as a useful point of departure. Assuredly Aristophanic is Gilbert's capacity to create in his plays worlds in which recognizable institutions—the legal system, the military, the rigid caste system of Victorian society—are transformed into absurdities. In *Trial by Jury*, the legal wrangling between the counsels of the jilted Angelina and the flirtatious defendant are resolved by the judgment of the judge—to marry Angelina himself. In *The Pirates of Penzance*, a pirate must first serve an apprenticeship, as though he were an artisan or skilled mechanic; furthermore, the pirate gang is pardoned of all their offenses because "they are all noblemen who have gone wrong." Also Aristophanic, though functioning in a different way, to be sure, are Gilbert's choruses—the sisters, cousins, and aunts of Sir Joseph Porter in *H.M.S. Pinafore*, the giggling schoolgirls of *The Mikado*, or the professional bridesmaids in *Ruddigore*—which serve to accentuate the ludicrousness of the situations.

The essential distinction, however, between the absurdities of Aristophanes and those of Gilbert is that for the Greek dramatist, the source of the comedy lay in some social or political aberration that he meant to expose, if not to correct. For Gilbert, on the other hand, though his plays are not devoid of social or political implications, the source of the comedy lies in the pursuit of some intellectual crotchet or paradox to its ultimate conclusion. The topsy-turviness of Gilbert's plays originates in legalisms and logic-chopping.

As a slave of duty, Frederic, the hero of *The Pirates of Penzance*, feels that he cannot betray his pirate comrades, loathsome though their trade is to him, until he is discharged of his indentures on his twenty-first birthday. Having been born on the last day of February in a leap year, however, he discovers that he is, in terms of birthdays celebrated, only a little boy of five. Similarly, through an ancestral curse, each baronet of Ruddigore must commit a crime daily or perish in unutterable agony. Failure to commit a crime is thus tantamount to committing suicide, which is itself a crime. Not only are the dilemmas of the characters resolved by similar sophistry, but also it appears that the complications have been conceived with no other purpose in mind.

One Gilbert and Sullivan work that does not quite fit this description is *Princess Ida*. This opera, however, is essentially a reworking of an earlier Gilbert play, *The Princess*, a "respectful perversion" of Alfred, Lord Tennyson's poem of the same name (1847), that odd composition whose central subject is the education of women. Even here, however, Gilbert treats the topic not as a timely social issue but as an occasion to explore the comic implications of the attempted isolation of one sex from the other. To say that Gilbert's plays take place in artificial environments hardly accounts for the intense intellectual pressure that has gone into their formation. The clash between the fairies and noblemen in *Iolanthe*, for example, originates in the play on the words "peri" and "peer." The officers of the dragoon guards in *Patience* readily abandon their military garb and their military bearing to become aesthetic poets, because only in that guise can they successfully woo the chorus of rapturous maidens.

Each opera enunciates a topsy-turvy premise, which is then examined. In *H.M.S. Pinafore*, it is the notion that "love can level ranks"; in *Patience*, it is that true love is disinterested; and in *Iolanthe*, it is that a race of immortal and insubstantial beings can exhibit all the characteristics of human beings. All these, it should be noted, are romantic notions derived very largely from literature. Gilbert's fancies are drawn as well from some of his own early works, particularly his parodies and *The Bab Ballads*. Very little seems to come from direct observation of life or reflection on personal experience, except for the minutiae, the little personal quirks and foibles that make a caricature. The result is a series of plays often quite rich in references or allusions to contemporary life but as remote from that life as animated cartoons are from the life of animals. The characters and plots have been reduced to formula.

Although some of the variations on them are quite subtle, the character types encountered in Gilbert's plays are almost as rigid as those in classical New Comedy. In addition to the fresh and innocent heroine and her equally ingenuous hero, there is the fastidious and querulous authoritarian (who usually gets to sing the patter song)—Sir Joseph in *H.M.S. Pinafore*, Major-General Stanley in *The Pirates of Penzance*, the Lord Chancellor in *Iolanthe*, King Gama in *Princess Ida*, Ko-Ko in *The Mikado*, and the Duke of Plaza Toro in *The Gondoliers*—as well as the elderly, decayed contralto, who is physically repulsive yet longing for affection—Buttercup in *H.M.S. Pinafore*, Ruth in *The Pirates of Penzance*, Lady Jane in *Patience*, Katisha in *The Mikado*, Dame Carruthers in *The Yeomen of the Guard*, and the Duchess in *The Gondoliers*. The easy classification of roles in these operas makes them particularly attractive to repertory companies.

For all the variety of locales in Gilbert's works, the most frequent form of action involves what has been called the invasion plot. That is, the territory of a more or less settled group is overrun by another, the situation demanding some kind of compromise, if not retreat. Sir Joseph Porter and his female relations board H.M.S *Pinafore*; Major-General Stanley's daughters innocently decide to picnic in the pirates' lair; the procession of peers invades the Arcadian landscape in act 1 of *Iolanthe*, only to have the fairies troop in force to Westminster in act 2. There is actual combat between military units in *Princess Ida*, and in *The Mikado*, the imperial retinue sweeps into Titipu, demanding of its inhabitants the appearance of conformity to decrees from on high.

This reduction of character and plot to a formula, although it is more commercially palatable (thanks to Sullivan's music) than the insipid paradoxes of Gilbert's earlier straight plays, does not initially seem conducive to the generation of enduring art. Yet in at least two ways, it has secured Gilbert's place in the theater, even if not as a dramaturge. First, it provided a vehicle for some of the most versatile metrical and verbal extravagances in the English language.

As a lyricist, Gilbert is unsurpassed in his ability to provide both singable *and* memorable words not only in arias, ballads, duets, and choruses but also to part-songs of considerable complexity and to patter songs for single and multiple voices. (Patter songs, which sound like tongue twisters sung at top speed, include "I am the very model of a modern Major-General," from *The Pirates of Penzance*.) The challenge produced the tuneful and rollicking songs familiar to almost everyone, such as "Faint Heart Never Won Fair Lady," from *Iolanthe*, or "For He Is an Englishman," from *H.M.S. Pinafore*. Yet it also produced tender and haunting songs, such as Ko-Ko's "The Titwillow Song" in *The Mikado* (which must surely have originated as a parody of Desdemona's "Willow Song" in William Shakespeare's *Othello, the Moor of Venice* (pr. 1604) and Jack Point's "I Have a Song to Sing, O" in *The Yeomen of the Guard*.

Moreover, it is in these lyrics, rather than in the large themes or preposterous situations of the operas, that Gilbert executes his greatest satiric thrusts. On the whole, like the audience for whom he wrote, Gilbert felt enormously pleased with the general state of things in the world around him and was vexed only by ideas, such as socialism or evolution, that threatened to rend society or by fads, such as aestheticism, that tended to distract it. Yet for all his conservatism, he did not wholly succumb to philistine complacency. In his songs, he frequently targets time-honored objects of satire: the abuse of privilege, the vanity in pride of ancestry, or the posturings of the *nouveau riche*. At the beginning of the second act of *The Mikado*, for example, Yum-Yum is adorning herself in preparation for her wedding day. She sings a song ingenuously identifying her with the world of nature, a song whose operation, like that of Alexander Pope's description of Belinda at the beginning of *The Rape of the Lock* (1712, 1714), simultaneously elicits wonder and censure at the fair creature. As in this song, Gilbert's satire is often ironically self-deprecating, requiring a good deal of attention to be understood.

This demand for attentiveness constitutes Gilbert's second significant contribution to the English theater. He educated a generation of middle-class theatergoers to listen carefully to what was being said onstage and to expect paradox at every turn. Though himself unwilling or unable to use the stage for serious mockery of social institutions, he made it possible for others to do so. He prepared audiences to receive the witty comedies of Oscar Wilde and the more intellectually provocative plays of George Bernard Shaw.

H.M.S. Pinafore • *Trial by Jury* demonstrated that Gilbertian humor could successfully be translated to the operatic stage; *The Sorcerer*, that Sullivan could actually compose for Gilbert. In *H.M.S. Pinafore*, the collaboration attained its full flowering. The first and least complicated of their more popular operas, it is also the most familiar.

The plot hinges on two threadbare conventions of comedy, a pair of lovers whose union is thwarted by their being of different social classes and a pair of babies, also of different classes, who have been switched in infancy. The discovery of the second circumstance conveniently resolves the difficulty of the first. Gilbert apparently believed in a fluid class structure: Josephine may marry up (although not too far up) but not down the social ladder, and Sir Joseph Porter, while his rise from office boy to First Lord of the Admiralty is a source of some amusement, is not repudiated, either as a cad or as a snob, for rejecting Josephine when she proves to be the daughter of a common seaman. His behavior is seen as quite understandable and serves to refute the absurd egalitarian sentiments he has uttered earlier, sentiments overwhelmed by the jingoistic sailors' chorus and glee.

As is usual in Gilbert, the satire against the ruling class is mild. It manifests itself through the self-revelation of an authority figure who is on the whole rather likable, however pompous. In the final analysis, such satire is seen as secondary to the larger purpose of amusement. Sir Joseph and his retinue of sisters, cousins, and aunts are there to provide a complication and a chorus.

The Pirates of Penzance • *The Pirates of Penzance* is, as many have observed, *H.M.S. Pinafore* brought to land. All the color of the nautical talk and the costuming has been preserved in the pirates, the female chorus of Sir Joseph's relations has become that of Major-General Stanley's daughters, and there is even an additional male chorus of policemen. Buttercup, who had been responsible for the mixup of babies in *H.M.S. Pinafore*, has metamorphosed into Ruth, whose blunder is to confuse words, apprenticing the young Frederic to a pirate instead of a pilot. There are distant echoes here of Shakespeare's *The Tempest* (pr. 1611) as Frederic, who has grown up knowing no women other than his nurse, Ruth, discovers the true nature of female beauty in Mabel. The complication is that, as a pirate, he is a sworn foe of legitimate authority, as represented by Mabel's father. Once again, the comic resolution undercuts any serious social criticism: Because they are really renegade noblemen, who owe fealty to Queen Victoria, the pirates surrender in her name and become suitable mates for the Major-General's daughters.

There is far less occasion for criticism of social institutions in *The Pirates of Penzance* than in *H.M.S. Pinafore.* Rather, Gilbert takes delight in puncturing romantic myths. Instead of a band of lawless Byronic outcasts, Gilbert's pirates are a guild of credulous, tenderhearted incompetents, whose evil purposes dissolve at once if their intended victim claims to be an orphan (a weakness that Major-General Stanley is quick to exploit). Their antagonists, the local constabulary, prove to be as unheroic as the pirates are unvillainous. Major-General Stanley, like Sir Joseph Porter, is a mere functionary. In the modern world, Gilbert seems to be saying, romantic idealization is no longer tenable, and the conflict between good and evil dwindles into banality.

Patience • Although *Patience* appears to be one of the most topical of Gilbert's works, taking aim at the whole aesthetic movement, the play's origins belie that contention. The central situation derives from "The Rival Curates," one of *The Bab Ballads*, in which two provincial clergymen compete for a title in abnegation or, in Gilbert's term, "mildness." Unlike the opera, the twenty-three-stanza ballad presents no motive for the eccentricity beyond that of a desire for reputation. The essential topsy-turvy premise of the opera, then, is that an affected mannerism extended to one's whole demeanor will excite admiration. Gilbert confessed that he had difficulty sustaining the conceit through the two acts of the opera without falling into bad taste or blasphemy, and this may account for the transformation of the rival curates into poets. The emergence of the young Oscar Wilde as a flamboyant exponent of aestheticism made him appear to be a perfect prototype of Bunthorne, the fleshly poet, an association that proved profitable both for Wilde and the three partners of the D'Oyly Carte Opera Company.

Love interest in the opera is supplied by Patience, a dairymaid sensible enough not to be attracted by bizarre behavior yet sufficiently innocent of passion to believe that love must be totally disinterested. It is through the characterizations of the fleshly and idyllic poets, however, that *Patience* achieved its popularity and has maintained its interest. Gilbert's attack was timely, to be sure, but somewhat off the mark. The eccentricity and languor of his poets are fair enough targets of satire, but he invests them as well with a kind of puritanism more appropriate to his curates. Elsewhere, Gilbert administers occasional mild jolts to middle-class complacency; in *Patience*, however, by portraying his poets not merely as fools but also as conscious hypocrites, he panders to philistine anti-intellectualism.

Iolanthe • *Iolanthe* brings together the world of Gilbert's earlier fairy plays and the world of reality, particularly legal and political reality. As in *The Pirates of Penzance*, Gilbert insists on looking at romantic matter in a matter-of-fact way. Like the Greek satirist Lucian, Gilbert endows his supernatural creatures not only with immortality, discretionary corporeality, and magical powers, but also with human emotions. The opening chorus of dancing fairies complains of boredom since the exile of Iolanthe for having married a mortal (Iolanthe is subsequently forgiven).

The offspring of that union, the shepherd Strephon (a fairy from the waist up), is in love with Phyllis, the ward of the Lord Chancellor, who intends to marry her himself. Needless to say, both the young and the middle-aged lovers are properly sorted out by the end of the opera, but not before several clashes have taken place between the romantic and pragmatic worlds. Phyllis, seeing Strephon in the company of his very youthful-looking mother, is driven to jealousy; he, backed by the powerful influence of the fairies, takes over Parliament, where he proceeds to confound the whole political system by instituting competitive examinations for admission to the peerage and by eliciting assent to all his proposals.

Iolanthe is quite remarkable for the good-naturedness of its critical observations on parliamentary democracy. At the beginning of act 2, Private Willis's song ponders the division of people into parties, by which they relinquish their private intellects and submit to the discipline of a leader on entering the House of Commons. Two songs later, Lord Mountararat extols the House of Lords for doing precisely nothing and doing it "very well": Britain's glory is contingent on the assurance that "noble statesmen do not itch/ To interfere with matters which/ They do not understand." Taken together, the two songs seem to express Gilbert's belief that, however riddled with anomalies, the British system of government works very well indeed.

The Mikado • *The Mikado* signaled a change of direction for Gilbert and Sullivan. With the exception of *Thespis*, whose setting is Olympus, and *Princess Ida*, which, like Tennyson's poem, is laid in a legendary atmosphere, all their operas up to *The Mikado* had been contemporary. However outlandish the premises or exaggerated the manners, they could be seen as obvious extrapolations of the familiar. Whether Gilbert felt that he had exhausted this vein or whether the possibility for more elaborate productions was the inducement, *The Mikado* initiated a movement away from the familiar. Though topical allusions abound, the last six operas all take place either in a locale definitely not English or at a time decidedly not the present. They are also characterized by more complicated plots. The simple invasion formula gives way to more intricate maneuverings, and the songs are made to carry a greater burden of exposition and development.

Though *The Mikado* may be no less popular than *H.M.S. Pinafore* or *The Pirates of Penzance*, it is more difficult to unravel and its satire is more oblique. Most obviously, in its portrayal of excessive ceremony and politeness masking bloodthirstiness and tyranny, *The Mikado* sardonically congratulates Englishmen for choosing not to belong to any other nation and laughs at the Victorian fascination for things Oriental. It is equally obvious, however, that Gilbert's Japanese have no more authenticity than his fairies: The opening choruses of *Iolanthe* and *The Mikado* are strikingly similar. In both, the singers proclaim themselves creatures of artistic convention, doomed to perform antics they know to be meaningless. The world of *The Mikado*, then, is one of stylized behavior, in which the law no longer serves society but enslaves it. The Lord Chancellor in *Iolanthe* had proclaimed, "The Law is the true embodiment/ Of everything that's excellent," but it remains for Ko-Ko, the Lord High Executioner, to have "a little list" of society's offenders who can be dispatched whenever a victim must be found, and for the Mikado himself to invent cruel and unusual punishments to "fit the crime." The plight of the thwarted lovers, Nanki-Poo and Yum-Yum, is central; what is topsy-turvy is their entire milieu, in which forms are preserved at the expense of substance.

The Yeomen of the Guard • *The Yeomen of the Guard* was Gilbert's response to Sullivan's repeated requests for more human situations, for characters less eccentric, and for songs whose sentiments were not continually undercut by irony. Though rich in comic turns, it aspires to the condition of grand, rather than comic, opera. It is quite likely that the setting—the Tower of London in the sixteenth century—with its potential for costuming and design, may have first suggested itself to Gilbert, and that only then did he begin to work on a plot.

Sergeant Meryll, a yeoman of the guard, and his son, Leonard, and daughter, Phoebe, plan to effect the escape of Colonel Fairfax, who is destined to be executed on trumped-up charges of sorcery. Meanwhile, Fairfax, knowing nothing of their scheme, is resigned to dying, but desires to marry first and thus thwart the plan of his kinsman, who concocted the charges in order to inherit Fairfax's estate. A hasty marriage is concluded with Elsie Maynard, a strolling singer. Fairfax, disguised as young Meryll, disappears from his cell, and his jailer, Wilfred Shadbolt, who in his love for Phoebe Meryll has unwittingly assisted the plot, is in danger of suffering the penalty in his stead. Shadbolt allies himself with the jester Jack Point, who, as Elsie's lover, has also been discomfitted by Fairfax's disappearance, and together, they concoct a tale.

Like that of Ko-Ko and Pooh-Bah in *The Mikado*, the explanation given for Fairfax's absence is filled with "corroborative detail, intended to give artistic verisimilitude to an otherwise bald and unconvincing narrative," maintaining that Shadbolt shot Fairfax dead as he tried to escape. Phoebe, in love with Fairfax and in distress at seeing him woo Elsie in the guise of her brother, reveals his true identity to Shadbolt. As Phoebe and Shadbolt are now in possession of each other's secret, they agree to marry in order to purchase each other's silence. Fairfax, who has actually been reprieved, is genuinely attracted to the wife he has acquired out of convenience, Sergeant Meryll pairs off with Dame Carruthers, the housekeeper to the Tower, and only Jack Point is left pathetically without a mate at the opera's conclusion.

The substitution of intrigue for topsy-turviness obviously distances *The Yeomen of the Guard* from *H.M.S. Pinafore*, yet the work is recognizably Gilbertian; for all their melodramatic pretensions, the characters have affinities with those of the other operas. Even Jack Point, who falls insensible as the curtain descends, is cousin to the Lord Chancellor and Ko-Ko. The plight of these characters, however, has been more poignantly imagined.

The Gondoliers • Composed in the midst of mounting strife between Gilbert and Sullivan, *The Gondoliers* is their last major theatrical success. In many ways it is the most colorful and lyric of the whole series. The richness of its foreign setting may be rivaled by that of *The Mikado*, but musically, it is unequaled; for this opera, Sullivan added to his usual array of arias, duets, part songs, and choruses the rhythms of Spain and Italy. Gilbert worked what must be the ultimate variation on the baby-swapping convention: Throughout the opera, the audience waits to find out which of the two gondoliers is the rightful king of Barataria, only to discover what may have already been guessed—that neither is. During the last few minutes of the opera, an even earlier switch is announced as having taken place, conveniently preventing the marriage of royalty with the lower orders.

It often appears that Gilbert is engaging in self-parody in *The Gondoliers*, for the situations of the earlier operas are here piled on one another. Topsy-turviness is present not merely in the mixup of the infants but also in the joint rule of the two gondoliers while they await the determination of their status and in their ludicrous attempts to introduce republican monarchy. In the antics of the Duke and Duchess of Plaza Toro, Gilbert is not repudiating the aristocratic ideal—the Grand Inquisitor sings persuasively of the need for degree in a stable society. Rather, Gilbert portrays in them examples of a decayed and venal aristocracy. Like Pooh-Bah in *The Mikado*, they have pride but no honor. For all its sprightliness, however, *The Gondoliers* lacks the integrity of the earlier operas: Themes and characters are introduced capriciously because they have worked before.

Other major works

SHORT FICTION: *The Lost Stories of W. S. Gilbert,* 1982.

POETRY: *The Bab Ballads,* 1869; *More Bab Ballads,* 1873; *Songs of a Savoyard,* 1898.

Bibliography

Crowther, Andrew. *Contradiction Contradicted: The Plays of W. S. Gilbert.* Cranbury, N. J.: Associated University Presses, 2000. Criticism and interpretation of the plays of Gilbert. Bibliography and index.

Finch, Michael. *Gilbert and Sullivan.* London: Weidenfeld and Nicolson, 1993. A look at the collaboration between Gilbert and Sir Arthur Sullivan. Bibliography and index.

Fischler, Alan. *Modified Rapture: Comedy in W. S. Gilbert's Savoy Operas.* Charlottesville: University Press of Virginia, 1991. Fischler begins his analysis with Gilbert's fiftieth theatrical work, *H.M.S. Pinafore,* because it both separated him from other Victorian playwrights and was the turning point in his comic dramaturgy. Gilbert's new approach to comedy appealed to bourgeois prejudices and provided his greatest popularity. Extensive notes and index.

Joseph, Tony. *The D'Oyly Carte Opera Company, 1875-1982: An Unofficial History.* Bristol, England: Bunthorne, 1994. A history of the opera company at which most of the Gilbert and Sullivan works were performed. Bibliography and index.

Orel, Harold, ed. *Gilbert and Sullivan: Interview and Recollections.* Iowa City: University of Iowa Press, 1994. A collections of interviews and essays remembering Gilbert and Sir Arthur Sullivan. Bibliography and index.

Stedman, Jane W. *W. S. Gilbert: A Classical Victorian and His Theatre.* New York: Oxford University Press, 1996. A look at Gilbert's life and works, including his collaborations with Sir Arthur Sullivan. Bibliography and index.

_____. *W. S. Gilbert's Theatrical Criticism.* London: Society for Theatre Research, 2000. A close examination of the criticism around Gilbert. Bibliography and index.

Wilson, Robin, and Frederic K. Lloyd. *Gilbert and Sullivan: The Official D'Oyly Carte Picture History.* New York: Alfred A. Knopf, 1984. Hundreds of photographs and designs from the 107-year history of the D'Oyly Carte Opera Company trace the evolution of the Savoy operas onstage in both England and the United States. Brief introductions to each section include biographical and critical information on Gilbert as it pertains to the opera company. Illustrations, bibliography, and index.

Ira Grushow,
updated by Gerald S. Argetsinger

Susan Glaspell

Born: Davenport, Iowa; July 1, 1876
Died: Provincetown, Massachusetts; July 27, 1948

Principal drama • *Suppressed Desires,* pr. 1915, pb. 1917 (one act; with George Cram Cook); *Trifles,* pr. 1916, pb. 1917 (one act); *The People,* pr. 1917, pb. 1918 (one act); *Close the Book,* pr. 1917, pb. 1918 (one act); *The Outside,* pr. 1917, pb. 1920 (one act); *Woman's Honor,* pr. 1918, pb. 1920 (one act); *Tickless Time,* pr. 1918, pb. 1920 (one act; with Cook); *Bernice,* pr. 1919, pb. 1920; *Plays,* pb. 1920 (includes *Suppressed Desires, Trifles, Close the Book, The Outside, The People, Woman's Honor, Tickless Time,* and *Bernice*); *Inheritors,* pr., pb. 1921; *The Verge,* pr. 1921, pb. 1922; *The Chains of Dew,* pr. 1922; *The Comic Artist,* pb. 1927, pr. 1928 (with Norman Matson); *Alison's House,* pr., pb. 1930; *Plays by Susan Glaspell,* pb. 1987 (C. W. E. Bigsby, editor; includes *Trifles, The Outside, The Verge,* and *Inheritors*)

Other literary forms • Susan Glaspell began her long career, which lasted almost four decades, writing short stories that appeared in such popular magazines as *Harper's Monthly, Good Housekeeping, American Magazine,* and *Woman's Home Companion.* The short stories, in the tradition of local-color writing, generally romanticized the Midwest and its people. Thirteen of her forty-three stories have been collected in *Lifted Masks* (1912). Although she enjoyed success as a short-fiction writer and a playwright, Glaspell regarded herself primarily as a novelist. Her nine novels include *The Visioning* (1911), *Ambrose Holt and Family* (1931), *Norma Ashe* (1942), and *Judd Rankin's Daughter* (1945). In addition, she is the author of a children's book, *Cherished and Shared of Old* (1940), several essays, and a biography of her first husband, George Cram "Jig" Cook, entitled *The Road to the Temple* (1926).

Achievements • Susan Glaspell received recognition in three of the genres that she employed. Several of her short stories were selected for E. J. O'Brien's yearly anthology, *Best Short Stories:* "Jury of Her Peers" in 1918, "Government Goat" in 1920, and "His Smile" in 1922. Her novel *The Morning Is Near Us* (1940) was a Literary Guild selection, and another novel, *Brook Evans* (1928), was made into the film *The Right to Love* by Paramount Pictures. In addition, she won in 1931 a Pulitzer Prize for her play *Alison's House.* Her greatest achievement, however, was the work that she did with the Provincetown Players, a group that she helped found. The Provincetown Players, whose stated purpose was to produce new plays by American playwrights, was extremely influential and changed the direction of modern American drama, providing a forum where none had existed. From its inception to 1922, the group's theater produced ninety-three new American plays by forty-seven playwrights. All but two of these playwrights had their first plays produced by the theater. Glaspell, who wrote eleven of her fourteen plays for the group, was, after Eugene O'Neill, the group's most important playwright.

Biography • Born July 1, 1876, to Elmer S. and Alice Keating Glaspell, descendants of pioneer settlers, Susan Glaspell grew up in Davenport, Iowa, and attended public schools. She went to Drake University in Des Moines, receiving her B.A. in 1899. While in college, she began writing stories and published her first one in the *Davenport Weekly Outlook* in 1896. After graduation, she spent two years working for *The Des Moines Daily News* and other newspapers as a reporter covering the court and legislative beats. She returned in 1901 to Davenport determined to become a writer. Her early stories, published in popular magazines, and her first novel, the best-selling *The Glory of the Conquered: The Story of a Great Love* (1909), were escapist, romantic, and conventional in form.

In 1907, Glaspell met Floyd Dell, future writer and social critic; George Cram Cook, a socialist writer; and Cook's feminist wife, Mollie. Cook and Dell established the Monist Society, a discussion group formulated to expose provincialism and to introduce avant-grade ideas to Davenport. Glaspell fell in love with Cook and encountered the disapproval of her friends and family. In 1909, in an attempt to end the affair, she traveled to Europe, using the royalties earned from her first novel.

On returning to the United States, she spent time in Colorado, Davenport, Chicago, and Greenwich Village. She also finished her second novel, *The Visioning*, which shows Cook's influence in the seriousness of the issues it introduced—trade unions, evolution, and divorce, to name a few—and began a third, *Fidelity* (1915), which explores small-town life in the Midwest and examines the limits placed on women by traditional gender roles. In 1912, she published *Lifted Masks*, a collection of short stories based on her experiences as a reporter. She and Cook, who had divorced his second wife, were married on April 14, 1913, in Weehawken, New Jersey. As a result of being exposed to his ideas, she grew more radical and less conventional in her fiction. Her writing moved away from the sentimental and began to focus on more contemporary themes: the conflict between morality and individual freedom, the hypocrisy of small towns, and the evolution of the "new woman."

Glaspell spent the summer of 1914 writing and acting in plays with friends in Provincetown, and the following summer the Provincetown Players was formed. Thus began a period of playwriting that lasted about fifteen years, from 1915 to 1931. She and Cook, who had a strong interest in drama, collaborated on the first play, *Suppressed Desires*, a satire on Sigmund Freud's ideas. Unable to get the play produced by the Washington Square Players, the first little theater in New York City, and encouraged by friends, Glaspell and Cook formed the Provincetown Players in 1915 as an outlet for American plays. In 1916, the group moved to Greenwich Village and, through its emphasis on new ideas and techniques and its support of new American playwrights, strongly influenced American drama. Cook became president and remained so until 1922, and Glaspell supported the endeavor primarily through writing plays but also through acting and directing, for the time being giving up her career as a novelist. She first wrote one-act plays; then in 1919, her first full-length play, *Bernice*, was produced, Glaspell performing the role of Abbie.

As the Provincetown Players became more commercial, Glaspell and Cook grew disillusioned, and in 1922, they moved to Greece, fulfilling a lifetime desire of Cook, who wanted to live in the land where great drama began. There, in 1924 in the ancient town of Delphi, Cook died. During the years Glaspell spent with Cook, she wrote one novel, seven one-act plays, four full-length ones, and twenty short stories, the stories written to achieve some financial security. After her husband's death, she returned to Provincetown.

Later, traveling in Europe, Glaspell met Norman Matson, a writer, whom she married in 1925. In 1928, she returned to writing novels: *Brook Evans, Fugitive's Re-*

turn (1929), and *Ambrose Holt and Family*, the latter adapted from *The Chains of Dew*, the last play she wrote for the Provincetown Players. She also wrote *The Road to the Temple*, a biography of Cook, in which she allowed, as much as possible, Cook's own words, garnered from letters, diaries, and other sources, to speak for him. She collaborated with Matson on a play, *The Comic Artist*, and wrote *Alison's House*, which received a Pulitzer Prize. In 1932, Glaspell was divorced from Matson. Her last play, "The Big Bozo," was not produced or published, and no copies are known to exist.

Glaspell did not see herself as a playwright and, without the Provincetown Players' demand for new plays and without Cook's encouragement, she ceased writing plays, although she retained an interest in the theater. In 1936, she went to Chicago to direct the Midwest Play Bureau of the Federal Theatre Project, where she selected plays and organized productions. Returning to Provincetown in 1938, she wrote three more novels: *The Morning Is Near Us*, *Norma Ashe*, and *Judd Rankin's Daughter*. She died on July 27, 1948, in Provincetown, of viral pneumonia.

Analysis • Although Susan Glaspell considered herself a novelist, she is best known for her plays. Her playwriting period lasted fifteen years, seven of which were during the time of her association with the Provincetown Players. In only one season, that of 1919-1920, did Glaspell not present at least one new play. Although her work in short fiction and the novel is somewhat conventional, her work in the theater is not. She experimented, taking risks with her plays. She was an early advocate of expressionism, the use of nonrealistic devices to objectify inner experience. She experimented with language, sometimes incorporating poetry into the dialogue, and her plays are more often about ideas—feminism and socialism—than they are about characters and plot. The general critical response of her contemporaries to her plays was praise for her realistic ones and a reaction of confusion to her more experimental ones.

(Library of Congress)

Her plays have a range of themes, but most concern the individual and the individual's need to find self-fulfillment. Specifically, she focuses on women who attempt to go beyond societal roles, searching for independence and autonomy. Often, however, these women pay a price: in love or acceptance by family and friends, in money, or, in the case of Claire Archer in *The Verge*, in mental health. Sometimes the search is for the "otherness" of life, that which makes life worth living and takes one beyond the trivial and the commonplace. This search is often aided by a guide or mentor who, some critics argue, is patterned after Cook.

Trifles • Glaspell's best-known and most anthologized play is the one-act *Trifles*, written for the Provincetown Players' second season, 1916-1917, to fill out a bill with Eugene O'Neill's play *Bound East for Cardiff* (wr. 1913-1914, pr. 1916, pb. 1919) and later rewritten as the short story "A Jury of Her Peers" (1917). In *The Road to the Temple*, Glaspell describes the origin of the play, writing that she sat in the empty theater until the image of a Midwest farm kitchen with its occupants appeared before her. *Trifles*, based on an event that Glaspell covered as a reporter in Des Moines, takes place in the kitchen of Minnie Wright, a woman accused of murdering her husband. Minnie Wright, in jail, remains offstage for the entire play. *Trifles* marked Glaspell's first use of the device of the absent protagonist, which would be employed again in other plays, most notably in *Bernice* and *Alison's House*. The play, with its grounding in realism and regionalism, is not representative of her later, more experimental plays, but it is said to be the best structured of her plays, and it is certainly the most often performed.

Trifles opens as five people enter a farmhouse kitchen. The three men—the sheriff (Mr. Peters), the county attorney (Mr. Henderson), and a neighbor (Mr. Hale)—are there to uncover evidence to link Minnie to the murder of her husband, John Wright, who was choked to death with a rope while he slept. The two women—the sheriff's wife and the neighbor's wife—are there to gather a few items to take to Minnie. As the men examine the kitchen, the bedroom, and the barn, the women remain in the kitchen. They notice the preserves Minnie had canned, the quilt she was sewing, things that the men belittle, but through their observations, the women solve the murder. The uneven stitching of the quilt indicates Minnie's anxiety, and when the women discover a canary with a broken neck, they know the motive. Minnie, who loved to sing as a young woman, was, in a sense, caged by John, cut off from her interests and isolated. She was figuratively strangled by John as the bird had literally been. After he killed what she loved, the only thing that gave her joy, she responded by choking him.

Although the women have information that could convict Minnie, they remain silent. Mrs. Hale, the neighbor, had already failed Minnie by not visiting her when she knew that Minnie's life was bleak, and she will not fail her again. Mrs. Peters, the sheriff's wife, understands from her own experience—she had lost her firstborn—what loneliness is, and she, too, will support Minnie. In a sense, they are the jury of her peers, peers because only they can understand her loneliness and desperation. They try and acquit her. The play, thus, is about sisterhood and the importance of women's sustaining one another in a culture that is dominated by patriarchal attitudes, attitudes that trivialize women and the work—canning, quilting, baking—that they may do.

The Verge • A more experimental play but one that also explores the limits placed on women is *The Verge*, a full-length play, produced in 1921 by the Provincetown Players. The play had a successful run at the New York MacDougal Street theater, but when it moved uptown to the Garrick Theatre, the audiences became more conventional and less receptive to the experimental and expressionistic play.

Claire Archer, a Faust-like figure, wants to create new life-forms, plants that transcend the boundaries of reality, reaching for "otherness." Claire has spent years in her laboratory developing her plants, but when one of them, the Edge Vine, regresses, she destroys it because it "doesn't want to be—what hasn't been." Similarly, when Claire's daughter Elizabeth accepts conventional attitudes, Claire rejects her, as she does with her sister Adelaide, who urges her to "be the woman you were meant to be." Tom Edgeworthy, one of Glaspell's mentors or guide figures, also fails Claire when he cannot commit to a complete relationship that would include both the spiritual and the physical. He does not reach for the "otherness" but instead attempts to restrain Claire: "I'm here to hold you from where I know you cannot go. You're trying what we can't do." She disagrees, "What else is there worth trying?" Because he refuses to accept the "otherness," she strangles him, destroying him as she did the Edge Vine. The play has strong feminist appeal in the character of Claire, who desires to go beyond the limits set by culture. She does succeed with her plant, the Breath of Life, but the price she pays is her sanity.

Alison's House • Glaspell's last produced play, *Alison's House*, presented by the Civic Repertory Theater in 1930, received a Pulitzer Prize. As she had in earlier plays—for example, *The Comic Artist*—Glaspell developed the theme of the artist and his or her obligation to society. Alison Stanhope, whose story is loosely based on the life of Emily Dickinson, has died eighteen years earlier, but some of her poems, which obviously deal with a love affair, have recently surfaced. Her relatives are torn between destroying them because they would reflect negatively on the family—the love affair was with a married man—and publishing them because of the public's right to have access to them.

The conflict is dramatized by the poet's brother, who wants the poems to remain unpublished, and his daughter Elsa Stanhope, who argues for publication. Elsa, who also had an affair with a married man, is forgiven by her father as they reach the decision that the publication of the poems should not be denied because of small-town morality and hypocrisy. In addition to these themes, the play exhibits other features common to Glaspell's plays: the absent main character and the setting of the small midwestern town.

Other major works

LONG FICTION: *The Glory of the Conquered: The Story of a Great Love*, 1909; *The Visioning*, 1911; *Fidelity*, 1915; *Brook Evans*, 1928; *Fugitive's Return*, 1929; *Ambrose Holt and Family*, 1931; *The Morning Is Near Us*, 1940; *Norma Ashe*, 1942; *Judd Rankin's Daughter*, 1945.

SHORT FICTION: *Lifted Masks*, 1912.

NONFICTION: *The Road to the Temple*, 1926.

CHILDREN'S LITERATURE: *Cherished and Shared of Old*, 1940.

Bibliography

Ben-Zvi, Linda. "Susan Glaspell's Contributions to Contemporary Women Playwrights." In *Feminine Focus: The New Women Playwrights*, edited by Enoch Brater. New York: Oxford University Press, 1989. Argues that Glaspell's plays represent the female experience and that through their structure, characters, and language, the plays help to create a woman-centered drama.

Bigsby, C. W. E. Introduction to *Plays by Susan Glaspell*. Cambridge, England: Cambridge University Press, 1987. Contains good biographical information and focuses on Glaspell's development as a playwright. Provides insightful critical comments on four of Glaspell's plays: *Trifles*, *The Outside*, *The Verge*, and *Inheritors*.

Ozieblo, Barbara. "Rebellion and Rejection: The Plays of Susan Glaspell." In *Modern American Drama: The Female Canon*, edited by June Schlueter. London: Associated University Presses, 1990. Explores why a playwright as influential as Glaspell had been to her contemporaries is excluded from many studies of drama and concludes that Glaspell was ignored because of her challenge to patriarchal attitudes.

_____. *Susan Glaspell: A Critical Biography.* Chapel Hill: University of North Carolina Press, 2000. A biography of the playwright.

Sarlós, Robert Károly. *Jig Cook and the Provincetown Players: Theatre in Ferment.* Amherst: University of Massachusetts Press, 1982. Although the focus of this book is on George Cram Cook, the author presents much useful biographical material about Glaspell. Good discussion of the influence of the Provincetown Players.

Waterman, Arthur E. *Susan Glaspell.* New York: Twayne, 1966. Primarily a critical-analytical study of Glaspell's novels and plays but also contains relevant biographical information. A chapter on the Provincetown Players describes the importance of the group and Glaspell's contribution to it. A bibliography contains both primary and secondary sources.

Barbara Wiedeman